Readings in
Child Development
and
Relationships

Russell C. Smart and Mollie S. Smart

Department of Child Development and Family Relations
University of Rhode Island

Readings in
CHILD
DEVELOPMENT
and
RELATIONSHIPS

SECOND EDITION

Macmillan Publishing Co., Inc.
NEW YORK
Collier Macmillan Publishers
LONDON

Macmillan Publishing Co., Inc.
866 Third Avenue, New York, New York 10022

Collier Macmillan Canada, Ltd.

Library of Congress Cataloging in Publication Data

Smart, Russell Cook, comp.
   Readings in child development and relationships.

   Includes bibliographies and indexes.
   1. Child psychology. 2. Adolescent psychology.
I. Smart, Mollie Stevens. II. Title.
BF721.S5714   1977   155.4'08   76-15956
ISBN 0-02-412110-X

PRINTING: 1 2 3 4 5 6 7 8   YEAR: 7 8 9 0 1 2 3

Preface

A child developmentalist is a person who invests in the future, because the next generation represents the future. Through studying children, the child developmentalist learns more about people in general, including himself. The study of child development is a liberal one, because it expands the student's understanding of human beings. The application of knowledge of child development has great practical value.

The child's development occurs through interactions on various levels, including physical, cognitive, and social. Therefore, the child is studied in relation to bodily growth and health, mental development, and family and community interaction. Cultural values include attitudes toward children. The values are expressed in behavior toward children. Child developmentalists are increasingly aware of the need to understand cultural values and their expression in regard to children.

From its beginning, the study of child development has been necessarily interdisciplinary. The child development movement in North America began in the 1920s, when Lawrence K. Frank gathered together a variety of specialists and guided them in establishing and directing centers for the study of children. The basic philosophy of this movement was, and still is, that the child is a whole person, living in relationship to other people who interact with him and support him in a widening series of inclusions. Although the study of growth had to be broken into manageable units, such as the growth of the mind and the growth of the body, students of child development recognized divisions as arbitrary and sought ways of studying the child as a whole and of putting the pieces back together after they had examined them. Because the child was recognized not only as a whole person but as a person-in-relation, it was essential to study parent–child relationships and to study the family. Because families are parts of communities, regions, and nations, these wider social networks are also pertinent to understanding the child.

The pioneer child-development centers gathered together specialists from a wide variety of disciplines in order to study the child, a whole person-in-relation. These centers were located in the Merrill-Palmer School in Detroit and at the universities of California, Cornell, Georgia, Iowa, Minnesota, McGill, and Toronto. The staff of the centers came from the fields of anthropology, education, medicine, nutrition, nursing, physiology, psychology, social work, and sociology. While focusing on common problems, these individuals educated each other, with the result that many professionals of varying backgrounds became specialists in child development. The first child development textbook, *Growth and Development of the Young Child*, was written by a nurse and social worker, Winifred Rand, a nutritionist and former dean of home economics, Mary Sweeny, and a psychologist, Lee Vincent.[1] Although Rand was primarily responsible for the parts on family and community, Sweeny for physical growth and nutrition, and Vincent for psychological development, the three authorities worked closely together to present an integrated account of living children interacting in human settings.

We had the privilege of beginning our professional lives at the Merrill-Palmer School (now the Merrill-Palmer Institute). Although we were not there when it began, we heard about the early days from those who started it. The first nursery school teachers had to be imported from England, because America had none. Mary Sweeny told about finding out how to feed young children. Nobody knew what was good for them and what they would eat. Miss Sweeny and her students worked in the kitchen, in the nursery school, and with parents to produce a body of knowledge that stands today. Longitudinal growth records were being collected. The Merrill-Palmer mental test for preschool children had just been standardized. The great people from other centers and other fields came often for meetings and speeches. Margaret Mead and Lawrence K. Frank were among them. The classwork was as integrated as the research and writing. Rarely was a class held with only one teacher. Even three or four might be present, each with a particular point of view and contribution to make. Students came with readings and observations. Class was a true sharing of knowledge and analysis of ideas and meanings. In staff meetings, the older and famous members taught us younger ones; they also listened to us.

Our field has grown enormously in terms of knowledge and personnel. During the past 20 years, psychologists have flocked to the child, recognizing early growth as a rich field for research. With the elaboration and sophistication of research in the many fields basic to child development, it is growing more and more difficult to keep the elements of mind, body, family, community, and world in focus. At the same time, it is growing more and more essential to educate child development specialists who can work to solve the human problems of today. Who will direct thousands of day-care centers in which children will have the means for optimal health and growth and where parents will be strengthened? Who will help floundering adolescents to achieve identity and integrity? Who will influence local and national governments to pursue policies that support sound human values? Such problems require the efforts of caring individuals equipped with broad knowledge of human development and relationships.

The readings in this book represent a sampling of the field of child development and relationships. The level of difficulty varies considerably from one reading to another. "Now the Nurse-Midwife," by Marion Steinman, is written for the intelligent public who read the *New York Times Magazine*. Research articles from the journal *Child Development* are likely to be more

---

[1] W. Rand, M. E. Sweeny, and E. L. Vincent, *Growth and Development of the Young Child* (Philadelphia: W. B. Saunders Company, 1930).

difficult to read, especially for the student who has not studied statistics. We include readings from the great masters, Piaget, Erikson, and Frank, because we want our readers to have direct contacts with them, instead of reading only other people's interpretations. Although content was our first consideration in the choice of articles, we have also tried to select a variety of authors, subjects, and sources. The selections include writings from most of the fields mentioned as integral to child development. Subjects of the studies include not only children from Canada and the United States but from a variety of other nations, including Australia, Great Britain, Guatemala, Israel, and New Zealand.

The first four parts are concerned with the infant, the preschool child, the school-age child, and the adolescent. At each age level, the readings reflect concern with the child as a physical, intellectual, emotional, and social being interacting with his family, peers, and community and being influenced by wider social spheres. Although we stress the normal and try to provide concepts of what most children are like, we also hope to make clear the uniqueness of every individual. We also want to interest North American students in children everywhere in the world. They will thus learn more about Americans, but what is more important, they will participate, we hope, to a greater degree as human beings in the human scene.

Part Five is called "Summary" but it can be read before the other parts. It consists of one chapter titled "An Overview of Human Life and Growth," and takes a brief look at man in relation to his biological setting.

Although the readings are supplementary to our textbook *Children: Development and Relationships*, they can, of course, be used with any text in child development.

R. C. S.
M. S. S.

Contents

Suggestions for the Student

Some of the readers of this book will be more familiar with textbooks than with research articles and reviews of research. Although some of the selections are as easy to read as textbooks, or even easier, we want to offer some suggestions. Some of our comments are general and some are specific as to how to study this book and how to learn from it.

Our personal conviction is that one cannot get the maximum amount out of a book such as this one by reading it and doing nothing more. Learning requires some kind of activity on the part of the learner. For most college students, reading is not a great effort. They quite easily get the general drift of what they read, but they may not grasp enough details in reading really to understand what they have read. However, when one takes notes concerning what he reads, the activity involved in phrasing the author's words usually results in the note taker making the ideas his own. Copying the words in the book is not what we mean by note taking. Although such copying is an active process, it exercises only the muscles used in writing and may not involve thinking or understanding. Note taking to us includes thinking about what the words say, picking out and rephrasing the important ideas, making sure that the new words have not made any important changes in the ideas. Note taking becomes a highly personalized skill, and there are many ways of doing it. (The two of us do it quite differently.) All good methods of note taking are the result of an active thinking process.

TAKING NOTES ON DIFFERENT KINDS OF READING   Those articles in this book that are reviews-of research and statements of theoretical positions require about the same kind of notes. There are usually not a great many main points, although some of them may have subsidiary points made in connection with them. Often these points are reiterated in a summary that may come at the beginning or the end of the selection. If there is no summary, the author may have omitted it because he thought he made his points so clearly that they would not be missed. In any case, assume the author had a message and ask yourself, "What does the author want me to learn? Why does he think it important? What evidence does he present for accepting the truth of his statements?"

The selections that are research reports are more specialized kinds of writing and therefore require a different kind or form of note taking. Here is an outline that we have developed over our years of teaching that students have found helpful.

How to Make an Abstract of Research Articles

Author, name of   The complete title of the article, as stated in the journal. Name of journal, year, volume, inclusive pages. (Month). For the selections in this book add the bibliographic reference for this book also, in the same form. Note that so far you have been copying, exercising your writing muscles. You should not do much more copying.

Purpose   State the purpose in the author's words if he has not been too verbose. Do you see why copying may be a good idea here? But make an active decision to copy. Do not just keep on writing.

Subjects   Name, ages, sex, socioeconomic status, hereditary factors, environmental factors, all the important identifying material that the author gives. Put it in tabular form if possible.

Apparatus and procedure   A brief description of any special apparatus, tests, or techniques. If a standard test is used, be sure to mention any deviations from the usual method of presentation or scoring. If the length of time the test continued or the number of determinations is important, be sure to include these facts.

Results   What the investigator found, in terms of scores, and so on. Put these in tabular form also if you can. Keep in mind that you are writing a summary, but do not leave out any important items. Also remember that you usually make abstracts for use over a long period of time, and that later you may want to know the results of this study for a purpose different from your present one.

Conclusions   How the author interprets his findings. Does he think his hypothesis is substantiated? What does he think is the "next step?" Does he tie his results into the main body of knowledge in his field?

Remarks   This is the place, and the *only* place, for you to say what you think. Is it a good study? Are there any points on which you disagree? Can you offer any interpretations other than those given by the author? What are the theoretical implications? Are there implications for practice? What further studies does this suggest to you?

The following questions are some of the points you should investigate under each of the major headings. All of them, of course, are not applicable to any one study, and there may be others in some instances. A beginning student will not have the background for answering all of them.

Purpose.   Does the author state the purpose clearly? Allowing for personal enthusiasms, was the purpose worthwhile?

Subjects.   Is the number adequate? Is the sample clearly described as to age, sex, SE status, education, race, and so on? Remember that in different studies different things are important. The two criteria here are whether the sampling is good and whether the sample is reproducible. That is, if you wanted to check the experiment, has the author given you enough information so that you could reproduce the group in all important characteristics?

Apparatus and Procedure.   As far as you can tell, did the investigator set up his procedure so that his results are not biased by it? Are factors controlled that might invalidate the results? Is there a better way of testing the same hypothesis? If statistics were used, are they adequate? Why did the investigator use the ones he did? If statistics were not used, why did he handle the data as he did? Do you approve of his methods? Why?

Results.   Are the results clearly stated? Are sufficient raw data given so that someone else could rework them? Would the results be different if better methods of handling the data had been used? What effect does the sampling have on the results? Do you know of any other studies that bear on this one, either substantiating it or contradicting it?

Conclusions.   Do the author's conclusions follow from the results he has stated? Do they bear any relation to his stated purpose? Do the conclusions as stated take into account any limitations in the sampling or method?

This is not the only way of keeping track of research articles. This outline, however, is as exhaustive as most people will need for ordinary purposes. Only occasionally, when you are engaged in writing a minute analysis of the literature on one topic, will you want to keep a more inclusive record of the details in an article. More often you will want to record less material than this outline requires. It is a lot of work to make a complete abstract, but when you have done it, your thinking becomes clearer and your files are that much more well stocked. Complete abstracts should not be neglected.

A Very Short Course in Statistics   Many students who read this book will not have had a course in statistics. Usually the authors of research articles interpret the statistics they use and state the conclusions that follow from them. But because you should not get into the lazy habit of skipping over the statistics, we include this section in order to help you to understand some of the important kinds of statistics.

Averages, or Measures of Central Tendency   What a non-statistician calls the average, a statistician calls the *mean* or the *arithmetic mean*. The average (mean) cost of your textbooks for this semester is the sum of what you paid for all the books divided by the number of books. A mean is a number that, mathematically, is most representative of a series of similar numbers.

Another kind of average is the *median*. A median is the middle number of a series of numbers that is arranged from small to large. There are two conditions under which it is used. The median is used when some of the numbers are much larger or smaller than the others. If you were able to get four used textbooks for $4.00, $4.75, $5.00, and $7.00, but had to spend $15.00 for a new edition, the mean cost would be $7.15. The median cost of $5.00 is more representative of the series of numbers. The median is also used when the unit of measurement is not divisible into smaller units. The mean number of children per family is an incorrect use of the mean, although it is sometimes reported, because there can be no such thing as a fractional child, and means rarely come out as integers. Since a median can be an integer, the average number of children per family should always be stated as a median.

Occasionally you may find other measures of central tendency in research articles. A statistics textbook will explain them.

Tests of Significance   In most research two or more groups are compared with each other. The important question is, "Are the differences the result of chance, or of a real difference in condition or treatment of the groups?" The researcher sets up the hypothesis (called the *null hypothesis*) that there is no true difference. He applies an appropriate statistical test, on the basis of which he decides to accept or reject the null hypothesis. He would accept the null hypothesis that there is no significant difference if the test showed that a difference as large as the one discovered could have arisen by chance. If the test showed that the difference could have arisen by chance less than five times out of 100 repetitions of the study, he rejects the null hypothesis and concludes there *is* a true, or significant, difference. The statistical notation for such a statement is $p < .05$, which is read, "the probability is less than five in 100." Occasionally a more stringent test of significance is used, which is written $p < .01$. This means that the result could be obtained by chance less than 1 per cent of the time. Note that a statistician does not say that a difference could *never* occur by chance, but that the probability of its occurring by chance is so many in 100.

There are many different kinds of tests of significance, depending on the kind of data being used. Some of the more usual are χ^2 (chi-squared), the t test, and the F test of analysis of variance. A test of significance always gives the basis for deciding whether the difference could have arisen by chance.

The t test and analysis of variance (ANOVA) are statistical tests that are similar: In the t test two conditions or situations can be compared; in a one-way ANOVA more than two (high, moderate, and no nutritional supplement, for instance) can be compared. A two-way ANOVA makes it possible to compare the effects of two variables (nutritional supplement and sex of subject) and also determine the effect of the interaction between the variables. In such a study, boys and girls would be included in the three nutritional supplement groups. All of the children would be measured for height at the beginning of the period of nutritional supplement and again at the end. The gains of all the children, both boys and girls, in each of the nutritional supplement groups would be compared; this would be a one-way ANOVA. Similarly, the gains in height of all the girls, regardless of level of supplement, would be compared with all the boys' gains; another one-way ANOVA. The analysis of variance is two-way, because it is possible, also, to find out if there is an interaction between nutritional supplement and sex of subject—do high-level boys react differently from high-level girls *and* from moderate-level and no-level boys? Because there are computers to do the immense number of calculations, there are three-variable and even four-variable ANOVAs reported in the literature, although they are rare, for very large numbers of subjects are necessary in order to make the subgroups big enough.

Correlation   A coefficient of correlation measures the degree to which two measures (height and weight, for instance) vary together—positive correlation if one measure gets bigger as the second one does, and negative correlation if one measure gets smaller as the other one gets bigger. Zero correlation means that there is no relationship between the two measures. Note that correlation coefficients do not say anything about causation. Heights and weights are positively correlated, but a person's weight does not cause her height, nor does her height cause her weight.

Coefficients of correlation range in size between $+1.00$ and -1.00. If the coefficient is .00, there is no relationship between the two measures. The closer it is to 1.00, either positive or negative, the closer is the relationship. If there was discovered to be a correlation of $+1.00$ between height and weight in a group of children, the tallest child would be the heaviest, the second tallest would be second heaviest, and so on to the shortest, the lightest. If you knew the height of one of these children in relation to the others, you could place him exactly in weight, in relation to the others. If a correlation coefficient is -1.00, the relationship is perfectly inverse. Suppose the coefficient between reading and arithmetic scores is .00 or not significantly different from .00. The best prediction of any child's reading test score, knowing what his arithmetic test score is, would be the mean reading score of the group of children. Such a prediction would not be very helpful, unless the score in arithmetic (the independent variable) is itself close to the mean.

Most often the correlation coefficient reported is the Pearson product-moment coefficient (r). Another coefficient that is often used is the rank-order coefficient (rho, or ρ).

Factor Analysis   As noted previously, correlation coefficients are measures of the degree to which pairs of scores vary together. Therefore, a set of coefficients can be used to obtain an indication of the *factors* underlying the co-variation of the scores. The method is called *factor analysis*. Since factor analysis was invented before there were computers, the number of calculations involved in the method prevented its wide use. If there are 50 variables to be correlated with each other, 1,225 correlation coefficients are necessary, and the computation of each coefficient involves several arithmetic calculations. Then many more calculations must be made on those coefficients in order to measure the factors. These kinds of repetitive calculations are what a modern computer does very well. More factor analyses are reported in the research journals now than were reported even five years ago.

A factor analysis yields from two up to nine or ten factors. Each variable (test) in the analysis has a loading on each factor. Loadings range from .00 up to .99. A loading that is not significantly different from zero means that that factor does not contribute anything to that test. The larger the loading, the more important is that factor in influencing the variability of the test scores.

When several tests or measures all have large loadings on a factor, there is evidence that all of them share something in common. The investigator then sets about naming the factor, by considering what it is that all members of the group have in common, and that the rest of the tests have not at all or in only small amounts. Unlike the calculation of correlation coefficients and factor loadings, the naming of the factors is not precise, since judgments have to be made about what the members of each subset share. Often, perhaps usually, the naming of the factors is obvious when the reader of the research considers what the original measures are. But sometimes an investigator has not considered all the possibilities of the meanings of the factors that the computer has extracted from his data.

Part One

INFANCY

1
Prenatal Development and Birth

While a single cell is transformed into an embryo, the embryo into a fetus, and the fetus into a baby, that organism interacts with the environment provided by the mother. She, in turn, is influenced in her reproductive performance by her own body and self, her husband (or partner) and family, and the community and world in which she lives. Within the brief space of the following three articles, we have included considerations of fetal development, the influence of the prenatal environment, new ways of conducting the birth process, and the stimulation of development in the premature baby.

In trying to understand what makes for excellent health and optimal development, researchers often study the abnormal, or what happens when growth processes go wrong. Thus, the first article, the title of which states the child's right to be normal, explores genetic abnormality. Positive treatment conditions are the subjects of the other two articles in this chapter.

Modern technology offers the means of assessing the normalcy of the fetus in an early stage of development. Carlo Valenti, a research obstetrician, describes the technique of amniocentesis and discusses its use in preventing the births of abnormal children, as well as its potential for correcting abnormalities. Mongolism is used to exemplify an abnormality detectable by amniocentesis. Every child developmentalist is faced by the philosophical and moral issues raised in this article.

Attitudes toward giving birth have changed as women defined themselves as more competent, and as the dangers of anesthesia have been recognized. While wanting control over their own bodies, women are also acknowledging their need for emotional support during labor and delivery. Although North American women have been getting such support more and more from their husbands, it is more usual throughout the world for women to get help and support from other women. The role of the nurse-midwife is described and discussed in the article by Marion Steinman. The author also gives a vivid description of labor and delivery in the new style.

Premature infants pose problems in development and care. They are also significant in a theoretical sense, in demonstrating a stage of development that is usually hidden. Are prematures more like fetuses or are they more like newborn babies? Are there some ways in which premature infants are equivalent to newborns? Many research studies deal with such questions. The present study by Ruth D. Rice explores the effects of tactile stimulation on weight gain, neurological functioning, and mental functioning. The article includes a discussion of the experiences of the premature baby.

The Child : His Right to Be Normal

Carlo Valenti

DOWNSTATE MEDICAL CENTER, STATE UNIVERSITY OF NEW YORK

In his new classic of modern biology, *The Person in the Womb*, Dr. N. J. Berrill makes this, among other, declarations:

> If a human right exists at all, it is the right to be born with normal body and mind, with the prospect of developing further to fulfillment. If this is to be denied, then life and conscience are mockery and a chance should be made for another throw of the ovarian dice.

In accord with this philosophy, I draw attention to some favorable prospects for "another throw."

About one in fifty babies is born with a greater or less degree of abnormality inherited from its parents. These weaknesses, more than 500 of them severe enough to be classified as diseases (diabetes, for example), are ordered by the genes carried on the chromosomes. No one has ever seen a gene, but we can identify chromosomes under the microscope. Every normal person has a complement of forty-six of them, paired in twenty-three sets. One of the twenty-three pairs determines sex. The determination is made by chance and occurs as follows (see Figure 1).

The female sex chromosomes are paired XX. In any division of the germ cell in preparation for mating with a male sperm, the female half of the marriage will therefore always be X.

The male sex chromosomes are paired XY. When the division of this germ cell occurs, the sperm may be X or it may be Y.

When a female egg is penetrated by an X sperm, the nuclei of the egg and the sperm will fuse XX and the offspring will be female.

When a female egg is penetrated by a Y sperm, the offspring will be XY, or male.

The choice is simple when everything goes well in the reproductive process. However, faulty working of the ovaries or testes sometimes produces fertilized XXX eggs (super-females, not always fertile), XXYs (outwardly male, but without sperm), XOs (outwardly female, but without ovaries and therefore without eggs), XXXXYs (typically defective mentally), and XYY's (typically defective mentally, often aggressive to a criminal extent).

The other twenty-two pairs of chromosomes suffer displacements when parents bring together certain genetic characteristics. The results can be very sad. For example, the chromosome pairs numbered 13-14-15 are catalogued by the letter D. Pairs No. 21 and 22 are catalogued by the letter G. Sometimes one chromosome of these two pairs is displaced in what is called a D/G translocation. What happens is that one of the No. 21 pair crosses over to and joins up with one of the No. 15 pair, riding piggyback as it were and giving that one No. 15 a lopsided appearance.

From *Saturday Review*, December 7, 1968, pp. 75–78. Copyright © 1968 Saturday Review, Inc. Reprinted by permission.

3

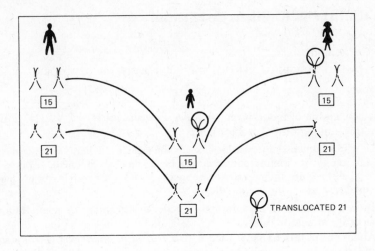

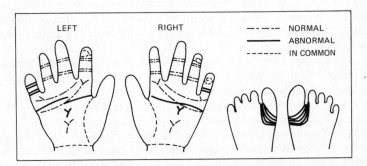

F I G U R E 1.   *How Mongolism is transmitted through a "balanced carrier" to an offspring is demonstrated above. Only two of the twenty-three sets of chromosomes—the No. 15s and the No. 21s—are shown. Note that whereas the father has the normal 21 pair, the mother has one 21 in its normal place and the other upside down on the lopsided No. 15. When chance deals the child the lopsided 15, he has three 21s and is doomed. Palm prints and sole prints of Mongoloid child are below.*

The person who bears this particular pattern of chromosomes is a balanced carrier for Mongolism. We say "balanced" because the total amount of genetic material on the chromosomes is normal, although the number of chromosomes is only forty-five. But the chromosomal pattern is thrown off balance when the balanced carrier's offspring inherits the lopsided chromosome from the carrier along with a 21 from the carrier and a 21 from the other parent. The total inheritance then is three 21s, two in the normal position and one on the lopsided chromosome. The three 21s doom their possessor to Mongolism.

Why focus on the Mongoloid?

A Mongoloid child—in medical terms, he is a victim of "Down's syndrome"—has folded eyes and a flat-rooted nose (the Mongolian-like features from which the popular name of the anomaly derives), small head, fissured protruding tongue, peculiarities in the lines of the palms of the hands and the soles of the feet, retarded intellectual development ranging from idiocy to a maximum prospective mental age of seven years.

Once given life, a Mongoloid is a poignant burden on its parents. For the Mongoloid appeals to all human instincts for companionship. He is cheerful, friendly, imitative, with a good memory for music and for details of situations he has experienced. A Mongoloid's life expectancy averages ten years—a decade of hopelessness, in most cases necessarily spent in a special institution.

Now it has been known for more than a dozen years that before a child is in finished form to leave his mother's womb the chromosomes of the prospective individual can be sampled and analyzed for aberrations. Dr. Fritz Fuchs, Danish-born chief of obstetrics and gynecology at Cornell University Medical College in New York, was able to pioneer such work in his native country because of the liberality of Denmark's laws governing therapeutic abortion.

The method developed by Dr. Fuchs and others is to obtain cells from the amniotic fluid, which is the stuff that every developing fetus floats in. Although the fetus derives almost all of its nourishment from rapidly pulsing blood fed from the placenta by way of the umbilical cord, the fetus before twelve weeks have passed by begins to swallow the amniotic fluid and excrete the fluid through its kidneys and bladder. In growing, the fetus sheds its skin gradually as we living persons shed ours, and other cells are dislodged from the mouth, bronchi, trachea, kidney, and bladder in the course of the swallowing and excreting. The fluid carrying all these cells must be sampled through the wall of the pregnant woman's abdomen by means of a hollow needle similar to those used to draw blood from a vein.

Where the needle enters the womb is of critical importance; if the wrong site were to be chosen, the placenta could be punctured or the fetus itself impaled. Either event could produce serious consequences.

To assure a safe choice, the exact location of the placenta and the floating head of the fetus is determined in the same way that submarines are located when afloat in sea water—that is, by sonar or echo-sounding. The method is feasible as early as the fourteenth week of pregnancy. A tiny portáble gun that fires waves at very high speeds is moved across the prospective parent's abdomen in sweeps proceeding successively downward until the entire belly has been scanned. A pattern similar to that seen on a radar screen emerges. With it as a guide, the entry point of the amniocentesis needle is fixed.

After a sample of the amniotic fluid has been removed through the needle, the sample is spun in a centrifuge. The liquid part of the sample is then discarded. A pellet of cells remains. In this pellet is the knowledge we seek.

Two groups of investigators have reported varying success in culturing the cells on nutritive media they have independently developed. Their techniques, described in the medical literature, did not yield good results in our obstetrics and gynecology laboratory here at State University of New York's Downstate Medical Center in Brooklyn. So Edward J. Schutta, Tehila Kehaty, and myself have worked out a culturing method of our own and with it have obtained twenty successes in twenty-four trials. All our failures occurred where the amount of amniotic fluid used was below a certain level. The twenty successful cell cultures yielded seventeen chromosome analyses, or karyotypes. The three failures apparently were due to bacterial contamination.

Two to six weeks of growth are required before the culture is ready to be karyotyped—that is, placed on a glass laboratory slide, dried, stained, and examined microscopically to determine the chromosome pattern.

Last April, a Boston medical colleague familiar with our work referred to us a twenty-nine-year-old mother from Massachusetts who was sixteen weeks pregnant. She knew her grandfather, her mother, her brother, and herself to be balanced carriers of the D/G chromosomal translocation. That is, all four were outwardly normal and healthy, but each carried within himself only one No. 21 chromosome in its normal pairing, while the other 21 was grafted onto one of the No. 15 chromosome pair. In short, although not themselves Mongoloid, three generations of the family carried the genetic threat of Mongolism.

The young New Englander had already experienced a spontaneous abortion, borne a daughter who was also a balanced carrier of the D/G chromosomal translocation, and borne a Mongoloid son who had lived for five months. She wanted another child, and sought our assurance that it would be normal. With the support of her husband, an engineer by profession, she requested a cytogenetic diagnosis on the unborn baby.

Amniocentesis was performed after a sonar sounding on April 15. The amount of amniotic fluid obtained proved inadequate for optimum cell growth. Amniocentesis was performed again on April 29, luxuriant cell cultures were available within two weeks, and satisfactory chromosome preparations were ready for analysis on May 21. The karyotypes showed a male pattern with the D/G chromosomal translocation characteristic of Mongolism. Our hospital's abortion committee authorized a therapeutic interruption of pregnancy on the grounds that, since Mongolism was certain, failure to interrupt could subject the young mother to unjustifiable psychiatric trauma. Notice of the therapeutic abortion was posted routinely on the staff bulletin boards, and the abortion was done on May 31. Autopsy findings and palmprint and soleprint patterns were consistent with our cytogenetic diagnosis.

The young woman who volunteered for this experience recovered and returned to her New England home within forty-eight hours. She is still eager for another child if she can have a healthy one. She has requested application of amniocentesis to all future pregnancies.

This woman now has a chance for "another throw of the ovarian dice," as Dr. Berrill put it. The British medical journal, *Lancet*, last July published news of her case in the form of a letter from Schutta, Kehaty, and myself. The *Journal of the American Medical Association* has since notified us that it has accepted for publication a longer formal report of the case. So far as I know, it is the first piece of such news to appear in the medical literature anywhere. It may not be sensational news because D/G chromosomal translocations account for only 2 per cent of all Mongoloid children. But to the individual women involved, it is a promise of release from fear and guilt.

Furthermore, the potential benefits of amniocentesis and karyotyping are applicable to the much greater percentage of Mongolism caused by trisomies. In these there are forty-seven chromosomes, including three No. 21s which appear as triplets in the place of the normal 21 pair (as opposed to the pair of 21s and the 21 contained in the lopsided chromosome of the D/G Mongoloids).

Trisomies are related to aging. Human eggs spoil with time just as other eggs do. . . . Every woman's supply of eggs has been nested in her ovaries since well before she herself was born. All else being equal, she begins releasing them, at the rate of one a month (except during pregnancy and subsequent nursing), when she is about thirteen years old, and continues the process for the forty-odd years that intervene before menopause. Overall, the chance of an American woman giving birth to a Mongoloid child is one in 680. To age twenty-five, the chance is one in 2,000; after age forty-five, one in fifty.

Our laboratory has made cytogenetic diagnoses of two women who feared their pregnancies might produce Mongoloid infants. One of these women was thirty-six years old, the other thirty-seven. Amniocentesis and karyotyping showed no chromosomal aberrations.

The potential of prenatal study of fetal cells obtained by amniocentesis is far greater than we have yet been able to explore. Three broad areas are open to investigation. In the first, a smear of the fetal cells can be made immediately after the cells are collected from the amniotic fluid. The smear shows presence or absence of the sex chromatin body (a condensation of nuclear material), which only female cells possess. The sex of the unborn child can thus be identified and sex-linked hereditary diseases, such as hemophilia and muscular dystrophy, can be diagnosed in the fetus. More than ten years ago, Dr. Fuchs in Denmark demonstrated the value of the technique by screening hemophilic pregnancies and interrupting those that would have resulted in male babies. Only males actually develop hemophilia; females carry the disease without being afflicted by it.

The second field of study of cells obtained by amniocentesis is the analysis of their chromosome complement, as illustrated by the case of the young woman patient described above. Advanced maternal age can cause a number of chromosomal errors in addition to the error that results in Mongolism. Anguish for the mothers involved can be avoided in some cases by interruption of pregnancy. The number of such cases is at the moment still uncertain. The certainty is that in the present state of knowledge we cannot correct chromosomal errors. In the future, however, we may be able to correct the effect of the errors by refining our methods, by applying the principle that each effect is due to a particular enzyme and that each enzyme is ordered by a particular gene. One step in the refinement is to map the locations of the genes on the chromosomes of man, as has already been done with the mouse.

The third area of endeavor in intrauterine medicine (treatment of the fetus in the uterus) is analysis of enzymes produced by the fetal cells that are taken from the amniotic fluid. There are hereditary diseases in which deficiency of given enzymes is known in the adult. Detection of the same deficiencies in the fetal cells may permit diagnosis of diseases in the unborn baby and possibly correction of the deficiencies and thus prevention of the diseases.

For example, one of the signs of Mongolism is flaccid muscles at birth. If the body of a Mongoloid baby is laid prone on the palm of the hand, the baby's head and limbs will flop downward like those of a rag doll. The weakness of the muscles has been attributed to absence of a chemical which can be made only in the presence of a particular enzyme. According to prevailing genetic theory, this enzyme must be missing from Mongoloid cells and the absence must be related to the existence in the cells of three No. 21 chromosomes instead of the normal pair of 21s.

In an English experiment, a chemical named 5-hydroxytryptophan was administered to fourteen Mongoloid babies ranging from a few days to four months in age. Within one to seven weeks later, normal muscle tone was restored to thirteen of these babies, who became able to raise their heads, arms, and legs. Clearly, a missing something had been supplied and had counteracted at least some part of the effect of the abnormal set of three No. 21 chromosomes.

The English researchers were careful to point out that there is yet no evidence that their treatment will improve the mental development of Mongoloid babies. It is conceivable, however, that if Mongolism were diagnosed sufficiently early in the development of the fetus and if the missing chemical could be administered then, the effect on the child might be remarkable.

A great many scientists the world over are now studying enzyme deficiencies in hereditary diseases in the adult human. As their reservoir of knowledge grows, the potential of amniocentesis widens proportionately.

A major determinant of the ultimate effectiveness of intrauterine medicine will be the public attitude on abortion. At present, the laws of many states do not allow therapeutic abortion on genetic grounds.* Genetic grounds are habitually construed as empirical statistical evaluations. Chromosomal analysis is not statistical but is direct and specific evidence of abnormality. As physicians, legislators, and the people come to understand the distinction, they will surely see that the law cannot be interpreted to exclude abortion based on chromosomal analysis. For a law that would compel a mother to give birth to a baby certain to be severely defective would be cruel and uncivilized.

* Note that this article was originally published in 1968. Ed.

Now, the Nurse-Midwife

Marion Steinman

Midwives joke that theirs is the second oldest profession, and most of the world's babies are still delivered by midwives. In the United States, however, in the early part of this century, the medical establishment forced midwives—who were then largely old-fashioned, untrained "grannies"—out of the childbirth business. Maternal and infant mortality was appallingly high in those days. As recently as World War I (according to the National Center for Health Statistics), more than 700 out of every 100,000 women died in childbirth, and 96 out of every 1,000 babies died before the age of 1. As the developing specialty of obstetrics attacked this problem, women were persuaded to have their babies in hospitals, and to be delivered by physicians. Today it is rare for a woman to die in childbirth, and infant mortality is down to 16.5 per 1,000 live births. And today there are only a handful of "granny" midwives left, still legally delivering babies, mostly in rural areas of the South and Southwest.

In the meantime, a different kind of midwife was evolving: the well-educated nurse-midwife. In 1931 the first school for nurse midwives in the United States was started, in New York City, by the Maternity Center Association. A few years later the renowned Frontier Nursing Service started a school for nurse-midwives in rural, mountainous eastern Kentucky. Up through the 1960's, however, there were still only a few hundred nurse-midwives in the country, and they were ministering mostly to the poor, in urban ghettos and in isolated rural areas. Today, there are about 1,200 nurse-midwives in the United States, and there are now 16 schools offering nurse-midwifery training programs (nine of them new since 1972), which turn out 150 new nurse-midwives a year.

More and more middle-class American babies are being delivered by these nurse-midwives. In Springfield, Ohio, a group of nine midwives, working with six back-up physicians, manages the labors and deliveries of 50 or 60 women a month. In Beckley, W. Va., two midwives have recently gone into private practice with two obstetricians. In Minneapolis, at the University of Minnesota hospital, four midwives are delivering a dozen or more babies each month. The United States Air Force now has some 40 midwives working in 15 base hospitals across the country; last year they delivered more than 1,000 women. And in New York City, at Manhattan's Roosevelt Hospital, five young midwives opened a private midwifery service about a year and a half ago which has proved so popular that they expect to do between 180 and 200 deliveries this year. Their clientele is largely educated, professional women: lawyers, nurses, teachers and even one doctor, a pediatrician.

A big step toward wider acceptance of nurse-midwives came in 1971, when the American College of Obstetricians and Gynecologists officially declared that in "medically-directed teams, qualified nurse-midwives may assume responsibility for the complete care and management of uncomplicated maternity patients." The college's statement was prompted by what, at the time, looked like an impending physician shortage. The birth rate was running so high that it seemed as if more midwives would be needed simply to deliver all the expected babies. Since then, the birth rate has fallen, and the college now believes that there are generally enough obstetricians. However, because women are now demanding more health-care services, the American College of Obstetricians and Gynecologists remains "enthusiastic" about nurse-midwives.

In recent years a rift has been developing between many American women and the whole United States system of obstetrical care. Women are vehemently criticizing both obstetricians and hospitals, contending that they are dehumanizing childbirth by viewing it as a disease rather than as a normal physiological process. Specific obstetrical practices—artificial induction of labor, the use of medication, episiotomy (surgical incision of the vagina), the use of forceps, the separation of mother and infant right after birth—have become the subjects of fierce debate between women and doctors. Some critics are even claiming that modern medical technology—such as the heavy use of anesthetics—actually damages babies. The modern nurse-midwives believe that they are uniquely qualified to help bridge this gap.

Today's nurse-midwives are far better educated than the old-time "grannies." To become a nurse-midwife, one must first graduate from a three-year or four-year nursing school and become a registered nurse. Next, one must get a year's experience in obstetrical nursing, and then take a course in nurse-midwifery at one of the 16 schools offering programs recognized by the American College of Nurse-Midwives. (These schools are Columbia and Downstate in New York City, Yale, Johns Hopkins, the Frontier School in Kentucky, Georgetown, Meharry in Tennessee, the Medical Center at Andrews Air Force Base in Maryland, St. Louis University, New Jersey Medical College and the Universities of Illinois, Kentucky, Minnesota, Mississippi, South Carolina and Utah.) The courses of instruction (which may last up to 24 months) include such subjects as normal and abnormal reproductive anatomy and physiology (both male and female), embryology, neonatology and genetics. Student midwives also watch or assist at as many as 40 or 50 labors and deliveries and will themselves manage (under supervision) a minimum of 20. This adds up to at least five years of training after high school. Some programs are open to nurses who do not have bachelor's degrees. An increasing number of nurses, however, who already hold bachelor's degrees, are obtaining master's degrees in midwifery—for a total of six years' training. After graduation, one must take a national certification examination, given since 1971 by the American College of Nurse-Midwives. Upon passing this, one is finally entitled to write the initials C.N.M.—for Certified Nurse-Midwife—after one's name. (Sex is no barrier. There are currently two male C.N.M.'s in the United States—one teaching in Pennsylvania, the other delivering babies in an Army hospital in Kentucky.)

For a long time many states had legal barriers against midwifery, inherited from the days when doctors were trying to drive the "grannies" out of business. Today, the various state laws determining where C.N.M.'s can and cannot practice are changing so rapidly that the College of Nurse-Midwives has a hard time keeping track of them. In the last five years—thanks in part to the statement of the American College of Obstetricians and Gynecologists—nearly half the states (including New York, New Jersey, Pennsylvania, Virginia, Colorado and California, plus the District of Columbia) have changed their laws affecting nurse-midwifery. As of now, nurse-midwives can deliver babies in all but three states: Alabama, Massachusetts and Wisconsin. Yet some strange, extra-legal situations persist. In Alabama, for instance, while "granny" midwives are still legally delivering babies under county-by-county permits, the attorney general has ruled that the practice of nurse-midwifery "violates the present Alabama laws." And in some 20 states without any legal bars against nurse-midwives, there are actually none practicing—because of resistance on the part of hospitals or physicians or nursing groups or simply lack of interest in the communities.

Nurse-midwives handle only normal deliveries, and they always work with an obstetrician backing them up. Midwives can prescribe painkillers, give local (but not general) anesthesia and cut and repair episiotomies. However, they call in the obstetraicn whenever a forceps delivery or a cesarean section seems necessary. The midwives' specialty, however, is supporting a woman psychologically, throughout labor and delivery, so as to minimize the amount of medication she needs. "The uniqueness of the midwife," says Dorothea Lang, who is both director of the New York City Health Department's Nurse-Midwifery Service Program and also current president of the American College of

Nurse-Midwives, "is that she knows how to support a mother, minute by minute, and also how to manage her delivery safely at the same time.

"An obstetrician could do this, but he doesn't always have the time. While the midwife's challenge is the normal, the physicians challenge is the abnormal. A normal obstetrical case is only one of his minor problems compared with the serious problems he's got waiting outside his door: complicated obstetrical cases, gynecological surgery, endocrinological problems, breast cancer. That's where his expertise lies. No one else can take care of those women. That's why the obstetrician-midwife team concept is really perfect."

New York City now has about 100 nurse-midwives delivering babies in 18 hospitals. The Roosevelt Hospital program—which was started by Dr. Thomas Dillon, Roosevelt's chief of obstetrics and gynecology, and its chief midwife, Barbara Brennan—is the only one in a private, voluntary hospital offering midwife deliveries to private patients. For a flat fee of $459, a woman gets a package deal covering all prenatal and postpartum visits and, at the time of her delivery, two nights in the hospital. The midwives try to respond to what women want. "Anything that they ask that is reasonable, that won't hurt them or the baby, is fine with us," says Barbara Brennan. Any one person— husband, mother, boyfriend—may stay with a woman throughout labor and delivery. "We don't give our patients anesthesia unless they want it, and if they don't want their legs up in stirrups or they don't want an episiotomy, that's okay."

One young couple, whom I'll call Renée and Sal Smith, recently came to the Roosevelt midwives for the delivery of their firstborn. For the Smiths, the low price was a factor: Sal, 29, teaches literature part-time at a city college while working on his own Ph.D. Renée, 24, a fine-arts major at Hunter, had first gone to an obstetrical clinic at another hospital, but "really hated" it. "The obstetricians weren't personal at all. They were very clinical and just totally medical. I was also afraid. I didn't know who would deliver me, or what they would allow." From Renée's first visit to the midwives, she was "very impressed. The midwife spent an hour with me, explaining things. Doctors some times tend to just say you're fine and not go into the medical details. The midwife would always explain whether my blood pressure was good or not, and what they were testing the urine sample for. It puts the responsibility on you to understand what's going on in your own body." Sal felt that Renée's whole attitude changed with her first visit to the midwives. "I couldn't believe it. Her tension really seemed to come down."

About 8 one Tuesday morning in the early summer, Renée and Sal arrived at the hospital. Renée's uterus was contracting at about five-minute intervals. Throughout her pregnancy, at each appointment, she had seen any one of the five midwives: Barbara Brennan, Eldra Simmons, Jeanne Kobritz, Mary Dowd or Dorinda Dew. This day Renée was greeted by Jeanne Kobritz—a cheerful, outgoing young woman only a few years older than Renée herself— who holds both a B.S. from the University of Maine and an M.S. from Columbia. Jeanne felt Renée's abdomen to determine the baby's position. It was lying head down—the normal way—but facing toward Renée's right side. "That's fine," Jeanne told her. "The head will probably turn to face the rear as it comes down." Jeanne also examined Renée. Wearing a mask and sterile gloves, she reached up into Renée's vagina until she could feel the cervix (the mouth of the uterus). Normally a thick structure, protruding into the vagina, the cervix had thinned and virtually disappeared, and it had also opened to a diameter of a good 6 centimeters (about $2\frac{1}{2}$ inches). It would need to dilate to 10 centimeters (about 4 inches) before the baby's head could pass through. Jeanne and an obstetrical nurse then attached a fetal monitor, strapping two belts, each with an electronic sensor, around Renée's abdomen. One sensor would pick up her unborn baby's heartbeat; the other would detect the frequency and duration of her uterine contractions. The monitor would continuously record this data, throughout Renée's labor, on a long strip of graph paper, and Jeanne would watch it, looking at the relationship of the baby's heartbeat to the stress of Renée's contractions—whether the heart rate dropped, and, if it did, whether and how fast it recovered. As Jeanne and Sal settled down by Renée's bedside in the labor room for the vigil, Sal confided, "We don't care whether the baby is a boy or a girl, but we think it is going to be a boy."

With each contraction, Renée lay back in bed and conscientiously breathed deeply, as she had been taught, to help her relax, while Sal timed the contraction by counting out the seconds, "15 . . . 30 . . . 40 . . . 50 . . ." Jeanne breathed with Renée, picking up her rhythm breath for breath, and Renée sighed gratefully, "It's nice to know that somebody's with me." Jeanne was prepared to spend all day, if necessary, coaching Renée through the unknown ordeal ahead. If all went well this Tuesday morning—if Renée's labor and delivery remained normal—she would have her baby without ever seeing a doctor.

Some women have become so angry at obstetricians and hospitals that they have been taking the extreme step of having their babies at home, attended only by friends or by self-appointed, underground (and illegal) "lay midwives" without any formal training. Women of a number of ethnic groups—Spanish-Americans, Chinese, gypsies—have long preferred, for reasons of modesty, to be delivered by other women and at home. Now the phenomenon is spreading. In a new book, "Immaculate Deception," Suzanne Arms passionately denounces hospitals and physicians and extols the "beauty" and "naturalness" of home birth. The New York City nurse-midwives get calls all the time asking them to do home deliveries—which is against the policy of the American College of Nurse-Midwives. In California, illegal midwifery has become so widespread that last year the state cracked down and arrested several women in Santa Cruz for practicing medicine without a license.

The trouble is, home delivery is risky. While some 95 percent of all births are indeed normal, significant complications can develop after the onset of labor. "A normal delivery is only normal retrospectively," points out Dorothea Lang. "At any minute a normal birth can turn into an abnormal one."

As we shall see.

By 10 a.m., after two hours of labor, Renée's contractions were stronger and coming every two or three minutes, and she was no longer interested in conversation. When Jeanne examined her for the second time, her membranes had ruptured, spilling out the amniotic fluid that surrounds and protects a fetus in the womb. Jeanne routinely checked to make sure that the fluid was not stained with the baby's fecal materal and that the umbilical cord was not appearing ahead of the baby—both signs of trouble. All was well. "You're a good 8 centimeters dilated," Jeanne reported, "and the baby's head seems to be coming down well. Youre moving right along; you went 2 centimeters in an hour and a half. You've got another 2 centimeters to go."

A few minutes later Renée was racked by nausea and threw up repeatedly. Jeanne explained that she had now reached the so-called "transition" stage between early labor and the more active, second stage of labor. "Transition is from about 7 centimeters to fully dilated. You've got all the signs. Your contractions are stronger. You're nauseous, and you probably feel sweaty. Transition is a different type of contraction, different frequency and intensity. And it hurts. It's the part that really bugs you."

11 am. Renée was still not fully dilated, and she was in such agony that she was glassy-eyed and tossing her head from side to side as she tried to breathe deeply through the contractions. "I feel so awful. I can't. I can't. I can't do it anymore."

"Yes, you can. Yes, you can," Jeanne encouraged her. "You're doing remarkably well." Jeanne also asked her if she wanted any medication, and Renée nodded gratefully. Jeanne then rigged an intravenous tube and injected Demerol directly into a blood vessel in Renée's arm so that the drug would work rapidly.

"When women are in transition," Jeanne explained later, "and the contractions come fast and close, they sometimes become almost psychotic. They have these feelings of impending doom, and they often say, 'I can't make it. I'm going to die." Renée only said "I can't do it" once or twice, but that's the beginning of a kind of panic that can set in.

"What you have to do is get them out of that right away, because if they get too far into that, it's harder for them to get back under control. If you can just help them with a little medication, to take the edge off the pain, they can do the breathing and relax. And you have to give a lot of encouragement. Renée is doing very well, but even if they aren't, you tell them that they are. Sometimes you're the only thread that they're hanging onto."

About noon, Renée was finally fully dilated, and it was time for her to begin actively pushing the baby out. Jeanne and Barbara Brennan, who had looked in and stayed to help, stood on either side of the bed, supporting Renée's legs while she braced her feet against their sides, as they had her—with each contraction—grab her knees, spread them far apart and bear down hard to try to expel the baby. It was hard work, and Renée screwed up her face each time with the effort. The two midwives kept up a running patter of instruction and encouragement. "Take a deep breath and hold it. Push down hard. Push. Push. Push. A longer push is more effective than a lot of short ones. Take another deep breath and hold it. Hold it. Hold it. Really push that baby's head down as far as you can. Excellent."

Renée had barely begun to push when she sank back on the pillows, exhausted, and moaned, "Please, I can't take any more pain. I don't have any strength left. Can I have something else?" Jeanne dissuaded her, telling her that "whatever you get the baby gets." Just at that point, Barbara was able to tell her, "I can see the baby's head!"

Now, however, ominously, the fetal monitor began showing that the baby's heartbeat was dipping. With each contraction, the heart rate was dropping from a normal 120 to 160 beats a minute to down below 100. The contractions apparently were reducing the blood flow—and thus the oxygen supply—to the baby's brain. The baby was in mild distress.

"I was beginning to sweat a little," Jeanne admitted later. "The fetal heart had been gorgeous throughout the whole labor, so we knew the baby was in good shape. The dip in the heart rate was not significant, really, but it was significant enough that the wheels started to turn. I was concerned enough to start thinking of alternatives."

The cesarean-section room at Roosevelt is only about 50 feet away from the labor rooms, and the midwives can have an obstetrician operating within minutes, if need be, to save a baby's life. "Although an emergency cesarean was in the back of my mind, I didn't really have to think about it with Renée, because she was far enough along that the baby could be delivered with forceps." Jeanne had also just seen the back-up obstetrician in the labor and delivery area, and knew he was already in scrub clothes. "Knowing that it would only be an instant meant that I didn't have to panic that much."

12:20 p.m. Aloud, Jeanne said to Renée, "When you get the next contraction, you've got to push like hell. The baby's heartbeat is a little low. There may be a loop of cord, so that every time you push, it tightens around the baby's neck or an arm or its chest. We want to get the baby out. An obstetrician can deliver it now with forceps, it looks like, if we have to." Jeanne also had the obstetrical nurse give Renée oxygen, to increase the oxygen supply to the baby, and she had Renée roll over on her side, between contractions, to shift the baby's weight. With these maneuvers, the baby's heartbeat picked up as soon as each contraction was over.

"We don't hide things from our patients," Jeanne told me later. "I didn't tell Renée every possible thing that I might be thinking could be going wrong, but I wanted her to be prepared. And that's when you really need to have the patient cooperative and in control, because if they aren't pushing then, you've got more of a problem. Every contraction they don't push means that there is that much more time the baby may be in distress.

"I would have been a lot more nervous if I'd been delivering that baby in somebody's living room. I don't know what I'd do, if I were in somebody's house, and the fetal heart was 60 and going. I just can't imagine how panicky I'd be. You might make it to a hospital, but if you do, what are you giving the parents? You might be giving them a brain-damaged child."

12:38 p.m. "Now don't push!" The midwives and the nurse quickly wheeled Renée out of the labor room and across the hall into the sterile delivery room, where they helped her onto the delivery table and lifted her legs into stirrups. The forceps delivery would not be necessary. Renée's eyes were dark and she was now whimpering with pain. 12:43. "A little teeny push, Renée." Jeanne—in cap, mask, sterile gown and gloves—quickly snipped a small episiotomy to prevent the vagina from tearing. 12:45. As Renée watched in an overhead mirror, the baby's head appeared, face down as predicted. Jeanne expertly slipped her hands down to see if the cord was looped around its neck. It wasn't. Then the rest of the baby slid out. It was a girl. A perfectly normal baby girl, about 6 pounds, letting out a healthy squall.

The tension broke. "I'm not really sure what made the heart go down," Jeanne said. "Maybe head compression." Sal was so excited he kept exclaiming over and over again, "We have a little girl! We have a little girl! I knew we'd have a little girl!"

When the baby was only a minute old, Jeanne laid her on Renée's abdomen and as Renée cradled her newborn, the infant immediately stopped crying and lay peacefully in her mother's arms. Renée's eyes were now luminous with delight. "That wasn't too bad. I was surprised it went so fast."

Premature Infants Respond to Sensory Stimulation

Ruth D. Rice

UNIVERSITY OF TEXAS, DALLAS

The newborn infant is not just a little pink, sleeping, unfeeling glob. Recent psychological findings have made us aware of how intensely the newborn responds to his or her environment.

We now know that each infant at birth has a distinctive personality determined in part by the mother's emotional condition during pregnancy and in the period immediately following birth.

A highly anxious mother subjected to a lot of stress will have a hyperactive, irritable, anxious baby, whose personality development after birth depends largely on minimal stress and maximal gratification of needs.

Failure to meet a baby's specific emotional needs at birth can cause psychosomatic symptoms within a few days or weeks after birth, including colic, hyperactivity, feeding difficulties and sleeping problems.

For premature infants and infants of low birth weight, these things are doubly important, since such infants suffer significantly more handicaps to begin with than do fullterm infants. It is well known that premature babies frequently have neurological, physical and mental defects and impaired motor and social functioning.

Despite numerous advances in scientific knowledge, premature and high-risk births are on the increase. And while new medical techniques have increased the survival rates for premature and high-risk infants, the incidence of morbidity has also increased.

Why is this so? Let's consider how unnatural and abrupt we have made the transition from the womb to life. The intrauterine environment is filled with the rich and varied sensations of the continual and progressive bombardment of activity that continues from the moment of conception to the moment of birth. Tactile-kinesthetic-vestibular stimulation is provided by the movements of the mother, the amniotic fluid, the muscular walls of the uterus, the placenta, and the fetal body itself. The fetus is massaged and stroked with each movement of

From *APA Monitor*, 1975, 6:11, 8–9. Copyright © 1975 by The American Psychological Association. Reprinted by permission.

the mother as she walks, bends, sits, and moves about. In his dark, watery cradle of amniotic fluid, the fetus swims gracefully about, weightless, as buoyant and active as an astronaut on a spacewalk, capable of free-floating movement and reflexive action. The amniotic fluid creates a whirlpool-like milieu, an environment that at once stimulates and protects the actively developing fetus.

The infant can hear the mother's heartbeat and may be imprinted by it. Other auditory stimulation is provided by the mother's digestive sounds and even by sounds outside the uterus.

The premature infant comes from the rich, close intimacy of the uterus with its constant stimulation to the incubator-isolette where little or no stimulation is provided. Hospital personnel are often reluctant to handle premature babies; many parents take their cues from this model and continue to hold or cuddle their premature infants less than they would a fullterm baby.

Indeed, it is highly probable that the premature child receives less stimulation throughout the entire developmental period than the fullterm child. Not only does this affect his neurophysiological development, but it places in serious jeopardy the mother/infant bonding and attachment relationship. The works by Klaus, Kennell*, Harlow, and others indicate that the attachment bond between mother and infant is based on tactile and sensory stimulation, not merely on feeding or caregiving. Humans are the only mammals that will tolerate the separation of newborn and mother. Other animals uniformly reject newborns from whom they are separated immediately after birth.

There is a significantly high number of premature births among the population of abused children, and the early and prolonged separation of mother and infant, deprived of the sensory bonding and attachment, may be one of the contributing causes.

All newborns need their mothers' close intimacy and frequent touch but the premature infant, cheated of the normal nine months of rich stimulation in the uterus, needs these things the most.

It is a lamentable fact that most hospitals do not allow mothers into their premature nurseries because of the fear of infection. The few studies that have been made in this area show that letting mothers into the nursery does not increase infection. Mothers, using if necessary the same sterile techniques that nurses use, could stroke, cuddle, talk to, feed and care for their babies while they are still in the incubator. Mothers should also be encouraged to provide breast milk for their incubator babies.

The study described below was designed to determine if neurological development and maturation could be facilitated through an increase in myelinization, cortical spacing and Nissl substance, and to determine if other cellular and endocrine functioning could be hastened in the premature infant. The nerve pathways from the skin are among the first to be sufficiently developed to activate and accelerate the rhythms and sequences of development. Since the neonate's responsiveness to tactile stimulation is greater than to other forms of stimulation, a tactile-kinesthetic stimulation treatment was developed to determine the effect on several variables of neurophysiological growth and development. Several variables were examined: (1) nine phylogenetic reflexes which

---

* See the article by Kennell, Klaus, and others that follows this one.

normally disappear by four months in fullterm infants. The disappearance of these primitive reflexes is a reliable index of maturation. They are: McCarthy, rooting, palmar-mental, crossed extensor, doll's eye, tonic neck, stepping automatic hand grasp and Galant; (2) two reflexes which normally appear with increasing cortical maturation and which normally are present in four-month old fullterm infants, and are also reliable indices of neurological maturation. These reflexes are the labyrinthine head righting reflex and the Landau; (3) weight, length and head circumference gain, and (4) mental and motor functioning.

Thirty prematurely born infants, who were 37 weeks or less in gestational age (determined by the Dubowitz neurological and physical assessment within 48 hours after birth) and whose birth weight was (2500 grams) or less were randomly placed in experimental and control groups. There were no significant differences in any birth variable or in sex. There was an equal distribution of race (Caucasian, black and Mexican-American) between the two groups and each included a set of twins. The infants were all born in a large city-county hospital in Dallas, Texas, and their mothers were all of a low socioeconomic status.

Treatment consisted of a sequential, caudocephalic progression of a precise method of stroking and massaging the infant's entire body. Public health nurses, were taught the treatment and they, in turn, taught the treatment to the mothers. They were instructed to provide the stimulation for 15 minutes, four times a day, for a period of 30 days beginning the day the infant came home from the hospital. Following each stroking treatment, the infant was rocked, held and cuddled for an additional five minutes. Each experimental infant received at least 120 such treatments during the first 30 days after release from the hospital nursery. The average stay of the infants in the hospital was two weeks.

Each mother was visited daily during the 30-day treatment period by a public nurse. Eighteen nurses were used in the study. The mothers were given timers to use with the treatments and weekly charts on which to record her observations about treatments.

When the mother of a control infant went home from the hospital, she received only the usual instructions for infant care given her by the attending physician. Control mothers were also visited by public health nurses, though not as frequently as the experimental mothers.

To insure that all infants, experimental and control, had sufficient nutrition during the experimental period, a four-month supply of formula was provided for each baby.

At four months of age, which was several weeks after treatment had ended, each infants' neurological, physical and mental/motor development was assessed by a pediatrician, a psychologist and a pediatric nurse who did not know which infant was experimental or control.

The results of the assessment indicated that stroking and rocking can accelerate maturation of cellular components insofar as neurological development can be measured by functional behavior. There were significant differences (p < .05) in favor of the experimental infants in the assessment of the phylogenetic reflexes. Six of the nine reflexes were not present in the experimental group at four months of age. There were significant differences (p < .001) in favor of the experimental infants in the assessment of the labyrinthine and Landau reflexes. A significant difference (p < .04) in weight gain occurred with the experimental infants, indicating an increase in enzymatic and endocrine functioning. And there were significant differences (p < .05) in mental functioning as measured by the Bayley Scales of Infant Development.

There were no significant differences in head circumference, body length or motor development, though the raw scores for each of these variables were greater for the experimental group.

Subjective findings indicated that the infants receiving the stroking and rocking were more socially adaptive and aggressive. Further, the nature of the treatment was such that the mother/infant relationship was enhanced and nurtured. This phenomenon could have far-reaching effects on the infant's continuing development of psycho-social-cognitive development and functioning.

It seems reasonable to predict from the findings of this study that a premature infant who achieves a more robust neurophysiological development would elicit a mother's more confident responsiveness, which in turn would set up a cyclic interaction of stimulus-response behavior. Some evidence of this cyclic interaction was noted when the mothers administered the treatments. Infants quieted, smiled, established eye contact and vocalized. Mothers observed this behavior with interest and pleasure, relating their belief that the "baby likes being stroked and held by me."

In short, the infants who were systematically stroked and rocked by their mothers for 30 days after arriving home from the hospital made significant gains in weight, neurological development and in mental functioning. In addition, it is suggested that they surpassed the rate of growth of normal, fullterm infants by virtue of age adjustment. A baby who was eight weeks premature at birth, and who was 16 weeks at examination date, would have an adjusted age of eight weeks total age. Thus, this infant would have made a 24-week gain in 16 weeks. In other words, at four months, chronological age, not only would this infant have "caught up" with a fullterm infant, but would have accelerated another eight weeks in developmental functioning. This was also evidenced in weight gain. The average weight gain for a fullterm infant is double his birth weight by four months. All the experimental infants more than doubled their birth weight in four months. One infant, who was 32 weeks gestational age and three pounds at birth, weighed over 15 pounds at four months of age—a gain of five times her birth weight.

2
Early Infancy

The following articles deal with the competencies of the newborn and very young infant, and the environments in which infants are able to put their competencies to use. Among the most fascinating topics in the field of child development are the recent discoveries of what infants can do in the way of perception, motor behavior, self-regulation, and relating to caregivers. Behavior immediately after birth may set the tone of the first affectional interactions.

Mothers, as well as infants, have resources for interacting very soon after delivery. John H. Kennell and his associates have studied spontaneous behavior of mothers in the first minutes and hours after birth. A follow-up study of mother-infant interaction indicates some lasting effects of these initial contacts.

In the course of mutual regulation of mother and infant, each responds to signals or cues given by the other. Results of research by Padraic Burns, Louis W. Sander, Gerald Stechler, and Harry Julia show that the distress signals of infants are related to the type of care given and to the constancy of the caretaker environment. In a responsive environment, the ability to signal distress is the infant's means of changing the environment.

Lewis P. Lipsitt is justly famous for his elegant experiments with infants, and for his precision and creativity in designing and carrying out research. In the following article, Lipsitt's description of apparatus and procedure serves as an example and explanation of the remarkable ways in which scientists explore response capabilities and the interrelationships between response characteristics.

Maternal Behavior One Year After Early and Extended Post-Partum Contact

John H. Kennell, Richard Jerauld, Harriet Wolfe, David Chesler, Nancy C. Kreger, Willie McAlpine, Meredith Steffa, and Marshall H. Klaus

CASE WESTERN RESERVE UNIVERSITY

INTRODUCTION

In the past decade, extensive observations in animals and a small number of careful studies in the human mother have suggested that the prevailing hospital policies which separate pre-term sick, and even full-term infants from their mothers may change a mother's attachment to her infant, resulting in an alteration of behavior toward her baby months or years after the birth (Leifer et al. 1969, Barnett et al. 1970, Klaus and Kennell 1970). After the long period of separation, usually associated with the care of the preterm or high-risk infant, there has been an increased incidence of mothering disorders which may counteract the beneficial effects of improved hospital care (Klaus and Kennell 1970). There is a disproportionately high incidence of pre-term births, ranging from 21 to 41 per cent, in studies of infants who fail to thrive in the absence of organic disease (Ambuel and Harris 1963, Shaheen et al. 1968). In reports in which the birth history has been recorded, the association of child abuse with either pre-term birth or serious illness, with mother-infant separation in the newborn period, varies from 24 to 39 percent (Elmer and Gregg 1967, Klein and Stern 1971). Since an infant's mental and emotional development is dependent upon his mother's behavior and care, the influence of separation on the mother and infant may be vital.

In certain animals, such as cattle and sheep, immediate separation of the mother and infant after birth for brief periods (one to two hours) may lead to clearly unusual mothering behavior; the mother may neglect her young, butt her own offspring away, or indiscriminately feed her own and other infants (Collias 1956, Hersher et al. 1958). In contrast, if mother and infant animal remain together for the first four days and are separated on the fifth day for the same period of time, the mother quickly resumes the characteristic mothering behavior of her species when she and her young are reunited. Klopfer and coworkers (1964) have shown that goats establish stable and specific mother-infant bonds in the first five minutes after birth. If the kid is in contact with the mother during this short period it will be recognised, accepted, fed, and protected. But if the kid is removed during the initial five-minute period and returned to the mother later, she will often reject it by butting and kicking, and will refuse to nurture or protect it. Thus there is a special attachment period immediately after delivery in some species of animals, and deviant

From *Developmental Medicine and Child Neurology*, 1974, **16**:2, 172–179. Reprinted by permission of Spastics International Medical Publications.

behavior may result if the animal mother is separated from her young during this period.

PRESENT STUDY   To test the hypothesis of a special attachment period existing in the human mother, two groups of primiparous mothers were studied. The control group comprised those who had the contact with their babies that is routine in American hospitals (a glance at their baby shortly after birth, a short visit at six to 12 hours after birth for identification purposes, and then 20- to 30-minute visits for feeding every four hours during the day). The extended-contact group consisted of mothers who, in addition to the contact mentioned above, were given their naked babies in bed with a heat panel for a period of one hour within the first three hours after birth and were allowed five extra hours with their babies for each of the first three days—a total of 16 hours more than the control group.

This report describes the differences in maternal behavior at one month and one year in these two groups of mothers, and presents observations which suggest that there may be a period shortly after birth which is of unique importance for mother-to-infant attachment in humans.

MATERIALS AND METHODS

There were 14 mothers in each group. Assignment to the groups depended on the day of delivery. Only mothers who were going to bottle-feed their babies were admitted to the study. The two groups were nearly identical with respect to mean age, social, economic and marital status, color, pre-medication, and days spent in hospital (Table 1). Mean birthweights were similar for both groups of infants.

In order to exclude any influence which might confuse the results, the nurses caring for the mothers adjusted their total daily time spent with them so that it was the same for both groups.

TABLE 1

Clinical Data of Mothers in the Two Groups

	EXTENDED-CONTACT GROUP ($N = 14$)	CONTROL GROUP ($N = 14$)
Black	13	13
White	1	1
Married	4	5
Mean age (years)	18.2	18.6
Days in hospital	3.8	3.7
Nursing time (minutes per day)	13	14
Mean birthweight of babies	3184g	3074g
Male/female infants	6/8	8/6

The first interview with the mothers was conducted 28 to 32 days following delivery and focused on the general well-being of the babies (such as the number of stools passed daily). Two questions about caretaking were scored by independent raters: 0, 1, 2, or 3. (The scores assigned for behavior were chosen arbitrarily to determine whether there were differences between the two groups, not to decide which was "best.")

The first question was: "When the baby has been fed and his diaper is dry and he still cries, what do you do?" Scores were given as follows: 0—mother always let the baby cry it out; 1—mother tended to let the baby cry it out; 2—mother tended to pick up the baby; 3—mother always picked up the baby. The second question was: "Have you been out since your baby was born? How did you feel." The scores were: 0—felt "good" while out; 1—thought about infant while out; 2—worried about infant while out; 3—didn't want to leave infant.

A second measure of maternal behavior was provided during a standardized examination of the infants in the presence of their mothers. Scores were given as follows: 0—mother remained seated and detached during the examination; 1—mother remained seated but watched; 2—mother sometimes stood and watched; 3—mother continuously stood and watched her baby during the examination. When the babies cried, maternal behavior was observed and scores given as: 0—ignored infant; 1—rarely soothed infant; 2—sometimes soothed infant; 3—always soothed infant.

Maternal behavior was also studied by the use of time-lapse films of the mother feeding their infants. All were aware that they were being photographed and they had an unlimited amount of time in which to complete the feeding. The actual filming was performed through a one-way mirror and took 15 minutes, at a speed of 60 frames per minute. The reactions of mothers and babies were then analyzed at one-second intervals. Analysers who did not know to which group the mothers belonged scored each of the first 600 frames for twenty-five specific activities, which varied from caretaking skills (e.g. position of the bottle) to measurements of the mothers' affection and interest (whether the mother's body was touching the infant's, whether she fondled her infant, and the amount of "en face"). "En face" is defined as the position of the mother's face held so that her eyes and those of her infant meet fully in the same vertical plane of rotation. Fondling refers to a spontaneous active interaction, not associated with feeding, initiated by the mother—such as stroking, kissing, bouncing and cuddling.

On finding apparent differences in the maternal behavior of the two groups at one month, we decided to follow-up the mother-infant pairs at one year in order to see whether the differences persisted. At the one-year examination, the mothers were observed by investigators who were not familar with the mothers in the study and none had had contact with the mothers during the 11-month interim.

These observers carefully monitored mother-infant interaction and the movements of the baby through a two-way mirror in seven separate situations: (1) an interview; (2) a physical examination of the infant, with weighing and hematocrit determination; (3) a separation of mother and infant, with the mother going behind a door, then re-entering for a reunion; (4) a picture-taking of the mother and infant; (5) free play; (6) a Bayley developmental testing of the infant; and (7) a filmed feeding of the infant. Verbal utterances were recorded on audiotape. Behavior was recorded by three methods, each of which permitted quantitative and continuous timed observations: (*a*) an analysis of a time-lapse film; (*b*) a direct check-list; and (*c*) a continuous-recording technique using a typewriter.

The standardized interview began with a question about how things were going. The mothers were then asked: "Have you worked or gone to school since the birth of your baby?" 13 mothers (six in the extended contact group, seven in the control group) answered "yes" and were then asked: "How did you feel?"

During the physical examination of the infants, an observer recorded, on a check-list, the location and activities of the mothers every 15 seconds. The mothers' reactions were recorded when their babies cried (for example, whether the mother struck the baby, criticized or scolded, ignored, or soothed her baby). Soothing was defined as three or more active attempts to comfort the baby within a 15-second period. Inter-observer reliability was calculated for individual behaviors. 70 per cent were greater than .85, and 91 per cent were greater than .80 (average = .84).

RESULTS

Analysis of the interview data at one month is shown in Table 2. The extended-contact group had scores of 2 or more, whereas mothers in the control group were at the lower end of the scale. (The chance of this occurrence is less than .05 with the use of the Mann-Whitney U test.)

Mothers in the extended-contact group more often picked up their babies when they cried, and tended to stay at home with their infants.

Observations during the physical examination of the babies revealed different scores for the two groups (Table 3). While no mother in the extended-contact group scored below 3, the scores of the control group ranged 1 to 6

TABLE 2
Maternal Scores from a Standardized Interview at One Month

| | NUMBER OF MOTHERS | |
MATERNAL SCORES	Control	Extended Contact
0	5	0
1	1	0
2	0	1
3	1	1
4	4	5
5	2	5
6	1	2
Total	14	14

SOURCE OF DATA: Klaus et al., 1972.

TABLE 3

Scored Observations of the Mothers Made During the Physical Examination of Their Infants at One Month

SCORE	NUMBER OF MOTHERS	
	Control	Extended Contact
1	1	0
2	4	0
3	3	1
4	2	1
5	2	4
6	2	3
Total	14	14

SOURCE OF DATA: Klaus et al., 1972.

(p < .02). The mothers in the extended-contact group significantly more often stood beside the examination table and soothed their babies when they cried.

Fondling and "en face" scores for the two groups are shown in Table 4. Although the amount of time the mothers looked at their babies did not significantly differ in the two groups, the extended-contact mothers were observed to have spent significantly more time "en face" and fondling their infants (p < .05).

When their infants were one year of age, the mothers in the two groups also proved to be significantly different in their answers to an interview question and in their behavior during a physical examination of the infants. The scores on the interview questions showed that, of the mothers who had returned to work or school, the extended-contact mothers were more preoccupied with their babies than were the control mothers (Figure 1). Only one of the control mothers said that she missed her baby, while five of the six mothers in the extended-contact group said that they worried about or greatly missed their babies. Six of the seven mothers in the control group did not mention the baby at all, but responded with more self-focused answers, such as "I was happy to be back at work, but I was on my feet all day." This discriminating orientation of the mothers either to their infants or to themselves was similar to the responses observed at the one-month evaluation.

TABLE 4

Filmed Feeding Analysis at One month, Showing Percentage of "En Face" and Fondling Times in Mothers of Both Groups

GROUP	"EN FACE"	FONDLING	TOTAL
Control	3.5	1.6	5.1
Extended Contact	11.6	6.1	17.7

SOURCE OF DATA: Klaus et al., 1972.

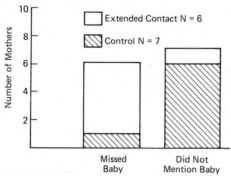

FIGURE 1.   *Maternal scores from a standardized interview at one year.*

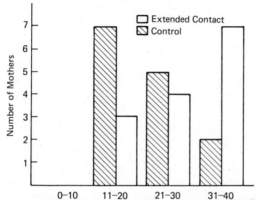

FIGURE 2.   *Scored observations of the mothers made during the physical examination of their infants at one year. Number of 15-second time periods spent at table-side assisting the physician.*

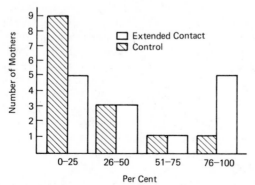

FIGURE 3.   *Scored observations of the mothers made during the physical examination of their infants at one year. Number of 15-second time periods spent soothing their infants in response to crying.*

Figure 2 shows that, in the 10-minute observation period during the physical examination, seven of the 14 extended-contact mothers spent 31 to 40 of the total 15-second time periods at the tableside assisting the physician, while only two of the mothers in the control group did so (p < .05). Half of the control mothers spent only 11 to 20 of the 15-second time periods assisting.

The mothers' responses to infant crying are seen in Figure 3. Note that six of the extended-contact mothers soothed in response to crying more than 50 per cent of the time, compared with two mothers in the control group. The majority of the control mothers spent less than 25 percent of the time soothing. Over-all, the mothers in the extended-contact group spent more time soothing in response to crying and were more likely to kiss their babies (p = .05).

The mother infant interactions during the developmental examination, interview, picture-taking, and free-play situations showed no significant differences between the two groups. The mean scores of the two groups for the Bayley mean developmental index were 98 for infants of extended-contact mothers and 93 for control infants (p > .05). Observations of the mothers during the feeding and separation studies were confused by the differing motor development of the infants at one year of age and could not be compared.

DISCUSSION

In view of the large number of factors affecting maternal behavior (Klaus and Kennell 1970), such as the mothers' genetic and cultural backgrounds, their relations with their husbands and families, the planning and courses of their pregnancies, their own mothering as infants, and their experiences in their families—the significant differences at one year in response to an interview question for 13 of the mothers, and in maternal behavior during the physical examination for the entire group, were not anticipated. We were surprised at the consistency of the differences over a span of 11 months, and wondered if only a few mothers in one or both groups had accounted for this. However, the ranking of the mothers within each of the two groups showed no significant correlation for the measures at the one-month and one-year examinations (that is, a mother ranking high in a certain activity at one month might be low at one year).

The differences between the two groups that were still present at one month after over 200 feeds, and over the first year after countless other encounters between mother and infant, may have significant effects on the infants. The evidence that differences in maternal attentiveness and responsiveness to the babies' cries continued through the first year assumes additional significance when seen in the light of Rubenstein's (1967) observations that increased maternal attentiveness facilitates later exploratory behavior in infants. A human mother's interaction with her baby, and therefore that baby's ultimate development, may be greatly influenced by early and extended contact.

The only comparable study is that of Leifer et al. (1972) who demonstrated significant differences in attachment behavior between mothers of full-term infants and two groups of mothers of preterm infants at one month. When mothers who were separated from their pre-term babies for the first three to 12 weeks (except for visual contact) were compared with mothers of pre-term infants permitted early tactile contact (two to three days after birth), Leifer and co-workers found no differences in observed behavior at one month. But they did discover that there were more divorces (five compared with none) and more infants relinquished (two compared with none) in the group of mothers with the prolonged separation from their babies.

Even though the social and economic status of the mothers in our study is different from the mothers of the full-term infants in the Leifer study, it is interesting that the same categories of maternal behavior observed during feeding at one month were surprisingly similiar in both studies (*ventral contact*, 77.2 per cent in the Leifer study compared with 64.8 per cent in our extended-contact group and 71.7 in the control group; *mother looks only at her infant*, 75 per cent in Leifer's study compared with 79.5 per cent in our extended-contact group and 72.9 percent in the control mothers).

Leifer noted that a "confluence of factors not all equally influential at any one point in time or over time" are involved in eliciting and maintaining maternal attachment behavior. From our studies, an important factor affecting attachment appears to be the period of time the mother spends in close contact with her baby in the first hours and days of life.

This is a preliminary study, and what appear to be striking findings need to be replicated in a larger study, but those who care for mothers and infants should be aware of the possible long-term effects—both positive and negative— of the early post-partum period.

SUMMARY

The observations of maternal behavior in 28 human mothers of full-term infants reported in this study are consistent with investigations in animals; measurable differences, lasting for as long as one year, are apparent between mothers with early and extended contact and those separated from their infants in the early hours after birth. The awareness of a special attachment period shortly after birth—during which brief periods of partial or complete separation may drastically distort a mother animal's feeding and caring for her infant—would lead a caretaker or naturalist to be extemely cautious about any intervention in the period after birth.

In the human mother, the disproportionately high percentage of mothering disturbances, such as child abuse and deprivation failure-to-thrive, which occur after a mother has been separated from her sick newborn infant, force a thorough review and evaluation of our present perinatal practices.

Acknowledgements This work is supported in part by the Grant Foundation and the Educational Foundation of America.

References

AMBUEL, J., HARRIS, B. (1963) "Failure to thrive: a study of failure to grow in height or weight." *Ohio Medical Journal*, **59**, 997.

BARNETT, C., LEIDERMAN, P., GROBSTEIN, R., KLAUS, M. (1970) "Neonatal separation: the maternal side of interactional deprivation." *Pediatrics*, **45**, 197.

COLLIAS, M. (1956) "The analysis of socialization in sheep and goats." *Ecology*, **37**, 228.

ELMER, E., GREGG, G. (1967) "Developmental characteristics of abused children."
Pediatrics, **40**, 596.

HERSHER, L., MOORE, A., RICHMOND, J. (1958) "Effect of post-partum separation of
mother and kid on maternal care in the domestic goat." *Science*, **128**, 1342.

KLAUS, M., KENNELL, J. (1970) "Mothers separated from their newborn infants."
Pediatric Clinics of North America, **17**, 1015.

―――― PLUMB, N., ZUEHLKE, S. (1970) "Human maternal behavior at the first contact
with her young." *Pediatrics*, **46**, 187.

―――― JERAULD, R., KREGER, N., McALPINE, W., STEFFA, M., KENNELL, J. H. (1972)
"Maternal attachment: importance of the first post-partum days." *New England
Journal of Medicine*, **286**, 460.

KLEIN, M., STERN, L. (1971) "Low birthweight and the battered child syndrome."
American Journal of Diseases of Children, **122**, 15.

KLOPFER, P. H., ADAMS, D., KLOPFER, M. (1964) "Maternal 'imprinting' in goats."
Proceedings of the National Academy of Science, **52**, 911.

LEIFER, A. D., LEIDERMAN, P. H., BARNETT, C. R., WILLIAMS, J. A. (1972) "Effects of
mother-infant separation on maternal attachment behavior." *Child Development*, **43**,
1203.

RUBENSTEIN, J. (1967) "Maternal attentiveness and subsequent exploratory behavior in
the infant." *Child Development*, **38**, 1089.

SHAHEEN, E., ALEXANDER, D., TRUSKOWSKY, M., (1968) "Failure to thrive—a retrospective profile." *Clinical Pediatrics*, **7**, 255.

Distress in Feeding: Short-Term Effects of Caretaker Environment of the First 10 Days*

Padraic Burns, Louis W. Sander, Gerald Stechler, and Harry Julia
BOSTON UNIVERSITY AND FRAMINGHAM STATE COLLEGE

This report is part of an extensive investigation into infant-caretaker adaptation
in the first 8 weeks of life. The study involved monitoring of a number of
variables involving infants and caretakers, and was designed to investigate the
development of regulatory processes in their interaction. The goal of this paper
is to illustrate the effect of replacement of the primary caretaker at 11 days of
life on a specific aspect of infant behavior, namely, "distress" or discomfort
during feeding. This "distress" behavior is viewed as a communication in the
interaction process by means of which the infant and caretaker reach a mutually
satisfactory adapted state.

From the *Journal of the American Academy of Child Psychiatry*, 1972, **11**, 427–439. Reprinted
by permission.

* This research has been supported by USPHS Grants Nos. K5–MH–20, 505, K–MH–18, 521,
HDO1766, 1–4, RO3–MH–15, 803–01. Both Dr. Sander and Dr. Stechler are Research
Scientists in the Research Development Program of the NIMH.
    Acknowledgment is made to Boston Hospital for Women, Lying-In Division, for the extended
use of their facilities, without which completion of the study would not have been possible.
Acknowledgment is also made to the Booth Memorial Home, and the Crittenton Hastings House,
and to their staffs, for their assistance in obtaining subjects. Special appreciation is expressed for
the contributions of Davida Pekarsky, M.A., for her help in collecting and preparing these data.

In a previous longitudinal study of early mother-infant interaction, Sander (1962) outlines a sequence of adaptive issues to be negotiated during successive 2–4-month periods in the first year. These are related epigenetically so that the success of one determines to some extent the base on which the next will rest. Successful negotiation of the first issue is achieved when the infant by the age of $2\frac{1}{2}$ months has established regularity in basic life processes such as eating and sleeping, which is coupled with evidence of comfort. This negotiation produces a corresponding feeling of satisfaction in the mother, who may then report that she has come to feel she now "knows" her baby, knows what he needs and how to satisfy him. The successful completion of an initial phase of adaptation readies the infant and mother for a next level of adaptation in the progressive development of social responsiveness and affective communication.

Of particular interest in this previous study was the finding (Pavenstedt and Sander, 1962) that, although there was considerable variation in the speed and success of the negotiation of the various issues, the successful negotiation of the initial adaptation was highly correlated with ratings of outcome of subsequent issues over the first 18 months of life. This observation suggested that the early organization of regulatory processes mediating between infant functions and caretaking activities may be of considerable significance for further development, and this suggested further and more precise investigation.

The conceptual model with which we approach this task includes the infant and primary caretaker (usually the mother) as components of a field or system interacting in an adaptive process, leading to an ever-developing synchronous organization of the field, within each and between the two main partners. A difficulty is generated by the fact that differences in central nervous systems and behavioral organizations are very great between the principals. They begin with a disparate organization and move toward coordination, on the basis of modifications in behavior of each, as their recurrent encounters become stabilized and predictable. For example, the child's sleeping rhythms and patterns only very gradually approximate those of the adult. Over the course of the first months we usually see the gradual development of longer sleep periods during the night and more awakening during the day, with the gradual establishment of a pattern that more or less fits that of the mother and the other family members. The young infant who tends to be wakeful and active at night and to sleep by day can disrupt the schedule of the mother and induce an uncomfortable sense of disorganization in her, or in the rest of the household, if she adapts to the baby. Certainly, asynchronization of interdependent life processes threatens to impose a strain on a family system.

We assume, therefore, that establishment of synchronization between intrinsic infant rhythms and stable regularities of the caretaking system (Sander et al., 1970) is the critical accomplishment of the earliest mother-infant interaction. The research problem is to determine the mechanisms on which synchronization depends. Work to date points to the possibility that the mechanisms may involve highly specific cues (Sander et al., 1970). For example, Wolff (1968) has shown that mothers respond differentially to (tape-recorded) cries of their infants, distinguishing a hungry cry or an exasperated cry from one resulting from a painful stimulus. They appear to differentiate the pain cry by the long rest period following the first long expiratory cry, indicating that "The temporal arrangement of vocalizations thus served an important signaling function even in the newborn period" (p. 5).

The cues used by infants and mothers to regulate interactional behavior have not been extensively studied, and are not well known. Cyclic functions of the infant, such as sleep-wake, hunger-elimination, are generated intrinsically and appear to be relatively independent in the newborn, and in early development become synchronized into regulated behavior. This suggests the need for studies of the specific relation of each major function of the infant to the infant-caretaker interaction. We need clues to specific control links which may regulate the subsystems. This paper will present some data as illustrative evidence bearing on this issue.

METHODS

DESIGN   The study sample consisted of 3 groups of 9 normal[1] infants each (Table 1). Two groups were composed of infants given up by their mothers for adoptive placement and cared for by surrogate mothers. Of these, infants in Group A spent the first 10 days in the newborn nursery being cared for by the usual nursery staff (multiple caretaking) on the usual fixed nursery schedule. These infants were then shifted to an individual rooming-in arrangement in a regular hospital room where each infant was cared for by a single caretaker on a demand schedule 24 hours a day for the next 18 days. At the end of the first 4 weeks, the infant was placed in a regular agency foster home and there followed for a second 4-week period.

The infants in Group B (also going to adoptive placement) went directly into rooming-in (usually 24 hours after delivery) where they had a first single caretaker from day 2 through day 10, and were shifted to a second caretaker

TABLE 1

Group	N	Caretaking Period I (0–10 days)		Caretaking Period II (11–28 days)	Caretaking Period III (29–56 days)
A	9	Nursery		Single Caretaker (X or Y) Rooming-in	Foster Home
B	9	Single Caretaker (X or Y) Rooming-in		Single Caretaker (Y or X) Rooming-in	Foster Home
		0–5 days	6–10 days		
C	9	Natural Mother Rooming-in	Natural Mother At home	Natural Mother At home	Natural Mother At home

[1] Normality was precisely defined and controlled by prenatal history, observation of delivery, and postnatal examination.

from day 11 through day 28. These infants were always on a demand schedule while cared for in the hospital. After the first 4 weeks they also went to foster homes, where we continued to observe them for a second 4 weeks.

Group C was composed of infants of experienced multiparous mothers. These infants were cared for by their own mothers, in rooming-in for 5 days, and then were followed at home for the remainder of the 8-week study period.

Groups A and B were designed to elicit differences in infants cared for *over the first 10 days* by multiple caretakers on a rigid schedule, or by single caretakers on demand schedule, with subsequent (day 11 onward) caretaking conditions being the same. Infant assignment to the 2 groups and to the 2 nurses who did most of the rooming-in surrogate mothering was unbiased. Group C provided a basis for comparison rather than a strict control group. Obviously, home rearing by a mother differs in many ways from hospital and foster home rearing. Group C was designed to provide normative data for the parameters measured, with which to understand the more closely monitored group A and B infant-caretaker pairs.

FEEDING OBSERVATIONS: "DISTRESS IN FEEDING"   During the 8-week period over which each infant was studied, extensive data were collected in areas such as sleep-awake, crying, motility, intervention, perception, and feeding (Sander, 1969; Sander et al., 1970). This paper is concerned with feeding observations, especially the behavior termed "distress in feeding." The findings are based on data from observations of more than 800 feedings of the 27 infants. In Groups A and B, one feeding was observed daily over the 4-week hospital period and twice a week for the foster home period. Group C infants were observed daily for the first 10 days, both in the hospital and at home, 3 times a week for the remainder of the first month, and twice a week thereafter. The single observer sat or stood 4 to 5 feet from the feeding infant, watching carefully and recording a number of variables, such as feeding time, nipple-in time, sucking time, state changes, time looking at caretaker, amount of milk taken, position change, stimulation, and distress, recorded mostly in real time on a portable 4-channel Rustrak recorder.[2] The material described in this paper covers only the small part of the feeding observation data related to distress variables; other of the feeding data have been presented elsewhere (Burns and Sander, 1967) or will be reported more fully in the future.

As we observed feedings, it became clear that some infant-caretaker interactions were smoother and better coordinated than others. This judgment was a complex one and the elements were hard to distinguish and define; the "distress" category served to document the grosser levels of infant disturbance. "Distress during feeding" was defined for this study to include grimacing, turning away from the nipple, spitting out the nipple, gagging, spitting up, fussing, and crying. Each such evidence of distress of disomfort was recorded by the observer, who made a discrimination and judgment as to the nature, quality, and intensity of the behavior. The milder forms of refusal or discomfort (including grimacing, turning away, spitting out the nipple, mild fussing) were

---

[2] Controlled reliability testing has indicated that the method was extremely reliable, with correlations (Pearson r) for 2 observing 20 feedings ranging from .68 to .99, with 7 out of 9 variables recorded being .9 or better. Correlation for the "distress" measure was .82.

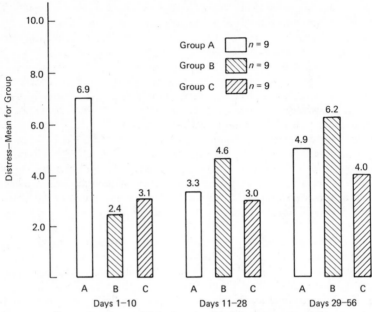

FIGURE 1.   *Distress scores: Caretaker groups x periods.*

given a score of 1 and the more intense (gagging, spitting up, crying) were scored as 2. A "distress" total score was then calculated for each separate feeding. These are the data considered here.

Crying or other distress during feeding is assumed to mean that some instability or incoordination exists in the feeding interaction. The caretaker uses such behavior on the part of the infant to regulate her own actions aimed at restoring him to greater comfort. There is considerable variation from infant to infant in the amount of distress shown. We assume that these variations are strongly influenced by individual differences in the makeup of the organism, as well as by external difference in the infants' environments. However, a distressed baby can usually be quieted by some appropriate comforting behavior by the caretaker. We have not yet been able to deal with the element of individual variation in feeding functions on the basis of initial measures. It is controlled here only by the nonbiased assignment of infants in the sample to the different groups and different caretakers.

FINDINGS

The "distress" measures for the three groups (A, B, C) for each of the 3 time periods (days 1–10, 11–28, 29–56) are shown in Figure 1. It can be seen that in the first time period (days 1–10), as might be expected, the infants in the newborn nursery (Group A), with multiple caretakers and a fixed 4-hour feeding schedule, showed considerably more "distress" events than did infants in rooming-in (Group B) or the Group C infants with their own mothers in the hospital and at home. Thus, it appeared that multiple caretakers and a fixed 4-hour feeding schedule were correlated with more evidence of discomfort and discoordination in the feeding process during the first 10 days.

In the second time period (days 11–28), the Group A infants, now in rooming-in, show a marked decrease in "distress" (t test, $p < .01$, 2 tailed), which appears to follow the shift from the less specifically responsive environment of the newborn nursery to a single rooming-in caretaker.

We were particularly struck by the finding that Group B infants shifted from low "distress" with their first rooming-in caretaker, to significantly higher "distress" with their second rooming-in caretaker (t test, $p < .02$, 2 tailed). Looking at Groups A and B alone in the first 2 time periods (first 4 weeks), an analysis of variance (two-way repeated measures) shows a significant difference between groups ($F = 4.68$, $p < .05$); no difference between time periods ($F = .38$), and a highly significant groups x periods interaction ($F = 11.95$, $p < .005$, df 1/16). This finding indicates that most of the variance is accounted for by the interaction, that is, related not primarily to the structure of the immediate situation (nursery vs. rooming-in), but to the sequence of environments. These findings are based on daily observations under highly uniform external conditions.

In the foster home period (days 29–56), with only 2 observations a week, the "distress" measures for both Groups A and B rose, Group B remaining higher than Group A. These increases are not statistically significant, probably because of both the greater variability in the environments of the foster homes and the relatively fewer observations.

Group C infants maintain a stable course through the 3 time periods with a slight, though not statistically significant rise in the second month, falling between Groups A and B in the first 10 days and slightly below them after day 11.

We were impressed by the increase in "distress" in the second period for Group B infants who had shifted from a first to a second caretaker. This suggested to us that in the first 10 days these infants had already established some organization, some degree of fittedness with the caretaker, in regulation of feeding function which led to distress, when violated by a new caretaker. In support of the idea that the increase is related to caretaker change, we noted that no such increase occurred at this time in Group C. We interpreted this finding as evidence that the degree of specificity of the caretaking environment in the first 10 days had affected the early organization of the infant so that those infants with early specific individual care were (or became) more sensitive to alterations in the caretaking environment.

We were able to pursue this hypothesis further with the same data because most of our sample babies had been cared for by 2 nurses who differed considerably in style of infant care. For Group A these 2 nurses cared for 7 of the 9 babies (over days 11–28), and for Group B cared for 7 of the 9 in days 2–10 (the first rooming-in period), and all 9 over days 11–28. These small groups of infants, although not adequate for statistical analysis, can be studied to see if different caretaking styles may influence "distress" patterns.

The differences in the caretaking styles of the 2 nurses were documented both by strongly agreed-upon clinical impressions and by quantitative difference registered in data on other areas of infant care (Sander, 1969; Sander et al., 1970).

Nurse Y appeared to give the more specifically infant-oriented care. She remained attentive to the infant's behavioral characteristics and insisted on giving priority to discovering individual differences and allowing them to guide her decisions about infant care. This included an ability to manifest her displeasure at interruptions or disruptions caused by the needs of the researchers to awaken or otherwise stimulate the infant in a way or at a time she felt was out of synchrony with the infant's needs.

Nurse X, on the other hand, was much more oriented toward the researcher and regular hospital staff, was very successful in making herself and all concerned comfortable, and even seemed to make the research task easier. At the same time it appeared clear that she did not see the infants so much as separate individuals and would say the same things about each baby.

When we now compare Group A infants with Group B infants first cared for in rooming-in by Nurse X and Nurse Y (Figure 2), it is clear that the infants first cared for by Nurse Y had the lowest "distress" in the first 10 days, followed by the greatest increase in the second period (when cared for by Nurse X), and again the greatest increase in the foster home. The infants first cared for by Nurse X show more "distress" in the first 10 days, but still less than those in the nursery. This score rises relatively less in the second period when they are cared for by Nurse Y, and then remains about the same in the foster home.

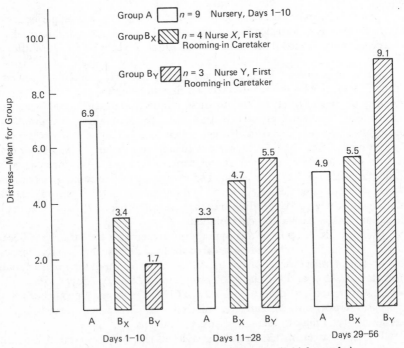

FIGURE 2.   *Distress scores: Caretaker groups (initial caretaker).*

DISCUSSION

"Distress" behaviors as defined for this study were quite specific infant behaviors which we judged to be evidence of some discomfort or incoordination in the feeding experience.

In our conceptual formulation of the mother-infant interaction and the developmental process, "distress" was viewed not only as a consequence of asynchrony in the interaction, but also as part of the process whereby the infant signals to the caretaker that something is wrong. In response to these signals, the caretaker may alter her behavior, perhaps experimenting with alternate behaviors, until she finds one that most comfortably maintains the infant. We know from the writings of Spitz (1945, 1946) and others (Fineman et al., 1971), and from our own observations of infants with "failure to thrive," that it is possible to "turn off" major aspects of an infant's signaling system. In the extreme examples referred to ("hospitalism," "spasmus nutans," and "failure to thrive"), this condition is generally caused by severe acute or chronic deprivation. The implication of our findings is that very early and what may be considered nonthreatening environmental influences may also significantly affect behavior and communication in the infant-caretaker interaction.

Let us review the findings. First: multiple caretakers and fixed feeding schedules in the newborn nursery result in comparatively high "distress" scores. When the baby is shifted to a single caretaker in rooming-in (days 11–28), this high level is reduced to approximately that of the normative comparison group. Second: a shift from a first single caretaker in the first 10 days to a second single caretaker, with no change in the structure of the rooming-in situation, leads to an increase in "distress" scores. Third: the more individually specific the care in the first 10 days, the more sensitive the infant appears to be to a change in caretaker. We are referring here to the increase in "distress" scores in Group B during the second period, and in particular to the scores of Group B infants initially cared for by Nurse Y.

This evidence indicates that those infants receiving the more individualized and specific care in the first 10 days are more sensitive to ensuing change. This may mean that they are more affected by it, or they may be better prepared to express "distress" in an unfamiliar and presumably asynchronous situation. It is important to note that Group C infants, with more natural mothering and no caretaking shifts, do not show any increase in "distress" over the first 4 weeks and no significant increase over the 8-week study period. We are therefore led to consider the hypothesis that the progressive increases, primarily in Group B infants initally cared for by Nurse Y, are related to the development of an early organization and subsequent interaction with shifting caretaking environments.

We believe that these data point up the importance of the earliest days of life in the establishment of expectations for key environmental features, and in influencing the sensitivity of a "distress signaling system" in its role as a regulating link in the infant-caretaker interaction. However, it is clear that we do not know much about the implications of these findings or their long-term significance. The epigenetic aspect of development implies that any factor with significant effect on early development inevitably affects all subsequent development.

However, it is clear that the question of what this effect will be requires much more information than we now have. It will require continued research, based on a recognition of the infant as a whole organism, and directed at determining how various behavioral systems become related to each other and how they become organized with the environmental context into a regulated total system.

The concept of "distress as a signaling system" within the mother-infant interaction, as discussed here, is one way of regarding the findings and is not demonstrated by these data. Neither do the data as presented elucidate the questions concerning the nature of the specific cues by means of which the infants identify and respond to the specific caretaking environment. We believe that these cues are perceived by the infant as auditory, visual, kinesthetic, and tactile perceptions, and that intensity, timing, pacing, and approach-withdrawal parameters affect the interaction. The feeding observations and other data from the study are being analyzed to see if such variables and their affects can be identified. For example, there is evidence in the feeding data that infants cared for by Nurse Y or by their own mothers spent more time looking at the caretaker during feeding than did infants cared for by Nurse X. We plan to continue these analyses in order to clarify the interrelation of functions, and to identify more specifically the cues that both infant and mother use to regulate and adjust their mutal adaptation. This study should document the origins of their role and signficance from the point of view of the genesis of a communication system in the dyad.

References

BURNS, P. & SANDER, L. W. (1967), Feeding patterns in early infancy and the assessment of individual differences in their organization. Presented at the Society for Research in Child Development, New York.

FINEMAN, J. B., KUNIHOLM, P., & SHERIDAN, S. (1971), Spasmus nutans: a syndrome of auto-arousal. *Journal of the American Academy of Child Psychiatry*, 10:136–155.

PAVENSTEDT, E. & SANDER, L. W. (1962), Progress report: mother-child interaction during first three years. Submitted to USPHS for Grant #M–3325, Sept., 1960–Dec., 1961, pp. 38–42.

SANDER, L. W. (1962), Issues in early mother-child interaction. *Journal of the American Academy of Child Psychiatry*, 1:141–166.

—— (1969), Regulation and organization in the early infant-caretaker system. In: *Brain and Early Behavior*, ed. R. Robinson. London: Academic Press, pp. 311–332.

—— STECHLER, G., BURNS, P., & JULIA, H. (1970). Early mother-infant interaction and 24-hour patterns of activity and sleep. *Journal of the American Academy of Child Psychiatry*, 9:103–123.

SPITZ, R. A. (1945), Hospitalism: an inquiry into the genesis of psychiatric conditions in early childhood. *The Psychoanalytic Study of the Child*, 1:53–74. New York: International Universities Press.

—— (1946), Hospitalism: a follow-up report. *The Psychoanalytic Study of the Child*, 2:113–117. New York: International Universities Press.

WOLFF, P. H. (1968), The role of biological rhythms in early psychological development. In: *Annual Progress in Child Psychiatry and Child Development*, 1968, ed. S. Chess & A. Thomas. New York: Brunner/Mazel, pp. 1–21.

The Synchrony of Respiration, Heart Rate, and Sucking Behavior in the Newborn*

Lewis P. Lipsitt
BROWN UNIVERSITY

In recent years, many advances have been made in the technical aspects of psychobiological recording. This new expertise has found its way into the maternity hospital where it is being used to monitor the condition of the mother and fetus prior to birth. Subsequently, it is used to explore the psychophysiology of the neonate in considerable detail. There is growing disenchantment among child psychologists with the traditional modes of behavioral assessment, especially the developmental test. This has facilitated the migration of developmentalists into the field of infant observation and experimentation with techniques that actually alter the baby's behavior rather than merely assess it. This has occurred in the context of a rising faith in, and indeed numerous demonstrations of, the great sensory capacities and learning proficiencies of the young child. This new appreciation, even of the neonate, has been facilitated by the social and medical interests of developmentalists. They see the possibility of appropriating these experimental techniques to more keenly detect sensory and neurological deficits in infants. Such experimental manipulative procedures can then be used to enhance developmental performance, particularly in those born with, or destined for, physical or social handicaps.

THE POLYGRAPHIC STUDY OF THE NEWBORN

The use of the polygraph for the documentation of infantile responsivity can facilitate the study of processes involving changes in the infant's condition over time, and in response to specific stimulation that may be administered in any sensory modality. Recent studies utilizing polygraphic recording of newborns' responses enable much finer detection of sensory and neurological capability. This is just as one would expect of techniques that are highly sensitive to individual differences. In addition, such procedures enable the simultaneous documentation of multiple responses, yielding a written record of the infant's response. Then the occasion of recording, and the stimulation associated with it, may be rehearsed afterwards to provide the opportunity for further statistical analyses of the episode.

We were concerned in the present studies with the interrelationships among several response characteristics, such as sucking, respiration, and heart rate. In addition, we wished to document the way in which sensory stimulation, taste in this case, serves to alter what might be called the basic congenital responsivity of the infant. In these studies, we have perhaps explored the earliest contributions of the environment to the newborn's response repertoire. The

From *Biologic and Clinical Aspects of Brain Development*. Mead Johnson Symposium on Perinatal and Developmental Medicine, No. 6. Evansville, Ind.: Mead Johnson and Company, 1975, Pp. 67–72. Reprinted by permission.

* Supported by USPHS Grant No. HD 03911.

circumstances in which we have accomplished this do not deviate sharply, of
course, from the range of stimulation which infants ordinarily experience within
the first few days of life, in the ecological niche which is the normal nursery of
the modern maternity hospital. Even so, the techniques are rather exquisitely
sensitive to individual differences in newborns. Thus, they enable the documentation both of commonalities among infants with respect to their response
to environmental change, and the stability of individual reactions over a period
of time.

Testing is done in a special crib, housed in a white sound-attenuated chamber
with temperature about 80°F. Ambient light is about 50 ft-candles. Breathing
is monitored by a Phipps and Bird infant pneumobelt around the abdomen.
Respiratton and body activity are recorded continuously on a Grass polygraph.
Hewlett-Packard electrodes are placed on the chest and leg, permitting polygraphic monitoring of the primary heart rate, which is integrated by a Hewlett-
Packard cardiotachometer and recorded on another channel. Figure 1 shows a
two-day-old child with the pneumobelt attached for the recording of respiration,
EKG electrodes for recording of heart rate, and the automatic sucking apparatus
in place for recording and for delivery of fluid contingent upon sucking behavior.

Sucking is recorded on another polygraph channel. The "suckometer"
consists of a stainless steel housing with a pressure transducer, over which a
commercial nipple is pulled. A polyethylene tube runs into the nipple from a
pump source and delivers fluid under the control of the experimenter and on
demand of the subject. When delivering, the pump ejects into the nipple-end a
.02 ml drop contingent upon the execution of a sucking response of preset
amplitude.

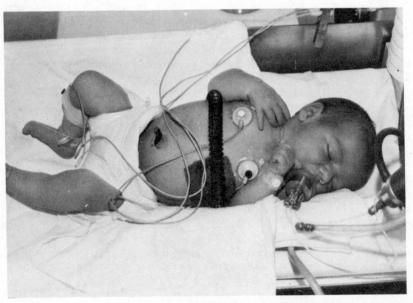

FIGURE 1.   A two-day-old infant in the testing situation.

In these studies, the situation may be arranged in such a way as to allow the infant to receive no fluid for sucking, or to receive a fluid such as sucrose or dextrose, in any desired concentration, contingent upon sucking, with one drop being ejected onto the tongue for each suck. A polygraph event marker records fluid ejections during fluid delivery periods, or the occurrence of a criterion suck during no-fluid conditions. To insure a constant acoustical environment, a 74 dB background white noise is produced from a noise generator continuously through a speaker enclosed in the infant chamber.

A nurse applies the electrodes and pneumobelt to the infant, who is then swaddled and placed on its left side. The nipple is then inserted, supported by a cushion to enable recording without touching the infant. During the first few sucking bursts on the nipple, no fluid is delivered and the equipment is calibrated. Preamplifier sensitivity is adjusted for each infant so the average sucking amplitude results in a 5 cm excursion of the polygraph pen. The threshold criterion is then set at 2.5 cm, so that only responses causing a pen sweep greater than 2.5 cm meet the criterion of a suck and are counted.

An exemplary polygraph record showing respiration, heart rate, the cardiotachometer transformation of the basic EKG, and sucking can be seen in Figure 2. Newborns characteristically suck in bursts of responses separated by

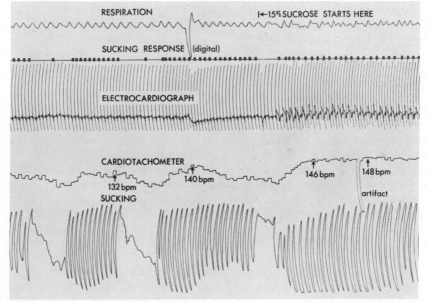

FIGURE 2.   *Exemplary polygraph record from 44-hour-old normal male, showing the last two bursts of no-fluid sucking preceding introduction of the sucrose-sucking condition without interruption. Total polygraph record shown runs for 1 minute. Top channel records respiration, pen marker shows digital representation of criterion sucks, which receive .02 ml drop of fluid during sucrose period. Next operating channel is the electrocardiograph (EKG), then the cardiotachometer transformation of the inter-beat intervals, followed by the sucking record. Long sucking bursts are characteristic of sucrose-sucking. No-fluid sucking occurs in short bursts of more rapid sucks. Heart rate during sucrose may be seen to go to a higher level (and remain there) than during no-fluid sucking.*

rests. The burst lengths and the rest lengths both constitute individual difference variables under no-fluid conditions. But, both of these parameters as well as the sucking rate within bursts (as will be seen later) are importantly influenced by the conditions which are arranged as consequences of the infant's own response. For example, with a change from a no-fluid condition to a fluid-sucking condition, or with a change from sucking for a less sweet solution to a sweeter solution, there is a tendency for the sucking bursts to become longer, for the inter-burst intervals to become shorter, and for the inter-suck intervals to become longer (i.e., for sucking rate within bursts to become slower). Because of these regularities of response in relation to the conditions imposed upon the infants during testing, it is possible to (a) explore the effects of one period of taste experience upon the response of the infant during a subsequent taste experience, and (b) investigate the interrelationships of these various sucking-response parameters with one another and with certain other response measures such as heart rate. The two studies reported here relate to those objectives.

SUCKING FOR SUCROSE, WATER, OR NOTHING

In a study by Kobre and Lipsitt (1972), the infants were first tested for two minutes on the nipple without any fluid delivery whatever. Subjects in this study were rejected for further study if they had a mean sucking rate lower than 30/minute during the two minute period. The 25 subjects remaining were divided into five groups. A total of 20 minutes of responding was recorded for each subject, four successive periods each of five-minutes duration. Between each period the nipple was removed for one minute to allow the tube to be flushed out with water and the child to be picked up.

The 25 infants, most in the third day of life, received one of five reinforcement regimens for the 20-minute period. One group (Suc-Suc) received only sucrose throughout the 20-minute period. A second group (H_2O-H_2O) received water throughout, and a third group (Suc-H_2O) received sucrose and water, alternated twice, in five-minute units. In a second portion of the experiment, one group (NF-NF) received no fluid throughout the four five-minute periods, and a second group (Suc-NF) received sucrose alternated with no fluid in five-minute periods.

It is of interest first to compare the frequency polygons representing the sucking behavior of the three groups which received a constant reinforcement condition throughout the 20-minute sucking period. These are the groups that got either sucrose, or distilled water, or no fluid for that 20 minutes. Figure 3 provides a graphical comparison of the three groups as represented by the computer-generated polygons which threw the inter-suck intervals accumulated during the 20-minute period into bins representing 100-msec intervals. This shows clearly that sucking rate within bursts slows down for a fluid-sucking condition relative to no-fluid sucking, and that sucking rate slows still further for sweet-fluid-sucking relative to sucking for distilled water. Thus there is an orderly progression from no fluid to plain water to 15% sucrose sucking, with the sucking response becoming slower and slower with an apparent increase in the incentive value of the reinforcement delivered consequent upon the response. It may also be noted, parenthetically, that under the sucrose condition the

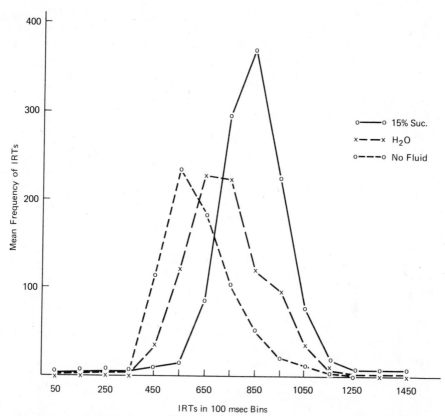

FIGURE 3.   *Mean incidence of interresponse times (IRTs) for each of the 100 msec bins. Each curve represents the combined IRT distribution for the five subjects in that group (Suc-Suc; H₂O-H₂O; NF-NF) over the 20-minute session. Sucking is slower for sucrose than for water, on average, and slower for water than under the no-fluid condition.*

infants invested a larger number of responses during a comparable period of time than under either the water or no-fluid condition. A somewhat larger number of responses was emitted for water, moreover, than for no fluid.

As has been indicated earlier, rather interesting interplays between various response parameters occur in neonates. For example, while infants suck more slowly within bursts for sweeter fluids, as if to savor them more, it is also the case that when sucking for sweet they tend to take shorter rests. Thus, they suck more times per minute for sweet than for non-sweet. This effect may be seen in Figure 4, wherein the comparison is shown of mean rates per minute for the group which got sucrose throughout with the groups which got water throughout. Then both of these are compared to the group that got sucrose and water alternated in five-minute blocks. Here it may be seen that the sucking rate per minute for the sucrose group is higher than for the water-sucking group. The trend shows that sucking rate over the 20-minute period is remarkably stable, and the difference between the two groups is a reliable one. More

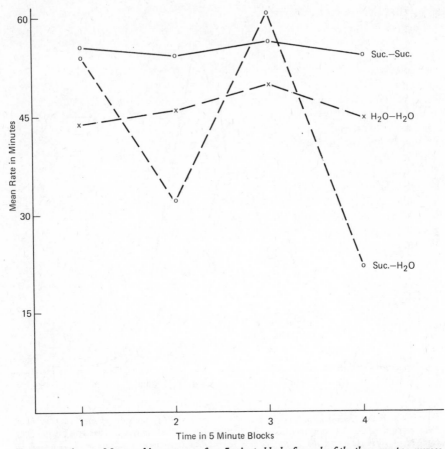

FIGURE 4. *Mean sucking rate over four 5-minute blocks for each of the three groups; sucrose alone (Suc-Suc), water alone (H_2O-H_2O), and sucrose and water alternated twice (Suc-H_2O). $N = 5$ in each group.*

important, however, is the obvious indication of an experiental effect in the alternated group. When sucking for sucrose, this group was essentially comparable to the group sucking for sucrose throughout. When switched to water, however, response rate during each of those five minute periods was significantly lower than their counterpart controls in the water-throughout group. Thus, when newborns have experience in sucking for sucrose, an immediately subsequent experience with water "turns them off." They display their apparent "aversion" for the water by a marked reduction in instrumental behavior which would put that fluid in their mouths. As can be seen from the figure, when the response consequent is changed, as from water to sucrose, response rate goes right back up to a normal level. There is even a suggestion there (though not reliable) of a positive contrast effect counterpointing the negative contrast effect shown during the second and fourth blocks (both of which effects are reliable).

The comparable comparison showing a similar effect in the relations between sucking for sucrose and sucking for no fluid is shown in Figure 5. This figure shows the no-fluid group to suck at an essentially constant rate of about 40 sucks per minute throughout the 20-minute testing session. The group alternated between sucrose and no fluid in successive five-minute blocks, however, goes from a sucking rate of almost 60 under sucrose to a rate of about 30 sucks per minute under the no fluid condition. This is a drop to a level significantly below that of the group receiving no fluid throughout. Thus the negative contrast effect occurs under conditions in which the lower-incentive condition involves either no fluid at all, or plain distilled water. There is no reason to suppose at this point that the phenomenon is not widespread throughout the range of incentive conditions and that it would occur whenever the infant is called upon to compare two levels of incentive, such as breast milk versus formula, or formula versus plain water.

More important from the standpoint of the psychologist interested in behavioral changes due to accruing experiences is the fact that the newborn is

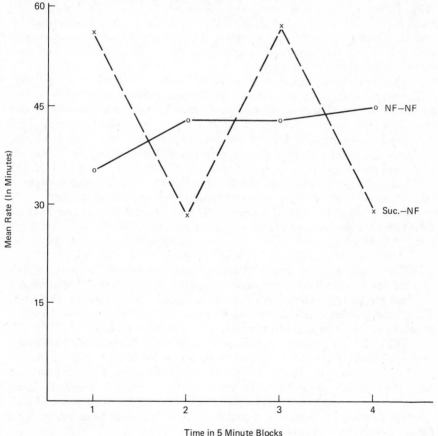

FIGURE 5.   *Mean sucking rate over four 5-minute blocks for each of two groups; no fluid (NF-NF), and sucrose and no-fluid alternated twice (Suc-NF). N = 5 in each group.*

strikingly affected in his subsequent behavior by his experiences within the immediately previous five minutes. Surely the negative contrast effect demonstrated here is one of the most rudimentary types of behavioral alteration, however temporary, due to experiential circumstances. As in the case of neonatal habituation to olfactory stimulation (Engen and Lipsitt, 1972), there is the strong suggestion that memorial processes are already working during the newborn period, such that there is a lasting impression made, admittedly of unknown duration, of the experience endured. These are the beginnings of learning processes.

RESPIRATION, HEART RATE, AND SUCKING

In a study involving 44 normal full-term newborns, 24 males and 20 females, testing was conducted on two consecutive days, using the polygraph recording techniques previously described. Mean age on initial testing (Day One) was 54 hours (27 to 120 hours) and, on Day Two, 78 hours (51 to 144 hours). All infants, 33 bottle-fed and 11 breast-fed, were seen between 8:30 a.m. and 9:30. Infants in this study were part of a long-term longitudinal study; only some aspects of the newborn data will be considered here. The procedures described here constituted only a portion of the total battery of testing done on each infant but they were administered, under identical standardized contitions, to all infants in the study.

A total of ten minutes of sucking was recorded for each infant immediately following calibration of the apparatus, five successive periods each of two minutes duration. Three of these were sucking for no fluid, followed by two periods of 15% sucrose-sucking. About 35 seconds intervened between periods during which a computer printed out the inter-response time data (IRT) for the preceding period. The nipple was not removed between periods. The infant continued sucking under the same condition as in the preceding period. The beginning of a period following the 35 second print-out was initiated after the infant stopped sucking for at least two seconds after the end of a burst.

At the end of the second sucrose period, the nipple was removed. There then ensued a two-minute period of polygraph recording during a "resting" state, defined as quiescent and with regular respiration, in which the infant neither sucked nor was stimulated in any way.

The results (Lipsitt, Reilly, Butcher, and Greenwood, in press) of this part of the longitudinal study have suggested a very interesting interplay between the sucking response, on the one hand, and heart rate, on the other. They further substantiate a process that suggests a "savoring mechanism" which seems to be present already during the newborn period.

The computer print-out at the end of each two-minute period provided a frequency distribution, for inter-suck intervals under two seconds, of sucking IRTs in 100-msec bins. The mean IRT could be calculated from the print-out, using the midpoint of the bin as its numerical representation. Figure 2, shown earlier, is a polygraph record from this study, showing the final phase of nonnutritive (no-fluid) sucking in comparison with the first phase of sucrose-sucking for an exemplary subject of this experiment.

Table 1 shows the five sucking parameters under the no-fluid and sucrose-sucking conditions. The mean and modal IRTs are greater when sucking is for sucrose than when sucking under a no-fluid condition, and the number of responses per burst is twice as large. Also, more rest periods (IRTs > 2 sec) occur under the no-fluid condition. Consequently, despite the faster rate of sucking within bursts under the no-fluid condition, more sucks per minute are emitted under sucrose. All those effects are reliable.

Table 2 compares the heart rate of infants during sucking periods with basal heart rate without the nipple. Very interestingly, the mean heart rate under no-fluid sucking was significantly higher than the basal rate. In turn the mean heart rate under sucrose-sucking was higher than under the no-fluid condition. Although sucking rate within bursts is *reduced* when the infant sucks for sucrose, then, heart rate nevertheless increases reliably.

TABLE 1

Comparison of the means (2-min units) of five sucking parameters under no-fluid and sucrose-sucking conditions over a two-day period, and correlation coefficients (r) comparing Day 1 and Day 2. From the initial group of 44 subjects, 3 failed to suck non-nutritively on Day 1, thus reducing the analyzable records to 41 for both days. In all, 4 subjects had non-analyzable sucrose-sucking records, 2 on Day 1 (these overlapping with the no-fluid failures), reducing the sucrose subjects to 40. The measures are based upon 2 min means, 3 for the no-fluid and 2 for sucrose condition.

	Day 1		Day 2		Day 1/Day 2	
	Mean	SD	Mean	SD	r	p^r
No-fluid sucking (N = 41)						
Total responses	88.3	23.2	96.6	30.9	.62	.001
IRTs 2" (rests)	8.1	2.6	8.7	2.8	.65	.001
Responses/burst	12.9	15.5	11.2	6.1	.79	.001
Mode IRT	620.3	99.0	572.8	61.9	.37	.05
Mean IRT	657.8	81.7	611.9	56.0	.42	.01
15% Sucrose sucking (N = 40)						
Total responses	103.0	28.2	106.2	27.6	.08	—
IRTs 2" (rests)	5.3	2.7	5.9	3.5	.13	—
Responses/burst	29.7	34.2	24.2	21.7	.03	—
Mode IRT	838.1	109.9	771.3	115.7	.63	.001
Mean IRT	855.8	105.3	786.9	85.8	.71	.001

TABLE 2

Heart rate (bpm) during resting and when sucking for no fluid or sucrose, and correlation coefficients (r) comparing Day 1 and Day 2. Failures to suck account for reductions of N from the initial group of 44, except in one case where the heart rate record during sucking was unreadable.

	N	Day 1		Day 2		Combined		Day 1/Day 2	
		Mean	SD	Mean	SD	Mean	SD	r	p^r
Basal	44	113.8	16.7	118.7	18.1	116.3	14.2	.29	.05
No-fluid sucking	40	124.0	14.5	123.4	13.6	123.8	12.2	.46	.01
Sucrose-sucking	39	145.7	15.5	147.4	12.3	146.6	13.1	.71	.001

CONCLUDING REMARKS

The more we study the human neonate under rather precise response-measurement conditions afforded by the polygraph and associated apparatus such as the computer, the more are we impressed, first by the fine interplay between the various congenital responses of the newborn, but secondly, by the extent to which the newborn's behavior and psychophysiological indices are affected by the environmental resources available to the infant at any given moment. Thus, the manual introduction of 10% sucrose into the infant's mouth in the presence of a refusal to suck will almost immediately generate sucking behavior which will persist even upon the subsequent withdrawal of that sucrose incentive. Similarly, and as has been demonstrated in the first experiment reported here, experience in sucking for a sweet substance for a five-minute period will affect the infant's subsequent behavior, at least for the next five minutes, when offered a less sweet incentive.

An important feature of the present experimental techniques is that the infant has been studied not just in the presence of stimulating features of the environment which were under the control of the examiner or experimenter, but also under conditions in which the infant is offered the opportunity to self-regulate. That is, our incentive conditions were such that we simply made available to the infant innocuous but variable reinforcing conditions, to which we studied the infant's response. The newborn through its instrumental or operant activity either made it happen or didn't, or did something in between. We think that we are at the beginning stages of a model for the interaction between an infant and its environment. Involved is not merely a stimulus-response relationship in which the environment or the infant's caretaker serves as stimulus, and the subject responds, or even one in which the infant serves as stimulus, and the environment responds. Rather, it is one in which there is constant reciprocity between the organism and environment, between the infant and the caretaker, in which each serves as a stimulus and each responds. Both operate at least in part according to incentive principles which can and will be discovered. This too simple view of human nature and human development will yield to more complex models as we learn more, but we can learn more only by starting at the beginning.

Finally, the techniques, tools, and results represented in the foregoing should have diagnostic significance in relation to the newborn, inasmuch as such normative findings can be utilized to assess "response deviation" in individual infants subsequently tested by the same techniques. The 24-hour test-retest stabilities of certain of these measures, given in Table 1, lend credibility to the utility of at least some of the measures for tagging the "deviant newborn." Research is in progress presently, involving both high-stress and low-stress newborns. The purpose is to determine the validity of these psychophysiological measures in assessing degree of fetal, obstetrical, or other perinatal distress. Ultimately, longitudinal studies must be done as well, to determine the long-term usefulness of such precise neonatal measures for purposes of assessing prognosis, or at least to determine the utility of these measures in identifying certain newborns for remedial or other special developmental follow-up.

References

ENGEN, T., and LIPSITT, L. P.: Decrement and recovery of responses to olfactory stimuli in the human neonate, Journal of Comparative and Physiological Psychology, 59: 2, 1965.

KOBRE, K. R., and LIPSITT, L. P.: A negative contrast effect in newborns, Journal of Experimental Child Psychology, 14:1, 1972.

LIPSITT, L. P.; REILLY, B. M.; BUTCHER, M. J., and GREENWOOD, M. M.: The stability and interrelationships of newborn sucking and heart rate, submitted for publication, 1974. in press.

3

Emerging Resources and Competencies

An infant reacts very much as a whole, showing many competencies in an environment favorable to their development and use. From the large number of articles on infant competency, we have chosen one that describes the development of the brain, the organ that directs not only behavior, but growth. The physical and psychological environments are related to behavior and development in the other two articles.

During the first two years of life, brain development is of very special importance, because this is the time of its major growth spurt. John Dobbing describes and explains brain development during the growth spurt and discusses its particular vulnerability at this time. He is cautious in relating brain structure to behavior. Dobbing's clear writing and graphic presentations make a difficult subject understandable to the reader who has little knowledge of this area.

Barry M. Lester's paper documents the wholeness of the infant, showing the effects of malnutrition upon behavior, mediated by the nervous system. By their crying and orienting behavior, infants indicate degrees of well-being. (In the previous chapter, Burns and his associates examined the newborn infant's ability to signal distress and to thereby interact constructively with a caregiver.) No doubt, sensitive parents and nurses interpret such signals intuitively, but research such as Lester's gives an objective basis on which to assess the meaning of behavior.

Psychologists have long believed that mental development was strongly influenced by an infant's experiences at home. But just what are the dimensions of the home learning environment? An instrument for observing and measuring these dimensions has been developed at the Center for Early Development and Education at the University of Arkansas. Using the instrument to measure home environment, mental test performance is related to home experience by Richard Elardo, Robert Bradley, and Bettye M. Caldwell.

Human Brain Development and Its Vulnerability

John Dobbing
UNIVERSITY OF MANCHESTER

THE VULNERABILITY OF THE BRAIN GROWTH SPURT

The growth of all tissues, and indeed of the body as a whole, does not follow a linear course with time. It always proceeds by means of one or more periods of transient rapid growth known as "growth spurts." The brain is no exception. Figure 1 traces the growth in weight of a rat's brain. It is a sigmoid curve, and the growth spurt can be expressed as a velocity curve as shown. There is a similar brain growth spurt in all mammalian species and it always occurs earlier than the general bodily growth spurt.

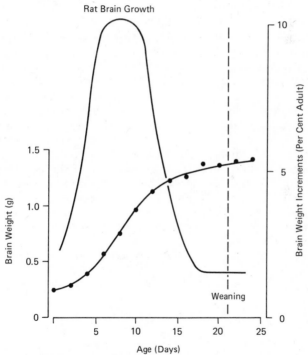

FIGURE 1. *The brain growth spurt. This occurs in all mammalian species, including man. Its special vulnerability is one of the main topics in this article. Here the brain growth spurt is shown for the rat, with a superimposed first order velocity curve.*

From *Biologic and Clinical Aspects of Brain Development.* Mead Johnson Symposium on Perinatal and Developmental Medicine, No. 6. Evansville, Ind.: Mead Johnson and Company, 1975. Pp. 5–12. Reprinted by permission.

The significance of the brain growth spurt for our present discussion is that this transient period of rapid brain growth seems to be one of particular vulnerability to growth restriction. We know this from experiments in animals whose bodily growth rates have been retarded at this time as well as beforehand and afterwards. It could not have been discovered in humans for obvious ethical reasons. However, since we are mainly interested in human children, we must also examine the whole problem of extrapolating experimental results from one animal species to another, including the human animal, and this has already given rise to much confusion.

Another major problem in our enquiry is our total ignorance of what constitutes the physical basis within the brain of higher mental function. We simply do not know how critical it is to have the correct quantity of nerve cells, or of synaptic connections between them, or of myelin or any other structure, nor even whether any of these things matter. Indeed, one is even sometimes left wondering to what extent higher mental function depends at all on the physical brain.

Let us first look at a very much oversimplified scheme of structural brain development, and see which structures are developing during the brain growth spurt which may be the ones whose physical vulnerability is so functionally important. Figure 2 shows such a scheme.

For humans the first three months of fetal life are a period of embryology when the brain is acquiring its adult shape. The same processes in the rat all occur within the first two *weeks* of fetal life. This period, which we can call "embryology" does not concern us here. Then there follows a period when cells which are destined to become nerve cells divide. Let us call this period one of "neuroblast multiplication." This is over by the time of birth in the rat and by about mid-pregancy in the human, except in certain special areas to be mentioned later. At the end of this early period of life we therefore possess our adult *number* of nerve cells, although much more development of them is yet to come.

It is not until about birth in the rat, following the period of neuronal multiplication, that the brain growth spurt begins: so we can assume fairly confidently that restrictions imposed during the growth spurt will not affect *numbers* of neurons except in those exceptional areas where neurogenesis occurs later. It may, however, affect their early development as discussed below.

The next easily measurable event (measured by estimating the increasing quantities of nuclear DNA in the tissue) is a period of tremendous multiplication

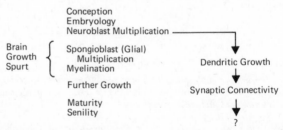

FIGURE 2.   *A greatly simplified scheme to describe the common mammalian pattern of brain growth.*

of the glial cells of the brain. These cells eventually heavily outnumber nerve cells and their multiplication period is consequently much more conspicuous. It occupies the first half of the brain growth spurt period, from about birth to about 12 postnatal days in the rat. This is the period shown as spongioblast (glial) multiplication in Figure 2. Almost nothing is known about the function of these mysterious glial cells in the adult. The only thing we definitely know about them is that during development many of them are concerned with the manufacture of myelin sheaths, those insulating, laminated, fatty coverings of the nerve fibre which help it to conduct impulses more quickly. Myelination itself can be measured by estimating the increasing quantities of myelin substances in the growing brain at this time, and it is easy to show (as might have been expected) that the most rapid phase of myelination occupies the second half of the brain growth spurt, having awaited the earlier arrival of the glial cells which make the myelin.

Glial cell multiplication, myelination and rapid increase in weight are, however, only three of the most easily measured components of the brain growth spurt, and they are not necessarily the most important from the functional point of view. In structural terms alone, many other things are happening at this time which we cannot so easily measure. Perhaps the most important of these is a very great outgrowth from the nerve cells (which had arrived before the beginning of the growth spurt) of their so-called dendritic tree. Figure 3 shows this process occurring in humans whose brain growth spurt is mainly postnatal, as will be discussed later. The great complexity of the dendritic arborisation is important because it is due to the dendrites that nerve cells are connected together in a very complex electrical circuit by means of the synaptic connections. Any single nerve cell may have as many as 10,000 such connections from other nerve cells. It is indeed much more likely that brain function, and even higher mental function, will be much more seriously affected by a restriction placed on dendritic arborisation during the brain growth spurt than by a moderate deficit in nerve cell number imposed before it begins. Unfortunately these later aspects of neuronal development are much more difficult to measure quantitatively than mere cell multiplication. Figure 3 expresses this difficulty and the fact that dendritic arborisation and developing synaptic connectivity are developmental processes which indeed belong to the brain growth spurt period, alongside the other more easily measured but functionally less important events. In addition at this time there is also a veritable revolution in the developmental metabolism of brain tissue. Radical changes in synthetic and degradative biochemical mechanisms occur, as the metabolic pattern of immaturity subsides, as that required for laying down new structure is transiently developed, and as metabolic preparation is made for maturing adult function. The secrets of the vulnerability of the brain growth spurt could as easily lie in a distortion of these biochemical developments as in disordered structural growth.

We will now consider the evidence for the existence of brain vulnerability during this phase of rapid growth of the organ. First we will describe the very simple experimental designs which have been employed, and then the evidence that quite moderate growth restriction at these times does produce lasting deficits and distortions of brain architecture and function.

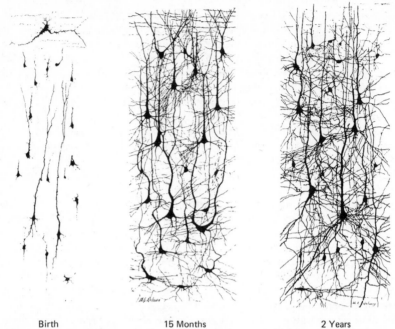

| Birth | 15 Months | 2 Years |

FIGURE 3.   *The increase of dendritic complexity in nerve cells of the human cerebral cortex in the first two years of postnatal life. This is the developing circuitry of the brain. Note how poorly developed it is at birth, although the nerve cells themselves are already present. Note also that it is still becoming more complex at two years of age. Adapted from the monographs of J. LeRoy Conel entitled, "The postnatal development of the human cerebral cortex."* (Reference: Conel, J. L. [1939, 1955 & 1959]. *The postnatal development of the human cerebral cortex.* Volumes 1, 5 and 6. Harvard University Press, Cambridge, Mass. Reproduced by kind permission of the publishers.)

EXPERIMENTAL DESIGNS

To test the proposition that the brain growth spurt period is one of enhanced vulnerability of the brain to growth restriction, all we need to do is to identify the timing of these stages in the normal early life of any animal species. We can then arrange to slow down the growth of the animal before, during or after that period, or in any combination of these three.

A convenient method of restricting growth of the fetus and suckling animal experimentally is by mild undernutrition either of the pregnant or lactating mother. Subsequently one can underfeed the weaned offspring. As well as an experimental growth-restricting device, undernutrition will also be directly studied by these methods and that, too, is a pressing world paediatric problem. It will be very important, since it is humans we are ultimately interested in, that the degree of undernutrition is not unrealistically severe compared with common human experience. Too much nonsense has been written by those who have extrapolated experimental results to humans from animal experiments in which the undernutrition has been grossly more severe than occurs even in times of famine in underprivileged human communities.

A convenient animal species is the rat. This is because the brain growth spurt is postnatal, and almost entirely confined to the first three postnatal weeks of life, which is the baby rat's suckling period (Figure 1). In this species birth conveniently occurs between the end of major neuronal multiplication and the beginning of the brain growth spurt (see Figure 2). Thus in the rat our three experimental periods are fetal life (before the growth spurt), the suckling period (during) and the postweaning period of growth by which time the growth spurt is over. Growth restriction in the first, fetal period, is imposed by underfeeding the pregnant mother; in the second by underfeeding the suckling mother; and in the third by directly underfeeding the growing weanling infant. In practice it is usual to foster the offspring at birth to new mothers. Both underfed and normally fed newborns are cross-fostered either to underfed or normally fed lactating foster-mothers. In this way there is a sharper separation at birth between different nutritional regimes.

One important result of such experiments is that growth restriction during the middle suckling period (that of the *brain* growth spurt) permanently affects the future growth of the whole animal although underfeeding during the first and third periods does not. However one tries to refeed or rehabilitate an animal growth restricted at the time of suckling (the first three postnatal weeks), it will always be small. Fetal undernutrition in the rat, provided the newborn is cross-fostered to a well fed lactating mother, and provided the growth restriction is not completely unrealistic in human terms, has little if any effect on subsequent bodily growth. Nor has postweaning growth restriction, in which complete bodily catch-up is available if properly rehabilitated. This last finding is particularly remarkable, since it is not until after weaning that the *bodily* growth spurt occurs, and at this time there is apparently no similar vulnerability of bodily growth. There is something about the successful accomplishment of *brain* growth which is necessary for the programme of proper subsequent *bodily* growth; and the secret is probably in the realms of endocrinology. Finally, in this experimental design, animals reared along these various trajectories of restricted growth are then rehabilitated on a full, *ad libitum* dietary intake until they are fully grown into adulthood, when their brains and their behaviour can be examined for any traces of their early, brain growth spurt restriction.

DEFICITS AND DISTORTIONS IN THE BRAIN FOLLOWING GROWTH RESTRICTION IN THE VULNERABLE PERIOD

We can now list some of the changes which can be found in the adult brain which have persisted since their early growth restriction. These are found only if the underfeeding has been timed to coincide with the brain growth spurt. They are not found following only fetal or postweaning undernutrition in the rat. As will be seen, the changes take the form of quantitative deficits, but there are also structural and functional distortions—and the latter may be the more significant.

Brain size   The adult brain size of previously underfed animals is permanently reduced. In addition it is reduced beyond the point which might have been expected from their reduced body size. Thus there is a permanent distortion of bodily configuration with a true, if slight microcephaly: a brain disproportionately small for the body size. When the brain is examined a little more closely, it is found that the organ is not uniformly reduced. One part of it, for example, the cerebellum, is much more reduced than is the rest of the brain. This has happened because, during the growth spurt of the whole brain, the cerebellum grows much the fastest of any region. And, since vulnerability in the brain appears to be related to speed of growth, the cerebellum suffers most. At all events here is another *distortion*, this time within the brain.

Brain cells   When measured by DNA estimation, the total number of brain cells of all types is reduced in about the proportion one would expect from the reduced brain size. In general it is thought that this deficit is at the expense of glial cells, not neurons, for reasons explained above. However, there is a certain special type of neuron in the cerebellum (the granular neuron) which is known to be an exception to the general rule that adult neuronal number is achieved before the brain growth spurt begins. These particular neurons divide later than the commencement of the brain growth spurt, and, as may have been expected, are found to be differentially deficient in the adult cerebellum following undernutrition at this time. All the other cerebellar neurons, which had already arrived, are present in proper quantity. This is yet another example of a distortion of the brain architecture, this time within the cerebellum which is not, therefore, merely small.

The cerebellar deficit and distortion is a particularly good example of the way in which the vulnerable period hypothesis is found to be justified. All depends on the timing of the growth restriction in relation to developmental events within the growth spurt period. It is also the only example so far discovered of a structural effect having definitely related functional consequences. The cerebellum has an important role in motor coordination: and these animals are found to be permanently clumsy. Perhaps it is significant that there are very large numbers of clumsy human children who are otherwise "normal," even in our own society, and this disorder does have a correlation with previous social disadvantage. This is discussed again later.

Another, somewhat unexpected distortion of cellular architecture has been found in the cerebral cortex. Neurons exist in layers in the cortex, having migrated there during development from their sites of origin. In adult rats who were previously undernourished, there is a small deficit in the deeper layers of the cortex, resulting in another distortion of the histological architecture. The significance of this arbitrary finding is not understood, but the distortion it exemplifies may well be functionally more important than a mere deficit.

Myelination   has already been mentioned as a major brain growth spurt process. Previously undernourished adult brains show a deficit in myelin quantity which is greater than would be accounted for by the reduced brain size: and this is, therefore, yet another example of distortion.

Synaptic Connections   Histological quantitation of brain structures is immensely laborious, since no useful mechanised techniques have yet been devised. Preliminary studies, however, have led to the claim that in some parts of the cerebral cortex there may be as many as *40 per cent* fewer synapses on each individual neuron. If this can be confirmed, we may be getting much nearer to a true physical basis for the distortions of higher mental function following early undernutrition.

Biochemical Distortions   There is already a number of reports that several enzyme systems which catalyse important brain reactions are also distorted. One of these concerns a permanent alteration in the activity of acetylcholinesterase, an enzyme greatly concerned with transmission of impulses at nerve endings. More recently, and perhaps even more significantly, a permanent alteration in the rate of synthesis of 5-hydroxytryptamine has been found in certain brain regions. 5-HT is thought to be one of the important neurotransmitter substances in the brain. Thus there is more than a suspicion that growth restriction permanently affects important brain biochemistry, provided it is correctly timed to the brain growth spurt period.

Permanent Alterations of Behaviour   A very large number of experiments have examined permanent differences in behaviour in animals following early undernutrition and subsequent rehabilitation. Although behavioural measures are ultimately much the most important criteria of whether physical deficits and distortions in the brain have any significance, they will not be discussed in any detail here, mainly because the relevance of such changes to human behaviour is much too large and difficult a discussion. However, permanent changes in animal behaviour which have been found include the clumsiness already mentioned, a tendency of the animals to overreact to stressful situations, and a demonstrable degree of possible "unsociability" in that they have an increase in aggressive and dominance traits. Many scientists have claimed to show deficits in learning ability, problem solving and memory, but although these are fascinating and exciting findings, their strict interpretation is extremely difficult, mixed up as it is with considerations of altered motivation for reward or altered reaction to punishment in the experimental situation.

There is no question whatever that the behaviour of these animals is profoundly and permanently affected. The major difficulty is in discussing these differences in meaningful, human terms.

A Single Opportunity for Brain Growth   Before attempting to extrapolate these findings to the human species, one final point must be discussed which has, of necessity, been discovered in animal experiment. It is that the timing of the brain growth spurt cannot be altered by altering the rate of growth. Whatever the rate of growth, the events within the developing brain which have been described for normal brain growth must occur at certain prescribed ages. Therefore, conditions must be good *at that time* for proper brain growth. There is no possibility of full recovery later if the opportunity to promote good brain growth is missed. This observation could have profound implications for human populations, both in normal times and at times of acute famine and disaster.

EXTRAPOLATION TO HUMANS

The applicability of the above experimental findings in animals to the human species is often seriously misunderstood and misinterpreted. There is no great difference between mammalian species in the pattern of brain development outlined in Figure 2. Even the individual unit structures of which the brain is composed, such as the nerve cells, glia and myelin sheaths, are remarkably similar both in composition and function from one species to another. For the present purposes, however, there is one important interspecies difference: that is in the *timing* of the vulnerable brain growth spurt period in relation to birth. In some precocial species, such as the guinea pig, sheep, cow, or horse, virtually the whole sequence occurs in fetal life, so that the animal is born neurologically very mature. In other species, such as the rat, mouse, and rabbit, the brain growth spurt is virtually entirely postnatal. In a third group, which includes the pig, birth occurs during the growth spurt period, some of it occurring before and some after birth. The important thing to grasp is that it is not important to the present discussion whether growth restriction is prenatal or postnatal. It is only important that it be imposed during the brain growth spurt, whenever that occurs in any particular species, if it is to produce the permanent changes described.

In view of the species' differences in timing, it therefore became vital to know when the human brain growth spurt occurred before we could guess the human implications of our experimental findings, and this has only recently been discovered and published.

About one hundred and forty complete human brains were collected from dead fetuses and children whose brain growth could be presumed to have been normal. By dissecting these into gross regions and analysing some of their constituents, it has been clearly shown that although the human brain growth spurt begins in fetal life, about the middle of gestation, it continues at least until the second birthday and probably beyond. This is in sharp disagreement with previous reports which, on the basis of an inadequate number of specimens inadequately examined, encouraged a text-book dogma that human brain development was virtually over by the fifth postnatal month. The recent finding that the human brain growth spurt occupies a long period of development, *and that most of it is postnatal,* has important practical implications. It is during this period that good brain growth should be actively promoted by ensuring good environmental conditions during its only opportunity to grow properly. It can even be conjectured that growth retarded human brains in babies with fetal growth retardation may be recoverable and compensated by urgent growth promotion after birth throughout at least the first two years. The possible implications for relief operations, as well as the organisation of food supplies in normal times in the Third World are obvious. The prolonged nature of the period of brain cell multiplication is shown in Figure 4, and the evidence that the all important growth of the dendritic tree of human cortical neurons is mainly postnatal has already been illustrated in Figure 4. Scrutiny of Figure 4 shows how little dendritic growth has occurred in humans by birth as well as the great degree of complexity which still has to develop, up to two postnatal years of age.

HUMAN NEURONAL MULTIPLICATION

This survey of human brain growth has also made it possible to determine the timing of the shorter period, before the growth spurt begins, when human

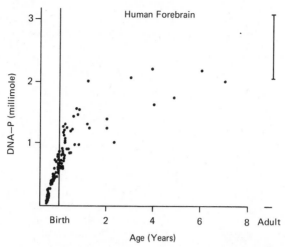

FIGURE 4.   *Graph showing the total numbers of cells of all types in the human forebrain from 10 weeks gestation to 7 years of life, and in adults. Each point represents one individual. The cells are 'counted' by chemical estimation of DNA on the assumption that each brain cell nucleus contains an equal quantity of DNA. Note how cell multiplication continues rapidly well into the second postnatal year. For important detail of the fetal period, see Figure 6.* (Reference: Dobbing, J. & Sands, J. [1973]. The quantitative growth and development of the human brain. *Archives of Diseases of Childhood* 48: 757–767.)

nerve cells multiply. Figure 5 shows this "mini-growth spurt" to be between 12 and 18 weeks of gestation. The biological importance of this as a period of vulnerability is reduced, however, by the fact that in humans the second trimester is thought to be a time in pregnancy when fetal growth is highly protected due to the smallness of the fetus in relation to the size of the placenta and mother. It is only in the last one third of pregnancy that fetal growth is normally threatened.

Nevertheless, there are hazards from which even the second trimester fetus is not protected. For example, the surprisingly sharp cut-off point between neuronal and glial cell multiplication at 18 weeks shown in Figure 5 bears a surprising resemblance to the cut-off point for producing microcephaly and mental retardation in the survivors of the nuclear attacks on Japan. All who were affected in this way were exposed to irradiation before the eighteenth week. Other examples of fetal hazard at this time which are known or are thought to harm the growing brain are maternal virus infection (for example, rubella), maternal medication, abnormalities of maternal metabolism (e.g., hyperphenylalaninaemia), X-rays, and even maternal fever. It is even possible that the more severe cases of mental retardation which, as mentioned at the beginning, show no damage to the brain except some degree of smallness, may be caused by something in the environment which interfered with this particular neuronal multiplication phase of brain growth between 10 and 18 gestational weeks. Only much more attention to the quantitative aspects of neurohistopathology (which is infinitely laborious) will help to confirm this conjecture.

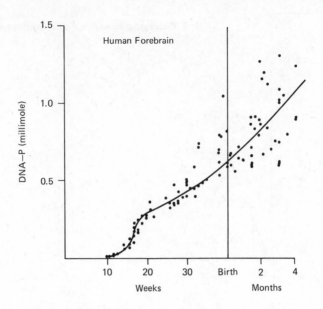

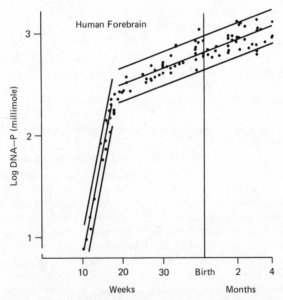

FIGURE 5A AND 5B.   *The upper figure shows the increasing numbers of cells in the human forebrain from 10 weeks of gestation to 4 postnatal months. The method of "counting" is explained in the caption to Figure 4. The lower figure plots the logarithm of the individual brain values in the upper figure. Notice the sharp cut-off point at 18 weeks between the earlier phase of nerve cell multiplication and the later phase of glial multiplication.* (Reference: Dobbing, J. & Sands, J. [1973]. The quantitative growth and development of the human brain. *Archives of Diseases of Childhood.* 48:757–767.)

HUMAN CEREBELLAR GROWTH

Figure 6 shows the shapes of the growth curves of cell multiplication in three major regions of the human brain. From this it can be seen that the human cerebellum has growth characteristics which are similar to those in the experimental animal. It grows much faster than the rest of the brain, but at the same time, and its growth spurt period is therefore much shorter. In the animals this led to a differentially much greater vulnerability of the cerebellum to growth restriction, leading to a much larger permanent reduction in cerebellar size and significant distortion of its histological architecture. More importantly it led to motor incoordination, or clumsiness. At the present time it must remain pure conjecture whether some of the very common clumsiness in our own children in Western Europe may be related to an environmentally-induced failure of cerebellar growth. It is possible that about five per cent of our children are clumsy. It is known that its incidence is statistically related to poor socio-economic circumstances. The question would not be impossible to investigate.

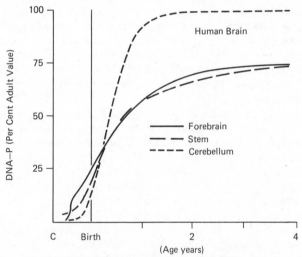

FIGURE 6.   *Numbers of brain cells of all types during development in three brain regions. Notice the much more rapid growth spurt in the cerebellum. The article discusses whether clumsiness in children could be due to the differential vulnerability of the cerebellum as occurs in animals.* (Reference: Dobbing, J. & Sands, J. [1973]. The quantitative growth and development of the human brain. *Archives of Diseases of Childhood.* 48:757–767.)

ENVIRONMENTAL EFFECTS ON HUMAN INTELLECT

The suggestion runs right through this article that the new vulnerable-period or growth-restriction pathology of the brain may be involved in a failure of large numbers of human people to reach their full genetic potential, even though their achievement may often be within the normal range. It is important, finally, to examine the possible size of the importance of these environmental restrictions, acting through an effect on physical brain growth.

Certain major considerations must be borne in mind. Firstly, as has repeatedly been stressed, we do not know anything about the physical basis, within the brain, of higher mental function. Secondly, we know quite certainly that the non-physical postnatal environment of the growing child has an enormous part to play in shaping his personality and intellect. Human emotional and intellectual development is astonishingly plastic. Tremendous improvement even in the severely mentally handicapped can be achieved through non-physical means, by increasing the child's experience of external stimulus. Presumably, similar alterations of achievement in normal children accompany comparable alterations of this environmental non-physical input. Indeed, the demonstrable effects of changes in the environment on the psychological development of the normal child are so great, that there seems little need to attach much importance of the comparatively insignificant effects of genetic inheritance.

Enthusiasts in our area of research must be prepared to accept that the intellectual consequences of physical brain growth restriction may also be small, even though the physical effects are clearly demonstrable in the brain. This is especially true of the proposed "deficit and distortion" pathology compared with the better known lesion pathologies. At first sight it may be relevant that the underprivileged world is not obviously populated by idiots. Only the minority whose malnutrition has been severe and clinically evident can be shown to have seriously and permanently diminished intelligence. And, in these children, it is difficult to distinguish between the physical causes of physically disordered brain growth and all the other gross disorders of their non-physical environment to which the malnourished children in a community are commonly exposed.

The following is therefore pure conjecture. Supposing we were able to break down the multitude of different environmental influences on developing intellect. Let us suppose that no single one of them amounted to more than a few per cent contribution (social class would be a much larger factor, but this is really a collection of very many single contributions). If you were then a mother (or a government) wanting to do the best to promote good child development, what would you do? There would be no simple, single factor which you could modify and improve. You would have to promote as many "plus scores" in the algebraic sum of factors contributing to achievement as you could identify. One major factor would presumably be the promotion of good brain growth. This can only be accomplished by achieving good bodily growth; and this in turn demands good socio-economic conditions and, above all, good nutrition. This is surely also true in our own privileged society as well as in the Third World.

It may finally be wondered, why should so much expensive research be necessary in order to come to the quite elementary conclusion that we must feed our children? The answer is that, if that were the whole story, research of this kind would not be necessary. But if, as has been indicated, there exists a particular, vulnerable period, a particular age of development during which the brain has its only opportunity to grow properly, it would be an important and urgent task for the developmental neurobiologist to identify this vulnerable period, so that irrevocably poor brain growth does not occur, and the very best brain growth can be economically promoted. Only when we have succeeded in doing this, by abolishing all forms of environmental restriction at this time, will we be likely to reveal the comparatively small contribution to the variance made by our individual heredity.

Further Reading

1. For a full description of the clinical implications of this subject, see Scientific Foundations of Paediatrics (1974). Edited by John A. Davis and John Dobbing; published by Heinemann, London & Saunders, Philadelphia. This also contains full account of the growth and development of all the other organ systems as well as the brain.
2. For more complete discussion of the behavioural implications, see Dobbing, J. & Smart, J. L. (1974). Undernutrition and the developing brain. *Brit. Med. Bull.* 30:164–168.

Behavioral Estimates of CNS Integrity in Infantile Malnutrition*

Barry M. Lester
UNIVERSITY OF FLORIDA

Abstract

Behavioral processes that have been used to estimate the integrity of the CNS were studied in 20 well-nourished and 20 malnourished 1-year-old male infants. Malnourished infants showed an attenuation of the cardiac-orienting response and an aberrant cry pattern characterized by an initial long sound that is high in pitch, low in intensity, arrhythmical with a long latency to the second cry sound. These results point to behavioral deficits in CNS-mediated processes associated with nutritional insult.

Although animal and human research has found both structural and biochemical abnormalities in malnourished brains[1] the behavioral correlates of these deficits are unclear. Most studies, especially with infants, have been confined to the use of standard developmental scales which provide a gross estimate of psychomotor performance but do not indicate specific behavioral processes that may be affected by nutritional insult.[2] In the present report specific behaviors that have been used to estimate the integrity of the CNS were compared in well-nourished and malnourished infants. Behavior studies were habituation of the cardiac-orienting response (OR) and temporal and acoustic measures of the cry response.

EXPERIMENT I

METHODS.   *Subjects*   Twenty well-nourished and 20 malnourished home reared 1-year-old male infants from the lower socioeconomic class of Guatemala City, Guatemala, served as subjects. Consent to participate in the study was

* Supported in part by National Institute of Child Health and Human Development Contract PH43–65–540.

obtained when the mother brought her infant to a government run medical clinic for the indigent for the infant's 1 year checkup. All infants were full term, clinically normal, single births of uneventful pregnancies and had suffered no major illnesses as of the time of testing. Differences in birth weight between the well-nourished ($\bar{X} = 2.52$, $SD = .37$) and malnourished ($\bar{X} = 2.57$, $SD = .38$) groups were not significant. None of the mothers were sedated during the birth of the infant and all infants had been breast-fed. No significant differences were found between the groups with regard to the socioeconomic variables of age or education of the parents or occupation of the father. The age and anthropometric characteristics of the sample are shown in Table 1. The malnourished infants were significantly lighter ($F = 98,44$, $df = 1,38$, $p <$ .001), shorter ($F = 23,50$, $df = 1,38$, $p < .001$), and had a smaller head circumference ($F = 14,29$, $df = 1,38$, $p < .001$) than the well-nourished infants. On the Gomez norms[3], based on a sample from Mexico City, the mean per cent of average weight was 66.4% (range of 56%–75%) for the malnourished infants and 94.4% (range of 89%–100%) for the well-nourished infants. According to the nutritional status categories suggested by Gomez, the malnourished infants were suffering from second- and third-degree malnutrition whereas the well-nourished infants were within the expected weight for age.

Procedure   The infants were presented with 20 trials of a pure tone stimulus in a sound-attenuated chamber. Within each nutrition group half of the infants were presented with 10 trials of a 750 Hz tone followed by 5 trials of a 400 Hz tone and 5 trials of the 750 Hz tone. For the other half of the sample this order was reversed. The tones were presented at 90 db for 5 seconds with a randomized intertrial interval having a mean of 20 seconds and a range of 15–25 seconds. All infants were in an awake and alert state when tested. Magnitude of heart rate deceleration was used to measure the OR. Previous work[4] suggests that HR deceleration is a component of the OR facilitating stimulus intake that may reflect the capacity of the nervous system to attend to and process new information.[5] Infant HR was monitored with a set of Beckman biopotential electrodes placed slightly above the infant's nipples and a ground located above the navel. Cardiac responses were recorded in an adjoining room with a Beckman type-R dynograph with cardiotachometer.

TABLE 1

Age and Anthropometric Characteristics of Well-Nourished and Malnourished Infants

GROUP	AGE (mo)	WEIGHT (kg)	HEIGHT (cm)	HEAD CIRCUMFERENCE
Well-nourished (N = 20)				
$\bar{X}$	12.38	9.44	72.19	45.48
SD	1.30	.87	2.87	1.34
Malnourished (N = 20)				
$\bar{X}$	12.28	7.02	67.77	43.87
SD	1.92	.65	2.89	1.35

Results and Discussion   No significant differences in prestimulus HR were found between the well-nourished and malnourished groups. A repeated measures analysis of variance showed no significant differences due to the order of tone frequency presentation. Accordingly, the order conditions were collapsed resulting in 20 subjects per nutrition cell. Figure 1 presents the mean HR decelerations to the pure tone stimuli for the well-nourished and malnourished infants. A repeated measures analysis of variance for trials 1–10 revealed a significant trials effect ($F = 3,42$, $df = 9,324$, $p < .001$) and a significant nutrition by trials interaction ($F = 5,61$, $df = 9,324$, $p < .001$). These effects were due to the larger mean HR deceleration on trial 1 in the well-nourished than in the malnourished group ($F = 48,99$, $df = 1,38$, $p < .001$). For trials 11–15 the analysis showed a significant trials effect ($F = 3,98$, $df = 4,132$, $p < .001$) and a significant nutrition by trials interaction ($F = 5,52$, $df = 4,132$, $p < .001$). The mean HR deceleration on trial 11 was larger in the well-nourished than in the malnourished infants ($F = 18,85$, $df = 1,38$, $p < .001$). Similarly, the analysis for trials 16–20 revealed significant effects for the trials factor ($F = 3,32$, $df = 4,132$, $p < .025$) and the nutrition by trials interaction ($F = 4,78$, $df = 4,132$, $p < .001$). The mean HR on trial 16 was larger in well-nourished than in malnourished infants ($F = 8,19$, $df = 1,38$, $p < .01$).

These results demonstrate an effect of nutritional status on the infant's ability to respond to and process a novel stimulus. Well-nourished infants showed a classic OR followed by rapid habituation to the repeated presentation of the stimulus. Moreover, qualitative changes in that stimulus produced response recovery or dishabituation which was followed by rapid habituation.

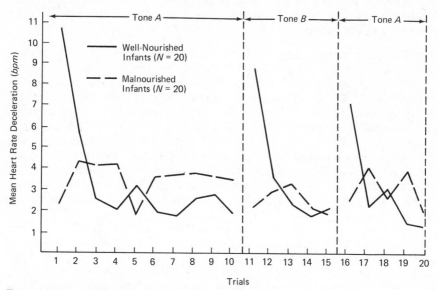

FIGURE 1.   *Mean heart rate deceleration on each trial to pure tone stimuli in well-nourished and malnourished infants. For each trial, heart rate deceleration was calculated by subtracting the mean of the two lowest beats during the 5-second stimulus onset period from the mean of the two lowest beats during the 5 seconds preceding stimulus onset.*

This suggests that the habituation of the OR was due to a neural inhibitory process rather than to peripheral adaptation of the receptor or to fatigue. In contrast, the malnourished infants showed an attenuation of the OR. Neither the repeated presentation of a stimulus nor qualitative changes in that stimulus produced anything but minimal responses in malnourished infants. Since OR evocation is thought to be a necessary precursor to centrally mediated attentional and cognitive processes, OR attenuation in malnourished infants strongly suggests CNS-mediated deficits in these important adaptive functions.

EXPERIMENT II

METHODS   Of the 40 infants, 24 (12 malnourished and 12 well-nourished) cried following the last habituation trial. Since previous studies have shown pathognomic cry patterns to be associated with brain damage[6,7] these cry sounds were subjected to both temporal and acoustic analyses for evidence of aberrant cry patterns. The cry sounds were recorded on a Sony portable tape recorder at a constant recording level at a distance of 1 meter from the mouth of the infant. The cry segment analyzed was the initial spontaneous cry sound following the offset of the last habituation tone. The analysis was performed with the experimenter blind as to the nutritional status of the infant.

Cry signals were analyzed with a model 1510 Real Time Spectrum Analyzer which plots a Fourier transformation of a signal on a cathode ray tube display. Five measures, two temporal and three acoustic, were taken from each cry segment. The temporal measures were the duration of the initial cry sound and the latency to the onset of the next cry sound. The acoustic measures were the fundamental frequency or basic pitch of the initial cry sound, the amplitude or intensity of the fundamental and the number of peaks or major shifts in the frequency of the initial cry sound.

RESULTS AND DISCUSSION   Table 2 summarizes the results of the analysis of variance for the cry measures. The analysis for the temporal measures showed that the duration of the cry and the latency to the next cry sound was longer in malnourished than in well-nourished infants. The analysis for the acoustic measures revealed that the cry of the malnourished infant was of a higher fundamental frequency and lower amplitude than the cry of the well-nourished infant. The number of peaks was also fewer in the malnourished infants than in the well-nourished infants. In other words, the cry of the malnourished infant can be characterized by a long initial sound that is high in pitch, and low in intensity with a long interval to the next cry sound. The malnourished cry also appears arrhythmical as indicated by the number of peaks in the initial cry sound.

Pearson product-moment correlations computed between all of the cry measures are shown in Table 3. Eight of the 10 correlations were significant, and all were in the expected direction. The correlations showed the association between a high fundamental frequency, low amplitude, few number of peaks, long initial cry and long latency to the next cry sound. Thus, both temporal and acoustic attributes of the cry seem to be similarly affected by nutritional insult.

The results from the cry analyses suggest that the cry pattern of malnourished infants is similar to the cry patterns found to be characteristic of some

TABLE 2

Results of Analysis of Cry Measures in Well-Nourished and Malnourished Infants

| | GROUP | | | | |
| | Well-Nourished ($N = 12$) | | Malnourished ($N = 12$) | | |
CRY MEASURE	$\bar{X}$	SD	$\bar{X}$	SD	$F(df = 1.22)$
Length of cry (sec)	1.52	.18	2.66	1.15	10.47*
Latency to next cry (sec)	.47	.26	1.8	.69	39.33**
Frequency of fundamental (Hz)	308.00	32.18	479.77	25.61	209.06**
Intensity of fundamental (dB)	50.31	7.0	38.16	5.47	22.48**
Number of peaks	4.5	1.2	2.25	.75	28.74**

* $p < .005.$
** $p < .001.$

brain-damaged infants. In fact, several investigators have pointed to the diagnostic utility of the cry as a sensitive measure of the integrity of the CNS.[8,9] Specifically, studies have found longer initial cry sounds, a longer latency to the second cry sound, higher pitch, and more arrhythmia to be associated with brain damage in infancy.[10,11] If aberrations of the cry pattern are indicative of CNS dysfunction, these findings may suggest that the regulatory function of the CNS is affected by malnutrition.

Finally, the results from the cry analysis can be compared with the HR data from the same subjects reported earlier. Table 4 shows the Pearson product-moment correlations between each cry measure and the magnitude of HR deceleration to the onset of the original stimulus (trial 1) and the two

TABLE 3

Intercorrelations Among Cry Measures

	1	2	3	4	5
1. Length of cry	1.00	—	—	—	—
2. Latency to next cry	.49**	1.00	—	—	—
3. Frequency of fundamental	.56**	.70†	1.00	—	—
4. Intensity of fundamental	−.33	−.50**	−.61**	1.00	—
5. Number of peaks	−.27	−.54**	−.70†	.43*	1.00

* $p < .05.$
** $p < .01.$
† $p < .001.$

TABLE 4

Correlations Between Magnitude of Heart Rate Deceleration and Cry Measures

	STIMULUS ONSET	DISHABITUATION STIMULUS 1	DISHABITUATION STIMULUS 2
Duration of cry	−.45*	−.64**	−.53**
Latency to next cry	−.65†	−.68†	−.52**
Frequency of fundamental	−.70†	−.62**	−.60**
Amplitude of fundamental	.63†	.33	.68†
Number of peaks	.50**	.46*	.46*

* $p < .05$.
** $p < .01$.
† $p < .001$.

dishabituation stimuli (trials 11 and 16). As can be seen in the table, 14 of the 15 correlations were significant and all were in the expected direction. The correlations with the temporal measures showed that longer initial cry sounds and a longer latency to the next cry sound are related to low magnitude HR decelerations on each trial. The correlations with the acoustic measures showed that high frequency, low amplitude, arrhythmical cries are related to low magnitude HR decelerations on each trial. In other words, both temporal and acoustic deviations from the normal cry pattern are associated with a low level OR. On the other hand, infants who evidence normal cry patterns show the expected OR to a novel stimulus.

CONCLUSIONS This study demonstrates that both orienting and cry behavior are similarly affected by nutritional insult. To the extent that these behaviors mirror the functional integrity of the CNS, the results indicate some of the specific behavioral correlates of CNS dysfunction due to malnutrition. Moreover, it seems reasonable to speculate that nutritional insult is most likely to affect those regions of the CNS responsible for the activation and modulation of behavior.

References

1. DOBBING, J.: Undernutrition and the developing brain. In W. Himwich, editor; Developmental Neurobiology, Springfield, Ill., Charles C Thomas. 1970, p. 502.
2. LESTER, B. M.: The consequences of infantile malnutrition. In H. E. Fitzgerald & J. P. McKinney, editors; Developmental Psychology: Studies in Human Development, Homewood, Ill., Dorsey Press, in press.
3. GOMEZ, F., CALVAN, R., FRENK, S., CRAVIOTO, J., CHAVEZ, R., & VASQUEZ, J.: MORTALITY in second and third degree malnutrition. Journal of Tropical Pediatrics, September; 77: 1956.
4. GRAHAM, F. K., & CLIFTON, R. K.: Heart rate change as a component of the orienting response, Psychological Bulletin, 65:305, 1966.
5. SOKOLOV, E. N.: Perception and the conditioned reflex. New York, Macmillan, 1963.
6. WASZ-HOCKERT, O., LIND, J., VVORENKOSKI, V., PARTANEN, T. & VALANNE, E.: The infant cry. Clinics in Developmental Medicine, 29: 1968.

7. KARCLITZ, S., & FISICHELLI, V.: The cry thresholds of normal infants and those with brain damage. *Journal of Pediatrics*, **61**:679, 1962.
8. PARMELEE, A.: Infant crying and neurologic diagnosis. *Journal of Pediatrics*, **61**:801, 1962.
9. ILLINGWORTH, R.: Crying in infants and children. *British Medical Journal*, **1**:75, 1955.
10. LIND, J., WASZ-HOCKERT, O., VVORENKOSKI, V., PARTANEN, T., THEORELL, K., & VALANNE, E.: Vocal response to pain stimuli in newborn and young infant. *Ann. Paediat. Fenn.* **10**:122, 1965.
11. WASZ-HOCKERT, O., LIND, J., VVORENKOSKI, V., PARTANEN, T., & VALANNE, E.: The infant cry. *Clinics in Developmental Medicine*, **29**, 1968.

The Relation of Infants' Home Environments to Mental Test Performance from Six to Thirty-six Months: A Longitudinal Analysis *

Richard Elardo, Robert Bradley, and Bettye M. Caldwell
UNIVERSITY OF ARKANSAS

In contrast to the large array of instruments available for the measurement of individual differences in children, there have been almost no techniques available to permit the precise measurement of the child's home learning environment. The present study involved the administration of a home environment inventory to a sample of 77 mothers and infants. Correlations between home inventory data and measures of infant development over a period of 30 months were higher than those typically reported relating infant tests or level of parental education to childhood IQ.

Several investigators (Bloom 1964: Plowden 1967; Walberg & Marjoribanks 1973) have produced evidence attesting to the fact that measures of various characteristics of the home environment contribute more strongly to the prediction of children's abilities than do social status or family structure indices. These studies have been cross-sectional in nature and have focused on children over 10 years of age. Walberg and Marjoribanks (1973), for example, interviewed the mothers and fathers of 185 11-year-old boys with a home environment inventory based on the theorizing of Bloom (1964). They reported that their inventory contributed the most to the prediction of a boy's verbal and numerical abilities, when compared with SES and family structure measures via canonical correlation.

From *Child Development*, 1975, **46**, 71–76. Copyright© 1975 by The Society for Research in Child Development, Inc. Reprinted by permission.

* This investigation was supported by grant SF-500 from the Office of Child Development, Department of Health, Education, and Welfare. A preliminary report was presented at the Southeastern Regional Meeting of the Society for Research in Child Development, Chapel Hill, North Carolina, March 1974. Copies of the Inventory of Home Stimulation may be obtained from Dr. Caldwell. Authors' address: University of Arkansas, Center for Early Development and Education, 814 Sherman Street, Little Rock, Arkansas 72202.

The present study involved the administration of a home environment inventory in infancy (Inventory of Home Stimulation [Caldwell, Heider, & Kaplan 1966]) in order to explore its ability to predict later mental test performance.

METHOD

Subjects   The subjects for this analysis were 77 normal infants, representing part of a larger sample of 135 infants who participated in a longitudinal observation and intervention study (Caldwell, Elardo, & Elardo 1972) which was designed to reveal the effects of different types of environments on infant development.

Excluded from the present sample were infants who received a program of educational intervention in the home and those for whom complete home environment and mental test data were not available. Additional descriptive information about the subjects is contained in Table 1.

Instrumentation   A decade ago, a group of persons working on the Syracuse Early Learning Project (Caldwell & Richmond 1968) began to devote considerable effort to the discovery of ways of assessing the subtle aspects of the young child's home environment in order to determine which specific features of it were most likely to influence development. The staff felt that it was imperative to develop a measure of the home environment that could warn of developmental risk before age 3. Their long-term goal was to produce a valid, reliable, easy-to-administer, observationally based inventory

TABLE 1
Characteristics of the Sample

FAMILY DATA ($N = 77$)

Welfare, 31; nonwelfare, 46
Father absent, 21; father present, 56
Maternal education (average no. of years), 12.1
Paternal education (average no. of years), 12.9
Paternal occupation: wide range of employment, but
on the average skilled labor to sales

CHILD DATA

Black males	$N = 29$, $\bar{X}DQ^* = $	94.4, SD = 21.7
White males	$N = 15$, $\bar{X}DQ = $	104.1, SD = 10.7
Black females	$N = 21$, $\bar{X}DQ = $	104.9, SD = 17.3
White females	$N = 12$, $\bar{X}DQ = $	102.6, SD = 22.6

* Refers to the average score obtained by the infants when tested at 6 months of age with the Mental Development Index of the Bayley Scales of Infant Development (Bayley 1969).

that would provide an index of the quality and quantity of social, emotional, and cognitive support available to a young child (from birth to 3 years of age) within the home setting.

A survey of empirical data, developmental theory, and expert opinion was conducted for clues to home characteristics that might be associated with favorable development during the early years of life. A list of environmental characteristics likely to foster early development in any setting was compiled and published (Caldwell 1968), and an instrument named the "Inventory of Home Stimulation" was developed and standardized from this list. The current version of the inventory contains 45 items representing the following six subscales: (1) emotional and verbal responsivity of the mother, (2) avoidance of restriction and punishment, (3) organization of the physical and temporal environment, (4) provision of appropriate play materials, (5) maternal involvement with the child, and (6) opportunities for variety in daily stimulation.

Scoring is based partly on observation and partly on answers to a semistructured interview administered in the home at a time when the child is awake and can be observed in interaction with the mother or primary care giver.

At an early stage of instrument development, consideration was given to the notion of including items based totally on observation of what transpired at the time of the visit. However, in order to cover certain important transactions not likely to occur during the visit, it was necessary to base about one-third of the items on parental report. All items are scored in a binary fashion (yes or no) and are phrased so that the total score equals the number of yes responses marked by the interviewer. The entire procedure takes approximately 1 hour.

At present, extensive standardization data do not exist for the inventory. Data have been gathered from 176 families in central Arkansas, however, and these data indicate that the instrument is sensitive enough to register a wide range of scores for families with identical social status designations.

In terms of reliability, raters can quickly be trained to achieve a 90% level of agreement. Internal consistency (KR-20) coefficients based on 176 cases range from .44 for subscale 6 to .89 for subscale 3. The internal consistency coefficient for the total scale was computed at .89. Using data from assessments made at 6, 12, and 24 months on 91 families, we computed test-retest correlations for each subscale and the total scale. Results indicate that the inventory has a moderate degree of stability across the 18-month period.

With regard to concurrent validity, Inventory of Home Stimulation scores for 91 families were correlated with seven socioeconomic status variables (welfare status, maternal education, maternal occupation, presence of the father in the home, paternal education, paternal occupation, and crowding in the home). Correlations between subscales and maternal education, presence of the father in the home, paternal education, paternal occupation, and crowding were moderate (.25–.55). Correlations between subscales and welfare status and maternal occupation were smaller in magnitude but still positive.

Procedure   Data collected from all subjects include scores on the Mental Development Index (MDI) of the Bayley Scales of Infant Development (Bayley 1969) at 6 and 12 months of age, and scores on the Stanford-Binet scale at 36 months. Each infant's home environment was assessed at 6, 12, and 24 months with the Inventory of Home Stimulation.

Several analyses were performed to determine which aspects of the early home environment were associated with the infants' mental test performance.

RESULTS

The Pearson product-moment and multiple correlation coefficients between home environment scores at 6 months and Bayley MDI scores at 6 and 12 months and Stanford-Binet scores at 36 months are presented in Table 2. An examination of these coefficients indicates that subscale 3 (organization of the physical and temporal environment) and subscale 6 (opportunities for variety in daily stimulation) have the strongest relationship to MDI scores at 6 months, $r = .22$ and $.20$, respectively. These subscales have a stronger relationship to mental test performance than even the total score on the inventory. The multiple correlation between all six subscales and the 6-month MDI is listed at $R = .31$.

The same general pattern of coefficients obtains between 6-month home environment scores and Bayley MDI scores at 12 months. To be specific, opportunities for variety in daily stimulation and organization of the physical and temporal environment are correlated with the criterion $r = .16$ and $.26$, respectively. The multiple correlation between all six scores and the 12-month MDI score is calculated at $R = .30$.

Correlations between 6-month home environment scores and 36-month Binet scores are generally higher than correlations between 6 and 12 months,

TABLE 2

Correlations Between 6-month Inventory of Home Stimulation Scores and Mental Test Scores Gathered at 6, 12, and 36 Months

	MENTAL TEST SCORES		
HOME ENVIRONMENT VARIABLES	6-Month Bayley MDI	12-Month Bayley MDI	36-Month Binet
1. Emotional and verbal responsivity of mother	−.008	.093	.254*
2. Avoidance of restriction and punishment	.005	.039	.244*
3. Organization of physical and temporal environment	.224	.263	.402**
4. Provision of appropriate play materials	.146	.067	.408**
5. Maternal involvement with child	.061	−.003	.325**
6. Opportunities for variety in daily stimulation	.204	.158	.305**
Total score	.141	.156	.500**
Multiple correlation†	.313**	.301*	.537**

* $p < .05$.
** $p < .01$.
† This represents the correlation of all subscales with mental test scores.

particularly the relationship between the total score and the 36-month Binet score, $r = .50$. In addition, provision of appropriate play materials, $r = .41$, and maternal involvement with child, $r = .33$, seem about as strongly related with 36-month Binet performance as do organization of the physical and temporal environment, $r = .40$, and opportunities for variety in daily stimulation, $r = .31$. The multiple correlation is given at $R = .54$.

Pearson product-moment coefficients and multiple correlation coefficients between 12-month home environment scores and 12-month MDI scores and 36-month Binet scores are shown in Table 3. The 12-month MDI scores seem most strongly related to provision of appropriate play materials, $r = .35$. A moderate relationship is also observed for organization of the physical and temporal environment, $r = .24$, and maternal involvement with child, $r = .22$. A multiple correlation of $R = .40$ was computed for all six subscales for this concurrent analysis.

Correlations ranging from $r = .24$ to $r = .56$ are observed between 12-month home environment scores and 36-month Binet scores, the highest being for provision of appropriate play materials, $r = .56$, and maternal involvement with child, $r = .47$. It is at this level that emotional and verbal responsivity also seems to show a strong relationship to mental test performance, $r = .39$. The correlation between the 36-month Binet score and the total home environment score obtained at 12 months is listed at $r = .55$, while the multiple correlation between the six subscales of the Inventory of Home Stimulation and the 36-month Binet scores is listed at $R = .59$.

In Table 4 the correlations between 24-month home environment scores and 36-month Binet scores are listed. Coefficients range from $r = .41$ for

TABLE 3

Correlations Between 12-Month Inventory of Home Stimulation Scores and Mental Test Scores Gathered at 12 and 36 Months

	MENTAL TEST SCORES	
HOME ENVIRONMENT VARIABLES	12-Month Bayley MDI	36-Month Binet
1. Emotional and verbal responsivity of mother	.176	.387**
2. Avoidance of restriction and punishment	−.008	.241*
3. Organization of physical and temporal environment	.241	.389**
4. Provision of appropriate play materials	.353*	.561**
5. Maternal involvement with child	.218*	.468**
6. Opportunities for variety in daily stimulation	.054	.283*
Total score	.252*	.551**
Multiple correlation†	.400**	.588**

* $p < .05$.
* $p < .01$.
*† This represents the correlation of all subscales with mental test scores.

TABLE 4

Correlations Between 24-Month Inventory of Home Stimulation Scores and Mental Test Scores
at 36 Months

HOME ENVIRONMENT VARIABLES	MENTAL TEST SCORES, 36-MONTH BINET
1. Emotional and verbal responsivity of mother	.495*
2. Avoidance of restriction and punishment	.406*
3. Organization of physical and temporal environment	.413*
4. Provision of appropriate play materials	.635*
5. Maternal involvement with child	.545*
6. Opportunities for variety in daily stimulation	.499*
Total score	.695*
Multiple correlation**	.718*

* $p < .01$.
** This represents the correlation of all subscales with mental test scores.

avoidance of restriction and punishment to $r = .64$ for provision of appropriate play materials. The total home environment score at 24 months and the Binet score at 36 months share almost 50% common variance, $r = .69$. The multiple correlation between the six subscales and the 36-month Binet scores is computed at $R = .72$. Correlations between Bayley and Binet scores are presented in Table 5.

TABLE 5

Correlations Between 6-Month Bayley MDI, 12-Month
Bayley MDI, and 36-Month Stanford-Binet Scores
($N = 77$)

SCALES	MDI-12	IQ-36
MDI-6	.410**	.283*
MDI-12	—	.319**

* $p < .05$.
** $p < .01$.

DISCUSSION

We begin with a note of caution. The analyses presented in this paper are based on only 77 cases. Therefore, it would be presumptuous to assume that highly similar results would be obtained from a more representative group of families. More accurate information may also be obtained by analyzing males and females separately. Nevertheless, the results of our analyses suggest that those aspects of home environment assessed by the Inventory of Home

Stimulation bear an important relationship to cognitive development during the first 3 years of life.

With our sample, the six home inventory subscale scores obtained at 6 months of age yielded a multiple correlation of .54 with the same subjects' Binet at age 3. The home scores obtained at 12 months yielded a multiple correlation of .59 with the Binet at age 3, while the multiple correlation between 24-month home scores and Binet scores at age 3 was .72.

These correlations are quite high; in general, they are higher than those reported in the McCall, Hogarty, and Hurlburt (1972) analysis relating infant tests and parental education to childhood IQ. They are also higher than Bayley-Binet correlations obtained from the same sample (see Table 5). The Inventory of Home Stimulation can thus be of value to those interested in the early identification of environmental factors detrimental to development. The work of Cravioto and DeLicardie (1972), which indicated that the presence of severe malnutrition was significantly associated with home stimulation, is illustrative of this. Cravioto and DeLicardie administered the Inventory of Home Stimulation twice yearly as part of their longitudinal investigation of environmental correlates of severe clinical malnutrition. From a sample of 229 infants, Cravioto and DeLicardie identified 19 infants who suffered from severe clinical malnutrition by the age of 39 months. From their total sample, they then assembled a matched control group for the malnourished infants and examined the distribution of scores on the Inventory of Home Stimulation for both groups. They found that the inventory administered at 6 months of age significantly discriminated between infants who were eventually to become malnourished and those who were not, thus delineating an important relationship between children's social environments and their physiological state.

Also illustrative is the cross-sectional study of Wachs, Uzgiris, and Hunt (1971). They employed the Inventory of Home Stimulation in an investigation designed to relate the home background of infants to the infants' cognitive development, as measured by the Infant Psychological Development Scale (Uzgiris & Hunt 1966). A total of 102 infants were involved in the study, ranging in age from 7 to 22 months. Two kinds of home circumstances were found to be most consistently related to infant development: intensity and variety of stimulation, and opportunities to hear vocal labels for objects, actions, and relationships. The first factor was at several ages negatively correlated with developmental test performance, suggesting the harmful effects of overstimulation or "stimulus bombardment." The second factor, concerned with the infants' verbal environment in the home, revealed several significant positive relationships to development beginning as early as 15 months of age. Wachs et al. (1971) present a convincing argument that certain types of environmental stimulation may be related in a curvilinear rather than a linear manner to psychological development. Their explanation for this type of relationship rests on Hunt's (1961) concept of "Hypothesis of the Match." These researchers see a need for longitudinal research to provide more information for understanding the complex relationships between home circumstances and indices of psychological development.

Our results indicate that home environment, when measured at a time when the infant is approximately 6 months of age, does not relate in any important fashion to the infant's performance on the Bayley Mental Development Index at 6 or 12 months of age; whereas the correlation between home environment as measured at 6 months and Binet performance at 3 years appears to be both significant and important, as do the correlations between home environment measured at 12 and 24 months of age and Binet performance at 3 years. These results suggest that the Inventory of Home Stimulation is measuring a complex of environmental forces which are perhaps prerequisites to later performance on cognitive tasks, and is measuring those forces at a time in the infant's life prior to the period in development in which such environmental forces have affected the infant's measured development. During the first year of life, the subscales dealing with organization of the physical and temporal environment and, to a lesser extent, opportunities for variety in daily stimulation seem most strongly related to mental test performance. However, beginning at 12 months, provision of appropriate play materials and maternal involvement with the child seem to show the strongest relationships. The meaning of these findings is uncertain. It may be that different aspects of the home environment are most salient at certain times in development. It may, on the other hand, suggest that certain home environment factors interact with mental capabilities in a complex fashion.

The data obtained after 12 months of age seem to indicate that perhaps the most enriching environments experienced by the children in our sample may be characterized as those in which a mother (or some other primary care giver) provided the infant with a variety of age-appropriate learning materials and likewise consciously encouraged developmental advances by talking to, looking at, and otherwise positively responding to and attending to her child.

In this study, as in the case with other correlational studies, several different hypotheses may be considered as plausible explanations of the results obtained: (*a*) a stimulating environment produces a bright child, (*b*) a bright child causes those in the environment to react in a more stimulating fashion, (*c*) some third factor affects both the child and the child's environment, and (*d*) various types of children interact differently with certain types of environments. Experimental investigation, or perhaps cross-lagged correlational analysis or path analysis, must be conducted to determine which of the four is the most plausible for each of the home environment variables assessed by the inventory.

For the present, for those who are of the opinion that the environmental forces assessed with the Inventory of Home Stimulation play primarily a causal role in development, the inventory has the potential for use in the differential diagnosis of strengths and weaknesses present in an infant's environment, thus assisting those concerned with prevention and remediation in their task of designing intervention strategies.

References

BAYLEY, N. *Bayley Scales of Infant Development.* New York: Psychological Corp., 1969.

BLOOM, B. S. *Stability and change in human characteristics.* New York: Wiley, 1964.

CALDWELL, B. M. On designing supplementary environments for early child development. *BAEYC* [*Boston Association for the Education of Young Children*] *Reports*, 1968, **10** (No. 1), 1–11.

CALDWELL, B. M.; ELARDO, P.; & ELARDO, R. The longitudinal observation and intervention study: a preliminary report. Paper presented at the meeting of the Southeastern Conference on Research in Child Development, Williamsburg, Va., April 1972.

CALDWELL, B. M.; HEIDER, J.; & KAPLAN, B. The inventory of home stimulation. Paper presented at the meeting of the American Psychological Association, New York, September 1966.

CALDWELL, B. M., & RICHMOND, J. B. The children's center—a microcosmic health, education, and welfare unit. In L. Dittman (Ed.), *Early child care: the new perspectives*. New York: Atherton, 1968.

CRAVIOTO, J., & DeLICARDIE, E. Environmental correlates of severe clinical malnutrition and language development in survivors from kwashiorkor or marasmus. In *Nutrition: the nervous system and behavior*. Scientific Publication No. 251. Washington, D.C.: Pan-American Health Organization, 1972.

HUNT, J. McV. *Intelligence and experience*. New York: Ronald, 1961.

McCALL, R. B.; HOGARTY, P. S.; & HURLBURT, N. Transitions in infant sensorimotor development and the prediction of childhood IQ. *American Psychologist*, 1972, **27**, 728–748.

PLOWDEN, B. *Children and their primary schools*. London: Her Majesty's Stationery Office, 1967.

UZGIRIS, I. C., & HUNT, J. McV. An instrument for assessing infant psychological development. Mimeographed. Psychological Development Laboratory, University of Illinois, 1966.

WACHS, T.; UZGIRIS, I.; & HUNT, J. McV. Cognitive development in infants of different age levels and from different environmental backgrounds: an explanatory investigation. *Merrill-Palmer Quarterly*, 1971, **17**, 283–317.

WALBERG, H., & MARJORIBANKS, K. Differential mental abilities and home environment: a canonical analysis. *Developmental Psychology*, 1973, **9**, 363–368.

4

Social and Personal Development

Social behaviors emerge as infants interact with adults and children. Although parents have long been considered the most important influences on children's social and emotional development, new evidence indicates that peers also play a vital role. Other adults are also salient in direct interaction with the baby and in their support to parents.

Prosocial or altruistic behavior in infants and young children is reported by Marion R. Yarrow and Caroline Z. Waxler. Using both mothers' reports and a battery of standard situations, they found infants showing that they observed and interpreted emotional behavior of others. Development of compassion and aggression is discussed.

Toddlers' behavior with one another is the focus of the study by Carol O. Eckerman, Judith L. Whatley, and Stuart L. Kutz. Reactions to a strange peer are different from reactions to a strange adult. Results of the study lead the authors to question what peers offer in contrast to familiar adults.

Day care and other supplements to home care are currently discussed and debated in North America. Many families need such care, and yet it is not universally available. Opponents of day care say that it will weaken the family in general. By learning how supplementary child care is done in other countries, a student gains understanding of alternative ways of meeting human needs.

The Israeli kibbutzim, which have long been of interest to North American child developmentalists, are different from one another, and change with time. Jeanette G. Stone describes and discusses present practices in three kibbutzim in her study guide for viewing films on kibbutz infancy. She refers to earlier practices and their relation to present ones. She makes the reader aware of the unity of the kibbutz culture. Child care practices are made possible, convenient, and even necessary by other practices that are parts of the kibbutz. This article gives a sense of the interdependency of children, parents, community, and nation.

The Emergence and Functions of Prosocial Behaviors in Young Children

Marion Radke Yarrow and Carolyn Zahn Waxler
NATIONAL INSTITUTE OF MENTAL HEALTH

The study of children's compassionate feelings and behaviors comprises a complex package for research. Compassion, altruism, prosocial behavior (the label is a problem) involve cognitions, principles, and judgments; they involve feelings and motives. We are well aware that not all of helping, sharing, and sympathizing arise out of identification with the feelings of or concern for the welfare of others, and aware that the phenomena of empathy, compassion, etc. are murky areas—philosophically and empirically. Despite this state of affairs, our research interest is in how compassion (concern for others) is born and bred. Our earlier research used experimental designs with nursery school children. We demonstrated differential changes in prosocial responding as a consequence of different types of modeling and reinforcement. Although these techniques increased the frequency of helping and sympathy (though increase was by no means assured), the helping response was expressed in such a variety of ways as to suggest very different meanings and feelings underlying the response.

The direction of our research program, therefore, shifted to the exploration of the phenomena of compassionate feelings and behaviors more generally. What are the precursors of prosocial inclinations and the very early capabilities of the child in this regard? To get a better grasp of these issues, it seemed important to explore more general questions about the inferential capabilities of young children, of very, very young children, inferences with regard to the affect and thoughts of others. With this kind of knowledge we could more readily ask, how does sensitivity and responsiveness to the needs of others develop? Where and how do they fit into a more general schema of the developing child, both with respect to his cognitive skills and his social behavior?

From three interrelated studies we are attempting to obtain a picture of the emergence and progression of prosocial behaviors, to investigate the cognitions, feelings, and motives involved. The subjects were 128 children, ranging in age from 10 *months* to 7 *years*.

In the first study, with the youngest children, the focus is on the child's emerging sensitivities to affective events in his environment, e.g., a parent's or child's anger or pain or fear or joy or anxiety. Our data are the child's responses to these events and, in turn, responses of others to the child. Three cohorts, of eight children each, were followed for 9 months; the youngest began at 10 months of age, the next cohort at 15 months, and the third cohort at 20 months. Mothers were trained to dictate detailed descriptions of day to day affective events. At three week intervals, investigators visited the home and simulated affective episodes (e.g., pain, anger, joy). Additional data were obtained on the child's development and the home environment.

Presented at meetings of The Society for Research in Child Development, Denver, 1975. Printed by permission of the National Institute of Mental Health.

The second and third studies began at age 3 with children in nursery school or coming back to the school setting for research purposes. Our purposes were (a) to investigate the development and relations of perspective-taking skills and prosocial behavior; and (b) to investigate the prosocial behavior in the life space of the child: the frequency, circumstances, and generality with which it occurs and its relation to its "opposite," "anti-social" behavior.

Through a battery of standard situations, we assessed the child's perspective-taking skills: That is, was the child able to recognize and identify correctly the perspective of the person in circumstances in which an object or event was encountered or experienced differently by the two of them? One set of tasks dealt with literal perspectives in a visual or tactile perceptual sense; a second set dealt with what we will call cognitive perspectives in the sense of comprehending self-other perspectives deriving from long-term differences in life experiences; and a third set dealt with affective perspective-taking. An example of each follows. Some of the tasks are adapted from Flavell; others are new. An example of literal perceptions is one with a child and another person seated on opposite sides of a table. Can the child indicate that a picture or object appearing upside-down to him would be viewed as right side up to the other, and vice versa? A cognitive perspective-taking task is illustrated by requesting the child to choose gifts for parents and opposite sex peer and for himself. Does his own preference pervade his choices? Emotional perspective-taking was tapped by the child's inability to differentiate between his own and another's immediate affective experiences in situations in which S experienced success and O, failure; S experienced pleasure with one object, but O experienced pleasure with a different object.

Prosocial behaviors (a child's potential helping, sharing, and comforting) were assessed in a series of six standard situations. On two occasions an adult accidentally spilled some materials in the context of play activities. In two other circumstances, there were limited supplies of snack or toys which might be shared. The child also had occasion to witness someone expressing pain (slamming her finger in a drawer) and to see and hear someone crying, ostensibly about a sad story. All of the experimental tasks were interwoven in meaningful contexts of play and interaction. In natural indoor and outdoor play settings, prosocial and aggressive interchanges were recorded. A measure of level of social activity was also obtained.

Our infant subjects supplied very provocative data on sensitivity to affective states of others. Responses were by no means universal. However very young children were often finely discriminative and responsive to others' need states. Children in the youngest cohort showed distress to parental arguments and anger with each other. Responses were sometimes marked: crying, holding hands over ears, comforting a distraught parent, or (punitively) hitting the parent perceived as the guilty one. Parental affection toward each other was equally arousing: Children of 1 to $2\frac{1}{2}$ years tried to join in or to separate the parents—even kicking the mother's leg. One child, from 15 months to 2 years, showed consistently different responses depending on whether mother or father initiated the affectionate hug or kiss. Initiation by the mother aroused no affect in the child, whereas with the father's (or grandfather's) initiation toward the mother, the child would "fall apart" (hitting, glaring, sucking her thumb).

While in the youngest children others' crying tended to elicit contagious crying as well as amusement, crying began to decrease, and as it waned, it was replaced by serious or worried attending. Around one year most of the youngest cohort first showed comfort to a person crying or in pain by patting, hugging, or presenting an object. Among $1\frac{1}{2}$ and 2-year-olds comforting was sometimes sophisticated and elaborate, e. g., fixing the hurt by trying to put a Band-aid on, covering mother with a blanket when she was resting, trying to locate the source of the difficulty. Children also began to express concern verbally, and sometimes gave suggestions about how to deal with the problem. Such precocity on the part of the very young gives one pause. The capabilities for compassion, for various kinds of reaching out to others in a giving sense are viable and effective responses early in life. How such behaviors develop and change in the process of socialization in various cultures and subcultures are issues to which science has addressed little investigation.

Lest one assume that we are ready to reformulate a theory about the innate goodness of man, it should be emphasized too that there were also many, many occasions on which benevolence was *not* forthcoming, and that early aggressions are equally impressive.

If by egocentric one means the translation of the environment in terms of one's own needs and body state in the face of different existing states of others, the data provide such evidence—namely, the child who tries to protect his own possessions when another child is being "robbed" of his, or the child who examines his own old injuries, hurts, and so on when someone else is injured, or verbal self-references—"look at my boo-boo"—as mother ministers to the real needs of an injured child. But the interesting point is that such self-references and self-considerations which have characteristically been conceptualized as the child's inability to take the point of view of the other, or preoccupation with one's own need state, may at times have a quite different function. They may also represent active attempts to *comprehend* (to form hypotheses about) others' affects by "trying them on," in this way trying to master (act positively on) the feelings in themselves which are aroused by others' affects. Support for such an idea is found in our data where it is not uncommon to observe self-referential responses followed by compassionate responses.

In our studies of 3 to 7 year olds, as described earlier, we explored children's perspective-taking (literal physical and psychological) in relation to their helping, sharing, and comforting behaviors. The children's abilities to successfully deal with another's perspective on the perceptual and cognitive tasks increased with age, the most substantial jumps occurring between $4\frac{1}{2}$ and 5 years of age. The prosocial behaviors by the same children showed no systematic developmental changes. Not surprisingly, then, there was no overall relation between perspective-taking abilities and prosocial interventions. This was true also at each given age level.

We expected the two kinds of responding to be related, since both (we assume) involve the capacity to make an inference about someone else's differential experience. Prosocial responding involves also the motivation to act on someone else's behalf. The lack of correspondence was of two kinds: children who succeeded on perspective-taking tests but did not respond prosocially, and children who helped, shared, or comforted, but failed on the perspective-taking tasks. This lack of correspondence raises a number of unsettling questions: Is the conceptualization of a common underlying process of perspective-taking incorrect or simplistic? Are the test-tasks that are presumed to measure self-other perspectives really not measuring these abilities well? Perhaps, especially in young children, the language components in the instructions may have an all-determining influence. In designing perspective-taking tasks for this study and in examining tasks that other investigators have used, we have become very aware of the difficulties in good task-construction. We have the strong impression that the child's capabilities are seriously underestimated by many experimental tasks assessing self-other perspectives.

Our third study extended our information to the functioning of these same children in their peer groups. With what frequency and consistency do they help, share, and comfort? How do these prosocial behaviors relate to aggressive peer interaction?

Prosocial behaviors occurred in almost every child. There was some consistency in relative frequency across natural and experimental settings in sharing and comforting responses. Sharing and comforting were significantly related to each other; neither was reliably associated with helping. Such data provide evidence of limited consistency in behaviors that involve sensitivity to others' feeling states. The relatively impersonal utilitarian "helping" of an inconvenienced person (as measured in our study) seems to tap a different kind of behavior from that involved in responding to the emotional needs, as in reacting to hurt or sadness. The data suggest that prosociality is not a unitary concept. Observations of responding to emotional states of others (here to sadness) documented the complexity in prosocial interventions. Our data indicate that merely tabbing a child as having (or not) shared or comforted another ignores significant variants in these responses: inhibitions, approach-avoidance conflicts, anxieties, sympathy, feelings of relief, success or satisfaction.

Compassion and aggression have long been positively linked in some psychological theories, but data are few. In the present study there were no simple relations between aggressive and prosocial behaviors. There was a single significant positive association (out of eight) only for girls. When level of social interaction is controlled, the significance disappears.

Associations between aggression and prosociality were re-examined, taking into account the absolute *level* of aggression. We reasoned that children with high frequencies of aggressive acts might be expressing qualitative as well as quantitative differences in aggression, e.g., hostile vs. assertive aggression. The sample was divided, therefore, at the mean on frequency of aggression and correlations were computed for each subsample, and data for boys and girls examined separately.

For boys *below* the mean on aggression, there was a significant positive association between aggression and sharing-comforting in peer interaction. In contrast, for boys *above* the mean on aggression the relation was negative. For girls, there was no such pattern. However, since the absolute level of aggression of girls is significantly lower than that of boys, the correlation between aggression and comforting-sharing for girls across the entire range of aggression is consistent with the findings for boys at the lower range of aggression. Controlling on level of social interaction did not materially alter the findings. One might hypothesize that moderately aggressive children are assertive more than hostile and that they are secure and competent in their peer groups. Assertiveness is a quality that might reasonably be expected to go along with the ability to intervene on behalf of another person.

These analyses have emphasized the aggressive behavior *expressed by* the child. There is another element of aggression, that expressed *to* the child. Among the boys and girls who were low to moderate in exhibited aggression, frequency of being the target of aggression and frequency of sharing-comforting behaviors were significantly positively related. In other words, among the relatively non-aggressive children, sensitivity to others' feeling states increased as the frequency of experiences of aggression from others increased. There was no such relation among children high on exhibited aggression. We will hazard a hypothesis: namely, aggressions experienced may contribute to the development of sensitivity to feelings when the child is himself not highly vulnerable and is secure in his relations with others. He may be able to learn from experiencing aggression from others and better understand the feelings and be better able to act empathically.

There is still a very modest accumulation of scientific knowledge regarding the human behaviors that qualify as prosocial. They are not a simple phenomenon. As scientists, we tend to give too little thought to cultural influences on the choice and definition of our research problems. It seems to us that research on prosocial behavior carries many overtones of these influences. In our society, the study of prosocial endeavors has been rather late in coming, compared with studies of aggression (and problems in our society), and compared with individual achievement and intellectual capacities, valued commodities by the society. Theories of prosociality, too, have frequently been formulated with materialistic or economic parallels, for example, cost-accounting theory, which represents a balancing of credit-debit ledgers of human relations. We are suggesting that it might be well to reflect more on our research emphases and theories of child development as products of the cultures and subcultures from which we come.

Growth of Social Play with Peers During the Second Year of Life *

Carol O. Eckerman, Judith L. Whatley, and Stuart L. Kutz
DUKE UNIVERSITY

To assess the social interactions between unfamiliar peers, 30 pairs of home-reared children—10 pairs in each of three age groups, 10–12, 16–18, and 22–24 months of age—were observed in an unfamiliar play setting with their mothers.

From *Developmental Psychology*, 1975, **11**, 42–49. Copyright © 1975 by the American Psychological Association. Reprinted by permission.

* This research was supported in part by a Duke University Research Council Grant. We thank Deborah Hotch for her services as an observer and Gregory E. Kennington for statistical advice.

The children contacted their mothers little and interacted more with toys and one another, exchanging smiles, vocalizations, and toys and imitating each other's actions. Contact of the same objects and involvement in the peer's activities with objects increased reliably with age. By 2 years of age, social play exceeded solitary play and the social partner was most often the peer. The results suggested that children generalize to peers behaviors developed through child–adult interaction, but that peers provide stimulation differing from that of familiar adults.

Scant attention has been paid to the social interactions between children under two years of age, despite the importance attached to early peer interactions by students of nonhuman primates (e.g., Harlow, 1969; Hinde, 1971) and despite repeated observations of human infants exchanging glances, sounds, smiles, and even toys (e.g., Bridges, 1933; Bühler, 1930; Vincze, 1971). Our knowledge of early human sociability remains limited in large measure to child–mother interactions and to children's initial reactions to unfamiliar adults (e.g., Rheingold & Eckerman, 1973; Schaffer, 1971). Yet the interactions between infant peers may mirror the social development occurring through child–adult interaction; and even more important, interactions with peers may contribute in their own right to early social development.

The most comprehensive prior study of interactions between children under 2 years of age is that of Maudry and Nekula (1939), conducted in a foundling home over 30 years ago. Pairs of children 6 to 25 months of age were placed together in a playpen, usually with only a single toy, and prompted into interaction. Although over 18 types of peer interaction were defined, the data were presented in such molar categories as positive and negative social behavior, precluding a description of what actually went on between the children. Maudry and Nekula (1939) concluded that infants at first fail to distinguish between each other and inanimate objects (6 to 8 months), later treat each other as obstacles to play materials (9 to 13 months), and only when approaching 2 years of age (19 to 25 months) view each other as social partners—a progression that differs markedly from that proposed for infant's interactions with adults (e.g., Schaffer, 1971). Their conclusion, however, was based upon viewing institutionalized children in a single, and probably unusual, setting. Although descriptions of the normally occurring interactions among peers reared together are available (e.g., Bridges, 1933; Bühler, 1930; Vincze, 1971), no such data exist for children reared in a nuclear family.

In the present study, pairs of normal, home-reared children were brought together in a controlled play setting which included their mothers. The children, similar in age and unfamiliar to one another, were left free to interact with several new toys, their mothers, or one another. The goals were (a) to describe the extent and forms of interaction that the children freely engaged in with one another, (b) to assess changes over the second year of life in their interactions, and (c) to compare their behavior with one another to that with their mothers and with novel inanimate objects. Such an examination of interactions among young peers is a prerequisite for reasoning about the role of peers in normal human social development.

METHOD

SUBJECTS   The subjects were 60 normal, home-reared children, drawn on the basis of age from the population of white infants born and residing in

Durham, North Carolina, an industrial city of moderate size. Over 90% of the mothers contacted by telephone agreed to participate.

The subjects were equally divided into three age groups, 10.0 to 12.0, 16.0 to 18.0, and 22.0 to 24.0 months of age, and paired within each group on the basis of age alone. Table 1 summarizes the characteristics of each age group.

Subjects came from homes characterized by above-average levels of education, the equivalent of 2 or 3 years of college for the mothers and 1 or 2 years of post-college training for the fathers; nevertheless, the range in education was considerable. About half of the children had a sibling, and all but 7 spent some time with peers outside the family. Only 4 children, or 7% of the total sample, received 50% or more of their daytime care outside the family.

Two additional pairs were observed at the two younger ages, but their records discarded: in one case, a mother repeatedly interrupted the play, and in the other, one child with a long history of hospitalizations lacked the motor abilities of his age-mates.

STUDY SETTING   The study took place in a room of moderate size (2.8 × 2.9 m), unfurnished except for a few animal pictures on the walls beyond the subjects' reach and several toys on the floor. The toys were a pulltoy with marbles enclosed in a clear plastic ball, a large plastic dump truck, and three 9-cm-square vinyl cubes decorated with pictures and letters; each toy was present in duplicate. Cushions on the floor in opposite corners along the room's

TABLE 1

Characteristics of the Subjects

	AGE GROUP		
ITEM	10–12	16–18	22–24
Age in months			
M	11.4	17.3	23.0
Range	10.4–12.0	16.3–18.0	22.0–23.8
Age difference in months			
M	.6	.6	.5
Range	.1–1.3	.0–1.9	.0–1.0
No. males	12	14	8
No. firstborns	8	13	14
No. having sibling(s)	12	7	9
Years of education			
Father			
M	17.5	18.4	17.3
Range	9–20	12–22	9–22
Mother			
M	14.4	15.3	14.6
Range	10–17	11–17	8–17
Hours/week with peers			
M	5.0	7.6	7.1
Range	0–24	0–45	0–36

length marked the mothers' positions; the toys were spaced along the wall opposite the mothers' positions. A one-way window behind the toys provided visual access: a microphone in the center of the ceiling, auditory access.

PROCEDURE   Each subject and his mother were escorted to a reception room where they met the other mother and child and the female experimenter. For approximately 5 minutes the children were left free to sit on their mothers' laps or to explore the room and the few toys it contained while the experimenter instructed the mothers in their role. They were asked to talk naturally with one another, allowing their children to do as they wished; they could respond with a smile or a word or two to the children's social overtures, but they were not to initiate interaction with them or direct their activities unless intervention was necessary to prevent physical harm.

The mothers carried the subjects into the study room, placed them on the floor before the toys, and sat at their positions on the floor. The experimenter then left the room, closing the door behind her, and the 20-minute session began. At the end of the session, the experimenter obtained from the mothers information about the family and the children's prior exposure to peers.

RESPONSE MEASURES   An observer behind the one-way window systematically sampled each child's behavior. He focused upon one child at a time and alternated 15-second periods of observation with 15 second periods of recording. Every four observation periods, or 2 minutes, the focus shifted from one child to the other. The resulting record thus was based upon 40 observations, 20 of each child. For each observation, the observer recorded whether or not each of 23 behaviors occurred; the frequency of the behavior within the 15-second period was not recorded.

Eighteen behaviors related to the peer's presence or activities were distinguished and defined on the basis of preliminary observations of children in the study setting. These behaviors, grouped into five categories, are defined in Table 2.

Additional measures provided a context for the study of the peer-related activities. Fussing (fretting, whining sounds), crying (loud continuous wailing), smiling (pleasant facial expressions with marked upturning of the corners of the mouth), and laughing (explosive sounds accompanying smiles) provided a measure of the affect engendered by the novel play setting as a whole. Contact of a mother (hugging or any physical contact for at least 3 continuous seconds) and attempts to engage a mother in play with the toys (offering a toy to her, playing with a toy in her lap) provided a measure of the activities directed toward the adults. Solitary play (all contacts with toys that lasted at least 3 seconds and did not involve either the peer or the mothers or qualify as same play) provided a contrast for social play.

A second observer simultaneously and independently recorded the behavior of 27 of the 30 pairs. Percentage of agreement, calculated by dividing the smaller of the two observers' measures by the larger and multiplying by 100, was obtained for each of the pairs on the measures subjected to analyses of variance. Median percentage agreement was above 90% for all measures except that of distant social response, and the lower agreement for this measure ($Mdn = 78\%$) may be attributed to the relative infrequency of the behavior and the slightly

TABLE 2

Behaviors Related to the Presence of Activity of the Peer

CATEGORY	DEFINITION
Watch	Continuous visual regard of the peer or his activities for at least 3 seconds.
Distant social response	One or more of the following six behaviors occurs.
Vocalize	A vocal sound or series of sounds, that may or may not be distinguishable as words, emitted while watching the peer.
Smile	Pleasant facial expression distinguished by a curved mouth with corners upturned, while watching the peer.
Laugh	An explosive sound of joy or amusement, while watching the peer.
Fuss	A fretting, whining, complaining sound emitted while watching the peer.
Cry	Loud continuous wailing while watching the peer.
Gesture	Wave at a peer as in greeting or departure; clap hands while watching the peer.
Physical contact	Touch and/or strike occurs.
Touch	Placing a hand upon the peer in a nonforceful manner, including patting, hugging, rubbing.
Strike	Forceful physical contact with the peer by either hand or foot, including hitting, pushing, or kicking.
Same play materials	Contact of the same toy as the peer or its duplicate for at least 3 continuous seconds without any direct involvement in the activities of the peer.
Direct involvement in peers' play	One or more of the following eight behaviors occurs.
Imitate	Duplication of the peer's activity, preceded by visual regard of the peer's activities. The peer's activity usually involves a toy or some other aspect of the inanimate environment, but it might consist of a distinctive motor response such as jumping.
Show a toy	Hold out a toy toward the peer, but out of his reach, while looking and/or vocalizing to the peer.
Offer a toy	Hold out a toy toward the peer within his reaching distance, while looking and/or vocalizing to the peer.
Accept a toy	Take a toy offered by the peer.
Take over a toy	Contact a toy released by the peer not more than 3 seconds previously.
Take a toy	Take an unoffered toy from the possession of the peer without a struggle.
Struggle over a toy	Both children attempt to gain sole possession of the same toy, including pulling, pushing, whining, etc.
Coordinate play	Act together with the peer to perform a common task, such as building a tower of blocks; or each child repeatedly takes turns performing an activity with attention to the other's activity, as when one child builds a tower of blocks, stands back and laughs as the other kicks it down.

differing perspectives from which the observers viewed the child's face. For three quarters of the pairs, the observers either did not disagree or they disagreed upon only a single instance of a distant social response.

METHODS OF ANALYSIS   The measures for the two children of each pair were summed, and the pair was treated as the unit of replication in analyses of variance. The study was conducted and initially analyzed in two parts. Fourteen of the pairs (Cohort 1) were first observed and predictions of age changes developed from analyses of variance performed on these observations: then the remaining 16 pairs (Cohort 2) were observed to test the predictions. The absence of any reliable cohort effects or Cohort × Age interactions for two-way analyses of variance indicated that the second set of observations replicated the first.

The data presented and analyzed in the present report are those for the total sample of subjects; pooling of the subsamples avoided the complexities involved in two-factor multivariate analyses of variance with unequal Ns and increased the precision with which age comparisons could be made. To assess changes in behavior with age, one-factor multivariate analyses of variance (Cramer, Note 1; further described in Clyde, Cramer, & Sherin, Note 2) were performed on selected related measures, followed by univariate tests.

The data of individual subjects were used to explore the effects of sex, birth order, and amount of prior exposure to peers on selected peer-related behaviors.

RESULTS

REACTIONS TO THE NOVEL PLAY SETTING   The subjects of all ages interacted with the toys and their peers, and they contacted their mothers little (see Figure 1). Interactions with the peer included any of the peer-related

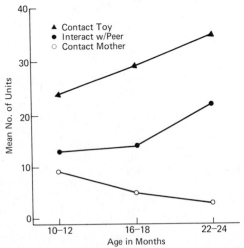

FIGURE 1.   *General reaction to the novel play setting.*

behaviors defined in Table 2 with the exception of the watch category. A multivariate analysis of variance on the three measures indicated a reliable change in behavior with age, $F(6, 50) = 3.42$, $p < .01$. Both the frequency of interactions with the peer and contact with the toy increased reliably with age, $F(2, 27) = 5.90$, $p < .01$; $F(2, 27) = 8.38$, $p < .001$; in contrast, contact with the mother decreased, $F(2, 27) = 7.73$, $p < .01$.

Fussing and crying occurred infrequently, during an average of only one of the 40 periods at each age; and at each age, smiling or laughing occurred more frequently ($M = 2.6$, 4.7, and 5.1 periods for the 10–12-, 16–18-, and 22–24-month groups, respectively). Some fussing or crying occurred in 14 pairs; smiling or laughing, in 22 pairs.

NATURE OF THE INTERACTIONS WITH THE PEER   The subjects attended to the peer (i.e., one or more peer-related behaviors occurred) in over 60% of the observations at each age. Table 3 summarizes the results for

TABLE 3
Frequency of Peer-Related Activities

	M FOR EACH AGE GROUP			RANGE FOR EACH AGE GROUP			
BEHAVIOR	10–12 Months	16–18 Months	22–24 Months	10–12 Months	16–18 Months	22–24 Months	F
Watch	18.3	19.2	15.9	12–26	12–30	7–23	< 1
Distant social response	3.5	3.9	5.2	1–9	0–11	0–14	< 1
Vocalize	1.7	1.5	3.1	0–6	0–5	0–12	
Smile	1.8	2.8	1.9	0–4	0–11	0–12	
Laugh	.0	.3	1.2	—	0–2	0–12	
Fuss	.0	.0	.1	—	—	0–1	
Cry	.0	.0	.0	—	—	—	
Gesture	.0	.1	.0	—	0–1	—	
Physical contact	2.0	.8	1.1	0–7	0–4	0–5	1.14
Touch	2.0	.5	.6	0–7	0–2	0–3	
Strike	.1	.3	.5	0–1	0–3	0–2	
Same play material	6.5	6.8	14.1	0–17	1–15	1–28	4.77*
Direct involvement in play	2.6	4.4	9.9	0–7	0–9	3–20	8.42**
Imitate	.9	1.3	2.0	0–4	0–4	0–8	
Show a toy	.2	.0	.3	0–1	—	0–2	
Offer a toy	.7	.8	.8	0–3	0–4	0–5	
Accept a toy	.3	.5	.2	0–1	0–3	0–1	
Take a toy	.1	.1	.6	0–1	0–1	0–3	
Take over a toy	.4	1.0	.8	0–1	0–6	0–5	
Struggle	.4	.8	3.2	0–2	0–3	0–13	
Coordinate	.0	.0	2.5	—	—	0–8	

* $p < .02$.
** $p < .001$.

each peer-related behavior. A multivariate analysis of variance of the five main categories of peer-related behaviors showed a reliable change with age, F (10, 46) = 2.06, $p < .05$. At all ages a prominent activity was watching the peer. Distant social responses were more frequent at each age than physical contact, but neither changed reliably with age. Vocalizing and smiling were the most frequent of the distant social responses; touching, the most frequent form of contact, especially at the youngest age. The behaviors related to the peer that changed with age were those that involved the play materials. The frequency of both contact with the same play material and direct involvement in the peer's play increased reliably, F (2, 27) = 4.77, $p < .02$; F (2, 27) = 8.42, $p < .001$, respectively.

Contact with the same play material was not simply the result of children playing with a single preferred toy. Analyses of the play material involved, available for the latter 15 pairs of subjects, showed that the pulltoys were involved for 9 pairs, the blocks for 11 pairs, the truck for 9 pairs, and other objects in the room for 3 pairs. Further, all except 2 pairs played with more than one toy in a synchronous manner; 4 played with all three toys synchronously.

Of the behaviors composing direct involvement in the peer's play, four showed orderly increases in frequency with age—imitation of the peer's activity, taking a toy from the peer, struggling over a toy, and coordinating activities with the toys. Five of the behaviors composing direct involvement in the peer's play—offering a toy, accepting a toy, taking a toy, taking over a toy, and struggling over a toy—concern the exchange or attempted exchange of play material between the two children. These exchange activities considered together occurred during an average of 1.9, 3.2, and 5.6 of the 40 intervals at the three ages and thus accounted for the greatest proportion of the activities composing direct involvement in play. Imitation by the focus child was the next most frequent activity across the ages, followed by coordinated play. Note, however, that imitation was recorded only when the focus child imitated the peer and not when the peer imitated him; the best estimate, then, of the frequency of imitation by either child is twice the frequencies tabulated, or 1.8, 2.6, and 4.0 periods at the increasing ages. Taking a toy and struggling—negative social responses according to Maudry and Nekula (1939)—together accounted for far less than half of the direct involvement in the peer's play at all ages.

Most of the peer-related behaviors were divided for purposes of comparison into Maudry and Nekula's (1939) positive and negative social reactions. Smile, laugh, vocalize, gesture, touch, show a toy, imitate, offer a toy, accept a toy, and coordinate toy activities comprise the positive reactions. Watching is excluded here, although included by Maudry and Nekula, since its high frequency at all ages would obscure comparison of the remaining behaviors. Fuss, cry, strike, take a toy, take over a toy, and struggle comprise the negative reactions. The ratio, in mean frequency, of the so-called negative reactions to positive reactions was 1.0 to 7.6, 2.2 to 7.8, and 5.2 to 12.6 for the 10–12-, 16–18-, and 22–24-month groups, respectively. At all ages, then, positive responses far outweighed negative ones, even when watching the peer was disregarded; and both positive and negative responses increased with age.

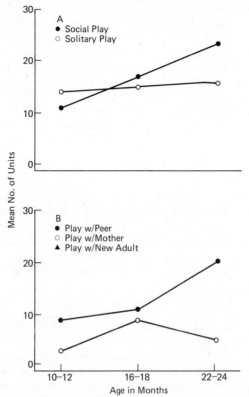

FIGURE 2. *The development of social play. (In social play, the child involves others—peer, mother, or new adult—in his activities with nonsocial objects.)*

GROWTH OF SOCIAL PLAY   Figure 2 contrasts the subjects' social play with solitary play. Social play includes the prior categories of same play material and direct involvement in play with the peer, as well as play with the mothers. A multivariate analysis of variance of solitary play and social play showed a reliable change in behavior with age. F (4, 52) $= 3.78, p < .01$. Solitary play occurred in slightly more than a third of the periods at all ages; social play, in contrast, increased reliably with age, F (2, 27) $= 5.42, p < .01$, until by 2 years it occurred in 60% of the periods. The increase in social play resulted from the reliable increase in play with the peer (see Figure 2B), F(2, 27) $= 10.86$, $p < .001$. Play with the mother reached a peak at 16 to 18 months. F (2,27) $= 3.28, p = .05$; play with the new adult, that is, the other mother, was rare. By 2 years of age, then, most of the children's activities, with toys also involved a person, and in this novel play setting, that person was more often the peer than the mother.

EFFECTS OF SEX, SIBLINGS, PRIOR EXPOSURE TO PEERS   Sixteen of the 30 pairs were composed of a male and female subject, 6 each in the 22–24- and 10–12-month groups and 4 in the 16–18-month group. In these pairs the effects of sex were examined upon 4 categories of peer-related behavior—watch, distant social response, physical contact, and direct involvement in play. A multivariate analysis of variance with sex as a repeated measures factor and age as an independent groups factor yielded no reliable effects of sex; the F values for univariate tests of the effect of sex were all less than 1.0.

The effects of siblings in the family and the amount of prior exposure to peers outside the family were explored by inspecting the data for pairs showing a contrast in these variables. No suggestive differences were found. Suitable pairs were too few and too irregularly distributed by age group to warrant statistical tests.

DISCUSSION

The results showed that during the second year of life, children in a novel play setting turned less to their mothers and more and more to inanimate objects and their peers. Further, the children increasingly integrated their activities with toys and peers until by 2 years of age, social play predominated. They touched the same objects as their peers, imitated their actions, exchanged toys, and coordinated their play to perform a common task or elaborate a social game.

The current study leads to conclusions about the developmental course of peer interactions quite different from those of Maudry and Nekula (1939). At 10 to 12 months, ages at which Maudry and Nekula characterize infants as treating each other as an obstacle to play material, the children of the present study smiled and vocalized to each other, offered and accepted toys, and imitated each other; only infrequently did they struggle over toys or fuss. Further, rather than episodic, qualitative changes in reactions to peers, the present results suggest an orderly increase in the variety and frequency of social interactions between children—both the so-called negative and positive interactions. Of the numerous differences in methodology that might account for the contrasting pictures of social development, the most salient difference appears to be Maudry and Nekula's prompting of the children into interaction and the accompanying restriction of toy materials and alternative activities. The contrasting conclusions emphasize the need for studying situational and experiential determinants of peer interactions, as has been done for mother–infant interaction. An infant of 10 months faced with a mother holding an attractive object might well pull at that object, directing all attention to obtaining it, but we would hardly conclude that infants of this age characteristically treat their mothers as an obstacle to play materials!

The integration of activities with toys and people during the second year of life highlights a central aspect of development. The responses we call social do not develop in a context devoid of inanimate objects; similarly those responses toward inanimate objects that we label exploration or play occur often in a social context. The mother, or attachment object, provides the setting for the infant's exploration of his inanimate world (e.g., Ainsworth & Wittig, 1969; Rheingold, 1969). Social objects, adults or children, also alter the stimulation that toys offer; they put toys in motion, make them do new things, and place them with other objects in new combinations. A toy on the ground does not equal a toy in the hand of a peer. On the other hand, nonsocial objects are vehicles for many forms of social interaction—for giving and taking, imitating, cooperating, or instructing. Smiling and vocalizing to persons or contacting them may be prominent early social behaviors, but other forms of social interaction require the child's integration of activites with things and people.

Questions remain about the determinants and function of the various forms of early interaction between peers. Are watching a peer's activities, looking, smiling, and vocalizing at him, and offering him toys functionally similar to other behaviors we label exploratory? Is the similarity perceived in matching one's activities to another's reinforcing? Do toy exchanges function to promote imitation and same play? Questions such as these await detailed study of the context in which the peer-related behaviors occur. Still, the present results establish several forms of peer interaction whose origins should be sought in infancy rather than the preschool years, and the behavioral descriptions of these interactions provide the starting point for studies of origins and function.

The children of all ages behaved toward one another not as children do with inanimate objects, but rather more as they do with familiar adults. The physical contact and manipulation characteristic of early activity with toys were minimal with the peer; rather the smiles, vocalizations, and offers of toys to the peer correspond to behaviors seen with mothers (e.g., Rheingold, 1973). A comparison, however, between play with the mother and direct play with the peer (the most nearly comparable categories of play) yields suggestive differences in the developmental course of these activities. At 10 to 12 months both were infrequent; by 16 to 18 months both were more frequent, but play with the mother exceeded that with the peer, and by 22 to 24 months, play with the mother had declined in frequency, while direct play with the peer increased markedly. Both the correspondence in forms of behavior toward the mother and the peer and the initial greater frequency of these behaviors toward the mother suggest that young children generalize to peers' responses developed through interaction with familiar adults.

By 2 years of age, however, the children of the present study interacted more with the peer than with their mothers. The restrictive instructions to the mother and the short duration of the play period may have contributed to this preference, but the fact remains that with increasing age primate young turn progressively more to their peers in play (e.g., Harlow, 1969; Heathers, 1955). The question of what peers offer in contrast to familiar adults is an important one for the fuller understanding of early social behavior. Peers and adults seem to differ in their persistence and affective involvement in children's play and the contrast shifts during the child's development. Mothers and fathers initially invest great persistence, affect, and imagination in attempts to engage their young infants in play, but later in development peers often seem more ready than parents to follow through on a child's playful overtures. Still, peers have two other characteristics that warrant study: Their actions and reactions may be more novel than those of parents, and the activities of peers may be more easily duplicated than those of adults, who only with difficulty behave as a child.

The present study, then, has demonstrated that home-reared children during the second year of life freely engage in a variety of social interactions with unfamiliar peers, interactions that resemble those with familiar adults more than those with inanimate objects. They smile, laugh, vocalize and gesture to one another, show and offer toys, imitate each other, struggle, and engage in reciprocal play. Thus, interactions with peers and with familiar adults appear closely intertwined in development. Yet as more and more of the children's play involved people, the social partner was more often the peer than the mother. This choice of the peer makes still more tenable the speculation that peers—even infant peers—make their own contribution to early human sociability.

Reference Notes

1. CRAMER, E. M. *Revised MANOVA program.* Unpublished manuscript, University of North Carolina at Chapel Hill, Psychometric Laboratory, 1967.
2. CLYDE, D. J., CRAMER, E. M., & Sherin, R. J. *Multivariate statistical programs.* Unpublished manuscript, University of Miami, Biometric Laboratory, Coral Gables, Fla., 1966.

References

AINSWORTH, M. D. S., & WITTIG, B. A. Attachment and exploratory behaviour of one-year-olds in a strange situation. In B. M. Foss (Ed.), *Determinants of infant behaviour IV.* London: Methuen, 1969.

BRIDGES, K. M. B. A study of social development in early infancy. *Child Development,* 1933, **4**, 36–49.

BÜHLER, C. *The first year of life.* New York: John Day, 1930.

HARLOW, H. F. Age-mate or peer affectional system. In D. S. Lehrman, R. A. Hinde, & E. Shaw (Eds.), *Advances in the study of behavior* (Vol. 2). New York: Academic Press, 1969.

HEATHERS, G. Emotional dependence and independence in nursery school play. *Journal of Genetic Psychology,* 1955, **87**, 37–57.

HINDE, R. A. Development of social behavior. In A. M. Schrier & F. Stollnitz (eds.), *Behavior of nonhuman primates: Modern research trends* (Vol. 3). New York: Academic Press, 1971.

MAUDRY, M., & NEKULA, M. Social relations between children of the same age during the first two years of life. *Journal of Genetic Psychology,* 1939, **54**, 193–215.

RHEINGOLD, H. L. The effect of a strange environment on the behaviour of infants. In B. M. Foss (Ed.), *Determinants of infant behaviour IV.* London, Methuen, 1969.

RHEINGOLD, H. L. Independent behavior of the human infant. In *Minnesota Symposia on Child Psychology* (Vol. 7). Minneapolis: University of Minnesota Press, 1973.

RHEINGOLD, H. L., & ECKERMAN, C. O. Fear of the stranger: A critical examination. In H. W. Reese (Ed.), *Advances in child development and behavior* (Vol. 8). New York: Academic Press, 1973.

SCHAFFER, H. R. *The growth of sociability.* Harmondsworth, England: Penguin, 1971.

VINCZE, M. The social contacts of infants and young children reared together. *Early Child Development and Care,* 1971, **1**, 99–109.

The Nature of Kibbutz Child Care

Jeanette G. Stone

Those who view the kibbutz from the outside often perceive its child care as the the mother giving her children over to a sort of institution. Today, kibbutz children are brought up jointly by their parents and by professional caregivers called *metaplot* (metapelet, in the singular). For the young infant, the mother is primary: a full-time mother. Later, she remains the central figure while giving the child less time as she resumes her work by easy stages. The metapelet's job is to provide skillful, affectionate and continuing care to children in the setting of the Children's House. She does not function as a substitute mother; rather she supplements the working parent. In the earlier, more austere days, the metapelet may well have been more dominant.

From earliest infancy through the preschool years, kibbutz children spend the greater part of their days in Children's Houses where they eat, bathe, nap, and where they are educated within the framework of informal learning and play. They also sleep at night in the Children's House, cared for by people on night-watch duty. Somtimes parents take turns sleeping in the Children's Houses. (In some ten percent of the kibbutzim, as in Kibbutz Gesher HaZiv, shown in the film *Day Care for a Kibbutz Toddler*, children sleep in their parents' apartments.)

In all kibbutzim, children spend a long "Children's Hour" with their parents in the family living quarters each day from about 4.00 P.M. on into early evening. Because the working day begins and ends early, and because meals, shopping, and laundry are taken care of by communal services, both parents are free to devote themselves to their children every afternoon—playing with them, swimming or hiking or gardening with them, reading to them, having tea together, feeding them a light supper. Israel works a six-day week. On the Sabbath, kibbutz children spend most of the day with their families.

The younger children are taken back to the Children's House and put to bed (by the parents in some kibbutzim and by metaplot in others) before the parents go to supper in the kibbutz dining hall. Older children may eat supper with their parents; these evening arrangements vary from family to family as well as from kibbutz to kibbutz.

There may be only one or two Children's Houses in a small kibbutz, with small separate age groupings under one roof. In a large settlement, there may be a whole cluster of Children's Houses. The infants and young children are grouped in small units of three to six individuals—each unit with its own metapelet and an assistant; older children are cared for in larger groupings.

Kibbutzim vary in the specific space arrangements and age groups in the Children's Houses. All have separate housing and different metaplot for each age level—babies, preschoolers, school-aged and older children. Some kibbutzim place infants and toddlers under one roof; for example, a House (as in Kibbutz

From *Study Guide for Three Films on Kibbutz Infancy*. New York: Institute for Child Mental Health, 1974. Reprinted by permission.

Ma'agan Mikhail in the film *Rearing Kibbutz Babies*) might have several small babies in one wing, with four or five toddlers in an adjacent wing, each wing with its own metapelet. These two wings usually share a common kitchen, bathroom, and storage area. In another kibbutz (like Kibbutz Dahlia in the film *Infant Development in the Kibbutz*) there would be a shift to a new House for toddlers.

When a newborn baby is brought from the hospital to the kibbutz Infant House, the mother is freed from her job, usually for about six weeks, to devote full time to her baby—to feed and bathe and care for the baby with no other responsibilities. She then resumes work, but on a part-time basis, gradually lengthened.

The mother continues her care for many of the baby's waking hours, all through the first six months, and their mutual attachment becomes strong. During the second six months of the baby's life, the mother gradually adds time to her working day until the end of the first year; by then she will have resumed full-time work and the metapelet will have assumed more care of the infant. (For women full-time work is 7 hours a day; for men it is from 8 to 8½ hours.)

The mother's schedule will be set up, during all of her children's early years and beyond, so that she can take time off every day to visit her children in their Houses. The contemporary kibbutz work schedule is based in part on consideration of children's need for close, continuous contact with their parents.

One often sees fathers (or other relatives) walking or biking through the kibbutz on an errand, stopping to see their children in the Children's Houses. A mother drops in to have a cup of coffee or a bite of fruit and to play with her child during an unscheduled break—this in addition to her scheduled breaks for nursing or visiting. Even after children reach school age, parents continue to visit them during the day.

In the same spirit of joint upbringing, metaplot continue the nurturing of kibbutz children. When the children begin formal schooling—which takes place within the Children's Houses for kindergarten and the first years of elementary education—they are taught by classroom teachers; however, the metaplot assigned to the school-aged children continue to function as general caregivers, and they assist the teachers during school hours, if need be. Before and after classes, the metaplot keep the children clean and fed and supervise their work and play.

Further information on kibbutz care of young children will be found in the references supplied. Very useful—and similar in outlook to our films—are the chapters by Frieda Katz and Gideon Lewin (Early Childhood Education) and Menachem Gerson (Oranim Pedagogical Center of the Kibbutzim) in the newly published volume by A. I. Rabin and Bertha Hazan.

IMPLICATIONS FOR CHILD CARE OUTSIDE THE KIBBUTZ

The films suggest that the kibbutzim have worked out a system of infant and child care in which children thrive with multiple caretakers without, apparently, losing primary connections to their own mothers and their own families. This should not astonish us if we think of such well-established parallel arrangements as the grandmother, or the regular baby-sitter who may care for a child for some hours each day, or the disappearing phenomenon of the amah, ayah, or nanny. So far as we know, such arrangements produce no sundering of the parental relationship.

Since the metapelet may change from time to time when the child shifts to a new Baby House or because the metapelet becomes pregnant or changes jobs, and since substitutes act for her during her various times off, the child's relationship to the metapelet is inherently less fixed than to the mother. And something in the way the metapelet operates—perhaps the presence of other children in her group—keeps the relationship from being as intense as the parental one.

For kibbutz child care (unlike grandmother or sitter or nanny) is *group* care. But in comparing it to other forms of group care, it is important to keep in mind the lavish kibbutz provision for staffing. In Kibbutz Dahlia (*Infant Development in the Kibbutz*) the basic ratio of children to adults is three to one. In Kibbutz Ma'agan Mikhail (*Rearing Kibbutz Babies*) the ratio is four to one; and in Kibbutz Gesher HaZiv (*Day Care for a Kibbutz Toddler*) the ratio is five to one. Even these ratios understate the case, since in each kibbutz, part-time assistants are added at mealtimes, bathtimes, etc. Moreover, as the narration of *Day Care for a Kibbutz Toddler* suggests, the overall size of the group appears to be just as important as the actual ratio in establishing the peaceful and intimate atmosphere of the kibbutz Infant House. For a young child (or for the adult caretaker) maintaining contact with three or four other babies of the same age and with one or two adults at a time is far less of a strain than interacting with, say, fifteen other babies and four or five adults—though the sheer ratio would be the same.

In terms of unit size, therefore, the Infant House arrangement most closely resembles what the United States has termed "family day care." Unlike family day care, however, the metapelet, instead of being on her own all day long, has the built-in institutional supports of other metaplot nearby, of substitute help, of central kitchens and laundries—and of time off during the day to visit her own children or to talk with grownups on an adult level. There is no comparable coffee-break or baby-break in our family day care system. In larger day care settings, separating large groups of children into clusters of four to five within the large group should be feasible. Perhaps as much as anything else, this would make for psychologically manageable family-size, rather than institutional-size, groupings. Note that this recommendation is not made for preschool children but rather for infants and toddlers. The kibbutz, itself, combines the children into larger multiples of the original foursomes as the children grow older.

Many of our child care institutions are marked by difference in status between parents and caregivers, which sometimes causes strain. The metapelet-parent relationship strikes a remarkably even balance: The metapelet is (more or less) professionally trained but she is the mother's equal, neighbor, and permanent co-member in the collective. They are familiar with each other. This may be one reason that the kibbutz appears to function best in its small village format: larger size or urban settings produce anonymity and personal and social distance. The extent to which such social balance can be brought into our own child care facilities needs more exploration. It should be noted, by the way, that the upbringing and schooling of all the children in the kibbutz is supervised by a rotating, elected Education Committee: both mothers and metaplot may be among its members.

Such organizational characteristics of the kibbutz may be hard to transfer to other countries or other kinds of infant and child care. The kibbutz is, after all, a collective which can mobilize such resources as it chooses to assign to child care, and it can deploy its members to those tasks deemed important by the entire community. Truly comparable child care provisions elsewhere would surely be very expensive. At best, we can but try to adapt as many of its important features as possible. What seems most transferable is a *kind* of caring—the metapelet's characteristically warm interest in her charges, knowledgeable interchange, unhurried ministering, and the kind of inventive stimulation caught by our camera in the unrehearsed hours of filming. It may be worth calling the attention of those working directly with children or those who are training such workers to examples in specific sequences in each of the three films discussed in the following sections.

Part Two

THE PRESCHOOL
CHILD

5

Personality and Body

Motor development is intimately related to other areas of development, as the readings in this chapter show. The stage of bodily growth and the condition of the body, of course, set limits upon possible movements and coordinations. The physical and social environments often acting in interaction, offer opportunities for various kinds of learning and expression.

Boys and girls differ in their use of space and in their choice between indoor and outdoor play. Lawrence V. Harper and Karen M. Sanders discuss reasons for their findings, weighing biological sex differences against differential gender socialization. These questions are important ones in the culture of present-day North America, where gender-role equality is an issue. An ethological interpretation is also offered, placing boys' and girls' modes of using space in perspective as inherited behavior patterns that had survival value in man's early environment.

Hyperactivity was studied in $2\frac{1}{2}$-year-old children and again when the children were $7\frac{1}{2}$ years old, by Charles F. Halverson Jr., and Mary F. Waldrop. Relationships were shown between behaviors at the two ages and between hyperactivity and bodily structure, cognitive performance, and social behavior. The unity of the child as body, mind, and social being is indicated by this study.

Perceptual development involves motor action and bodily experience as well as cognitive operations. Arthur Lefford, Herbert G. Birch, and George Green studied finger localization and finger movement of children from ages 3 to 6. Performance is related to sensory and cognitive behavior. The authors see practical implications for understanding learning disabilities.

Severely malnourished children usually come from environments that are low in social and intellectual stimulation, as well as those that are physically inadequate. After nutritional rehabilitation, children often have to return to the poor social and intellectual environment. Myron Winick, Knarig K. Meyer, and Ruth C. Harris report on a group of previously malnourished children who were adopted into excellent environments. The study analyzes the contributions of nutritional and social environments upon previously deprived and non-deprived children.

Preschool Children's Use of Space: Sex Differences in Outdoor Play *

Lawrence V. Harper and Karen M. Sanders
UNIVERSITY OF CALIFORNIA AT DAVIS

Abstract

Over a two-year period time-sampled observations were made of the free-play behavior of 65 children between 3 and 5 years of age in a half-acre nursery school complex. In both years, the boys used more space and consistently spent more time playing outdoors than did the girls. Consideration of the possible determinants of this sex difference led to the conclusion that endogenous factors could account for the data as readily as traditional models of socialization.

According to Wynne-Edwards (1962), in most mammals, males range more widely than females. Studies of the free play of primate (Crook, 1966) and human young (Terman and Tyler, 1956) indicate that males expend more physical energy than females. Garai (1970) states that boys are less concerned than girls with security and are more likely to seek large areas for exploration and play. The sex difference in activity level in human children cannot be explained by the greater incidence of perinatal insult in males because Pedersen and Bell (1970) observed that, in a sample carefully screened to exclude perinatal or congenital abnormality, boys still displayed more gross motor output and more frequent changes in activity than girls. According to Money and Ehrhardt (1972), a preference for outdoor pursuits is one of the elements of "tomboyism" in human females who were masculinized anatomically as the result of synthetic progestins administered to their mothers during early pregnancy.

Several recent studies have provided evidence that boys are more likely than girls to wander afield. In laboratory settings, 13-month-old girls played nearer to the mothers than did boys (Messer and Lewis, 1972). Between preschool and grammar school, boys spent more time away from thir teachers, covering more ground per minute than did girls (Omark and Edelman, 1973). Among the !Kung Bushmen of Africa, male children were more likely than females to stray from the central campsite (Draper, 1973). Early studies using self-reported behavior preferences of American children indicated that boys were more likely than girls to engage in outdoor activities (Terman and Tyler, 1956). However, there exists a paucity of observational data directly comparing the sexes with respect to the spontaneous use of indoor and outdoor space.

Thus, quantitative data on the spontaneous behavior of children in settings allowing them free access to buildings and open areas have considerable

Extended report of a paper by the same title published as a "Brief Report" in *Developmental Psychology*, 1975, **11**, 119.

* This study was supported by a grant from the California Agricultural Experiment Station. The authors wish to express their thanks to Dr. E. E. Werner for her comments and suggestions on this manuscript, and to Ms. Jane Welker, director of the Early Childhood Education Center, for her cooperation and encouragement.

theoretical as well as practical value. The following report is based upon a 2-year observational study of pre-school children's free-play use of space and play equipment in a half-acre nursery school compound.

METHOD

Subjects   Children enrolled in the University of California, Davis laboratory nursery school during the 1971–72 and 1972–73 academic years served as subjects for this study. Admission to the nursery school was limited to children between 3 and 5 years of age. An attempt was made to keep the population mixed with respect to sex, and ethnic and socio-economic background; however, a majority of the children were from middle-class, white families. The total number of children attending at any one time was limited to 30, but with quarter-to-quarter turnover as many as 40 different children were enrolled throughout the course of an academic year. Children with gross physical or behavioral abnormalities were usually excluded from the nursery school program.

We observed the behavior of 65 apparently normal, English-speaking children, 16 girls and 16 boys in 1971–72, and 16 girls and 17 boys in 1972–73. Despite the fact that a child may attend for two consecutive years, only one boy upon whom observations were reported from 1971–72 was represented in the 1972–73 sample. As of January 1972, the mean ages of the 1971–72 sample were 53.2 months for the boys and 53.8 months for the girls. In January 1973, for the 1972–73 group, the boys averaged 46.9 months of age and the girls 44.2. The age differences between the two yearly samples were significant at the .05 level ($t_{31} = 2.30$) for the boys and at the .001 level for the girls ($t_{30} = 4.21$). The sex differences in age within samples were not statistically significant. Sample size varied from one season to the next because a number of children did not attend for the entire year; the data reported here are from children who were present during at least 75% of the season under discussion.

Setting   The nursery school facility included a "main building" (1,340 ft^2 floor space available to the children) in which the children deposited belongings and kept a dry change of clothes. In addition to the locker area there were two bathrooms, a kitchen, two craft areas, a music area, a "nature study" area, a room with a toy kitchen, a "book" room, and an area in which puzzles were stored. A second building, the "block house," (678 ft^2 available for use) had two rooms for block play, a room with craft tables, a "book" room, and a kitchen. A third, smaller, building served as a research house for faculty and graduate students; it was not available for free play.

These structures were surrounded by about 19,000 ft^2 outdoor space landscaped with trees and shrubs. The open region was divided from north to south by a long, low, unlighted storage shed (180 ft^2) and a 3 ft-high wooden fence, running from the shed toward the main building, partially separating the main building from the regions to the southeast. The space directly in front (south) of the main building, (620 ft^2), including the steps and porch, was covered by a corrugated plastic roof extending about 15 ft from the main building to the storage shed. A small, paved, fenced courtyard (1335 ft^2)

separated the main building from the block house. The fully open spaces included a sandy region (3900 ft²) in front of the main building in which there were two jungle gyms, a farm tractor, a 3-swing set, and a sandbox. East of the shed there were two large lawns (4800 and 1500 ft²). The larger contained an open, raised platform with a ladder and a fireman's pole, and, as of early spring 1972, a tire swing suspended from a tree. Various large oil drums, packing crates and modular climbing toys were available in this region. The smaller grassy space faced the larger one; late spring 1972 an enclosed climbing structure was erected in this region and by fall 1973 a pen and shelter were constructed behind the research house for rabbits, chickens, and guinea pigs. Directly in front of the block house, separated from the large lawn by a cement pathway was a smaller lawn (512 ft²) in which there was a tree swing. The remaining outdoor space included shrubbery around the buildings and along the south fence, a paved patio between the research house and the block house, and paved pathways around the large lawn and between the various buildings. During free play, few restrictions were placed upon the children's access to these spaces although the block house was occasionally closed.

Procedure   Each child was observed once each week during free play from the time he or she arrived in the morning (around 9:00 a.m.) until snack time, at about 10:00, or until 35–50 minutes' observation were completed. Each observer followed one child per day recording his or her location and activity every 15 seconds on a prepared checksheet. Recording intervals were signaled by portable, battery-powered, timing devices that delivered an audible click to the observer through an earphone. All play areas were designated by a number posted in a conspicuous location. In 1971–72, areas were defined in terms of specific fixed structures (e.g., the sand box), or for large, apparently homogeneous regions, on an *a priori* basis, in terms of roughly equal sized central and peripheral segments. For 1972–73 several of the latter areas were redefined according to the patterns of use observed in 1971–72; the indoor areas remained the same.

The observers' presence had little effect on the subjects; the nursery school served as a demonstration laboratory for students enrolled in child development and related fields, and the children rapidly habituated to the presence of a large number of adults. Throughout both years there were six to seven observers; thus, each of 30 selected subjects was observed at least once each week and each observer was paired with every other observer to conduct at least one reliability check every week throughout the course of the study. Inter-observer agreement on time spent in each area, as indicated by the number of agreements divided by the number of agreements plus disagreements averaged over 90% over both years for all areas to be discussed in this report.

RESULTS

Since the first four to six weeks of the fall quarter were characterized by warm, sunny weather, the year was divided into three seasons: "Fall" weather extended until the end of the last consistently "warm" (at least 60°F; range 60–90°F) week. "Winter" weather lasted until the end of the rainy season and until temperatures consistently remained above 60°F (range 38°–70°F). "Spring" weather was characterized by temperatures consistently above 60°F (range 60–100°F) and predominantly sunny days. The data were analyzed for the year as a whole, and by each season.

As column 1 of Table 1 indicates, the children spent nearly half their time indoors. The boys spent more time outdoors than did the girls. A tally of the number of indoor and outdoor areas in which the boys' total scores exceeded the girls' showed that, for both the 1971–72 and 1972–73 observations, the boys

TABLE 1

Proportions of Free-Play Time Spent Out of Doors According to Sex, Region, Year, and Season

			MEAN TOTAL TIME OUTSIDE ÷ TOTAL TIME OBSERVED	MEAN TIME OUTSIDE IN "NEAR" REGION ÷ TOTAL TIME OUTSIDE	MEAN TOTAL OBSERVATION TIME
Total for Year	71–72	Boys $N = 12$ $p^* < .001$	.552	.594	20.26 hrs
		Girls $N = 13$	.288	.621	20.01
	72–73	Boys $N = 10$ $p < .002$	.609	.658	18.08
		Girls $N = 8$	.400	.678	17.55
Fall	71	Boys $N = 15$ $p < .02$	.642	.673	5.33
		Girls $N = 13$	.411	.671	5.08
	72	Boys $N = 12$ $p < .01$	.665	.682	4.82
		Girls $N = 11$	.467	.645	4.35
Winter	71–72	Boys $N = 13$ $p < .002$	.316	.614	6.33
		Girls $N = 13$	.120	.631	7.57
	72–73	Boys $N = 13$ $p < .001$	.491	.683	8.22
		Girls $N = 11$	.235	.645	7.88
Spring	72	Boys $N = 13$ $p < .0001$	.687	.531	8.62
		Girls $N = 15$	.371	.533	7.59
	73	Boys $N = 14$ $p < .005$	.744	.605	5.47
		Girls $N = 12$	.580	.676	5.43

* Mann-Whitney Test.

used more outdoor areas than did the girls in every season. The yearly totals showed the boys dominating 43 of 54 outdoor areas that were used in 1971–72 ($p < .0001$, binomial approximation) and 39 of 51 used in 1972–73 ($p < .005$, binomial approximation). The girls dominated the indoor areas; in the first year they spent more time in 19 of the 22 indoor areas ($p < .001$, binomial test) but in the second, they dominated only 14 of the 22 (N.S.). Another measure of area use, the ratio of time spent playing outside to total play time, was computed. For all seasons of both years, the boys spent significantly more of their time outdoors than did the girls (See Table 1, column 1). Since the outdoor areas generally were considerably larger, it follows that the boys used more space than the girls. A rough estimate of the amount of space utilized was obtained by multiplying the per cent of total time spent by each sex in each area by the per cent of total space (inside plus outside) covered by each area. As expected, this total "score" for each season, for both years, favored the boys ($p < .05$, binomial test). According to this measure, the boys used between 1.2 (Spring, 1973) and 1.6 (Winter, 1972–73) times as much space as the girls.

Given that the boys spent more time outside and thus used more space than the girls, it seemed important to see whether there existed a qualitative difference; that is, whether the boys used different regions proportionately more than the girls. Since the enclosed patio and sandy region directly south of the main building were most obviously accessible to the "home base," a ratio of total time in these areas to total time spent outdoors was computed. None of the sex differences were significant; both sexes spent slightly less than two thirds of their outdoor play time in the region directly communicating with the front door of the main building. Recalling that nearly half their time was spent in the main building, for both years, the children thus spent three quarters of their time in about one third of the total space available to them.

Over the course of the 1971–72 school year there was a tendency for the children to spend progressively more outdoor time in the spaces beyond the sandy regions (See Table 1, column 2). Compared to fall, in 1971–72, 11 of 12 boys spent proportionately less time in these areas in spring ($p < .006$, binomial test), but in 1972–73 only 6 of 9 boys showed the same decline (N.S.). Similar trends were apparent for the girls: 11 of 12 showed less outdoor time in the sandy area in spring 1972 as compared to fall 1971 ($p < .006$), but for the 1972–73 year, only 4 of the 8 girls showed a comparable shift. This difference most probably reflects the introduction of the tire swing and fort in the grassy areas in early spring 1971–72; no comparable changes in the physical setting were made in 1972–73.

As is evident from Table 1, bad weather kept the children indoors more (although the staff was instructed to be permissive in this regard). For both years and both sexes, the proportion of time spent outdoors in fall and spring was greater than in winter; almost every child spent less time outdoors in winter (all within-sex p's $\leq .05$, binomial tests). Between fall and spring 1972–73 the boys increased their outdoor time significantly (8 of 9, $p < .05$, binomial test) but the difference for boys in 1971–72 was non-significant; the girls showed no comparable changes in either year.

To further evaluate the existence of qualitative differences in the children's use of space, an analysis was conducted area by area. The individual records were scanned to determine the number of areas that accounted for 75–85% of each child's time for each season of the year. Only those areas that were thus determined to be among the most frequently used by at least three children of one sex were subjected to further analysis. On this basis, the sexes were compared for their use of 40 (of 75) designated areas for 1971–72 and 42 (of 74) areas for 1972–73. Sex differences were evaluated by Mann-Whitney or Chi-square tests. See Table 2 for a summary of the results.

For fall 1971, there were eight areas for which there were significant sex differences in usage at the .05 level or better; in winter 1971–72, there were 12, and by spring 1972 there were 15 areas that received significantly different utilization by the sexes. Over the entire year there were 20 areas in which the sex differences were statistically significant. The only "outdoor" area used more by girls was the sheltered porch in front of the main building. The indoor areas receiving more use by the boys were confined to the equipment shed and the block room of the block house. The areas in which significant sex differences occurred were those in which the boys spent 59% and the girls spent 62% of their time over the year.

In 1972–73, despite a younger group, a new head teacher, and new assistants, the same pattern emerged. In fall, the boys dominated the equipment shed and four of five outdoor areas in which significant sex differences were found; the girls dominated the remaining indoor area. While the fall season was short, winter 1972–73 was long and the rainiest on record for a decade. During this period, the boys spent more time than the girls in all of the 10 outside areas for which there were significant differences and the shed; five of the remaining six significant inside differences favored the girls. The boys' tendency to dominate the block room in the block house only approached significance ($p < .10$). In spring 1973 the girls "took over" the swings, but the boys predominated in the other seven outdoor areas for which there were significant differences. Again the boys' only indoor area was the storage shed while the girls spent more time in the remaining two indoor areas for which there were differences. Over the entire year there were 11 significant differences; the boys dominated the outside areas, the storage shed and block room of the block house while girls dominated the remaining inside areas. The areas in which significant sex differences occurred during 1972–73 accounted for 58% of the boys' and 59% of the girls' free play time.

In addition to the time spent in the different areas, a record was kept of the amount of time during which the children were "in transit" from one area to another (defined as entering three or more areas within a single 15-second period). In 1971–72 the boys spent more time in transit than the girls in every season; the yearly total difference was significant ($p < .05$, Mann-Whitney). In 1972–73, the boys spent significantly ($p < .05$) more time in transit than the girls only in winter; they also spent more time in transit than the girls for the year as a whole but the difference was not statistically significant. A simple tally of the number of areas entered at least once showed the boys entering more areas in spring 1972 ($p < .01$) and for the entire 1971–72 observation year ($p < .001$). In 1972–73 the boys entered more areas in winter ($p < .01$) and for the year as a whole ($p < .01$).

Wherever possible, within-sex comparisons were made to determine whether age or prior experience were related to the children's use of space.

Fewer significant differences than would be expected by chance were found, although it must be emphasized that the subsamples were uniformly small.

DISCUSSION

Consistent with Omark and Edelman's (1973) findings that nursery school children spent more of their free-play time indoors than did older children, even our male subjects spent nearly half their time indoors. Perhaps due to the small size of the subsamples or the limited age ranges, we found no evidence for an age-related increase in the amount of outdoor play. Of possible practical significance is the observation that much of the available space received relatively little use by either the boys or the girls. However, this finding should be viewed with caution given the fact that several structural features of the outdoor regions presented physical, and, insofar as they defined an area "belonging to" the main building, perhaps psychological barriers to free movement. We are currently pursuing this question further.

Our findings support the views that males are more attracted to the outdoors (Money and Ehrhardt, 1972) while females spend more time in sheltered areas (Garai, 1970). Although our data do not bear directly upon the question of the mechanisms underlying the development of sex differences in childrens' use of space, several of our incidental observations during the course of the study and two *post hoc* analyses are pertinent. Whereas cultural expectations of female "passivity" and selective reinforcement for conformity to sex-role stereotypes may account for some of the observed differences (Kagan, 1964), our data do not support such an interpretation. During both years of this study, the nursery school staff was composed of women who held liberal, egalitarian views; there was no reason to suspect that the children were under pressure to conform to traditional expectations. Indeed, on the basis of the 1971–72 findings, deliberate attempts were made by the staff to entice the girls outdoors during 1972–73. Thus if girls actually tend to rebel at adult demands for traditional sex-role behavior (Kagan, 1964), sex differences should have been minimized in this permissive atmosphere.

However, it is still possible that pressures exerted by parents at home could have accounted for the observed differences. To evaluate this possibility, an attempt was made to assess the existence of sex-typed socialization pressures on the basis of questionnaire responses submitted by the children's parents. In 1972–73, parents of each child enrolled in the nursery school were required to fill out a questionnaire concerning, among other things, five things they "enjoyed doing" most and least with their child and five things about the child they liked most and least. These questionnaires were collected and the items such as "friendliness," "dirtiness," and so on, were listed. These items were rated as in keeping with either the traditional "male" or "female" stereotypes by 71 students in an advanced class in Child Development. Items receiving over 75% agreement were taken as areas of potential parental pressure. Giving "male" items a score of -1 and "female" items a score of $+1$, and assigning parental enjoyment or liking a positive sign and parental dislike a negative sign, each child was assigned a "socialization pressure" score. These "scores" were then compared with the proportion of time that the children spent outdoors.

TABLE 2
Areas in which Sex Differences in Use Occurred: By Year and Season

Within each period the upper line gives Boys: Mean % Time (with p indicated by significance markers) and the lower line gives Girls: Mean % Time.

Period	Sex	3 Wooden Climbing Gym	4 Tractor	5 Swings	5a†† Sand Adjacent to Swings	6 Sandbox	7 Sand	8 Sand by Shed	9 Sand by Porch	9a†† Central Sandy Area	10 Tool Table	12 Porch	14 Equipment Shed	16 Bushes	22 Grass	23 Grass/Fort	26§ Grass/Tree Swing
Fall 1971	Boys		4.45 **			1.68 **	2.79 †	10.23 *					2.11 **				
	Girls		.57			.17	.14	3.27					.36				
Winter 1971–72	Boys	2.73 *				1.04 †	.75 **	2.04 **					.45 *		.42 **	2.47 *	
	Girls	.56				.01	.04	.97					.11		.03	.07	
Spring 1972	Boys	2.67 *	1.77 *			.68 *		5.71 †					1.33 †			1.94 **	
	Girls	.88	.45			.08		.27					.22			.55	
Year 1971–72	Boys	2.27 **	1.95 **			1.18 †	2.27 †	5.98 †			3.62 *	.75 *	1.29 †		.53 †	2.14 †	7.75 *
	Girls	.66	.42			.06	.39	1.23			1.61	1.34	.22		.17	.47	3.38
Fall 1972	Boys		2.99 *					8.61 †			1.87 *		1.78 **			2.95 **	
	Girls		.61					1.26			1.77		.39			1.45	
Winter 1972–73	Boys	1.83 †	1.74 **	3.35 *	.87 **	.24	.98 *	4.70 †	1.78 *	5.05 **	3.45 **		2.03 **	1.43 *			
	Girls	.12	.37	.64	.24	.05	.13	.36	.62	1.40	.98		.35	.06			
Spring 1973	Boys			1.43 *	1.61 **	3.33 *			1.94 **				1.32 †		.35 *	1.94 *	
	Girls			8.00	.39	.83			.45				.36		.35	.76	
Year 1972–73	Boys		2.12 **		1.74 **			8.02 †		4.65 *			1.85 **	.37 **			3.91 *
	Girls		.22		.22			.65		2.53			.35	.05			1.53

	27	34	43	53§	61	63	64	65	66	67	70	72	73	75	76	77	77††
	CENTRAL GRASS AREA	GRASS	PAVED COURT	FORT	LOCKERS	TABLE ACTIVITY	TABLE ACTIVITY	MUSIC	NATURE STUDY	PLAY HOUSE	BOOK ROOM	CABINETS	PUZZLES	BATHROOM	KITCHEN	BLOCK ROOM	BLOCK ROOM
Boys: Mean % Time Fall 1971 *p*						3.43 **	4.51 *			3.50 *							
Girls: Mean % Time						9.05	10.46			8.66							
Winter 1971–72	1.30 *	1.10 *				6.20 **		1.08 **	2.64 *			1.07 *		.64 **			
	.40	.47				18.04		4.31	6.80			2.64		1.58			
Spring 1972	2.61 †						2.13 *		2.85 *	1.02 *			1.50 *	.92 *	1.72 **		
	.50						6.44		7.34	2.88			5.23	1.61	3.85		
Year 1971–72	.25 *					5.82 **		.61 †	2.60 †			.56 †	4.16 **	.79 **	1.40 *	6.32 *	
	.49					13.12		2.50	6.91			1.98	8.91	1.56	3.27	3.10	
Fall 1972													2.99 **				
													10.38				
Winter 1972–73			.43 **		2.23 *	5.39 **	6.20 **				6.39 *			.25 †	4.90 **		
			.01		4.00	14.71	14.61				2.82			1.51	10.76		
Spring 1973				1.83 *		1.78 †									4.25 *		.86 *
				.74		9.80									5.73		.21
Year 1972–73						3.86 **	4.12 **										
						11.17	8.92										

* $p \le .05$ ** $p \le .01$ † $p \le .001$ †† Designated only in 1972–73   § Structure erected spring 1972

107

For the seven girls for whom both maternal reports and year-long data were available, the *rho* was $-.348$; that is, in the opposite direction predicted by socialization theory. There were too many ties to permit the use of *rho* among the nine boys for whom adequate data were available; however, a median split indicated no relationship. Further, a comparison of the socialization pressure scores for these boys and girls (whose outdoor usage differed significantly; $p < .005$, Mann-Whitney) revealed only a non-significantly greater tendency for girls (mean $= +4.71$) to receive more pressure than boys (mean $= +3.33$; $t_{14} = 1.457$, $p < .10 > .05$). An additional check of the items revealed that only 4 of the 9 boys' parents mentioned liking to take their children "on walks" while 3 of the 7 girls' parents did so and, in addition 2 girls' parents who did not mention walks and one who did, listed hiking or going on outdoor trips as being activities they enjoyed doing with their daughters. Thus, there was little evidence of overt parental pressure to conform to sex-stereotyped behavior in general, and no indication of differential encouragement of outdoor activity.

If such pressures did exist covertly it was thought that they might be expressed indirectly by discouraging the girls' getting dirty and encouraging them to "look nice," and that they would be reflected in the clothing typically worn by the girls. Thus we compared the proportion of outdoor play of girls who consistently wore dresses with that of those who consistently wore jeans, etc. The distribution of scores according to attire was essentially random; combining extreme groups across years, there was only a non-significant tendency for the *dress-wearers* to spend more time outside.

It is possible that the nature of the activities or apparatus favored the girls' staying indoors and the boys' going outside. However, such reasoning accepts the premise that boys are more attracted than girls to gross motor activity, without attempting to account for it. Furthermore, analyses of the locations in which popular, movable equipment was used suggest that the observed sex differences reflect more than toy location. For example, containers such as pots, bowls, etc. were used by the boys outdoors 81% of the time *vs* 16% of the time outdoors for the girls in 1971–72; for 1972–73 the corresponding percentages were 66 and 38 respectively. Of 15 classes of items that could be used either indoors or outdoors, the boys played more outdoors than the girls with 13 ($p < .02$, Binomial test) in 1971–72, and with 11 ($p < .06$, Binomial test) in 1972–73. Thus it seems that portable items were often moved to favored play-spaces; their location did not necessarily determine the children's choice or use of space.

In summary, we found little evidence that the behavior of the nursery school staff, the expressed concerns or the overt practices of the children's parents, or the nature of the available apparatus could account for the observed sex differences in behavior. Explanations invoking endogenous factors are consistent with our data. Terman and Tyler (1956) suggest that the greater muscle strength and vital capacity of boys might account for their more vigorous activity as compared with girls. Recent studies of the effects of androgens on the behavior of primates and humans indicate that prenatal exposure to male sex hormones predisposes genetic females to engage in male-typical behaviors, including a preference for vigorous, outdoor activity even in the absence of continued androgenic stimulation. (See Money and Ehrhardt, 1972, for review.) Our finding that there was no sex difference in the relative proportion of time spent in the outdoor regions beyond the sandy areas might appear to contradict the idea that endogenous factors such as androgens could account for the data. However, experiments with infrahuman mammals (Beach, 1971) and observations of the effects of hormonal influences on human behavior (Money and Ehrhardt, 1972) indicate that prenatal androgenic stimulation leads to sex differences in the frequency or intensity of behavior rather than to qualitative differences. Thus our data are consistent with the hypothesis of endogenous causation.

The greater outdoorishness of males might be attributed to the fact that they have a higher basic metabolic rate (BMR) than do girls (Tanner, 1970). Assuming that their lower BMR would render girls more sensitive to cold, our finding of an intensification of sex differences in outdoor activity in the long and relatively severe winter of 1972–73 would seem to support such a hypothesis. However, the fact that the same pattern of sex differences was apparent during the spring and early summer months of both years, when temperatures were consistently in the neighborhood of 75–85°F, suggests that females' possibly greater sensitivity to cold is insufficient to account for our data. The greater activity level of the boys, as represented by their greater time in transit, could reflect any of several factors: higher BMR, greater muscle strength and vital capacity, a direct androgenic influence on motor output, or greater biological immaturity (cf. Tanner, 1970) and hence, relatively lower capacity to sustain a particular focus (Kagan, 1971). However, Money and Ehrhardt's (1972) observation of greater vigor in prenatally androgenized females supports the hypothesis of a central, hormonal effect, since these girls also tended to be intellectually precocious, and thus presumably suffering no attentional deficits.

Our data are thus more consistent with hypotheses implicating the role of endogenous factors than with a hypothesis of environmental determination of sex differences in children's use of space. In particular, they support hypotheses involving the effects of androgenic stimulating during the first trimester.

However, from a biological perspective (Blurton-Jones, 1972) the analysis of the proximate mechanisms such as androgenic stimulation or differences in muscle strength represents only part of the picture; a complete account should also consider the possible selective pressures leading to the evolution of such mechanisms. That is, one should be able to indicate how a greater tendency for males to move about—in unsheltered regions—would confer an advantage upon the species.

While the details of man's prehistory are still the subject of debate, a plausible explanation can be offered if one accepts the view that many significant features of human evolution were the result of man's adopting a hunting-gathering way of life (Lee and De Vore, 1968). According to Watanabe (1968), among contemporary hunter-gatherers, the male's (hunter's) geographical range of food-seeking activity is considerably greater than the female's (gatherer's), whose collecting tends to be concentralized in the vicinity of the group's base camp. Assuming that the exigencies of the hunting-gathering strategy, *per se*, forced such a division of labor upon humans, a selective advantage might well have accrued to groups in which there developed endogenous predispositions toward appropriate behavior [particularly if there already existed sexual dimorphism in size and activity as that which now exists among many old-world primates (Crook, 1966; 1972)]. As a result of these predispositions, the males would have become more familiar with the group's home range, hunting grounds, and with the habits of available prey, thereby enhancing the likelihood of successfully obtaining game.

Furthermore, endogenous tendencies for males to undertake the more risky enterprise of hunting large game makes "biological sense" in view of the generally accepted principle that the potential "cost" to a population of accidentally losing a male (child) is less; that a stable population is more dependent upon the number of females, and that, other things being equal, the number of males may vary more radically without severely threatening the ability of a population to maintain itself (Wynne-Edwards, 1962). Given the greater expendability of males, and assuming that camps tended to serve as safe or protected sites in an otherwise dangerous or hostile environment, another benefit would have derived from the males' tendency to range afield and to be more "on the move." The males' activity would have provided a screen of expendable individuals about the periphery of the camp in the same way that young Japanese monkey males provide an outer defense perimeter for the females and infants who congregate at the center of the group (Imanishi, 1963).

Thus, the greater centrifugal movement of males would have maximized their opportunities to become successful hunters and, at the same time, provided an early warning or buffer zone around the periphery of the group while the more centripetal tendencies of the females would have caused them to remain in areas of relatively greater safety. Groups in which these patterns did not exist, or were reversed, presumably would have been more at risk biologically and therefore would have been at a reproductive disadvantage.

In conclusion, our findings indicate the existence of a marked sex difference in preschool children's tendency to play in unsheltered areas. Our data are more compatible with explanations based upon the existence of endogenous determination of gender-dimorphic behavioral traits than with explanations based upon the existence of sex-role expectations. An argument is presented in support of the hypothesis that natural selection may have favored the development of such sex differences in man. The problem for future investigations is to specify the nature of and the ways in which the environmental factors co-act with endogenous sensitivities to produce behavioral differences.

References

BEACH, F. A. Hormonal factors controlling the differentiation, development, and display of copulatory behavior in the ramstergig and related species. In E. Tobach, L. R. Aronson and E. Shaw (Eds.) *The biopsychology of development.* New York: Academic Press, 1971. Pp. 249–296.

BLURTON-JONES, N. G. Characteristics of ethological studies of human behaviour. In N. G. Blurton-Jones (Ed.) *Ethological studies of child behaviour.* Cambridge: Cambridge University Press, 1972. Pp. 3–33.

CROOK, J. H. Gelada baboon herd structure and movement. A comparative report. In P. A. Jewell and C. Loizos (Eds.) *Play, exploration and territory in mammals.* New York: Academic Press, 1966. Pp. 237–258.

CROOK, J. H. Sexual selection, dimorphism and social organization in the primates. In B. Campbell (Ed.) *Sexual selection and the descent of man 1871–1971*. Chicago: Aldine, 1972. Pp. 231–281.

DRAPER, P. Crowding among hunter-gatherers: The !Kung bushmen. *Science*, 1973, **182**, 301–303.

GARAI, J. E. Sex differences in mental health. *Genetic Psychology Monographs*, 1970, **81**, 123–142.

IMANISHI, K. Social behavior in Japanese monkeys, *Macaca fuscata*. In C. H. Southwick (Ed.) *Primate social behavior*. New York: Van Nostrand, 1963. Pp. 68–81.

KAGAN, J. Acquisition and significance of sex typing and sex role identity. In M. L. Hoffman and L. W. Hoffman (Eds.) *Review of child development research*. Vol. 1. New York: Russell Sage, 1964. Pp. 137–167.

KAGAN, J. *Change and continuity in infancy*. New York: Wiley, 1971.

LEE, R. B. & DeVore, I. (Eds.) *Man the hunter*. Chicago: Aldine, 1968.

MESSER, S. B. & LEWIS, M. Social class and sex differences in attachment and play behavior in the year-old infant. Merrill-Palmer Quarterly, 1972, **18**, 295–306.

MONEY, J. & EHRHARDT, A. A. *Man and woman, boy and girl*. Baltimore: Johns Hopkins, 1972.

OMARK, D. R. & EDELMAN, M. Peer group social interactions from an evolutionary perspective. Paper presented at the biennial meeting of the Society for Research in Child Development. Philadelphia, Pa., March, 1973.

PEDERSEN, F. A. & BELL, R. Q. Sex differences in preschool children without histories of complications of pregnancy and delivery. *Developmental Psychology*, 1970, **3**, 10–15.

TANNER, J. M. Physical growth. In P. H. Mussen (Ed.) *Carmichael's manual of child psychology*, Third Ed., Vol. 1. New York: Wiley, 1970. Pp. 77–155.

TERMAN, L. M. & TYLER, L. E. Psychological sex differences. In L. Carmichael (Ed.) *Manual of child psychology*, Second Ed. New York: Wiley, 1956. Pp. 1064–1114.

WATANABE, H. Subsistence and ecology of northern food gatherers with special reference to the Ainu. In R. B. Lee and I. DeVore (Eds.) *Man the Hunter*. Chicago: Aldine, 1968. Pp. 69–77.

WYNNE-EDWARDS, V. C. *Animal dispersion in relation to social behaviour*. New York: Hafner, 1962.

Preschool Hyperactivity: Social and Cognitive Relations in Middle Childhood [*]

Charles F. Halverson, Jr., and Mary F. Waldrop
NATIONAL INSTITUTE OF MENTAL HEALTH

Abstract

The relations between preschool hyperactivity and school age behavior were explored. Consistent clusters of observed behaviors were associated with teacher ratings of hyperactivity; namely, two independent and replicated factors, Activity

A paper presented at the meetings of The Society for Research in Child Development, Denver, 1975. A different version appears in *Developmental Psychology*, 1976, **12**, 107–112. Printed by permission.

[*] The authors wish to thank Gale Inoff and Richard Q. Bell for their help on various aspects of this study.

Level and Social Participation. These two factors and the hyperactivity ratings were significantly related to behavior at $7\frac{1}{2}$. For both boys and girls, hyperactivity showed considerable stability over five years. Hyperactivity expressed by high activity levels is negatively related to various measures of cognitive and intellective performance at $7\frac{1}{2}$. Hyperactivity as expressed in social participation is positively related to the same measures of intellectual performance. The activity level component is highly related to an index of minor physical anomalies, while the social participation component is not.

There has been some evidence and considerable speculation that early hyperkinetic and impulsive behavior is implicated in the development of cognitive style differences and related social behavior in children. For example, Kagan, Moss, and Sigel (1963); Witkin (1963); Sigel, Jarman, and Hanesian (1967); and Pedersen and Wender (1968) have speculated that high magnitude activity level may be an important antecedent of various intellectual and social behaviors. The general hypothesis has been that high levels of activity and impulsivity tend to interfere with the development of behaviors conducive to cognitive and social development. For example, Kagan (1971) has presented evidence that children with "fast tempos" (short attention span and impulsive) do not maintain an active involvement in hypothesis verification when confronted with a new event. They act quickly on the first hypothesis and go on to a new situation. What generally has been lacking are longitudinal data on early high-activity behaviors and their relations to later cognitive functioning.

High levels of impulsive play activity are presumably one index of this impulsive cognitive processing which interferes with a more complete examination of alternate hypotheses about new events. In the present paper, therefore, there are two major emphases; (a) the assessment of impulsive, hyperactive play in unselected, non-clinical samples of preschool children and, (b) the implications of that preschool hyperactivity for later cognitive and social functioning. Because this investigation concerned results obtained on non-clinical, unselected samples of children, the term "hyperactive play" must be interpreted as not referring to a clinical syndrome but as a convenient summary term for a set of behaviors shown to a greater or lesser degree by most children in free, unrestrained situations.

Hyperactivity was initially assessed in this sample by a rating system developed by Bell, Waldrop, and Weller (1972). These ratings have been condensed by factor analysis to form an internally consistent and highly reliable rating factor describing hyperactive play behavior in nursery school settings. It was felt that further understanding of the structure of hyperactivity could be obtained by identifying and subjecting to analysis the *observed* behaviors that related to the rating factor. Before assessing the implications of early hyperactivity for later cognitive and social functioning, we first examined the stability of both rated and observed hyperactivity between age $2\frac{1}{2}$ and $7\frac{1}{2}$ years.

METHOD

PRESCHOOL STUDY   At the preschool phase, relations between the rating factor of hyperactivity and independently observed samples of play and social behavior were assessed. The children were 60 boys and 60 girls ranging from 30 to 34 months of age with a mean age of 32 months. All children were white and from middle-class intact families living in the suburbs of Washington, D.C. (Hollingshead index classes II, III, and IV). They attended a research nursery school in same sex groups of 5 or 6 for five weeks.

The setting was designed to make the children as comfortable and at ease as quickly as possible. Play and social behavior was coded daily in a free-play setting indoors, a quiet room for rest, and a free play setting outdoors. Except for free play outdoors, observations were made by two independent observers from behind one-way vision glass. The behavioral codes consisted essentially of the cumulative time spent in various categories of activity and frequency counts of specific types of behaviors such as opposes peer, water play, running. A total of 6 days of observation distributed over a 1-month period was obtained for each child. Interobserver reliabilities were all above $r = .90$ for measures used in the present study and odd-even stabilities were consistently above $r = .60$. Details of the procedures can be found in Bell, Weller, and Waldrop (1971).

A male and a female teacher were with the children in all settings, and two days each week, independently, made six ratings concerning hyperactive behavior. The ratings were on 11-point scales and dealt with frenetic play, spilling and throwing, nomadic play, aggression, inability to delay, and induction of intervention. The children were given composite scores based on the six ratings using the procedure described by Bell et al. (1972).

Because the observational codings were not directed toward the description of hyperactivity per se but were, rather, focused on general play and social variables across all settings, an empirical strategy which would guard against chance correlates was devised to assess the observation correlates of rated hyperactivity. The sample was divided into two subsamples of 60 children each (30 boys and 30 girls in each subsample). For each subsample intercorrelations were computed between the hyperactivity rating factor and all reliable observation codes. Six behavioral variables from indoor free play, five from outdoor free play, and two from the rest period replicated as being significant in their relation to the hyperactivity rating and were, thus, retained for further analysis. These 13 measures were then subjected to a principal component factor analysis with two factors being rotated by the varimax procedure. The result was two orthogonal observation factors which related significantly to the hyperactivity rating. Table 1 lists the variables and their loadings on the two orthogonal factors. The first observation factor, Activity Level, had high loadings on running, walking, and a pedometer measure of activity level; negative loadings on inactivity. The second factor, termed Social Participation, had positive loadings on positive peer interaction, squealing, and following games; negative loadings on watching peers and stationary watching. These two factors emerged for both subsamples. Between-sample comparisons (Ryder, 1967b) of the two factors yielded high correlations (Factor 1, $r (58) = +.88, p < .001$; Factor 2, $r (58) = +.78, p < .001$). These two observational factors together, however, only accounted for 43% of the variance associated with the rated hyperactivity factor, indicating considerable non-shared variance. For this reason, the longitudinal analyses were done on all three factors: the observational factors of Activity Level and Social Participation as well as the rating factor of hyperactivity.

TABLE 1

Varimax Rotated Observation Factors of Hyperactivity Replicated Across Two Samples

VARIABLES	FACTOR 1 ACTIVITY LEVEL	FACTOR 2 SOCIAL PARTICIPATION
Activity Recorder (O)	.83	−.11
Runs (O)	.67	−.08
Opposes peer (I)	.59	.15
Up and about (R)	.55	.34
Direct walking (I)	.55	.38
Squeals (O)	.21	.53
Positive interaction (I)	.14	.42
Water play (I)	.01	.36
Withdraws from peer conflict (I)	.00	−.48
Stationary watching (I)	−.18	−.72
Follows game (R)	−.37	.61
Watch peer (O)	−.44	−.70
Sustained play (O)	−.72	−.24

(I) = Indoor free play.
(R) = Rest period.
(O) = Outdoor free play.

FOLLOW-UP STUDY AT AGE 7½　　Sixty-two of the children from the preschool sample were studied at a follow-up five years later (35 boys and 27 girls). The setting for the follow-up study was a well-equipped playroom in which mother and child were observed together for 20 minutes. During that time, each child was free to play while the mother was occupied with a questionnaire. A narrative account of the child's behavior was recorded by an observer from behind one-way vision glass and subsequently coded for number of play shifts and rate of shifts. These two variables measured the amount of sustained, directed play. In addition, 9 general behavioral ratings of the child were done by a person who had not known the child in the earlier preschool study, (interrater reliabilities of the 11-point scales ranged from $r = .70$ to $r = .94$, with a mean of $r = .82$). These ratings covered such concepts as Frenetic Play, Inability to Delay, Cooperativeness, and Vigor. Later, while the child was being given tests of intelligence and cognitive style, including the WISC, the Children's Embedded Figures Test (Karp & Konstadt, 1963) and the Sigel Sorting Task (Sigel et al., 1967), the mother was interviewed about her child's social behavior. The mother's detailed diary account of the child's social contacts for the prior week was discussed. From the mother's diary account and from the observations of the child's social interactions, three summary ratings were made regarding the child's social ease, dominance in peer relations, and tendency to play with a group of children vs. play with close friend (Extensity). Further analyses of peer data can be found elsewhere (Waldrop & Halverson, 1975).

From the three cognitive tasks that were administered individually, the following classes of measures were obtained:

Verbal and Nonverbal Intelligence   This was assessed by the Wechsler Intelligence Scale for Children (WISC).

Categorization-Style   The Sigel Sorting Task (Kagan et al., 1963) was used to evaluate conceptual style. The test consists of 12 arrays containing four pictures each, a stimulus picture and three response pictures. After the children identified the stimulus picture, they were asked to pick out one response picture that was most like the stimulus picture. They were then asked to give reasons for making the choice. The three response pictures were designed to elicit one of three "styles" of responding—the *analytic*, involving pairings based on objective attributes, the *relational*, response selections based on functional relations between pictures, and the *inferential*, responses based on a conceptual category. Items were scored using the child's verbal statement. Interrater agreement was adequate ($r = .94$), and the split-half reliabilities ranged from $r = .70$ to $.80$ for the three categories of response.

Field Dependence–Independence   This was measured by the Children's Embedded Figures Test (CEFT), developed by Karp and Konstadt (1963). The test is a downward extension of the Witkin (1950) Embedded Figures Test suitable for children as young as 5 years. It contains 25 items arranged approximately in order of increasing difficulty in a format essentially similar to the adult form. Karp and Konstadt reported adequate internal consistency and, for children 9 years of age and older, high-order correlations with the adult form of the Embedded Figures Test.

In addition to the behavioral measures, each child was assessed for the presence of multiple minor anomalies (Waldrop & Halverson, 1971) and administered the Lincoln-Oseretsky Motor Scale (Sloan, 1955). This latter scale is an objectively scored series of items pertaining to fine and gross motor coordination and development. Earlier research (Waldrop & Halverson, 1971; Halverson & Victor, 1975) has consistently shown minor physical anomalies and motor coordination problems to be related to other indices of hyperactivity in young children.

RESULTS

Data will be presented first with respect to the longitudinal stability of hyperactivity and then with respect to the longitudinal and concurrent implications of hyperactivity for cognitive and social functioning. Analyses of the cross-stage correlations done separately for the sexes revealed no significant differences, therefore, all correlational analyses are presented for the combined sample of 62 children.[1]

Stability of Hyperactivity   To assess as closely as possible the same rating construct of hyperactivity at $7\frac{1}{2}$ as was rated at $2\frac{1}{2}$, three highly intercorrelated

[1] An intercorrelation matrix of the follow-up variables and the preschool hyperactivity variables is available from Dr. Halverson.

ratings at $7\frac{1}{2}$ were summed together to form a hyperactivity rating composite: Frenetic Play, Inability to Delay, and Cooperativeness (negatively weighted). These ratings were defined and rated to match as closely as possible the same ratings done at $2\frac{1}{2}$. The concurrent correlations of this factor at age $7\frac{1}{2}$ and longitudinal correlations are presented in Table 2. The $7\frac{1}{2}$ rating cluster of hyperactivity showed a highly significant correlation with the preschool rating of this dimension (r (62) $= .57$, $p < .001$), indicating a fair degree of stability over 5 years. Of the two observation components of preschool hyperactivity, Activity Level showed some predictability over 5 years while Social Participation is only marginally related to later hyperactivity. The two observation codings of fast-paced behavior at $7\frac{1}{2}$ (shifts in play and rate of shifts) related positively to hyperactivity at both age periods.

The correlates of the other general behavior ratings done at $7\frac{1}{2}$ are listed in Table 1 and they reveal considerable consistency in the pattern of relations as well. Children high on rated and observed hyperactivity at $2\frac{1}{2}$ tended to be rated as animated, vigorous, and excitable at follow-up.

TABLE 2

Longitudinal and Concurrent Relations of Hyperactivity at $7\frac{1}{2}$

	MEASURES AT $7\frac{1}{2}$	MEASURES AT $2\frac{1}{2}$		
	Hyper-activity Factor (Rating)	Hyper-activity Factor (Rating)	Activity Level Factor (Behavior)	Social Participation Factor (Behavior)
Hyperactivity Factor	—	.57†	.31*	.14
Inability to delay	—	.56†	.33**	.00
Frenetic play	—	.49†	.47†	−.04
Cooperativeness (negative)	—	−.33**	−.32**	.00
Free Play Observations				
$\overline{X}$ number of shifts	.49†	.34**	.33**	.00
Rate of shifts	.39**	.38**	.35**	.13
General Behavior Ratings				
Animation	.48†	.25*	.11	.20
Dependency	−.18	−.26*	−.28*	−.27*
Vigor in play	.62†	.42†	.29*	.26*
Coping	−.20	−.04	.13	.17
Fearfulness	−.20	.00	.13	−.22
Excitability	.82†	.47†	.32**	.18
Lincoln Oseretsky Motor				
Scale	−.50†	−.54†	−.44†	.12
Minor Physical Anomalies	.44†	.51†	.37**	−.03

* $p < .05$.
** $p < .01$.
† $p < .001$.

Two other variables gave added importance to the hyperactivity measures at $2\frac{1}{2}$ and $7\frac{1}{2}$. Performance on the Lincoln-Oseretsky Motor Scale showed significant negative correlations to both concurrent rated hyperactivity and to hyperactivity measured at $2\frac{1}{2}$. These correlations indicate that children who score high on hyperactivity in terms of ratings and observed activity level tend to be less coordinated. Further evidence of the importance of the hyperactivity dimension over time comes from the positive relations of $2\frac{1}{2}$ and $7\frac{1}{2}$ hyperactivity to an index of minor physical anomalies assessed at age $7\frac{1}{2}$. The relations between aspects of hyperactivity and anomalies as well as the stability of rated hyperactivity associated with anomalies have also been reported earlier (Waldrop & Halverson, 1971). The relations of hyperactivity to anomalies suggest that there is a possible congenital factor (anomalies being present from birth) contributing to the stability of this dimension in early childhood, particularly as referenced by the Activity Level factor.

Cognitive Correlates of Hyperactivity   Relations of cognitive performance at $7\frac{1}{2}$ years of age with concurrent and antecedent hyperactivity are presented in Table 3. Both $2\frac{1}{2}$ and $7\frac{1}{2}$ hyperactivity ratings are significantly and consistently negatively related to FSIQ, VIQ, and PIQ on the WISC. The observation factor of Activity Level is also negatively related to intellectual performance. These findings are similar to the relation between preschool hyperactivity and performance on the CEFT at $7\frac{1}{2}$. High levels of rated hyperactivity and high levels of the observation factor of Activity Level were related

TABLE 3
Hyperactivity Correlates of Cognitive Variables

	Measures at $7\frac{1}{2}$	Measures at $2\frac{1}{2}$		
	Hyper-activity Factor (Rating)	Hyper-activity Factor (Rating)	Activity Level Factor (Behavior)	Social Par-ticipation Factor (Behavior)
WISC				
Full scale IQ	−.31*	−.38**	−.47†	.14
Verbal IQ	−.21	−.29*	−.38**	.24*
Performance IQ	−.33**	−.33**	−.40**	−.05
Children's Embedded				
Figures Test	−.28*	−.34**	−.34**	.25*
Sigel Sorting Test				
Relational	.20	.22	.11	.00
Analytic	.00	.03	.23	.12
Inferential	−.24	−.31**	−.30*	−.08

* $p < .05$.
** $p < .01$.
† $p < .001$.

to *field dependent* behavior on the CEFT. These findings are consonant with cross-sectional data reported by Witkin (1963) who reported field dependent behavior to be associated with impulse control problems. It should be noted, however, that the observation factor of Social Participation is *positively* related to VIQ and was associated with a tendency toward field *independent* behavior.

Relations between hyperactivity and the cognitive style data differed from our expectations: hyperactivity was unrelated to both relational and analytic functioning, at $2\frac{1}{2}$ and $7\frac{1}{2}$ years of age. There were only modest negative correlations with inferential responding. When IQ was partialed out of these correlations, no relationship remained. In general, then, early hyperactivity was not found to be an important antecedent of the analytic style as Kagan et al. (1963) hypothesized.

Social correlates of Hyperactivity   An examination of the relations of the rated hyperactivity factor and social behavior at $7\frac{1}{2}$ reveals only one significant relation, a correlation of $+.41$ between the preschool hyperactivity rating and dominance in peer relations at $7\frac{1}{2}$. Interestingly, it is not the observed Activity Level component that is important but rather observed Social Participation. The Social Participation component of hyperactivity at $2\frac{1}{2}$ was related to social behavior at $7\frac{1}{2}$, as shown by positive relations to social ease (r (60) $= +.49$, $p < .001$), the tendency to play with groups of children (r (60) $= +.36$, $p < .01$), and dominance with peers (r (60) $= +.40, p < .01$). These relations show, perhaps not surprisingly, some predictability of the Social Participation component of hyperactivity to peer relations at $7\frac{1}{2}$ but only marginal predictability for other facets of hyperactivity as examined in the present study. It should be remembered that the children were seen individually at $7\frac{1}{2}$ and in groups at $2\frac{1}{2}$. Therefore, at $7\frac{1}{2}$ there are no observed social measures.

T A B L E   4
Social Correlates of Hyperactivity

	MEASURES AT $7\frac{1}{2}$	MEASURES AT $2\frac{1}{2}$		
	Hyper-activity Factor (Rating)	Hyper-activity Factor (Rating)	Activity Level Factor (Behavior)	Social Participation Factor (Behavior)
Extensity	$-.02$	.03	.07	.36**
Social ease	.15	.08	.00	.49†
Dominance	.18	.41†	.14	.40**

** $p < .01$.
† $p < .001$.

DISCUSSION

The data in the present study provide longitudinal evidence confirming the importance of hyperactive behaviors for the development of differences in intellectual and social behavior in young children. There is, for both boys and girls, stability of rated impulsive and hyperkinetic behavior over five years. Even though all of the variables comprising both observational factors correlated individually with rated hyperactivity, these two factors relate to different criterion behaviors at $7\frac{1}{2}$. The observed preschool factor of Activity Level replicates most of the relations obtained with the rating alone while the concurrent social behaviors associated with rated preschool hyperactivity only showed implications for later social behavior. While both factors correlate with preschool rated hyperactivity (Activity Level r (60) = .62, p < .001; Social Participation r (60) = .39, p < .01) it is the Activity Level factor which carries the negative implications for later intellectual functioning (as does rated hyperactivity). It is, then, motoric hyperkinesis and not high levels of positive social interaction which seem to affect negatively those behaviors important for the development of intellectual functioning. In fact, the social behaviors identified with hyperactivity in preschoolers tend to be positively related to verbal intelligence and field independence in this sample.

The relations between hyperkinesis and intellectual functioning closely paralleled the findings reported by Kagan et al. (1963). In the Fels data, they found rated hyperkinesis for ages 3 to 6 to be negatively correlated with adult intellectual mastery for both males and females. These results and the data from the present study strongly suggest that the inability to inhibit motor behavior during early childhood is inimical to the development of sustained involvement in cognitive skills.

The findings in the present study also corroborate Witkin's (1963) contention that impulsive, hyperactive behaviors are related to field dependent functioning on the Embedded Figures Test. These data did not replicate, however, the findings of Kagan et al. (1963) that hyperkinesis is one class of behavior negatively related to analytic responding. In general, it was only the inferential-categorical style which was related negatively to hyperactivity, and this correlation appears due to the high relation of IQ and inferential-categorical responding, (r (60) = +.61, p < .001).

The longitudinal relations of preschool Social Participation reveal straightforward predictability to social behavior at age $7\frac{1}{2}$. High activity level, however, was not related to the aspects of social functioning measured at $7\frac{1}{2}$. Added significance of the positive relations of preschool Social Participation with Social Ease and Dominance at age $7\frac{1}{2}$ may be found in Ryder's (1967a) canonical reanalysis of the Fels data reported by Kagan and Moss (1962). Ryder found Dominance in peer relations and Social Ease with peers from ages 6–10 to be predictive of adult achievement orientations. It is possible that data in the present study may have identified one potential early preschool antecedent, Social Participation, to this developmental line from early childhood to adulthood.

Finally, the results of the present study are consonant with Kagan's (1971) contention that there is a stable disposition of play tempo in early childhood, and, further, that play tempo, as indexed by variations in play activity levels, has important consequences for social and intellectual functioning in the young child.

References

BELL, R. Q., WALDROP, M. F., & WELLER, G. M. A rating system for the assessment of hyperactive and withdrawn children in preschool samples. *American Journal of Orthopsychiatry*, 1972, **42**, 23–34.

BELL, R. Q., WELLER, G. M., & WALDROP, M. F. Newborn and preschooler: organization of behavior and relations between periods. *Monographs of the Society for Research in Child Development*, 1971, **36**, (Whole No. 142).

HALVERSON, C. F., Jr., & VICTOR, J. B. Minor physical anomalies and problem behavior in elementary school children. *Child Development*, 1976, **47**, 281–285.

KAGAN, J. *Change and continuity in infancy*. New York: Wiley, 1971.

KAGAN, J., & MOSS, H. A. *Birth to maturity: a study in psychological development*. New York: Wiley, 1962.

KAGAN, J., MOSS, H. A., & SIGEL, I. Psychological significance of styles of conceptualization. In J. C. Wright and J. Kagan (Eds.), Basic cognitive processes in children. *Monographs of the Society for Research in Child Development*, 1963, **28**, (2, Serial No. 86): 73–112.

KARP, S. A., & KONSTADT, N. L. *Manual for the children's embedded figures test*. New York: Cognitive Tests, 1963.

PEDERSEN, F. A., & WENDER, P. H. Early social correlates of cognitive functioning in six-year-old boys. *Child Development*, 1968, **39**, 185–193.

RYDER, R. G. Birth to maturity revisited: a canonical reanalysis. *Journal of Personality and Social Psychology*, 1967, **7**, 168–172. (a)

RYDER, R. G. Computational remarks on a measure for comparing factors. *Educational and Psychological Measurement*, 1967, **27**, 301–304. (b)

SIGEL, I. E., JARMAN, P., & HANESIAN, H. Styles of categorization and their intellectual and personality correlates in young children. *Human Development*, 1967, **10**, 1–17.

SLOAN, W. The Lincoln-Oseretsky motor development scale. *Genetic Psychology Monographs*, 1955, **51**, 183–252.

WALDROP, M. F., & HALVERSON, C. F., Jr. Minor physical anomalies and hyperactive behavior in young children. In J. Hellmuth (Ed.), *Exceptional infant: studies in abnormalities. Vol. 2.* New York: Brunner/Mazel, 1971.

WALDROP, M. F., & HALVERSON, C. F., Jr. Intensive and extensive peer behavior: longitudinal and cross-sectional analyses. *Child Development*, 1975, **46**, 19–26.

WITKIN, H. A. Discussion of psychological significance of styles of conceptualization. In J. C. Wright and J. Kagan (Eds.), Basic cognitive processes in children. *Monographs of the Society for Research in Child Development*, 1963, **28** (2, Serial No. 86): 118–122.

WITKIN, H. A. Individual differences in ease of perception of embedded figures. *Journal of Personality*, 1950, **19**, 1–15.

The Perceptual and Cognitive Bases for Finger Localization and Selective Finger Movement in Preschool Children [*]

Arthur Lefford, Herbert G. Birch, and George Green
ALBERT EINSTEIN COLLEGE OF MEDICINE

This study reports the development of the ability of 167 children from 3 to 6 years of age to selectively oppose fingers to the thumb and to localize digits. 12 tasks were administered. The data indicate a clearly defined age-specific developmental course for digital competence over the preschool years. First, different sensory modalities are effective as guides for selective action; then, intersensory transfer develops as an effective guide for action at a later stage; and finally, the ability to use representational information as a guide for behavior is demonstrated. Findings are discussed in relation to the development of body schemata and to neuropathological conditions. The tasks investigated may have diagnostic potential for preschool children at risk for learning disabilities.

This study reports the development of the ability of children from 3 to 6 years of age to selectively oppose their fingers to the thumb and to localize the fingers. It derives from two different traditions in research. The study of development of finger-thumb opposition is related to the tradition of normative studies of psychomotor development in children (Gesell & Amatruda 1947; Kuhlman 1939). The impetus to pursue the course of finger differentiation derived from the observation in clinical examination in neurology by Gerstmann (1924, 1958) that finger agnosia was associated with right-left disorientation, dyslexia, agraphia, and acalculia.

The disturbance of finger awareness was part of a syndrome which involved disturbances in such primary education skills as reading, writing, and arithmetic (Critchley 1953; Nielson 1938; Stengel 1944) in adults who had acquired them but lost them after suffering some form of brain damage. The phenomenon has also been studied in normal and defective children (Benton 1955, 1959; Benton, Hutcheon, & Seymour 1951; Kinsbourne & Warrington 1963a, 1963b; Mathews & Falk 1964; Orton 1937; Strauss & Carrison 1942; Strauss & Werner 1938, 1939). With the exception of the Kinsbourne and Warrington study (1963b), detailed examination of the preschool child's developing awareness of the fingers of his hand has not been forthcoming. The findings suggest that in many subjects disturbances in finger awareness or agnosia are associated with deficiencies in scholastic skill, or what now is called learning disabilities. In view of the numerous and diverse disorders of intellective and

From *Child Development*, **45**, 335–343. Copyright © 1974 by The Society for Research in Child Development, Inc. Reprinted by permission.

[*] This study was supported by the National Institutes of Health, National Institute of Child Health and Human Development (HD 00719), and by the Association for the Aid of Crippled Children. This report is being published after the untimely and tragic death of Dr. Herbert G. Birch. Reprints may be obtained from Arthur Lefford, Ph.D., Yeshiva University, Ferkauf Graduate School, 55 Fifth Avenue, New York, New York 10003. An extended description of procedures is available on request. George Green is now at Saint Dominic's Home, Blauvelt, New York.

scholastic functions with which finger awareness has been associated, it appeared essential to have more detailed norms of the normal development of these functions with a view to exploring their potential as an index of normal and aberrant development of the central nervous system. Because it would be of value to have the earliest indication of normal or pathological development, an attempt was made to study finger differentiation from the age at which it first starts, 3 years, to the age of school entry, 6 years.

In an earlier study (Birch & Lefford 1967) evidence was found to suggest that the control of voluntary action was dependent at least in part on the child's ability to utilize sensory information and to integrate information from the different sense modalities. The present study therefore also represents an examination of the effects of different conditions of indication or stimulation of the fingers and conditions for performance on the ability of preschool children to selectively oppose fingers and thumb and to localize them by pointing.

METHOD

The ability of the child to differentiate among his fingers was studied by examining three modes of response. Selective finger-thumb opposition required the child to oppose his thumb to a particular digit when both thumb and digit have previously been indicated by the examiner. Finger localization on the child's own hand involved the demand that the child point to his thumb and to a finger of his own hand which the examiner had previously indicated. Finger localization on a drawing required that the child point to the thumb and finger which pictorially represented the pair previously indicated by the examiner on the child's own hand. Conditions of indication of the fingers were varied systematically for each type of response. This resulted in a set of 12 tasks administered in the serial order in which they are described below. All tasks were presented twice. The second presentation of the series was administered immediately after the first presentation in reverse order to the first presentation to control for practice effects. The children were required to respond with their preferred hand. Only three children preferred the left hand.

All children were tested individually either in a separate room, or, if preferred, in an isolated section of the normal nursery school room. Interest was high, and all children readily participated in the "new game." The tasks were given in the order in which they are described below.

1. Visual imitation of finger-thumb opposition (V Imit). In this task, the examiner said to the subject: "We are going to play a game. Let me see if you can bring your fingers together in the way that I bring mine together." The demonstration was then given of the finger-thumb opposition with the palmar surface of the hand up and alongside the corresponding level of the child and held until a response was made.

2. Nonvisual imitation of finger-thumb opposition (nV Imit). This task was administered in exactly the same manner as the previous one except that now an 8 × 10 card was interposed between the subject's hand and eyes.

3. Visual-tactual finger-thumb opposition (VT FTO). In this task the subject was required to make the particular finger-thumb opposition

movements on the basis of the examiner indicating the fingers to be opposed by heavily touching the subject's thumb and fingers while the subject visually observed what was being done.

4. Visual finger-thumb opposition (V FTO). This task was given exactly in the same manner as the previous test except that the examiner pointed to the fingers without touching them.

5. Tactual finger-thumb opposition (T FTO). The finger to be opposed to the thumb was indicated to the subject by the examiner touching the finger to be opposed. The child's view of the hand was obstructed by interposing an 8 × 10 card between the subject's hand and his eyes. (The card was removed before the subject responded.)

6. Tactual-nonvisual finger-thumb opposition (T nVFTO). This task was the same as the T FTO test just described except that the subject was not permitted to see his own hand while attempting to respond.

7. Visual-tactual pointing to self (VT Self). On this examination the thumb and other fingers were indicated as in VT FTO. The subject was then required to point with this contralateral hand to the fingers which had been indicated to him.

8. Visual pointing to self (V Self). The thumb and finger were indicated to the subject as in V FTO, and he was required to point to the fingers which had been indicated to him by pointing to them with his contralateral hand.

9. Tactual pointing to self (T Self). On this test the thumb and finger to be localized by the subject were indicated to him as in T FTO. The subjects were required to respond as in the previous localization tests.

10. Visual-tactual pointing to model (VT Mod). The subject's fingers in this test were stimulated as in the VT Self task. He was required to respond, however, by designating the previously indicated fingers by pointing with his other hand to the fingers represented by a line drawing of the hand. The picture of the hand was placed in line with and just above the hand which was stimulated. The model was in view of the subject during indication and at all other times during the examination by this procedure.

11. Visual pointing to model (V Mod). The subject was stimulated as in the V Self task. He was required to respond as in the above task.

12. Tactual pointing to model (T Mod). The fingers were indicated to the subject as in the T Self task and he was required to respond as above.

Subjects   The subjects for the study consisted of a total of 167 nursery school children from the Bronx, New York. Four nursery schools participated in this study with a pupil population drawn from lower- and middle-class communities of mixed ethnic and religious backgrounds. Boys and girls were approximately equal at each age level. None of the subjects selected for study showed any signs of deviant intellectual or social development, as noted by pediatrician, parents, teachers, or examiners.

Scoring   The first finger-thumb opposition or finger-thumb localization made by the child was taken as his response to the demand. Any changes made by him were not scored. The score was a simple quantitative measure and consisted of the sum of numbers of correct responses made on the two trials. Since the thumb and another finger on the hand were stimulated on each trial and two trials were given for each finger-thumb combination, scores ranging from 0 to 8 were possible. For the needed χ^2 tests it was necessary to develop a criterion measure of pass or fail. A child was judged to have passed the task if each of the four different finger-thumb combinations had been correctly opposed or identified for a given condition on a given trial.

RESULTS

The data were analyzed in two ways. First, the findings were considered with respect to the adequacy with which finger-thumb opposition and finger-thumb localization developed with age as reflected in the average number of correct responses made by the subjects at each half-yearly interval. Second, the effect of the various experimental conditions on response competence was considered. In order to statistically evaluate these differences, age-specific fourfold

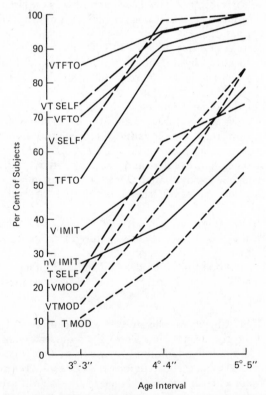

F I G U R E 1.   *Percentage of children at the different age intervals who succeeded to criterion under the various conditions of stimulation and response.*

tables at yearly levels across pairs of conditions were tested by the McNemar χ^2 test for correlated proportions (McNemar 1955). These values are shown in Table 3. Because of the large number of χ^2s calculated, the 1% level was used. This procedure resulted in three age groups: 3-, 4-, and 5-year-old. The number of subjects who correctly opposed or identified all the finger-thumb combination of the hand at least once on the two series was used to construct the fourfold tables. From these data, it was also possible to calculate the percentage of subjects who successfully met the aforementioned criterion measure at each year level. These data are represented in Figure 1 and reflect the development of age-related competence.

The Development of Finger-Thumb Opposition   The performances of children ranging in age from 3 years to 5 years 11 months, on tasks which demand that they selectively oppose the fingers of the hand to the thumb, are summarized in Table 1, which shows the mean number of correct responses made under the different conditions. The least difficult tasks are VT FTO and V FTO. Next, in order of greater difficulty, are the T nVFTO and the T FTO tasks. Visual Imit and nV Imit are the most difficult tasks. The percentage of

TABLE 1

Age Differences in FTO Competence under Different Conditions of Testing

	AGE					
CONDITION	3–0 to 3–5 ($N = 15$)	3–6 to 3–11 ($N = 31$)	4–0 to 4–5 ($N = 30$)	4–6 to 4–11 ($N = 36$)	5–0 to 5–5 ($N = 30$)	5–6 to 5–11 ($N = 25$)
Visual-tactual FTO:						
M	6.00	7.16	7.53	7.81	7.90	7.92
SD	2.17	1.61	1.33	.62	.40	.40
Visual FTO:						
M	5.67	6.35	7.28	7.08	7.70	7.96
SD	2.65	2.32	1.04	1.84	.79	.20
Tactual FTO:						
M	4.71	5.32	7.07	7.22	7.43	7.80
SD	2.83	2.76	1.39	1.07	1.10	.50
Visual imitation:						
M	4.05	5.13	5.43	5.78	6.57	6.88
SD	2.25	1.98	2.06	1.87	1.45	1.42
Tactual-nonvisual FTO:						
M	4.71	5.87	7.03	7.43	7.73	7.76
SD	2.59	2.51	1.33	.97	.78	.66
Nonvisual imitation:						
M	3.14	4.32	4.88	5.36	5.76	6.64
SD	2.31	1.94	2.07	1.73	1.56	1.50

TABLE 2

Finger Localization Scores

CONDITION OF INDICATION	AGE					
	3–0 to 3–5 ($N = 15$)	3–6 to 3–11 ($N = 31$)	4–0 to 4–5 ($N = 30$)	4–6 to 4–11 ($N = 36$)	5–0 to 5–5 ($N = 30$)	5–6 to 5–11 ($N = 25$)
	On Self					
Visual-tactual:						
M	5.00	6.32	7.67	7.54	7.87	7.96
SD	3.26	2.68	.55	1.27	.35	.20
Visual:						
M	4.48	5.90	7.33	7.11	7.67	8.00
SD	3.28	2.95	.84	1.79	.66	.00
Tactual:						
M	2.57	3.81	5.23	5.46	5.53	7.24
SD	1.99	2.48	1.83	2.06	1.98	1.05
	On Model					
Visual-tactual:						
M	1.67	2.87	4.87	5.67	6.37	7.40
SD	1.83	2.75	2.30	2.01	1.27	.76
Visual:						
M	.95	2.90	5.33	5.44	6.10	7.28
SD	1.75	2.95	2.23	1.87	1.60	.84
Tactual:						
M	.52	1.94	3.80	4.19	5.17	5.64
SD	.93	2.21	2.46	1.92	1.84	1.78

children who correctly oppose every finger of the hand to the thumb is shown in Figure 1. Although the trends for each condition are different, statistically significant differences by the McNemar χ^2 test (see Table 3) were found at all ages only between the V Imit and the VT FTO and the V FTO at beyond the 1% level. Only at the 3-year age level was the VT FTO different from the T FTO beyond the 1% level. Though the children performed very slightly better on the T nVFTO task than on the T FTO task, no significant statistical difference was found. As seen in Figure 1, considerably fewer children succeeded on the nV Imit task than on the V Imit; however, the differences were not found to be significantly statistically different.

The Development of Finger Localization   Age difference in the subjects' competence to localize by pointing to the fingers on their hands and on the model in terms of mean number of correct responses is presented in Table 2. The percentage of subjects at the three yearly age levels is presented in Figure 1.

TABLE 3

McNemar χ^2 Values for Correlated Proportions at Three Annual Age Levels for Different Conditions

	AGE (YEARS)		
CONDITION	3 ($N = 46$)	4 ($N = 66$)	5 ($N = 55$)
VT FTO vs. V FTO	4.08*	1.13	.00
VT FTO vs. T FTO	11.53**	1.13	2.25
VT Self vs. T Self	19.05**	17.39**	12.07**
V Self vs. T Self	12.50**	20.05**	12.07**
VT Mod vs. T Mod	.25	4.51	11.13**
V Mod vs. T Mod	2.25	11.12**	11.13**
V FTO vs. V Imit	8.52**	15.61**	7.69**
T FTO vs. T Self	7.56**	13.47**	5.79**
VT FTO vs. T. Self	4.17*	.17	.00
V Self vs. V. Mod	18.05**	24.07**	7.11**
T Self vs. T Mod	4.90*	13.79**	6.27**
VT Self vs. VT Mod	23.31**	30.31**	7.11**

* $p < .05$.
** $p < .01$.

Localization on Self   The subjects' ability to localize their fingers and thumbs by pointing to them on their own hands was well developed when VT and V indication of the fingers to be localized were used. The T Self task proved to be far more difficult than the two previous conditions. The differences between the T condition of indication and the two other conditions were statistically significant beyond the 1% level at all age levels, as indicated in Table 3.

Localization on Model   Requiring the subjects to localize the finger and thumb on a model of the hand proved to be the most difficult set of tasks, as can be seen from mean number of correct responses made, as shown in Table 2, and the percentage of subjects who met the criterion, as shown in Figure 1. There were statistically significant differences between the visual and tactual indication at the 4-year level and between VT, V, and T indication at the 5-year level, as seen from Table 3.

Other Differences in Performance   At all age levels more children could effectively use T information as an indicator for finger-thumb opposition than could use it for correctly pointing to their own fingers. The difference is statistically significant beyond the 1% level, as indicated in Table 3.

Localization of the fingers on the subject's own hand and localization on the model involved a basic difference with respect to whether the terminus of the action was on the subject's own body or on a representation of it. Fewer subjects at all ages were able to localize the fingers on the model than were able to do so on their own hands. This difference was statistically significant, as shown in Table 3, for all three conditions of indication, V, T, and VT.

The localization on the model and the imitation of finger-thumb opposition are similar in that they involve the translation of information from the examiner's hand as a model to the subject's body or from his own body to a model, the drawing of the hand; V Imit and V Mod differences were not statistically significant.

Finger Individuation   Successful finger-thumb opposition and localization do not develop uniformly in all fingers. To evaluate the differential rates of development, the percentage of subjects able to correctly oppose or localize a given finger was ranked at each 6-month interval and for each condition, and the ranks were summed across the age intervals. The differences among the sums of ranks for each of the fingers were then evaluated by Friedman ANOVA for ranks. Statistically significant differences about the 2% level of confidence were found only for those tasks requiring the subject to point to the model and to imitate the finger-thumb opposition demonstrated by the examiner. Under all conditions of indication, pointing to the little finger and thumb was most frequently correctly indicated on the model; the index finger and thumb, the middle finger and thumb, and ring finger and thumb followed in that rank order. For V Imit and nV Imit, the fingers were most successfully opposed to the thumb in the following rank order: index finger, little finger, middle finger, and ring finger. Generally, it appeared that the index and little fingers are differentiated first, followed by the middle and ring fingers.

DISCUSSION

The observations of the study provide evidence delineating certain factors which underlie the emergence of skilled differentiated action and the development of the body schema using the hand as a microcosm. The findings of finger-thumb opposition development indicate that it is not the lack of motor ability which makes the child unable to direct a given finger and thumb to each other. What is lacking is sensory and perceptual discrimination among the fingers. By 6–9 months the child can oppose the forefinger and thumb in picking up a small object. By 3 years 2 months, most children can imitate finger-thumb opposition to each finger in succession (Kuhlman 1939). Motor ability required for the task is present, but perceptual discrimination among the fingers appears to be lacking. When tactual stimulation of the fingers is used only 52% of the 3-year-old children selectively discriminate among all the fingers, and when visual indication is used, only 70% of the 3-year-old children correctly oppose the fingers and thumb.

By 1½ years, children can point to familiar pictures or objects when asked to do so. However, when the children are asked to point to their fingers which are visually indicated, only 63% of the 3-year-old children respond correctly. Since they can make a pointing movement, it would appear that at that age they do not yet fully discriminate differentially among the fingers. It appears, therefore, that one factor which determines a correct movement of one part of the body to another, by finger-thumb opposition or pointing, is the sensory differentiation of the point or locus which is the goal of the movement. The movements as actions are already possible among the 3-year-old children; it is a lack of orientation to the locus or place to which the movement is to be made which is lacking.

A second factor which is critical in making a movement or action possible is that of intersensory integration. When the fingers are stimulated tactually and the subject must point to the fingers of his own hand or to those on the model, the movement is guided visually. This involves an intersensory integration of the two sense-modalities schemata. That there may be intrasensory differentiation but a lack of intersensory integration is suggested by the fact that the T Self task is statistically significantly more difficult than both the T FTO task and V Self task at all age levels. Of the 3-year-old children, 52% showed evidence of tactual differentiation and 70% showed visual differentiation. However, only 26% of the children passed the T Self task, suggesting that 26% lacked intersensory integration. Among the 4-year-olds, 27% lacked intersensory integration, and among the 5-year-olds 17% of the children still lacked the integration. To pass the T Self task the Ss must be able to distinguish which fingers were stimulated tactually and translate the tactual information into a visual equivalent which guides the localization on the subject's own hand. The lack of intersensory equivalence would make a correct response not feasible.

Another factor implicated in the attainment of a successful action in several of the tasks presented the children is the ability to understand representation or symbolization (i.e., the functional equivalence of two different objects). Both in the imitation of the examiner's FTO movements and in the pointing to the fingers on the drawing of the hand, visual equivalence or representations have to have been established for a correct response. In the case of imitation, the children must understand that the fingers on the examiner's hand symbolize or represent the equivalent fingers on their own hand. When the Ss are required to point to fingers on the drawing of the hand, they must also understand that the drawing symbolizes or represents the fingers of their own hand. The V Imit task is significantly more difficult than the V FTO task, and the V Self is significantly easier than the V Mod task. There are no statistically significant differences between the percentage of subjects who succeed to criterion on V Imit and the V Mod at any age level. The ability to understand representation and correspondence of the fingers increases between the third and fifth years. By the fifth year about 80% of the subjects succeeded, and by extrapolation it might be expected that all children would succeed at these tasks by 7 years of age.

The most difficult task in the battery was the T Mod task. This task involves both intersensory equivalence and representation. The fingers are indicated to the Ss tactually, and they must visually identify the fingers on the model as well as guide their pointing fingers visually. To complete this task successfully, the Ss must be able to discriminate among the fingers within a sense modality; intersensory equivalence must have been established between the visual and tactual senses; and the representation of the fingers on the model to those on the children's own hands must have been understood.

With respect to the problem of body image, the development of finger differentiation and control may be taken as a microcosm in which the processes and developmental changes underlying the development of bodily adaptation as a whole are reflected. Thus, the data we have analyzed have relevance for the concepts of body schema and body image which have been considered both in the context of development (Benton et al. 1951; Schilder 1950) and of neuro-pathology (Critchley 1953).

Despite the fact that the concept of body image was first advanced as an explanatory idea in neurology almost a century ago, little is still understood of its origins. Henry Head (1926) suggested that body image was composed of sche-mata which represented the organized "storehouse of past impressions" which affect the organization and interpretation of incoming sensory impulses. Benton (1959); Birch, Proctor, and Bortner (1961); and Oldfield and Zangwill (1942) have all viewed such schemata as learned organizations of sensory inputs and sensory integrations. Bartlett (1932) was the first to recognize in an explicit way that "schemata are built up chronologically." Both he and Schilder (1950) as well as Benton (1955) subscribe to the view that developmental factors were instrumental in the emergence of the body scheme. However, these speculations have remained unaccompanied by any serious developmental investigation of underlying processes.

The processes of intrasensory differentiation, intersensory integration, and symbolic representation we have described as underlying the development of finger selection and opposition in young children can be considered as the emerging developmental competences from which the schemata of Bartlett (1932) and Head (1926) derive. Such processes emerge in the preschool years (or earlier) and provide a basis for the organization of experience out of which body image can be acquired. The data suggest that in the early stages of development there are independent schemata for the particular sense systems. This finding supports the speculation advanced by Bartlett (1932) that intra-sensory schemata are the first to emerge in the course of development. Our findings also suggest that he was right in anticipating that such sensory system schemata soon interrelate and acquire an intermodal structure. At a later stage the schemata intrinsic to the body itself become linked to the perceptions of other bodies and objects in the external world which are first-order representations. When a child correctly designates his own fingers on the drawing of a hand or is able to oppose selected digits on the basis of another person's movements, he is treating the external environment as the equivalent of stimuli deriving from his own body surface. How he acquires these equivalences and the nature of the learning process which is involved in their acquistion remain unknown but represent fruitful areas for subsequent investigation.

PRACTICAL IMPLICATIONS

The explication of the developmental course of such a typically human behavior as finger-thumb opposition and differential finger awareness provides a simple and useful evaluative technique for neurologic intactness and develop-mental progress in preschool children. The behavior is particularly intriguing because manual functioning is a ubiquitous human activity whose emergence may be relatively unaffected by particular social and cultural settings. If this is the case it may be a useful method for the comparative evaluation of develop-ment across cultures and provide a relatively culture-free basis for the evaluation of developmental course.

The method of examination may be of particular potential value for the early identification of children at later risk of school failure. The early studies of

Orton (1937), Strauss and Carrison (1942), and Strauss and Werner (1938, 1939) suggest that finger agnosia may be associated as a clinical finding with difficulties in such primary educational skills as reading, writing, and arithmetic. The demonstrations by Benton et al. (1951) and Strauss and Carrison (1942) suggest, too, that children of school age have the ability to successfully engage in finger selection which has a consistent relationship with mental age. It is possible therefore that an earlier evaluation of digital competence may well be one basis for the early identification of subnormality.

References

BARTLETT, F. C. *Remembering: an experimental and social study.* London: Cambridge University Press, 1932.

BENTON, A. L. Development of finger-localization capacity in school children. *Child Development,* 1955, **26**, 225–230.

BENTON, A. L. *Right-left discrimination and finger localization.* New York: Hoeber-Harper, 1959.

BENTON, A. L., HUTCHEON, J. F., & SEYMOUR, E. Arithmetic ability, finger-localization capacity and right-left discrimination in normal and defective children. *American Journal of Orthopsychiatry,* 1951, **21**, 756–766.

BIRCH, H. G., & LEFFORD, A. Visual differentiation, intersensory integration and voluntary motor control. *Monographs of the Society for Research in Child Development,* 1967, **32**(Serial No. 110).

BIRCH, H. G., PROCTOR, F., & BORTNER, M. Perception in hemiplegia, IV: Body surface localization in hemiplegic patients. *Journal of Nervous and Mental Disease,* 1961, **113**, 192–202.

CRITCHLEY, M. *The parietal lobes.* London: Arnold, 1953.

GERSTMANN, J. Fingeragnosie: eine umschriebene Störung der Orientierung am eigenen Körper. *Wiener Klinische Wochenschrift,* 1924, **37**, 1010–1012.

GERSTMANN, J. Psychological and phenomenological aspects of disorders of the body image. *Journal of Nervous and Mental Disease,* 1958, **126**, 499–512.

GESELL, A. E., & AMATRUDA, C. S. *Developmental diagnosis.* (2d ed.) New York: Hoeber-Harper, 1947.

HEAD, H. *Aphasia and kindred disorders of speech.* London: Cambridge University Press, 1926.

KINSBOURNE, M., & WARRINGTON, E. K. Developmental factors in reading and writing backwardness. *British Journal of Psychology,* 1963, **54**, 145–156. (a)

KINSBOURNE, M., & WARRINGTON, E. K. The development of finger differentiation. *Quarterly Journal of Experimental Psychology,* 1963, **15**, 132–137. (b)

KUHLMAN, F. *Tests of mental development.* Minneapolis: Educational Test Bureau, 1939.

McNEMAR, Q. *Psychological statistics.* (2d ed.) New York: Wiley, 1955.

MATHEWS, C. G., & FALK, E. D. Finger localization, intelligence, and arithmetic in mentally retarded subjects. *American Journal of Mental Deficiency,* 1964, **69**(1), 107–113.

NIELSON, J. M. Gerstmann syndrome: finger agnosia, agraphia, confusion of right and left acalculia. *AMA Archives of Neurology and Psychiatry,* 1938, **39**, 536–560.

OLDFIELD, R. C., & ZANGWILL, O. L. Head's concept of the schema and its application in contemporary British psychology. *British Journal of Psychology,* 1942, **33**(Pt. 2), 58–64.

ORTON, S. T. *Reading, writing and special problems in childhood.* London: Chapman & Hall, 1937.

SCHILDER, P. *Image and appearance of the human body*. New York: International Universities Press, 1950.

STENGEL, E. Loss of spatial orientation, constructional apraxia and Gerstmann's syndrome. *Journal of Mental Science*, 1944, **90**, 753–760.

STRAUSS, A., & CARRISON, D. Measurement and development of finger schema in mentally retarded children. *Journal of Educational Psychology*, 1942, **33**, 252–264.

STRAUSS, A., & WERNER, H. Deficiencies in finger schema in relation to arithmetic disability. *American Journal of Orthopsychiatry*, 1938, **8**, 719–724.

STRAUSS, A., & WERNER, H. Finger agnosia in children. With a brief discussion on defect and retardation in mentally handicapped children. *American Journal of Psychiatry*, 1939, **95**, 1215–1225.

Malnutrition and Environmental Enrichment by Early Adoption: Development of Adopted Korean Children Differing Greatly in Early Nutritional Status Is Examined

Myron Winick, Knarig Katchadurian Meyer, and Ruth C. Harris
COLUMBIA UNIVERSITY

Numerous studies conducted in several different countries have demonstrated that malnutrition during the first two years of life, when coupled with all the other socioeconomic deprivations that generally accompany it, is associated with retarded brain growth and mental development which persist into adult life (1–3). What is not clear is the contribution of the malnutrition relative to that of the other social and cultural deprivations. When malnutrition has occurred in human populations not deprived in other ways the effects on mental development have been much less marked (4). Animal experiments have shown that early isolation results in the same type of persistent behavioral abnormalities as does early malnutrition (5). A stimulatory environment has been shown to counteract the untoward behavioral effects of early malnutrition in rats (6). These observations have led to the hypothesis that malnutrition and environmental deprivation act synergistically to isolate the infant from the normal stimulatory inputs necessary for normal development (6). In addition, they suggest that enriching the environment of previously malnourished children might result in improved development. To test this hypothesis, we have examined the current status of a group of Korean orphans who were adopted during early life by U.S. parents and who had thereby undergone a total change in environment.

From *Science*, December 1975, **190**, 1173–1175. Copyright 1975 by the American Association for the Advancement of Science. Reprinted by permission.

EXPERIMENTAL SAMPLE

The sample was drawn from records of children who had been admitted to the Holt Adoption Service in Korea between 1958 and 1967. The following criteria were established for inclusion in the sample:

1. The child must be female. This was decided in order to eliminate sex differences; and because many more female than male infants were brought to the agency they provided a larger adoptive sample to choose from.

2. Date of birth and results of physical examination at the time of admission to Holt care, including height and weight, must be available on the records.

3. The child must have been less than two years old when first admitted to Holt care and less than three years old when adopted.

4. The child must have been reported to be full term at birth.

5. The physician's examination at time of initial contact must have revealed no physical defect or chronic illness.

6. The child must have been followed by the adoption service for at least six years and must be currently in elementary school (grades 1 to 8).

7. The child must have a current mailing address in the United States.

From 908 records chosen at random 229 children were found who met all these criteria. We divided these 229 into three groups, as follows, on the basis of how their height and weight at time of admission to Holt related to a reference standard of normal Korean children of the same age (7): group 1, designated "malnourished"—below the 3rd percentile for both height and weight; group 2, "moderately nourished"—from the 3rd through the 24th percentile for both height and weight; group 3, "well-nourished" or control—at or above the 25th percentile for both height and weight.

There were 24 children, randomly distributed through the three groups, whose height and weight were not in the same percentile grouping. These were eliminated from the sample. The remaining 205 consisted of 59 children in group 1, 76 in group 2, and 70 in group 3.

A letter was sent by the Holt Adoption Service to the parents describing the general objectives of the study and asking their cooperation. It was followed by a letter from us explaining the study in more detail and asking for permission to request information about the child from the school. Where possible, the parents were called by telephone so that any questions they had about the study could be answered. For various reasons, 64 children could not be followed—17 in group 1, 24 in group 2, and 23 in group 3. Most of this loss resulted from inability to reach the parents, from an inadequate response, or from parental refusal. The final sample thus consisted of 141 children—42 in group 1, 52 in group 2, and 47 in group 3.

Information on health, growth and nutrition, and family socioeconomic background was obtained from the families of these 141 children by means of a checklist questionnaire (8). Information about scores on standardized tests of intelligence and school performance for the years 1971 to 1973 was requested from the schools on a mailed form constructed for this purpose.

TABLE 1
Number of Cases in Each Group

		NUMBER MEASURED FOR			
GROUP	TOTAL NUMBER	Current Height	Current Weight	IQ	School Achievement
1	42	41	41	36	40
2	52	50	51	38	38
3	47	47	47	37	37

The outcome data presented here consist of current height, which was obtainable for 138 children; current weight, obtainable for 139; current IQ (9), for 111; and current achievement scores, for 115. Table 1 shows the number of children in each group about whom these data were obtained.

RESULTS

As may be seen in Tables 2 and 3, all three groups have surpassed the expected mean (50th percentile) for Korean children in both height and weight. There is a tendency for the children in groups 1 and 2 to be smaller and lighter than in group 3, but the differences are statistically significant only between the mean heights of children in groups 1 and 3 (Table 2). Although all three groups are heavier and taller than would be expected if they had remained in Korea, their means all fall below the 50th percentile of an American standard.

The mean IQ of group 1 is 102: of group 2, 106; and of group 3, 112 (Figure 1). Only the difference between groups 1 and 3 is statistically significant ($P \leq .005$). All the groups have reached or exceeded mean values of American children. When the data are converted to stanines (Table 4) the results are the same as with the IQ scores.

TABLE 2
Current Height (Percentiles, Korean Reference Standard): Comparison of the Three Nutrition Groups. F Prob. Is the Probability That the Calculated F Ratio Would Occur by Chance

GROUP	N	MEAN PERCENTILE	S.D.	F PROB.	CONTRAST GROUPS	t-TEST t	P
1	41	71.32	24.98	.068	1 vs. 2	1.25	.264
2	50	76.86	21.25		1 vs. 3	2.22	.029*
3	47	82.81	23.36		2 vs. 3	1.31	.194
Total sample	138	77.24	23.41				

* Statistically significant.

TABLE 3

Current Weight (Percentiles, Korean Reference Standard): Comparison of the Three Nutrition Groups. F Prob. Is the Probability That the Calculated F Ratio Would Occur by Chance

Group	N	Mean Percentile	S.D.	F Prob.	Contrast Groups	t-Test t	t-Test P
1	41	73.95	24.60	.223	1 vs. 2	1.24	.218
2	51	79.94	20.78		1 vs. 3	1.61	.141
3	47	82.11	22.66		2 vs. 3	.49	.624
Total sample	139	78.91	22.68				

TABLE 4

IQ Stanines: Comparison of the Three Nutrition Groups. F Prob. Is the Probability That the Calculated F Ratio Would Occur by Chance

Group	N	Mean Percentile	S.D.	F Prob.	Contrast Groups	t-Test t	t-Test P
1	37	5.25	1.32	.005	1 vs. 2	1.42	.160
2	38	5.74	1.62		1 vs. 3	3.45	.001*
3	37	6.46	1.66		2 vs. 3	1.91	.061
Total sample	112	5.82	1.61				

* Statistically significant.

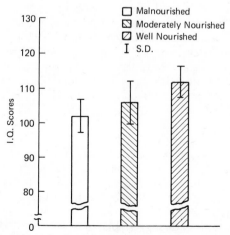

FIGURE 1.   *The IQ's of the three nutrition groups—means and standard deviations (S.D.).*

TABLE 5

Achievement Stanines: Comparison of the Three Nutrition Groups. F Prob. Is the Probability
That the Calculated F Ratio Would Occur by Chance

| | | | | | | t-TEST | |
GROUP	N	MEAN PERCENTILE	S.D.	F PROB.	CONTRAST GROUPS	t	P
1	40	5.07	1.51	.002	1 vs. 2	2.12	.038*
2	38	5.79	1.47		1 vs. 3	3.60	.001*
3	37	6.48	1.89		2 vs. 3	1.80	.080
Total sample	115	5.76	1.72				

* Statistically significant.

Results for achievement scores (Table 5) are similar to those for IQ's. All the groups have achieved at least to stanine 5 (the mean for U.S. school children of the same age). There is a highly statistically significant difference between group 1 and group 3 ($P \leq .001$). Differences in achievement between groups 1 and 2 just reach the level of statistical significance. All the groups are doing at least as well as would be expected from an average U.S. population.

DISCUSSION

In the studies referred to earlier which showed persistent retardation in children malnourished during the first two years of life (1–3), after successful nutritional rehabilitation the children were sent back to the environment from which they came. Even by comparison with nonmalnourished siblings or other children from similar socioeconomic environments their growth and development were retarded (3). Thus severe malnutrition itself during the first two years of life appears to exacerbate the developmental retardation that occurs under poor socioeconomic conditions. What happens to the child from a high socioeconomic background who becomes malnourished early in life? In the few such cases that have been studied (children with cystic fibrosis or pyloric stenosis) the children have shown a much smaller degree of retardation in growth and development and have tended to catch up with time (4). What has not been determined yet and what is a much more important practical problem is the fate of a malnourished child from a poor socioeconomic background who is subsequently reared in the relatively "enriched" environment of a higher socioeconomic stratum.

In a few instances attempts have been made to modify the subsequent environment either by keeping the child longer in the hospital in a program of environmental stimulation or by sending the child home but enrolling him or her in a special preschool program designed to provide a variety of enriching experiences. Improvement in development has been noted with both these approaches but there have been reversals as soon as the special program was discontinued (10). The data suggest that if a severely malnourished child is subsequently to develop adequately, any program of environmental enrichment must be of long duration. In the present study, severely malnourished children were compared with moderately malnourished and well-nourished children after all had undergone a radical and permanent change in their environments by being adopted into primarily middle-class American homes. (The adoptive parents had no knowledge of the previous nutritional status of the child, and the distribution of these children into their adoptive homes was entirely random.) The results are in striking contrast to those obtained from similar groups of children returned to the environments from which they came (1, 2). Even the severely malnouished adopted Korean children have surpassed Korean norms of height and weight. Moreover, the marked initial size differences between the malnourished and the well-nourished infants have almost entirely disappeared, leaving only a small difference in height. None of the groups reach mean values for American children of the same age. This may reflect either genetic size differences between Korean and American children or the effects of chronic undernutrition extending for several generations in developing countries such as South Korea.

Perhaps even more striking and less in accord with previously reported experience is the fact that the mean IQ of the severely malnourished children is 102 and slightly skewed to the right. It is about 40 points higher than that reported in similar populations that were returned to their early home environments (1, 3). In addition, achievement in school for the severely malnourished group is equal to that expected of normal U.S. children. However, the stigmata of malnutrition had not entirely disappeared by the time these children were studied. There are statistically significant differences between the previously malnourished and well-nourished children in IQ and achievement scores. Whether these are permanent differences it may be too soon to judge. It should be noted, however, that the initially well-nourished children attained a mean IQ and achievement score higher than that of middle-class American children. It may be that these attainments (and those of the other two groups as well) reflect the select character of adoptive parents and of the environment they provide to their adopted children.

In this study all the children came to their U.S. homes before the age of three—the mean age was 18 months. Thus they spent a major portion of their early developmental years in their adoptive homes. It would be important both theoretically and practically to determine whether adoption at later ages produces similar results. Such studies are being planned.

References and Notes

1. M. B. STOCH and P. M. SMYTHE, *Arch. Dis. Child.* **38**, 546 (1963): H. G. Birch. *Am. J. Public Health* **62**, 73 (1972).
2. J. CRAVIOTO, E. R. DE LICARDIE, H. G. BIRCH. *Pediatrics* **38**, 319 (1966).
3. M. E. HERTZIG, H. G. BIRCH, S. A. RICHARDSON, J. TIZARD, *ibid.* **49**, 814 (1972).
4. J. D. LLOYD-STILL, paper presented at the annual meeting of the Society for Pediatric Research, San Francisco, May 1974; P. S. Klein, G. B. Forbes, P. R. Nader, *Pediatrics*, in press.
5. S. LEVINE, in *Stimulation in Early Infancy*, A. Ambrose, Ed. (Academic Press, London, 1969), p. 21: V. Denenberg, *ibid.*, p. 62.
6. D. A. LEVITSKY and R. H. BARNES, *Science*, **176**, 68 (1972).

7. CHANG YU HONG, *Pediatric Diagnosis and Treatment* (Yongrin, Korea, 1970).

8. A publication showing the questionnaire is in preparation.

9. Results of only four tests of mental ability, all of them group tests, were used in this study: Lorge-Thorndike Intelligence Test, Otis-Lennon Mental Ability Test, Cognitive Abilities Test, and California Test of Mental Maturity. Each of these tests has a mean of 100 and a standard deviation of 15; they were chosen, on the advice of two consulting educational psychologists, because of their equivalency. Results of the following achievement tests were used: California Achievement Test, California Test of Basic Skills, Metropolitan Achievement Test, Stanford Achievement Test, and SRA Achievement Series. To facilitate comparison of ability and achievement scores both were converted to stanine scores, the former by chronological age, the latter by school grade. In stanine scores 9 is high, 1 is low, and the mean is 5. The conversion to stanine scores was done by two educational psychologists who had no knowledge of the nutrition group assignments.

10. D. S. McLAREN et al., *J. Ment. Defic. Res.* **17**, 273 (1973); H. McKay and A. McKay, paper presented at the Western Hemisphere Conference, Mayaguez. Puerto Rico, October 1970.

11. Acknowledgment is made to the Agency for International Development and the Grant Foundation for support of this research. We thank J. Justman and M. Sontag for consultations on how to evaluate the school data, L. Burrill for help with converting the IQ and achievement scores into standard stanines, B. Miller for technical assistance with the sampling and mailing, and G. Raabe and B. Milcarek for computer programming.

6

Development in Cognition, Imagination, and Language

New studies question accepted beliefs about children's thinking, such as the principles on which children categorize and the conditions under which young children are egocentric. Child developmentalists have always maintained that play is essential for healthy development, but now research is clarifying the role of play in language and cognitive development. Similarly, parent-child interaction is known to be important for language development, but now the actual processes are being analyzed.

One approach to exploring children's cognitive behavior is to ask them to sort objects or pictures into groups. Eleanor Rosch and Carolyn B. Mervis maintain that there are natural categories, based on human experience in the world. They show how young children can use these categories as well as adults, and that only in superordinate classification does performance improve with age.

Spatial egocentrism means inability to differentiate between what one perceives from what another person perceives. Spatial egocentrism decreases as the child organizes space and his relationships within it. Peter B. Pufall explores these processes with kindergarten children, showing the gradual construction of spatial reference systems.

A child learns his mother-tongue largely from his mother. Do mothers have special qualifications as language teachers? Ernst L. Moerk studied mothers' utterances in relation to those of their children. He found that mothers adjusted their comments sensitively to the complexity of their children's utterances.

Children's Sorting: A Reinterpretation Based on the Nature of Abstraction in Natural Categories [*]

Eleanor Rosch and Carolyn B. Mervis

UNIVERSITY OF CALIFORNIA, BERKELEY AND CORNELL UNIVERSITY

Abstract

The previous developmental finding that young children do not group objects taxonomically (i.e., because they are the same kind of objects) was argued to be an artifact of the use of stimuli which are related only at a level of abstraction superordinate to the level at which basic structure exists in the real world. In the present studies, a total of 180 subjects at ages 3 years, 4 years, kindergarten, grades 1, 3, 5, and adult were divided into two groups, one of which was given an opportunity to sort sets of color pictures of common objects such as animals, vehicles, and clothing into groups at the hypothesized basic level of abstraction, the other of which was given the same pictures but in sets cross-cutting the basic level so that taxonomic sorting would necessarily be at the superordinate level. Experiment 1 was administered in the form of oddity problems, Experiment 2 with standard sorting procedures. Results were that subjects at all ages, in both designs, sorted the basic level groups taxonomically. The usual developmental trend was observed only for superordinate classifications. These results were not simply effects of vocabulary development. Implications for theories of categorization and of development were discussed.

There is a long tradition of sorting research in the developmental literature which indicates that young children and adults use different principles when classifying objects. Adults, when given instructions to "put together the things that go together" tend to put things together taxonomically (e.g., objects that belong to the same category); whereas, the younger the child, the more likely he is to sort on the basis of associations, stories, chains, and by means of other non-taxonomic criteria. A particularly well-known example of such a finding is given in Bruner, Olver, and Greenfield (1966); however, research of this nature spans over 30 years (for example, Annett, 1959; Garrettson, 1971; Goldman & Levine, 1963; Thompson, 1941). It is the contention of the studies to be reported here that most of the findings of this research tradition are artifacts of the items which have been used in the sorting studies; an error which has been due to an exclusive focus on cognitive developmental factors internal to the

Portions of this paper were presented at meetings of The Society for Research in Child Development, Denver, 1975. Printed by permission.

[*] This research was supported in part by a grant to the first author (under her former name Eleanor Rosch Heider) by the National Science Foundation GB-38245X, in part by a grant from the Grant Foundation, and in part by a grant from the National Institute of Mental Health 1 RO1 MH24316–01. Portions of this data were presented in a paper delivered at a meeting of the Society for Research in Child Development, Denver, 1975. We wish to thank Meriska Huynen and Carol Simpson for help in testing and the students and staff of the University of California nursery school and the Pacific Grove public schools for their kindly cooperation.

Carolyn Mervis is now at Cornell University. She was a National Science Foundation predoctoral fellow during performance of the research.

child and a neglect and lack of understanding of the actual structure of objects in the real world and of the reflection of that structure in psychological categories.

The developmental research in the sorting studies to be reported is based on a general theory of human categorization which has been elaborated in previous work (Rosch & Mervis, Note 1; Rosch, Mervis, Gray, & Simpson, Note 2). The basic argument of the theory is that categorizations which humans make of the concrete world are not arbitrary classes which the child must be taught to impose upon the environment in a rote manner; rather, the categories themselves have an internal rationale which renders them highly determined. Categories are structured because the real world is structured. Real-world attributes, unlike the sets often presented laboratory subjects, do not occur independently of each other; they occur in correlated (redundant) clusters. (For example, creatures with feathers are more likely also to have wings than creatures with fur.) Categorization occurs in order to reduce the infinite differences between stimuli to behaviorally and cognitively useful proportions; therefore, the basic category cuts in the world should be those which yield the most information for the least cognitive load. Basic categories should, thus, be the most inclusive categories which can follow the correlational structures perceived in the world.

In a series of converging experiments, we found that there is, in fact, a basic level of abstraction in adult human categorizations of concrete objects. Basic level objects were the most inclusive categories which were found to have the following properties: (a) Clusters of attributes occur which subjects agree are possessed by members of the category. For example, chairs (a basic level category) have seats, legs, you sit on them, etc., whereas, furniture (a superordinate) has virtually no common attributes, and kitchen chair (a subordinate) has basically the same attributes as chair. (b) Sets of common motor movements are made when using or interacting with objects of that type. This finding may be particularly important developmentally, since it means that basic level objects are the most inclusive categories for which a sensory motor schema (Piaget, 1952) can be formed. (c) Commonalities in the shape, and, thus, the overall look, of objects occur. (d) It is possible to recognize an average shape of an object of that class. (e) It is possible to form a concrete image of a typical member of the class (Rosch, Mervis, & Miller, Note 3).

In terms of developmental applications, basic level objects should be those first learned by means of visual perception and sensory motor interaction with the object and, thus, should be the first divisions of the world at which it might make sense to a child to put things together because they are the same type of thing. However, in *all* previous sorting studies, the possible taxonomic categories were invariably at the superordinate level; e.g., the child would have to put together a cat and a dog as animals rather than two cats as cats.

In our studies, subjects at each of the following ages—3 years, 4 years, kindergarten, grades 1, 3, and 5, and adult—were divided into two groups, one of which was given an opportunity to sort sets of color pictures of common objects such as animals, vehicles, clothing, and furniture into groups of basic level objects, the other of which was given the same pictures but in sets cross-cutting the basic level so that taxonomic sorting would necessarily be at the usual superordinate level. The 3- and 4-year-olds received only two categories, and the task was administered in the form of oddity problems; the older groups received four categories, and the standard sorting task and instructions.

EXPERIMENT 1

While children below the age of 6 years may have difficulty understanding instructions in the standard sorting task (Bruner et al., 1966; Nash, Note 4), oddity problems can be comprehended at much younger ages (Gelman, 1972). Thus, in order to be able to include nursery school age children in our experimental design, the first experiment employed an oddity problem format.

METHODS.   SUBJECTS   Subjects were 40 nursery school children, 40 elementary school children, and 20 adults. The children included 20 3-year-olds, 20 4-year-olds, 10 kindergartners, 10 first graders, 10 third graders, and 10 fifth graders. In each age group, exactly half of the children were males and half females. Mean ages at the time of testing, for each age group respectively, were: 3 yr. 5 mo.; 4 yr. 7 mo.; 5 yr. 7 mo.; 6 yr. 5 mo.; 8 yr. 8 mo.; and 10 yr. 7 mo. The adult subjects (6 males, 14 females) were undergraduates who participated in the experiment for course credit. Socioeconomic status of the subjects was unknown.

STIMULI   Stimulus materials were color photographs of animals and vehicles. Four categories of animals—cats, dogs, butterflies, and fish—and four categories of vehicles—cars, trains, motorcycles, and airplanes—were used. Pictures were selected from a pool of 125–200 for each of the eight categories according to the procedure described in Rosch et al. (Note 2). Four pictures were used for each basic level category. Two sets of triads were used: one which could be correctly paired at the basic level, and one which could be correctly paired only at the superordinate level.

To prepare the basic-level triad set, four pairs of pictures from each basic level category were made yielding 16 pairs per superordinate. Pictures were paired with the restrictions that each of the four available pictures per basic-level category be used twice and that the two pictures in a pair not be the same color. The third member of the triad was chosen from the other superordinate category by the following procedure: there were four pairs of pictures within each basic level category. Each of the pairs was combined with one picture from each of the four different basic level pairs of the other superordinate. Thus, from the four pairs of cats, one pair was combined with a car, one with a truck, one with a motorcycle, and one with an airplane. The four pairs of fish were combined with a different car, truck, motorcycle, and airplane. This procedure was repeated for all eight categories, yielding 32 different triads.

To prepare the superordinate triad set, each picture from a basic level category was paired with one picture from each of the other basic level categories within the same superordinate. Thus, each car was paired with one train, one motorcycle, and one airplane. Again, the restriction was used that the two pictures in a pair not be the same color. This procedure yielded six sets of four pairs for each superordinate. Each pair was combined with one member from the other superordinate category according to the procedure described for basic level pairs. There were 48 triads in the superordinate set. For both the basic level and superordinate sets, all pictures were used an equal number of times.

PROCEDURE   For the two nursery school groups, triads were presented to the child, one at a time. The three pictures were put on the floor, and the child was told to put together (point to) "the two that are alike, that are the same kind of thing." After the child had gone through the entire set, the last six triads were shown to the child, one at a time. He was reminded which two pictures he had put together and was asked why they belonged together. If the child gave any reason other than a taxonomic one, he was asked if there were any other reason why the two pictures belonged together. Triads were presented in a different random order to each subject, and the order of pictures within triads were shuffled between subjects. Half the subjects in each age group (10 subjects) performed the task with the basic level set and half with the superordinate set. The nursery school children and the adults participated in the entire experiment as outlined above. Because a ceiling in correct sorting of both basic level and superordinate pairs had been reached by age four, and because a ceiling in giving taxonomic reasons for sorts for the basic level had also been reached by age four, the other subjects (elementary school children) were required to sort only six randomly chosen superordinate triads, for which they were asked to give the reason for their sort.

RESULTS AND DISCUSSION   The results were quite clear. At all age levels, basic level sorts were virtually perfect; for the 3-year-olds, the percent correct for basic level sorts was 99, and for 4 years and older, basic level sorts were perfect. Performance was considerably lower for the youngest age group, however, on sorts of the triads which could only be paired at the superordinate level: 3-year-olds, 55% correct; 4-year-olds, 96% correct.

There were no sex differences; data for both sexes were, therefore, combined in the analyses reported. A three-way Analysis of Variance (ANOVA) was performed on the pairing responses for the triads. Between-subject factors were Grade (3-year-olds, 4-year-olds, and adult) and Type of category (basic or superordinate). Category (animal or vehicle) was nested within Type of category. The dependent variable was per cent of correct responses. The effects of primary interest were that of Type of category and the interaction between Type and Grade. Our prediction that basic level sorts would be correct significantly more often than superordinate sorts was confirmed, $F(1, 54) = 26.58, p < .01$. Because a ceiling in performance on these simple triads had been reached essentially by age 4, a significant interaction could be expected between Type of category and Grade; that result was also obtained, $F(2, 54) = 18.54, p < .01$. These two results show that there do exist objects which even small children will classify in the same manner as adults. Basic level sorts are equally easy for all age groups; it is only superordinate level sorts which improve with age.

Not unexpectedly, the main effect of Grade was also significant: $F(2, 54) = 20.9, p < .01$. The effect of Category (animal or vehicle) was not significant—$F(1, 54) = .49$, ns.—and no interaction other than that between Type of category and Grade was significant. A Tukey test confirmed that 3-year-olds performed significantly worse than either 4-year-olds or adults, while there was no difference in performance between the latter two groups.

From the results of the sorting alone, it might be argued that the findings are simply a function of language development; that is, that children learn the names for basic level objects before those for superordinate categories, and that items are put together when the child knows they have the same name. Two pieces of evidence from the present study argue against such an interpretation.

Subjects' reasons for six of their sorts were obtained for all age levels. These reasons were classified into taxonomic reasons (giving the name of the two items placed together) and all other reasons such as giving attributes or autistic responses. To demonstrate the failure of naming to account for sorting results, results for percent of correct names for superordinate sorts are shown in Figure 1. Adults are omitted because they were perfect in both sorting and naming.

Two points are made clear by Figure 1. For all ages, correct sortings were superior to correct namings. (This was true also for the basic level names at the youngest age; correct sorts for 3-year-olds were 99%, correct names 65%; however, a ceiling was reached for basic level names by age 4). Since a difference

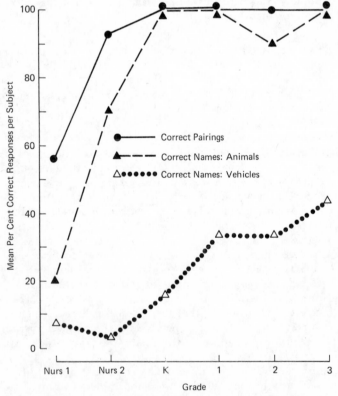

FIGURE 1.   *Correct sorting and correct reasons in the triads test.*

between sorting and naming could conceivably have been due partly to guessing (correct sorts could sometimes have been produced by chance but correct names had to be generated from an infinite set of linguistic responses), we compared correct names for the animal and vehicle categories. As already reported, there were no differences in percent of correct sorts between the animals and vehicles; however, as Figure 1 shows, animal pairs were named correctly far more often than vehicles at all age levels except the youngest, in which names for both were poor, and adults, in which names for both were perfect. The significance of this finding was tested by the Sign test (correct responses for animals versus vehicles for each child). Separate analyses were performed for each age level. The difference between animals and vehicles was not significant for the 3-year-olds or adults but was significant for all other age levels: 4-year-olds, $p < .035$; kindergarten, $p < .004$; grade 1, $p < .004$; grade 3, $p < .016$, grade 5, $p < .016$.

In summary: pictures of objects classifiable into basic level categories were classified in an adult taxononic manner by children at all ages, including 3-year-old children. Only the sorts of superordinate level objects showed the usual improvement with age. Evidence was presented that these results are not simply due to difference in knowledge of names for basic and superordinate level categories. Thus, our basic hypothesis concerning the effect of stimulus sets on sorting was confirmed.

EXPERIMENT 2

Experiment 1 used a simplified oddity problem format in order to create a meaningful task for 3- and 4-year-old children. However, all of the previous studies have used a different sorting procedure. In order to use a task directly comparable to that of previous studies, and in order to have a task difficult enough to show sorting differences for children older than 4 years, we performed a second study based on the same logic as Experiment 1, but using a standard sorting format.

METHODS.   SUBJECTS   Subjects were 64 children and 16 adults. The children were 16 kindergartners, 16 first graders, 16 third graders, and 16 fifth graders. In each group, exactly half the children were males and half females. Mean age at the time of test, for each group respectively, was: 5 yr. 7 mo.; 6 yr. 5 mo.; 8 yr. 4 mo.; and 10 yr. 7 mo. Adult subjects (6 males, 10 females) were undergraduates who participated in the experiment for course credit. Socioeconomic status of the subjects was unknown.

STIMULI   Stimulus materials were color photographs of clothing, furniture, people's faces, and vehicles. Four categories of each were used. They were: *clothing*—shoes, socks, shirts, pants; *furniture*—tables, chairs, beds, dressers; *people's faces*—men, women, young girls, infants; *vehicles*—cars, trains, motorcycles, airplanes. Pictures of items were chosen in the manner described in Experiment 1.

There were four sets of stimuli which could be sorted at the basic level and four sets which could only be sorted taxonomically into superordinate categories. Basic level sets consisted of one of the basic level categories from each of the four superordinates. For example, one subject might receive four shoes, four chairs, four men's faces, and four cars. Two subjects at each age level received each basic level set. To form the superordinate sets, each picture within the basic level sets was numbered arbitrarily 1, 2, 3, or 4. For a set, all of the like numbers were combined. For example, one subject received shoe 1, sock 1, shirt 1, pants 1, table 1, chair 1, car 1, etc. Two subjects at each age level received each superordinate level set.

PROCEDURES   The pictures in a set were shuffled and laid in front of the subject in random order. Instructions were: "Here are some pictures. (The experimenter called the child's attention to each picture by pointing to each in turn.) Put together the ones that go together, the ones that are the same kind of thing." The child was encouraged to include all of the pictures in his groupings. If his first sort was not taxonomic, the pictures were returned to a random order and he was asked if he could find another way to put them together. When the child had finished each sort to his satisfaction, he was asked why those pictures went together.

RESULTS AND DISCUSSION   A child was considered to have sorted taxonomically if either his first or second sort was broken into four groups of four pictures corresponding to the four categories built into the stimuli. The pattern of results was very similar to that obtained in Experiment 1. As in Experiment 1, there were no sex differences. For the basic level categories, all but one child in kindergarten and all but one child in the first grade sorted in an adult taxonomic fashion. For superordinate level sorts, however, only half of the children in each of those grades sorted taxonomically. All of the children in the older group (grades 3 and 5) and all of the adults sorted taxonomically for both basic level and superordinate sets. Because the results for kindergarten and first grade were identical, those two groups were combined for a χ^2 comparison of the difference between basic level and superordinate sorts. Results confirmed that for this group, basic level sets were sorted taxonomically significantly more than superordinate sets: $\chi^2 (1) = 3.64, p < .05$. Thus, as had been the case for the oddity problems of Experiment 1, children of all ages were virtually perfect when sorting the basic level stimuli, and only showed the usual developmental trend in sorting the superordinate level categories.

The children's reasons for their sorts were divided into taxonomic and nontaxonomic reasons following the procedures of Experiment 1. The comparison of taxonomic sorts and reasons are shown in Figure 2. The production of taxonomic reasons lagged behind taxonomic sorting responses. Separate χ^2 tests were performed for grades kindergarten and 1 and for grades 3 and 5 for the difference between the number of children giving taxonomic reasons versus the number giving taxonomic sorts. Both tests were significant: for the younger group, $\chi^2 (1) = 18.66, p < .001$; for the older group, $\chi^2 (1) = 3.79, p < .05$. In the present experiment, the probability of correct sorting by chance was extremely small (unlike the 1/3 correct guessing probability for the triads of Experiment 1). Thus, the difference between taxonomic sorts and taxonomic reasons indicates that the sorts were based on principles other than simple knowledge of the category names.

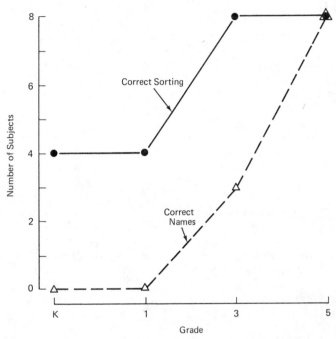

FIGURE 2.   *Correct sorting and correct reasons in the sorting task.*

In summary: for a traditional sorting task, as well as for the oddity problems of Experiment 1, it was shown that even kindergarten children sorted in an adult taxonomic manner when given categories which could be sorted at the basic level. Developmental changes in sorting occurred only for sets which could be grouped solely at the superordinate level.

GENERAL DISCUSSION   The general argument of the study has been that understanding the child's cognitive processes in classification can occur only within a general framework for understanding human categorization. Previous studies of children's sorting behavior have concluded that young children do not group objects because they are the same kind of object but use, as a basis of grouping, other connections between objects. However, these studies have used objects which we believe (Rosch & Mervis, Note 1; Rosch et al., Note 2) are not the same kind of thing for young children. In both of the present experiments, when children at very young ages (3 years for an oddity problem procedure, kindergarten for a sorting procedure) were presented with categories which previous research indicated mirrored the structure of the environment, items from those categories were classified in an adult taxonomic fashion. Only grouping into categories superordinate to these basic classifications demonstrated the usual developmental trends.

From these findings, we do not intend to argue that the logic of categorization does not change with age. The present research did not examine the meaning of categories as such to the child and the consequent logic of class inclusions. The studies do, however, suggest that classification by taxonomic identity (putting things together because they are the same kind of thing) is a far more primitive principle than has been supposed. Evidence that this is the case can also be derived from the very early occurrence of a stage in language development in which the child requests the names of things ("What that?") which is correlated with rapid development in the child's vocabulary of nouns (Brown, 1974). Evidence, somewhat more far afield, may be derived from the fact that stimulus generalization, a response which, by definition, treats non-identical stimuli as equivalent, is apparent in the earliest behavior patterns of infra-human organisms.

The results of the present study have both substantive and methodological implications. Substantively, the fact that basic level objects were sorted taxonomically at the earliest ages supports our claim for the primacy of categorizations at this level of abstraction. Furthermore, that our subjects did group taxonomically when given the right kind of objects indicates that grouping things by the kind of thing they are is a logically more primitive function developmentally than has been supposed. In terms of method, the study should serve as a general caution. Whenever classification tasks are used—for example, in memory research and cross-cultural investigations as well as in developmental studies—the cognitive operations of subjects cannot be considered apart from the nature and logic of the stimuli used.

Reference Notes

1. Rosch, E. & Mervis, C. B. *Basic objects in natural categories: I. Attributes and motor movements.* Manuscript submitted for publication, 1975.
2. Rosch, E., Mervis, C. B., Gray, W., & Simpson, C. *Basic objects in natural categories: II. Shapes of objects.* Manuscript submitted for publication, 1975.
3. Rosch, E., Mervis, C. B., & Miller, R. S. *Imagery of basic level, superordinate, and subordinate categories: A priming study.* Unpublished manuscript, 1975. (Available from the first author.)
4. Nash, S. C. The use of free recall to infer cognitive organization in three, four and five year olds. Unpublished MA thesis, University of Pennsylvania, 1973.

References

Annett, M. The classification of instances of four common class concepts by children and adults. *British Journal of Educational Psychology*, 1959, **29**, 223–236.
Brown, R. *A first language.* Cambridge, Mass.: Harvard University Press, 1974.
Bruner, J. S., Olver, R. R., & Greenfield, P. M. *Studies in cognitive growth.* New York: Wiley, 1966.
Garrettson, J. Cognitive style and classification. *Journal of Genetic Psychology*, 1971, **119**, 79–87.
Gelman, R. The nature and development of early number concepts. In H. Reese (Ed.) *Advances in child development and behavior.* (Vol. 7). New York: Academic Press, 1972.
Goldman, A. E. & Levine, M. A development study of object-sorting. *Child Development*, 1963, **34**, 649–666.
Piaget, J. *The origins of intelligence in children.* New York: International Universities Press, 1952.
Thompson, J. The ability of children of different grade levels to generalize on sorting tests. *Journal of Psychology*, 1941, **11**, 119–126.

Egocentrism in Spatial Thinking: It Depends on Your Point of View*

Peter B. Pufall

SMITH COLLEGE

Abstract

Sixty-three kindergarten children were tested on a spatial perspective task in which they had to copy the location and orientation of objects when the model and response spaces were aligned or one was rotated 90 degrees or 180 degrees. There were very few errors when the spaces were aligned, and there were significantly more errors on the 180 degrees than the 90-degree rotations. Egocentric responding dominated spatial responding on the 180 degrees but was infrequent on the 90-degree rotations. These findings are explained as due to the symmetry relations between space and self for each perspective difference.

An impediment to children's spatial thinking, and particularly spatial perspective taking, is its egocentricity. In general, egocentricity refers to the inability or failure to differentiate the subjective from the objective aspect of knowing. In the case of perspective taking, it is the failure to understand that perspective is relative, and this failure is evident when the child represents, in whole or in part, another perspective as identical to his own.

Although egocentricity is most frequently thought of as a property of preoperational thinking, it is clear from much of the reported literature that the preoperational child's thought is not exclusively egocentric (Fishbein, Lewis, & Keiffer, 1972; Laurendeau & Pinard, 1970; Piaget & Inhelder, 1956; Pufall & Shaw, 1973). Preoperational children do represent some aspects of space objectively while representing other aspects of the same space egocentrically. Moreover, egocentricity does not appear to be restricted to the preoperational period. Pufall and Shaw (1973) note that 10-year-old children not only reflected egocentricity in their spatial thinking but did so to a greater degree than the younger children for certain spatial layouts. In this same study it was clear that the 10-year-old children had achieved the level of operational thought. In contrast to younger children who preserved an isolated relation egocentrically, the older children organized large portions of space egocentrically. Thus, they did logically multiply spatial relations but failed to compensate for perspective difference.

Data such as these do not fit comfortably into a model of development which explains the shift away from egocentricity in terms of the development of abstract structures such as operational systems of logical multiplication.

These observations have led Pufall (Note 1) to distinguish two aspects of spatial thinking. One aspect is operative and deals with the development of structuring activities which constitute reference systems for organizing spatial

From *Developmental Psychology*, 1975, **11**, 297–303. Copyright © 1975 by The American Psychological Association. Reprinted by permission.

* The present research was supported by the Sloan Foundation. Thanks are due to Ann Pufall for help on data collection and Susan Lathrop for data analysis.

arrays and mapping perspectives into each other. Piaget and Inhelder's (1956) theoretical work specifying the development of infralogical structures gives one model of the development of the operative aspect of knowing. The more abstract operative systems act upon particular spaces and particular features within that space. The second aspect of spatial knowing, then, is the discrimination of distinctive features or relations such as parallel to. The empirical and theoretical work of the Gibsons (E. J. Gibson, 1969; J. J. Gibson, 1966) seems to be directed toward understanding this aspect of spatial knowing and its development.

Egocentric thought does not appear to fit comfortably as a property of either aspect of spatial thought. Egocentricity does not specify a structure or system but certainly can specify the relations to be structured; for example, the relations of right, left, near, and far can be multiplied into a two-dimensional system similar to a geographic system: far, far right, right, etc. Nor is egocentricity a property of an object to be discriminated since it is a relation between self and space. This relation is special because it does not change in functional importance as the child's structuring of space and discrimination of spatial features change.

Any theory of spatial thinking has to account for the development of organizational systems, discrimination of spatial properties, and the relation of these two to the functioning of egocentric thought. The latter problem involves specifying the conditions under which egocentric thought would function when perspectives need to be coordinated. If positions within a space were defined like squares in a patchwork quilt, each marked by topographically distinctive features, then positions would not be discriminated by relating them to other positions. As a consequence there would be few errors and no apparent egocentric involvement no matter what perspectives need to be coordinated. The more likely case in nature, and more interesting case to study, involves spaces in which positions have to be defined relationally because topographic features are repeated. Due to the repetition of features within a space, some perspectives would be more similar than others, and, of course, some egocentric descriptions of each perspective would be more similar.

The relation among perspective and egocentric description can be referred to as a symmetry relation. If perspective A and A' are symmetrical with respect to self, then one would expect the child, or even the adult, to describe the spatial relations egocentrically. In the limiting case, if the two perspectives are identical then positions of objects are frequently referred to as the far-right, far-left, etc., objects. Symmetry relations, in varying degrees, can be identified when there are perspective differences. For example, in the present study identical trees are located in one pair of diagonal quadrants and a barn and house are in the other diagonal pair. When the perspective differences are 180 degrees there is a symmetry with respect to the trees; there is a far-right tree and a near-left tree. When the perspective difference is 90 degrees there is no symmetry because the far-left tree now corresponds to the far-left house.

This analysis can be generalized to realizations intrinsic to space, for example, parallelness. The objects to be positioned were longer than they were wide and were often positioned so that they were parallel to a topographic property of the space. When there is no perspective difference or it is 180 degrees, the objects are not only parallel to that spatial feature but also continue to be parallel to an egocentric projection, for example, they project near to far. When the difference is 90 degrees, the parallel relation between the object and edge is preserved only if the relation to self is not. The symmetry relation in the first case might yield accurate positioning but the orientation of the object might be egocentric; that is, the child might preserve the orientation as looking toward him even though under a 180-degree transformation it should look away. If the asymmetric relation is preserved on the 90-degree perspective difference, then if there is an error of orientation it can not be egocentric.

In summary, the symmetry analysis predicts that egocentric functioning, rather than accuracy in spatial reasoning, is influenced by perspective difference, at least during the preoperational period. It is also assumed that the symmetry relations influence independently global and local descriptions of spatial relations. As a consequence the child might correctly discriminate what feature a position is adjacent to but egocentrically discriminate among those many positions about that feature.

METHOD

SUBJECTS   Sixty-three kindergarten children ranging in age from 5.5 to 6.0 years were tested. This age children were tested because they could be expected to express some degree of egocentricity and because they would not have mastered completely the perspective problem. The sample consisted of 30 girls and 33 boys; all attended parochial schools in Washington, D.C., and came from lower-middle- to middle-socioeconomic-status familes. All of the children were Caucasian.

MATERIALS   The basic equipment consisted of two 60 × 60 cm displays simulating a farm scene, two pairs of animals (lambs and rabbits), and a wooden screen 50 × 50 cm. Each landscape was divided into quadrants by a road running near to far and a stream running left to right. The stream ended in a pond on the right when a subject viewed it in its standard position. An object was located in the center of each quadrant: a house in the upper left, a tree in the upper right, a barn in the lower right, and a tree identical to the other tree in the lower left. Two objects, the trees, were repeated and also were symmetrical with no distinctive feature differentiating one side from another. Two objects were unique, the house and the barn, both in the sense of not being repeated but also in the sense that they were asymmetrical with distinctive features differentiating the four sides of each.

PROCEDURE   There were nine trials, three when the two displays were in the same orientation, three when one was rotated 90 degrees, and three when one was rotated 180 degrees. On each trial a screen was placed between the two displays. On the nonrotation trials the experimenter placed his animals on one display and then instructed the subject to place his animals on his display so that they were "in the same spot as mine [the experimenter's] and facing the same way as mine [the experimenter's]." On the rotation trials the experimenter rotated the display first and then placed his animals. On these trials the experimenter reminded the subject that the display had been rotated and to remember that fact when locating and orienting the animals. Another instruction used to sensitize the subject to the effects of rotation was to remind the subject that the two displays "should look the same when turned around again." After the subject had made his placements, the experimenter removed the screen and if necessary rerotated the display; then the experimenter pointed out whether or not the placements were correct.

Each child went through a two- or three-trial warm-up period, during which the child was familiarized with the instructions and the act of placing the animals. Corrections were made if necessary but they were needed infrequently.

PLACEMENT TYPES   There were six different placements, three for each animal. One placement by each tree (placement type: by a repeated feature), one placement by each building (placement type: by a unique feature), and two by the road (placement type: by an edge). The objects were oriented so that they were parallel to a side of the building or edge of the road. All six placements were approximately 1.88 cm from the adjacent object. On each trial the animals were located in adjacent quadrants. The placement types and perspective difference conditions were randomized with the following restrictions: On each trial two of the three placements were represented; the three perspective differences occurred within each block of three trials; and the same positions were not used on adjacent trials.

RESULTS

Placements were analyzed in terms of the relations to be preserved intrinsic to the space. As can be seen in Table 1, location and orientation were analyzed separately. Each of these was analyzed in terms of the type of feature (repeated, unique, or edge) next to which the placement was to be made. Location responses were scored in two ways. At a global level they were analyzed with respect to the "quadrant" in which the animal was located. And at a local level when placements were adjacent to either a repeated or unique feature, responses were scored in terms of their position "about a feature." This second measure was inappropriate when the animal was located next to the road. In those cases, switching from one side of the feature to the other involved

TABLE 1
Percentage of Error and Egocentric Responses

PERSPECTIVE DIFFERENCE	LOCATION					ORIENTATION		
	Quadrant			About a Feature				
	Repeated	Unique	Edge	Repeated	Unique	Repeated	Unique	Edge
90° Ego	8	0	24	37	2	43	4	13
Total	36	2	45	70	12	66	30	52
180° Ego	52	10	36	63	34	45	52	60
Total	53	11	51	79	37	74	66	63

changing quadrants as well. To score placements about a feature, the area around the feature was divided into four wedges with the feature at the center. As a consequence one position was correct, one preserved the egocentric relation, and two were incorrect for other reasons. Orientations were scored within a system similar to compass headings. The gaze of the animal was recorded as north, north-northeast, east, etc. One orientation was correct, one preserved egocentric relations, and six were incorrect for other reasons.

Table 1 contains the percentage of responses that were errors (total) and the percentage that were egocentric. Both percentages were based on all of the responses made by each child. As a consequence, when the two percentages are equal, it indicates that all errors were egocentric in kind. For example, children failed to discriminate a quadrant when it contained a repeated feature on 53% of the trials, and 52% of their responses were egocentric; therefore, 98% of the erroneous responses were egocentric.

There were very few location or orientation errors on the nonrotation trials: quadrant (1%); about a feature (1%); and orientation (5%). Obviously, these children could comprehend and duplicate the spatial relations when perspective was not a factor. Therefore, the errors in the two rotation conditions are due to the problem of compensating perspective differences. The subsequent analyses analyze performance on the 90-degree and 180-degree perspective difference problems. Due to the fact that the important contrasts are all within subjects, no overall analyses could be done. The differences in performance on the two rotation conditions were analyzed by a sign test.

The major questions asked in the present study were: (a) Does the type of spatial relation to be duplicated influence its discrimination? and (b) what influence does the degree of perspective difference have on performance? A visual appraisal of Table 1 indicates quite clearly that the type of placement as well as the degree of perspective to be compensated influence performance. In general, fewer errors are made when placements are adjacent to a unique feature and also when the smaller perspective difference is to be compensated. However, it is equally clear that there are interactions between types of placements and perspective differences. These interactions appear to be different for total versus egocentric errors. Consequently, each is reported separately and in turn.

TOTAL ERRORS   The children made the fewest errors discriminating quadrants when the placement was adjacent to a unique feature ($p < .01$). Errors on the other two placements did not differ significantly from each other. This pattern holds for both perspectives. The degree of perspective difference influences performance reliably only when the placement to be duplicated is by a repeated feature ($p < .01$). In that case children made fewer errors on the 90-degree perspective.

The type of placement also influenced discrimination performance about a feature. For both the 90-degree and 180-degree rotation, children made fewer errors when the placement was to be made by a unique feature ($p < .01$). Perspective difference influenced performance when placements were by a unique feature ($p < .01$) but not when they were by a repeated feature. In the latter case performance was poor on both perspectives.

Type of placement also influences orientation performance. On 90-degree perspective differences, children made significantly fewer errors of orientation when placements were to be made by a unique feature ($p < .01$), with no significant performance differences when placements were by a repeated feature or edge. There were no reliable differences in performance across placement types when the perspective difference was 180 degrees. Perspective difference had an effect only when placements were to be made adjacent to a unique feature. In that case children made fewer errors when the rotation was 90 degrees.

EGOCENTRIC ERRORS   Analyses of egocentric errors indicated reliable differences in discriminating quadrants among all placement types ($p < .01$) for both perspective differences. The children made fewer egocentric errors on 90-degree than 180-degree perspective differences when the placements were to be made adjacent to a repeated feature ($p < .01$) but the differences were not significant for placements in a quadrant by a unique feature or an edge.

The differences in performance in placing objects about a feature are significant for both perspective differences ($p < .01$). In each case children made fewer egocentric placements about a unique feature than they did about a repeated feature. The effect of perspective difference was significant for both placements by a unique and by a repeated feature ($p < .01$).

Egocentrism in orienting the animal was also affected by placement type and perspective difference. When perspective difference was 90 degrees, the differences in performance among placement types were significant ($p < .01$), but none of the differences were reliable when the rotation was 180 degrees. Differences in perspective influenced performance in orienting an object by a unique feature or an edge ($p < .01$) but not by a repeated feature. Children made very few egocentric errors on the 90-degree condition in the two former cases.

In the final set of analyses, performance on location and orientation was compared. Of the 63 children tested, 57 made more orientation than quadrant errors, and 59 made more orientation than about a feature errors. Similar results were found for egocentric errors; 53 children made more egocentric errors in orienting the animal than in locating it about a feature. In each case the distribution is significantly different from chance ($p < .01$).

DISCUSSION

In general, the data are consistent with the symmetry analyses suggested in the introduction; more specifically, the local symmetry relations were more important than the global ones. Children did make significantly more egocentric errors when the perspective difference was 180 degrees; however, their spatial thinking on the 180 degree trial was neither exclusively egocentric in this condition nor was it exclusively nonegocentric when the perspectives differed by 90 degrees.

The fact that children made fewer errors on 90-degree as compared to 180-degree differences and fewer location than orientation errors might be related to symmetry as well. Perhaps the assymmetry affords a disequilibrium that not only motivates the child to abandon an egocentric perspective but also to detect relations intrinsic to the space. The improvement was restricted to discriminating between the two trees and about the house or barn. The former suggests that the children coordinated spatial properties within a system. However, if such a system existed, it would be expected that the children would also better differentiate positions by an edge and positions about a tree, both of which are possible only if the positions are organized into a coordinate system. Perhaps it is more parsimonious to conclude that these children were at best more likely to detect distinctive features. This would account for the clear reduction in errors made about the unique features which were distinctively marked on all four sides and it also accounts for the discrimination between trees because one was by a pond while the other was not.

Orientation also seems to be influenced by local symmetry relations. In those cases where the animal was parallel to an edge or side of a building, the children conserved this relation (85%). When the perspective difference was 180 degrees, the parallel relation from both perspectives was symmetrical with respect to self, for example, the parallel lines projected along the near-far axis. Conserving parallelness was then consistent with egocentric thought on the 180-degree difference but not on the 90-degree difference. The tendency to conserve this relation accounts for the fact that children rarely oriented the animals egocentrically if the perspective difference was 90 degrees. However, when parallelness to any immediately adjacent feature was not an aspect of the orientation, perspective differences did not differentially affect how the animal was oriented. For both perspective differences, approximately 76% of the errors of orientation were egocentric.

The fact that perspective differences were significant for orientations by a unique feature is interesting and seems consistent with the equilibration hypothesis offered above. When there was asymmetry, the children would abandon an egocentric orientation and become more sensitive to spatial relations intrinsic to the space. In many cases they apparently detected the distinctive features which marked the sides of each building and projected the orientation towards them, for example, toward the silo. When there was symmetry the children were less likely to detect or use this information, probably because in this case the egocentric orientation appeared to be so similar to the objective orientation.

The most obvious difference in orientation and location performance was when placements were next to a unique feature. Children were much more likely to locate the animal on the correct side of that feature than to orient it correctly. Perhaps location was easier because the sides of these buildings differed in many ways; thus, location was redundantly marked, whereas orientation had to be projected onto a specific feature. The difficulty the children had detecting distinctive features toward which to orient the animal was reflected in the difficulty they had orienting the animals correctly by an edge. Another possibility was that orientation was initially not analyzed as having a direction but only as an angular relation between edges. Thus, children might accept conservation of an angular relation as a sufficient description of an orientation. This appears to be reasonable explanation for the children's efforts to orient the animal by an edge when the perspective was 90 degrees. They were correct on half of the trials, which is at chance level if they were randomly choosing direction but conserving the parallel relation with the appropriate edge. It is possible that both interpretations are valid. Perhaps the children's first level of analysis was to conserve the angular relation and the second level was to examine the features onto which the animal gazed. If distinctive features were nearby, the children were likely to use them, but if they were at some distance, they might not have been detected or used them. Nevertheless, even if they are proximate and detectable, their functional value depends on whether or not there was a symmetry relation between self and the two perspectives.

The symmetry hypothesis has been offered as an explanation for the dynamic relation among spatial reference systems (Pufall & Shaw, 1973). It follows from this hypothesis that objective and self-referential systems coexist in the young child's thought, and perhaps in thought at all levels of development. When the systems are asymmetric, the child is motivated to explore cognitively or act on the relations intrinsic to that particular space. Presumably, through such activity the pre-operational child not only differentiates topographic and projective spatial properties (E. J. Gibson, 1969; J. J. Gibson, 1966) but also abstracts or constructs operational systems of reference from actions of co-ordination applied to space.

The development of these two aspects of knowing marks the beginning of concrete operational thought. However, especially during the early operational thought, structuring activities are intimately linked with topographic cues. When topographic information is reduced, thus increasing symmetry among descriptions of surface features, there is increased egocentric thinking even among children as old as 10 years of age when they have to mentally transform a space (Pufall & Shaw, 1973). Egocentrism in this case reflects the operational level of thought as the child multiplies egocentric relations differentiating identical objects because they are far left, far right, etc. Older, but not younger, operational children perform almost errorlessly if they are given relatively brief experiences with this type of space, suggesting that they detect abstract spatial relations which reduce symmetry relations (Pufall, Note 1). Thus, during the concrete operational period, children learn to detect abstract spatial properties and this expanded sensitivity to distinctive features means that asymmetry would become more the rule than the exception.

Reference Note

Pufall, P. B. Developmental relations between egocentrism and coordinate reference systems. In D. Shelton (Chair). *Development of spatial reference systems.* Symposium presented at the meeting of the Society for Research in Child Development Philadelphia, 1973.

References

Fishbein, H. D., Lewis, S., & Keiffer, K. Children's understanding of spatial relations: coordination of perspectives. *Developmental Psychology*, 1972, **7**, 21–33.

Gibson, E. J. *Principles of perceptual learning and development.* New York: Appleton-Century-Crofts, 1969.

GIBSON, J. J. *The senses considered as perceptual systems.* Boston: Houghton-Mifflin, 1966.

INHELDER, B., & SINCLAIR, H. "Learning cognitive structures." In P. H. Mussen, J. Langer, M. Covington (Eds.) *Trends and Issues in Developmental Psychology.* New York: Holt, Rinehart and Winston, 1969.

LAURENDEAU, M., & PINARD, T. *The development of the concept of space in the child.* New York: International Universities Press, Inc. 1970.

PIAGET, J., & INHELDER, B. *The child's conception of space.* London: Routledge and Kegan Paul, 1956.

PUFALL, P. B., & SHAW, R. E. Analysis of the development of children's reference systems. *Cognitive Psychology,* 1973, **5,** 151–175.

Verbal Interactions Between Children and Their Mothers During the Preschool Years

Ernst L. Moerk

CALIFORNIA STATE UNIVERSITY, FRESNO

Twenty children and their mothers were observed while interacting verbally in an unstructured situation. The 10 boys and girls ranged in age from around 2 to 5 years. Quantitative as well as categorical aspects of the interactions were analyzed. Both types of dependent variables were found to change with the age and the language level of the children. Close mutual adaptation of both partners for the quantitative as well as the qualitative dimension were demonstrated. The correlation patterns between the types of utterances allow the abstraction of a "primitive" and an advanced cluster of language-teaching/learning behaviors. The stability and generalizability of these trends were discussed in comparisons with other recent studies on this topic.

In contrast to previous assertions, recent evidence indicates that mothers provide language input highly suited for their preschool children (Snow, 1972; Drach, Note 1; Pfuderer, Note 2; Frank & Seegmiller, Note 3). It has also been reported that mothers adapt their language behavior to the capacities of their children as the children progress in their language skills (Phillips, 1973; Snow, 1972; Baldwin, Note 4). The detailed changes in the types of interactions and the possible consequences for language learning, however, have been only minimally explored (Moerk, 1974; Nelson, 1973; Baldwin, Note 4; Moerk, Note 5). Single suggestive findings on this topic have been reported: Slobin (1968) indicated that with increasing age of the child, the frequency of imitations and expansions declines. Shipley, Smith, and Gleitman (1969) also found a decline in imitation with increasing verbal maturity of the child. These early leads have recently been substantiated by Kemp and Dale (Note 6), Nelson (1973), and Bloom, Hood, and Lightbown (1974).

From *Developmental Psychology,* 1975, **11,** 788–794. Copyright © 1975 by The American Psychological Association. Reprinted by permission.

The existing evidence suggests several specific aspects of the verbal inter-actions between mothers and their children that need detailed study: (a) The influence of the age and language level of the child on types of verbal behavior of both members of the dyad has to be further explored. (b) The achievement of the calibration between mother and child has to be investigated. It appears that Moerk (1972) has to date made the only attempt to subject this topic to a detailed analysis. (c) The interrelationships between the various types of language behavior of children and their mothers have to be explored by means of contingency or correlational studies.

The present investigation is oriented toward these three aspects of dyadic interactions. Quantitative as well as categorical measures are included as dependent variables.

METHOD

SUBJECTS   The subjects were 10 girls and 10 boys with their mothers from normal middle-class homes. The ages of the girls ranged from 1 year 9 months to 5 years 0 months, and those of the boys from 2 years 4 months to 5 years 0 months. When the children were placed in rank order according to their ages, the modal difference between 2 adjacent children was 2 months. For both sexes there was one maximum difference of 12 months; between 2 boys there was also a minimal difference of 0 months. All three extremes appeared at the limits of the age range, the maximum difference at the upper age limit. English was the main language, although a second language was used in some homes and under-stood by the child. The 20 pairs were selected from over 30 dyads; length of protocol and normalcy of interaction were the selection criteria. Protocols with less than 100 utterances per member and those that provided evidence of tense and affected behavior were excluded. Observers were trained psychology students who had been previously acquainted with but were not related to the observed dyads. Each dyad had a different observer, who, as a familiar person, could blend unobtrusively into the behavior setting before he began the recording.

PROCEDURE   The design of the study is cross-sectional. Only one inter-action of each mother–child pair, lasting 1 hour, was analyzed. The home was chosen as the setting for the observation and only mother–child interactions were analyzed. The behavior setting was described at the beginning of the observation, and whenever changes occurred they were recorded. Mothers and children followed their usual routines while their language interactions were tape recorded. The accompanying nonverbal behavior of both partners was recorded by the observers as completely as possible in written form, and both types of information were included in the transcribed protocols.

ANALYSIS OF DATA   The average length of utterance, in syllables, was calculated for each child as an index of his linguistic level. The utterances of both interaction partners were classified into categories according to their communicational functions. Only categories for which high interrater reliability of categorization could be obtained were used. The indices of reliability (Scott, 1955; Scott & Wertheimer, 1962) ranged from .76 to .93.

RESULTS AND DISCUSSION

Discussed first is the correlation between the age of the children and their mean utterance length, as well as the mutual adaptation of the verbal behavior of both partners in its quantitative aspect, as expressed by the length of utterances. A high correlation was found between the age of the child and his mean utterance length, $r(19) = .82, p < .01$. In contrast, the age of the child was not significantly related to measures of the mother's utterance length. A much better predictor of the mean length of the mother's utterances is the mean statement length of the child. The correlation between these two variables was highly significant, $r(19) = .69, p < .01$. Significant correlations were also found between the modal and maximum utterance length of both partners, $r(19) = .44, p < .05$ and $r(19) = .54, p < .01$; this also indicates that mothers and their children have developed congruence in specific aspects of interaction.

Correlations represent only relative similarity; the absolute differences between the obtained values could still be very great. These differences between the child's and mother's utterance length appear to be of special importance because the child has to analyze the mother's model in order to learn from it; these differences are reported in Figure 1.

The mean utterance length of the mother exceeds that of the child in all 20 dyads. Since the difference between the mean utterance length of both partners is small, the mother probably provides an optimal amount of incitement for the child to master this higher linguistic level. The mothers' mean utterance length increases less over the age span studied than does that of the children, which results in a decrease in the difference between the means. A comparison between the mothers' mean and the children's maximum provides evidence that the complexity of the mothers' utterances lies well within the range of competence of the child. When the curve of the mothers' maximum utterance length is considered, it is seen that almost all mothers maximally tax the capacities of their children. The only instance in which the maximum utterance length of the child exceeds that of the mother by two syllables is probably due to chance, since only a small number of interactions were sampled in 1 hour of observation. The high correlation between the mothers' and the children's maximum utterance length suggests that mothers are aware of sentence length as one aspect of their children's linguistic competence. The absolute difference between both maxima indicates, furthermore, that mothers know that the capacity to comprehend linguistic messages somewhat surpasses the capacity to produce them.

Large differences exist between the maximum, mean, and modal utterances of the mother. The differences between the mother's maximum length utterances and the child's mean and modal ones are even larger. Since the mother's maximum length utterances were usually comprehended by the child, the differences express the gap between the maximum performance potential and the average performance and between the performance in comprehension versus that in production, respectively. The impact of these discrepancies on the interactions of individual dyads and on the language acquisition of the child may be important. Figure 1 shows that despite the general age trend, large differences between individual dyads exist. Some mothers seem to be more prone than others to maximally tax the capacity of their children to process long sentences.

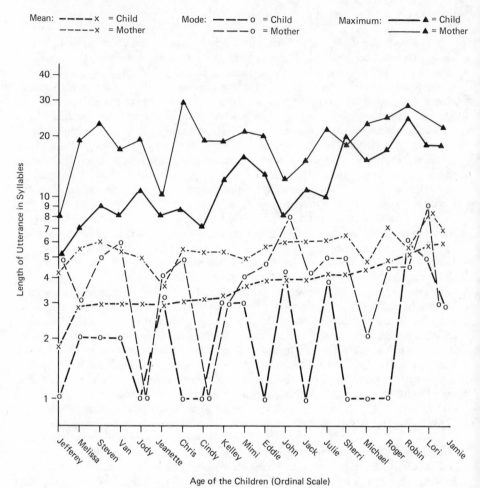

Mean: – – – × = Child   Mode: – – – o = Child   Maximum: ▬▬▬ ▲ = Child
– – – – – × = Mother   – – – o = Mother   ▬▬▬ ▲ = Mother

FIGURE 1.   *Changes in the measures of utterance length with increasing age of the child.*

The pattern of modal length statements, which is greatly subject to chance influences in small samples of interactions, is more irregular. Yet again, with one exception, the modal utterance length of the mothers is equal to or longer than that of their children.

More important than the quantitative aspects of language acquisition may be the changes in the type of interactions between mother and child when the child advances in age and language skills. Frequency counts of types of interaction were performed, and the raw frequencies were transformed into percentages of the total number of utterances of mother and child respectively. Since no significant differences between boys and girls were obtained, the data for both sexes were collapsed.

Eight categories for the verbal behavior of the mother and nine for that of the child could be reliably differentiated. Their mean frequencies and the standard deviations in percentages are presented after the label for each category. The mother's interactions fall into three larger content groups: (a) One group encompasses all those variables that represent a translation of objective/environmental/pictorial configurations into the verbal medium. These are: "Mother models from picture book" ($M = 5.02$, $SD = 6.68$); "mother describes an object or event" ($M = 5.41$, $SD = 3.86$); "mother describes her own acts" ($M = 1.03$, $SD = 1.04$); and "mother describes child's acts" ($M = 1.30$, $SD = 1.32$). (b) The next group, consisting of "mother gives corrective feedback" ($M = 4.18$, $SD = 4.83$) and "mother answers a question" ($M = 5.17$, $SD = 6.73$), deals with responses of the mother to verbal behavior of the child. (c) The third group, "mother guides child's action" ($M = 2.60$, $SD = 2.58$) and "mother gives an explanation" ($M = 3.54$, $SD = 2.54$), is somewhat in contrast to the first one because environmentals given are not translated into language, but language has to be translated into external or internal actions. The latter two categories are relatively sophisticated and their frequencies increase most with the age and language level of the child.

The nine categories of the child's verbal behavior seem to fall into four groups. "Child imitates" ($M = 5.54$, $SD = 6.99$) represents a special phenomenon and should probably be classified separately. The next three variables, "child asks a question" ($M = 9.62$, $SD = 6.88$), "child expresses a need" ($M = 10.81$, $SD = 5.97$), and "child answers a question" ($M = 16.98$, $SD = 9.02$), serve primarily as information exchange. The categories "child encodes from picture book" ($M = 8.34$, $SD = 11.39$), "child describes an object or event" ($M = 6.36$, $SD = 3.67$), and "child describes his own acts" ($M = 3.07$, $SD = 2.17$) parallel those of the mother in that external circumstances are translated into language. Finally, two categories, "child describes a past experience" ($M = 2.71$, $SD = 2.41$) and "child describes his plans" ($M = 3.43$, $SD = 2.88$), represent a translation of cognitive representations into the linguistic medium. The last two phenomena are more advanced cognitively, and their frequencies increase most distinctly with the linguistic level of the child.

This functional description of the categories suggests that these interactions could provide opportunities to teach and learn language. Moerk (1972) has provided some support for this suggestion. A summation of the means shows that approximately 25% of the mother's utterances and 65% of those of the child are accounted for by the above categorizations. With an average total of 300 and 200 utterances for mother and child, respectively, at least 75 and 130 utterances of the mother and the child, respectively, could be conductive to the teaching or the acquisition of language skills.

Changes in the form of interaction are more closely related to the mean statement length of the child than to his age or to the mean statement length of the mother. The discussion will, therefore, center on the correlation between the types of interaction and the mean statement length of the child. Four types of relationships can be distinguished:

1. An inverse relationship between the language level of the child and the frequency with which a type of interaction is used; this is expressed

in negative correlations. The correlations and regression equations used to predict the interactional category (Y) from the mean length of utterance of the child (X) are: "Mother models from picture book": $r(19) = -.61$, $p < .01$, $Y = 19.27 - 3.77 X$; "mother gives corrective feedback": $r(19) = -.61, p < .01$, $Y = 14.42 - 2.71 X$; "mother describes child's acts": $r = -.44, p < .05$, $Y = 3.34 - .54 X$; "child imitates": $r(19) = -.48$, $p < .05$, $Y = 17.45 - 3.15 X$; "child encodes from picture book": $r(19) = -.61, p < .01$; $Y = 32.80 - 6.47 X$.

2. A significant positive relationship between the mean utterance length of the child and the type of interaction is found in two instances. The same data are supplied as above. "Child describes a past experience": $r(19) = .57, p < .01$, $Y = -2.20 + 1.30 X$; "child describes his plans": $r(19) = .60, p < .01$, $Y = -2.66 + 1.61 X$. The correlation approaches significance in the case of "mother guides child's action": $r(19) = .39$, $.05 < p < .10$, $Y = -.92 + .93 X$.

3. The third group of interactional categories does not appear to be related to the level of the child's language. This independence is expressed in low and insignificant correlations.

4. Finally, the frequency of three interaction forms appears to be related curvilinearly to the age and mean utterance length of the child. Since this relationship is most distinct in regard to the age of the child, the correlation ratio, eta, in relation to age was computed. For "mother answers a question": $\eta(4, 15) = .64, p < .01$; for "child asks a question": $\eta(4, 15) = .66, p < .01$; and for "child answers a question": $\eta(4, 15) = .35$ (ns). These three correlation ratios are considerably higher than the corresponding correlation coefficients, $r = .29, .38$, and $-.21$, respectively; none of the latter reached significance.

A last aspect of the present analysis centers on the interrelation of the various forms of interaction. The complete correlation matrix is composed of three different submatrices: (a) the intercorrelations of the mother's forms of interaction; (b) the intercorrelations of interactional forms of the child; and (c) the correlations between the forms of interaction of the mother and those of the child as an expression of dyadic dynamics. Only the following three significant correlations were obtained between the interactional categories of mothers: Between "mother gives corrective feedback" and "mother describes child's acts," $r(19) = .59, p < .01$; between "mother answers a question" and "mother gives an explanation," $r(19) = .46, p < .05$; and between "mother guides child's action" and "mother gives an explanation," $r(19) = .55, p < .05$. These correlation patterns seem to represent a cognitive didactic interaction style of mothers.

The larger number of significant intercorrelations of the interactional behaviors of the child allow the abstraction of two clusters: (a) A cluster of "primitive" interactional forms, which are positively correlated with each other and negatively correlated with more mature forms. The following variables belong to this first cluster: "Child imitates" and "child encodes from picture books." (b) A cluster of more mature forms of interaction includes the variables "child describes his plans," "child describes a past experience," "child describes his own acts," and "child describes an object or event." The variables pertaining to the latter cluster are negatively correlated with those of the first cluster.

When the correlations between the forms of interaction of the mother and those of the child are inspected, the same dichotomy can be seen: the child's primitive forms, that is, imitation and encoding from picture books, are positively correlated with the mother's modeling from picture books and her corrective feedback. The correlations with imitation are: $r(19) = .77, p < .01$ and $r(19) = .44, p < .05$. Those with encoding from picture books are: $r(19) = .69$, p $< .01$ and $r(19) = .41, p < .10$. The child's use of picture books is also negatively correlated with the mother's more complex forms of interaction: "Mother gives an explanation," $r(19) = -.52, p < .01$, and "mother describes an object or event," $r(19) = -.47, p < .05$. On the other hand, the child's more mature forms of interaction are highly and significantly correlated with the mother's more sophisticated categories: "answers a question," "guides child's actions," "gives an explanation," and "describes an object or event." The correlation pattern between the primitive as well as the mature interactional forms of both partners again provides striking proof of the high level of calibration achieved between the partners even when the qualitative aspect of their interactions is considered.

In summary, the present findings are in accord with those of Pfuderer (Note 2), Moerk (1974, Note 5), Phillips (1973), and the reports of the group associated with Baldwin (Note 4) in indicating a gradual increase in the complexity of the speech of both mothers and children. All the authors affirm that the speech of the mother is always somewhat above that of the child in complexity, that is, the mother seems to "pace" the child's linguistic performance.

Similarities also appear between the few studies that deal with qualitative changes in interactions. Nelson (1973) reported the frequency of mothers' descriptions of objects to be around 7% while in the present study a mean of 5.41 and a standard deviation of 3.86 is found for this category. All researchers reported a decline in imitation with the language level of the child beginning around the age of 2 years. Nelson (1973) demonstrated that at the age of 2 years, the asking of questions by children is positively related to all language indices. The curvilinear relationship of question asking with age, as found in the present study, also suggests that question asking at this early age fulfills a productive function for language acquisition. A decline of this type of interaction from 26% at 2½ years of age to 21% at age 5 was also reported by Baldwin (Note 4). These two reports are in conflict with Moerk's (1974) finding that question-asking behavior increases up to the age of 5 years. However, when Moerk (Note 5) reported data of a larger sample, he also found some indication of a decrease in this behavior when the children reached the highest level of language skills. Since all of the above-discussed studies included only a relatively small number of dyads, Seegmiller's (Note 7) observation may explain the differences. She indicated that wide differences between dyads exist in the amount of question–answer interaction. The same fact has also been observed in the present sample. Chance factors of sample selection may therefore account for the differences encountered in published reports.

Baldwin's (Note 4) conclusion that children progress from labeling to conversations about materials and activities is also supported by the present results. The more frequent descriptions of objects, events, and actions together with the steep increase in the discussion about past experiences and future plans represent the relevant evidence. In a related manner, Sigel (1971) discussed the "distancing function" of language, and Lewis (1973) and Morris (1938) offered some cognitive-evolutionary explanations for its development during early childhood.

Besides these specific points of correspondence, in all the relevant studies a close calibration between mother and child has been found for all channels of communication (Escalona, 1973). Accordingly, mothers seem to be discriminately, albeit perhaps without full awareness, involved in the language-teaching process. In all of the present protocols it was impressive to observe how "mothers frequently and opportunistically seized upon the present situations and materials to get in a bit of teaching" (Seegmiller, Note 7, p. 7). Since much teaching and learning can result from such interactions that continue over several years, the instructional activities of parents deserve closer attention in every attempt to explain first language acquisition.

Reference Notes

1. DRACH, K. M. The language of the parent: A pilot study. In K. Drach, B. Kobashigawa, C. Pfuderer, & D. Slobin (Eds.), *The structure of linguistic input to children* (Language-Behavior Research Laboratory, Working Paper 14). Unpublished manuscript, University of California, Berkeley, January 1969.
2. PFUDERER, C. Some suggestions for a syntactic characterization of baby-talk style. In K. Drach, B. Kobashigawa, C. Pfuderer, & D. Slobin (Eds.), *The structure of linguistic input to children* (Language-Behavior Research Laboratory, Working Paper 14). Unpublished manuscript, University of California, Berkeley, January 1969.
3. FRANK, S. M., & SEEGMILLER, M. S. *Children's language environment in free play situations.* Paper presented at the biennial meeting of the Society for Research in Child Development, Philadelphia, March 1973.
4. BALDWIN, C. P. *Comparison of mother–child interactions at different ages and in families of different educational level and ethnic backgrounds.* Paper presented at the biennial meeting of the Society for Research in Child Development, Philadelphia, March 1973.
5. MOERK, E. L. *Changes in verbal interactions of child–mother dyads with increasing language skills of the child.* Paper presented at the 20th International Congress of Psychology, Tokyo, Japan, August 1972.
6. KEMP, J. C., & DALE, P. S. *Spontaneous imitations and free speech: A developmental comparison.* Paper presented at the biennial meeting of the Society for Research in Child Development, Philadelphia, March 1973.
7. SEEGMILLER, B. *The norms and patterns of mother–child interaction in free play.* Paper presented at the biennial meeting of the Society for Research in Child Development, Philadelphia, March 1973.

References

BLOOM, L., HOOD, L., & LIGHTBOWN, P. Imitation in language development: If, when, and why. *Cognitive Psychology*, 1974, **6**, 380–420.
ESCALONA, S. K. Basic modes of social interaction: Their emergence and patterning during the first two years of life. *Merrill-Palmer Quarterly*, 1973, **19**, 205–232.

LEWIS, M. M. The beginning of reference to past and future in a child's speech. *The British Journal of Educational Psychology*, 1937, **7**, 39–56.

MOERK, E. L. Principles of dyadic interaction in language learning. *Merrill-Palmer Quarterly*, 1972, **18**, 229–257.

MOERK, E. L. Changes in verbal child–mother interactions with increasing language skills of the child. *Journal of Psycholinguistic Research*, 1974, **3**, 101–116.

MORRIS, C. W. Foundations of the theory of signs. In O. Neurath, R. Carnap, & C. W. Morris (Eds.), *International encyclopedia of unified science* (Vol. 1). Chicago: University of Chicago Press, 1938.

NELSON, K. Structure and strategy in learning to talk. *Monographs of the Society for Research in Child Development*, 1973, **38**, (1, 2, Whole No. 149).

PHILLIPS, J. R. Syntax and vocabulary of mother's speech to young children: Age and sex comparisons. *Child Development*, 1973, **44**, 182–185.

SCOTT, W. A. Reliability of content analysis. The case of nominal scale coding. *Public Opinion Quarterly*, 1955, **19**, 321–325.

SCOTT, W. A., & WERTHEIMER, M. *Introduction to psychological research.* New York: Wiley, 1962.

SHIPLEY, E. F., SMITH, C. S., & GLEITMAN, L. R. A study in the acquisition of language: Free response to commands. *Language*, 1969, **45**, 322–342.

SIGEL, I. Language of the disadvantaged: The distancing hypothesis. In C. Stendler-Lavatelli (Ed.), *Language training in early childhood education*. Urbana: University of Illinois Press, 1971.

SLOBIN, D. I. Imitation and grammatical development in children. In N. S. Endler, L. R. Boulter, & H. Osser (Eds.), *Contemporary issues in developmental psychology*. New York: Holt, Rinehart & Winston, 1968.

SNOW, C. E. Mother's speech to children learning language. *Child Development*, 1972, **43**, 549–565.

7

Emotional and Social Development

Through interactions with other people, children acquire knowledge of others and of themselves and techniques for dealing with other people. Social interactions have a feeling side. Children learn to recognize and express their own emotions and to interpret and react to the emotions of others, using their cognitive resources as well as their emotions. Processes underlying social behavior are examined here.

Nonverbal communication occurs when one person reacts to another's nonverbal signals, such as facial expressions, posture, gestures, and distancing. Gail A. Wasserman and Daniel N. Stern analyzed the nonverbal signals given by preschool children as they approached a peer. Their behaviors indicated that children were aware of their own sex and that of the other child, since they made closer approaches to peers of their own sex. Nonverbal signals are thought to give more accurate information about children's attitudes toward peers than do their answers to questions.

Conceptual perspective-taking, or taking the point of view of another person, enables the first person to know or to make a good guess as to what the second person is thinking. Psychologists have paid a great deal of attention to the question of whether preschool children can take the point of view of another person. Piaget placed this ability in the stage of concrete operations, which begins at around 7 years of age. In the previous chapter, Pufall investigated children's ability to take another spatial perspective. Here Daniel G. Mossler, Mark T. Greenberg, and Robert S. Marvin have devised situations in which younger children can take the conceptual perspective of another.

Empathy refers to being able to perceive how another person is thinking and feeling, often with an emphasis on the feeling side. Helene Borke has investigated empathy in preschool children, both Chinese and American, and both middle-class and disadvantaged. Thus, she was able to test influences of culture and socioeconomic level in addition to showing age-level differences.

Social interaction is affected by individual differences in temperament, according to Jeannie L. Lewis. Rating children on nine dimensions of temperament, she related temperamental characteristics to social behavior at school and at home.

The family is, of course, the arena in which basic social-emotional interaction patterns are acquired. With the contemporary family changing as it is, the effects of new family forms upon children are relatively unknown. Therefore, an ongoing study at the University of Virginia is very important. A preliminary report of this research, by E. Mavis Hetherington, Martha Cox, and Roger Cox, gives insight into the impact of divorce on children, mothers, and fathers.

Approach Behaviors Between Preschool Children: An Ethological Study*

Gail A. Wasserman and Daniel N. Stern

NEW YORK HOSPITAL–CORNELL MEDICAL CENTER

The ethological approach to the study of nonverbal communication promises to further our understanding of interpersonal events. However, at this point, not enough is known about the development, in young children, of the components of nonverbal signal systems, such as distancing, postural orientation, facial expressions, and hand and head gestures.

Many aspects of the child's motivational state, such as fear, aggressiveness, affiliation and curiosity are communicated through these signal systems. Additionally, the child's differential use of such behaviors can serve as an index of the degree to which he differentiates such salient dimensions of his relationship to his peers as their sex as compared to his own, their dominance status, their familiarity, and their perceived aggressiveness, fearfulness, or friendliness. Accordingly, the study of these signal systems may provide us with new and powerful tools for examining various developmental issues related to normal and abnormal peer interactions.

This paper is part of an ongoing study of the ontogeny of such kinesic communications systems, as they operate in dyadic interactions. Previous work by Stern and Bender (1974) has documented the existence, in preschool children, of nonverbal signals which are organized into functionally meaningful clusters and are used differentially, depending on the situation in which the child finds himself. Specifically, Stern and Bender found consistent differences in the behavior of 3–5-year-old children approaching a strange adult. Depending upon the age and sex of the child and the degree of threat presented by the adult, children showed consistent differences in how close they would approach to the adult, the degree to which they oriented their faces and bodies away from the adult, and their usage of hand gestures, such as hand to mouth and hands behind back, as well as in their performances of facial expressions, particularly smiling and apprehensive mouth behaviors.

The current study extends these observations to peer interactions, rather than child–adult interactions, and examines nonverbal behavior between approaching peers, as a function of the child's age, sex, relative dominance–status, aggressiveness, and sex of the other interacting peer. We would also wish to document the presence of kinesic signals which are specific to sex related and dominance behaviors and to trace their emergence in the young child.

Presented at meetings of The Society for Research in Child Development, Denver, 1975. Printed by permission.

* The authors would like to express their appreciation to the following individuals and schools for their assistance in this research: Maryann Ford, Kathy Kappy Lewis, Larry Jordan, Andrea Consales, Helen Hall, Claire Jasinski, Miyako Namikawa, Margaret Pratesi; Mount Tom Country Day School, New Rochelle, N.Y.; Pengilly Day School, New Rochelle, N.Y.; Saxon Woods Country School, Mamaroneck, N.Y.; Ridge Street Country School, Portchester, N.Y.; Yonkers Jewish Community Center, Yonkers, N.Y.

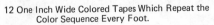

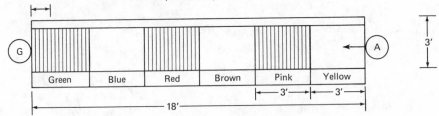

FIGURE 1.   *Approach carpet.*

Ss were 134 white 3–5-year-old children. Children from all the experiments I will describe are all middle-class preschoolers from the same suburban area. Children were met in their classroom by the experimenter and asked to participate in a study of how boys and girls walked. Children were brought, 4 at a time, 2 boys and 2 girls, to a familiar room in the school. Two children waited outside, while the other 2 entered the room. One child, whom we call the goal ("G"), was asked to stand on the end of a long rug, which was 18 feet long and 3 feet wide, and was marked with 12 different-colored, 1 inch wide strips of colored tape, which repeated the color sequence every foot. The second child, whom we call the approacher ("A"), was asked to stand at the other end of the

TABLE 1
ANOVA: Log of Approach Distance + 1, Peer Approaches

SOURCE	df	MS	F
Age (A)*	2	3.093	2.800
Sex (A)	1	.514	.465
Order	1	.067	.060
Age (A) × Sex (A)	2	.487	.441
Age (A) × Order	2	.951	.861
Sex (A) × Order	1	.625	.566
Age (A) × Sex (A) × Order	2	.211	.191
Error	122	1.105	
Sex (G)**	1	2.260	6.775†
Age × Sex (G)	2	.141	.423
Sex (A) × Sex (G)	1	.104	.312
Order × Sex (G)	1	.596	1.788
Age × Sex (A) × Sex (G)	2	.153	.458
Age × Order × Sex (G)	2	.332	.995
Sex (A) × Order × Sex (G)	1	.109	.325
Age × Sex (A) × Order × Sex (G)	2	.684	2.050
Error	122	.334	

  * (A) = Approaching child.
** (G) = Goal child.
  † $p < .025$.

rug. The experimenter then said, "Now, 'Johnny,' walk up to 'Susie,' and stop in front of her." A second experimenter scored the approach behavior. The approacher and goal then changed places, for a second run. Cycling in the waiting children, each child approached two other children of the same age as himself, one of the same sex, and one of the opposite sex. The order of approaches was counterbalanced.

TABLE 2

ANOVA: Angular Distance, Peer Approaches

SOURCE	df	MS	F
Age (A)*	2	1.282	.172
Sex (A)	1	6.794	.913
Order	1	2.318	.311
Age × Sex (A)	2	1.968	.264
Age × Order	2	7.943	1.067
Sex (A) × Order	1	4.409	.593
Age × Sex (A) × Order	2	8.320	1.118
Error	122	7.441	
Sex (G)**	1	7.469	6.179†
Age × Sex (G)	2	.701	.580
Sex (A) × Sex (G)	1	1.301	1.076
Order × Sex (G)	1	17.200	14.229††
Age × Sex (A) × Sex (G)	2	1.231	1.019
Age × Order × Sex (G)	2	.214	.177
Sex (A) × Order × Sex (G)	1	1.789	1.480
Age × Sex (A) × Order × Sex (G)	2	1.330	1.101
Error	122	1.209	

* (A) = Approaching child.
** (G) = Goal child.
† $p < .025$
†† $p < .001$.

Two positional behaviors were recorded: 1) how close the approacher came to the goal ("approach distance"), and 2) the degree to which the approacher avoided directly facing or fully squaring off with the goal ("angular distance").

We expected that if dominance were one of the relevant dimensions of children's approach behavior, and if this dimension were more salient for boys, as some have suggested, then boys should stop further away from boys and should angle their bodies away more from boys.

Looking at the top half of Figure 2, which shows the graphs for approach distance, the upper right-hand figure indicates that children stop significantly further from opposite-sexed goals than from same-sexed goals. The bottom two figures are for angular distance, and as you can see from the graph on the right, children orient their bodies significantly further away from opposite-sexed goals than from same-sexed goals. There were, however, no differences as a function of the sex of either the approacher or the goal, rather, the relevant dimension was whether the goal was of the same or opposite sex as the approacher. As a

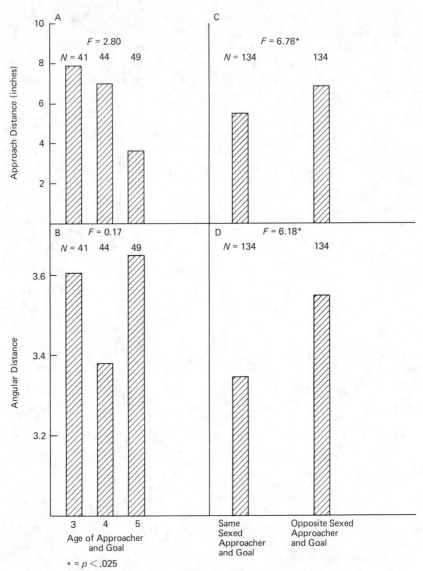

* = p < .025

FIGURE 2.   *Approaches between children of the same age.*

footnote from the upper left-hand graph, you will notice that older children approach somewhat closer than younger children. This has been a consistent finding in our work, but it will not be commented upon further here. There are no age changes in angular distance.

Clearly, the major determinant of the approach behaviors here was not any hypothesized dominance related to sex, but rather a differentiation of the child's own sex relative to the sex of the goal child.

We then attempted to structure the situation so that the dominance–related aspects would be more salient for the child. We asked nursery school teachers to rank order the children in their classes by aggressivity. From each class list we picked the two most aggressive and the two least aggressive children. Taking each sex and classroom separately, then, every child both approached and served as the goal for two other children: one who ranked next to him on the class list and one from the other end of the scale with order counterbalanced. Here we had 26 boys and 28 girls.

Statistics for both approach distance and angular distance revealed no significant effect of either sex or aggressivity of approacher or goal. It would appear then, from these negative findings, that aggressiveness is not a component of the dominance relation, at least as measured by our approach situation.

Having ruled out aggressiveness, at least as reflected in teacher ratings, what other child characteristics might meaningfully be considered as components of dominance relations? The most obvious one, it seemed to us, would be age-status. This is likely to be a very salient dimension for young children, especially in a nursery school with age-graded classes, where issues such as which children take naps and who is taught to read, depend on which class a child is in.

Our next step, then, was to have 4-year-old children approach 3-, 4- and 5-year-olds of the same and opposite sex. On the first day of testing, subjects were asked to approach, one at a time, a 4-, a 3-, and a 5-year-old child, in that order, all of either the same or opposite sex. At a later session, between 1 and 4 weeks later, the child was asked to approach the 3 children of the remaining sex. The order 4, 3, 5 was chosen because we assumed that this would start off with a *known* peer, and only gradually work up to a less-known, higher status child. Here we used 8 4-year-olds of each sex as approachers, and 16 3-year-olds, 20 4-year-olds, and 15 5-year-olds as goals. Some of the 4-year-old goals were also used as approachers.

For this experiment, we videotaped the behavior of the approacher and the goal. The videotape record was later scored for a variety of facial expressions and hand gestures.

Once again, if dominance (as represented by the age or grade of the goal) were relevant here, we would expect more distancing and body aversion when children approach older goals than when they approach younger goals. Looking first at the two figures on the left of Figure 3, with the age of the goal plotted on the horizontal axis, we can see that there is no significant age of goal effect for either approach distance or angular distance. The most consistent finding was, again, as shown on the two figures on the right, that approachers of both sexes stopped further away from opposite-sexed goals and oriented their bodies more away from opposite-sexed goals than they did from same-sexed goals, regardless of age-status differentials. This is the same result we noted above.

Although we observed no sex differences per se in the positional behaviors studied, a finer analysis using the videotapes revealed some interesting sex differences in facial expressions and gestures of both the approacher and the goal. As seen in Figure 4, there was a trend for smiles to be more characteristic of approaches involving females, and for apprehensive mouth behaviors to be more characteristic of approaches involving males. This may perhaps be

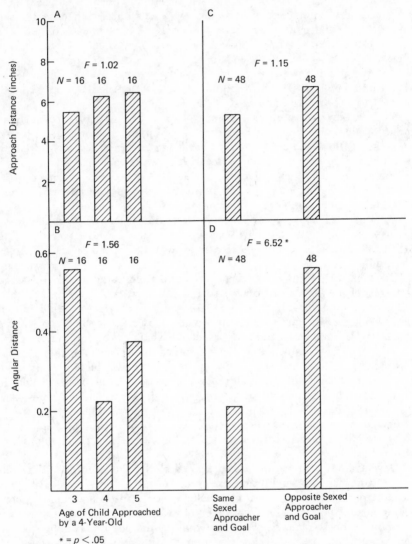

FIGURE 3.   *Approaches of 4-year-old children to 3-, 4-, and 5-year-old children.*

evidence for some sort of dominance signaling between the boys, and possibly more affiliative behavior in the girls.

I don't have the time to discuss these differences further, but I do want to return to our major findings.

First, with the possible exception of our findings on facial expression, there is no evidence of dominance hierarchies based on sex, teacher ratings of aggressiveness, or on age-status within a year of the approacher's status. We do feel that our method of demonstrating dominance behavior is valid, because signs

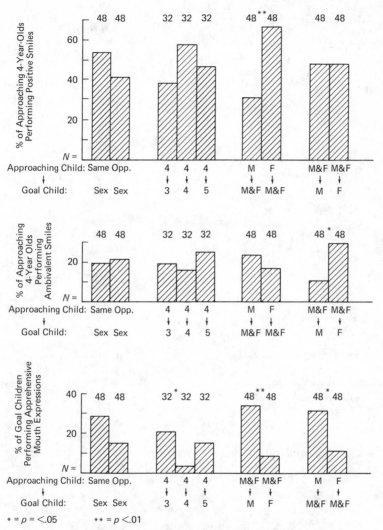

FIGURE 4.   *Sex differences in approach behaviors.*

and signals *are* components of dominance relations in adults, and we believe that the absence of any differences in these systems along the dimensions of sex, aggressiveness, or age-status means that such dominance relations are not yet present at the ages we have studied. This is in keeping with observations reported by Blurton-Jones (1967), in which he finds no evidence of a dominance hierarchy in children age 5 and younger. Further, Omark, Omark, and Edelman (1973), observing 4–8-year-olds, report very little relationship between observed dominance behavior on the playground and which child, of a pair, takes charge in solving a joint task. Who grabs toys, or who wins fights, may at this age very well be indications of some system other than that of a dominance hierarchy.

TABLE 3
ANOVA: Approach Distance, Age Status Differential

SOURCE	df	MS	F
Sex (A)*	1	2.344	.056
Order	1	162.760	3.882
Sex (A) × Order	1	10.010	.239
Error	12	41.927	
Age (G)**	2	5.469	1.015
Sex (A) × Age (G)	2	8.469	1.573
Order × Age (G)	2	26.135	4.853†
Sex (A) × Order × Age (G)	2	8.635	1.603
Error	24	5.385	
Sex (G)	1	14.260	.484
Sex (A) × Sex (G)	1	33.844	1.150
Order × Sex (G)	1	.094	.003
Sex (A) × Order × Sex (G)	1	270.010	9.171†
Error	12	29.441	
Age (G) × Sex (G)	2	11.698	.965
Sex (A) × Age (G) × Sex (G)	2	11.906	.982
Order × Age (G) × Sex (G)	2	6.781	.559
Sex(A) × Order × Age(G) × Sex(G)	2	1.073	.088
Error	24	12.128	

* (A) = Approaching child.
** (G) = Goal child.
† $p < .025$.

Our second, and probably most important finding, is that children stay further away and orient their bodies away from opposite-sexed children. This was true, in the two experiments that employed cross-sexed approaches, for approachers of *both sexes and at all ages*.

There are two conclusions which I think we can draw from this finding. The first is that by age 3, children seem to have acquired a sex label for themselves, and the second is that by age 3, children can discriminate the sex of their peers. The first finding is consistent with the work by Money (Money, Hampson & Hampson, 1957), and by Gesell (Gesell et al., 1940) on the acquisition of gender identity. It is usually assumed, however, that a correct assessment of other children's sex comes rather later than we have found it. At this age, the utilization of a nonverbal measurement such as we have reported, may prove more sensitive than direct questioning in assessing children's awareness of the sex of their peers.

Just as intriguing and perhaps more so, is that children consistently *avoid* children of the opposite sex. This is in keeping with findings that, in this age range, children direct more positive social reinforcement to same-sexed peers (Charlesworth and Hartup, 1967) and that they stay further from opposite-

TABLE 4

ANOVA: Angular Distance, Age Status Differential

SOURCE	df	MS	F
Sex (A)*	1	.094	.223
Order	1	1.760	4.190
Sex (A) × Order	1	.010	.025
Error	12	.420	
Age (G)**	2	.948	1.560
Sex (A) × Age (G)	2	1.156	1.903
Order × Age (G)	2	1.135	1.869
Sex (A) × Order × Age	2	.635	1.046
Error	24	.608	
Sex (G)	1	1.260	2.729
Sex (A) × Sex (G)	1	3.010	6.519†
Order × Sex (G)	1	.260	.564
Sex (A) × Order × Sex (G)	1	1.760	3.812
Error	12	.462	
Age (G) × Sex (G)	2	1.823	3.107
Sex (A) × Age (G) × Sex (G)	2	1.698	2.893
Order × Age (G) × Sex (G)	2	1.135	1.935
Sex(A) × Order × Age(G) × Sex(G)	2	.135	.231
Error	24	.587	

* (A) = Approaching child.
** (G) = Goal child.
† $p < .025$.

sexed peers in the playground (Langibis et al., 1973; Omark et al., 1973). This avoidance is not generally thought to begin until much later, in middle childhood, after which it becomes intense in preadolescence. In our study, however, there were quite a few instances in which the children verbally expressed their contempt for children of the opposite sex, so the intense avoidance may very well be present long before we would expect it.

From the ethological point of view, we consider these findings relevant to the origin and the ontogeny of the nonverbal signal systems regulating that very important sphere of human activity: interaction between the sexes. We are now planning to chart the development of these behaviors, as well as that of facial expressions and gestures, through middle childhood and adolescence, to observe and describe the changing signal systems which constitute inter-sex behavior.

References

BLURTON-JONES, N. in D. Morris (Ed.), *Primate Ethology*. London: Weidenfeld Nicholson, 1967. Pp. 347–368.

CHARLESWORTH, R. & HARTUP, W. W. Positive social reinforcement in the nursery school peer group. *Child Development*, 1967, **38**, 993–1002.

Gesell, A., Halverson, H. M., Thompson, H., Ilg, F. L. Cosiner, B. H., Ames, L. B., & Amatruda, C. S. *The first five years of life: A guide to the study of the preschool child.* New York: Harper & Row, 1940.

Langibis, J. H., Gottfried, N. W., & Seay, B. The influence of sex of peer on the social behavior of preschool children. *Developmental Psychology,* 1973, **8,** 93–98.

Money, J., Hampson, J., & Hampson, J. Imprinting and the establishment of gender role. *Archives of Neurology and Psychiatry* 1957, **77,** 333–336.

Omark, D. R., Omark, M., & Edelman, M. Dominance hierarchies in young children. Paper presented at the International Congress of Anthropological and Ethnological Sciences, Chicago, 1973.

Stern, D. & Bender, E. An ethological study of children approaching a strange adult: sex differences. In R. Friedman, R. Richart, & R. Vandewiele (Eds.) *Sex differences in behavior.* New York: Wiley, 1974. 233–258.

The Early Development of Conceptual Perspective-Taking

Daniel G. Mossler, Mark T. Greenberg, and Robert S. Marvin
UNIVERSITY OF VIRGINIA

Role-taking or perspective-taking refers to the "... process by which the individual somehow cognizes, apprehends, or grasps ... certain attributes of the other person" (Flavell et al., 1968, p. 5). These attributes can include another persons' visual percepts, thoughts, desires, intentions, etc. The focus of this investigation was on conceptual rather than perceptual perspective-taking. Our aim was to find out when children correctly infer what another person *thinks* or *knows* rather than what another person *sees* or *hears*. Specifically, the purpose of this study was to determine the age at which children are able to engage in a simple form of conceptual perspective-taking.

The literature is unclear as to when children are first able to infer another person's state of knowledge. Some of the research has found that children younger than 7 years of age are not able to take another's perspective. Typically, young children respond egocentrically; they do not differentiate their viewpoint from another's viewpoint. For example, Flavell (Apple-dog story, 1968) and Chandler (Droodles task, 1973) used tasks in which the child had access to information not available to the other person, and in which the child was required to make an inference about the other's restricted conceptual viewpoint. They found children unable to engage in non-egocentric perspective-taking until ages 9 and 7, respectively. The younger children egocentrically inferred that the other person's knowledge of the story was the same as his own.

This body of research has been criticized for using complex stimuli and response demands which are beyond the capabilities of young children (Borke,

Presented at meetings of The Society for Research in Child Development, Denver, 1975. A brief report, titled "Conceptual Perspective-Taking in 2–6-Year-Old Children," appeared in *Developmental Psychology*, 1976, **12,** 85–86. Printed by permission.

1971; Marvin, 1972). Thus, in these complex tasks, an egocentric response could indicate either a lack of perspective-taking skills, or a lack of some other cognitive skill required by the task. Using less complex stimuli and less complex response demands, a few studies have found evidence of basic perspective-taking abilities in children as young as three or four years of age. For example, Borke (1971) had children select a picture to match the affective state of a child in a story. She found that children as young as three years of age correctly anticipate the actor's feelings in certain simple contexts. Some of these studies have in turn been criticized on the grounds that they in fact may not be measuring perspective-taking. As Chandler states, "Non-egocentric thought, in the sense intended by Piaget (1956), is not simply a synonym for accurate social judgment but implies the ability to anticipate what someone else might think or feel precisely when these thoughts and feelings are different from one's own. Without this important qualification, egocentric and non-egocentric thought result in the same outcome and their measurement is hopelessly confounded" (1972, p. 105).

Therefore, to ensure that perspective-taking is required for correct performance, the task must be constructed such that the child's perspective is *demonstrably* different from that of the other. The task must contain a minimum amount of "shared cultural perspective." According to Chandler (1973) the term "shared cultural perspective" refers to the amount of shared knowledge between the subject and the other person. For example, a young child can accurately predict that a person at a birthday party will be happy. He need not engage in perspective-taking to correctly anticipate the other's feelings, since it is part of our shared knowledge that anyone at a birthday party (including the child himself) is probably happy.

Although Chandler presented this as an absolute quality, which is either absent or present, it is more useful to think of shared knowledge as a continuum along which perspective-taking situations may vary. Any such situation must involve a minimum of shared knowledge. Clearly, the child must attribute some shared qualities to the other person, i.e., that the other can think, that the other can hear, that the other can speak, and so on.

In a review of the social-cognition literature, Shantz (in press) concludes that the simpler the tasks are made, the earlier investigators are able to find evidence of these abilities. However, she questions whether these investigations are actually measuring perspective-taking or some other related abilities. In other words, the research which is most clearly measuring perspective-taking, by having demonstrably different viewpoints, is confounded with the use of complex stimuli and response demands. On the other hand, the research using stimuli and less complex response demands may not really be measuring perspective-taking at all.

These considerations are taken into account in this study. We investigated young children's abilities to engage in conceptual perspective-taking using a less complex variation of Flavell's privileged-information situation. While maintaining the requirement of demonstrably different viewpoints, we used short videotaped stories requiring the child to make a yes-no inference about the other's restricted viewpoint. To make the task as naturalistic as possible, the task was administered in the child's home using the mother as the other person.

Eighty middle-class children between the age of $2\frac{1}{2}$ and $6\frac{1}{2}$ years balanced for sex were used in this study. The subjects included 10 2-year-olds ($\bar{X} = 2:8$), 20 3-year-olds ($\bar{X} = 3:5\frac{1}{2}$), 20 4-year-olds ($\bar{X} = 4:6$) 20 5-year-olds ($\bar{X} = 5:6$), and 10 6-year-olds ($\bar{X} = 6:4$).

The children were presented with two videotaped stories containing one or two bits of information. In one story, the videotape showed a boy walking into a house; the audio stated, "This boy is going into his grandmother's house." In the second story, the videotape showed a boy getting up from a table and walking up to his mother; the audio contained his direct request for a cookie. The order of presentation of the stories was counterbalanced. The actual procedure was as follows.

The experimenter spent 20–30 minutes playing with the child and showing him the equipment. Then the experimenter told the child that they were going to play a T.V. game. The experimenter asked the mother to wait in the other room. With the mother out of the room, the child was shown one of the stories. He was then questioned to make sure that he understood and knew the correct bit of information about the story. Interestingly, when asked "What happened on the T.V.?", most children said, "It went off!" The child was then asked, "Was the boy going into the house?" and "Whose house was the boy going into?"

The experimenter then went into the other room and brought back the mother. The child was told; "Now you and mommy are going to watch the story again, but this time I am going to turn the sound down." The experimenter made sure that the child watched as he turned the sound down. The child and the mother were then shown the same story without the audio portion. The experimenter then said to the child, "Now I am going to ask you some questions about what your *mommy* thinks." The child was questioned about his mother's knowledge of both the audio and video portions of the story. With respect to the grandmother story, the child was asked; "Does your mommy think the boy was going into a house?" and "Does your mommy know whose house the boy was going into?" The child was then asked to justify his response. "How does your mommy know that?" or "How come she doesn't know?" The same full procedure was repeated for the second story. At the end of the questioning procedure for the last story, the child was asked. "Did your mommy see the same thing that you saw?" and "Did your mommy hear the same thing that you heard?"

The child's responses were coded as either egocentric or non-egocentric on the following basis. A child was given a non-egocentric score for the grandmother–house story if he realized that his mother knew the boy went into a house (yes), but that she did not know whose house (no). For the cookie story, a child was given a non-egocentric score if he realized that his mommy knew the boy was sitting at a table (yes), but that his mother did not know what the boy asked for (no). For the last set of questions, a child was given a non-egocentric score if he realized that his mother saw the same thing that he saw (yes), but that she did not hear the same thing that he heard (no). The justifications were scored as correct if the child said that his mother did not know because either the sound was turned down, or she was out of the room.

Since the questions were highly correlated (Tetrachoric coefficients .90–.93), they were collapsed across to give one overall egocentric or non-egocentric score. If the child answered none or only one of the three questions non-egocentrically, he was scored as egocentric. If however, the child answered either two or three of the questions non-egocentrically, he received a non-egocentric overall score. Additionally, a child received a justified or unjustified overall score depending on whether or not he answered a greater than chance proportion of the justifications correctly.

A five by two chi-square analysis was performed on both the perspective-taking questions and the justifications. With respect to the perspective-taking questions, a chi-square value of 50.72, p < .001 demonstrated that children of different ages performed differentially on the task.

None of the 2-year-olds performed non-egocentrically.[1] Only one of the 20 3-year-olds answered two or more questions non-egocentrically. However, 13 of the 4-year-olds and 18 of the 5-year-olds responded in a non-egocentric fashion. All of the 6-year-olds responded non-egocentrically. Thus the major age difference in this task was at 4 years of age, with more than half of the 4-year-olds answering in a non-egocentric fashion.

Age trend with respect to the justifications was somewhat different. A chi-square value of 34.55, p < .001 indicated that children responded differently depending on their age. None of the 2- or 3-year-olds correctly justified his answer. Eight of the 20 4-year-olds responded correctly as did 12 of the 20 5-year-olds. Nine of the 10 6-year-olds justified their responses correctly. Thus, the shift for veridical performance on the perspective-taking questions was more rapid and complete compared to the shift for correct performance on the justifications.

Since we used a simplified task with minimal memory constraints and minimal response demands, we can be more confident that a failure to perspective-take was not due to the task complexity. On the other hand, we have constructed a situation with demonstrably different perspectives between the child and his mother. Therefore we can be more certain that a child who is characterized as non-egocentric has some basic perspective-taking skills.

The results of this study indicate that a majority of children as young as four years of age are able to make inferences about another's conceptual points of view, i.e., about another's thoughts or states of knowledge. Obviously in any

TABLE 1

Responses to Perspective-Taking Questions and Justification Questions

	AGE IN YEARS					
RESPONSES	2	3	4	5	6	
Egocentric	10	19	7	2	0	$\chi^2 = 50.72; p < .001$
Non-egocentric	0	1	13	18	10	
Unjustified	10	20	12	8	1	$\chi^2 = 34.55; p < .001$
Justified	0	0	8	12	9	

[1] Six of the 10 2-year-olds were administered only one videotape sequence as they could not follow the task at all.

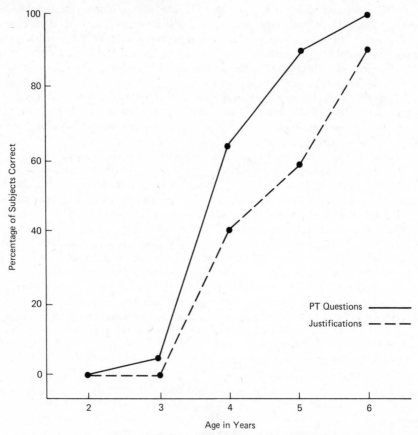

FIGURE 1.   *Responses to audio-visual task.*

situation there are a wide variety of cues that children can use as a basis for making inferences about others' perspectives. These cues may be, among others, spatial, temporal, verbal, or non-verbal, or they may be purely situational. In our research we are currently attempting to isolate the kinds of cues that children use in this particular perspective-taking situation. The kinds of questions we are concerned with are: Do children use a multiplicity of cues? Does the reliance on any one type of cue change with age? What are the first cues used by children in perspective-taking?

In concluding, we would like to examine the results of this study in the light of certain aspects of Piaget's theory. Piaget (1956) described perspective-taking as a concrete operational ability which involves reversibility and co-ordination of perspectives. According to Piaget, these abilities are typically unavailable to children younger than 7 years of age.

However, Piaget describes the sub-period between 4 and 7 years of age as the "intuitive period." Children in this subperiod periodically decenter and show a gradual co-ordination of representative relations.

Almost all of our 4-, 5- and 6-year-old children could be so characterized. A further problem is that the ability to perform correctly on a perspective-taking task does not in and of itself constitute concrete operations. The hallmark of concrete operations is the formation of highly organized representational cognitive structures which are reversible, and are integrated with other, similar, structures. With reference to the difference in results between correct perspective-taking and correct justification, it appears that a majority of the 4-year-olds in this sample, and almost all of the 5- and 6-year-olds in this sample, possess at least the ability to engage in reversible representational operations, and further that a majority of these children are able to integrate their perspective-taking into a justified, explanatory framework. There is, however, a sizable minority of 4- and 5-year-olds who do not integrate their perspective-taking into a justified explanatory framework. This suggests two things: first that operational reversibility may be a necessary, but not sufficient, criterion for concrete operations; second, that the criterion of numerous operations being organized *together* may be a more valid criterion. In other words, it may be necessary to reassess our notions of the intuitive and concrete operational periods, and of the transition from one to the other.

References

BORKE, H. Interpersonal perception of young children: Egocentrism or empathy? *Developmental Psychology*, 1971, 5, 263–269.

CHANDLER, M. J., and GREENSPAN, S. Ersatz egocentrism: A reply to H. Borke. *Developmental Psychology*, 1972, 7, 104–106.

CHANDLER, M. J. Role-theory and developmental research. Paper presented at the American Psychological Association, Montreal, 1973.

FLAVELL, J. H., BOTKIN, P. T., FRY, C. L., WRIGHT, J. W., and JARVIS, P. E. *The Development of Role-Taking and Communication Skills in Children*. New York: John Wiley & Sons, 1968.

MARVIN, R. S. Attachment- exploratory- and communicative-behavior of 2, 3, and 4-year-old children. Unpublished Ph.D. Dissertation, University of Chicago, 1972.

PIAGET, J. *The Psychology of Intelligence*. London: Routledge and Kegan Paul, 1950.

PIAGET, J. and INHELDER, B. *The Child's Conception of Space*. London: Routledge & Kegan Paul, 1956.

SHANTZ, C. U. The development of social cognition. In *Review of Child Development Research*, Vol. 5, in press.

The Development of Empathy in Chinese and American Children Between Three and Six Years of Age: A Cross-Culture Study *

Helene Borke

CARNEGIE-MELLON UNIVERSITY

A series of social interaction situations representing the four emotions of happy, afraid, sad, and angry were administered to 288 American children and 288 Chinese children. Twenty-four girls and 24 boys, half from middle-class families and half from disadvantaged families, were tested at 6-month intervals between 3 and 6 years of age. Children from both cultural groups exhibited similar overall trends in their ability to recognize other people's emotional responses. By 3 years of age, the majority of American and Chinese children could differentiate between happy and unhappy reactions in other people. Perception of afraid, sad, and angry feelings developed somewhat later and appeared to be influenced by social learning. This cross-cultural study confirms the results of a previous investigation that very young children are capable of empathic responses. The awareness of other people's feelings by young children from very different cultural backgrounds suggests that empathy may be a basic human characteristic related to social adaptation.

Empathy in its most advanced stage is the ability to perceive the world from the perspective of the other. Although awareness of another person's view point is essential for effective interpersonal communication, very little is known about the early development of empathic ability. Until recently, most of the available evidence suggested that young children are primarily egocentric and that sociocentric thinking seldom appears before early adolescence (Burns & Cavey, 1957; Chandler & Greenspan, 1972; Flapan, 1968; Flavell, Botkin, & Fry, 1968; Freud, 1965; Gollin, 1958, Piaget, 1926, 1928, 1967; Werner, 1948).

In two previous papers (Borke, 1971, 1972), the present author questioned the conclusion that young children are egocentric and unable to take another person's perspective. Data from an earlier study (Borke, 1971) indicated that by 3 years of age children are capable of differentiating between happy and unhappy responses in other people and can recognize social situations associated with these responses. An alternate hypothesis was proposed that the development of empathy is a continuous process which proceeds through a series of hierarchical stages closely related to cognitive development. Empathy is manifested in very young children as a conscious awareness that other people have feelings which are different from their own and culminates during adolescence in what Piaget describes as truly relativistic thinking, thinking that involves the ability

From *Developmental Psychology*, 1973, 9, 102–108. Copyright © 1973 by The American Psychological Association. Reprinted by permission.

* The author would like to thank Hwang Chien-hou, Chairman of the Psychology Department, National Taiwan Normal University, and Sarah Su, Professor of Child Development, National Taiwan Normal University, for their help in collecting the data for this study and for the valuable insights they provided on the early socialization of Chinese children. This investigation was supported by United States Public Health Service Grant MH 17778–01.

to put oneself in another person's place and see the world through that person's eyes.

Since the original research was based on a small sample of middle-class American children (Borke, 1971), the effects of cultural and social class variables were not investigated. A cross-cultural study which controlled for social class differences was conducted to provide information about (*a*) the relationship between the development of empathic ability and specific social class and cultural influences and (*b*) the universality of development of empathic awareness. The study compared very young Chinese and American children. Both the Chinese and American cultures emphasize the central importance of the family, but in each of these societies socialization occurs within the context of very different cultural traditions. The Chinese family encourages mutual dependence and social conformity, whereas the American family stresses self-reliance, and individual freedom (Murphy & Murphy, 1968).

METHOD

Several steps were taken to insure that the instrument employed to measure empathy would be as free as possible of cultural bias. First, American kindergarten children in the United States and Chinese kindergarten children in Taiwan were asked to describe the kinds of situations that might make them feel happy, afraid, sad, or angry. The children's spontaneous comments were tape recorded and categorized. Responses common to both groups were used as the basis for constructing two sets of stories: (*a*) stories describing general situations that might make a child feel happy, afraid, sad, or angry and (*b*) stories describing situations in which the child being tested does something that might cause another child to feel happy, afraid, sad, or angry.

These two sets of stories were then administered to 87 Chinese and 96 American second graders. The children were asked to indicate how another individual might feel in each situation by selecting one of four stylized faces depicting the emotions of happy, afraid, sad, or angry. Ekman, Sorenson, and Friesen's (1969) study, indicating pancultural elements in the identification of emotions from facial expressions, provided the research basis for presenting the stylized faces. A chi-square analysis was used to determine which stories had responses that differed from a random-classification pattern. The four stories which showed the highest agreement among children's responses in both cultural groups were selected for each of the affective categories (i.e., happy, afraid, sad, and angry). Also selected were four situations which showed high agreement among children's responses in one cultural group but not in the other and three situations which showed high variability of responses for the children in both cultural groups.

The final set of 23 stories was administered to 288 Chinese and 288 American children. Half of the children in each group were from middle-class families and half were from disadvantaged families. The children were also equally divided between the two sexes. Twelve girls and 12 boys from similar socioeconomic and cultural backgrounds were tested for each 6-month interval between 3 and 6 years of age (i.e., 3–3.5, 3.5–4, 4–4.5, 4.5–5, 5–5.5, 5.5–6).

The 3- to 5-year-old American and Chinese middle-class children who participated in this study all attended private nursery schools. The children in the 5- to 6-year old range were selected from public school kindergartens in predominantly middle-class neighborhoods. The American 3- to 5-year-old children in the disadvantaged group attended either Head Start or child care programs supported by federal funds. The 5- to 6-year-old American youngsters went to kindergartens in the same elementary schools that provided the educational programs for the younger children. The Chinese preschool children described as lower class attended special workers' preschools supported by the government. The 5- to 6-year-old Chinese youngsters were selected from schools located in working-class neighborhoods.

The task was administered individually to the children in their schools. The American children were tested by graduate students under the supervision of the principal investigator; the Chinese children were tested by college psychology majors in their senior year. Sarah Su, Professor of Child Development, National Taiwan Normal University, translated the test materials, established liasons with the cooperating schools, and supervised the students who did the testing.

The testing procedure used by all of the examiners consisted of first asking the children to identify drawings of faces representing the four basic emotions of happy, afraid, sad, and angry. After helping the children identify each of the faces, the examiners presented the first set of stories. Each story in this set was accompanied by a picture of a child with a blank face engaged in the described activity. The children were asked to complete the pictures by selecting the face that best showed how the child in the story felt. The faces were presented in random order, and with each presentation the examiners again identified the emotions for the youngsters. The same procedure was followed for the second set of stories involving peer interactions except that a single picture of a youngster standing was used for all of the stories.

RESULTS

Chinese and American children between 3 and 6 years of age were compared for number of correct perceptions of happy, afraid, sad, or angry social situations. An analysis of variance design was used to evaluate the relative effects of six variables: sex, status, nationality, age, emotion, and test part. Five of the six variables, sex, status, nationality, age, and emotion, contributed significantly to the variance ($p < .01$). There were no significant differences between the two test parts. The first-order interactions significant at the .01 level were status and emotion, nationality and emotion, nationality and age, and emotion and age. The significant second-order interactions were status, nationality, and emotion; and status, nationality, and age (see Table 1).

American and Chinese children demonstrated similar overall trends in their ability to identify happy, afraid, sad, and angry situation (see Table 2). Recognition of these four types of emotional situations generally increased with age (see Figure 1). Perceptions of happy situations showed only a small increment since by 3 to 3.5 years of age over 90% of the American and Chinese middle- and lower-class children perceived the happy situations correctly (see Tables 3 and 4).

TABLE 1

Analysis of Variance Comparing Effects of Sex, Socio-economic Status, Nationality, Test Part, Emotion, and Age on the Ability to Perceive Other People's Feelings in Social Situations

SOURCE	df	MS	F
Sex (A)	1	3.84	9.86**
Status (B)	1	13.24	34.02**
Nationality (C)	1	5.49	14.10**
Test part (D)	1	.76	1.94
Emotion (E)	3	177.65	456.43**
Age (F)	5	15.91	40.87**
A × B	1	.16	.41
A × C	1	.05	.13
A × D	1	.01	.01
A × E	3	.27	.71
A × F	5	.38	.97
B × C	1	1.42	3.66
B × D	1	1.64	4.22
B × E	3	1.97	5.06**
B × F	5	1.11	2.86
C × D	1	.14	.35
C × E	3	1.65	4.23**
C × F	5	2.06	5.30**
D × E	3	1.23	3.16
D × F	5	.08	.21
E × F	15	3.82	9.81**
A × F × C*	1	1.42	3.66
B × C × E	3	8.25	21.19**
B × C × F	5	1.20	3.07**
Residual	4533	.39	
Total	4607		

* Only three-way interactions with mean squares substantially above those for the higher-order interactions were included. The remaining were pooled into the residual term.
** $p < .01$.

Identification of fearful situations showed the greatest improvement with age. Recognition of fearful situations increased from an average of 50% correct responses between 3 and 3.5 years of age to over 90% correct responses by age 5 (see Figure 1). There was considerable variation in the younger children's ability to recognize fearful situations. Seventy percent of the Chinese middle-class children correctly identified the afraid situations as early as 3 to 3.5 years of age, as compared with only 40% of the American middle-class children in this youngest age group. The American middle- and lower-class children caught up with the Chinese middle-class youngsters by age 4 to 4.5, but the Chinese lower-class children remained behind in their ability to recognize fearful situations until 5.5 to 6 years of age (see Tables 3 and 4).

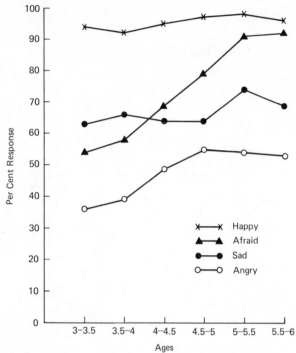

FIGURE 1.   *Percentage of correct responses of American and Chinese children at various age levels to social interaction situations.*

The children's recognition of sad situations appeared to increase only slightly with age (see Figure 1). The apparent lack of improvement in the children's accuracy of perception of sad situations stemmed from cultural and social class differences which cancelled each other out when the data from the American and Chinese children were combined. In the youngest age group, 3 to 3.5 years, middle-class and lower-class Chinese children correctly identified

TABLE 2

Percentage of Correct Responses by American and Chinese Children to Social Interaction Situations

NATIONALITY	SOCIAL CLASS	INTERACTION SITUATION			
		Happy	Afraid	Sad	Angry
American	Middle	96	73	79	51
	Lower	97	75	58	54
	Average	96	74	69	53
Chinese	Middle	96	80	66	51
	Lower	93	68	70	36
	Average	95	74	68	44

TABLE 3

Percentage of Correct Responses by Middle- and Lower-Class American Children at Various Age Levels to Social Interaction Situations

| | SOCIAL INTERACTION SITUATION | | | | | | | |
| | Happy | | Afraid | | Sad | | Angry | |
AGE	Middle Class	Lower Class	Middle Class	Lower Class	Middle Class	Lower Class	Middle Class	Lower Class
3.0–3.5	93	97	40	52	57	52	32	47
3.5–4.0	91	96	48	63	78	52	40	48
4.0–4.5	97	97	71	74	77	52	57	52
4.5–5.0	97	97	84	78	84	53	65	62
5.0–5.5	98	98	96	93	88	74	60	54
5.5–6.0	99	95	97	91	88	63	53	59

67% and 76%, respectively, of the sad situations as compared with American middle-class and lower-class youngsters of the same age who recognized the sad situations only slightly more than 50% of the time. At the older age levels, American middle-class children showed a dramatic improvement in their ability to identify sad situations reaching 88% accuracy by 6 years. The Chinese children, in contrast, showed a slight decrease with age in the accuracy of their perception of sad situation (see Tables 3 and 4).

Chinese and American children consistently perceived angry responses less accurately than any of the other emotions (see Figure 1). There was, however, a significant increase with age in the children's ability to identify angry situations. The Chinese lower-class children had more difficulty recognizing the angry

TABLE 4

Percentage of Correct Responses by Middle- and Lower-Class Chinese Children at Various Age Levels to Social Interaction Situations

| | SOCIAL INTERACTION SITUATION | | | | | | | |
| | Happy | | Afraid | | Sad | | Angry | |
AGE	Middle Class	Lower Class	Middle Class	Lower Class	Middle Class	Lower Class	Middle Class	Lower Class
3.0–3.5	96	91	70	54	67	76	38	27
3.5–4.0	93	90	68	52	76	84	40	28
4.0–4.5	94	91	75	52	69	55	51	38
4.5–5.0	98	96	83	71	61	62	58	38
5.0–5.5	96	99	94	82	53	79	62	42
5.5–6.0	96	94	87	94	67	59	57	44

situations than the children in any of the other groups (see Tables 3 and 4).

In both cultures, girls were more accurate than boys in their ability to perceive social situations ($\bar{X} = 1.44$ for girls and 1.39 for boys). There were no significant interactions between sex and any of the other variables (i.e., nationality, status, age, or emotion). Separate analyses of the four emotions—happy, afraid, sad, and angry—also showed no significant differences between girls and boys.

DISCUSSION

A comparison of very young American and Chinese children revealed basic similarities between the two groups in the early development of empathic awareness. Chinese and American children by 3 to 3.5 years of age were able to differentiate easily between social situations which evoke happy and unhappy responses in other people. These results are consistent with the findings reported in a previous study (Borke, 1971) and provide further evidence that the capacity for social sensitivity and empathic awareness develops at a very early age.

Recognition of afraid, sad, and angry emotions appeared to be influenced to a considerable extent by the interaction of social class and cultural factors. Chinese middle-class youngsters between 3 and 3.5 years of age were far more accurate in identifying fearful situations than Chinese lower-class children or American middle- or lower-class children in the same age range. This increased awareness of fearful situations by very young Chinese middle-class children may reflect the overprotective tendencies of Chinese middle-class parents, who frequently set limits on their youngsters' active exploratory behavior because they are afraid the children will hurt themselves. American middle-class children between 3 and 3.5 years of age experienced the greatest difficulty recognizing fearful situations. This finding would be consistent with the attitudes of American middle-class parents, who encourage active play and self-reliance in their young children and tend to minimize the possibility of danger or getting hurt. The rapid increase with age in the ability of American middle-class children to recognize fearful situations supports the results of a previous study (Borke, 1971). In this earlier paper, it was suggested that as middle-class American children grow older, they learn about situations which evoke fear responses through exposure to books and television as well as their own experiences. Interestingly enough, the Chinese lower-class children, for whom books and television are least accessible, lagged behind the other youngsters in their recognition of fearful situations.

The ability of Chinese middle-class and lower-class youngsters between 3 and 4 years of age to recognize sad situations more accurately than American middle- or lower-class children of the same age possibly reflects the emphasis within the Chinese culture on feeling "shameful" or "losing face." The American middle-class children showed a considerable increase with age in their ability to recognize sad situations. This trend was also observed in previous studies (Borke, 1971; Borke & Su, 1972) and may be related to the greater social acceptability of feeling sad between 4 and 7 years of age when American middle-class children, more so than the children in any of the other three groups, are actively engaged in the task of developing inner controls over their unacceptable feelings.

American and Chinese children at all age levels had the greatest difficulty identifying angry situations. Since young children certainly experience anger, these results suggest that in both the American and Chinese societies children become aware of the unacceptability of expressing angry feelings at a very early age. The greater inability of lower-class Chinese children to perceive angry responses in others as compared with middle-class Chinese children and middle-class and lower-class American children may be related to the extreme subservience expected of lower-class individuals in the Chinese society. The socialization of lower-class Chinese children to accept this role apparently begins quite early.

An analysis of the children's incorrect responses to the sad and angry situations indicated that the majority of American and Chinese youngsters gave "angry" as their alternate response to sad situations and "sad" as their alternate response to angry situations. Only 10% of all incorrect responses to the sad and angry situations fell in other categories. The children's inability to differentiate sharply between sad and angry situations also occurred in a previous study (Borke, 1971). At that time, three possible explanations were suggested: (a) ambiguity in the stories selected, (b) stronger conflict associated with feeling sad and, especially, angry in our society as compared with feeling happy or afraid, (c) individual differences in responding to frustration, with some people having a greater tendency to react with anger and others to react by feeling sad.

Although in the present study every effort was made to select situations which the majority of the children in both cultural groups would perceive as predominantly sad or angry, there was still considerable overlap in the perception of these two emotions. The cumulative evidence from this and previous investigations (Borke, 1971; Borke & Su, 1972) suggests that any situation which has the potential for either a sad or angry response generally has the potential for both (i.e., an individual might initially feel sad because someone close was leaving but later experience anger over the frustration caused by the separation). The greater difficulty experienced by the children from both cultural backgrounds in identifying angry situations as compared to happy, afraid, and sad situations supports the possibility that stronger conflict is associated with feeling angry in both the American and Chinese societies. There was also evidence that some individuals respond to frustration primarily by feeling angry and others by feeling sad. Twenty-four percent of the American and Chinese children gave "sad" as their primary response to all of the sad and angry stories and 7% gave "angry" as their primary response. This indicates that almost one third of the youngsters had a previously established set which influenced their perception of sad and angry situations. The multiplicity of factors operating in the perception of sad and angry responses suggests that the ability to differentiate between sad and angry reactions in other people is a considerably more complex process than the identification of happy or fear responses.

The relationship of empathic ability to sex differences has been considered in a number of studies. The results are contradictory with some researchers reporting differences (Dimitrovsky, 1964; Gollin, 1958) and other finding no difference (Borke, 1971; Feshback & Roe, 1968; Rothenberg, 1970; Walton 1936). In the present study, sex differences appeared as a significant variable but contributed the least to the overall variance. One possible conclusion is that any significant relationship which might exist between empathic ability and sex is very small and can easily be affected by slight variations in the populations from which the samples are drawn.

This cross-cultural research supports the results of previous studies showing that very young children are capable of empathic awareness. The ability to differentiate between happy and unhappy responses in other people appears to be well established in both Chinese and American youngsters by 3 years of age. Some of the social class and cultural differences in the children's perceptions of fearful, sad, and angry reactions seem to indicate that social learning is an important factor in the ability to recognize other people's feelings. The presence of empathic awareness in young children from very different cultural backgrounds suggests that empathy may well be a basic human characteristic related to social adaptation.

References

Borke, H. Interpersonal perception of young children: Egocentrism or empathy? *Developmental Psychology*, 1971, 5, 263–269.

Borke, H. Chandler and Greenspan's "ersatz egocentrism": A rejoinder. *Developmental Psychology*, 1972, 7, 107–109.

Borke, H., & Su, S. Perception of emotional responses to social interactions by Chinese and American children. *Journal of Cross Cultural Psychology*, 1972, 3, 309–314.

Burns, N., & Cavey, L. Age differences in empathic ability among children. *Canadian Journal of Psychology*, 1957, 11, 227–230.

Chandler, M. J., & Greenspan, S. Ersatz egocentrism: A reply to H. Borke. *Developmental Psychology*, 1972, 7, 104–106.

Dimitrovsky, L. The ability to identify the emotional meanings of vocal expressions at successive age levels. In J. R. Davitz (Ed.), *The communication of emotional meaning*. New York: McGraw-Hill, 1964.

Ekman, P., Sorenson, E. R., & Friesen, W. V. Pan-cultural elements in facial displays of emotion. *Science*, 1969, 164, 80–88.

Feshbach, N. D., & Roe, K. Empathy in six and seven year olds. *Child Development*, 1968, 39, 133–145.

Flapan, D. *Children's understanding of social interaction*. New York: Teachers College Press, 1968.

Flavell, J. H., Botkin, P. T., & Fry, C. L., Jr. *The development of role-taking and communication skills in young children*. New York: Wiley, 1968.

Freud, A. *Normality and pathology in childhood*. New York: International Universities Press, 1965.

Gollin, E. S. Organizational characteristics of social judgment: A developmental investigation. *Journal of Personality*, 1958, 26, 139–154.

Murphy, G., & Murphy, L. B. *Asian psychology*. New York: Basic Books, 1968.

Piaget, J. *The language and thought of the child*. New York: Harcourt-Brace, 1926.

Piaget, J. *Judgment and reasoning in the child*. New York: Harcourt-Brace, 1928.

Piaget, J. *Six psychological studies*. New York: Random House, 1967.

Rothenberg, B. Children's social sensitivity and the relationship to interpersonal competence, intrapersonal comfort, and intellectual level. *Developmental Psychology*, 1970, 2, 335–350.

WALTON, W. E. Empathic responses in children. *Psychological Monographs*, 1936, 48(1, Whole No. 213).

WERNER, H. *Comparative psychology of mental development*. New York: International Universities Press, 1958.

The Relation of Individual Temperament to Initial Social Behavior

Jeannie L. Lewis
THE OHIO STATE UNIVERSITY

Though the area of peer relations has been considered important for social adjustment, it has rarely been an area for research into individual differences— particularly in its very early stages. I conducted, in 1973, an exploratory study to search for a relation between a child's behavioral individuality or temperament in the home setting and his initial adjustment to peers in a pre-school setting.

Individual temperament, the "how" of behavior—as conceptualized by the research team of Thomas, Chess, and Birch—has been found to relate to the development of pathology, match between parent and child, and style of school performance (Thomas, Chess, and Birch, 1963, 1968; Gordon and Thomas, 1967; Ross, 1966). Thomas, Chess, and Birch distinguished the "difficult" pattern of behavior (predominantly non-adaptable, intense, and tending to withdraw from novelty) which was found to antedate the development of behavior disorders. The "slow-to-warm-up" child (low in activity level, intensity, with withdrawal tendency) typically took some time to adapt to new experiences. Thus, temperamental characteristics have been found significant for the child's capacity to adapt to environmental changes and the quality of his reactions to novelty and stress. I expected individual differences in the child's style of behavior to be evident in the manner with which he adapted to the pre-school peer group—as a novel and potentially stressful setting. This study was also expected to shed light on cross-setting continuities and discontinuities in behavior, as well as what forms of social behavior prove to be meaningful psychological variables.

My subjects were fourteen children enrolled in Montessori pre-schools in the Columbus, Ohio, area. They ranged from 2 years 5 months to 3 years 10 months of age and were of upper-middle class background. Only three of the fourteen had had previous structured group experience—in short-term day care programs. From interviews with their mothers, I gathered data on each child's typical behavior in a variety of areas at home, within the concurrent six-month

Paper presented as part of the Symposium "Nature and Development of Early Peer Relations," Meetings of the American Psychological Association, New Orleans, 1974. Printed by permission.

period. According to the guidelines of Thomas, Chess, and Birch (1963), this material could be rated along the nine dimensions of temperament—activity level, rhythmicity, approach/withdrawal, adaptability, intensity, threshold, mood quality, distractibility, and persistence. I wanted to preserve the continuous nature of temperament, and so used the percent of ratings at one extreme of each dimension as the final score for each child. This had been done in a project related to the original Thomas, Chess, and Birch project (Terestman, 1964).

The three classrooms in which the subjects were enrolled had a teacher/child ratio of about 15/2. The observational data were collected after each child had attended pre-school for about two weeks. Data were taken for thirty-minute periods on four separate days during free play periods. Data consisted of time samplings (15 second intervals) of the social behavior of each individual subject —social distance and nature of activity. Through event sampling within these intervals, any social behaviors in visual, physical, and verbal modes were recorded. The visual behaviors included looking and watching. Physical behaviors recorded were approaches and actions toward other children (including giving, touching, pushing, taking). Verbal behavior included talking and play noises. To record these behaviors I chose to use a symbol system similar to that used by Blurton-Jones and other ethological researchers who have studied and catalogued pattern of children's social behavior (Blurton-Jones, 1972; McGrew, 1972; Leach, 1972). Each of the classes of behavior mentioned was given a 2–3 letter symbol and a notation as the object of the behavior (child or teacher). As an example, an approach to a child would be recorded "Apr-C." In the data analysis, behaviors toward children and teachers were separated. An average percent-time score for all these classes of behavior was derived for each subject. Also noted were expressions of positive mood and duration of continuous activity with materials.

It was possible, in looking at the results, to get an idea which classes of behavior might be meaningful psychological variables. I felt that the visual behaviors, in view of their lack of positive relationships to either temperament or other social behavior, plus the difficulty in recording them, were less crucial. Social distance (isolation versus proximity) proved to be highly related to both temperament and other behavioral variables, and was quite easy to record via time-sampling.

Three dimensions of temperament were found to be especially significant in relation to social behavior. These were activity level, approach/withdrawal tendency, and sensory threshold. The high activity level child, in addition to showing a great deal of physical activity, was also socially active toward both children and teachers. Children high on approach tendency were similarly attracted and active toward social objects. It seemed in general that the "easy" temperament characteristics (approach orientation, adaptability, and positive mood) were associated with high social proximity. The sensitive, low threshold child, conversely, tended toward isolation, social and physical restraint.

Physical activity level and approach tendency were found to be highly correlated across home and school setting. Distractibility at home was associated with many variations in activity and generally erratic social contact in pre-school. Regularity and persistence at home were associated with stable, constructive activity and a high level of verbal communication in the peer group. Expressions of positive mood showed a not quite significant correlation across settings. However, persistence at home was not related to a tendency to persevere in activities at school. Neither adaptability, intensity, or mood were found to be related to the classes of social behavior. It is likely that if qualitative measures of behavior had been chosen—such as the intensity of behavioral reactions, from mild to strong—these dimensions might have been found more significant.

The findings showed that individual characteristics of the child influence the nature of early social behavior, aside from previously researched factors of age, sex, and previous pre-school experience. The relations of temperament to competent, precocious behavior complement the volume of findings relating temperament to pathology.

The child's style of behavior may influence both his immediate reaction to novel setting and social objects, as well as the nature of past experiences he has accumulated. For example, the very active child is likely to have sought and experienced a multitude of social contacts in the past (probably building his level of social skill), as well as exhibiting a great deal of current energy and mobility in initial response to the pre-school setting. The vulnerability of the low threshold child to massive, novel stimulation may have restricted the extent of his past social experience, as well as currently fostering a reaction of withdrawal to block out overwhelming input.

Earlier research has focused on energy or activity level and sensitivity threshold as characteristics important in adaptation. These characteristics act to determine the magnitude of behavioral output, the processing of input, and individual tolerance level. This exploratory study suggests in addition that the typical direction of behavior (approach versus withdrawal) may be a further adaptive factor.

These results could also be looked at in terms of individual differences that predispose to precocity in social development. Edward Mueller (of this symposium) has proposed that early social contacts are object-centered—that interest in play objects may be the initial social attractants. If so, then high activity level or approach-oriented children could be expected to accumulate in greater quantity and intensity the experiences with materials that induce social interaction with peers. They would achieve social competence earlier and with less need for intervention or warm-up than the more inactive, withdrawn children.

So these results have implications for the theoretical contribution of individual differences to the course of social development. On the practical side, an understanding of temperamental contributions to social adjustment could help parents and educators to anticipate a child's reaction to the pre-school experience and aid in treatment.

Clearly this study must be interpreted and generalized cautiously in light of small sample size, limitations in the measures, and restricted social class range of the subjects. It is also possible that the special Montessori setting had an influence on the findings, as some emphasis on independent activity was apparent in the approach. It would be interesting to have follow-up information on the adaptation of the more sensitive, withdrawn children to determine whether their behavior reflected reactions to novelty or a more lasting style of social restraint. Though the sensitive child was weak on social participation, it did not appear that he was completely uninvolved. Sensitivity was associated with a great deal of watching behavior. Thus, these children in their own way appeared to be absorbing with interest what was happening around them. They were usually responsive to social overtures made by others, but took little initiative themselves. It seems likely that the focus on initiated behavior in this study (as opposed to social responsiveness) has given a rather one-sided picture of the sensitive child's social competence.

A larger sample size would permit a clearer look at possible sex differences in the pattern of results, as well as the effects of age and previous group experience.

This exploratory study has found that individual differences in the style of behavior have an impact upon the child's initial adaptation to a peer group. At the same time that many advances are being made in the general knowledge of early social development, the study of individual differences may illuminate some of the bases for such changes for emerging patterns of adjustment.

References

BLURTON-JONES, N., Categories of child-child interaction, in Blurton-Jones (ed.), *Ethological Studies of Child Behaviour*, Cambridge University Press, London, 1972, pp. 97–128.

GORDON, E. and THOMAS, A. Children's behavioral style and the teacher's appraisal of their intelligence, *Journal of School Psychology*, (5) #4, 1967, pp. 292–300.

LEACH, G. M., A comparison of the social behavior of some normal and problem children, in N. Blurton-Jones (ed.), *Ethological Studies of Child Behaviour*, Cambridge University Press, London, 1972.

McGREW, W. C., Aspects of social development in nursery school children with emphasis on introduction to the group, in N. Blurton-Jones (ed)., *Ethological Studies of Child Behaviour*, Cambridge University Press, London, 1972, pp. 129–156.

Ross, D. C., Poor school achievement; a psychiatric study and classification, *Clinical Pediatrics*, (5), #2, 1966, pp. 109–117.

TERESTMAN, N., Consistency and change in mood quality and intensity studied as aspects of temperament in preschool children, unpublished doctoral dissertation, Columbia University, 1963.

THOMAS, A., CHESS, S., and BIRCH, H., *Behavioral Individuality in Early Childhood*, New York University Press, New York, 1963.

THOMAS, A., CHESS, S., and BIRCH, H., *Temperament and the Development of Behavior Disorders in Children*, New York University Press, New York, 1968.

Beyond Father Absence: Conceptualization of Effects of Divorce

E. Mavis Hetherington, Martha Cox, and Roger Cox
UNIVERSITY OF VIRGINIA

It may seem rather odd that the first paper on a symposium on fathers is dealing with fathers who are absent rather than present. However, I believe a fruitful way of studying the role of the father and the impact of the father on mothers and children is to examine changes in family interaction and functioning following a divorce in which the mother has been granted custody of the child.

If you examine the literature on father absence carefully you will be struck by how little we know of factors that mediate differences found between children with absent or present fathers. We tend to rely very heavily on explanations based on modeling. How can children, particularly boys, be expected to exhibit normal cognitive and social development or sex-role typing or self-control, if they don't have the field independent, quantitative, problem solving, instrumental, self-controlled, masculine model of the father to imitate?

Undoubtedly the lack of a male model is an important factor in the development of children. However there may be less direct but equally powerful ways in which father absence effects children.

Following a divorce in which custody has been granted to the mother, the mother–child relationship may become more intense and salient. The father is infrequently present to moderate or mediate in the interaction. The mother must most of the time take over parenting roles assumed by both the mother and father in intact families, and this often imposes considerable stress on the mother. There are fewer time outs in the parenting game in one-parent families.

In addition to pressures associated with lack of paternal support in child rearing following divorce, the divorced mother has other stresses to cope with. The lack of the paternal support system is also felt in economic needs, needs for intimacy and sexual gratification, restrictions in social and recreational activities and contacts with adults. How she copes with these stresses will impact on the development of the child.

It would be just as unfortunate to view the effects of father absence solely in terms of the effects of absence of a father on mothers and their related effects on children, as it is to lean too heavily on modeling as an explanation for these effects. Divorce affects the whole family system and the functioning and interactions of the members within that system. To get a true picture of the impact of divorce, its effects on the divorced father living out of the home and on the mother and children must be examined. Because of time limitations, I am going to restrict my presentation today to a discussion of changes in functioning of mothers and fathers following divorce. I am not going to present any of our

Paper presented as part of the Symposium "Beyond Father Absence: Conceptualizations of Father Effects," Society for Research in Child Development, Denver, 1975. Printed by permission.

findings on changes in the behavior of children following divorce although this was a main focus of our project.

The findings I am going to report today are part of a two-year longitudinal study of the impact of divorce on family functioning and the development of children. The goals of the study were first to examine the response to the family crisis of divorce, and patterns of reorganization of the family over the two-year period following divorce. It was assumed that the family system would go through a period of disorganization immediately after the divorce, followed by recovery, reorganization, and eventual attainment of a new pattern of equilibrium. The second goal was to examine the characteristics of family members that contributed to variations in family processes. The third goal was to examine the effects of variations in family interaction and structure on the development of children.

The original sample was composed of 36 white, middle-class boys and 36 girls and their divorced parents from homes in which custody had been granted to the mother, and the same number of children and parents from intact homes. The final sample was 24 families in each of the groups, a total of 96 families. Sample attrition was largely due to remarriage in the divorced families, to families or a parent leaving the area, and to eight families who no longer wished to participate in the study. Families with stepparents were excluded, since one of the interests in the investigation was seeing how mothers and children functioned in father absent homes and how their functioning might be related to deviant or nondeviant behavior in children. In the analyses to be presented today, families were randomly dropped from groups to maintain equal sizes in groups.

When a reduction in sample size occurs from 144 families to 96 families, one immediately becomes concerned about bias in the sample. On demographic characteristics such as age, religion, education, income, occupation, family size, and maternal employment there were no differences between subjects who dropped out or were excluded from the sample and those who remained. In addition when a family was no longer included in the study, a comparative analysis was done of their interaction patterns and those of the continuing families. Some differences in these groups will be noted in the course of this presentation. In general, there were few differences in parent-child interactions in families who did or did not remain in the study. However, there were some differences in the characteristics of parents who remarried and how they viewed themselves and their lives.

The study used a multimethod, multimeasure approach to the investigation of family interaction. The measures used in the study are presented in the first table. The parents and children were administered these measures at two months, one year, and two years following divorce.

In this presentation I am going to restrict my discussion mainly to the findings based on parent interviews and the observations of the parent and child in a structured interaction situation in the laboratory, although I will occasionally refer to related findings on other measures. Therefore only these two procedures will be presented in detail.

As was found by Baumrind using some similar measures, the parent-child interaction patterns in the home observations and in the free play and labora-

TABLE 1

PARENT MEASURES	CHILD MEASURES
Interview	Unstructured observations in the home
Unstructured observations in the home	Observations of free play
Observations of free play with parent	with parent and child in the
and child in the laboratory	laboratory
Observations in structured task	Observations on structured task
situation with child	situation with parent
Diary record	Observation in nursery school
Personality measures:	Peer nomination
State-Trait Anxiety Inventory	Teacher ratings
CPI Masculinity-Femininity Scale	Problem checklist
Draw a Person	It Test
Personal Adjustment Scale	Draw a Person
(Adjective Checklist)	
Socialization Scale CPI	
Rotter I-E Scale	

tory sessions were remarkably congruent. For example, parents who were nurturant, who made high use of positive or negative sanctions, or who had good control over their children tended to be so across situations. Children who were compliant, oppositional, or affiliative also tended to maintain these behaviors across situations.

Parents were interviewed separately on a structured parent interview schedule designed to assess discipline practices and the relationship with the child; support systems outside the family household system; social, emotional, and heterosexual relationships; quality of the relationship with the spouse; economic stress; family disorganization; satisfaction and happiness; and attitudes toward the self. The interviews were tape recorded. Each of the categories listed in Table 2 were rated on scales by two judges. In some cases the category involved the rating of only a single 5- or 7-point scale. In others it represents a composite score of several ratings on a group of subscales. Interjudge reliabilities ranged from .69 to .95 with a mean of .82. The interviews were derived and modified from those of Baumrind, Sears, Rau, and Alpert, Becker, Martin and Hetherington, and others.

Each parent was observed separately interacting with the child in the laboratory in a half-hour free-play situation and in a half-hour structured situation involving puzzles, block building, bead stringing, and sorting tasks. The interaction sessions with the mother or father were on different days, separated by a period of about a month. Half of the children interacted with the mother first and half with the father first. Behavior was coded in the categories in Table 3. The coding procedure was similar to that used by Patterson and his colleagues where the observation period is divided into 30-second intervals and an average of about five behavior sequences of interactions between the subject and other family members were coded in the 30-second interval. Two raters

TABLE 2

Control of child	Economic stress
Maturity demands of child	Family disorganization
Communication with child	Problems in running household
Nurturance of child	Relationship with spouse
Permissiveness-restrictiveness with child	Emotional support in personal matters
Negative sanctions with child	Immediate support system
Positive sanctions with child	Social life and activities
Reinforcement of child for sex-typed behaviors	Contact with adults
	Intimate relations
Paternal availability	Sexuality
Maternal availability	Number of dates
Paternal face-to-face interaction with child	Happiness and satisfaction
	Competence as a parent
Maternal face-to-face interaction with child	Competence as a male/female
	Self-esteem
Quality of spouse's relationship with the child	Satisfaction with employment
	Conflict preceding divorce
Agreement in treatment of the child	Tension preceding divorce
Emotional support in child rearing from spouse	

rated all sessions. Interjudge agreement on individual responses averaged .83 per cent.

A repeated measures analysis of variance involving test session (two months, one year, two years), sex of subject, sex of parent, and family composition (divorced versus intact) was performed for each measure on the interview and structured interaction tasks. In addition, correlational analyses of all variables within and across subgroups was performed.

What kind of stresses are likely to be experienced by members of a divorced couple? How might these be related to parent–child relations?

Greater economic stress in divorced couples was apparent in our sample. Although the average income of the divorced families was equal to that of the intact families, the economic problems associated with maintaining two households for divorced couples led to more financial concerns and limitations in purchasing practices in divorced couples. It has been suggested by Herzog and Sudia that many of the deleterious effects of father absence on children could be eliminated if economic stability was provided for mothers with no husband in the home. However, in our study the number of significant correlations was not above chance between income or reported feelings of economic stress and parents' reported or observed interactions with their children or with behavior of the child in nursery school. It may be that in our middle-class sample with an average family income of about $22,000 the range is not great enough to detect the effects of economic stress. In a lower-class sample, the greater extremes of economic duress might be associated with variations in parent-child interaction or the development of the child.

A second area in which stresses are experienced by divorced couples are in social life and in meaningful, intimate interpersonal relationships. Divorced

TABLE 3

Interaction Coding

PARENT BEHAVIOR	CHILD BEHAVIOR
Command (positive)	Opposition
Command (negative)	Aversive opposition
Question	Compliance
Nonverbal intrusion	Dependency
Ignore	Negative demands (whining, complaining,
Affiliate (interact)	angry tone)
Positive sanctions	Aggression (tantrum, destructiveness)
Negative sanctions	Requests
Reasoning and explanation	Affiliate
Encourages	Self-manipulation
Dependency	Sustained play
Indulgence	Ignore
Opposition	
Compliance	
Encourages independence	

adults often complain that socializing in our culture is organized around couples and being a single adult, particularly a single woman with children, limits recreational opportunities. Both the interview findings presented in Table 4 and the diary records kept by parents indicate that social life is more restricted in divorced couples and that this effect initially is most marked for women. Divorced men go through a period of active social life one year after divorce; however by two years the social activities of divorced fathers have declined. Divorced mothers report having significantly less contact with adults than do the other parents and often commented on their sense of being locked into a child's world. This was less true of working than nonworking mothers.

Heterosexual relations play a particularly important role in the happiness and attitudes toward the self of both married and divorced adults. Happiness, self-esteem, and feelings of competence in heterosexual behavior increased steadily over the two year period for divorced males and females, but they are not as high even in the second year as those for married couples. It should be noted, however, that the subjects who later remarried and were shifted from this study of divorce and father absence to a stepparent study scored as high on happiness, although lower on self-esteem and feelings of competence, as did parents in intact families. Frequency of sexual intercourse was lower for divorced parents than married couples at two months, higher at one year, and about the same frequency at two years. Divorced males particularly seemed to show a peak of sexual activity and a pattern of dating a variety of women in the first year following divorce. However the stereotyped image of the happy, swinging single life was not altogether accurate. One of our sets of interview ratings attempted to measure intimacy in relationship. Intimacy referred to love in the Sullivanian sense of valuing the welfare of the other as much as one's own, of a deep concern and willingness to make sacrifices for the other, and strong

TABLE 4

Mean Ratings of Parental Variables of Intact and Divorced Couples of Preschool Children

VARIABLES AND TIME AFTER DIVORCE	INTACT		DIVORCED	
	Father	Mother	Father	Mother
Social life and recreation				
Two months	21.60	20.98	14.21	12.27
One year	21.85	21.17	22.25	15.56
Two years	21.13	21.17	16.96	16.94
Family disorganization				
Two months	15.73	13.17	23.83	20.31
One year	15.15	12.96	22.60	22.85
Two years	15.29	12.75	19.19	17.56
Parental control				
Two months	31.7	30.6	21.7	19.3
One year	29.9	30.6	18.6	15.3
Two years	30.7	30.0	24.0	23.3
Positive sanctions				
Two months	6.00	7.35	7.90	5.42
One year	6.04	7.29	7.63	4.42
Two years	5.96	7.23	4.88	6.08

attachment and desire to be near the other person. Intimacy in relationships showed strong positive correlations with happiness, self-esteem, and feelings of competence in heterosexual relations for both divorced and married men and women. Table 5 shows that in the divorced but not in the married sample if subjects were divided into those above and below the median in terms of intimacy in relationships, happiness correlated negatively with frequency of intercourse in the low intimacy group and positively in the high intimacy group. The same pattern held for self-esteem. This was true for both divorced males

TABLE 5

Correlations Between Frequency of Sexual Intercourse and Happiness in High and Low Intimacy Divorced Groups

	HIGH INTIMACY		LOW INTIMACY	
	Male ($N = 24$)	Female ($N = 24$)	Male ($N = 24$)	Female ($N = 24$)
Two months	+ .40*	+ .43*	− .09 (n.s.)	− .42*
One year	+ .49**	+ .47**	− .41*	− .46*
Two years	+ .54**	+ .52**	− .48**	− .57**

* $p < .05$.
** $p < .01$.

and females. The only nonsignificant correlation was for low intimacy males immediately following divorce. Many males but few females were pleased at the increased opportunity for sexual experiences with a variety of partners immediately following divorce. However, by the end of the first year both divorced men and women were expressing a want for intimacy and a lack of satisfaction in casual sexual encounters. Women expressed particularly intense feelings about frequent casual sexual encounters, often talking of feelings of desperation, overwhelming depression, and low self-esteem following such exchanges.

Thus far we have been focusing mainly on changes in the divorced partners in the two years following divorce. We will now look at differences in family functioning and in parent–child interactions as measured both in the interview and in direct observations in the structured interaction situation.

One of the sets of interview scales was family disorganization, which dealt with the degree of structure in proscribed household roles, problems in coping with routine household tasks, and the regularity and scheduling of events. The fathers' scales dealt with similar problems but focused on those in his life and household. It can be seen in Table 4 that the households of the divorced mothers and fathers were always more disorganized than those of intact families, although this disorganization was most marked in the first year following divorce and had significantly decreased by the second year. Children of divorced parents were more likely to get pick-up meals at irregular times. Divorced mothers and their children were less likely to eat dinner together. Bedtimes were more erratic, and the children were read to less before bedtime and were more likely to arrive at nursery school late. These results were found both in interviews and in the structured parental diaries.

The interaction patterns between divorced parents and children differed significantly from those in intact families on almost every variable studied in the interview, and on most of the parallel measures in the structured interaction situation. On these measures the differences were greatest during the first year and a process of re-equilibration seemed to be taking place by the end of the second year, particularly in mother–child relationships. Some of the findings for fathers must be interpreted in view of the fact that divorced fathers become increasingly less available to their children over the course of the two year period. Although at two months divorced fathers are having almost as much face-to-face interaction with their children as are fathers in intact homes who, as has been demonstrated in Biller's work, are often highly unavailable to their children, this interaction declines rapidly. At two months, about one quarter of the divorced parents even reported that fathers in their eagerness to maximize visitation rights were having more face-to-face contact with their children than they had before the divorce.

Because of time limitations the results of the parent–child interactions cannot be presented in detail. However I will try to summarize some of the more important findings and present a few tables to give the flavor of the results. In almost all of the parent–child relations data I am going to present there were significant third or fourth order interactions. The tables I will present will be the highest level interaction for those variables. I will present mainly tables from the interview data but the findings dealing with parallel variables from the observational data are similar.

TABLE 6

Mean Ratings of Parental Variables of Intact and Divorced Couples with Preschool Boys and Girls

VARIABLES AND TIME AFTER DIVORCE	INTACT				DIVORCED			
	Girl		Boy		Girl		Boy	
	Father	Mother	Father	Mother	Father	Mother	Father	Mother
Maturity demands								
Two months	26.6	31.4	32.8	32.2	17.8	19.9	18.4	20.0
One year	25.8	31.0	33.2	32.3	13.0	14.8	16.3	13.7
Two years	26.3	31.9	33.3	33.0	20.9	24.1	28.7	24.7
Communication								
Two months	15.0	17.1	14.9	17.3	11.3	11.1	10.7	9.0
One year	15.5	17.5	15.3	18.1	11.7	9.8	9.8	11.9
Two years	15.5	18.3	16.0	18.7	12.0	15.9	8.3	12.9
Nurturance								
Two months	33.1	33.4	30.3	32.8	32.0	29.5	31.5	25.7
One year	33.0	32.9	30.6	32.5	29.4	24.3	22.0	23.6
Two years	33.2	32.1	30.3	32.3	24.6	30.9	25.7	27.1
Consistency								
Two months	20.1	19.7	18.4	18.3	14.3	15.8	13.0	12.7
One year	20.1	20.0	19.3	18.5	10.7	11.0	10.5	9.9
Two years	20.2	20.5	20.0	20.0	17.5	17.8	14.1	16.6
Negative sanctions								
Two months	15.13	10.54	17.08	14.00	8.29	18.71	10.33	20.38
One year	14.88	10.71	18.00	13.67	8.46	22.88	13.29	24.04
Two years	14.67	10.29	18.71	12.88	13.13	15.38	15.50	17.75

It can be seen in Table 6 that divorced parents make fewer maturity demands on their children. Although this changes over the two years after divorce, they are demanding less self-sufficient, autonomous, and mature behavior of their children than are parents in intact families. Note the curvilinear shape of the function over time which can be seen particularly for mothers.

Table 6 shows that divorced parents communicate less well with their children. That is, they are less likely to solicit the child's opinion and to use reasoning and explanation than are the parents in intact families. This effect is more marked with boys than with girls.

In Table 6 it can be seen that there is a steady decline in nurturance of divorced fathers with their children. For divorced mothers there is a marked drop by the end of the first year which we assume is a period of reorganization and a marked increase by the end of the second year as the family re-equilibrates.

On Table 6 we also see that divorced parents are less consistent than parents in intact families with the most marked decline in consistency occurring at the end of the first year and increased consistency in the second year.

Table 4 shows that the lack of consistency is reflected in the lack of control divorced parents have over their children. Again we see the increase in control following the drop in the first year. This same pattern was obtained when the per cent of parental commands to which the child complied was examined in the structured interaction situation. For divorced parents its lowest point was at one year with a marked increase in successful commands at two years.

Table 4 shows that the lack of control in the divorced parents seems to be associated with very different patterns of relating to the child for mothers and fathers. The divorced mother tries to control the child by being more restrictive and giving more commands which the child ignores or resists. The divorced father wants his contacts with his children to be as happy as possible. He begins by initially being extremely permissive and indulgent with his children and becoming increasingly restrictive over the two year period, although he is never as restrictive as fathers in intact homes. The divorced mother uses more negative sanctions than the divorced father does or than parents in intact families do. However by the second year her use of negative sanctions is declining as the divorced father's is increasing. In a parallel fashion, Table 4 shows that the divorced mother's use of positive sanctions increases after the first year as the divorced father's decreases. The "every day is Christmas" behavior of the divorced father declines with time. The divorced mother decreases her futile attempts at authoritarian control and becomes more effective in dealing with her child over the two year period. Effectiveness in dealing with the child is related to support in child rearing from the spouse and agreement with the spouse in disciplining the child in both divorced and intact families. When support and agreement occurred between divorced couples, the disruption in family functioning appeared to be less extreme and the re-stabilizing of family functioning occurred earlier, by the end of the first year.

When there was agreement in child rearing, a positive attitude toward the spouse, low conflict between the divorced parents, and when the father was emotionally mature as measured by the CPI socialization scale and the Personal Adjustment Scale of the Adjective Checklist, frequency of father's contact with the child was associated with more positive mother–child interactions. When there was disagreement and inconsistency in attitudes toward the child, and conflict and ill will between the divorced parents, or when the father was poorly adjusted, frequent visitation was associated with poor mother–child functioning and disruptions in the children's behavior. Emotional maturity in the mother was also found to be related to her adequacy in coping with stresses in her new single life and relations with children.

Other support systems such as that of grandparents, brothers and sisters, close friends, or a competent housekeeper also were related to the mother's effectiveness in interacting with the child in divorced but not in intact families. However they were not as salient as a continued positive relationship of the ex-husband with the family.

In summary, when a father leaves the home following divorce the family system is in a state of disequilibrium. Disorganization and disrupted family functioning seem to peak at one year and be re-stabilizing by two years following the divorce. Stresses in family functioning following divorce are reflected not only in parent–child relations but in the changes in life-style, emotional distress, and changes in attitudes toward the self of the divorced couple. These changes in the parents may be mediating factors in changes in the child's behavior. A want for intimacy seems to be a pervasive desire for both males and females and the attainment of intimate relations seems to be associated with positive adjustment and coping behavior.

Since this study only lasted two years, it is impossible to state whether the re-stabilizing process in the divorced family had reached an asymptote and was largely completed at two years or whether this readjustment would continue over a longer period of time until it would ultimately more closely resemble that in intact families.

8

Supports for the Development of
Young Children

The educational experiences of young children have far-reaching influences upon them. An objective of research is to specify the particular effects of different kinds of experience on cognitive, social, and personal development. This chapter samples a variety of educational influences, a theory and its application, a special program of education for a special kind of subgroup, and the use of television.

Although an excerpt from Piaget's work is included elsewhere in this book, we believe that students can also profit from interpretations of Piaget. Millie Almy's writings have introduced many teachers and students to Piaget's thinking. Almy has helped teachers to make Piaget a basic part of their teaching. Her recent article, "Piaget in Action," is a very lucid account of what Piaget's theory and findings have to offer to the education of young children.

Minority groups exist in almost all nations. In addition to possessing different customs and cultural values, they often speak a different language. How shall the children of minority groups be educated into the mainstream without damage to their self-esteem and ability to learn? Connie R. Sasse reviews research and describes and explains bilingual education with special reference to Mexican-Americans. She brings out the fact that social, legal, and judicial issues are involved in bringing about equality of educational opportunity through bilingual education. Thus, the child is seen as influenced not only by his family and school but by the whole of society.

Dorothy G. Singer and Jerome L. Singer are well known for their work on children's imagination. When they undertook to investigate the impact of television on children, they were especially interested in how television might contribute positively to socialization. The research reported here involves effects on imaginative play.

Piaget in Action

Millie Almy
UNIVERSITY OF CALIFORNIA, BERKELEY

As word about Piaget has spread, psychologists, teachers, and others have tried to accommodate to ideas that often run counter to the behaviorist tradition in which most of us were brought up. Not surprisingly, we have assimilated Piaget's concepts to our own cognitive structures in ways that have often distorted and changed the concepts. It should also be noted that Piaget, although not altering the basic grand design of the theory that he began to sketch some fifty years ago, has explored new problems, made discoveries, modified some of his views, and strengthened others. Meanwhile investigators have conducted research, some of which is strongly supportive of the theory and expands on it, and some of which calls certain elements into question. Perhaps one can say that the theory is dynamic and does not stand still for the educator who wishes to put it to use in the classroom. Despite this, I think certain elements of the theory are basic and can provide some guidance to teachers.

Educators often identify Piaget as a learning theorist. This is an example of the way we tend to assimilate new ideas to old structures. Piaget's basic concern is not with learning (that is with changes in behavior that cannot be attributed to maturation) but rather with the development of knowledge. Accordingly, he cannot be identified with the majority of psychologists who have influenced American education.

Once the educator grasps the fact that Piaget's concern is with knowledge, or with knowing, and not with learning, the further distinctions that Piaget makes may only gradually be understood. For example, *physical knowledge*, knowledge that can be inferred directly from observation of the physical world, differs from *logico-mathematical knowledge*, knowledge that individuals construct from their own actions on the physical world. Again, it may be some time before the distinctions between *figurative* and *operative knowledge* become clear. *Figurative knowing* is static and tied to immediate perception. *Operative knowing* transcends the immediately given and can deal systematically and logically with transformations. It is the latter kind of knowing that, for Piaget, marks the mature intelligence, and in the long run enables the individual to deal more and more effectively not only with physical knowledge but with social and moral knowledge as well.

Whatever difficulty many educators have had with the different kinds of knowledge postulated by Piaget, most have, I think, had less trouble accommodating to the idea that the mature intelligence evolves through a series of stages, and that the thinking of the child differs from that of the adult, not merely in the quantity of concepts available but qualitatively as well. Even here, however, there is evidence that the theory has been assimilated to the traditional

Reprinted by permission from *Young Children*, Vol. XXXI, No. 2 (January 1976). Copyright © 1975, National Association for the Education of Young Children, 1834 Connecticut Avenue, N.W., Washington, D.C. 20069.

ways of schooling. Piaget's research has undoubtedly more often been used to determine the sequence in which concepts should be presented to children than to determine the nature of the classroom experience the children should have. In other words, educators have more often called on Piaget to determine *what* children should be taught rather than *how* they should be taught. It is the *how* that is most important if we are to see Piaget truly in action in the classroom.

Out of the hundreds of articles and books Piaget has written, only a few deal with matters of education. These suggest that the *how* is to be derived from an understanding of the factors that are involved in the child's transitions from the sensorimotor period of infancy to the concrete-operational thinking of childhood and finally to the formal operations that characterize the thinking of the mature adult.

Piaget identifies four factors that contribute to these transitions. The first three—maturation, action on the physical environment, and social interaction—are all involved in the fourth—the process of equilibration or self-regulation.

The fact that maturation is one factor influencing the way the child's knowledge develops does not imply, as many psychologists and educators have assumed, that Piaget espouses an emerging curriculum dictated only by the current interests and capabilities of the child. It does suggest, however, that certain kinds of curricular activities are more appropriate for certain ages than for others.

As Piaget has put it,

> We must recognize the existence of a process of mental development; that all intellectual material is not invariably assimilable at all ages; that we should take into account the particular interests and needs of each stage. It also means . . . that environment can play a decisive role in the development of the mind; that the thought contents of the ages at which they occur are not immutably fixed; that sound method can therefore increase the students' efficiency and even accelerate their spiritual growth without making it any less sound. (Piaget, 1966, p. vi).

Just as the recognition of the factor of maturation does not mean a curriculum that is tied to what the child can do today, so an emphasis on the child's action on the physical environment does not mean a curriculum that is only manipulative. The child grows in understanding of the world by testing the ways it responds to investigations and by observing the effects the child's own actions have. Such manipulation is essential in developing real comprehension. I am convinced that the reason most children are as intelligent as they are in the all too prevalent "look and say" curriculum found in most kindergartens and first grades and in too many preschools comes from the fact that they do actively explore their environment when they are outside the four walls of the classroom. On the other hand, children left entirely to their own devices miss many opportunities to derive fuller meaning from their experience. Social interaction is essential to move an ordinary experience with the physical environment to what Hans Furth calls "higher level" thinking.

The teacher who sees that the child who has just observed that "big" things float soon has an encounter with a big thing that sinks, contributes to the child's development, even if not a word is said. But words may also facilitate development, as when the teacher, having observed an older child arranging and rearranging a set of cubes in different patterns, inquires as to what the child found out through the manipulations. The teacher in the traditional classroom spends much time *telling* children about the world and then questioning them to see whether they have remembered what they have been told. Piagetian theory seems to call for a teacher who listens more than she or he tells and whose questions are designed to promote reflection and further inquiry on the part of the child.

Piagetian theory also emphasizes the importance of the child's interaction with other children. As children confront the beliefs of those who see things differently, as they adapt their wishes to others or vice versa in ongoing socio-dramatic play, as they contest with each other in structured games, they become less egocentric and better able to take other viewpoints.

The influence on the child's development of maturation, of experiences with physical objects, peers, and adults, are all subsumed under the process of *equilibrium* or *self-regulation*. This aspect of Piaget's theory has given both psychologists and educators difficulty. The process, Piaget maintains, is continuous with other organic functions. To American psychologists who have been trained to think more like physicists than biologists this concept has seemed incomprehensible. To the educator who has come to think of schooling as a process in which a competent teacher moves a group of children from one grade level to the next, proving the accomplishment by the results of achievement tests, the concept has been anathema.

Essentially, equilibration, from the viewpoint of the child, is a "do-it-yourself" process. A child may need much or little physical experience or confrontation with peers or questioning by teachers in order to accommodate existing cognitive structures to a new idea, and the way that idea is assimilated depends on what the child already knows or believes considering his or her own life history. Piaget does not suggest that because it is the child who is ultimately in control of his or her own cognitive development the teacher is thereby freed from responsibility. But he does caution with regard to logico-mathematical structures, "Children have real understanding only of that which they invent themselves, and each time that we try to teach them something too quickly we keep them from reinventing it themselves" (1966, p. vi).

As I reflect on the complexities of Piaget's theory, I wonder not that so few teachers have tried to put it in action but rather that so many are doing so. When they do, they opt to focus not on behavior which is readily observable, but on development which can only be inferred. They choose to have classrooms that are filled with a variety of objects and for children who are actively engaged with them, rather than tidy classrooms where pencil, paper, and workbooks can be neatly stored and children sit quietly in their seats. Their classrooms will inevitably hum with conversation and discussion. The essential difference between their classroom and others, however, lies not so much in the ways they appear or sound as in the teacher's awareness of the ways each child thinks and the provisions made to support and facilitate that thinking. Such provision goes beyond the narrowly cognitive and takes into account each child's concerns and interests as well.

How do teachers who want to put Piaget's theory into action go about it? Furth says that teachers prefer to begin trying certain activities with children rather than getting into the theory. I suspect that is generally, although not always, true. But what activities? The answer to this, I presume, depends not only on the teacher's personal intellectual predilections, but also on which of the many interpreters of Piaget's theory he or she encounters. Some interpreters stay close to the theory and rely on it almost to the exclusion of other developmental theories. Others are more eclectic, calling, for example, on Erikson and Werner for further illumination of psychological processes and on Dewey and Whitehead for amplification of the pedagogical. Some interpreters believe that a good place for teachers to start is with the tasks that Piaget has posed children. Some have even incorporated such tasks into the curriculum. For others, as for some of my colleagues at the University of California, Berkeley, the tasks are a means of getting the teacher tuned in to the thought of children. In their program, student teachers, whether destined to teach at the early childhood, elementary, or secondary levels, conduct Piagetian interviews with children at all the levels.

To put Piagetian concepts into action requires, above all else, a thinking teacher. He or she looks beyond the child's verbalizations and manipulations and tries to understand what they mean to the child. This way of looking at and thinking about children is far from easy. It adds, however, a new and satisfying dimension to teaching.

References

PIAGET, J. *Science of Education and the Psychology of the Child.* New York: Orion Press, 1970.
PIAGET, J. Foreword to *Young Children's Thinking* by Millie Almy and others. New York: Teachers College Press, 1966.

Bilingual Education in the Southwest : Past, Present, and Future

Connie R. Sasse
TEXAS TECH UNIVERSITY

In February 1974, the U.S. Commission on Civil Rights issued the sixth and final report of its Mexican American Education Study. Entitled *Toward Quality Education For Mexican Americans,* the report identifies three basic principles that provide a focus for improving the education of Chicano students.

1. The language, history, and culture of Mexican Americans should be incorporated as inherent and integral parts of the educational process.
2. Mexican Americans should be fully represented in decision-making positions that determine or influence educational policies and practices.

From *Texas Tech Journal of Education,* 1974, **1,** 65–83. Reprinted by permission.

3. All levels of government—local, State, and Federal—should reorder their budget priorities to provide the funds needed to implement the recommendations enumerated in this chapter (1974, p. 187).

A number of specific recommendations covering curriculum, student assignment, teacher education, counseling, and Title VI are included to support the three basic principles identified above. One specific recommendation concerning curriculum is that "state legislatures should enact legislation requiring districts to establish bilingual education or other curricular approaches designed to impart English language skills to non-English-speaking students while incorporating into the curriculum the children's native language, culture, and history. These programs should be instituted for each group of students whose primary language is other than English, and who constitute five percent of the enrollment or number more than 20 in a given school" (1974, p. 204).

The U.S. Commission on Civil Rights is a temporary, independent, bipartisan agency established by Congress that has power only to recommend courses of action; thus, it has no power to enforce compliance with its recommendations. Under these circumstances, the purpose of this paper is to assess the probability of the above specific recommendation being implemented in the public schools of the Southwest. To accomplish this, I intend to review the background and current status of bilingual education, outline the rationale for bilingual education, discuss research findings relevant to the benefits of bilingual education, and summarize the legal status of bilingual education—both legislative and judicial aspects. Finally, I will attempt to predict the conditions under which the above recommendation could be implemented.

WHAT IS BILINGUAL EDUCATION   Bilingualism is the ability of an individual to use, primarily to understand and speak, two languages. Bilinguals may be classified according to their skill in two languages along a more or less infinite scale, with some bilinguals having one dominant and one secondary language, while others are reasonably balanced in two languages. Some bilinguals switch easily from one language to another, whereas others find it extremely difficult and confusing to do so. In many cases, children entering the public school system are considered bilingual when in fact they are monolingual in their mother tongue.

If there is some ambiguity in the literature over the definition of who is a bilingual, there is less confusion (at least in the professionals' minds) over what constitutes bilingual education. Most authors in the field use the definition of bilingual education found in the Draft Guidelines to the Bilingual Education Program under Title VII of the Elementary and Secondary Education Act. The guidelines (Andersson and Boyer, 1970, vol. 2, p. 8) state that "bilingual education is instruction in two languages and the use of those two languages as mediums of instruction for any part of or all of the school curriculum. Study of the history and culture associated with a student's mother tongue is considered an integral part of bilingual education."

In amplifying this definition, Benítez (1971, p. 500) suggested that in order to be considered truly bilingual, an English-Spanish program must contain four basic areas: (1) English language skills, (2) Spanish language skills, (3) subject matter (mathematics, science, social studies), and (4) culture of both target groups. He further emphasized that in a bilingual program English must be taught as a second language, but that teaching English as a second language (ESL) does not automatically assure a bilingual program, because to be truly bilingual the program must also be bicultural.

There is a very curious paradox associated with the development of bilingual education in our country. Throughout the course of history, in this country and abroad, the ability to speak two or more languages has been a mark of the educated man, an elitist, if you will. Many dollars are spent to develop language programs at the secondary or postsecondary level, yet the schools seemingly make conscious efforts to force all elementary students to be monolingual. Gaarder (1965) contended that bilingualism can be either a great asset or a great liability, depending upon the education the child receives in both languages. In our public schools millions of children have been damaged or cheated or both by well-intentioned but ill-informed educational policies that have made their bilingualism an ugly disadvantage (Nedler, 1971). Yet, at the same time, we honor and respect the educated diplomat who is at ease conversing in another language.

RATIONALE FOR BILINGUAL EDUCATION   The public conscience has gradually become sensitive to the predicament of the minority population, and new theoretical models have been developed and implemented, so that educational leaders have come to the point of view that initial school experiences should capitalize on the child's home language and culture. While granting that a person living in a society, the language and culture of which differ from his own, must be equipped to participate meaningfully in the mainstream of that society, it should not be necessary for him to sacrifice his rich native language and culture to achieve such participation (Board of Regents of New York Department of Education, 1972, p. 144).

The child's mother tongue is not only an essential part of his sense of identity, it is an important aspect of his self-image and his sense of dignity about himself and his family. Schools can, and should, maintain and strengthen the sense of identity that a non-English-speaking child brings to school, and should build on that sense of identity to give the child skills that will enable him to function in the mainstream society. It appears that young children have an impressive capacity to learn, and especially in the case of language learning, children learn the sound system, the vocabulary, and the basic structure of a language more easily and better than do adults or adolescents. Moreover, considerable evidence indicates that initial learning through a child's non-English home language does not hinder the learning of English or of other school subjects. In addition, as Andersson and Boyer (1970, vol 1, p. 49) pointed out, bilingual education holds the promise of helping to harmonize various ethnic elements in a community into a mutually respectful and creative pluralistic society.

With this solid rationale for bilingual education, it is interesting to speculate why it has taken so many years for bilingual education to become accepted and promoted. There are perhaps two reasons why it has taken so long to overcome the traditional monolingual instructional approach to non-English-speaking children: ambiguities in the evaluation of bilingualism and the misdirection of bilingual programs in the schools.

Although there is a long history of research investigating and evaluating bilingual education, much of it has been contradictory or inconclusive. Because children taught in their native language could not be shown to have marked improvement in English language skills, it was felt that there was little use to "waste time" on instruction in the mother tongue when the schools' goal was to bring the students to proficiency in English. It has only been within the past few years under the impetus of the humanistic education movement that educators have begun to consider the affective aspects of instruction in the mother tongue. In fact, a number of authors (Andersson and Boyer, 1970; Herbert, 1972; John and Horner, 1971; Levenson, 1972) have suggested that an improved self-concept, a sense of adequacy, and a cultural identity are perhaps the most important outcomes of bilingual education for the non-English-speaking child.

The second background factor that has hindered the development of bilingual-bicultural programs as defined above has been the concept of compensatory education as remediation for perceived inequality of educational opportunity according to Arciniega (1973, p. 178). Although the goal of equal educational opportunity has long been espoused by most people, there are two differing views of what constitutes equality (see Figure 1). The "equal-access-to-schooling" view, the more traditional, contends that equal educational opportunity is said to be attained when it can be demonstrated that different segments of the population have a roughly equal opportunity to compete for the benefits of the educational system. In contrast, the "equal benefits" view focuses on the distribution of the results or benefits of the system. In other words, equality of opportunity exists only when the range of achievement is approximately the same for the various groups being served by the system.

Traditionally, and especially during the 1960's and the era of the "culturally deprived," educators have viewed minorities (whether racial, ethnic, or economic) in terms of deprivation. They assumed that the implementation of education to "make up the deficit" would bring about equality of educational opportunity. The limitations of this model, the experiences with compensatory education in the 1960's, and the emergence of minority professionals have led to the development of an alternate scheme for achieving equality of educational opportunity.

Instead of being perceived as deficiencies, cultural differences are perceived as strengths to be enhanced and promoted. These strengths serve as a base for the Culturally Democratic Learning Systems Approach. The implementation of this model theoretically results in the elimination of institutional racism, cultural bias, and discrimination in the schools and leads to equality of educational opportunity through the equal benefit view. Programs of bilingual-bicultural education as described above clearly fit this emerging model.

Another way of comparing the two approaches to bilingual education is through *cultural assimilation versus cultural pluralism* models. The traditional aim has been assimilation, centering almost exclusively on methods to insure that students would be assimilated into the English language culture as rapidly as possible. If the native language was used as a medium of instruction, it was used

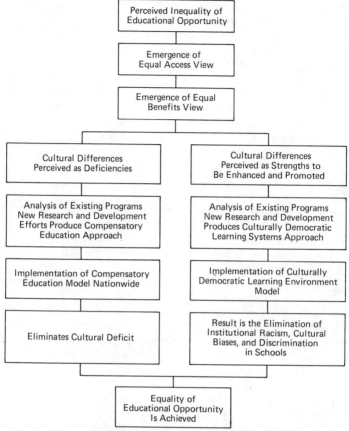

FIGURE 1.   *Schematic of alternative responses to the equal benefits view.* (From Arciniega, 1973.)

only as a bridge to English—one to be crossed as rapidly as possible and then destroyed (Kjolseth, 1973, p. 13).

The pluralistic model includes instruction in both English and non-English with each language receiving equal time and equal treatment. The developmental trend of the program is toward maintenance of both languages. In the assimilation model the ethnic language is being exploited, whereas in the pluralistic model the ethnic language is being cultivated (Kjolseth, 1973, p. 16). Again, bilingual-bicultural education fits the pluralistic model.

PAST AND PRESENT STATUS OF BILINGUAL EDUCATION   The existence of bilingual education in the United States falls into two separate and distinct eras. The first began in 1840 with German and English being the languages in which instruction was given. This era lasted until 1919 when all German instruction in elementary schools and almost all in secondary schools was eliminated as a result of World War I hysteria. From 1920 until 1963, bilingual education essentially disappeared from the United States. The modern era in bilingual education commenced in 1963 when the Coral Way Elementary School in Miami, Florida, offered a choice between the traditional all-English program and a bilingual program that included instruction in Spanish by experienced Cuban teachers.

Although bilingual education holds promise for both English-speaking and non-English-speaking students, full bilingual programs as defined earlier are seldom found. The Southwest is the geographical region of the country with the largest concentration of Spanish-speaking people, which should make it fertile ground for bilingual programs in Spanish and English; however, they are infrequently initiated. Only 6.5 percent of the Southwest's schools have bilingual programs and these are reaching only 2.7 percent of the Mexican-American school population—only one student out of nearly 40 (Uranga, 1973, p. 166).

In more narrowly conceived programs based on the compensatory approach to bilingualism, English as a second language (ESL) is taught with the objective of making non-English speakers more competent in English. In these transitional programs, no effort is made to present related cultural material. Although considered a less desirable program than full bilingual education, only an estimated 5.5 percent of the Mexican-American students in the Southwest receive some kind of instruction in ESL (Uranga, 1973, p. 166).

Even more narrowly conceived than ESL are the remedial reading programs offered in some schools. Using a strictly monolingual approach, remedial reading has been much more accepted than either bilingual education or ESL. More than half of the Southwest's schools offer remedial reading courses, yet only 10.7 percent of Chicano students are enrolled in these classes (Uranga, 1973, p. 167).

It is obvious that current programs are simply not adequate to meet the needs of Mexican-American youth. Only 2.7 percent of all Mexican-American youth are enrolled in programs that have been identified as truly bilingual. Another 16.2 percent are receiving instruction in narrowly conceived ESL or remedial reading programs, which leaves 81.1 percent of all Chicano students with no access to programs that might facilitate their school performance and achievement.

RESEARCH ON BILINGUALISM AND BILINGUAL EDUCATION

Regarding bilingual education, Fishman (1965, p. 227) noted that few behavioral science fields have been plowed as frequently, and fewer yet have produced more contradictory findings, than the relationships among bilingualism, intelligence, and language learning. The controversy and contradictory claims are not surprising in an area with political overtones that make it difficult for researchers to be objective, inasmuch as their research can affect the lives of a number of people (Turner, 1973, p. xiii). Furthermore, many contradictory findings in the literature frequently stem from differences in methods of investigation and the difficulty of separating the alleged language handicap from educational retardation, cultural and socioeconomic conditions, emotional concomitants, or any combination of the above factors (Darcy, 1963, p. 259). In general, however, the early work in this country found that bilingual students were handicapped in terms of intellectual functioning. In a review of research on Spanish-English bilinguals in the Southwest and in New York City from 1950 to 1960, Darcy (1963) found that bilingual subjects received lower but inconsistent scores on verbal and nonverbal group and individual intelligence tests. However, she reported that when bilinguals and monolinguals were matched for socioeconomic status their mean scores on a nonverbal test of intelligence did not differ significantly.

One study during this early period in bilingual research that did find bilingualism to be an advantage was conducted by Malherbe (reported in Zintz, 1969, p. 399) concerning bilingualism in South Africa. Malherbe tested about 18,000 students who had been educated in three types of secondary schools. One group was educated in English-speaking schools, another in Afrikaans-speaking schools, and a relatively small, third group was educated in Afrikaans-English bilingual schools. The data showed a small but statistically significant advantage in favor of the bilingual school in regard to language attainment in both English and Afrikaans at all intelligence levels.

Despite Malherbe's findings, in the early 1960's, the prevailing attitude was that bilingual students were mentally disadvantaged. This myth was shattered in 1962 by Peal and Lambert in their classic study of 10-year-old school children from six French schools in Montreal, Canada. Balanced bilingual children were compared with monolingual children on intelligence, attitude, and achievement. The samples were matched on socioeconomic class, sex, and age. One strength of this study over many of the previous ones was that tests standardized in the native language were used. Moreover, data were collected from several assessment devices rather than one or two. Peal and Lambert found that French and English-speaking bilinguals performed significantly better than French-speaking monolinguals on both verbal and nonverbal intelligence tests, and appeared to have a greater mental flexibility, a superiority in concept formation, and a more diversified set of mental abilities. The bilingual students were found to be further ahead in school than the monolinguals, and they achieved at a significantly higher level than did their classmates in English study, as might be expected, and in school work in general. The monolinguals saw their own group (French-Canadians) as being superior, whereas the bilinguals held more favorable attitudes towards the English than towards the French.

Modiano (1968, pp. 34–43) studied three tribal areas in the Mexican highlands. Students who were native speakers of two of the indigenous languages of Mexico were studied in 26 schools. An equal number (13) of Federal and State schools were matched on demographic data with bilingual schools of the National Indian Institute. In the Federal and State schools, reading was taught in the national language, Spanish, whereas in the Indian Institute Schools, reading was first taught through the vernacular prior to instruction in Spanish. The purpose of the study was to determine which group of schools produced the greater measure of literacy (specifically, greater reading comprehension) in Spanish. In all three tribal areas, a significantly larger $(P = .001)$ proportion of students from the bilingual schools were selected by their teachers as being "able to understand what they read in Spanish," than were selected from the all-Spanish State and Federal schools. In addition, in each tribal area, students who had first learned to read in their mother tongue read with greater comprehension in Spanish (as measured by standardized tests) than did those who had received all reading instruction in Spanish.

In the area of Spanish-English bilingualism, a project in the El Paso Public Schools found that Mexican-American first grade students receiving instruction in both Spanish and English scored as well on English language proficiency tests as the control groups, which were instructed in English only. And, their proficiency in Spanish was far superior to that of the students who were taught monolingually (Olstad, 1973, p. 52).

A similar project involving 4,000 children in the San Antonio Independent School District found that children receiving instruction in both Spanish and English made more gains in English vocabulary and grammar than did children in the English-only program. Children receiving bilingual instruction tested higher in English proficiency. They also made greater gains in IQ (as measured by the Goodenough-Harris Draw-a-Man Test) than did those in the English-only program (Olstad, 1973, pp. 52–53).

In another project (Bates, 1970, pp. 77–78), first grade children participated in a bilingual program in which the bilingual teacher worked for two hours daily with each class, with half the time spent in instruction in Spanish and half in English. The instruction for the remainder of the day was in English. There was no significant difference in mean gain in English verbal ability between the total experimental group and the total comparative group; thus the time spent on Spanish language development in the bilingual program had not penalized the pupils in English verbal ability. The Mexican-American pupils in both groups had a greater mean gain than the Anglo-American pupils; they began and ended with less English verbal proficiency than the Anglo-American pupils, however.

Politzer and Ramírez (1973, p. 60) obtained speech samples from Mexican-American children who attended a monolingual school ($N = 67$) and Mexican-American children attending a bilingual school ($N = 59$) in the same school district. The children watched a silent movie and then audiotaped the story of the movie. The errors from standard English were counted and categorized. Politzer and Ramírez found that the spoken English of Mexican-American children who had spent approximately three years in a bilingual program was no worse than that spoken by the children who had been instructed for three years in a monolingual program. In addition, they found that bilingual education and the use of Spanish at school had positive effects on Mexican-American children's attitudes toward Spanish and toward their Mexican-American background.

In another study Hickey (1972, pp. 25–26) hypothesized that some of the widely used tools for measurement of intelligence and verbal learning ability were functionally ineffective with Mexican-American bilinguals. His study focused specifically on structural and functional differences in the language that could affect test scores. Hickey tested 100 monolingual (Anglo-American) and 100 bilingual (Mexican-American) Head Start students with the Peabody Picture Vocabulary Test (PPVT). He found that 20 percent of the PPVT consists of words ending in "ing" and that the Mexican-American children consistently missed these items. He found that there were no sex differences in the scores, and that the "ing" words were the only differences between the two groups. Accordingly, Hickey modified the PPVT to eliminate the "ing" endings; he then tested 30 students from each lingual group and found no differences between the monolingual and bilingual students.

The final research reported in this review is that of Lambert and Tucker in a six-year longitudinal bilingual study in Canada (Lambert and Tucker, 1972; D'Anglejan and Tucker, 1971). In 1965, a group of English-speaking Canadians enrolled their first-grade children in an experimental class taught only in French except for two half-hour periods daily in English language arts. These children were matched with two control groups, one taught in English and the other in French, in nearby neighborhoods. Children were assessed for intelligence; socioeconomic status and parental attitudes toward French-Canadian people and culture were matched. Each spring of the study, the experimental and control classes were given a battery of tests to assess their intellectual and cognitive development and attitudinal status. Approximately 100 different measures were administered to all children each year.

After six years, the program has not resulted in any intellectual confusion or retardation among the subjects. In fact, the experimental children performed as well as the control groups in mathematics tests via English and French, indicating that they had no difficulty in using their mathematical concepts acquired via French when called upon to work in English. There was no evidence of a lag in English language skills, either active or passive, when the experimental children were compared with the control group of monolingually instructed English-speaking children. The productive skills in French of the experimental children were not equal to those of the French-speaking control class, their speech tending to be less fluent and to contain more grammatical errors than that of native-speaking children. However, they had attained French language skills that the researchers judged to be far beyond the level that they would have attained through traditional second language teaching methods—and at no cost to their English language ability.

Another interesting result emerged from assessment of the children's attitudes toward their own and other ethnolinguistic groups. The product of this program appeared to be essentially a new type of individual (neither exclusively English nor French), who possessed a sensitivity and a positive outlook toward both ethnolinguistic groups.

LEGAL STATUS OF BILINGUAL EDUCATION

As recently as the mid-1960's, 21 states, including California, New York, Pennsylvania, and Texas, had laws requiring that all public school instruction be in English. In seven states, including Texas, a teacher risked criminal penalties or the revocation of his license if he taught bilingually.

FEDERAL LEGISLATION   In the mid 1960's Chicanos in the Southwest and members of other groups mounted a widespread campaign for bilingual-bicultural education, which culminated in 1967 when bills were introduced in

Congress to amend the Elementary and Secondary Education Act of 1965 to provide for bilingual education programs. On 2 January 1968, President Lyndon B. Johnson signed into law the Bilingual Education Act, Title VII of the Elementary and Secondary Education Act of 1965 as amended in 1967. The Act begins with this declaration of policy:

> In recognition of the special educational needs of the large numbers of children of limited English speaking ability in the United States, Congress hereby declares it to be the policy of the United States to provide financial assistance to local educational agencies to develop and carry out new and imaginative elementary and secondary school programs designed to meet these special educational needs. For the purpose of this title, "children of limited English-speaking ability" means children who come from environments where the dominant language is other than English. (As cited in Andersson and Boyer, 1970, vol. 2, p. 1)

Programs under the Bilingual Education Act are intended primarily for children of limited English-speaking ability between the ages of three and 18, and English-speaking children are expected to have an opportunity to learn the non-English mother tongue of their classmates. Another feature of the Act is the poverty clause, which restricts grants to school districts "having a high concentration of such children from families (A) with incomes below $3,000 per year, or (B) receiving payments under a program of aid to families with dependent children under a state plan approved under Title IV of the Social Security Act."

The original authorization for the bill was $400 million, to be spent over a period of six years; however, only $117 million of that money has been spent. The authorization for fiscal year 1973 was $135 million, but after much haggling between the administration and Congress, the actual expenditure was approximately $35 million, which supported 213 projects in 32 states and territories and involved 19 languages other than English. Of the estimated 100,222 students enrolled in Title VII projects, 91,138 are in Spanish-English bilingual programs.

There has been a steady decline in the number of new proposals received for funding under the Bilingual Education Act. In 1970, 315 proposals were received in the Bilingual Education Programs Branch of the U.S. Office of Education. In 1971, 195 were received, and in 1972, only 150 new proposals were received (Andersson, 1971, p. 435).

In 1972, the Emergency School Aid Act reserved 4 percent of its total appropriation for bilingual education, which made $9 million available to fund 40 projects in 1973. The ESAA program does not stipulate that the children come from impoverished backgrounds, but communities seeking ESAA funds must be under a comprehensive desegregation plan acceptable to the Office for Civil Rights (Wright, 1973, p. 184).

There are a number of other federal laws that make provisions for bilingual education. The Education Professions Development Act (now incorporated into the National Center for Improvement of Educational Systems) has funds available for training bilingual teachers and counselors. Bilingual projects are authorized for migrant education (Title I—Migrant, ESEA) and Indian education (Indian Education Act of 1972). Other funds are available through the Ethnic Heritage Program (Title IX of ESEA), and through the Head Start and Follow Through programs of the Economic Opportunity Act (Wright, 1973, p. 184).

It may be that the federal laws governing bilingual education will soon be changed. Both Senator Joseph Montoya and Senator Edward Kennedy have bills pending that would revise current federal programs. However, even if Congress makes changes in bilingual education legislation, the effects on non-English-speaking children will be slight unless more money is appropriated (Wright, 1973, p. 185).

STATE LEGISLATION   In 1971, Massachusetts became the first state to *require* school districts to provide bilingual programs for children whose first language is not English. The Massachusetts Transitional Bilingual Act calls for the use of both a child's native language and English as mediums of instruction and for the teaching of history and culture associated with a child's native language. It authorizes state expenditures of up to $4 million a year to help districts meet the costs of bilingual programs exceeding the average per pupil expenditure in the district as a whole (Kobrick, 1972b, p. 56).

Although the Massachusets statute requires school districts to provide bilingual programs, participation by the children and their parents is voluntary. The major weakness of the statute is that it is silent on whether English-speaking children may be enrolled in bilingual programs. Therefore, it does not contain safeguards against the isolation of minority children in such programs (Kobrick, 1972b, p. 57).

Other states, such as Pennsylvania, mandate bilingual education without providing the necessary funds, or provide funds without compelling bilingual instruction, as do New Mexico, New York, and Washington. Within the past year, Texas passed legislation that established bilingual education as state policy for non-English-speaking students and budgeted $700,000 for 1973 and $2 million for 1974, after which the funds will come from general education monies. California appropriated $5 million in 1972 for an experimental two-year program. One unusual aspect of the California law is that at least one-third of a class must be proficient in English in order to insure that the class is actually bilingual. Louisiana recently has established a program to preserve the French-speaking heritage of its Cajun population (Wright, 1973, p. 185).

JUDICIAL ACTION   Although the number of cases that have been tried in the courts concerning bilingual education has been small, the impact of these cases has been felt widely, and will continue to be felt if others take advantage of the precedents that have been set.

In the case of Serna versus Portales Municipal Schools (351 F. Supp. 1279, 1972), a class action suit, it was asserted that the school district had discriminated against Spanish-surnamed students by failing to provide learning opportunities that satisfied both their educational and social needs. The plaintiffs claimed deprivation of due process and equal protection guaranteed by the Fourteenth Amendment to the United States Constitution and of their statutory rights under Title VI of the Civil Rights Act of 1964, specifically Section 601.

The court ruled that the Spanish-surnamed children did not in fact have equal educational opportunity and that a violation of their constitutional right to equal protection existed. The Portales school district was ordered to reassess and enlarge its program directed to the specialized needs of its Spanish-surnamed students in all four elementary schools and to recruit and hire more qualified Spanish-speaking teachers and teacher aides in each of the district's schools. In a similar case against the school district of San Felipe Del Rio, Texas, the district judge ruled that bilingual programs must be instituted to accommodate the needs of the Mexican-American students.

The most recent judicial decision came on 21 January 1974, when the Supreme Court of the United States ruled on the case of Lau versus Nicols (U.S. 94 S. Ct. 786, 1974). This case concerned the failure of the San Francisco school system to provide English language instruction to approximately 1800 students of Chinese ancestry who do not speak English. It was claimed that this denied them a meaningful opportunity to participate in the public educational program and thus violated Section 601 of the Civil Rights Act of 1964, which bans discrimination based "on the ground of race, color, or national origin," in "any program or activity receiving federal financial assistance," and the implementing regulations of the Department of Health, Education, and Welfare. The original decision had gone against the plaintiffs in the U.S. District Court for the Northern District of California and in the United States Court of Appeals for the Ninth Circuit.

In reversing the decision of the lower courts in Lau versus Nichols, the Supreme Court noted that it seemed obvious that the Chinese-speaking minority received from the school system fewer benefits than did the English-speaking majority. In 1970, HEW issued clarifying guidelines for the implementing regulations of the Civil Rights Act of 1964. In part, these stated:

> Where inability to speak and understand the English language excludes national origin-minority group children from effective participation in the educational program offered by a school district, the district must take affirmative steps to rectify the language deficiency in order to open its instructional program to these students. (Lau versus Nichols, p. 789)

Because the San Francisco school district had agreed to comply with Title VI of the Civil Rights Act of 1964 as part of its contractual agreement in receiving federal monies, the Court used this agreement as a basis for its landmark decision.

SUMMARY AND IMPLICATIONS—THE CASE FOR IMPLEMENTATION OF BILINGUAL EDUCATION FOR MEXICAN-AMERICAN STUDENTS

The intent of this paper has been to survey the evidence available, and then attempt to predict the probability of bilingual education being incorporated into the schools of the Southwest that serve Mexican-Americans, whose native tongue is Spanish.

Although a number of highly respected educators feel that bilingual education for both English-speaking and Spanish-speaking students would be a valuable direction for schools to take, it is doubtful that this type of program will ever attain anything but limited availability in the Southwest. Whereas Lambert's longitudinal study in Canada provides evidence that English-speaking children would not suffer in terms of their English language skills if they enrolled in a program in which instruction was in Spanish, and in fact, would gain fluency in Spanish as well as a favorable attitude toward Spanish and the Spanish culture, it is not likely that this evidence will be considered. It seems that the majority of Americans are so ethnocentric that they would see little value in being fluent in another language and comfortable in another culture. The change in attitude that would be required for all pupils to be enrolled in bilingual programs is simply too great for this alternative to be viable for large numbers of people at this time.

Regarding bilingual education for Spanish-speaking students, the prospects appear more promising. Although researchers have not been able to demonstrate conclusively that a Mexican-American child can become literate in English best by first becoming literate in Spanish, research shows that instruction in Spanish does not retard English language skills. In addition, a number of authors have pointed out that the affective aspects of instruction in the mother tongue are tremendously important in the development of self-concept, self-esteem, and a sense of adequacy in Mexican-American students.

Another promising sign has been the change in the attitude of both educators and the public over the last decade. As recently as 1967, it was illegal to give bilingual instruction in a number of states, whereas today many states have legislation supporting or mandating bilingual education.

Of course, the most important event relating to the future of bilingual education was the Supreme Court decision in Lau versus Nichols that failure to provide a child who does not speak English with English language instruction is clearly a violation of the 1964 Civil Rights Act. Even though the court did not prescribe what type of program should be instituted to remedy the situation, it clearly stated that some type of special program must be provided for non-English-speaking students, and that school districts have an affirmative duty to rectify the language deficiencies of non-English-speaking students in order to open the instructional program to these students.

There are still obvious obstacles to be overcome. Many communities doubt that the maintenance of non-English languages is desirable. It is possible that some individuals could even misinterpret Lambert's longitudinal data to support their contention that Mexican-American children would do as well to attend English-speaking schools, inasmuch as the Lambert experiment involved a home/school language switch. However, the Lambert experiment was conducted under conditions that are not directly generalizable to the Southwest. The province of Quebec contains approximately a 1:1 ratio of English and French-speaking citizens. The experiment was designed to support the maintenance of the weaker language (French), that is, the one most likely to be lost. From the perspective of the maintenance of the weakest language, the Lambert data would support the maintenance of Spanish in the Southwest through bilingual programs.

Another obstacle is the lack of qualified teachers. A survey cited by Light (1972) of teachers of English as a second language found that such teachers are almost totally unprepared for their work. In a sample of elementary and secondary school teachers, it was found that 91 percent had no practice teaching in ESL. Eighty-five percent had no formal study in methods of teaching ESL, while 80 percent had no formal training in English syntax. Sixty-five percent had no training in general linguistics. Teacher preparation institutions are only beginning to realise that new and better programs are urgently needed to educate qualified teachers in the numbers required. In these days of the over-supply of teachers, it may be that the shortage of qualified bilingual teachers will end due to the laws of supply and demand, but it is likely that it will be a number of years before there is any appreciable number of certified bilingual teachers. In fact, recent California Legislation (Wright, 1973, p. 185) excuses bilingual teachers from certification—which may be an indicator of the measures necessary to create a cadre of bilingual teachers. Along with the lack of qualified teachers, there is a lack of adequate materials, and an oversupply of inadequate evaluation methods and instruments.

With all the problems attendant to a widespread initiation of bilingual education, it appears that Lau versus Nichols has opened the door. Given the reluctance of the educational system to move itself and the lag between edu-cational theory and school practice, it may be that those who stand to benefit most from bilingual programs will have to force the issue. Minority language speakers, primarily Spanish-speaking in the Southwest, who are unable to get bilingual programs established will have to be willing to take the issue to the courts. A school district under court order to provide some type of special instruction for non-English-speaking students will be in no position to delay initiation of a program. In the Southwest, it will be up to Mexican-Americans to provide this legal impetus, if necessary, and to be in positions on the local, state, and national levels to have input into the kind of programs established.

It seems ironic that legally the stage is set for minorities to demand full bilingual programs, yet many of the programs that are evolving with the label "bilingual" are half-way measures that at best can be considered transitional programs. It appears that only as Mexican-Americans in the Southwest gain the political power necessary to have access to the decision-making process, and only as they are willing to use the legal tools available to them, will bilingual-bicultural programs be established to meet the needs of all students.

References

ABRAHAMS, ROGER D., and TROIKE, RUDOLPH C. (Eds.), *Language and Cultural Diversity in American Education*. Englewood Cliffs, New Jersey: Prentice-Hall, Inc., 1972.

ANDERSSON, THEODORE. "Bilingual Education: The American Experience." *The Modern Language Journal* 55 (November 1971), 427–437.

ANDERSSON, THEODORE, and BOYER, MILDRED. *Bilingual Schooling in the United States*. 2 vols. Washington, D.C.: U.S. Government Printing Office, 1970.

ARCENIEGA, TOMÁS A. "The Myth of the Compensatory Education Model in Education of Chicanos." In Garza, Rudolph O. de la; Kruszewski, Anthony; and Arceniega, Tomás A. (Eds.), *Chicanos and Native Americans*. Englewood Cliffs, New Jersey: Prentice-Hall, Inc., 1973, pp. 173–183.

BATES, ENID BUSWELL. "The Effects of One Experimental Bilingual Program on Verbal Ability and Vocabulary of First Grade Pupils." Unpublished doctoral dissertation, Texas Tech University, 1970.

BENÍTEZ, MARIO. "Bilingual Education: The What, the How, and the How Far." *Hispania* 54 (September 1971), 499–503.

Board of Regents of New York State Department of Education. "Emphasis on Bilingual Education." *Intellect* 101 (December 1972), 144–145.

CARLISLE, JOHN. "A Closer Look at the Bilingual Classroom." *Hispania* 56 (May 1973), 406–408.

CARROW, ELIZABETH, "Comprehension of English and Spanish by Preschool Mexican-American Children." *Modern Language Journal* 55 (May 1971), 299–305.

CROSS, WILLIAM C., and BRIDGEWATER, MIKE. "Toward Bicultural Education for the Southwestern Mexican-American." *Education* 94 (September/October 1973), 18–22.

D'ANGLEJAN, ALISON, and TUCKER, G. R. "Academic Report: The St. Lambert Program of Home-School Language Switch." *Modern Language Journal* 55 (February 1971), 99–101.

DARCY, NATALIE T. "Bilingualism and the Measurement of Intelligence: Review of a Decade of Research." *The Journal of Genetic Psychology* 103 (1963), 259–282.

FISHMAN, JOSHUA. "The Status and Prospects of Bilingualism in The United States." *Modern Language Journal* 49 (March 1965), 143–155.

GAARDER, A. BRUCE. "Teaching the Bilingual Child: Research, Development, and Policy." In *Bilingualism and the Bilingual Child, A Symposium*. Reprinted from *The Modern Language Journal* 47 (March and April 1965), 165–175.

GARZA, RUDOLPH O. DE LA; KRUSZEWSKI, Z. ANTHONY; and ARCENIEGA, TOMÁS A. *Chicanos and Native Americans*. Englewood Cliffs, New Jersey: Prentice-Hall, Inc., 1973.

GUERRA, MANUEL H. "Educating Chicano Children and Youth." *Phi Delta Kappan* 53 (January 1972), 313–314.

HERBERT, CHARLES E. JR. "The Bilingual Child's Right To Read." *Claremont Reading Conference Yearbook* 36 (1972), 51–58.

HICKEY, TOM. "Bilingualism and the Measurement of Intelligence and Verbal Learning Ability." *Exceptional Children* 39 (September 1972), 24–28.

IANCO-WORRALL, ANITA D. "Bilingualism and Cognitive Development." *Child Development* 43 (December 1972), 1390.

JOHN, VERA P., and HORNER, VIVIAN M. *Early Childhood Bilingual Education*. New York: Modern Language Association of America, 1971.

KJOLSETH, ROLF. "Bilingual Education Programs in the United States: For Assimilation or Pluralism?" In Turner, Paul R. (Ed.), *Bilingualism in The Southwest*. Tucson, Arizona: The University of Arizona Press, 1973, pp. 3–28.

KOBRICK, JEFFREY. "A Model Act Providing for Transitional Bilingual Education Programs in Public Schools." *Harvard Journal of Legislation* 9 (January 1972a), 260–300.

KOBRICK, JEFFREY W. "The Compelling Case for Bilingual Education." *Saturday Review* 55 (April 29, 1972b), 54–58.

LAMBERT, WALLACE E., and TUCKER, G. RICHARD. *Bilingual Education of Children*. Rowley, Massachusetts: Newbury House Publishers, Inc., 1972.

Lau versus Nichols, 94 S. Ct. 786 (1974).

LEVENSON, STANLEY, "Spanish and Portuguese in the Elementary Schools." *Hispania* 55 (May 1972), 314–319.

LIGHT, RICHARD L. "On Language Arts and Minority Group Children." In Abrahams, Roger D., and Troike, Rudolph C. (Eds.), *Language and Cultural Diversity in American Education*. Englewood Cliffs, New Jersey: Prentice-Hall, Inc. 1972, pp. 9–15.

MODIANO, NANCY. "National or Mother Language in Beginning Reading: A Comparative Study." *Research in the Teaching of English* 2 (April 1968), 32–43.

NEDLER, SHARI. "Language, the Vehicle; Culture, the Content." *Journal of Research and Development in Education* 4 (Summer 1971), 3–8.

OLSTAD, CHARLES. "The Local Colloquial in The Classroom." In Turner, Paul R. (Ed.), *Bilingualism in the Southwest*. Tucson, Arizona: The University of Arizona Press, 1973, pp. 51–66.

PEAL, ELIZABETH, and LAMBERT, WALLACE E. "The Relation of Bilingualism to Intelligence." *Psychological Monographs* 76 (1962) Whole No. 546.

POLITZER, ROBERT, and RAMÍREZ, A. G. "An Error Analysis of the Spoken English of Mexican-American Pupils in a Bilingual School and a Monolingual School." *Language Learning* 23 (June 1973), 39–61.

Serna versus Portales Municipal Schools, 351 F. Supp. 1279 (1972).

STENT, MADELON D.; HAZARD, WILLIAM R.; and RIVLIN, HARRY N. *Cultural Pluralism in Education: A Mandate For Change.* New York: Appleton-Century-Crofts, 1973.

TUCKER, G. R., and D'ANGLEJAN, ALISON D. "Some Thoughts Concerning Bilingual Education Programs." *Modern Language Journal* 55 (December 1971), 491–493.

TURNER, PAUL R. (Ed.), *Bilingualism in the Southwest.* Tucson, Arizona: The University of Arizona Press, 1973.

URANGA, SUSAN NAVARRO. "The Study of Mexican-American Education in the Southwest: Implications of Research by the Civil Rights Commission." In Garza, Rudolph O. de la; Kruszewski, Z. Anthony; and Arceniega, Tomás A. (Eds.), *Chicanos and Native Americans.* Englewood Cliffs, New Jersey: Prentice-Hall, Inc., 1973, pp. 161–172.

U.S. Commission on Civil Rights. *Toward Quality Education for Mexican Americans.* Report VI: Mexican American Education Study. Washington D.C.: U.S. Government Printing Office, 1974.

WRIGHT, LAWRENCE. "The Bilingual Education Movement at the Crossroads." *Phi Delta Kappan* 55 (November 1973), 183–186.

ZINTZ, MILES V. *Education Across Cultures.* Dubuque, Iowa: Kendall/Hunt Publishing Company, 1969.

Family Television Viewing Habits and the Spontaneous Play of Pre-School Children *

Dorothy G. Singer and Jerome L. Singer
UNIVERSITY OF BRIDGEPORT AND YALE UNIVERSITY

In most families in this country and, increasingly, throughout the world, it can probably be said that television is indeed very much a member of the family. Surveys suggest that in most homes where there are young children, from toddlers to early adolescents, the television set is on much of the time during the day and well into the night and is viewed with different degrees of concentration by all members of the family. Like an imaginary companion, "Big Brother," it is there providing stimulation and talking to the smallest child in a way that has never been a part of human experience before. Viewed from this vantage point, it seems almost a national disgrace that so little attention has been paid by appropriate governmental or private agencies to the direct impact of the

From *American Journal of Orthopsychiatry*, 1976, 46, 496–502. Copyright © 1976 the American Orthopsychiatric Association, Inc. Reproduced by permission.

* This research was supported in part by the Yale Child Study Center, the Yale Institute of Social and Policy Studies and Family Communications, Inc.

television set on the socialization of children. The major thrust of formal research until fairly recently has been to examine possible influences of television upon overt aggressive behavior. The relevant reviews of this literature (Singer, 1971; Murray, 1973) show that exposure to aggressive material on television will have the effect of increasing the level of aggression in children, particularly those already showing tendencies toward overt aggressive behavior. The serious implications of such findings are clear but have not yet been fully faced by either the networks or various mental health agencies. If only 20 per cent or 30 per cent of all pre-school children show a predisposition to aggressive behavior in the sense of being inclined to direct physical attacks on other children, the extensive exposure of such children to the large amounts of direct violence on television, whether in cartoons or live form, is likely to generate a sizable upsurge in the occurrence of acts of overt violence by these children in the short run at the very least. This certainly constitutes a national mental health problem and one that calls for serious attention. We should like also to point out more subtle and as yet relatively little studied effects of aggressive material on television. The spate of detective and police shows on television, while generally representing the side of law and order, almost always end up with the good guys shooting the bad guys to death. Obviously the writers' intentions are merely to wind the story up quickly and dramatically but the message in many subtle ways is being communicated to the vast millions viewing that it's okay for the police to shoot down "alleged perpetrators" rather than go through all the trouble of arresting them and bringing them to trial.

Our primary concern in the present paper is to examine more extensively possible ways in which the television medium may be put to use for what might be termed pro-social or constructive social goals as part of the overall socialization process. The presentation here represents essentially a case report on a two-month experience with the children and parents of a day care center in a small industrial city in Connecticut with the subsequent follow-ups carried on over almost a year as part of consultation to the parents of the center. The major focus of our intervention was the study of spontaneous imaginative play shown by the children during the course of the free-play periods in the day care center. The position we took and which will not be detailed here at length was that while all children show a certain amount of pretend or make-believe or socio-dramatic play as an inevitable part of cognitive growth, what Piaget called ludic symbolism, there are interesting differences in the extent to which children engage in such games and interesting consequences for children of the differences in predisposition to imaginative play. For example, a study carried out by Biblow (Singer & Singer, 1973) indicated that children already pre-disposed to make-believe and fantasy play showed less likelihood of aggressive behavior when frustrated and also after viewing an aggressive television show. Children more predisposed to aggressive play were somewhat inclined to increase the level of aggression following the exposure to the aggresive TV presentation.

The major thrust of our research study was to examine the ways in which exposure to a children's television show, specifically "Misterogers' Neighborhood," would enhance the spontaneous imaginative play of children after several weeks of exposure and would also perhaps increase the level of positive emotionality in the course of play. Briefly, the formal experiment itself which has been extensively described elsewhere (Singer & Singer, 1974) involved a comparison of control group with children watching "Misterogers" daily for two weeks in a group, a second group watching the same program but with an adult serving as a kind of intermediary and translator, and the third group which viewed no television but was provided with a live adult teacher who engaged in a variety of make-believe exercises with the children. The results of this study indicated pretty clearly that exposure to the live adult model had the largest impact on increasing the spontaneousness of the behavior of the children as measured in post-experimental free play periods. Exposure to the "Misterogers" show with the adult intermediary showed the next largest increment, while mere exposure to the television show alone (particularly since the show is slanted at the individual child and there were fifteen viewers in the group) led to only more small increments in make-believe play. By comparison, the control group children showed, if anything, a drop in the occurrence of make-believe play over a six-week period.

In order to carry out this investigation, we felt that it was important to involve ourselves and our staff of eight raters who were unfamiliar with the experimental hypothesis as fully as possible with the school and its director to establish a sense of rapport and to provide the parents with as much opportunity for informed consent concerning their children's participation in the study. This, therefore, included regular meetings with the parents before, during and subsequent to the experimental phase of the study. These meetings afforded us the opportunity to obtain data by the use of questionnaires on television viewing habits and on personal attitudes towards sex role in child rearing and towards the personal and social self-worth on the part of the parents.

While we do have more formal statistical data, our approach in this presentation will be concerned with the general qualitative indications that emerge from our contact with approximately seventy parents whose children attended the day care center. The families involved were all in their twenties and thirties and might be classified best as American-ethnics. That is, they represented persons working in blue-collar or lower level white-collar positions with strong sub-cultural ties to Italian, Ukrainian, Polish, and Irish backgrounds. In most cases the mothers worked at least part time and viewed the day care center as an absolute necessity. Following are some of the more general outcomes that emerged from the questionnaire responses describing children's and family television favorites and extent of viewing. Our data also included self-ratings on child-rearing attitudes, sex role, and a particularly interesting measure of personal and social self-worth, an adjective checklist based on the work of Carlson and Levy (1968).

The general indications were that these families tended to view by far the most popular television shows such as "All in the Family," "I Love Lucy," and the various popular detective/police shows such as "Mannix," "Kung Fu," and so on. A typical family pattern involved the children's viewing of television in the late afternoon on return from school and staying up relatively late so that many of the children viewed a number of the prime time more aggressive television shows, generally in the company of their parents. One mother who by many standards would seem to have been more educated nevertheless reported gleefully how much she enjoyed watching "Creature Features," a monster movie show, with her four-year-old. Because of the nature of the location of the city, educational television was not easily available and so most of the parents and children have never seen "Misterogers" nor "Sesame Street," although they had heard a little bit about these shows, and, as our research went on, parents quickly began to at least say the right things about the value of this type of programming. It seemed quite clear initially that the major import of our survey and interview with the parents was how little thought or attention these basically well-intended and responsible parents paid to the content or extent of television viewing by their children.

When we divided the groups into those whose children showed a greater amount of spontaneous imaginative play compared with those whose children showed the low median scores on spontaneous make-believe play, we found interesting differences both in the mothers' self-reports of style and the quality of television programming viewed in the family. On the self-worth checklist, for example, the mothers of those children who showed more imaginative spontaneous make-believe play tended to significantly more often rate themselves high in Personal Self-worth rather than Social Self-worth. They rated themselves higher on traits such as "ambition," "confidence," "creative," "energetic," "fair-minded," or "idealistic." The mothers of the children who showed significantly less spontaneous imaginative play were more likely to have rated themselves high on variables such as "attractive," "compassionate," "considerate," "cooperative," "friendly," "generous." If we then looked at the television viewing patterns, we found that the parents of the less imaginative children reported both the child's favorite programs and their own as involving aggressive or violent components. Programs such as "Daktari," "Hogan's Heroes," "Kung Fu," and "Gunsmoke" were more likely to be the favorite viewing of both parents and children where the mothers reported higher Social rather than Personal Self-worth scores and also where the children shared lower spontaneous imaginative play.

In other words, there seemed to be a general configuration that emerged in our admittedly small but fairly intensively studied sample. Mothers whose self-orientation was built around major emphasis on independence, thoughtful or internally oriented values tended in some subtle way to communicate this pattern to their children. As other researches we have carried out suggest mothers foster make-believe play through storytelling, and through allowing the children privacy. In addition, such mothers tended to take a more active role in monitoring the TV viewing habits of the children and placed greater emphasis on programming that was less likely to be directly aggressive or violent. Parents whose Self-worth orientation was built more around their relationship to others tended to be less supportive or fostering of imaginative play in their children and also tended to be less concerned about the quality of programming that children viewed or about the likelihood of the children's exposure to aggressive content.

The second phase of our investigation involved watching the children more directly in their response to various of the "Misterogers" programs to see if we could get some clue as to the kinds of materials that particularly held the children's attention. Viewing in a group as large as fifteen is not the ideal situation for the "Misterogers" program, quite frankly. "Misterogers" himself talks directly to the individual child, one presumably viewing alone or with one or two others in a home atmosphere. At the day care center, the groups of fifteen were naturally more restless and less able to concentrate at the slow pace of a program like the "Misterogers" one. Nevertheless the level of concentration was moderately high for three and four year olds for all of the programs. Particularly effective were programs that involved make-believe animals and puppets. What seemed clear was that the building of tension and indeed even moderate aggression as in the "Jack in the Beanstalk" puppet show that took up part of one of the programs will hold attention, produce positive emotional reactions that can be easily recorded, and will reduce the likelihood of overt aggressive behavior in the children. For groups as large as this, the more low-keyed programs such as the one that dealt with books and reading while stimulating a good deal of imaginative play in the children during the program itself failed to hold their attention to the set and in that sense was somewhat less accessible for this type of large audience. Our experience based on analysis of the pattern of the children's behavior as observed by raters during each of the programs used suggests that there are distinct advantages to the use of television with an available adult intermediary as part of day care or nursery facilities provided that the viewing groups are limited to perhaps no more than six and ideally three or four. In settings such as those with the adult initially present and then gradually phasing himself or herself out the gentle message of "Misterogers" and the stimulating quality of his Neighborhood of Make-Believe for imaginative play seems decidedly to be an important positive way in which television can have an impact.

A final phase of this modest form of community intervention included the establishment of parent groups that met through the following year under the direction of one of the authors. What emerged amongst other things from these group meetings with parents was the sense that modestly educated young parents are eager for help in learning how to use the television medium more effectively. They're not always sure that they can control the set. The inevitable family fights over viewing of sports activities necessarily emerge. Nevertheless there seems to be considerable interest in the possibility that help might be forthcoming in deciding on what might be the most appropriate types of television shows for various age levels of children. Parents also needed help with facing some of their own social attitudes. For example, the low-keyed gentlemanly "Misterogers" was perceived by many women and particularly those who took a strongly traditional feminine orientation on one of the scales we employed of sex-role identification as being perhaps too "effeminate"; they felt it wasn't a good idea to expose their sons to this type of programming. It was clear that parents need help in understanding the difference between homosexuality and gentle humanity. For this group of parents anything that smacked of homosexuality was terribly distressing and it required some help for them to see that whatever their prejudices might be they were irrelevant to the quiet and thoughtful approach that "Misterogers" took to the children. But it became quite clear to us in the course of the study that even relatively "liberated" women were inclined to feel that their sons would be in some way distorted in their growth if they were not exposed to vigorously active or aggressive male figures on television. Perhaps one implication of our experience with this group around the "Misterogers" show was that if women's liberation is to become a reality in the more ideal sense, women are going to have to pay more attention to accepting the gentleness in their own sons and to preparing them for more of the tenderness and sensitivity that in the past has been so exclusively emphasized for women.

IMPLICATIONS

The general implications of our experience in this particular mixture of formal experiment with community intervention on a small scale has led to some important directions in which we feel research ought to go in the future. We believe that it is quite feasible to study the ongoing viewing patterns of children to a variety of programming and to rate the children by the use of trained observers on a variety of affective reactions as well as indications of degree of concentration and overt aggressiveness. We believe it is desirable to compare the pattern of viewing and enjoyment of particular programs with response to other programs and also to examine the subsequent outcomes in spontaneous play behavior of persistent viewing of a variety of programs. One obvious question we have has to do with the differential impact of shows such as "Misterogers" with more popular and better known "Sesame Street." There seems little question that the quick cut and lively theatricality of "Sesame Street" may hold children's attention more, particularly if viewed in groups. What remains to be studied more extensively is the degree to which the "message" whether cognitive or attitudinal is grasped by the child. Recent studies of the use of the Fat Albert spots by children indicated that techniques are available for evaluating the degree to which the particular pro-social message may be grasped by a youthful audience. It would seem that little by little psychologists will have to take the trouble to evaluate the socialization impact of widely viewed programs and use this information to feed back suggestions both to parents and producers.

Another implication that grew clearly out of our contact with the parents in the group was the desirability of building into either regular clinical or educational facilities or to consultation programs for parents of children in nursery schools, kindergartens or day care centers some regular systems of obtaining information on parents' viewing habits and then feeding back to the parents suggestions on approaches to monitoring the TV, to viewing the television closely with children and serving as intermediaries or translators. Parents also need to learn methods of clearly limiting the children's exposure. Many parents were genuinely surprised to realize that allowing children to view late night shows might actually increase the possibility of nightmares or overt aggressive behaviors for some of them. Once confronted with some of the research evidence in this connection or with the reasonable alternatives available, parents seemed only too eager to rethink their approach to the children's viewing habits.

One of our theoretical hypotheses that as yet bears more intensive testing has to do with the possibility that children who have been encouraged to develop more extensive imaginative play tendencies are likely to be less influenced by negative content and more capable of integrating pro-social messages perceived from television. It remains to be seen whether this hypothesis can be supported in more formal research, but it appears to us that there is a whole variety of questions of this kind that need to be asked about the interaction of predispositional variables, general parental atmosphere and the response to specific pro-social types of television content (see Appendix).

In conclusion, our position based on this and related experience in observing pre-school children and their response to teaching and television viewing is that there is still a tremendous opportunity for increasing the scope and flexibility of socio-dramatic and imaginative play in most children. Television provides both an exciting viewing situation and interesting and elaborate content which can later be incorporated by children into make-believe play. The problem is that what tends to get incorporated by many children are the more violent aspects of the television content since those are so much the focus of the adult oriented programming to which we found so many really young children exposed. Our position is that interesting and elaborate make-believe themes using both realistic and puppet or fantasy characters abound in life and these can be used in programming or in direct make-believe training for children so that they can be incorporated into the play behavior of the children subsequently. Such imaginative play along with some of the other pro-social kinds of exposure such as the cooperativeness or positive alternatives to aggression in frustration situations that have been dealt with by Stein and Friedrich (1973) seem to us important parts of socialization for all children. Rather than approaching television which is clearly here to stay as a member of our family with negative attitudes either of censorship or helpless scorn, we believe that it is up to psychologists to examine the parameters of the child's imaginative capacities and then find ways in which systematic viewing with adult help can enhance growth possibilities in a variety of constructive areas.

References

CARLSON, R. & LEVY, N. A brief method for assessing social-personal orientation. *Psychological Reports*, 1968, **23**, 911–913.

CBS/Broadcast Group. A study of messages received by children who viewed an episode of "Fat Albert and the Cosby Kids." Office of Social Research, CBS, 1974.

MURRAY, J. P. Television and violence. *American Psychologist*, 1973, **28**, 472–478.

SINGER, J. L. & SINGER, D. G. Fostering imaginative play in pre-schoolers: Television and Live Adult Effects. Paper read at American Psychological Association Convention, New Orleans, 1974.

SINGER, J. L. The influence of violence portrayed in television or movies on overt aggression. In J. L. Singer (Ed.), *The Control of Aggression and Violence*. New York: Academic Press, 1971.

SINGER, J. L. *The Child's World of Make-Believe: Experimental Studies of Imaginative Play*. New York: Academic Press, 1973.

SPRUELL, N. Visual attention, modelling behaviors and other verbal and non-verbal meta-communication of pre-kindergarten children viewing Sesame Street. *American Educational Research Journal*, 1973, **10**, 101–114.

STEIN, L. & FRIEDRICH, L. K. Television content and young children's behavior. In J. P. Murray, E. P. Rubenstein, & G. Comstock (Eds.), *Television and social behavior*. Vol. 2. *Television and Social learning*. Washington, D.C.: U.S. Government Printing Office, 1972.

APPENDIX

THE COMPONENTS OF RESEARCH ON TELEVISION
AND CHILDREN

I. Which processes related to TV can we measure
   A. Attention of child to content
      1. Looking behavior
      2. Ongoing behavior
      3. Restlessness or diversion from screen
   B. Affect of the child while watching and after
      1. Ratings of emotion of expressiveness (TV monitor of face—e.g., Ekman)
         Motor tendencies—thumbsucking, gestures, masturbating, sleepiness or boredom, anger
         e.g., evidence of fear as well as aggression or enjoyment
         Mixed emotion—approach-avoidance or puzzlement
      2. Affect after watching
         e.g., liveliness, restlessness, attitude toward following program
      3. Interaction with other children and with set (Misterogers on screen) vs. child alone and with adults [their role]
      4. Predispositional variables—High vs. Low anxiety children, High Fantasy vs. Low Fantasy children, Aggressive vs. Nonaggressive, boys vs. girls, age and stage levels and affective reaction
      5. Imitation as a function of positive or negative affect vs. neutral
      6. Does liveliness hold interest in itself or must there be conflict, danger, aggression, cognitive disconfirmation or novelty, suspense
   C. Cognitive elements
      1. Level of language usage
      2. Complexity of stimuli
      3. Children's comprehension of content [modeling cues—acquisition—imitation/disinhibition/counter imitation
      4. Measures of concept formation and cognitive levels at outset—age levels—predispositional variables (Boehm test)
      5. Changes in convergent and divergent processes [Piagetian notions—animism, conservation] cognitive aspects of humor
II. Outcome measures
   A. Cooperative
      1. Retention of material
      2. Generalization and conceptual level
      3. Insights into conflicts; self-awareness and body image and reality vs. fantasy
      4. Symbolic transformation (e.g., emergence in dreams or spontaneous play)
      5. Vocabulary and language changes and communication (verbal and nonverbal) [Meichenbaum studies on reflective and impulsive children] [Smilansky—critical and injunctive vs. descriptive] Self-references and alternations of role
      6. Imagery evidences—Reyher's semantic elaboration

      7. Competence and mastery level; task persistence
      8. Organization—structuring capacity
  B. Affective
      1. Joy and interest—positive affects, humor and playfulness
      2. Modifications of anger and alternatives to aggression—modeling of coping mechanisms in conflict situations
      3. Fear reduction—dentist, doctor, animals, hair cuts, dark, sleep, separation, strangers
      4. Tenderness, loving-warmth and love for animals, open affection
      5. Empathy, identification of own and others' emotions
  C. Socialization
      1. Cooperative behavior
      2. Sharing [Liebert's modeling and cooperation]
      3. Change in "ethical" level
      4. Self-control and delay
      5. Competence and mastery level
      6. Sociodramatic play—role playing and role reversal
      7. Tolerance for self and others—racial, handicapped
II. Parent and teacher training
  A. Delineation of major training areas
      1. Awareness of cognitive level differences, e.g., vocabulary, grasp of situations
      2. Awareness of stage in social development
      3. Identification of conflicts and negative affects
      4. Communication of positive affects
      5. Awareness of environmental reinforcement contingencies (careful observation)—monitoring behavior
  B. Specific training
      1. Role playing of techniques for conflict resolution or reinforcement
      2. Imaginative games
      3. Expression of own positive affect and awareness of own styles—touching and physical contact
      4. Developing specific dependency or independence
      5. Preparation for specific life situations
        a. Separation and attachment
        b. Sibling rivalries
        c. Need satisfaction and delay of gratification
        d. Doctors, dentists, operations
        e. Refusal to eat, toilet training, sleep resistance, regressive behavior, temper tantrums, social withdrawal, shyness, timidity, sadness
        g. General and specific aggression situations
        h. Natural phenomena—storms, dark
        i. Phobias and compulsions
        j. Development of competencies and failures (e.g., athletics)

Part Three

THE SCHOOL-AGE
CHILD

9

Physical Characteristics and Skills

Physical development, health and motor coordination are all closely interrelated, affecting each other and also influencing the child's learning, social relationships, and attitudes toward himself. In planning either research or programs for children, it is essential to take into account the child's body, growth, health, and activity patterns.

From David Sinclair's book, Human Growth After Birth, we have selected a detailed description of one system, the skeletal system. Much is known about the different types of growth involved in bone growth, and Sinclair makes these processes very vivid. The study of bones is significant not only because the skeleton plays a prominent role in posture, locomotion, and the formation of blood, but because bones form a sensitive record of health and disease, as well as of growth.

Children differ in their ability to fight infection and to recover quickly and completely from illness. The article by Gerald T. Keusch describes the interaction between malnutrition and infection, including the role of immunity. Keusch shows how poverty leads to malnutrition, infection, and retarded growth. He points out that the problem is economic and political more than it is medical.

Optimal growth and health require large amounts and varieties of physical activity. Academic learning, social development, and personal growth are enhanced by adequate physical exercise. D. A. Bailey documents children's need for sufficient vigorous activity and points out that Canadian children are exposed to a sedentary life. United States children may be even more sedentary. Bailey describes a French experimental program in physical education that has been enormously successful in stimulating healthy development of the whole child.

Cartilage and Bone

David Sinclair

PERTH MEDICAL CENTRE

The skeleton contributes about 14 per cent to the weight of the adult body, and, along with the fibrocartilaginous intervertebral discs, something of the order of 97–98 per cent of the total height. (The remaining 2–3 per cent is due to the thickness of the scalp and the fibro-fatty pad of the heel, together with the thickness of the articular cartilages in the lower limb and in the atlanto-occipital joint.)

A great deal more is known about the growth of bone than about the growth of any other tissue, because of the accessibility of bone to investigation in the living person by means of radiology. It is therefore possible to discuss the processes involved in some detail.

FORMATION AND GROWTH OF CARTILAGE

Towards the end of the first month of fetal life the embryonic connective tissue in the region of the future skeleton begins to show signs of differentiation. The primitive connective tissue cells become more closely packed, and lose the processes which up to now have radiated from them. Later they begin to lay down a matrix rich in chondroitin sulphate (cartilage is about 70 per cent water, and, of the dried residue, 80 per cent is collagen and chondroitin sulphate), and this gradually separates the cells from each other again. The cells round the developing cartilage begin to form two layers: in the outer one they differentiate into fibroblasts, and coincident with this collagen is laid down. The cells of the inner layer remain more or less undifferentiated and capable of division to produce cartilage cells. The two layers together are called the perichondrium.

The newly-formed cartilage grows larger in two ways, by interstitial growth and by appositional growth. Interstitial growth occurs because the cells in the centre of the developing mass do not immediately lose their power to divide. The new cells which they form join with the older ones in laying down more and more matrix, and the whole tissue grows rather as dough does in bread-making. Obviously this process depends on the matrix being pliable, and after a short while the matrix becomes too rigid for much interstitial growth to occur, and the second mechanism, appositional growth, takes over.

In this process the cells of the deeper layer of the perichondrium divide: some of the offspring remain as stem cells, and others differentiate, so that more and more cartilage is laid down on the surface of the existing mass [FIGURE 1]. The differentiated cells surround themselves with matrix in the usual way, and are in turn overlaid by successive new layers so that they gradually sink into the depths. As the mass increases in size, the surface area of the perichondrium expands to cover it and an increasing number of stem cells is therefore required.

From *Human Growth After Birth*. 2nd ed. London: Oxford University Press, 1973. Pp. 48–58. Reprinted by permission.

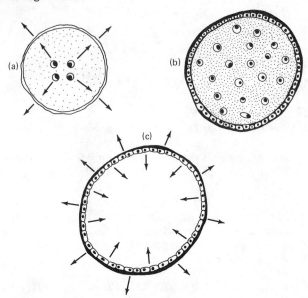

FIGURE 1.   *Interstitial and appositional growth. (a) Interstitial growth. The cells in the centre of the mass divide and the whole mass increases in size as a result. The matrix is still spongy and elastic. (b) The matrix is now too rigid to allow further expansion by interstitial growth. (c) Appositional growth. The cells of the inner layer of the perichondrium divide, so adding successive layers of cartilage to the surface of the mass and progressively pushing the active layer itself further away from the centre of the mass.*

OSSIFICATION

During the second month of fetal life, bone formation begins. In a few bones, such as the clavicle and the bones of the vault of the skull, ossification begins directly in the connective tissue of the embryo, and such bones are said to be ossified "in membrane." The remaining bones of the skeleton are ossified "in cartilage," which means that the same sort of process takes place after the connective tissue has become converted into a sort of cartilaginous template: the only difference is that cartilage bones have to go through this extra stage.

The points at which bone formation begins are known as "primary centres" of ossification, and these centres appear in different bones at different times, the first usually being either the mandible or the clavicle, at about the fifth week of fetal life. In a membrane bone, the first sign of ossification is the penetration of a blood vessel to the spot, bringing with it specialized cells called osteoblasts and osteoclasts. Around the osteoblasts collagen fibres are deposited, and on these fibres calcium and other inorganic salts accumulate. The osteoclasts, which are large multinucleated cells, have the task of shaping the growing bone tissue by removing unwanted material. There has been a great deal of controversy about the exact methods employed by the osteblasts and osteoclasts, and the matter is too complicated to go into in a book of this size. It is generally accepted, however, that osteoblasts are in some way concerned with bone deposition and osteoclasts with its removal.

In the primary centre of a cartilage bone, the first sign of ossification is that the cartilage cells swell up, and arrange themselves in columns. At the same time calcium salts are deposited in the matrix of the cartilage, so converting it into what is known as "calcified cartilage." A blood vessel now grows into the region from the perichondrium, bringing with it osteoblasts and osteoclasts as in the case of membrane bones. The osteoclasts remove some of the calcified cartilage, collagen fibres appear round the osteoblasts, and gradually the calcified cartilage is replaced by true bone.

GROWTH OF SHORT BONES

The subsequent growth of a short bone such as one of the cuneiform bones of the foot can be illustrated by a diagram [FIGURE 2]. In the centre of the cartilage, which is by now taking up the shape of the adult bone and is therefore known as the "cartilaginous model," there is a steadily enlarging core of bone. At the same time the original cartilage is itself growing appositionally, by the deposition of more cartilage on its surface. A kind of race develops between the two processes of cartilage deposition and bone formation, and this continues until the adult stage of development is reached, at which time the bone formation "catches up" with the deposition of cartilage so that the cartilage disappears, except for a thin rind which is left on the surface wherever the bone takes part in a joint with its neighbours. Because the perichondrium has come to surround bone and not cartilage, we now call it periosteum, but it retains the same two layers.

The perichondrium covering the cartilaginous joint surfaces disappears in the course of development. Such surfaces do not stop growing with the attainment of maturity, for they are exposed to considerable wear and tear which has to be made good, but reparative growth in this region is necessarily interstitial, since there can be no contribution from the perichondrium. Similar

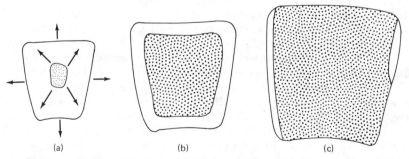

(a)   (b)   (c)

FIGURE 2.   *Growth of short bone. (a) The core of newly formed bone in the centre of the cartilaginous "model" increases in size at the expense of the cartilage. At the same time the cartilaginous model itself grows by activity of the perichondrium. (b) Growth of new bone proceeds faster than growth of cartilage, so that a greater proportion of the developing structure is composed of bone. (c) Bone formation has outstripped cartilage formation and the whole structure is now composed of bone with the exception of a large cartilaginous articular facet on one surface and a smaller one on the opposite surface. This is the adult condition for this particular bone, and growth now ceases.*

considerations apply to the articular cartilages at the ends of the long bones, which may retain a thickness of 5–6 mm. in the larger joints.

GROWTH OF LONG BONES

The growth of the long bones of the limbs is more complicated. The primary centre appears in the cartilaginous shaft of the future bone in exactly the same way as in a short bone. But, about the same time, bone begins to be formed on the surface of the shaft, due to the appearance of osteoblasts in the perichondrium, which now becomes the periosteum. The active cells in the deeper layer of the periosteum cause the shaft to grow in thickness. At the same time the bone formed in the primary centre is eroded away by osteoclasts, leaving a cavity which is not built in by osteoblasts, and forms a convenient storage place for the blood-forming cells and fat which constitute the bone marrow. As ossification proceeds, so the marrow cavity extends along the shaft of the bone and at the same time grows in diameter because of osteoclastic activity in its walls. The bone continues to grow thicker by appositional growth on the outside of the shaft, but as it does so the destruction on the inner surface keeps pace, and in this way the ratio of the total diameter of the shaft to the thickness of its walls is maintained more or less constant until maturity.

While these events are taking place, the expanded ends of the cartilage model grow, at first by interstitial, and later by appositional growth. As time goes on, other centres of ossification appear in the cartilage masses at the ends of the future bone [FIGURE 3]. In some instances there may be several such "secondary centres," which may eventually fuse together to form one large centre. Some secondary centres appear before birth, but the majority appear later, at a time characteristic of the individual bone; many do not begin their activity until puberty. The mass of bone formed by a secondary centre or an agglomeration of secondary centres is called an epiphysis, and, because of their calcium content, these epiphyses are readily seen in radiographs, where they show as a dense shadow separated from the shaft by a translucent zone of still growing cartilage. This zone of cartilage is known as the "epiphyseal plate," and it is a vital factor in the growth in length of the bone.

Cartilage cells in the epiphyseal plate increase its thickness by interstitial growth at the same time as ossification proceeding outwards from the shaft is destroying it and manufacturing bone. The result is that a race similar to that which occurs in the short bones takes place, and eventually the cartilaginous plate is overwhelmed, and becomes replaced by bone, which therefore unites the epiphyseal mass with the bony shaft. This "closure" of the epiphysis terminates the growth in length of the bone, and in most of the long bones this event occurs at about the age of 16 to 18 in the female and 18 to 21 in the male. It is interesting that in rats the epiphyses of the long bones never close, but merely become inactive; such a quiescent zone of growth may be reactivated by various stimuli in fully adult animals. For example, rats can be made to grow at any time during their lives by injections of somatotrophin. This is not possible in man once the epiphyses have closed.

One of the earliest things to be discovered about the growth of a limb bone was that interstitial growth in length does not occur. This was shown by Stephen Hales, and subsequently by John Hunter, who made marks on the

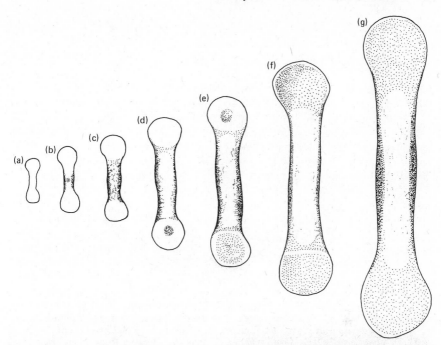

F I G U R E 3. *Growth of long bone. (a) Cartilage model. (b) Primary centre appears in the shaft and a collar of compact periosteal bone surrounds it. (c) The shaft is ossified but the ends remain cartilaginous. (d) The marrow cavity appears in the shaft and progressively enlarges. A secondary centre eventually appears at one end of the bone. The walls of the shaft are made of compact bone. (e) Another secondary centre has appeared. The first has now formed an epiphysis of cancellous bone covered by cartilage and separated from the bony end of the shaft by a cartilaginous epiphyseal plate. (f) The second epiphyseal plate is overwhelmed by the ossification proceeding into it from the shaft and has been converted into bone. Growth at this plate has ceased and the epiphysis is said to be "closed." (g) The cartilaginous epiphyseal plate at the "growing end" of the bone continues to grow in thickness for some time, but eventually it too is replaced by bone and growth in length comes to a halt. Throughout the whole process of growth in length, growth in thickness of the shaft has proceeded steadily by apposition from the periosteum.*

shaft of a bone, allowed the animal to grow, and subsequently found that the distance between the marks remained constant. Similar evidence can now be obtained by radiology after embedding two pellets of metal in the substance of a growing bone. Radiology is indeed the chief method of studying the growth of human bone, but other methods can be used with animals. For example, pigs readily eat the plant madder (*Rubia tinctoria*), which contains a compound similar to the dye alizarin. This is deposited where bone is being laid down and stains it pink. If an animal is given madder to eat for a known period, it can then be killed and the bones can be examined; all bone formed during the time of madder feeding will be stained pink, and will stand out from the normal white bone [FIGURE 4]. In more recent years further observations have been made using tetracycline, which is deposited mainly in the periosteal growing region, in the epiphyseal plate, and in the region at the end of the shaft. Other workers have used radio-isotopes such as strontium.

FIGURE 4.   *Shaft of the tibia of a pig fed on madder. The madder was omitted from the food for 30 days before the animal was killed, and the bone formed during that time is white, while the previously formed bone is stained red (indicated by stippling).* (Drawn from a photograph by Brash, J. C. (1934), *Edinb. med. J., 41*, 305–19; 363–87.)

In man, more growth always takes place at one end of a long bone than at the other, and the more active end is sometimes known as the "growing end" of the bone. This is perhaps misleading, since both ends grow, but the term does serve to indicate the end at which an injury might result in more disturbance in the growth of the limb. In the upper limb, the "growing ends" of the bones are at the shoulder and the wrist: in the lower limb, they are at the knee. There are further important differences in the rates of growth of individual bones. Thus, the growing end of the femur puts on length roughly twice as fast as the growing end of the tibia. Injury to the epiphyseal plate at the lower end of the femur is thus much more serious in its effects on growth than damage to the plate at the upper end of the tibia. If the growth at one end of a long bone is experimentally prevented, there is an increase in the rate of growth at the other end, but so far there is no explanation for this observation.

Just why one end of a bone should grow faster than the other is not known: the various influences which determine bone growth would be likely to affect both ends equally, and there appears to be no histological or biochemical difference between the epiphyseal plates of the two ends. It is similarly curious that in all long bones except the fibula the secondary centres which appear last are the first to fuse with the shaft. Occasionally, as in the rat, fusion does not take place at all, and the epiphyseal plate remains visible on a radiograph as a radiotranslucent line separating shaft from epiphysis. In such cases growth usually stops at or about the normal time.

As in most living things, the pressure exerted by the growth process is enormous, and it has been estimated that in order to stop growth at an epiphysis in a human limb it is necessary to apply a force of some 400 kg. Pressures less than this do not entirely stop growth, but they may impede it, and if the pressure is applied at an angle to the line of growth, deformities may result through the growth being misdirected. It has been suggested that certain deformities may be the result of faulty sitting or sleeping postures in small children; for example, that the prone knee-chest sleeping position may give rise to bow legs through pressure being applied at an angle to the epiphyses at the knee.

At the ends of the bones, where growth is rapid, spongy bone tends to be produced. This has a honeycomb structure, in which thin plates of bone criss-cross each other, enclosing in their meshes little cellular spaces in which is packed the marrow. The directions taken by these plates, which are called trabeculae, depend on the stresses thrown on the particular bone, and it seems that the collagen fibres, on which the inorganic salts are deposited, are laid down in such a way as to resist the pressure and tension lines of force in the bone. The most celebrated example in the body is afforded by the head and neck of the femur, in which the stresses can be compared to the stresses in a crane head [FIGURE 5]. It appears that the trabeculae may at first be laid down at random, but that those which are inclined obliquely to the shearing forces in the bone are moved out of the way by these forces. Trabeculae which happen to lie in the direction of a pressure or tension line will be comparatively undisturbed, since along these lines there is no shearing force. Nevertheless, a genetic factor is also involved, since bone removed from the body and grown in nutrient medium will also show similarly oriented trabeculae.

In the shaft of the bone, where growth is relatively slow, the bone produced by accretion is compact and dense. It has in fact been suggested that rapid bone growth always produces spongy bone, and slow growth produces compact bone.

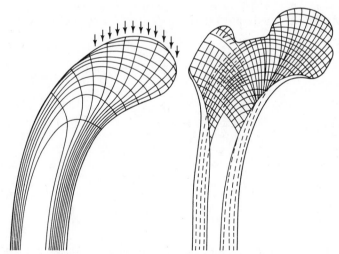

FIGURE 5.   *Lines of stress in cancellous bone. The upper end of the femur (right) compared with lines of stress in the head of a crane (left).* (From Thompson, D'Arcy W. (1942), *Growth and Form*, 2nd ed., London, Cambridge University Press, by kind permission of the publishers.)

Whatever the reason, the compact bone of the shafts of the long bones is thickest where it has to withstand the maximum stresses; in general, this is about the middle of the shaft.

Moulding and rearrangement is not confined to the interior of the growing bone. As growth proceeds, it is necessary that some of the existing surface material should be removed if the characteristic shape of the bone is to be preserved [FIGURE 6], and this is done by the osteoclasts. If anything goes wrong with the moulding process, the ends of the bones will be clumsy, thickened, and inadequately suited for their purpose. Some of the external moulding of a bone depends on the pressures and stresses exerted by the local soft tissues—for example, the pull of muscles attached to the bone, or the pressure of a neighbouring nerve trunk. But these effects can only be considered as a kind of "fine adjustment," and a bone grown in tissue culture, with no such influences acting on it, will still assume a shape not too different from the normal adult configuration.

Unlike the bone itself, the fibrous periosteum which covers it increases in surface area by general interstitial growth, and therefore some sliding has to take place between the two structures. Since the muscles have their primary attachment to the periosteum, which is in turn attached to the bone by Sharpey's fibres, it follows that considerable local reajustments must occur in the case of muscles attached where much sliding takes place. The attachments of muscles have also to be rearranged because of the continuous process of moulding of the prominences or depressions to which they are fixed.

Bone also undergoes internal reconstruction during growth. The distribution and arrangement of the trabeculae alter continuously to maintain the pattern induced by external stresses, and the Haversian systems of compact bone which is undergoing moulding are removed and reorganized.

Once bone has been formed it is by no means inactive; it is constantly being destroyed and reformed, and the picture presented by radio-isotope studies is

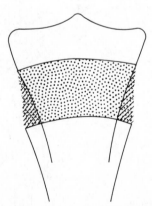

FIGURE 6.   *External modelling of bone. The diagram shows the upper end of the tibia, the outline of the adult bone being superimposed on the outline of the 14-year-old stage of its development. The total amount of bone laid down by the epiphyseal plate during the time interval is shown by the stippling, and the amount of this bone which has to be removed in order to keep the contour of the bone constant is shown by the cross-hatching.*

one of an intensely busy tissue, in which the maximal rate of structural change occurs round about the age of $2\frac{1}{2}$ years. In young adults there is a relatively low turnover of material in bone, and later in life the amount of destruction gradually comes to predominate over the amount of replacement, so that bone tends to become rarified and weakened in old age.

Malnutrition and Infection : Deadly Allies

Gerald T. Keusch

MOUNT SINAI HOSPITAL, NEW YORK

I noticed the first red spot on my daughter's face just after we had cleared the health and customs inspections at the airport in Mérida, Mexico. While we were waiting for our luggage, the first lesion was joined by several others, and soon three-year-old Lyssa—feeling sick and feverish—was spotted like a leopard. That evening at dinner she was apathetic and fidgety and had no appetite. The rash had changed its character, and now I could see small, glistening fluid-filled blisters sitting in the center of each red spot, the classical "dew drop on a rose petal" rash of chickenpox.

In the morning, the original spots were crusting, but since new ones were appearing, we stayed in Mérida for the day. Lyssa rode around town in a horse-drawn cab and enjoyed the swings in an empty playground. On the third day of her illness, Lyssa's temperature was only slightly elevated and there were fewer new spots. We decided to visit the Maya antiquities in the Yucatan as planned. For the next three days we hiked, climbed the ruins of ancient temples, and rode a Land Rover to the more remote ruins in the Puuc hills. Lyssa, with her crusting rash, looked the worse for wear, but she hiked and climbed, enjoyed and fussed, like any three-year-old without chickenpox.

At the same time, Maria, a three-year-old Maya living in the highlands of Guatemala, stopped eating, developed fever, and began to have diarrhea. By the time the rash of chickenpox broke out, she had been ill for more than two days and was losing weight. When signs of pneumonia appeared the following day, Maria's alarmed parents decided to bring her to the regional hospital. After walking six miles, they reached the highway where they could hail a bus. And so, five hours after leaving home in the arms of her father, Maria was in the hospital being treated for severe chickenpox and malnutrition. She remained critically ill and continued to lose weight for the first ten days of her hospitalization. Then, somewhat miraculously, she improved: the fever and diarrhea finally subsided and she showed a slight weight gain. Still, when she was discharged after three weeks in the hospital, Maria had not regained her preillness weight or general state of health.

Reprinted, with permission, from *Natural History* Magazine, November, 1975. Copyright © The American Museum of Natural History, 1975.

At this point my family and I arrived in Guatemala, where I was to study at the Institute of Nutrition of Central America and Panama (INCAP). And while Lyssa enrolled in a nursery school, Maria entered a nutritional rehabilitation center.

What was the difference between the response of these two children to the same common childhood illness? Was it simply a matter of luck, a difference in the virulence of the two virus strains involved, or perhaps a genetically determined resistance factor? What was to become consummately clear to me during that summer of study was the incredible toll in morbidity and mortality due to malnutrition and infectious diseases, which often operated together in a spiral course that led to permanent physical and psychomotor retardation, if not early death.

In developing countries, the heartrending sight of pediatric wards filled with children suffering from complications of infectious diseases, principally because they are malnourished when stricken, usually leads to a simplistic, well-intentioned, charitable effort to provide food for these youngsters. Interventions, however, are neither simple to devise nor simple to implement. The problem is rooted in the social, cultural, political, and economic morass of national development policies and in the international relationships of nations. And beyond that, efforts to preserve and improve the health of children in developing nations (often burdened with incredible population growth rates, even in the face of excessive infantile and childhood mortality) are, on the surface, counterproductive because they increase the number of survivors competing for the same limited food sources.

Malnutrition is a problem of human ecology that can only be understood through careful examination of each of the factors that interact in the complex. Infection is one such factor, with a multiplicity of cause and effect repercussions. My purpose in exposing this spectrum of interlaced contacts—both direct and circuitous, overt and covert—between malnutrition and communicable diseases is that we may better comprehend the priorities of national planning and development for programs of action. Based on a basic premise I hold both as a physician and a medical scientist—that an understanding of the mechanisims of disease is the essential beginning of its eradication—I will focus on the physiology of the problem, rather than extant injustices. Such a premise does not beg the moral question since the results of this approach can be as striking and revolutionary as revolution itself—and often less destructive.

Infection is the end result of an intimate joining of the paths of two biological entities, the host and the agent, occurring under specific environmental conditions. These same three factors—host, agent, and environment—are the classic elements of the science of epidemiology, or the impact of diseases in populations. To understand what happens to an individual or to a population of individuals, we must first understand the environment in which we live—we must examine the ecosystem in its natural state. To do this, we must leave the pediatric ward and enter the community.

The ravages of malnutrition are most profound on the young and thus, most poignant. In some areas mortality rates are so high that half the live born die before their seventh birthday, their deaths usually caused by or associated with, an infection. These children are sick with infections so often that it may seem that they are more or less continuously infected. In Santa Maria Cauque, Guatemala, for example, forty-five newborns were studied for their first three years of life. During that short period, they experienced nearly 2,500 episodes of a variety of infectious diseases. Diarrheal diseases accounted for more than two-fifths of the illnesses, with a peak incidence during the second year of life. Although we tend to think of newborns and young infants as particularly vulnerable, the experience in nearly every developing country demonstrates that the situation actually worsens for children one to four years old. The age at which this vulnerability becomes apparent usually corresponds to the age of weaning; with decreased intake of breast milk and no compensatory increase in other foods, the weanling becomes particularly susceptible to gastrointestinal illnesses, a syndrome known as "weanling diarrhea."

The interaction of malnutrition and infection can be succinctly stated: each makes the manifestations of the other worse. Regardless of the starting point, the two factors contribute to a never-ending cycle of infection to malnutrition to infection. What are the contributing mechanisms to this cycle? Broadly, these can be divided into the effects of infection on nutrition, the effects of malnutrition on infection (for example, effects on the manifestations of illness, as well as on defense mechanisms of the body against infectious agents), and occupying a middle ground, the effects of cultural responses to these main factors. Cultural practices can either mitigate or worsen these effects.

How does infection affect nutritional status? Perhaps the most readily documented and directly visible event during febrile infections is a generalized wasting of body tissues. People obviously lose weight during acute infectious illnesses, for the body literally begins to consume itself as muscle protein is degraded to its constituent amino acids. These, in turn, are released into the bloodstream and redistributed from there to other organs, such as the liver. A degradative process, such as breakdown of muscle mass, is called catabolism, and during infection, catabolic processes seem to be triggered by fever. As the protein is being broken down, it is also being wasted in body secretions, to be permanently lost via urine, feces, and sweat (a frequent consequence of fever). All humans, regardless of their state of nutrition, lose protein nitrogen during an infection, but some can afford it less, and some cannot ever replenish the loss. The infected individual is a two-time loser, for in addition to the excessive loss of protein nitrogen, he is also taking in fewer essential nutrients. As we have all experienced, loss of appetite often accompanies infections. Whereas a healthy, uninfected individual can reduce urinary nitrogen loss to compensate for diminished intake, this reactive mechanism does not operate during the fever phase of an infectious disease.

If the infected individual is a small child with marginal nutritional status at the outset, he may become a three-time loser, for acute manifestations of protein-calorie malnutrition frequently develop in this setting. This is the disease of the bloated, apathetic child we have all seen in photographs of regions afflicted by famine, drought, or war. And the condition frequently terminates in death.

At the same time that the body's stores of nitrogen are being wasted, other constituents of the fluid interior compartment of cells—potassium, magnesium, phosphorus, zinc, and sulfur—are also being lost. No doubt, the loss of these minerals has important consequences, but we do not yet understand their full physiological significance.

Occurring simultaneously with these breakdown phenomena are what are called anabolic processes: the manufacture of body constituents, such as cells, tissues, and proteins. Many of these anabolic processes are part of the mobilization of the body's defenses to fight the infection, and are, of course, beneficial. Increased production of scavenger white blood cells, for example, which confront, ingest, kill, and digest invading bacteria, is crucial if the infected individual is to survive. Nevertheless, such production is in competition with the body's maintenance and growth requirements for the limited stores of protein and energy. When tissue damage has also occurred, the need to repair the normal architecture means using protein and energy to repeat a task already accomplished once before.

In addition to white blood cells, the body synthesizes antibodies and other proteins. Among these are the antiviral substance interferon and a vital group of serum proteins that make up the complement system, whose function it is to augment and amplify the body's normal defensive response. There is no doubt that these proteins are necessary, for without them, severe and recurrent infections would occur. But when nutritional status is marginal, any need for the body to turn protein synthesis to production of these proteins represents a diversion from the growth or maintenance of normal tissues and organs.

This "rob Peter to pay Paul" principle can be seen in the altered growth curves of children who, suffering some degree of protein-calorie malnutrition, also become infected. Weight loss and delayed resumption of growth, often resulting in permanent stunting, typically are part of acute febrile infections. And what can be seen and measured in physical growth stunting appears to mirror similar effects on brain and neurological growth, with permanent retardation of psychomotor development.

However disastrous the consequences, these anabolic processes do have a discernible purpose—augmentation of the body's defense mechanisms. But a variety of other anabolic events occur that do not have an obvious purpose, at least as far as is now known. Among these processes are increased synthesis of certain liver enzymes and of a group of proteins known collectively as acute phase reactants. In a malnourished individual, synthesis of acute phase reactant proteins represents a diversion of amino acids from other building processes and body functions.

This is not the body's only apparently unwise decision. In addition to diversion, two other types of "functional wastage of nutrients" occur. One of the most characteristic responses to infection, in fact, one of the cardinal manifestations of disease, is fever. From the physiological point of view, the purpose of elevated temperature in restoring the well-being of the body's ecosystem has never been clear. True, in isolated instances raised temperature alone can eradicate an offending microorganism, such as the bacteria responsible for gonorrhea or syphilis. In fact, in the days when there were no antibiotics, physicians would transmit malaria to patients with venereal disease, in the hope that the periodic rigors and fevers of malaria would cure them. (This strategy of fighting fire with fire led someone to muse that the wages of sin is the cure in hell.)

But in most instances fever does not seem to serve a discernible purpose. Therefore, the energy utilized to generate the heat, the depletion of carbohydrate stores from the liver, the utilization of amino acids from muscle to make new sugar in the liver, and the mobilization of stored fat all represent functional wastage.

Finally, during febrile diseases iron, zinc, and several trace metals are taken up by cells of the liver and locked, as it were, into a strongbox. This sequestration of iron removes it from the bone marrow, where iron is used to synthesize hemoglobin, the oxygen-carrying protein of the red blood cells. Anemia, which frequently develops during chronic infection, is due in part to this sequestration of iron. Furthermore, iron serves a critical role in several enzymes in the scavenging white blood cells: iron deficiency may thus create deficient functioning of these cells.

Infection in the gastrointestinal tract, which is frequently the case in malnourished children, often has direct effects on the intestinal mucosa that can alter its absorptive function. This malabsorption, which means that ingested food is used less efficiently, can persist long after the acute infection subsides. During some of these infections, excessive numbers of cells fall off the intestinal surface and are passed out of the body. Since each cell is a protein packet, this further depletes the body's protein stores and poses an additional problem— replacement of the lost cells. Other protein packets—pus cells—are mobilized to fight the infection, and they too, are excreted along with intestinal cells.

As for cultural responses to infection, when a child has profound gastrointestinal symptoms and no appetite, his parents, whether in a developing country or an industrialized nation, often withdraw foods suspected of being difficult to digest. These usually include spices and condiments, but protein-rich foods are often included as well. At a time of increased protein loss from body stores and diminished efficiency of absorption from the intestinal tract, a greater than normal protein intake would be required just to maintain balance or simply to minimize losses. Yet just the opposite occurs.

In Central America, for example, the Indians prepare *atole*, a bland, watery drink made from corn, deeming it the only food fit to feed a sick child. In recent years a totally nonprotein cornstarch has been used for this purpose. As a volume replacement for real food, it is likely that cornstarch has precipitated many fatal cases of acute kwashiorkor; still, vitamin-supplemented cornstarch is actively promoted by commercial companies as a nutritious foodstuff. In our culture, too, the same kind of response occurs in the form of the tea and toast regimen to "rest" the intestine. But some populations can afford this form of dietary indiscretion less than others.

Infection, then, is a stress on anybody. But for those of us who are well nourished and basically healthy, the stress is short-lived. Aided by an elaborate system of defense mechanisms, we can quickly recover and recoup our nutrient losses. The malnourished child is not so fortunate; not only does he suffer far more from such stress, but his protective mechanisms are also deficient as a result of his poor nutritional status. To understand this complex interaction, it is first necessary to look at the mechanisms themselves.

Surrounded as we are by organisms invisible to the naked eye, in fact, outnumbered in our human cell population by the aggregate number of bacterial cells in our intestinal tracts alone, we have evolved a variety of protective systems. Some mechanisms are entirely nonspecific, some are exquisitely and elegantly precise.

The nonspecific mechanisms, although rarely considered, are very effective. The simple luxury of an intact skin, for example, represents a major barrier to invasion by potentially pathogenic bacteria that reside on the skin or that can be picked up by contact with infected people or contaminated objects in the environment. This is easily demonstrated by the frequency of infections that develop whenever the cuticle is broken, even in otherwise healthy, well-nourished individuals. Any nail chewer will confirm that paronychia is an occupational hazard.

The malnourished child, however, does not have an intact skin. Almost invariably, his skin is broken by fissures, sores, cuts, and ulcers—with oozing and crusting of serum and pus. These breaks in the integrity of the skin provide ready portals of entry for many types of bacteria.

The mucosae that line the nose, throat, and upper respiratory passages are thinner and more delicate than the thick, keratinized skin surface, and these membranes require additional protective mechanisms. They are lined with ciliated epithelial cells bearing multitudes of motile hairlike projections, which beat in unison in a wavelike fashion, a pattern sometimes likened to "wind in a wheatfield." These cilia rapidly move particles away from the lungs toward the mouth and the outside world, thus minimizing the chance of inhaled particles reaching the sensitive lungs. Mucus secreted by specialized cells scattered along the membranes aids in this process. Bacteria, dust, and other pollutants—rolled up and packaged in little balls of mucus—are propelled up toward the mouth by the beating cilia. From there, they may be spat out or swallowed. We do not know for sure, but it seems likely that since this process depends on energy, nutritional deprivation could adversely affect the functioning of cilia.

Within the stomach these mucus balls, together with ingested and swallowed bacteria, encounter hydrochloric acid. The purpose of this acid is not simply to cause indigestion, as television advertisements would have you believe, but to create favorable conditions for the action of digestive enzymes and to kill many bacteria unable to survive an acid environment. During the recent cholera outbreak in Europe and the Middle East, investigators in Israel found that patients developing the disease had abnormally low gastric acid production. This allows greater numbers of live organisms to pass into the susceptible small intestine, where the greater the number of organisms, the greater the likelihood of disease. Malnutrition may lead to, and is frequently associated with, gastritis, which results in diminished gastric acid secretion. Thus, poor nutritional status could directly impair this important body defense.

Leaving the general protective mechanisms, we come to the body's circulating defense system, which is far more specific. This system involves four major cell types and several proteins that circulate in the blood. Known as the complement system, these substances augment the functioning of the four cell types: the T-lymphocyte (T-cell), the B-lymphocyte (B-cell), the polymorphonuclear leukocyte (PMN), and the monocyte (MC). Like soldiers in an army, the cells have different jobs when confronted with an enemy, in this case, infectious agents, but their functions interrelate and, ultimately, they must work as a unit.

The B-cell, the workhorse of circulating immunity, makes antibodies—proteins in the blood or serum that antagonize foreign substances such as microorganisms—when stimulated to do so by contact with the inciting material. The T-cell cannot make antibodies, but responds to a specific stimulus by producing small protein molecules that encourage the activity of the other killer cells. Under proper conditions, the PMN and the MC recognize, ingest, and kill bacteria. Activated MCs, in fact, are called "angry monocytes," for they will ingest and kill almost anything they recognize as foreign, be it a different microorganism or an abnormal, malignant cell.

Perhaps the simplest system involves the PMN, a cell that is born and matures in the bone marrow, circulates briefly in the blood, and then passes out into the tissues; from there it is lost to the body via the urine and the intestinal tract. This passage is a one-way journey; the circulating cell pool represents the front line of defense, with the bone marrow a reserve force. In response to invading bacteria, particularly bacteria in tissues rather than those that circulate in the blood, PMNs must recognize that they are needed and move to the site of developing infection, a process called chemotaxis. Once at the site, the PMN must recognize the organism in order to ingest it (phagocytosis, literally, "eating the cell"). In order to be recognized, the invading organism must be prepared by a process called opsonification (from the Greek, "to buy victuals" or "to prepare for eating"). The process involves coating the bacterial cell with certain substances, opsonins, derived from the complement system or a specific antibody. Since many pathogenic bacteria are virulent by virtue of their ability to resist being phagocytized, opsonization is essential.

How does nutritional status affect this microbial world? Many of these responses are stimulated or influenced by the complement system. And this system is strongly affected by the body's state of nutrition. In a malnourished child, components of the complement system are deficient, adversely affecting chemotaxis, opsonization, and bacteria-killing systems. Even when there are normal opsonins and the offending organism is coated so that it can be recognized, the malnourished PMN seems to kill ingested bacteria more slowly.

This is a bigger problem than it may at first seem. To reduce the rate at which the PMN kills bacteria does not just add a day or so to the length of illness; rather, it can allow the disease to develop in the first place, instead of being stopped in its tracks before symptoms appear.

The T-cells, too, are exquisitely sensitive to nutritional insult. The malnourished child has fewer T-cells, and these function less effectively, which means that all defenses dependent upon them are markedly impaired. This type of response is particularly important in such infections as tuberculosis and typhoid fever.

As for the B-cells and the MCs, they may be relatively spared. In my laboratory, we caused animals to develop protein-calorie malnutrition, then studied the MCs in the test tube. We exposed them to certain pathogens and watched the MC-immune response, which was largely normal. But in the real test, in the intact animal, where MCs have to work in conjunction with T-cells and the complement system, both of which are markedly abnormal, they cannot function adequately. Since many of the mechanisms involved in the immune system have overlapping domains, small qualitative abnormalties in several areas can add up to a major problem.

An understanding of the interaction between malnutrition and infection is not simply an abstract exercise; it has therapeutic value in the pediatric wards where Maria and thousands of others like her are being treated. In the past, for example, a child hospitalized for protein-calorie malnutrition was immediately given iron to correct this deficiency. Yet if he had an infection, which was likely, this could be the worst thing to do. Since the iron-binding protein in a malnourished child is low, all iron added to the blood is freely available to the infecting organism, which may grow better and become more virulent as a result (like fertilizing a weed-filled garden). We now know that we must first replace protein before correcting for iron deficiency.

These findings also influence our understanding of disease prevention. Many countries have embarked on large, expensive, and well-intentioned programs of disease prevention through immunization of children. In theory, by vaccinating a child with live pathogens (which are, of course, attenuated), you cause his immune system to form antibodies to the agent. Thus, if he is exposed to the pathogen in the future, the successfully immunized child will not develop the disease. Such procedures have been responsible for wiping out most of the dreaded childhood infections—yellow fever, measles, polio, and others. Yet the malnourished child, with his immune deficiencies, may not be able to respond to these live pathogens in a normal fashion; if he is vaccinated, the organisms, which may live quite happily in his body for many years, could cause serious problems in the future.

Not only have we begun to understand that what is considered classical pediatric care in the developed countries may at times be inappropriate in the Third World, but studies in a Guatemalan village have also served to focus our attention on a new group. In the past, nutrition and health programs, including those of UNICEF and various charities, were aimed at school-age children, not because they needed such attention more than other groups, but because they were logistically reachable. Focus on weanling diarrhea pushed concern back to the vulnerable preschool child. We now believe that the most important group to reach is the growing fetus. Contrary to the belief that the developing infant could successfully parasitize the mother for whatever nutrients were needed for growth, our studies show that newborns in the village are not normal—they are small at birth, weighing an average of $5\frac{1}{2}$ pounds, and nearly 20 percent show evidence of subtle intrauterine infection.

Although there are legal and ethical considerations in defining when "life" begins, it is certainly not at birth. The Chinese, recognizing this long ago, call an infant one year old at birth. It could be that intrauterine malnutrition and infection affect prenatal growth and birth weight. Birth weight, in turn, significantly affects the growing infant's development: the smaller the newborn, the greater the incidence and severity of postnatal problems. Here then is a new target group for health intervention—a group that can be reached through the pregnant woman, who is an identifiable and often reachable person in the community.

What then does all this mean? Obviously, the ultimate answers to problems of malnutrition and infection lie in efforts to feed the world's population, to improve hygiene, and to control environmental sanitation. Unfortunately, these are political questions more than they are medical problems, and realistically, their resolution will take a long time. It will require the active input of physicians and medical scientists to help politicians, economists, and development planners set proper priorities. Physicians must be heard, and to do this, we will have to leave the laboratory and enter the political arena.

Immediate steps can be taken in the form of improved sanitation, education, immunization programs to control infectious diseases, and proper therapy when prevention has failed, but the entire public health approach must be reassessed, placing medical problems in the larger context of the ecology of poverty. To break the cycle of malnutrition and infection is a lofty goal, but if the Marias of Guatemala are to have the same chances as the Lyssas of New York to reach their full intellectual genetic potential, attainment of this goal is worth all the effort we can give it.

The Growing Child and the Need for Physical Activity

D. A. Bailey
UNIVERSITY OF SASKATCHEWAN

INTRODUCTION

This paper will attempt to provide some substantiation for the belief that in our sedentary post-industrial society of today, growing children must be provided with wider opportunities to participate in vigorous programs of physical activity. Canadian children today are entering a society characterized by sedentary living patterns, emotional stress, poor dietary habits, and lack of physical activity. And yet, many of the programs of physical activity being offered currently both in and out of school, tend to deprive a great many youngsters of their normal childhood instincts for play, and in fact discourage those very children who need activity the most.

WHY PHYSICAL ACTIVITY FOR CHILDREN?

On the basis of research findings to date we can say:

1. Physical activity is necessary to support normal growth in children.

2. Inactivity as a youngster can have a bearing on mature functional capacity and consequently may be directly related to a number of adult problems.

3. The basic orientation toward experience is established early in life. If we want adult participation in physical activity it should be remembered that motivation towards activity is probably laid down at a very early age. "As the twig is bent, so grows the tree."

From J. G. Albinson and G. M. Andrew (Eds.) *Child in Sport and Physical Activity*. Baltimore: University Park Press, 1975, Pp. 81–93. Reprinted by permission.

4. Learning inside the classroom may be enhanced and supported by activity outside the classroom. "All work and no play makes Jack a dull boy."

There are probably a number of other reasons for physical activity for the child which can be scientifically supported. In particular, in the psychological area, there is evidence that a positive enjoyable exposure to physical activity during the formative years has a great deal to do with self concept, confidence, and adult adaptability. This, however, is best left for others who are more expert in the psychological area to deal with. The present paper will limit itself to a discussion of the four listed reasons for activity.

1. PHYSICAL ACTIVITY TO SUPPORT NORMAL STRUCTURAL GROWTH

Reviews on the effect of exercise on structural growth have recently appeared in the literature (Elliott, 1970; Malina, 1969) which update earlier reviews published in 1960 (Rarick, 1960; Espenschade, 1960). Rarick (1973) has recently edited a book entitled "Physical Activity—Human Growth and Development" which delves deeply into the subject. These reviews all reach the general conclusion that a certain amount of physical activity is necessary to support normal structural growth.

Exercise is known to increase bone width and mineralization while inactivity decreases mineralization. Inactivity as a result of prolonged periods of recumbency, periods of immobilization in casts, and more recently prolonged space flights, leads to decalcification of bones. Resumption of normal activity corrects the imbalance, although sometimes it takes several years to restore loss of calcium due to immobilization (Kottke, 1966). Demineralized bones, of course, are weaker and more brittle. Athletes in good condition tend to have stronger bones and muscles and as a consequence their bones are less easily broken. In this context, a statement by Dr. C. Stuart Houston, Professor of Diagnostic Radiology, University of Saskatchewan, Saskatoon, is worth quoting.

> Bones are not solid unchanging structures as people once thought. Instead, a bone, like any other organ in the human body, is a *dynamic* structure. New cells are laid down and old cells are taken away. New calcium ions enter the scaffolding as old calcium ions return to the blood. The body has a very precise balancing mechanism to maintain normal levels of calcium and phosphate in our blood. For this reason, it takes extreme deficiency of calcium or vitamin D in our diet, or a marked abnormality of the parathyroid glands to cause demineralization of bone. Yet only one week of inactivity often causes noticeable demineralization—loss of half the calcium from a bone. So the amount of activity we get is much more important than the amount of milk we drink. If we are active, our bones will be well minera-lized and both bones and muscles will be strong. This is true in children, true in adult life and true in old age. As a radiologist, I see almost every day, dramatic changes appearing in bones and muscles from disuse. It seems obvious that continued exercise is necessary for the maintenance of normal bone and muscle strength—and normal health. This is not new or original but it is important. In-activity is very harmful.

Applying the research in this area to the growing child, it can be accepted that weight bearing and physical activity are not only important but necessary in terms of healthy growth.

2. Physical Activity, Functional Growth, and Adult Capacity
The question of what, if any, are the effects of exercise on the functional growth
of children, and on functional capacity when maturity is reached, has increasing
relevance today. We live in a country where cardiovascular diseases are the
cause of every second death. Recently, as interest has been focused on the
possible role of inactivity as a factor in the increasing incidence of cardiovascular
disease, we are finding more and more adults becoming interested in exercise.
This is good, but exercising throughout life particularly during the growing
years may be of primary importance. Just as many cases of adult obesity have
been linked to childhood nutrition, so adult health problems related to inactivity may possibly be linked to sedentary childhood activity patterns. As
Astrand has said speaking about physical activity. "Anything neglected during
adolescence can in many cases not be made up later on" (1972).

The importance of looking at the child when trying to identify basic causes
of degenerative cardiovascular disease in adults is best emphasized by a paper
by Kenneth Rose (1973). Rose documents the developmental history of arterio-
sclerotic disease in man. The first signs appear around age two and the disease
process is reversible until the age of 19. At about 19, the process of the disease is
essentially irreversible, and from then on it inexorably progresses until it
becomes clinically manifest usually in the 40's.

John Kimball, noted University of Colorado cardiologist has stated that
"Evidence is growing stronger that the earliest bodily changes leading to heart
disease begin early in life." He notes that more and more autopsy reports on
children show that their blood vessels have already begun to clog with fatty
deposits that can eventually lead to heart attack. Clearly, the importance of
proper diet and adequate exercise during the growing years cannot be over
emphasized.

Nathan Smith (1972), talking about the increasing incidence of obesity in
children has stated,

> If infants and children are not to be obese, there must be family activity and home
> activity patterns developed from infancy that will effectively increase energy
> expenditure. Restricted play pens can contribute as much to obesity as a high
> calorie, unsupervised diet. Mothers and families need our guidance from the birth
> of their infant in developing activity life styles that are going to provide a healthy
> energy expenditure.

Biochemical Studies on Exercise and Functional Growth   A recent approach
that has been taken in studying the effect of exercise on functional growth
is biochemical in nature. Researchers have been investigating growth at the
cellular level using biochemical techniques which are based upon the recognition that for most tissues the amount of DNA per cell nucleus is constant.
This provides a chemical unit which can be applied in studying the growth
phenomenon, whereby DNA per gram of tissue can be used as an index of
cell number and the protein to DNA ratio can be used as an estimate of
cell size.

These studies (Widdowson, 1970; Winick, 1971; Cheek et al., 1970;
Knittle and Hirsch, 1967) have shown that the rate of cell division and the
ultimate number of cells that comprise a particular tissue or organ are

determined not only by instrinsic (genetic) factors but also may be influenced by extrinsic (environmental) factors. The state of nutrition, prenatally and neonatally, either under-nutrition or super-nutrition, has been shown to be one such factor.

The question arises, are there other extrinsic factors that may influence cellular growth? What about a factor like exercise, particularly if it is introduced during a period of active growth? Skeletal muscle tissue would appear to be a tissue of particular interest in this respect because it has been shown to be in an active state during adolescence. As Cheek (1969) has said,

> The usual growth pattern for most organs is that the period of hyperplasia or cell division eventually stops and does not begin again. However, skeletal muscle is a striking exception. Most muscle hyperplasia occurs in fetal life and early postnatal life, but during adolescence, presumably under the influence of androgens, hyperplasia of muscle cells undergoes marked resurgence.

A valid working hypothesis would seem to be that just as nutritional insults at a given time during growth have permanent repercussions throughout life, perhaps the lack of strenuous exercise or the excess of it during the growing years may affect the ultimate adult complement of cells and hence the functional capacity to perform as an adult.

Studies by Buchanan and Pritchard (1970), Cheek (1971), and an investigation conducted in our own laboratory, Bailey et al. (1973) on the effect of exercise on skeletal muscle tissue in growing rats would seem to provide some backing for this hypothesis. Obviously work of this type must be continued, but if these studies can be substantiated by further animal work, and verified in man, the impact will be profound. What it will mean is that adult capacity may be a function of activity during the growing years in addition to genetic determinants.

Some knowledgeable people closely related to sports have been speculating along these lines for a number of years. Roger Bannister (1968), the first man to break the four minute mile, has said.

> Recently, as the average age of record breakers has fallen, I have realized that another factor is at work. If "interval" training is started when the athlete is young enough, his body can be 'stretched' physiologically and anatomically to a degree that is impossible if the training starts after maturity when growth has ceased.

Physiological Studies on Exercise and Functional Growth   A more traditional approach to study the influence of exercise or physical activity on functional growth has been to compare athletes with non-athletes, or to compare subjects classified according to various levels of physical activity. In the Saskatchewan Child Growth and Development Study (Bailey, 1968) children were followed on a longitudinal basis for 10 years from ages 7–16. A variety of measures were taken annually to try and find out if physical activity was related to growth in any way. Children were grouped into physical activity categories (very active, active, sedentary, etc.) on the basis of parental questionnaires and teacher interviews. On measures of strength, suppleness, and stamina (aerobic power) very active boys were significantly superior to sedentary boys at all ages (Bailey, 1973). These findings are in agreement with a similar longitudinal study on boys ages 11 to 18 reported by Parizkova (1972) who reported body composition as well as functional differences between boys classified according to activity.

A study of the best young girl swimmers in Sweden who were extensively studied over a period of years starting at age 14, showed that large functional capacities in lung volume and heart size were maintained into adult years. In commenting on this study, Astrand (1967: 760) speculated,

> During adolescence there may be a second chance to improve those dimensions which are of importance for the oxygen-transport system. This is an interesting problem, especially with regard to physical education in school. It may not be possible to repair later in life what is neglected during the adolescent years.

These and other studies confirm that physical activity and exercise are basically beneficial. But such comparisons do not establish what comes first. Are active children functionally superior because they are active, or are they active because they are functionally superior?

Ekblom (1970) used a dimensional approach to try and answer this question. He noted that if physical training is started in a grown man there is an upper limit in functional capacity over which one cannot go, even if the physical training is very hard and extended over many years. He investigated the effect of physical training on boys during adolescence to try to answer the question—when in life is this upper limit set? Is it strictly genetic or can it be influenced by physical training before and during puberty? He followed a training group of boys and a control group for six months and concluded that heart volume and functional capacities like maximal oxygen uptake increased in the training group more than could be expected from normal growth. Apparently an extrinsic environmental factor like exercise was involved along with intrinsic genetic growth factors.

Bailey et al. (1974) applied a similar dimensional approach to eight years of longitudinal growth data on boys aged eight to 15. Expected and actual changes in aerobic power as a result of increasing linear dimensions were calculated. Presently data on very active boys and very sedentary boys are being compared to the expected base line and the results of this analysis should provide further information on the influence of physical activity on functional growth.

Do functional changes as a result of training during youth persist into adult years? A study by Saltin and Grimby (1968) provides evidence to support this contention. They compared the adjustability to effort of three groups of subjects in the age group 50–59 years. One group consisted of men who were former athletes who had given up all sport 20 years earlier, and followed a sedentary occupation. A second group comprised men who had achieved the same athletic performances in their youth as their former colleagues in cross-country running or long distance skiing, but had kept up regular training during the adult years. A third group consisted of men who were non-athletes during youth. The results confirm the hypothesis, maximal oxygen uptake was 30 ml/min/Kg body weight in the men who were non-athletes during youth, 38 ml for the former youthful athletes who followed sedentary adult living patterns and 53 ml for the former athletes who had kept up regular activity in the adult years. Generally speaking, functional capacity as an adult appeared to be partially a function of activity during the growing years.

Obviously, many questions regarding exercise and functional growth remain unanswered but as the above studies indicate, data is now coming in and long overdue investigations are now being undertaken. On the question of whether physical training as a youth can affect mature functional capacity, the evidence while not yet clear cut is suggestive and indicates that an increase in physical activity for children is advisable not only for the immediate effect on the child, but also over the long term as it applies to adult health.

Before leaving this discussion of adult health, the study by Leaf (1973) on long lived people is of interest. He evaluated the living patterns and life style of very old people living in three geographic locations in the world where longevity of the people has been documented to be well above normal expectations. The one common link between the old people of the three communities was a high degree of physical activity.

> The old people of all three cultures share a great deal of physical activity. The traditional farming and household practices demand heavy work, and male and female are involved from *early childhood* to terminal days. Superimposed on the usual labor involved in farming is the mountainous terrain. Simply traversing the hills on foot during the day's activities sustains a high degree of cardiovascular fitness.

3. POSITIVE CHILDHOOD EXPERIENCE IS IMPORTANT   As adult health problems associated with sedentary living patterns become more pronounced, the importance of physical activity not only for children but for adults as well becomes increasingly important. The human body is built for action, not for rest. This used to be a historical necessity. The struggle for survival demanded good physical condition. Optimal function of the human body can only be achieved by regularly exposing the heart, circulation, muscles, skeleton, and nervous system to some loading, that is to say, physical work. In earlier times the body got its exercise both in work and in leisure. However, in our modern society machines have taken over an ever increasing share of the work which was formerly accomplished by muscle power alone. Too often even our leisure time is spent watching rather than doing. Our lifestyle has changed to such a degree that it seems now to be dominated by lying, sitting, and riding.

As a result of this situation we have recently seen a mounting campaign on behalf of governments and other agencies to increase public awareness concerning the need for increased physical activity. Through the use of the mass media, advertising campaigns of the type sponsored by Participaction have urged Canadians to participate in more physical exercise in order to attain a generally higher level of physical fitness.

The long term success of approaches of this nature depend, at least in part, on the motivation towards physical activity that is established at an early age. One way of assuring adult participation in physical activity is to make sure that all young children receive positive, enjoyable exposures to activity.

A study by Orlick (1970) provides substantiation for this premise. Extensive interviews were conducted with eight or nine year old organized sport participants and non-participants. The findings of this study showed that by eight or nine years of age many children had already been either turned on to or turned off sports. Many non-participant (and drop out) children in this study indicated that they never (or never again) would go out for a sports team, whereas, the vast majority of the participant children indicated that they would always want to go out for a sports team. As Orlick says, "If one is to seriously think about maximizing adult participation in sports and physical recreation, it seems imperative that all young children receive positive, enjoyable exposures to physical activity."

This then is another reason why physical education in our schools is so important. Along with parents, it is the school that must play a decisive role in leading people to physical activity. It is the school where recreative skills should be taught and where facts concerning the positive health benefits of physical activity should be imparted. It is in the school where opportunities for fun, self expression, discovery, and the chance to succeed physically should be provided for all children.

Unfortunately, many schools have failed the children in this regard. School curricula tend to reduce the time available for physical activity rather than increase it. In Canada at the elementary level the time devoted to physical education as compared to the time spent in intellectual pursuits during a school week amount to about six per cent of the total class time. The time allocation for physical education in the school day in Canada ranks among the lowest in the civilized world. Is there any rationale for this situation?

The UNESCO Council (1964) concerned with setting guidelines for education in emerging countries recommends the following.

> An individual, whatever his ultimate role in society, needs in his growing years a due balance of intellectual, physical, moral and aesthetic development which must be reflected in the educational curriculum and time table . . . Between $\frac{1}{4}$ and $\frac{1}{6}$ of the total time table should be devoted to physical activity.

But, in Canada over the last quarter century we have seen the steady erosion of the time available for organized physical activity within the school setting. At the upper secondary level the overemphasis upon academic education is so pronounced that in some cases it becomes almost total. This situation has developed because educational authorities have adopted the premise that learning will progress as a direct function of the amount of time spent behind a desk. Evidence in industry tells us this is not the case. There comes a point of diminishing returns beyond which productivity drops as working time increases.

Along these lines, there may be some lessons to be learned from the "$\frac{1}{3}$ time" school experiments in Europe, which seem to indicate that academic learning progresses better if proportionately less time is spent behind the classroom desk.

4. PHYSICAL ACTIVITY TO SUPPORT ACADEMIC LEARNING ($\frac{1}{3}$ TIME SCHOOLS)   The following material on the Vanves school in France has been drawn from a paper by MacKenzie (1974).

> Vanves is situated in the southern suburbs of Paris, France. The Vanves Primary School has nine classes of children, ages 6 to 11 years. The staff now consists of nine classroom teachers, who teach everything except swimming, dance and part of the games and gymnastics; plus two part time specialist physical education teachers, plus the principal (directrice), Mme. Boes. Since 1951, this

little school has been the focus of bold new education practices that now, almost 20 years later, are about to sweep across that nation's schools.

Both before and after World War II, many French doctors and educators were concerned about the heavily overloaded intellectual (i.e., academic) program in the schools. In the elementary (primary) schools, only two hours per week were devoted to physical education, plus three hours of recreation, compared with 23½ hours per week of academic work, with homework in addition. Increasingly, medical and educational opinion indicated that such an unbalanced program was not in harmony with what was known about the nature and growth of children, that it was not good for their healthy development. Many French headmasters had drawn attention to the inefficiency of afternoon intellectual work for most of the children in elementary schools.

As a result of these evaluations from the medical and teaching professions, several experiments were set up in Vanves (and later, in other regions), beginning in 1951, by the Ministry of Education. These were aimed at obtaining a better balance between the pupils' physical and intellectual activities, thereby arriving at a much more effective way of educating children. This was done by selecting certain classes in the Vanves school, revising quite significantly their daily program, and then comparing intellectual, physical, cultural, social, and other educational components with those of carefully paired controlled classes which continued under the normal school schedules. The whole series of experiments took place over a ten year period. Essentially, the experimental classes did their academic work in the mornings, and devoted the afternoons to physical education (daily), art, music, and supervised study. No written homework was assigned for the evenings. The time spent on academic education was reduced to about four hours per day, and that devoted to physical education raised to one to two hours per day (seven to eight hours per week).

By 1960, the results of the experiments more than confirmed the basic hypothesis. Not only were the health, fitness, discipline and enthusiasm superior in the experimental schools, but the academic results surpassed those of the control classes. It appeared that a better balance in educational activities resulted in better performance all around. Similar experiments were then repeated in Brussels and Japan, with similar results.

At the beginning of the Vanves experiments, the parents' concerns were mainly two-fold:

1. That their children would fall behind academically.

2. That (with the outdoor emphasis upon physical education) pupils would catch colds, etc., and miss school.

Neither of these actually occurred; in fact, the reverse.

Figure 1 (opposite) indicates the 1969 weekly timetable used in Vanves (actually used since 1961).

The results of extensive research in these schools—which have come to be known as "⅓ time" schools because nearly one-third of the daily or weekly timetable is devoted to physical education—are indicated in the following summary as expressed in an interview in 1969 with Dr. H. Perie, Chief of the Medical Services in the Ministry of Youth and Sports in Paris.

1. Doctors and educators in France now think alike—physical education is an integral part of education, perhaps even the main part.

	Monday	Tuesday	Wednesday	Thursday	Friday	Saturday
8:30		Academic		N	Academic	
9:30		10 Minute Exercise		o	Break	
10:30		Academic		S	Academic	
11:30				c		
12:30		Lunch		h	Lunch	
1:30	Games and Gymnastics	Swimming	Games and Gymnastics	o		N o
2:30				l	Dance	
3:30	Free Time		Rec ────────		───── reation	S c
4:00	Supervised Study — Art — Music				S.S. Projects	h o
5:00	Continuation for				Older Pupils	o l
5:30						

No Written Homework in Evenings

2. Scientific research into the effects of physical education establish that:

a) It promotes the growth of children.

b) Those taking physical education have better health and much less trouble.

c) Motor development is better, and is better balanced.

3. Those taking $\frac{1}{3}$ time physical education had better performances academically and less susceptibility to stress. Differences have shown up markedly in intellectual development. We wouldn't conclude that those taking physical education are more intelligent, but the *tools of intelligence* are much keener. As the physical education pupils have less problems, their minds are more open, and they will receive more from their teachers. This is why school results are better.

4. Study between the experimental and control groups showed:

a) The $\frac{1}{3}$ time physical education pupils mature more quickly, and are more independent.

b) The physical education groups will accept the social way of life better. By playing with and against others in a good setting, children learn the "life game" better than those who don't.

c) Aggressions can be controlled better by physical education opportunities.

Mme. Boes, the Principal of Vanves School, outlines the main benefits of $\frac{1}{3}$ time physical education in her school as follows:

1. Pupils can enter the secondary school at least as well as pupils from other schools.

2. They are in better health, stronger, not so tired, keener.

3. They are happier, have better attitudes, and less stress.

4. Discipline is better—very few problems.

5. It is easy for them to change to other schools.

6. The "esprit de corps" among the teachers is improved—things are better for all.

Despite this impressive research, the number of classes in France which adopted this Vanves way of education grew only slowly during the 1960's, perhaps to 1,500 classes. Many people hoped the Vanves example would become general in France, but many also felt that only if and when the Ministry *made* the plan general, would it in fact become so. Some of the reasons for the limited growth of the plan were attributed to tradition, inertia, increased costs, and a shortage of well trained elementary physical education teachers—the "resources don't follow" (although the idea might be good).

However, a dramatic breakthrough came in October, 1969. As of that date, the Ministries of Education, and Youth and Sports have specified "$\frac{1}{3}$ time" physical education for elementary schools in France—that is, to Grade VI— amounting to about six hours per week. (At the same time, the Ministries have also inserted five hours of physical education per week in the French secondary schools, dependent upon personnel and equipment.)

Two obvious questions face us here in Canada, in view of this research and development in Europe.

a. What are the implications for our schools?

b. What evidence do we have that our present distribution of educational experiences, and arrangement of the school day is the best we can provide for our children?

CONCLUSION

An attempt has been made to emphasize the importance of physical activity for all children. Physical activity is necessary to support normal growth in children, it is important for children to be active to ensure a healthy childhood. The importance of physical activity in terms of preventive medicine is also becoming clearer. Our present way of life can no longer spontaneously satisfy the biological need for physical activity, as in the past. Clearly, it is important to get people interested in regular physical activity at an early age. Anything that is neglected in youth in many cases can not be made up later on. Positive early experience is essential for all children if we hope to change adult life styles.

Unfortunately, as this paper has shown, school curricula have tended to reduce rather than increase the available time for physical activity and recreation within the school day. This is regrettable since it is during the school years that young people acquire the motivation, understanding and skills necessary for effective adult living. Hopefully, as a result of this conference, changes will be made in a system of education that constrains our children during the vulnerable period of active growth to bend over books and desks five and one-half hours a day without providing them with the time and resources to discover and use their physical faculties.

References

ASTRAND, P. O.
1967   Commentary—Symposium on physical activity and cardiovascular health. *Canadian Medical Association Journal* 96: 760.
1972   *Health and fitness.* Scandia Insurance Co., Stockholm.

BAILEY, D. A.
1968   *The Saskatchewan child growth and development study.* University of Saskatchewan, Saskatoon.
1973   Exercise, fitness and physical education for the growing child—a concern. *Canadian Journal of Public Health* 64: 421.

BAILEY, D. A., BELL, R. D., and HOWARTH, R. E.
1973   The effect of exercise on DNA and protein synthesis in skeletal muscle of growing rats. *Growth* 37: 323.

BAILEY, D. A., ROSS, W. D., WEESE, C. H., and MIRWALD, R. L.
1974   Maximal oxygen intake (VO_2 max) and dimensional relationship in boys studied longitudinally from age 8 to 15. *VI International Symposium on Pediatric Work Physiology*, Prague.

BANNISTER, R.
1968   Limits of human performance, *Documenta Geigy*. Basle, p. 18.

BUCHANAN, T., and PRITCHARD, J.
1970   DNA content of tibialis anterior of male and female white rats measured from birth to 50 weeks. *Journal of Anatomy* 107: 185.

CHEEK, D. B., HOLT, A. B., HILL, D. E., and TALBERT, J. L.
1969   In: *Problems of Nutrition in the Perinatal Period.* Report of the Sixtieth Ross Conference on Pediatric Research. G. M. Owen (ed). Ross Laboratories, Columbus.

CHEEK, D. B., GRAYSTONE, J. E., and READ, M. S.
1970   Cellular growth, nutrition and development. *Pediatrics* 45: 315.

CHEEK, D. B. et al.
1971   Skeletal muscle cell mass and growth: the concept of the deoxyribonucleic acid unit. *Pediatric Research* 5: 312.

EKBLOM, B.
1970   Physical training in normal boys in adolescence. *Acta Paediatrica Scandinavica Supplement* 217: 60.

ELLIOTT, G. M.
1970   The effects of exercise on structural growth. *Journal of the Canadian Association for Health, Physical Education and Recreation* 36: 21.

ESPENSCHADE, A.
1960   The contributions of physical activity to growth. *Research Quarterly: American Association for Health, Physical Education and Recreation* 31: 351.

KNITTLE, J. M., and HIRSCH, J.
1967   Infantile nutrition as a determinant of adult adipose tissue, metabolism and cellularity. *Clinical Research* 15: 323.

KOTTKE, F. J.
1966   The effects of limitations of activity upon the human body. *Journal of the American Medical Association* 196: 825.

LEAF, A.
1973   Getting old. *Scientific American* 229, 3: 45.

MACKENZIE, J.
1974   ⅓ time physical education. *Saskatchewan Movement and Leisure* 1: 6.

MALINA, R. M.
1969   Exercise as an influence upon growth. *Clinical Pediatrics* 8: 16.

ORLICK, T. D.
1970   Children's sports—a revolution is coming. *Journal of the Canadian Association for Health, Physical Education and Research* 39: 12.
PARIZKOVA, J.
1972   Somatic development and body composition changes in adolescent boys differing in physical activity and fitness: a longitudinal study. *Anthropologie*, X/1.
RARICK, G. L.
1960   Exercise and growth. In: *Science of Medicine of Exercise and Sports*. Harpers, New York.
RARICK, G. L. (ed).
1973   *Physical Activity: Human Growth and Development*. Academic Press, New York.
ROSE, K.
1973   To keep the people in health. *Journal of the American College Health Association* 22: 80.
SALTIN, B., and GRIMBY, G.
1968   Physiological analysis of middle aged and old former athletes, comparison with still active athletes of the same ages. *Circulation* 38: 1104.
SMITH, N.
1972   The challenge of obesity. *Maternal and Infant Nutrition Seminar, Atlanta*.
UNESCO
1964   International Council of Sport and Physical Education: Declaration on sport. Place de Fontenoy, Paris.
WIDDOWSON, E. M.
1970   Harmony of growth. *Lancet* II: 901.
WINICK, M.
1971   Cellular growth during early malnutrition. *Pediatrics* 47: 969.

Mental Development

What is the nature of school-age children's thinking, reasoning, memory, and language? How are these processes interrelated? The subject matter of this chapter deals with these questions. Piaget's theory has provided rationale for one of the two articles.

"Children's Concepts of How People Get Babies," by Anne C. Bernstein and Philip A. Cowan, is fun to read because of all the quotations of naïve comments about sex. It is also a convincing support for Piaget's explanations of the ways in which children assimilate information to the cognitive level on which they are operating. Furthermore, the article scientifically justifies the classic advice of sex educators to parents, that they should answer children's questions simply and honestly, taking cues from the child as to how much information to give.

Current interest in school learning and related problems has stimulated research on the processes of memory. Patricia E. Worden's article deals with some of the conditions under which children are most successful in recall. She presents evidence that recall is improved by previous sorting of stimuli into categories.

Children's Concepts of How People Get Babies *

Anne C. Bernstein and Philip A. Cowan
UNIVERSITY OF CALIFORNIA, BERKELEY

Twenty boys and girls at each of 3 age levels (3–4, 7–8, 11–12) were given a newly constructed interview focusing on their concepts of how people get babies (social causality). They were also given Piaget-type tasks assessing physical

From *Child Development*, 1975, **46**, 77–91. Copyright © 1975 by The Society for Research in Child Development, Inc. Reprinted by permission.

* This paper was based upon a dissertation by Anne Bernstein, submitted in partial fulfillment of the requirement for a doctoral degree in psychology at the University of California, Berkeley. The authors wish to thank Professors Ken Craik, Joseph Kuypers, and Margaret Singer for their guidance. Thanks also to Sonne Lemke for making available her social identity task, and to Carolyn Cowan for her constructive comments on this manuscript. We extend our gratitude to the Children's Community Center of Berkeley, and to the children and parents who cooperated in this study.

conservation-identity (Clay), physical causality (Origin of Night), and a new social identity task (Lemke, 1973). Performance on all tasks systematically increased with age, intercorrelations were high, and children tended to perform at the same absolute cognitive level on each task. Children's concepts of how people and babies appears to follow a Piagetian development sequence embedded in a matrix of social and physical causality and identity concepts. There also appears to be a consistent developmental lag in which physical causality precedes physical conservation-identity, which in turn precedes social identity: the Origin of Babies appears to be the most developmentally difficult of the 4 tasks. A qualitative analysis supported Piaget's interactive theory of development. Sex information is not simply taken in by children; it is assimilated (transformed) to the child's present cognitive level.

What do children think about how babies come to be? Almost 5 decades ago, Piaget (1929) suggested that children's ideas about the cause of babies should follow the same sequence of cognitive developmental stages as their concepts of physical causality. Despite the testability of the hypothesis and the importance of the topic, only three subsequent studies have provided an empirical developmental assessment of what children think about the origin of babies.

A study by Conn (1947) used doll play as an interviewing technique with 100 4–11-year-old children. Analysis of the data was confined to summary descriptions of the child's response content. Conn concluded that "it is inconceivable to the child of preschool age that the baby may be in the mother." He also concluded that sex information is beyond the grasp of the intelligent child of 7 or 8 and that not until 9 or 10 do children first notice and discuss the mother's distended abdomen during pregnancy. It is possible that these results were biased in part by the doll-play method or the particular sample chosen; it is certainly our impression, 25 years later, that younger children are more knowledgeable than Conn suggested.

Two more recent studies directly examined Piaget's hypothesis (Kreitler & Kreitler, 1966; Moore & Kendall, 1971). Both studies question Piaget's conclusion, but the age range of the subjects was narrow (4–5½, 3–5½), and the interviewers used a standardized format rather than Piaget's more flexible clinical method.

Both practical and theoretical considerations make further studies absolutely necessary. Sex educators and the general public are locked in bitter dispute concerning what children should be taught and what they already know (Breasted, 1971). Personality theorists, beginning with Freud ([1908] 1963), have based important conclusions on data obtained from patients' or college students' reconstructions of childhood. Child analysts now obtain data from their patients (A. Freud, 1965), but the literature contains only anecdotal reports filtered through theorists' eyes. There appears to be no shortage of adult opinions on the subject. The present study, within a cognitive developmental framework, represents a new attempt to gather systematic normative data directly from children. In part, it shifts the emphasis away from the prevailing views which assume that changes in children's concepts of procreation are a function of what they themselves observe, of peer and adult (mis)information, and of physiological growth related to libidinal or sexual functioning.

It seems to us that the cognitive concepts most relevant to the origin of babies are those concerning causality and identity. It is only when the child begins to perceive that events and phenomena have causes that he can attempt to investigate what they are; it is only when the child recognizes that he himself and other persons are continuous beings, conserving identity despite the transformations in appearance due to maturation, that he can think about his own origins or those of his siblings.

In the present study children from the ages of 3 to 12 were presented with four tasks. A newly constructed social causality questionnaire examined their concepts of the origin of babies. An analogous questionnaire about the origin of night developed by Laurendeau and Pinard (1962) represented an index of physical causality. The development of social identity was investigated with an as-yet unpublished task (Lemke, 1973), and the development of physical identity was inferred from children's performance in the traditional conservation interview. If children's concepts concerning how people get babies are embedded in a cognitive developmental matrix, then scores on the four tasks should be correlated within and between age levels. There should also be instances of systematic developmental ordering in which performance on some tasks is more advanced than on others (i.e., décalages), but previous theoretical and empirical evidence was not conclusive enough to make specific predictions. Finally, this study provides a qualitative analysis of children's concepts of how people get babies, in part to provide more information about what children think, and in part to provide data for speculation about the cognitive processes involved.

METHOD

SUBJECTS   Sixty children participated in this study, 10 boys and 10 girls at each of three age levels (3–4, 7–8, 11–12). It was expected that performance would range from preoperational to a level transitional between concrete and formal operations in Piaget's system.

Given the hesitance of many parents to have their children questioned about sexual matters, random sampling was not attempted in this study. The final sample, referred by our acquaintances, consisted primarily of upper-middle-class Caucasian children who had at least one younger sibling and thus would have had to comprehend the entrance of a younger child into their families. Since most of the children were from two-child families, there was no confounding of age of subject and number of siblings. Because the study focused on establishing invariant sequences of performance and within-individual developmental cohesion, the lack of random sampling was not considered a serious drawback at this stage of our knowledge.

MEASURES   Social and physical causality and identity concepts were measured by four different tasks. Each task adopted a clinical interview format in which standardized questions were followed up with interviewer probes designed to clarify the meaning of the child's response and to locate the response more precisely at a particular developmental level. All tasks were scored on a seven-point scale; an attempt was made to establish the same score for the same developmental stage level on each task. Interrater reliability was established at 75%–90% on a random selection of half the protocols for each task.

1. PHYSICAL CONSERVATION-IDENTITY: MANIPULATION WITH CLAY AND WATER
The children's ability to conserve nonsocial objects was assessed by the familiar tasks involving transformations of clay. They were asked to judge the equality or inequality of amount in two clay balls, one of which was changed in shape and then divided in two. Those who succeeded in conserving amount with these initial tasks were given two volume-conservation problems. In the first the experimenter placed one clay ball in a glass of water and asked the child to estimate the height of water if an identical clay ball were placed in a second glass. In the next volume task the experimenter transformed the shape of the second clay ball and then repeated the question.

Level 0: No answer or all incorrect answers.
Level 1: Preoperational. Incorrect answers with perceptual explanations ("It looks bigger or it's larger"), or correct answers with no explanations.
Level 2: Transitional. Satisfactory explanations on one but not both conservation-of-amount tasks (e.g., "It's longer but its thinner").
Level 3: Concrete operations. Conservation of amount in both tasks with adequate explanations. No conservation of volume.
Level 4: Transitional. Correct predictions of water height but explanations on a concrete level (e.g., "It will rise to the same height because it's the same amount").
Level 5: Transitional. Correct predictions and adequate explanation in only one of two volume tasks.
Level 6: Formal operations. Successful conservation of amount and volume with explanations reflecting the fact that volume is conserved despite transformations in appearance.

Initially the physical conservation task had been chosen as an index of children's concepts of physical identity. We subsequently found that Piaget (Piaget & Voyat, 1968) had clarified the two concepts, showing that physical identity is concerned with transformations in which one of two objects remains unchanged. It appears that physical identity concepts slightly precede conservation and are necessary for conservations to occur. We will, therefore, refer to the task as "physical conservation-identity" in order to emphasize potential parallels with the social identity task.

2. SOCIAL IDENTITY   Lemke (1973) had developed a measure of the child's sense that an individual's identity continues through time despite changes in physical appearance. It also assesses the child's ability to identify individuals on the basis of their relationship to others. In the present study, Lemke's measure was interpreted as an index of the child's ability to "conserve" social objects.

Each subject was presented with two photographs of an eight-member family taken several years apart. After discussion established that the pictures came from the same family, the child was presented with six photos of that family from both earlier and later periods, asked to identify the individuals in each picture, to provide his rationale for making the identifications, and to arrange the photos in their proper time sequence. The subject was then asked to explain why a younger female child was not in the earliest picture. If the subjects did not volunteer the information that she was not yet born, they were asked a series of questions concerning her whereabouts (e.g., "Do you think she was taking a nap?"), ending with the direct question, "Do you think she was born yet?"

Because Lemke had not administered this measure to children over the age of 9, it was not anticipated that successful completion of this task would occur as late as 11–12 years. Two additional transition stages were added to Lemke's original rating schedule. The rating schedule as amended includes the following stages:

Level 0: An initial stage in which any individual may be any other individual without clear distinctions based upon sex or race or general physical characteristics.

Level 1: Identity of a person in the different photos is denied except where all qualities are the same. Attention to alterations in appearance due to clothing, etc., interfere with judgments of identity.

Level 2: Static identifications, based on same size, hair style, hat. Fewer errors. Beginning to grasp principle of ordering and to realize younger children in late photos could not yet have been in the first one.

Level 3: Transitional stage. Fewer errors than above. All grasp that youngest siblings not yet born in early photos.

Level 4: Correct identifications but the relationships of individuals within the family are not firmly grasped and identity is based solely on appearance. Principle of ordering established.

Level 5: Transitional stage, distinguished from the preceding in that the use of context, or the relations of individuals within the family, is becoming more established in the child's reasoning, but is still not firmly held or consistently applied.

Level 6: Systematic operational thinking. Implications for individual identity include identification by relation of unit to other units and to the whole.

3. PHYSICAL CAUSALITY: THE ORIGIN OF NIGHT   Laurendeau and Pinard's (1962) standardized version of Piaget's questions concerning the origin of night was chosen to represent a physical causality task. All children were asked to tell the interviewer what night is, why it is dark, where the dark comes from, and what makes it night. Children usually attribute the origin of night to sleep, to clouds, or to the disappearance of the sun. A further set of standardized questions followed up whatever answers the child gave. All children were asked if "we can make the night in this room," and if pulling the blinds down would make it dark. Finally, they were asked where the dark in the room comes from and to explain what makes it day.

Laurendeau and Pinard developed a scale to rate the child's level of reasoning about the origin of night and, by inference, about problems of physical causality.

Level 0: No understanding of question; refusal to answer.

Level 1: Absolute finalism (e.g., it becomes dark so we may go to sleep).

Level 2: Explicit artificialism mixed with finalism (e.g., it becomes dark because God calls the dark, or Mother puts the light out).

Level 3: Artificialism disguised as physicalism; fabricating agent necessary but uses natural, physical elements. Animistic elements (e.g., the moon opens his eyes, he blows the sun away and he blows the night in).

Level 4: Additional stage not delineated by Laurendeau and Pinard. Physical explanations mixed with strong animistic and finalistic elements (e.g., when the sun turns the other way, it's real dark, when the moon comes).

Level 5: Physicalism with taints of finalism or animism (e.g., it becomes dark because we need rest and the sun goes to the other side of the world).

Level 6: Absolute physicalism (e.g., it becomes dark because the sun is shining on the other side of the world).

4. SOCIAL CAUSALITY: THE ORIGIN OF BABIES   The clinical method provided the experimenter the opportunity to assess the child's understanding of her questions as well as an opportunity to go beyond mere rote-learned, parroted answers. All concepts and terms describing reproduction were introduced by the child himself; only after the child indicated the trend of his thinking was the line of questioning by the interviewer determined. Each answer was probed until the child's thinking became as explicit and as detailed as he or she was able to make it, following through on the implications of the initial explanation. It was not assumed that the child's use of any given word necessarily meant that he comprehended its common usage definition.

Each interview included the following questions: "How do people get babies?" "What does the word 'born' mean?" "What does it mean to say someone [e.g., you] was born?" "How do mothers get to be mothers?" "How did your mother get to be your mother?" "When did she start being your mother?" "How do fathers get to be fathers?" "How did your father get to be your father?" "When did he start being your father?" "How was it that [name of younger sibling] came to live in your family and be your sister/brother?"

In addition, younger children were asked: "What if some people who lived in a cave in the desert, where there weren't any other people, wanted to have a baby. Because they had never known any other people, they didn't know how people get babies. What if they asked you for help? If they asked you what they should do if they wanted a baby, what would you tell them?"

Older children were asked: "What did you think about how people get babies before you understood it as well as you do now? What did you think when you were little?"

Pilot protocols were used to create a scale which, while following the structural outline of the Laurendeau and Pinard scale, dealt specifically with the application of similar levels of cognitive development to the problem of the origin of babies.

Level 0: Lack of comprehension of questions.

Level 1: Spatial causality. Question is perceived as spatial, not causal, i.e., "Where do people get babies?" Child assumes that babies have always existed; the problem is to discover where the baby was before it was present in the family, no need to explain how.

Example: MIKE (3-8). You go to a baby store and buy one. JACK (3-2). From tummies.

Level 2: Artificialism, including finalism and animism. Child answers the "how" questions as such. Egocentric interpretation of body parts and processes involved, which are limited to those they themselves have experience with, e.g., the "digestive fallacy," where the baby gets into the tummy by being ingested and exits as in elimination. Artificialism, the origin of natural phenomena described as if produced by a process of manufacture, here entails only natural materials. Emphasis on purpose rather than process, although need for explanation is assumed.

Example: JANE (3-7). [How does the baby get in the tummy?] Just make it first. [How?] Well, you just make it. You put some eyes on it. . . . Put the head on, and hair, some hair all curls. [With?] You make it with head stuff. [How?] You find it at a store that makes it. . . . Well, they get it and then they put it in the tummy and then it goes quickly out.

Level 3: Transitional. Explanations are semiphysical, semipsychological, semi-artificialistic, but only technically feasible operations are given credence; e.g., "agricultural fallacy," or concretization of the metaphor of "planting a seed." Animistic distortions: anthropocentric and zoocentric, i.e., subautonomous organic units are endowed with the will and the physical motility of people and animals. Moral causality: social convention treated as an immutable given.

Example: JANE (4-6). The sperm goes into the Mommy to each egg and puts it, makes the egg safe. So if something bump comes along it won't crack the egg. [Where does the egg come from?] From the Daddy. [Then what happens?] It swims in, into the penis and then it . . . I think it makes a little hole and then it swims into the vagina. [How?] It has a little mouth and it bites a hole.

Level 4: Explanations are primarily physical although still tinged with finalism and egocentrism. The attributes of the fabricating agent, heretofore either God or man, are now given over to nature or social convention. This level is distinguished from 5 and 6 in that the child, while aware of the physical processes involved in procreation, cannot explain why these processes must occur, i.e., he knows the "facts of life" but does not understand what about these processes causes the new life to begin.

Example: LARA (7-9). The man and the woman get together, and then they put a speck, then the man has his seed and the woman has an egg, and then I guess, that's all I know really. [Why do the seed and the egg have to come together?] Or else the baby, the egg won't really get hatched very well. [How does the baby come from the seed and the egg?] The seed makes the egg grow. [How?] It's just like plants. If you plant a seed a flower will grow.

Level 5: Preformation. This level is distinguished from the preceding in that the child explains what there is about the seed and the egg coming together that produces the child. It is distinguished from Level 6 in that the child still does not conceive of any stage before the baby's existence; it is a latent form that can be transferred (e.g., from one person's body to another). But its original substance is invariable. There is no perceived need for a final cause.

Example: PATRICK (12-9). The lady has an egg and the man has a sperm, and they, sort of he fertilizes the egg, and then the egg slowly grows, the sperm grows into a baby inside the egg. . . . [Fertilize?] It means it gets inside the egg, the sperm. It just sort of goes in. The egg before the sperm goes in is sort of like, well, I guess, it doesn't have anything in it to grow, it just has food and I guess a shell on the outside. . . . It's sort of the beginning of the baby. It has to happen, because otherwise the sperm would just die because it has no shelter on the outside to keep it alive, no food, nothing. And then the egg, there's nothing in it to grow, I guess. It has no . . . no . . . no . . . living animal in there.

Level 6: Physicalism freed from precausality. Physical explanations of this physiological process. Psychological and moral connotations, while taken into account, are not given determinist status. Distinguished from Level 5 in that the exchange of genetic materials during fertilization is seen as the point of origin of the new being.

Example: TINA (11-11). [Fertilize?] Well, it just starts it off I guess. . . . Mixes the genes or, well, puts particles or something into the egg. [Genes?] Genes are the things from the father and the mother, you know, and they put a little bit of each into the baby so the baby turns out to be a little bit like the mother or father or something.

DEVELOPMENTAL SCORING   Each task was scored on a seven-point (0–6) scale, in which higher scores were assumed to represent higher developmental levels. In physical conservation-identity and in physical causality tasks it has been traditional to assume that scores correspond to Piaget's developmental stages: preoperational, concrete, and formal operations, and the transitions between them. Table 1 presents a summary of the scoring criteria for all four tasks. It indicates our best estimate of the comparable structural-stage level represented by each score. It reflects our intentions to compare task performance rating not only in terms of relative rank (correlation) but also in terms of absolute levels (χ^2).

PROCEDURE   Children were tested individually in their homes. The Origin of Babies interview was given first, and the following three tasks were administered in random order. The testing period lasted between 30 and 60 minutes.

In sum, four tasks assessing concepts of physical conservation-identity (Clay), social identity (Family Pictures), physical causality (Origin of Night), and social causality (Origin of Babies) were administered to 20 boys and girls at each of three age levels (3–4, 7–8, 11–12). The study attempted to establish a Piagetian sequence of children's concepts of procreation; it examined the place of this sequence within a matrix of physical and social concepts.

RESULTS AND DISCUSSION

In the first part of this section we will present a quantitative analysis of the four tasks and their interrelationships. In the second part we include a selection of qualitative data in order to convey a more concrete sense of children's concepts of procreation.

QUANTITATIVE ANALYSIS   *Developmental Data.*   A frequency distribution of children's responses to the Origin of Babies interview is presented in Table 2. Responses scored as belonging to initial developmental stages were in fact more often given by the younger children, while the oldest children were consistently rated near the top of the stage hierarchy. A slight deviation from this pattern in the 7–8-year-olds will be discussed below. Except for this 7–8-year-old deviation, frequency distributions for the other three tasks were virtually identical to Table 2. The consistent increase in stage scores with

TABLE 1

A Developmental Comparison of Scoring Systems

PIAGETIAN STAGE	TASK			
	Physical Conservation-Identity (Volume of Clay)	Social Identity (Family Pictures)	Physical Causality (Origin of Night)	Social Causality (Origin of Babies)
Preoperational	0: No answer or all wrong	0: Arbitrary identifications	0: No answer or incomprehension	0: Lack of comprehension
	1: Preoperational	1: Insistence on sameness	1: Finalistic interpretations	1: Spatial answers, absolute precausality
		2: Static identifications	2: Artificialistic beliefs	2: Artificialism, including finalism and animism
Transitional	2: Transitional	3: Transitional	3: Semiartificialistic and semiphysical interpretations	3: Transitional between artificialism and physicalism
Concrete	3: Conservation of clay but not when displacing water	4: Intuitive personal identity reversibility but little use of context	4: Physicalism with no artificialism but some finalistic or animistic constructions	4: Physicalism with lacunae
Transitional	4, 5: Conservation of clay in water, reasoning inadequate	5: Inconsistent use of context in making identifications	5: Physicalism with taints of finalism	5: Physicalism with preformation
Formal?	6: Conservation with reference to volume consistently made in explanations	6: Systematic operational thinking; individual identity linked to relation of unit to other units and the whole	6: Physicalism freed from all precausality	6: Physicalism freed from precausality, insistence on a final cause

increasing age supports the hypothesis that the concepts are ordered in a developmental sequence.

Separate two-way analyses of variance (age × sex) were performed for each of the four measures (the results are summarized in Table 3). In all tasks F ratios for age were statistically significant ($p < .01$) while those for sex differences or interactions were not. Again, age increases are accompanied by regular increases in cognitive performance.

TABLE 2
Percent Distribution of Subjects by Age and Development
Stage Scores: Social Causality Task

		STAGE						
AGE	N	0	1	2	3	4	5	6
11–12	20	0	0	0	0	10	50	40
7–8	20	0	30	0	40	20	5	5
3–4	20	5	60	30	0	5	0	0
Total	60							
Mean age		3-6	5-1	4-7	7-10	8-9	11-8	11-7

An additional analysis of variance was made for the social causality Origin of Babies measure, since it appeared from examination of the raw data that a real difference between boys and girls in the 7–8-year-old group was being masked by combining the 2–year levels. This second analysis of variance, which treated each age year as a separate group, produced an F ratio significant at $p < .05$ for variance attributed to difference in sex, with girls showing higher scores, especially in the 7-year-old group. Despite the larger difference at one age level, the interaction between age and sex was statistically insignificant. It is the sex difference in the 7–8-year-old group that is responsible for the deviation from gradually ascending gradations on the frequency distribution measure (Table 2).

Between each pair of tasks correlations were calculated in order to determine whether age increases in one task were accompanied by age increases in another. Table 4 shows the value of Pearson correlation coefficients for each pair of measures, both for the sample as a whole and for each age group. All six whole-sample correlations were statistically significant ($p < .01$, $df = 58$) and ranged between .73 and .83. Four of the six correlations between pairs of tasks in the 3–4-year-old group were statistically significant, two of six were significant in the 7–8-year-olds, and only one in the oldest group. Thus, the whole-sample

TABLE 3
Analysis of Variance of Four Tasks: Age × Sex

SOURCE	df	PHYSICAL CONSERVATION- IDENTITY	SOCIAL IDENTITY	PHYSICAL CAUSALITY	SOCIAL CAUSALITY
Age	2.54	97.70*	92.65*	49.00*	75.98*
Sex	1.54	1.15	3.92	2.61	3.92
Interaction	2.54	2.30	.49	.87	1.47

*$p < 0.1$.

T A B L E 4

Correlations between Tasks: Within-Age and Total Sample

	PHYSICAL CONSER-VATION-IDENTITY (CLAY)	SOCIAL IDENTITY (FAMILY PICTURES)	PHYSICAL CAUSALITY (NIGHT)	SOCIAL CAUSALITY (BABIES)
Physical conservation:				
3–4*		.36	.62†	.68†
7–8*		.18	−.19	.21
11–12*		.53†	.13	.08
Total**		.83‡	.80‡	.73‡
Social identity:				
3–4			.49†	.23
7–8			.26	.38†
11–12			.02	−.01
Total			.79‡	.76‡
Physical causality:				
3–4				.50†
7–8				.70‡
11–12				.03
Total				.74‡

*$df = 18$.
** $df = 58$.
† $p < .05$.
‡ $p < .01$.

trend is supported best within the youngest sample. The scores of the 3–4-year-olds showed most variance. With older subjects the lower variance and a ceiling effect probably combined to reduce the statistical association among tasks.

The data indicate that task scores were consistently related to age (Table 3, analyses of variance) and that the relative rate of development in each task was similar (correlations). The results are consistent with the hypothesis that there is an invariant necessary sequence of development in the four tasks, but they do not provide conclusive evidence. Only longitudinal studies can determine definitively whether each child must progress through each level in the given order.

Décalage   Piaget's concept of the décalage (Piaget & Inhelder, 1969) is an elusive one. It posits developmental lags in the application of a child's cognitive structure to particular content areas in order to account for the fact that children do not arrive simultaneously at the same stage in all concepts or tasks. A first step in examining the issue of décalage was to find out whether children performed at the same absolute level on each task. Table 5 presents the χ^2 tables constructed for each pair of measures. Subjects' performance was categorized as preoperational (p) or at least concrete operations (o) on each task.[1] Fisher Exact Tests for each 2 × 2 table produced values of χ^2 that were all statistically significant ($p < .001$). From 68% to 93% of the subjects were at

[1] The dividing line occurred between scores of 2 and 3 for physical conservation-identity and between 3 and 4 for the other three tasks (see Table 1).

TABLE 5

Chi-Square Tables for Pairs of Tasks: Performance Either Preoperational
(p) or Concrete Operational (o)

	Physical Causality				Physical Causality				Physical Causality	
		p	o			p	o			p	o
Physical Conservation	p	14	4	Social Identity	p	13	11	Social Causality	p	14	19
	o	0	42		o	1	35		o	0	27

	Physical Conservation				Physical Conservation				Social Identity	
		p	o			p	o			p	o
Social Identity	p	17	7	Social Conservation	p	18	15	Social Causality	p	22	11
	o	1	35		o	0	27		o	2	25.

exactly the same developmental level in both tasks. It is evident that there is an absolute as well as a relative association among the tasks.

An examination of the χ^2 tables indicates that the relatively low number of exceptions to perfect agreement appear to follow a pattern. For example (top left), four subjects were operational in physical causality but not in the physical conservation task, while none was at a high level on conservation but not causality. And (top middle) 11 subjects were operational on physical causality but not social identity, while one showed the reverse trend. These results suggest that in addition to a strong correlation between tasks there is also a developmental ordering which could be conceptualized as a rough Guttman scaling. Of the total of 60 subjects, 46 were at or beyond concrete operations in physical causality (Origin of Night), 42 in physical conservation-identity (Clay), 36 in social identity (Family Pictures), and 27 in social causality (Origin of Babies).

This rough ordering was further explored in analysis of variance comparisons among tasks as a function of age and sex; these comparisons incorporated the total range of scores rather then the two-step χ^2 division of levels. No statistically significant main effects or interactions with sex were found. In addition to the significant age effect, $F(2,54) = 149.5$, $p < .001$, there was a significant task effect, $F(3,162) = 24.4$, $p < .001$, and a significant age × task interaction, $F(6,162) = 9.7$, $p < .001$. The relevant means are presented in Table 6. Again, the Origin of Night task was the easiest (4.40), followed by the Clay task (3.87), the Family Pictures (3.48), and the Origin of Babies task (3.18). All differences were statistically significant (*t* tests, $p < .01$). Subjects performed at a higher level on both physical objects tasks than on the social object tasks. Causality was the easiest task in its physical form (Night) and most difficult in its social form (Babies), so no generalizations concerning the relative difficulty of causality and identity concepts could be made.

In general, the trends were similar but not as marked within each age group. The clearest physical-social concept difference occurred in the 7–8-year-

TABLE 6

Average Developmental Scores (0–6) on Four Tasks: Within-Age and Total Sample

	PHYSICAL CAUSALITY	PHYSICAL CONSERVATION- IDENTITY	SOCIAL IDENTITY	SOCIAL CAUSALITY
3–4	2.50	1.25	1.10	1.40
7–8	5.00	5.00	4.00	2.85
11–12	5.70	5.25	5.35	5.30
Total	4.40	3.83	3.48	3.18

old sample. We have noted before that at this age in the Origin of Babies task the 7-year-old boys produce particularly low scores.

The evidence from both χ^2 and analysis of variance clearly indicates that the logical structures underlying concrete operations are applied to the four tasks in a consistent order, that is, there is clear evidence of a décalage. While Piaget has found it theoretically and empirically necessary to acknowledge the existence of décalages, explanations of the phenomenon are far from clear.

Generally, three types of variables have been suggested by Piaget to account for a décalage: the child's experience, the role of affect, and the nature of the task itself. All three may be operative in the present case.

1. Experience. Among the four tasks under consideration, the social causality Origin of Babies questionnaire produced the lowest developmental level of performance. In our culture it is likely that experience in the form of verbal discussion would be least in this area. In addition, experience in the form of direct physical-sensorimotor contact with the phenomenon is least possible. Finally, in terms of Piaget's concept of logicomathematical experience— experience with operating upon and transforming things and ideas—again, the origin of babies is least accessible to children of the four concepts under discussion.

2. Affect. Piaget's writings in the area of affect are often sketchy (see Piaget, 1967). He views the affective and cognitive aspects of development as inseparable and irreducible, with affectivity constituting the "energetics of behavior patterns whose cognitive aspect refers to the structure alone" (Piaget & Inhelder, 1969). Usually, Piaget notes affect as an intrusion factor which promotes lower levels of performance in a particular area.

In the present study, 7-year-old boys were at a significantly lower level of reasoning about human reproduction. This was the only task and the only age at which clear sex differences emerged. Perhaps the affective intrusion was simply the embarrassment of 7-year-old boys talking to a female interviewer "about sex." Perhaps, though, more complex factors were involved. The Freudian concept of latency should be considered at this point.

Latency is described as a time of decreased sexual interest but increased interest in the development of masculine and feminine sex roles. In the present sample many of the 7–8-year-old boys were occupied with stereotypically "boyish" things, while many of the girls had rooms replete with doll babies and playhouse furnishings. Thus a combination of affective-libidinal and experiential factors may have led to the girls' higher scores in this age range.

3. The nature of the task. Piaget often comments that some tasks more than others seem to "resist" assimilation to a particular structural level. The tasks were obviously different in method of presentation, for example, two were verbal, while two were presented with concrete stimuli. This particular variable does not appear to account for performance differences, since the verbal tasks (Night and Babies) showed the highest and lowest levels of performance, but it is certainly possible that other aspects of what has been called "method variance" may have led to developmental discrepancies in performance.

What may have been centrally important in producing a décalage was the nature of the transformations involved in each task. The tasks with physical referents (Clay, Night) were clearly easier than tasks with social referents (Family, Babies). Both physical tasks involved transformations of the physical world which were reversible, while the social tasks both involved irreversible transformations. Piaget and Voyat (1968) in a study of identity found that an irreversible transformation, even in a physical object, makes the problem of conservation-identity more difficult.

It appears, then, that experience, affect, and task variables may all interact to produce the obtained décalage. Exactly how this occurs must be the subject of future research.

Summary of quantitative findings   The quantitative data indicate that children's concepts of how people get babies show a Piagetian developmental sequence. They are highly correlated with conservation, causality, and identity measures, but all the tasks show some important absolute differences. Children attain concrete operations first on physical causality, then physical conservation, then social identity, and finally social causality. Physical concepts appear to develop before social concepts. Concepts of physical causality appear to develop before conservation or identity concepts, but social causality, at least on the topic of how babies are born, comes relatively later. Before discussing these trends in more detail, we will present some descriptive data concerned with children's concepts of procreation.

QUALITATIVE ANALYSIS   We wish to convey to the reader a concrete sense of what and how children think about the origin of babies. To meet obvious needs for abbreviation, we focus on children's answers to only one of the questions in the interview. "How does the baby happen to be inside the mother's body?" generated the most comprehensive answers and was the single most important question in terms of differentiating between cognitive levels.

Level 1   Most 3–4-year-olds believe that a baby has always existed, but they have several different notions concerning how it comes to be in the mother's body. Some believe it was always there, others assume it was located somewhere else in the same form and then somehow came into the mother, and still others speculate about a series of transformations.

[How did the baby happen to be in your Mommy's tummy?] It just grows inside.
[How did it get there?] It's there all the time. Mommy doesn't have to do any-

thing. She waits until she feels it. [You said that the baby wasn't in there when you were there]. Yeah, then he was in the other place in . . . in America. [In America?] Yeah, in somebody else's tummy. [In somebody else's tummy?] Yeah, and then he went through somebody's vagina, then he went in, um, in my Mommy's tummy. [In whose tummy was he before?] Um, the, I don't know, who his, her name is. It's a her.

At Level 1, children appear to be assimilating directly from their own experience. There is no "first cause." If something comes out, it can go back in.

Level 2   Children at this level begin to attribute babies to some cause, primarily a person or persons who function as manufacturers. Laura described how people get babies.

Maybe they just paint the right bones. . . . Maybe they just paint the bones and paint the blood, and paint the blue blood. . . .

Similarly Tom, a 4-year-old boy, suggested that a woman who wants a baby to grow in her stomach should "maybe get a body" at a store; she could then "put it all together" with "tools" to "produce a baby." This child, described by his mother as having received no religious training, was one of two children, both Level 2 boys, to mention God in his account of how people get babies. According to Tom, God makes Mommies and Daddies "with the little seed":

He puts it down . . . on the table . . . then, it grows bigger. The people grow together. . . . He makes them eat [the seed], then they grow . . . to be people . . . then they stand up and go someplace else, where they could live . . . [the seed] makes them into people [from] skeletons [which were at] God's place.

Note that 4-year-old Tom assumes that a baby is bought at the store, but that his Mommy and Daddy were made by God from seeds. It is as if the remoteness of his parents' childhood requires a more remote cause. Especially for young children it may be necessary to explore differences and similarities in their concepts of parent origin, self origin, and their own future role in producing offspring. Note also that despite differences in content the manufacturing analogy was present in both explanations. Tom was the only child who attributed the role of manufacturer to God, a startling contrast to Conn's study in which half of the children in the entire sample and the great majority of the preschoolers attributed a decisive role to the Deity.

A few children at Level 2 connect a father with the birth process, but assimilate what they have been told to a mechanical process. A girl responds:

[If the seed is in the Daddy, how does it get on the egg?] I don't know. Cause he can't really open up all his tummies. [Then how?] It rolls out. [How does it get to the egg?] Well, I think that the Daddy gets it. [How?] Puts his hand in the tummy. [Whose?] His tummy. [Then?] He puts it on the bottom of the Mommy and the Mommy gets the, gets the egg out of her tummy, and puts the egg on top of the seed. And then they close their tummies . . . and the baby is born. . . .

For her the seed and the egg can only come together by manual means. She expressed some doubts that her version of the story could be accurate, but her experience provided her with no real alternatives and she very conscientiously tried to confine her description to physical processes and causes.

Two Level 2 children had an apparently oblique approach to questions about procreation:

[How would the lady get a baby to grow in her tummy?] Um, get a rabbit. 'Cause one day I saw a book about them, and . . . they just get a duck or a goose and they get a little more growned . . . and then they, turn into a baby. [A rabbit will turn into a baby?] They give them some food, people food, and they grow like a baby. [If I asked you to tell me just one way that people get babies, what would you say?] I would say, a store, buy a duck, and a duck. [A duck?] Yeah. [Who told you that? How'd you find out about the duck?] I saw it in a book, and my Mommy told me it. [Your Mommy told you that ducks turn into babies?] No, I just saw, find out from this book.

This story of the duck transformed into a baby highlights one of the difficulties children have with books that attempt to teach them about human reproduction by analogy with other animals. Often such books will start out with how other animals mate and give birth, working up the animal kingdom until they reach human beings. When unable to account for a given aspect of human reproduction, the child assimilates details from other sections of the book, details which for him are no more fantastic in their adopted contexts than they were as originally stated.

This example, and others we will cite, begins to illustrate a general point: "knowledge" about babies and sex is not simply a matter of information and misinformation. It is difficult to believe that children have somehow been told the answers they give. Rather, it appears that children who wonder about, or are asked about, the origin of babies, *make up* answers. These answers represent assimilations both from the context of experience and from the structure of thought.

Level 3.   Children giving Level 3 responses appeared to have isolated three major ingredients in the creation of babies: social relationship (some affective and/or marital bond between man and woman), the external mechanics of sexual intercourse, and the fusion of biological-genetic materials. They conceptualize these ingredients in a more sophisticated way than Level 2. However, consistent with the general description of children in transition between preoperations and concrete operations, they are unable to coordinate any of the variables in a coherent system.

Sometimes, children attempting to relate two areas may themselves be aware of the hazy link between them.

[How does the father give "the stuff" for the baby?] Well, he puts his penis right in the place where the baby comes out, and somehow it comes out of there. It seems like magic sort of, 'cause it just comes out. Sometimes, I think the father pushes maybe.

There is no preformation in either sperm or egg: this child clearly stated that the egg is not a baby until the father gives his part, but she was somewhat vague and rather concretistic in describing why his contribution is necessary:

If he didn't then a baby wouldn't come. [Why?] Because it would need the stuff that the father gives. [Why?] I don't know. [What does it do?] Helps it grow. . . . I think that stuff has the food part, maybe, and maybe it helps protect it. . . . I think he gives the shell part, and the shell part, I think, is the skin.

Another example of how one variable becomes assimilated to the other can be seen in Frank's responses. His mother reports that he was taught "sperm/egg physiology" and about "intercourse as a function of procreation and a love relationship." It would seem that 8-year-old Frank has absorbed more about the "love relationship" than about the physiology.

> It's like when people are naked, and they're together, and they're together, and they just lie together, I guess. Like they're hugging. Some men give hickies, except my Dad don't. They're just ... together. [What does that have to do with getting babies?] I don't know. I guess it's like mothers and fathers are related, and their loving each other forms a baby, I guess. [How?] I don't know. It's just there's love and I guess it just forms a baby, like I said before. ...

Thus, he described love as a relationship quality that substantively forms the developing baby.

Some children at Level 3 seem as if they are beginning to keep the variables separate, but the variables still run together. For example, one girl was becoming aware that intercourse and "baby making" are not synonymous. However, her method of birth control was still tied to the mechanics of intercourse:

> Well, I think, when you get married, you go on your honeymoon ... and you fuck on your honeymoon, you know, then that makes it so you've got each other's germs, and then when you do it again you've got a baby. But sometimes you don't do it like for long enough or something like that; although I'm not sure, and then it doesn't, you don't get a baby.

Level 4. Table 1 noted our assumption that Level 4 represented a qualitatively new stage: concrete operations. Thus, there should be a different kind of reasoning as well as a different content of response. In fact, Level 4 is the first of three levels which rely completely on physical causes of conception. All artificialism and mechanical manufacturing theories of Levels 1 and 2 are rejected. Variables are coordinated in a biological system. Level 4 is distinguished from Levels 5 and 6 because at this stage the child cannot provide an explanation of the *necessity* of uniting genetic materials. Karen, when asked why the seed and the egg have to come together replied:

> Or else the baby, the egg won't really get hatched very well. [How does the baby come from the egg and the seed?] The seed makes the egg grow. [?] It's just like plants; if you plant a seed a flower will grow. [There's no egg with plants.] No, it's just a special kind of seed, that makes an egg hatch. ... [Why must seed touch egg for the baby to grow?] The egg won't hatch. [What about its coming together makes a baby?] I don't know. Well, I don't think. ... I don't know. [Can the egg grow into a baby without the seed?] I don't think so. [Can the seed grow into a baby without the egg?] I don't know.

She had absorbed the information that seed and egg are necessary to create a new life and that they must come together to begin the process of development, but she had no clear idea of why this was so. She had, however, in another part of the interview, integrated the sperm and egg system in the notion of intercourse.

Level 5. The protocols at this level included a concept of the baby as inherent in either the sperm or the egg; thus, the embryo is preformed in one germ cell and sexual intercourse merely provides necessary and sufficient conditions for development to occur. In the history of embryology, preformation is used to refer to growth without differentiation, that is, the preexistence in miniature of all living creatures in the germ cells of animals and the seeds of plants. In this section it will be used to refer to both ovism—the preexistence of the embryo in the egg—and animalculism—the preexistence of the embryo in the sperm.

Four of the 11 Level 5 children might be called ovists. These children described the sperm as a catalyst, energizing or giving life to the latent embryo in the egg. They all referred in some manner to sexual intercourse. When asked what that had to do with getting babies, most replied that the egg was fertilized during sexual intercourse. Asked to define fertilization, they revealed their "ovist" tendencies:

> [Then, what does "fertilize" mean?] Kind of give it food and things like that. . . . [How is it that the baby starts growing when the sperm goes into the egg?] I guess when it gets in there it just does something to the egg, and it makes it start growing. . . . [Can egg grow if no sperm goes into it?] I don't think so. [Can sperm grow with no egg?] No, that doesn't have the baby; it's the egg that would have the baby in it.

In contrast to ovism, animalculism consisted of the belief that genetic parenthood was exclusively a paternal matter. This belief was an ancient one. Four of the Level 5 children were explicit animalculists; the protocols of two others were laden with implications of the preformation of the embryo in the sperm, although there were no explicit statements about how preformation works. For these children, the sperm is "real tiny and has to go into the lady" where it "grows into a baby." Sexual intercourse is necessary in order to transfer the sperm from its point of origin in the father to an environment more conductive to development in the mother. Responding to the question "How do fathers get to be fathers?" Kathy said:

> Well, if they're the man that made love to your mother, then they're your father because you really originally came out of him, and then went into your mother. [More?] Well, you were a sperm inside of him, there. So that you're the, you're really his daughter or son. 'Cause he was the one that really had you first. [Why must the egg be there for the sperm to develop into a baby?] 'Cause otherwise the sperm will have, uh, nothing to nourish it, or sort of keep it warm or, you know, able to move or something. Just has, it's not, just has to have the egg to be able to do something, develop. It just dies if it doesn't have the egg.

Thus, the egg is described as having the female cultural role of providing warmth and nourishment for the developing fetus.

These explicit explanations of ovism and animalculism demonstrate two important points. First, the 11–12-year-olds have a preformist notion of conception. But, in contrast with 3- and 4-year-olds, this notion is embedded in a much more complex causal theory. Like other aspects of Piaget's theory, development seems to occur in a spiral rather than a straight line. Children "circle back" to the same issues, but deal with them on a more differentiated and integrated structural level. Second, these explanations suggest that children may recapitulate part of the history of the science of embryology in trying to make sense of human reproduction. The next step after Level 5, historically and ontogenetically, is the realization that the genetic material for the embryo is furnished by *both* parents and that the system is interactive rather than additive. Contrary to popular usage, the child is not a simple composite of "his mother's eyes," "his grandfather's ears," and "his father's temper." It is possible that formal operations may be necessary for Level 6 explanations of the origin of babies.

Level 6.   Children rated at Level 6 had to include in their physiological explanations of reproduction the ideas that the embryo begins its biological existence at the moment of conception and that it is a product of genetic materials from both parents.

The most scientifically accurate description of conception was provided by Michael:

> The sperm encounter one ovum, and one sperm breaks into the ovum which produces, the sperm makes like a cell, and the cell separates and divides. And so it's dividing, and the ovum goes through a tube and embeds itself in the wall of the, I think it's the fetus of the woman.

Vera referred to the role of genes in the inheritance of parental traits. She explained the function of fertilization in embryonic development:

> Well, it just, it starts it off, I guess. You know, well . . . mixes something or, you know. [?] Mixes the genes or, well, puts particles or something into the egg, to make it, you know, fertilized. And so it will, you know, have genes and different kind of blood and stuff like that I guess. Because if it didn't it would be more like the mother, I guess. [What do genes have to do with it?] Well, genes are the things from the father and the mother, you know, and they put a little bit of each into the baby so the baby turns out to be a little bit like the mother or father or something. Not always, but a little bit.

Other explanations of the necessity for the union of the reproductive cell were not as extensive. Children in this group offered such statements as "The two cells meet and start growing," and "The fluids have to be together to make the baby." The highly complex scientific technical knowledge of some children at Level 6 caps a trend evident in all of the qualitative examples we have cited and the many others that were collected. We have described the Origin of Babies interview as focusing on an aspect of social causality. But the children's explanations rely heavily on notions of physical causality (especially biochemical-genetic) and social and physical identity (through transformations). Explanations concerning the origin of babies clearly involve, at the very least, all four of the conceptual dimensions we have been considering. The qualitative data from the Origin of Babies task alone indicate clearly that the observed quantitative intercorrelations among the four tasks were not accidental.

Summary of Qualitative Results.   Children's concepts concerning the origin of babies follow a development sequence and are embedded in a matrix of cognitive-structural variables. At Level 1, children are preformist and, in essence, do not see the need for a "cause" of babies. In Level 2 the causes are assimilated from notions of people as manufacturers. Children at Level 3 isolate two or three main factors: social, sexual, and biological—but do not coordinate them in a true system. With the advent of concrete operations, children at Level 4 do coordinate the variables in a system of physical causes but fail to come to grips with genetic transmission. Level 5 children are quite familiar with genetic transmission but conceptualize it as additive rather than interactive. Thus, they enter a new level of preformism, becoming ovists or animalculists. Finally, at Level 6, children provide a reasonably sophisticated scientific theory of how people get babies. We should note, at the close of this section, that not all questions on this topic have been answered. Most notably, in its ultimate form, the question of how babies come to be raises the issue of the origins of life itself. At this time, we can only wonder whether an answer will ever be attained.

Implications.   This study is an example of what will likely become a common research strategy in the area of cognitive development. It is an attempt to take some known developmental task "anchors" (Night, Clay) as indices to locate a previously unexplored area of children's thought. Presumably the Piagetian sequence will be found in many such content areas important to both children and adults. Each study, like this one, will raise more questions concerning the necessary "components" of thought in a particular area, and also concerning the explanations of particular developmental lags or décalages.

The findings of this investigation support the hypothesis that children's understanding of human reproduction proceeds through a Piagetian developmental sequence, embedded in a matrix of physical and social causality and identity concepts. Qualitative data illustrating the content of the concepts concerning how people get babies also demonstrate their interdependence with the matrix of causality and identity concepts. The qualitative data also provide illustrations supporting an interactive theory of development. Specifically, "sex information" is both taken in (accommodated) and radically transformed (assimilated) on the basis of the child's experience, affect, and cognitive structural level.

This last conclusion indicates that the study has important practical implications. Sex education of children is an increasing controversial area. Our results suggest strongly that children actively construct their notions about babies; they don't wait to be told about procreation before they have an idea of how it occurs. What is often taken as misinformation may largely be a product of their own assimilative processes at work on materials with too complex a structure for them to understand. This account of children's six levels of understanding may provide a beginning guideline in the assessment of their present level.

Further study is obviously needed before it is possible to guide children along the path from their present level to a more differentiated picture of human conception. Studies of moral development by Turiel (1969) provide a model for assessing the effects of educational materials on children at different levels of cognitive functioning. He suggests that concepts one level beyond the child's original stage of functioning will be assimilated, while prior stages will be rejected and later stages distorted or not comprehended. We expect that similar findings will be obtained in assessing the impact of educational materials about procreation. The highly politicized and controversial nature of this topic makes it plain that not all of the issues can be resolved by empirical research.

References

BREASTED, M. *Oh, sex education*. New York: New American Library, 1971.

CONN, J. M. Children's awareness of the origins of babies. *Journal of Child Psychiatry*, 1947, **1**, 140–176.

FREUD, A. *Normality and pathology in childhood: assessments of development*. New York: International Universities Press, 1965.

FREUD, S. On the sexual theories of children. 1908. In P. Rieff (Ed.), *The collected papers of Sigmund Freud.* New York: Collier, 1963.

KREITLER, H., & KREITLER, S. Children's concepts of sexuality and birth. *Child Development*, 1966, **37**, 363–378.

LAURENDEAU, M., & PINARD, A. *Causal thinking in the child*. New York: International Universities Press, 1962.

LEMKE, S. Children's identity concepts. Unpublished doctoral dissertation, University of California, Berkeley, 1973.

MOORE, J. E., & KENDALL, D. C. Children's concepts of reproduction. *Journal of Sex Research*, 1971, **7**, 42–61.

PIAGET, J. *The child's conception of the world*. New York: Harcourt, Brace, 1929.

PIAGET, J. *Six psychological studies*. D. Elkind (Ed.). New York: Random House, 1967.

PIAGET, J., & INHELDER, B. *The psychology of the child*. New York: Basic, 1969.

PIAGET, J., & VOYAT, G. Recherche sur l'identité d'un corps en développement et sur celle du mouvement transitif. In *Epistémologie et psychologie de l'identité*. Paris: Presses Universitaires de France, 1968.

TURIEL, E. Developmental processes in the child's moral thinking. In P. Mussen, J. Langer, & M. Covington (Eds.), *New directions in developmental psychology*. New York: Holt, Rinehart & Winston, 1969.

The Development of the Category-Recall Function under Three Retrieval Conditions *

Patricia E. Worden

UNIVERSITY OF CALIFORNIA, SAN DIEGO

First, third, and fifth graders sorted pictures of animals and household items into either 2 or 6 categories. Subjects were then given a standard "free" recall (free), were reminded of the categories (informed), or were required to recall items from one category at a time (blocked). Recall was found to be a function of number

From *Child Development*, **45**, 1054–1059. Copyright © 1974 by The Society for Research in Child Development, Inc. Reprinted by permission.

* Preparation of this paper and the research reported were supported in part by NSF grant GB 20798 and NIMH grant MH 24492. I wish to thank Dr. George Mandler and Dr. Jean Mandler for their kind help in preparation of this manuscript. I also thank the San Diego City School District for its cooperation in providing subjects for this study.

of categories in the sort, and there were no differences in recall among the free, informed, and blocked retrieval conditions. These results suggest that the sorting procedure provided subjects with a strong categorical organization for retrieval which was not affected by further organizational constraints at output.

The present experiment is concerned with certain input and output variables in children's recall of lists of categorized words. It was designed to study (a) two levels of categorization at the time of stimulus presentation and (b) three kinds of retrieval schemes at the time of recall. The major question under study concerns the relative importance of categorical organization at input compared with the effects of various output strategies.

The level of organization at input was varied by requiring subjects to sort the stimulus items into either two or six categories. Prior research with adults (Mandler 1967) has shown that the number of categories into which the stimulus set is sorted bears a strong relationship to the number of items recalled, with increasing numbers of sorting categories (up to seven) directly related to increased recall. On the other hand, evidence of such a category-recall function has not been found with children younger than 13 years (Mandler & Stevens 1967).

The failure of Mandler and Stevens to find a category-recall relationship suggests that children's recall may be much less related to organizational factors than is the recall performance of adults. However, the investigation of the category-recall function was only of secondary interest to Mandler and Stevens, and the number of categories used by their subjects was not systematically varied. Observation of any effect on recall of number of categories may have been obscured by the nature of their experimental design. The present experiment is a more direct investigation of the category-recall relationship with children.

In addition, this study compared the effects of three different retrieval schemes on recall performance. Previous research has shown that children in a "teaching" condition, who were taught to recall items from the same category together, performed significantly better than subjects who were not "taught" (Moely, Olson, Halwes, & Flavell, 1969; Shultz, Charness, & Berman, 1973). However, the improvement of children in the teaching condition could not be attributed solely to a superior retrieval strategy, since teaching subjects received category information at the time of presentation and control subjects did not.

Scribner and Cole (1972) gave subjects in all conditions category information at the time of input, thereby restricting the investigation to retrieval strategies alone. After three trials, subjects who were required to recall in category blocks performed significantly better than subjects who were merely reminded of the category names at the time of retrieval. Lange (1973) replicated the superiority of blocked recall over other kinds, but contrary to Moely et al. and Shultz et al., Lange found no difference between subjects who were reminded of category names and those who were allowed free recall.

In light of these conflicting studies, it is evident that the role of categorical organization in retrieval has yet to be clarified. The most consistent result, found by Cole, Gay, Glick, and Sharp (1971), Scribner and Cole (1972), and Lange (1973), is that blocked category output represents a superior aid to retrieval. The advantage of category-informed recall for children, however, has not been consistently found.

In the present experiment, free, informed, and blocked retrieval schemes were compared under conditions in which all subjects had knowledge of the categorical structure of the stimulus items before they began the recall task. It was necessary to limit the experiment to one trial, since the subjects' knowledge of their retrieval condition would make it impossible for the experimenter to control the subjects' organization of the input on any subsequent trials. These constraints of a single trial and consistency of category information at input insured that any improvement found in subjects' recall in a particular retrieval condition could be attributed solely to processes occurring at the time of output.

Three age groups were studied in order to investigate any developmental trends for the two input and three output conditions. The study is not concerned with improvement of recall as age increases but rather is interested in the interaction of age with the input and output manipulations. Therefore, the difficulty of the problem was equated for all subjects by varying the number of stimulus items given to each age group. The size of the stimulus list given to a particular age group was determined by pilot research. The list length given to subjects at each grade level was adjusted so that all subjects would recall approximately the same percentage of items.

In summary, a sorting technique was used to give children two levels of categorical organization at input in an attempt to find a relationship between number of sorting categories and recall. Additionally, the amount of organizational constraint at output was manipulated in order to determine the effect of retrieval strategies on amount recalled.

METHOD

Subjects and Design.   Subjects were children from the first, third, and fifth grades in a predominantly white middle-class elementary school in San Diego, California, who participated with their parents' permission. The mean ages of the children in each grade were 6-4, 8-3, and 10-2 respectively. Both sexes were equally represented in all conditions.

The experiment consisted of a $3 \times 2 \times 3$ factorial design: three grade levels, two levels of category sorting, and three retrieval conditions. The entire design thus contained 18 cells with six subjects per cell, for a total of 108 subjects.

Materials.   The experiment was conducted in a mobile laboratory equipped with a small table and two chairs. Stimulus items were simple line drawings on individual cards approximately 4 inches square. Subjects recalled verbally, and their output was written down by the experimenter.

The stimulus lists consisted of between 12 and 24 easily recognizable pictures belonging in two general categories, "animals," and "things you find at home" (as they were described to the subjects). These two categories could be divided further into three subcategories each: "zoo animals," "they live on the farm," "pets"; and "things you wear," "things to eat with," "furniture." This set of pictures was used for both the two-category and the six-category conditions.

The first-grade subjects received 12 pictures: chair, bed, dress, shirt, fork, glass, lion, monkey, chicken, cow, dog, and goldfish. Third graders were presented with six additional pictures: couch, shoes, cup, bear, horse, and cat, for a total of 18 items. Fifth graders received six additional items: table, coat, spoon, camel, pig, and turtle—24 pictures in all. In this way, the number of categories (either two or six at any grade level) remained the same, but the number of items per category was increased for the third graders and again for the fifth graders.

Procedure.   Subjects were informed that they would be shown a number of pictures and that they would be asked to recall the pictures later. The set of stimuli appropriate to each grade level was then shown to the subject in a predetermined random order with the restriction that no two-category members were adjacent in the presentation order. The subject named each item in turn; if the picture was given a different name than the one intended by the experimenter ("sofa" for "couch"; "jacket" for "shirt"), the subject's label was used as the correct name for the rest of the experiment.

As the subject named each item, the experimenter named the category label associated with the picture, for instance, "Shirt, yes that's something you wear." The experimenter then placed the card face up on the table. The cards remained on the table until all had been presented, and pictures belonging to the same category were grouped spatially. When all the pictures had thus been presented, the experimenter said, "As you can see, the pictures belong in two [six] groups," and then named each category while pointing to it. She then said, "Now, I'm going to pick them all up and give you another set of these same cards, and I'd like to see if you can put the pictures into exactly the same groups as I did." A second set of the same pictures was given to the subject and he sorted them into categories, naming each card in turn. No subject in any grade failed to sort correctly the second time. The experimenter rewarded the subject by saying, "Very good! You did that *exactly* right!"

The pictures were then removed. As a short-term memory buffer the subject was asked to give the following information: spell his name, give his birth date, the date, and his teacher's name—filling approximately 30 seconds.

Next, the experimenter said, "Now I would like to see how many of those pictures you can remember." Subjects in the free condition were further told, "You tell me their names, and I'll write them down." Subjects in the informed condition were reminded that the pictures had consisted of either two or six groups, and the category labels were repeated for the subject at this time. Subjects in the free and informed conditions who asked if their recall must proceed according to the categories presented were told that they could recall in any order they wished. Subjects in the blocked condition were required to recall category members as prompted by the experimenter: "Now tell me the zoo animals; now tell me things you wear," etc. The categories were prompted in random order.

When all subjects had indicated that they were finished, or were silent for 15 seconds, they were prompted by the experimenter: "Can you think of any more?" For subjects in the blocked condition the experimenter asked, "Can you think of any more from any of the groups?" After another 15-second pause, the experiment was terminated.

RESULTS

Number of pictures recalled was submitted to an analysis of variance, with grades, number of categories, and retrieval conditions as main effects. Mean number of items recalled for the first, third, and fifth grades, respectively, was 9.08, 13.33, and 18.46; $F(2,90) = 180.69$, $p < .01$. The result, of course, was produced by giving more stimulus items to subjects in each higher grade level. In contrast, the mean percentage of items recalled out of the total possible for each grade was .76, .74, and .77, suggesting that the manipulation of list lengths resulted in a comparable level of difficulty of the problem for all subjects.

There were no significant differences among retrieval conditions, with free, informed, and blocked conditions yielding 13.03, 13.75, and 14.11 mean words recalled. This variable did not interact significantly with any other main effect, nor was the grades × categories × retrieval triple interaction significant.

Output clustering was measured by a procedure which takes into account the number of adjacent category members, the number of items recalled, and the number of categories recalled. This measure, the relative ratio of repetition (RRR) is discussed in detail in Mandler (1969) and is similar in nature to other commonly used clustering measures. The RRR varies from .0, in the case of no output clustering, to 1.00 in the case of perfect clustering.

Recall clustering was uniformly high in nearly all conditions, with a grand mean for all subjects of .85. The mean clustering scores for the free, informed, and blocked retrieval conditions, respectively, were .75, .81, and .98; $F(2,90) = 11.79$, $p < .01$, with only the blocked condition significantly different from the others by an individual comparison test. This effect was experimentally produced by requiring subjects in the blocked condition to cluster their recall.[1] The importance of this result is that increased clustering was not associated with increased recall in the blocked retrieval condition.

For the number-of-categories variable, subjects who sorted the stimuli into six groups averaged 15.94 items recalled, compared with 11.31 items for those who sorted into two groups, $F(1,90) = 131.41$, $p < .01$. In addition, table 1 summarizes the significant interaction between grades and number of categories, $F(2,90) = 5.44$, $p < .01$; the slope of the category-recall function increased significantly as age increased. This interaction is difficult to interpret since the

TABLE 1
Mean Recall Under Two Sorting Conditions at
Three Grade Levels

	NUMBER OF CATEGORIES	
GRADE	2	6
1	7.33	10.83
3	11.39	15.28
5	15.22	21.72

[1] The mean for this condition is slightly less than the perfect 1.00 because subjects were given a chance to recall items from any category at the end of the blocked recall.

potential steepness of the slope at each grade level was limited by the number of items given to different-aged subjects.

Analysis of the recall of words per category (WPC), as presented in Figure 1, further illustrates the strong relationship found between the number of categories employed in sorting and the number of words subsequently recalled. Since the number of items per category given to subjects varied, each subject's WPC must be compared with the maximum possible in that condition. The dashed lines in Figure 1 represent the total possible and the solid lines show the actual WPC attained by subjects in each condition. It is evident from the graph that the six-category subjects performed nearly perfectly, while subjects in the two-category condition fell short of attaining the maximum WPC.

Output clustering in the number-of-categories condition was measured using RRR, with no significant difference found between the two-category and six-category means of .83 and .87. An additional measure, "RRR-inverse," yielded mean clustering scores of .48 and .81, respectively. The RRR-inverse represents a measure of the sub- or supercategorization reflected in the output order of subjects in each of the two conditions. In the two-category condition, RRR measures the degree to which subjects grouped animals together and household things together. The RRR-inverse further measures the degree to which the animals, for instance, are grouped into pets, zoo animals, and farm animals. For the six-category subjects, RRR-inverse measures the degree to which the pets, farm animals, and zoo animals were output as one supercategory of animals. Subjects in the blocked retrieval conditions were not included in the RRR-inverse analysis, since the order of output of sub- or supercategories was determined by the order in which the categories were cued by the experimenter.

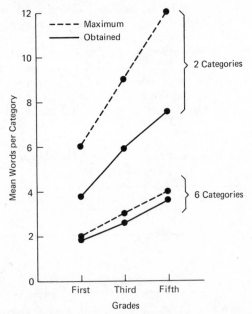

FIGURE 1.   *Words per category recalled by subjects in two sorting conditions.*

Since the subjects were not informed of the sub- or supercategories in the list, the RRR-inverse measure reflects the degree to which subjects spontaneously organized their output according to sub- or supercategories. The six-category subjects, whose RRR scores indicated that their output was highly clustered according to the six categories, were also found to be ordering the six categories into the two supercategories. That is, they grouped the three subcategories of animals together, and also the household objects. On the other hand, the two-category subjects also clustered according to the two supercategories, but failed to order the items within each into the three subcategories belonging to each supercategory. That is, zoo animals were not clustered separately from farm animals and pets. An analysis of variance showed the two-category RRR-inverse score (.48) to be significantly lower than that of the six-category subjects (.81), $F(1,60) = 38.15, p < .01$.

DISCUSSION

A direct relationship was found between number of categories in the sorting phase and subsequent recall. Subjects who sorted into six categories recalled significantly more words than those who sorted into two categories. The WPC analysis (Figure 1) additionally showed that the six-category subjects recalled a much higher proportion of words per category than did the two-category subjects. Overall, the children in this experiment were found to gain approximately one to $1\frac{1}{2}$ words per sorting category. Adults have been found to recall five more words for each additional category (up to seven) in the sort, but under conditions where the total number of words was much greater than in this study (Mandler, 1967). It was not possible to give the six-category subjects more items per category without requiring the two-category subjects to learn an unmanageable number of items per category. However, the near perfect WPC recall of the six-category group suggests that subjects in this condition might have been able to recall even more words per category if given a chance to do so. For this reason, any comparison of the one to $1\frac{1}{2}$ word per category gain in this study to the five word gain for adults would be premature. Further experimentation which controls for ceiling effects associated with large numbers of sorting categories will be necessary to determine the extent of the category-recall relationship at any given grade level.

Since clustering as measured by RRR was equally high for both the two-category and the six-category subjects, it appears that increased recall was not related to an increase in the amount of output organization. However, while the two-category subjects clustered their two given categories, these subjects failed to organize their output according to subcategories The six-category subjects were found to subcategorize *and* to supercategorize their output, indicating a more tightly structured categorical output than that of the two-category subjects.

It appears that children, like adults, find it easier to memorize words which are organized into many small groups rather than few large groups. Apparently, once a subject retrieves a single category item, he can easily retrieve the others, if the set is small enough. In addition, the six-category subjects in this experiment did not forget entire categories, a problem when the number of categories is large, because they were able to organize the categories further into two supercategories. Children as young as the first grade were found to use this strategy, which suggests that under the proper conditions even young children can benefit from use of a sophisticated categorical organization.

Retrieval Strategies.   No differences were found in the recall of subjects in the free, informed, and blocked retrieval conditions. This result is surprising in light of previous research in which blocked recall was found to be superior to other retrieval conditions (Scribner & Cole, 1972). In light of these negative results, it is interesting to compare the present experiment with that of Scribner and Cole. They found blocked recall to be superior to informed recall after three trials. The difference between subject's recall in the blocked and informed conditions after the first trial, however, was less dramatic. Perhaps the subjects' knowledge of their retrieval condition influenced their organization of the input on trials 2 and 3. Thus, any facilitation of blocked retrieval could be attributed to improved organization at both input and output. Indeed, in light of the present experiment where all subjects were given the same opportunity to organize at input, it appears that increased organization at the time of output alone is not sufficient to improve recall.

Another difference between the study of Scribner and Cole and this experiment is the input procedure itself. Scribner and Cole presented items individually, for a fixed amount of time, in random order, and subjects were informed of the list categories. In contrast, the sorting method used here insured that each subject began the recall phase with a stable categorical organization of the items to be remembered. The two procedures thus give subjects a different amount of categorical structure (although the same amount of category information) at input. It is likely that subjects who actively participate in the formation of a category structure (as in sorting) are better prepared to use that organization to aid recall than are subjects who are merely informed of categories. The sorting presentation probably gave subjects as strong an organization as they would be able to use, and no further benefit was realized from additional organizational constraints at output.

Such an explanation would clarify the finding that recall did not increase in spite of significantly higher clustering for the blocked retrieval group. The clustering of subjects in the free and informed groups was remarkably high, indicating a strong tendency of subjects to use the organization acquired at input to structure their recall. When this initially high level of clustering was increased further in the blocked retrieval condition, there were no "extra-facilitating" effects. The proposal that the sorting procedure gives subjects a stronger organization than does the standard presentation should, of course, be tested by comparing the two methods of presentation directly in a single experiment.

References

Cole, M.; Gay, J.; Glick, J. A.; & Sharp, D. W. *The cultural context of learning and thinking.* New York: Basic, 1971.

Lange, G. The development of conceptual and rote recall skills among school age children. *Journal of Experimental Child Psychology*, 1973, **15**, 394–406.

MANDLER, G. Organization and memory. In K. W. Spence & J. T. Spence (Eds.), *The psychology of learning and motivation*. Vol. 1. New York: Academic Press, 1967.

MANDLER, G. Input variables and output strategies in free recall of categorized lists. *American Journal of Psychology*, 1969, **82**, 531–539.

MANDLER, G., & STEVENS, D. The development of free and constrained conceptualization and subsequent verbal memory. *Journal of Experimental Child Psychology*, 1967, **5**, 86–93.

MOELY, B. E.; OLSON, F. A.; HALWES, T. G.; & FLAVELL, J. H. Production deficiency in young children's clustered recall. *Developmental Psychology*, 1969, **1**, 26–34.

SCRIBNER, S., & COLE, M. Effects of constrained recall training on children's performance in a verbal memory task. *Child Development*, 1972, **43**, 845–857.

SHULTZ, T. R.; CHARNESS, M.; & BERMAN, S. Effects of age, social class, and suggestion to cluster on free recall. *Developmental Psychology*, 1973, **8**, 57–61.

11

Working toward Competence

Research on schoolchildren yields information that can help teachers to understand better how their pupils learn and how they feel about themselves, their school, and their achievement. Some studies also stimulate teachers, administrators, and parents to think critically about their values, the goals they hold for children, and the price of their demands upon children. Results of many studies show sex differences, indicating that girls and boys cannot be lumped together in planning educational experiences that will be optimal for all.

As seen in the previous chapter, children assimilate information to their own cognitive structures. The questions they ask are, of course, products of their own particular levels of cognitive development. Hildy S. Ross and Rita H. Balzer have investigated the effects of answering questions on children's remembering information and on their asking more questions. The results have implications for teaching.

Kennedy T. Hill's paper is from a symposium on negative evaluation and feedback in which the participants examined the effects of adults' criticisms on children. Hill found that adults adjusted their feedback to the maturity of the child and that developmental level was an important factor in the ways in which children react to negative feedback. Responses of highly anxious children differed from the responses of children who were not anxious.

The results of Audrey M. Borth's research call for an examination of the proper role of the school in society. In studying what it takes to succeed in school, she analyzed characteristics and responses of children in schools in two socioeconomic settings. She found oppressive effects of school experiences on children, especially girls.

Determinants and Consequences of Children's Questions[*]

Hildy S. Ross and Rita H. Balzer
UNIVERSITY OF WATERLOO

Children from grades 1, 3, and 5 were exposed in pairs to a series of slides accompanied by descriptive statements, and invited to ask questions. Questions were answered for one member in each pair. Providing answers significantly increased the frequency of questions among Answer Ss. In addition, Answer Ss remembered significantly more than did No Answer Ss, three days after the presentation of the stimuli.

Questioning, long considered an indicant of curiosity (e.g., Smith & Hall, 1907; Woodworth, 1921), has recently been characterized as "a form of *epistemic behavior,* that is, behavior directed toward, and reinforced by the acquisition of knowledge . . . motivated primarily by epistemic curiosity" (Berlyne & Frommer, 1966, p. 178). Consistent with this definition Berlyne and Frommer found that stimuli high in the collative variables (e.g., novelty, uncertainty, incongruity, and surprisingness) generally induced more questions. However, they failed to find consistent differences in the number of questions asked by children whose questions were either answered or not answered. The provision of answers increased the number of questions asked by grade 3 children, but not by children in grades 1 and 5. This second unexpected result is difficult to comprehend if questioning is motivated by epistemic curiosity and reinforced by the acquisition of knowledge. Thus the primary purpose of the current study was to re-examine the relationship between questioning and the provision of answers.

Several features of Berlyne and Frommer's study may account for their failure to find a consistent effect for answering children's questions. First, the overall frequency of questioning was low (averaging fewer than two questions per stimulus item) making any condition differences difficult to detect. In the hope of inducing more questions in the current study, the stimuli selected were relatively novel and complex, and practice stimuli were used to ensure that all Ss asked some questions. Second, Ss in Berlyne and Frommer's study were tested individually. To highlight the contrast between Answer and No Answer Ss in the current study, they were tested in pairs consisting of one subject from each condition. Finally, the questions of the Answer Ss in Berlyne and Frommer's study were generally answered after all questions concerning a particular stimulus item had been asked. Thus answers were not only delayed (a factor which itself may have diminished their value as reinforcers) but additional questions further delayed the answers to previous ones. Here all questions asked by the Answer S were answered immediately.

From *Child Development,* 1975, **46,** 536–539. Copyright © 1975 by The Society for Research in Child Development, Inc. Reprinted by permission.

[*] This research was supported by Canada Council Research Grant No. S71-2015. The authors would like to thank Sister Elise Diemont and the students of St. Daniel Separate School, Kitchener, Ontario, for participating in this study and Michael Ross, for his suggestions and comments.

293

A second issue examined in the current investigation was the retention of the information provided in the answers to the questions. It has been proposed that questions serve to prepare the individual for the reception of answers, by directing his attention toward that which is relevant (Symonds, 1936; Woodworth, 1922). Studies of questions posed chiefly by others verify that they facilitate the retention of information (Berlyne, 1954; Finley, 1921; Rothkopf, 1967); however, questions asked personally should have an additional beneficial impact on memory for the answer. If questions are motivated by epistemic curiosity, a state of uncertainty that is directed toward and resolved by the acquisition of knowledge, then the questioner should be uniquely receptive and attentive to the information he seeks. Moreover, Bruner (1961) has suggested that information is more easily retained and retrieved if it fits into pre-existing cognitive structures. Answers to questions inspired by one's own uncertainty should be more easily integrated into existing cognitive structures than answers to questions posed by others. In the current research Ss were tested for their retention of the information obtained by the member of each pair whose questions had been answered. It was hypothesized that the S who had himself asked the questions would provide more accurate answers to them than the one who had merely heard both the questions and their answers.

METHOD

Subjects Ss were 10 boys and 10 girls from each of grades 1, 3, and 5. Their mean ages were 6.6 (range: 6.2–7.0), 8.7 (range: 8.0–9.0), and 10.7 (range: 10.0–11.2). All attended an urban Catholic separate school in Kitchener, Ontario.

Procedure Ss were seen in same-sex, same-grade pairs; one was assigned to the Answer and one to the No Answer condition. Ss were told that they were going to play a detective game in which they could ask questions about the pictures they would see. Furthermore, since "being a detective is not easy work" they were told of a "rule" which stated that not all questions could be answered. This "rule" allowed E not to answer the questions of the No Answer S concerning the test stimuli.

The stimuli consisted of eight slides developed from pictures found in children's books and accompanied by brief descriptive statements. For example, the first test stimulus pictured Eskimo children performing the Mexican Hat Dance. E said: "These children live in the far North. They are playing a new game which they just learned in school." A practice stimulus preceded the test stimuli for which all questions were answered and prompting and explanations were used until each S had asked a minimum of three questions.

There were five test stimuli each of which was exposed for 3 minutes following E's descriptive statement. The No Answer S received an answer for only his first question on stimulus one. E responded immediately to each of the Answer S's questions. Answers were based on a set of materials about each question which was supplemented by E's improvised answers to any questions that were unrelated to these prepared notes. Thus answers were, as far as possible, consistent across all Ss. Regardless of whether E answered a question, she established eye contact and smiled at the questioner if he turned to look at her. All sessions were tape recorded; the microphone was placed on a desk directly in front of the Ss.

Following the presentation of the five test stimuli, Ss were each given a rating sheet which asked whether they enjoyed playing the game, whether they would like to play it again, and whether they liked the lady who played it with them. "Happy face" drawings were used as response choices to each question, i.e., a smiling, indifferent, or frowning face indicated positive, neutral, and negative feelings, respectively. Grades 3 and 5 Ss completed the ratings independently; for grade 1 Ss, E explained the task and read the questions with them. Ratings were completed anonymously, and later labelled by E.

Two additional stimuli were then shown. All questions were answered, including those from the No Answer S, who also received liberal praise for his questions. This procedure was designed to compensate for any possible negative feelings due to the experience of not having had questions answered.

Three days later each S was seen individually by the same E. They were told that they were going to be asked questions about the pictures they had seen, because "good detectives remember things."

Questions were selected from those asked by the Answer S in session 1 and now asked of both members of the respective pair. Whenever possible, three questions were asked about each of the five test stimuli. The descriptive statements used to introduce the stimulus were repeated prior to each set of questions, and E always made certain that S remembered the picture referred to. S's open-ended responses were recorded. This procedure took from 5 to 10 minutes.

RESULTS

Number of Questions   The mean number of questions asked by each S was 22.1, or 4.4 per stimulus. In all, the 60 Ss asked 1328 questions.

The influence of the treatment conditions (Answer vs. No Answer) and the grade and sex of the Ss were evaluated using analysis of variance. Treatment was considered a within-subject variable, as two subjects (one from each condition) were seen simultaneously, while grade and sex were considered between-subject variables.

Providing an answer significantly increased the number of questions asked over all stimuli ($F (1, 24) = 5.6, p < .026$). Table 1 shows that Ss in the Answer Group asked an average of 26.3 questions while those in the No Answer Group asked 18.0. Neither the grade nor the sex of the Ss affected the frequency of questions, nor was any interaction among the factors significant.

Furthermore, as the session progressed the differences between the Answer and the No Answer Groups in the frequency of asking questions increased; the difference was .9 questions on stimulus one, and increased to 2.8 questions on stimulus five (Table 1). A linear trend analysis showed that this increase was significant ($F (1, 24) = 5.3, p < .05$) and uninfluenced by the grade or sex of the Ss.

Subjects' Ratings of Session 1   On a 3-point scale (positive, neutral, negative responses), 82% of the responses selected were positive, indicating

TABLE 1
Mean Number of Questions

| GROUP | STIMULUS | | | | | |
	1	2	3	4	5	TOTAL
Answer	4.4	5.1	5.7	4.8	6.2	26.3
No-Answer	3.5	3.7	4.2	3.1	3.4	18.0
Difference	.9	1.4	1.5	1.7	2.8	8.3

that subjects enjoyed playing the game, would like to play it again, and liked the lady who played it with them. Ss in the Answer Group gave positive responses to 83% of the questions while those in the No Answer Group gave positive responses to 81% of the questions, a nonsignificant difference.

Retention of Answers Ss in the Answer Group, who had themselves asked the questions that were used in the retention test, averaged 61% correct, while those in the No Answer Group, who had heard both question and answer in session 1, averaged 49% correct. This difference was statistically significant $(F(1, 24) = 10.4, p < .004)$. For both males and females, and in all three grades, the Answer Group Ss gave a greater percentage of correct responses than did the No Answer Group. No sex or grade differences were significant; however, the Sex × Treatment interaction approached significance $(F(1, 24) = 3.5, p < .07)$. The differences in retention between the Answer and No Answer Groups were greater for females (65 versus 45 per cent correct) than for males (57 versus 52% correct).

DISCUSSION

In the current study a clear reinforcing effect of providing answers to children's questions was found. This finding, although contrary to Berlyne and Frommer's results, supports Berlyne's (1970) theory. Questioning appears to be appropriately defined as an epistemic behavior directed towards the acquisition of information. The many procedural differences between the current study and Berlyne and Frommer's study make it impossible to attribute the differences in the findings to any one factor. However, the current findings justify accepting the assumption that the provision of answers should influence the number of questions asked. Berlyne and Frommer's grade 1 and 5 subjects may be considered exceptions to this rule. The problem thus becomes one of explaining a limited set of data, rather than revising theoretical accounts of the motivational basis of questioning.

Several alternative suggestions can be made concerning the mechanism whereby the provision of answers influenced questioning. First, the information provided in the answers may have directly reinforced and hence increased the frequency of questioning by the Answer Ss. Alternatively, the No Answer Ss may have learned that they could get more information by allowing the Answer

Ss to ask questions, and in that case the frequency of questions asked by the No Answer Ss would have decreased. Unfortunately, the constant order of the stimuli for all Ss, and the effects of increasing familiarity with the experimenter and the experimental situation make these separate trends impossible to analyze; yet the complete absence of any tendency for the questioning of No Answer Ss to decline makes the second possibility unlikely. In addition, one could argue that providing answers was primarily socially reinforcing, indicating to the Ss that one member of the pair was being a "good detective," while the other was not. If this were true, however, Ss who felt unsuccessful might be expected to view the game as less fun, to have less desire to play it again, and to like the experimenter less. The rating scales did not reflect any differences in attitudes between answered and unanswered Ss, which tends to weaken this alternative explanation of the results.

The current findings on retention also substantiate the proposition that questioning is an epistemic behavior. Questioning activity was related to the retention of information; the child who asked the question was presumably more curious about and attentive to the answer, and consequently remembered it more accurately than the child who had merely heard both question and answer. The information received in the answers to the child's own questions may have been more easily integrated into his pre-existing cognitive structures, as is suggested by Bruner's (1961) reasoning.

In summary, the current study demonstrated that within a relatively brief period, the provision of answers influenced the number of questions children ask. It seems likely that this effect would be even more dramatic when repeated daily in the child's natural environment. Berlyne (1970) has stated that "the degree to which parents and teachers encourage a child's questions and answer them patiently and fully will, we must suppose, have lasting effects" (p. 973). If answers to questions posed personally are better retained than answers to questions posed by others, as is suggested by the current findings, and if even the questions posed by others facilitate retention, as is suggested by previous work, then eliciting and answering questions seems an excellent means of promoting the acquisition and retention of information.

References

BERLYNE, D. E. An experimental study of human curiosity. *British Journal of Psychology*, 1954, **45**, 256–265.
BERLYNE, D. E. Children's reasoning and thinking. In P. H. Mussen (Ed.), *Carmichael's Manual of Child Psychology*, Vol. *1*, New York: Wiley, 1970.
BERLYNE, D. E. and FROMMER, E. D. Some determinants of the incidence and content of children's questions. *Child Development*, 1966, **37**, 177–189.
BRUNER, J. S. The act of discovery. *Harvard Educational Review*, 1961, **31**, 21–32.
FINLEY, C. W. Some studies of children's interests in science materials. *School Science & Mathematics*, 1921, **11**, 1–24.
ROTHKOPF, E. Z. Selective facilitative effects of interspersed questions of learning from written materials. *Journal of Educational Psychology*, 1967, **58**, 56–61.
SYMONDS, P. E. *Education and the psychology of thinking*. New York: McGraw Hill, 1936.
WOODWORTH, R. S. *Dynamic psychology*. New York: Columbia University Press, 1922.

Developmental Changes and Individual Differences in Children's Reactions to Negative Evaluations *

Kennedy T. Hill
UNIVERSITY OF ILLINOIS, URBANA-CHAMPAIGN

It seems clear that a child's ability to make effective use of negative evaluations from adults becomes an increasingly important determinant of his academic and social development. Today I would like to examine several developmental changes either in children's interpretation of, or reactions to, evaluative feedback from adults. Then I will relate these developmental changes to individual differences in children's sensitivity and reactions to negative evauation.

Let us turn first to research suggesting developmental changes in children's interpretation of different kinds of adult feedback. Crandall (1963), for example, found that junior high school age children reacted quite differently to adult nonreaction depending upon what overt feedback preceded it. If nonreaction followed positive reactions, children responded as if the nonreaction was a negative evaluation. In contrast, nonreaction following negative feedback was responded to as if the nonreaction was positive in meaning. Thus a contrast effect was present: Nonreaction was interpreted as meaning the opposite of whichever overt feedback it followed.

Montanelli and I (Montanelli & Hill, 1969) found quite different results for younger children in the late elementary school years. For these younger children, the effects of preceding positive or negative feedback were not reversed during subsequent nonreaction from an adult. Nonreaction seemed to have little informational value. On the other hand, if the adult switched from either positive or negative feedback to opposite overt feedback, for example, from positive to negative, then the children responded very strongly to the second kind of feedback they received. I might mention as an aside that, consistent with the research just summarized by Redd, children responded initially more strongly to negative than positive feedback and also more strongly to the negative feedback when it came second.

These studies taken together suggest that within the context of what feedback came previously, young children appear to interpret only overt negative feedback from adults as indicating negative evaluation, while older children may respond to neutral adult reactions as being negative in nature depending on what previous feedback has occurred. We would speculate further that for still older children and adults, it is possible that a shift to a mild form of the same overt feedback or to less frequent overt feedback of the same kind may be

Presented as part of the Symposium "Negative Evaluation and Feedback: Impact and Implications for the Agent and Recipient," Society for Research in Child Development, Denver, 1975. Printed by permission.

* The research reported here was supported in part by Research Grant Number OEG-0-72-0882 from the National Institute of Education, Department of Health, Education, and Welfare, and by Public Health Service Traineeships (HD-00244) from the National Institute of Child Health and Human Development, United States Public Health Service.

reacted to as having opposite meaning to the initial overt feedback. Thus an adult receiving rather frequent positive evaluation and later somewhat less frequent positive feedback from the same individual may interpret the less frequent but still positive reactions as indicating a negative assessment. Changes in facial expression and vocal cues may also cause the person being evaluated to interpret feedback as changing in meaning. For example, criticism no longer given in a harsh voice or with a frown may be interpreted as being a change toward a more positive assessment from the teacher, parent, or other evaluating adult.

So far we have been discussing children's and adult's reactions to *changes* in an adult's evaluative reactions. Let us turn now to the absolute nature of the feedback being given. A second hypothesized developmental change is that as children become older, feedback they interpret as being negative is objectively given in an increasingly positive manner. Young children may respond only to overt criticism as meaning negative evaluation. Older children may interpret the adult's failure to respond as indicating a negative assessment. And for adults, mild positive reactions may be interpreted and function as negative evaluation, the familiar "damning with faint praise." Or perhaps in this era of grade-inflation and letter-of-recommendation inflation, we should say "damning with considerable praise."

Why might this be? Why would young children only respond to overt criticism as indicating negative evaluation while older children and adults interpret neutral or even somewhat positive feedback as being negative evaluation? Perhaps the answer lies in how adults provide feedback to children of different ages, so that in all cases the children are simply responding to feedback in terms of its functional use by adults. Adults often may express their positive and negative reactions to children freely and directly. For the young child and his parents, a spade is a spade whether the child is "being good" or misbehaving. But adults may find it increasingly difficult to provide direct overt feedback as children become older and reach adulthood, especially negative feedback in highly evaluative interpersonal situations. Such negative evaluation may be as aversive for the adult trying to give it as for the older child or adult receiving it, or perhaps it is more accurate to say trying not to receive it. Moreover, young children typically do not question the legitimacy or right of the parent or other adults to provide negative evaluations. Older children and adults, in contrast, may challenge either the appropriateness or the validity of negative feedback from an adult.

We are suggesting, then, that adults may provide negative feedback in different ways to children of different ages, being more overt and direct with young children and more indirect and even positive with older children. The same reaction from an adult may then be correctly interpreted by the recipient as meaning different things at different ages. Children thus would make increasingly subtle discriminations of adult evaluative reactions at older ages. Consider nonreaction: To a young child nonreaction may mean nothing. To an older child, nonreaction may be neutral in meaning, and to adults, nonreaction may typically be interpreted as being negative in nature. The next time a colleague gives you a paper to react to, give him a kind of noncommittal neutral reaction and see if he doesn't respond as if you don't think much of his paper or starts probing to learn what you didn't like about it.

So far we have discussed developmental changes in children's interpretation of different kinds of adult feedback or changes in feedback. A third developmental change relevant to the theme of this paper concerns how children at different ages respond to negative feedback in terms of problem solving strategies. Allen (1966) and others have found that criticism disrupts younger elementary school-age children's performance and causes them to leave a task quickly. In direct contrast, for older elementary school-age children, criticism facilitates the child's trying new solutions and strategies for performing at a task and results in greater persistence than does positive feedback (Allen, 1966). Younger children thus respond to negative (and positive) feedback as would be expected from a straightforward reinforcement model, performing better and persisting longer under praise but doing less well and leaving sooner under criticism. Older children, however, process the same feedback quite differently. This may be due in part to the contingencies used by adults in providing negative feedback to children. For young children, adults may more often than not use disapproval when they wish a child to terminate a behavior, e.g., to stop hitting another child. As children become older, negative feedback from adults may often be used in an attempt to modify the child's behavior, especially in achievement and problem-solving situations, in which standards of excellence are nearly always involved. Thus negative adult evaluation may often signal young children to stop what they are doing but older children to change their behavior. As Allen notes, older children appear to change their problem-solving activities in response to criticism in an apparent effort to find a more correct solution to gain approval. Younger children do not appear to relate criticism to their performance strategies or change them. Within Redd's framework, one might expect a criticizing adult to have strong negative valence for younger children, since aversive feedback is being experienced but does not lead to positive gains in performance; for older children, a criticizing adult might have either a positive or negative valence depending on the usefulness of the criticism in helping the child improve performance on a meaningful task.

We are suggesting, then, that older children differ from younger children both in what is construed as negative evaluation and in their inclination or ability to use that negative feedback to effectively modify performance strategies to achieve greater subsequent success. Let us turn now to an individual difference variable, children's level of evaluation anxiety, which appears to play a major role in children's development of more mature reactions to negative feedback and to their response to some of the factors discussed by Redd and Dweck. The hypotheses discussed here are related to a theory we have proposed elsewhere (Hill, 1972) about the motivational dispositions of children of varying levels of evaluation anxiety. Briefly, we have suggested that both the motives to obtain approval and success and the motives to avoid disapproval and failure increase as level of evaluation anxiety increases, but the increase is especially apparent for the avoidance tendencies. Thus low anxious children are relatively more concerned about succeeding and obtaining approval whereas high anxious children are relatively more motivated to avoid failure and criticism, although both approach and avoidance tendencies are high for these latter children. Children with strong evaluation anxiety, then, may be overly responsive to evaluative reactions of adults, and especially to negative feedback.

Anxious children's dominant motives to avoid disapproval and failure leads them to respond to criticism and disapproval in much the same way as younger children, as we discussed earlier. Under criticism, anxious children may leave evaluative situations quickly, perform less efficiently and more slowly and cautiously, and accept the negative feedback without changing performance strategies at a task to obtain positive outcomes (Hill, 1972), much like Allen (1966) found for kindergarten children. Low anxious children, in contrast, show the tendencies Allen found for older grade school children—persistence under negative evaluation and flexibility in changing problem-solving strategies in order to arrive at correct solutions.

On the basis of our theoretical analysis, anxious children should also respond more to the general effect entailed in negative evaluation and be less able to process and use the information communicated by the feedback. Anxious children should then develop a strong negative valence toward adults providing negative feedback. Less anxious children, because of their ability to process the information involved in negative evaluation and use that information to enhance their performance to eventually gain positive outcomes, should develop a relatively more positive valence toward the adult providing criticism.

Because of their strong motivation to avoid disapproval and failure, it is also predicted that children with strong evaluation anxiety will be less likely to interpret ambiguous feedback as being negative in meaning. For example, junior high school age high anxious children may be less likely to interpret nonreaction following positive feedback as being negative, as Crandall found in general for children of this age. Such a tendency would help the anxious child avoid the immediate aversive experience of failure but of course only at the expense of losing the informational value of indirect negative feedback which would help the child improve his subsequent performance. Anxious children would then lag developmentally behind their low anxious counterparts in their willingness or ability to correctly interpret nonreaction, mild positive reactions, and other relatively subtle forms of negative evaluation given by adults to older children and other adults (see Hill, Emmerich, Gelber, Lazar, & Schickedanz, 1974). High anxious children may respond only to overt negative feedback much like younger children. Indeed, hesitancy of anxious children to interpret correctly negative evaluations communicated in increasingly subtle ways as the child becomes older may account in part for his increasingly poor classroom learning and achievement, again since the anxious child does not recognize or use the informational value of the feedback in his learning activities.

The anxious child's strong motives to avoid disapproval and failure should also result in several additional preferences related to the work of Redd and Dweck discussed earlier in this symposium. First, the anxious child should prefer a situation in which the adult feedback is noncontingent on his performance rather than contingent, since the former should be less likely to signal evaluation and possible failure and further disapproval from the adult. Second, the child with a high level of evaluation anxiety should prefer tasks involving luck rather than ability (see Dweck, 1975), again to avoid negative assessment of his performance and possible adult disapproval. Finally, the anxious child's strong general responsivity to adult reactions will cause the child to avoid or perform poorly in situations involving simply the *potential* for adult feedback, such as when an adult is present and monitoring performance but not responding, or absent but may return later to evaluate the child's work on the basis of a performance outcome or record.

What can be done to help high anxious children deal effectively with adult feedback? Our analysis suggests several ways of changing evaluation practices which could promote younger and anxious children's effective use of negative feedback to improve their performance. Such changes would involve increasing both the child's ability to process the information contained in negative feedback and his positive motivation in evaluative situations. For example, Redd's finding that a combination of positive and negative feedback produces a greater valence for the evaluating adult than just negative feedback should hold especially for older anxious children as well as for younger children in general. A mixture of success and failure or approval and disapproval, perhaps with a predominance of positive outcomes and feedback, should especially help anxious children by bringing into play their strong motives to attain success and gain approval, as well as the even stronger motives to avoid failure and disapproval which negative evaluation alone would trigger. Dweck's suggestion that adults use explicit, unambiguous feedback and provide an explanation of the basis of a child's failure and strategies for enhancing successful performance should be particularly helpful for young children and older anxious children since these youngsters are less likely to interpret criticism appropriately and use that information in their subsequent problem-solving efforts. The theory and research suggested in our symposium, then, are suggesting ways in which adults can provide negative as well as positive feedback to children to optimize different children's learning and performance and to enhance the positive valence of learning and other evaluative situations.

References

ALLEN, S. The effects of verbal reinforcement on children's performance as a function of type of task. *Journal of Experimental Child Psychology*, 1966, **3**, 57–73.

CRANDALL, V. C. Reinforcement effects of adult reactions and non-reactions on children's achievement expectancies. *Child Development*, 1963, **34**, 335–354.

DWECK, C. S. The role of expectations and attributions in the alleviation of learned helplessness. *Journal of Personality and Social Psychology*, 1975, **31**, 674–685.

HILL, K. T. Anxiety in the evaluative context. In W. W. Hartup (Ed.) *Young Child, Vol. II.* Washington, D.C.: National Association for the Education of Young Children, 1972, pp. 225–263.

HILL, K. T., EMMERICH, H. R., GELBER, E. R., LAZAR, M. A., and SCHICKEDANZ, D. Children's interpretation of adult non-reaction: a trial-by-trial self-report assessment and evidence for contrast effects in an observational context. *Journal of Experimental Child Psychology*, 1974, **17**, 482–494.

MONTANELLI, D. S., and HILL, K. T. Children's achievement expectations and performance as a function of two consecutive reinforcement experiences, sex of subject, and sex of experimenter. *Journal of Personality and Social Psychology*, 1969, **13**, 115–128.

Sex Differences in Coping and Defending in Two School Contexts

Audrey M. Borth
LAKE FOREST COLLEGE

This is the report of an analysis of sex-related student differences in styles of coping and defending in two school contexts. The purpose of the larger inquiry of which this analysis was but a part, *Coping and Defending in Black Classrooms*, focused on non-intellective correlates of achievement in a special social context: an all black urban elementary school.

Data were collected on a Student Interview Schedule administered orally in small groups in grade 5, and from school records. The performance variable standing for achievement (and by which children are ability tracked in this urban system) was the latest recorded standardized reading score.

Following a Lewinian model (Lewin, 1935) describing behavior as a function of the interaction of person and environment, we clustered non-intellective correlates in three categories: Background or Descriptive Variables (sex, race, social class, age, I.Q., and family structure); General Psychological Variables (motives and defenses); and specifically School Related Variables (learning climate and style, norms, and sentiments toward school.)

Viewing achievement on the continuum of all scores available for the Metropolitan Achievement Tests in reading, we regressed our psychological and school-related variables plus age and I.Q. on it. We also factor analyzed the data in terms of shared variance to describe what we refer to in this study as typical strategies for responding to the demands and expectations of the school situation (coping and defending strategies).

At the outset we had hoped to characterize achievers in this social setting in enough specificity to enable us to develop a model for intervention in the early school life of children who were not succeeding in the system as it is now constituted.

The underlying assumption with which we began our study was that the achievement level of almost all students, regardless of race, sex, social class, or family background, *can* be raised within the school context. We questioned both the narrow conception of "fixed limits" of student attainment (Hunt, 1962), and the necessity, though not the existence, of the overwhelming effects of family background on school success (Coleman, 1966).

Our assumption was sorely tried by two years of intimate contact and research with fifth graders in the urban black school hereafter referred to as Southside.

It was to some measure supported by a less extensive comparative study in a nearby University School.

Although the backgrounds of the children at University School were certainly "richer" in many respects than those of the children at Southside, and their achievement motivation higher, it was not so much the differences

Presented at meetings of The American Psychological Association, Chicago, 1975. Printed by permission.

between populations as the residual similarities which we speculate belong to the general role of elementary school student that interested us. In many respects, the basic characteristics of "studenthood" (high Deference, Endurance, Dependency, Work scores; low Autonomy, Dominance, Aggression and Flight-Fight scores) remained the same in both school contexts, as did the age-graded, teacher dominated control structure of classrooms. (Table 1).

Having analyzed the data in search of correlates of achievement (Table 2) and in the hope of identifying related coping and defending strategies for successful students in the two schools, we used again the same procedures to analyze by sex. We found the sex-related student characteristics also followed

TABLE 1

Variable Means for Total Fifth Grade Southside and University School Samples

PSYCHOLOGICAL VARIABLES	SOUTHSIDE		UNIVERSITY		DIFFERENCE*	
	Mean	Error	Mean	Error	Mean	Significance
Achievement	5.62	.14	6.20	.21	.58	.05
Aggression	3.79	.19	3.44	.28	.35	NS
Autonomy	3.97	.15	4.76	.24	.79	.01
Deference	5.88	.15	5.76	.31	.12	NS
Dominance	3.72	.16	4.07	.30	.35	NS
Endurance	6.98	.16	5.78	.28	1.20	.01
Work	12.43	.20	15.13	.34	2.70	.01
Flight	7.20	.24	6.16	.36	.04	NS
Fight	8.19	.27	5.20	.31	2.99	.01
Dependency	12.45	.25	11.62	.34	.83	NS
Pairing	9.74	.18	10.89	.30	1.15	.01
Control	23.55	.20	26.73	.32	3.18	.01
Anxiety	19.74	.20	16.62	.35	3.12	.01
Self-Satisfaction	5.26	.07	5.60	.12	.34	.01

SCHOOL-RELATED VARIABLES	Mean	Error	Mean	Error	Mean	Significance
Sentiment toward school	16.55	.20	17.40	.21	.85	.01
Concept of ability	12.13	.27	12.84	.34	.71	NS
Class discussion	2.75	.05	2.91	.04	.16	NS
Seek teacher's help	2.79	.05	2.76	.08	.03	NS
Teacher affect	2.74	.06	2.71	.07	.03	NS
School fun	2.66	.06	2.49	.08	.17	NS
Cooperation	2.60	.07	2.67	.07	.07	NS
Hard work	2.88	.04	2.78	.07	.10	NS
Social standard	2.52	.07	2.78	.06	.26	.05
Learning style	9.38	.18	11.04	.19	1.66	.01

* Two-tailed t-tests used to determine level of significance.

TABLE 2
Regression Results for University Sample

MULTIPLE R = .73	F 3.35	SIGNIFICANCE .01	DF 11/33
Independent Variables			
Concept of ability	6.29	.05	1/33
School work fun	4.63	.05	
Pairing	−4.35	.05	
Fight	4.12	.05	
Sentiment toward school	−3.30	NS	
I.Q.	2.60	NS	
Teacher affect	2.06	NS	
Number of children	−1.79	NS	
Autonomy	−1.61	NS	
Family structure	−1.25	NS	
Always work hard	1.19	NS	

a general pattern regardless of school attended: at both Southside and University the boys in our studies described themselves as "more self-satisfied," "aggressive," "dominant," and "work oriented," and more interested in the norm that "it is just as important to get along with others as to do school work" (male "bonding" appears to develop early) than did the girls.

Regardless of which school they attended, the girls responded that they were from families they perceived as "more interested in their schooling," that they "liked school" more; that they favored "a friendly cooperative learning style;" and that "it is good to participate in class discussion" to a greater extent than boys did. In other words, by fifth grade boys seemed to perceive themselves as more independent and peer-oriented while girls seemed more dependent on family and teacher feedback and approval.

TABLE 3
Regression Results for Southside Fifth Grade Population

MULTIPLE R .57	F 6.12	SIGNIFICANCE .01	DF 8/103
Independent variables			
I.Q.	19.91	.01	1/103
Age	6.77	.05	
Flight	6.40	.05	
Teacher affect	3.71	NS	
Deference (negative)	−2.26	NS	
Class participation	2.14	NS	
Anxiety (negative)	−1.82	NS	
Family structure	1.75	NS	

Overall, however, *boys and girls* were more likely to respond similarly to classroom expectations (andronomously) at University School, and to respond differently (more in accord with traditional sex role stereotypes) at Southside Elementary. The sex differences were wider in the lower class black school sample than in the same age group at middle-class, racially mixed University School.

RESULTS OF THE REGRESSION ANALYSIS FOR BOYS AT SOUTHSIDE

All of the variables, background, psychological, and school-related (as represented by Table 1) were regressed on the performance variable, Metropolitan reading score. Approximately 67% of the achievement variance among boys is accounted for in the multiple regression.

Aggression, Deference, Work, Endurance, and Number of children in the family were found to be *negatively* related to achievement in the multiple regression for boys. I.Q., Family structure (intact), preference for a "friendly, cooperative classroom learning style," Flight, the belief that "it is just as important to get along with others as to do school work," and Age were positively related to achievement. In the step down analysis, the only variables significantly positively related to achievement were I.Q. (.01), Family structure (0.1), and Classroom Learning Style (.05).

Since I.Q. was most highly correlated with achievement among the fifth grade boys in this school it is interesting to note how other variables were related to I.Q. in the correlation matrix. Positive sentiments toward school (.21), Aggression (.26), and Flight (.30) as well as Reading Score (.60) were positively correlated with I.Q. Negatively associated with I.Q. were Deference (−.35) and Pairing (−.43). It is particularly interesting to note that Aggression is *negatively* associated with achievement but positively associated with I.Q. Deference, the strategy the majority of our subjects, both boys and girls tell us is important in the classroom (factor analysis) is *negatively* associated with both I.Q. and achievement among boys.

RESULTS OF REGRESSION ANALYSIS FOR GIRLS AT SOUTHSIDE

Using the same procedure we found approximately 31% (less than half that of the boys) of the variance among girls is accounted for by our variable clusters. That, in itself, tells us something about the differential approach to schooling of boys and girls.

Positively associated with achievement for girls were the belief that "the teachers should try to understand how students feel," "feelings of control over the environment," the belief that "it is good to help others with school work except during tests," and the number of children in the family. In the step down analysis only the idea that "teachers should try to understand how students feel" is significantly positively related to achievement (.05).

In the correlation matrix this variable is not related to any of the other independent variables.

REPORT OF FACTOR ANALYSIS FOR BOYS AT
SOUTHSIDE—COPING AND DEFENDING STRATEGIES

Psychological and school related variables, plus age and I.Q. were entered into the factor analysis. The resultant factors are clusters of variables which help explain the data in terms of common factor variances. They help us to locate and identify the unities underlying responses for boys. The factors were tentatively interpreted on the basis of the researchers' knowledge of all the data analyses. We looked for constructs that might help to explain variances in style of coping and defending boys purport to value in this setting.

Factor loadings for the first five factors of the nine factor rotated structure are reported here. They account for 61% of the variance.

Factor I which accounts for 14% of the variance loaded highest on general psychological variables; Aggression and Fight vs. Endurance and Work. This bipolar factor described two opposing clusters: one, the type of student who is high on Aggression and Fight but correspondingly low on Endurance and Work; two, the boy who is high on Endurance and Work but low on Aggression and Fight. We know from previous analysis of the data that the majority of these boys choose Endurance and Work values over Fight and Aggression. However, in the regression analysis, Aggression, Endurance, and Work are all negatively related to achievement, belief in work orientation significantly so. Fight and Aggression, though clearly not encouraged in this school context *was* positively associated with I.Q.

Factor II, accounting for 13% of the variance, was another bipolar factor of mixed psychological and school related variables. Positive sentiments toward school and Concept of Ability vs. Flight. This factor seemed to describe the kind of boy who is either "in it" or "out of it" in school. In this context it is the boy who opts "out" through Flight, a psychological defense against environmental press, who is the highest achiever. In the regression analysis Flight was positively related to achievement while Sentiments toward School and Self-Concept of Ability, school related variables, dropped out of the analysis.

Factor III (12%) loaded highest on three school related variables (norms): "It is good to help others in school"; "You should always work hard"; and "It is good to ask the teacher for help." This factor described the boy who is socially oriented and believes in conforming, at least verbally, to both peer and teacher expectations. He may be a pleasant class member but it doesn't help him at all as far as achievement is concerned.

Factor IV (12%), a mix of psychological and school related variables, is again a bipolar factor describing the inverse relationship of I.Q. to Pairing and Age. It describes the type of younger, bright boy who achieves on the basis of his measured intelligence or the older peer oriented boy who uses friendship as a defense. I.Q. and Achievement are most highly correlated in boys (.50).

Factor V (11%) loaded highest on Self-Satisfaction (Psychological) and the idea that "school work should be fun" (school related). This boy's coping strategy also seems to be socially oriented: he sees school as an occasion for fun and feels good about himself.

What this factor analysis of the data shows most clearly is that there is no necessary relationship between the motives, values, or perceived expectations of the student role held by most of the boys in this setting and their academic achievement. In fact, the attributes the majority of boys value are often counter-productive for academic achievement. The boy who believes Work Orientation and Endurance constitute appropriate strategy for coping with school demands will be among the lowest achievers. We have shown in the regression analysis that both variables are negatively related to achievement. The boy who likes school and thinks he is doing well and in turn rejects Flight as a defense, also works against his own achievement. Flight as a defense against classroom interaction is positively related to achievement. In summary, it is the most sociable "in it" boy who achieves least. The withdrawn "out of it" student who depends primarily on his measured intelligence on entrance is the one who achieves best in school.

FACTOR ANALYSIS—GIRLS

The first five factors of the nine–factor, rotated structure, reported here account for 64% of the variance among girls' responses.

Factor I (14%) loaded highest on psychological variables and was made up of the same bipolar components as Factor I for boys: Work and Endurance vs. Fight. (The Aggression variable did not emerge with Fight in the girls' analysis). Obviously the school has conveyed to most students, regardless of sex, the value of Work Orientation and "sticktoitiveness." Few girls are high on Fight scores; but when they are they will be correspondingly low on Work Orientation and Endurance. Neither of these strategies, however, are related to academic outcomes for girls. As mentioned earlier, the only psychological variable related to achievement among girls in this school was "feelings of control over one's self and life chances" (autonomy). Only the belief that "the teacher should try to understand how students feel" (school related) was significantly related to achievement.

Factor II (13%) also loaded highest on psychological variables unrelated to actual achievement. This bipolar factor, Need Achievement and Deference vs. Aggression and Autonomy, described two kinds of girls: those (the majority) who are desirous of achievement and who see giving up aggressive and autonomous feelings for deference as an appropriate way of fulfilling achievement needs; those (few) who would rather perceive themselves as assertive and independent by eschewing Deference and Achievement motivation if it costs them their autonomy.

Factor III (13%) loaded highest on school-related variables: the idea that "a friendly, cooperative learning style is best"; belief that "it is good to ask the teacher for help." Socially oriented toward peers and dependent on the teacher's good offices, this kind of girl uses an interactive strategy which undoubtedly makes her a good student role incumbent but helps her not at all in producing academically.

Factor IV (13%) also loaded high on classroom norms: "It is good to take part in class discussion" (i.e., the teacher likes it): "School work should be fun most of the time." Unfortunately, at this school, girls who think school work should be pleasant are losers. This variable is *significantly negatively* associated with achievement in the regression analysis for girls.

Factor V (12%) like Factor IV for boys was a bipolar factor which loaded highest on background variables, Age vs. I.Q., but does not show Pairing or friendship as does the boys' factor. I.Q. was not related to achievement among girls.

In none of the first five factors did the type of girl who is most likely to achieve—the one who believes that "the teacher should really try hard to understand how students feel" appear. Her apparently uncommon, but productive strategy is, we conjecture, to identify with the teacher and to try to get the teacher to understand how she feels by feeling most like the teacher. It is probably this mutually reinforcing interaction (in which the boys are unlikely to be interested) between the teacher and this kind of girl which help her achieve.

As is usual in social psychological research as it is now designed, our data had far less explanatory power for girls than for boys. This is most clear in the fact that variables in the regression for boys account for 66% of the variance while the same variables entered into the regression for girls accounted for only 31%. As a further example, Reading score and I.Q. are highly correlated (.50) in the data for boys, insignificantly (.18) in the data for girls.

The highest positive correlation among all the variables (Background, Psychological, School-related, Performance) entered into the correlation matrix for girls was between reading achievement and the belief that "the teacher should try hard to understand how the students feel" (.36).

RESULTS OF ONE-WAY MANOVA

To test the significance of the differences observed between boys' and girls' strategies at Southside, we performed a multivariate analysis of variance to test the null hypothesis of no difference between groups, using I.Q. and Age as covariates.

The overall F ratio for the multivariate test of equality of mean vectors was 2.17 with 28 and 81 degrees of freedom. The F was significant with a p of less than .004. The null hypothesis was rejected. We found a multiple combination of variables that significantly discriminated between boys and girls at Southside.

Girls' scores were significantly *higher* than boys on Sentiments toward School (they like it more); Deference (stereotypical); and preference for "a friendly, cooperative learning style" in the classroom when Age and I.Q. were controlled.

Boys' scores significantly exceeded girls' on Work Orientation; Pairing (friendship as a defense); the belief that "it is just as important to get along with others as to do school work."

I.Q. and age aside, the picture that begins to emerge from the data on coping and defending differences between boys and girls at the fifth grade level seems predictive of later sex-role differences as they are perceived by the wider society. What is learned in school appears to bear much better relationship to role socialization than to instrumental achievement. In short we might say that girls relate to authority and learn to like it, boys relate to Work and depend on their peers for support.

Our sample in the University School study was too small for the powerful Manova procedure. However, as we noted at the outset, girls from both schools reported that they were from families more interested in their schooling; that they had more positive sentiments toward school; that they favored a friendly cooperative learning style, and that "it is good to participate in class discussion" to a greater extent than boys did.

Boys from both schools exceeded girls on "Self-satisfaction," Aggression, Dominance, Work Orientation; and the idea that "it is just as important to get along with others as to do school work." Background variables—race, class, age, I.Q., family structure—on which the two school populations were significantly different, seemingly have little impact on sex role differences as we have looked at them in these school contexts.

CONCLUSION

This research investigated the relationship between socialization and achievement in elementary school. Its findings suggest that the relationship is antithetical; that school has oppressive effects on children, particularly girls, in a society which uses institutions to perpetuate inequality and stereotyping and then rationalizes its stratifications by blaming the victim. "Current educational problems stem not from the fact that the schools have changed, but from the fact that they continue to do precisely the job they have always done" (Greer, 1969). What they have always done is to stream and train according to the needs of the prevailing social structure and in conformity with its stereotypes of age, sex, class, and socioeconomic status.

If social psychological research is to be of pragmatic as well as scholarly value, it must ask questions about the organization, nature, and purpose of schooling in its social context and as it has historically operated. Continuing research effort should be directed at questioning the validity of the stated goals of social institutions. At the inception of the research discussed here, for example, we too, in best university style, accepted a conventional sociological definition of the function of an elementary school. "An elementary school is a social organization primarily concerned with the encouragement of activities in which children demonstrate how well they can achieve; adult members assign specific tasks to nonadult members who in turn are expected to perform and submit results for evaluation" (Dreeben, 1968). At its conclusion we concurred rather that "the picture of educational disadvantage which emerges with examination of achievement data is a clear indication of the failure of school systems" (Stodolsky and Lesser, 1967).

What *is* being learned in school, consciously or unconsciously, is the student role defined in these data by expectations for defensiveness, dependency, sticktoitiveness, passivity, and conformity. In most children we found aggressive achievement motives come into conflict with student role expectations, particularly in relation to the authority figure of the teacher. This conflict seems to be resolved by the majority of student role incumbents in favor of complementarity—that is—that there is but one dominant, autonomous, aggressive, role in the classroom and that one is institutionally prescribed for the teacher.

Such role expectations are differentially detrimental according to sex, socioeconomic status, and caste. Blacks, the poor, and females are least likely to break out of the belief system perpetrated by schooling because the power structure and social stratification of the wider society work to keep them in their place while the next generation of white, middle-class males (and even a few black males) are being selected out to advance to favored positions in society.

Our hope is that the findings reported here, in collaboration with other such studies, will lead us to re-examine *au fond* our current assumptions about the function of schooling and the nature of the student role.

As a socializing institution the school seems uniformly successful in the lessons of self-abnegation, dependency, deference, endurance, and passivity; far less successful in producing healthy human beings equipped with coping strategies conducive to instrumental achievement and personal integration.

SIGNIFICANCE OF THE STUDY

The primary importance of this study is that it adds to the accumulating evidence that schooling, as an institution, reflects and enforces the bias of the wider society; most particularly, that schooling, as it is now structured, is based on the ascendance of ascribed authority over individual aspirations and achievement. Being a student, like being female, being black, or being poor is a repressed state against which role incumbents must fight in order to achieve scholastically, economically, or socially. Is it any wonder that given such contrary signals between being a "good student" and being an achiever, the accomplishments and the mental health of so many young persons, male and female, are impaired?

These data along with other such studies, may hopefully provide educators, particularly those involved in teacher training, with a background against which to ask further questions about the nature of the student role and its relation to academic achievement in the conventional classroom.

12

Social Development and Interpersonal Relationships

Children grow up in a broad social environment that expresses the values and beliefs of the culture. At school age, children are not confined to what parents and siblings think and believe, but learn also from a variety of sources, including peers, older children, teachers, other adults, books, movies, and television. Family members, of course, continue to exert influence on social and personal development.

The first article by Russell C. Smart and Mollie S. Smart compares values and attitudes of groups of children in Australia, Canada, England, New Zealand, and the United States. Similar in ethnic derivation, these groups differ as to physical and psychological environment. Significant differences were found in depiction of happiness, hostility, humor, cooperation, competition, work, sports, fantasy, adults, and family.

Generosity and helping have been found to increase with age during the elementary school years. Kenneth H. Rubin and Frank W. Schneider analyze the relationship between moral judgment and altruistic behavior, and the role of egocentrism and decentration as basic to increasing altruism.

Important as sibling interaction seems to be for many aspects of development, studies on this topic are infrequent, probably because many combinations of siblings are possible. One particular effect of having an older brother was explored by Langdon E. Longstreth, Gayle V. Longstreth, Christopher Ramirez, and Gloria Fernandez. By asking teachers to nominate children who were extremely physically active and extremely physically passive, they established a relationship with the absence or presence of a big brother.

Group Values Shown in Preadolescents' Drawings in Five English-Speaking Countries *

Russell C. Smart and Mollie S. Smart
UNIVERSITY OF RHODE ISLAND

A. INTRODUCTION

Studies of group values through analyses of children's drawings have been carried on in many cultures by Dennis (3) and his colleagues (4, 5). Dennis has presented evidence to show that when preadolescent boys are asked to draw a man, any kind of man they wish, they most often draw the types of men they admire and that the contents of their drawings reflect social values. The incidence of smiling pictures, for example, indicates the degree to which happiness is a value in the culture. Although children's drawings are also used for testing intelligence and for clinical diagnosis, Dennis' method is not concerned with individual children but with the frequency with which certain concepts are expressed by a group. Gardiner (5) has assembled frequencies of the depiction of hostility in many of the same groups for which Dennis gives data in other categories; he interprets hostility shown in drawings as including expression not permitted through other modes. The frequency with which hostility is pictured may be an indication of the frequency with which the subjects experience hostile feelings, or the extent to which hostile behavior is typical of the society.

The present study is an attempt to compare five English-speaking countries in terms of the values reflected in preadolescents' drawings. The groups compared are from England, Canada, United States, Australia, and New Zealand. England is the "mother country" of the other four whose populations have been augmented by immigration largely from Northern and Western Europe. Non-Caucasian individuals have been excluded from the samples.

We hypothesized that the differentiation of the four daughter countries from the mother country would reflect the length of time since the split occurred, as well as the condition of life prevailing at the present time. In addition to comparing the five samples on smiling, hostility, and other indications of values and interests through the drawing of a man, we wanted to tap attitudes toward cooperation, competition, and other ways of relating to people.

From *The Journal of Social Psychology*, 1975, **97**, 23–37. Reprinted by permission of the Journal Press, 2 Commercial Street, Provincetown, Mass. 02657.

* The New Zealand phase of this research was supported by the New Zealand-United States Educational Foundation and Massey University. The Australian phase was supported by the Australian-United States Educational Foundation and Melbourne University. We are grateful for the cooperation of teachers, principals, and superintendents in all the schools we visited in Ballarat, Australia; Chatham, Ontario, Canada; Berkhamsted, England; Wanganui, New Zealand; and South Kingstown, Rhode Island, U.S.A. In administering tests, we were assisted by Jan Bogrow, Alta Gordon, Liz Lamberton, Mary Lou Roman, and Ellen Smart. Alta Gordon in New Zealand and Barbara Bland in the United States helped with scoring. We acknowledge our debt and gratitude to Dr. Wayne Dennis.

Dennis suggested in a personal communiction that we ask the child to draw himself and another person. We therefore collected two drawings from each subject. While Dennis and Gardiner have published frequencies of categories from boys' drawings only, the present study includes 100 girls from each country, as well as 100 boys.

We predicted that New Zealand children would indicate more cooperation and less hostility than American children. Social welfare measures in New Zealand provide many supports to health. Adults' concern with children's well-being can be documented by studies comparing New Zealand parents and teachers with those in the other countries. For example, high levels of parent-child interaction have been found, perceived by both boys and girls as coming from both mothers and fathers (8). Attitudes, beliefs, and perceptions of teachers were compared in 12,000 teachers representing New Zealand, Australia, England and the United States (1). New Zealand teachers were significantly lower and American teachers significantly higher than teachers from the other countries in emphasis on punishment, discipline, and control in the classroom and on belief in punishment as an effective motivator. New Zealand teachers ranked highest in the belief in rewards as motivators. From this information, as well as from more general conditions, we would expect New Zealand children to rank lower than Americans in hostility.

Canadians also show many evidences of concern for child and family welfare, through the Vanier Institute of the Family, children's allowances, comprehensive health care plans, and a high economic priority on education. Canada, Australia, and New Zealand are uncrowded and unspoiled ecologically, as compared with the United States and England. Conditions of life in the latter countries are not as beneficial as in New Zealand. Canadians and Australians might be expected to fall between Americans and New Zealanders in evidences of hostility and cooperation.

England is old and crowded with a relatively rigid class system and a lower standard of living than the other countries. However, an extensive social welfare system provides for excellent physical care and education for all children. Adams' (1) cross-national study of teachers showed English teachers ranking highest in their belief that rules should be established by the teacher and not by pupils or by teacher and pupils together. English teachers believed less than other teachers in rewards as motivators and in intrinsic motivation. We predicted more hostility and competition and less cooperation in English children than in the other British groups.

Dennis found the highest incidence of smiling (75%) in Old Americans and the lowest in more recently arrived ethnic groups. Northern European groups were still lower and below them were Middle Eastern groups and, showing fewest smiles, were the groups least touched by the modern world. We therefore predicted that our American sample would draw more smiling figures than would the others, that Canadians would be second and English last.

Having frequently noticed in casual observation that Canadian and New Zealand children are more active in sports and games than are Americans, we predicted that the United States would rank last for depicting sports and games. Because of Bronfenbrenner's (2) comments on the paucity of interactions between American adults and children, we expected that Americans would draw the smallest number of pictures showing an adult with the child. On the basis of known concern of New Zealanders with the physical and mental health of children, and our own findings on high interaction levels between parents and children (8) we predicted that their children would draw a relatively large number of pictures showing an adult with a child.

B. METHOD

1. SUBJECTS   One thousand drawings were obtained from 100 boys and 100 girls in one town in each of five countries, Australia, Canada, England, New Zealand, and United States of America. The children were 11 and 12 years old. They came from publicly supported schools in towns of between 10,000 and 30,000 population. The towns consisted of relatively stable, settled populations, with no appreciably sized ethnic groups of recent arrival. We cannot claim that they accurately represent the populations of their respective nations. Efforts were made in consultation with school officials to use schools that drew on a broad representation of the population of the five towns. When a school was selected, all the children in the appropriate grade or form were tested. When more than the required number of drawings were obtained, the first 100 complete drawings were scored. Black children's drawings were eliminated, since there were not enough of them to score separately. In New Zealand, Maori children's drawings were scored separately and those results have been reported (7).

2. PROCEDURE   The principal introduced the examiner to the teacher, who was then free to leave the room. Dennis' procedures were followed. One of the authors, or a trained assistant (not the teacher) was always in charge of the class while the children were drawing. Classes varied in size from about 15 to 30. Subjects were given sheets of typing-size paper and told, "I want you to draw a picture of a man. You may draw any kind of man you wish, but draw a whole man, not just the head and shoulders." When the man was finished, we said, "Now turn the paper over and draw a picture of yourself and somebody else. It can be anyone you like, a friend, teacher, brother or sister, mother or father, anyone you wish. Draw yourself and this person doing something, anything you like." When the drawings were collected, the examiner asked about the person and activity depicted when they were not clear.

The drawings were completed in about half an hour. Then the examiner offered to answer any questions. A lively period invariably followed, moving quickly away from the test to the examiner's experiences in other countries.

3. SCORING   For the pictures of the man, smiling and humor were scored according to Dennis' (3) guidelines which are, in essence, that both corners of the mouth turn up. Hostility was scored according to Gardiner's directions (5) which were actually developed in collaboration with Dennis. Gardiner stated his criteria as including "presence of weapons (any figure with a gun, knife, sword, etc.), figures of boxers, wrestlers, soldiers or other persons shown in

TABLE 1

Contents of Drawings of Man and Dyad by Children in Five Countries

PERCENTAGES	AUSTRALIA		CANADA		ENGLAND		NEW ZEALAND		UNITED STATES		TOTAL	
	BOYS	GIRLS	BOYS	GIRLS	BOYS	GIRLS	BOYS	GIRLS	BOYS	GIRLS	BOYS	GIRLS
On man												
Smiling	43	46	65	57	29	41	51	59	56	52	48	50
Hostility	8	2	3	5	9	2	9	0	13	0	8	2
Humor	24	18	12	1	15	11	17	8	12	17	16	11
Fantasy	0	0	2	0	2	2	6	0	11	5	4	1
On dyad												
Smiling	37	55	61	77	35	43	40	56	75	80	50	62
Hostility	18	3	11	0	16	0	16	1	17	7	15	2
Cooperation	21	19	28	44	16	21	32	32	8	12	21	26
Competition	30	5	29	8	42	12	24	7	3	1	26	7
Work	2	3	5	12	4	10	11	11	2	0	4	7
Games & Sports	56	33	58	49	52	41	53	40	16	14	47	35
Adults	5	0	9	4	11	2	14	7	9	5	10	4
Family	7	10	20	12	13	6	17	12	6	15	12	11

a posture preparatory for physical struggle—i.e., bared fists or kicking—representations of death or injury, and the delineation of insignias (badges, emblems, medals) commonly associated with cowboys, military figures, etc." (5, p. 261). Humor was scored by referring to Dennis' text and examples (3). Fantasy was our category in which we placed depictions of unreal creatures, situations, and activities. The dyad was scored on smiling and hostility, on whether the other person was adult or child, family or nonfamily, and on themes of competition, cooperation, games and sports, achievement, and work. Competition was scored plus when competitive games were shown or when people compared products, such as holding up the fish they had caught to see which was bigger. Cooperation was noted in any situation where people helped each other, such as practicing catching a ball, paddling a canoe, putting a Bandaid on a wound, and setting the table together. Thus a depiction of a sport or game might also be scored as competitive, cooperative, or neither. For example, a picture of two people holding fish poles and lines was scored as a sport, but as neither cooperative nor competitive. Most dyads showed the self with a like-sexed peer. Scoring the presence of an adult was usually unambiguous. To determine whether the other person was a family member, it was necessary to see the label or to ask the child.

Two or three people (one or two of the authors and one of two assistants) scored all the drawings separately. When the first two scorers disagreed on any item, they discussed the scoring until they either came to an agreement, or called in the third scorer, who made the decision. It was rarely difficult to reach consensus, discrepancies usually being the result of one person failing to see an item that was readily observed when pointed out.

C. RESULTS

1. DRAWING OF A MAN: CROSS-NATIONAL COMPARISONS   Table 1
shows percentages of boys and girls in samples from five countries whose drawings indicated smiling, hostility, humor, and fantasy.

a. Smiling   Table 2 places the obtained boys' frequencies for smiling in relation to Dennis' data. The American sample falls between Dennis' various American groups, as do also the Canadian, Australian, and New Zealand samples. The English sample is very close to Dennis' Scottish sample. Tests of significance of differences between percentages showed that the English boys' sample produced fewer smiles than each of the others ($p < .01$ for Canadian, U.S., and N.Z.; $p < .05$ for Australia).

Although cross-national differences among the girls were smaller, the English girls made fewer smiling pictures than did the New Zealanders and Canadians ($p < .05$).

b. Hostility   Table 2 also shows frequencies of hostility shown by boys in the present study in relation to samples obtained in other parts of the world by Dennis and others. England, Australia, and New Zealand cluster closely,

TABLE 2

Percentages of Drawings by Boys Portraying Smiles* or Some Form of Hostility

Smiles

75 Old Americans	42 Brooklyn Yeshiva	20 Mexico City
—	Boys	19
—	41 Brooklyn Hassidim	18 Heidelberg
—	40	17
65 *Canada*	39	16 *N.Z. Maori** (*N = 25*)
—	38	15
—	37 Nonorthodox Israelis	14 Navahos
—	36	13
59 Brooklyn W.	35 Gothenburg	12 San Cristobal
Christian	34	11 Beirut
58	33 Brooklyn Negroes	10 Ankara
57	32	9 Teheran, Armenian
56 *South Kingstown, R.I.*	31 Japanese Village	Lebanese
(W)	30	8 Mississippi Negroes
—	29 *England*, Taipei I	7 Orthodox Israelis,
—	28	Athens, Lebanese
—	26 Edinburgh	villages I
51 *New Zealand (W)*	26	6
—	25	5 Chiapas Indians
—	24 Taipei II	4 Lebanese villages II
—	23	
43 *Australia*, Brooklyn	22 Kyoto	
public school Jews	21 Cambodia	

Hostility

35 Thailand	—	6 Mexico (Ladinos),
34	16 Yugoslavia	Mecca, U.S.
33	16	Negroes (Mississippi)
32 *N.Z. Maori**	15 Algeria* (*N = 73*)	5 Lebanon
(N = 25)	14	4
—	13 Sweden*(*N = 40*)	3 Syria* (*N = 91*),
—	*South Kingstown,*	Mexico City,
	R.I. (W)	*Canada*
26 Germany	12	2
25 Taiwan I	11 Turkey	1 Israel Orthodox Jews*
24	10 Scotland	(*N = 79*)
23	9 *England, New*	Japan* (*N = 68*)
22 Taiwan II	*Zealand*, Kuwait	0 Cambodia, Mexico
—	8 *Australia*	(Chiapas Indians)
—	7	

* In each sample, with the exception of * items, $N = 100$. Countries in italics indicate sample collected by Smarts. Others collected by Dennis and Gardiner.

with U.S.A. higher and Canada lower. All of the present samples rank in approximately the lower third of the list. The only significant differences among the present five samples is that Canada ranks lower than U.S.A. ($p <$ .01) and lower than Australia ($p <$ .05). Girls produced so few signs of hostility that tests of differences are not possible.

 c. Humor Australian boys drew the largest number of drawings with humor, exceeding Americans and Canadians at the .05 level. Australian girls also ranked highest in humor, differing significantly from Canadians ($p <$ .01) and New Zealanders ($p <$ .01). Canadian girls' humor was less than American and English ($p <$ .01) and also less than New Zealand ($p <$ .05). Boys produced many more humorous drawings than girls.

 d. Fantasy Although numbers of drawings showing fantasy are small, American boys exceeded both English and Canadian boys ($p <$ .01). The Australian boys drew no pictures with fantasy. Of the seven girls who employed fantasy, five were American, two English.

2. Drawing of a Dyad: Cross-National Comparisons Table 1 shows percentages of boys and girls in the five samples whose drawings of a dyad depicted smiling, hostility, cooperation, competition, work, games and sports, adults, and family members.

 a. Smiling United States boys and girls drew more smiling faces than did any other groups. Differences were all significant at the one percent level except for American-Canadian.

 b. Hostility No significant differences were shown.

 c. Cooperation New Zealanders and Canadians ranked high, Americans low. New Zealand boys were higher than English and American, ($p <$ .01). American boys were lower ($p <$ .01) than New Zealand, Canadian, and Australian. Canadian girls scored significantly higher than English, Australian, and American. New Zealand girls were significantly above Australian and American.

 d. Competition English children ranked highest in competition. Differences were significant for boys but not for girls. English boys scored higher ($p <$ .01) than New Zealanders and Americans. Americans were significantly lower than all other groups.

 e. Work Work was seldom depicted, but New Zealand boys showed more of it than other groups and significantly more than English and American ($p <$ .01). American girls drew no pictures with work themes. Canadians, New Zealanders, and English were similar in frequencies, exceeding Australians significantly ($p <$ .01 for Canadians, $p <$ .05 for New Zealanders and English).

    f. Games and Sports   American boys and girls drew pictures of sports and games less often than their age mates in the other four countries ($p < .01$). Otherwise, the only significant difference between groups was that Canadian girls exceeded Australian at the five percent level.

    g. Adults   Few pictures showed adults. New Zealand children ranked highest, Australian lowest. The only significant difference was between boys in New Zealand and Australia ($p < .05$).

    h. Family   Among boys' groups, Canadians and New Zealanders included family members more than did Australians and Americans ($p < .01$). Among girls, the only significant difference was that Americans drew more family members than did English ($p < .05$).

3. OVERALL SEX DIFFERENCES   More significant differences were found between boys' groups (39) than between girls' groups (27). With differences at the one percent level, the totals were 32 for boys and 19 for girls. For drawing the man, the numbers of differences at the one percent level were 7 for boys, 3 for girls; on the dyad, these figures were 25 and 16.

    In a comparison of all 500 girls with all 500 boys, boys scored significantly higher ($p < .01$) in hostility, humor, and fantasy on the man drawing. Similarly, for the dyad, boys exceeded girls in competition, games and sports, hostility and adults. Girls drew more smiles ($p < .01$) and more work ($p < .05$). Differences were not significant in frequencies for cooperation and family.

D. DISCUSSION

1. DRAWING OF A MAN   The results for frequency of smiling are consistent with Dennis' findings and generalizations on geographic and cultural characteristics of groups drawing high numbers of smiling men. Table 2 shows the four English-derived groups clustered between Dennis' Old Americans and Brooklyn Jews, while the English group is placed close to the Scottish group. Dennis has noted that Americans draw a high incidence of smiling men, as compared to groups in all other parts of the world, and that among Americans, the highest frequencies are drawn by "Old Americans," white Christians whose ancestors have been in the United States for several generations. The more recently-arrived the ancestors, the fewer smiles American boys tend to draw. Our Canadian sample ranks next to Dennis' "Old Americans" and indeed the Canadian children were from an area settled over 150 years ago by British people and since joined by a few Northern Europeans. Our results for Maori boys (7) are also consistent with Dennis' (3) conclusion that there is a gradient extending from the Old Americans of European descent, through groups presently living in Northern Europe and Israelis of relatively recent European ancestry, to persons who have only recently begun to be "Westernized." If it is assumed that Dennis' interpretation is correct, our four English-derived groups have followed the expected pattern in holding hedonistic values to a high degree, as compared with the rest of the world, including the English

groups. The low level of the English groups is also consistent with the findings of Adams and associates in their research on teachers. English teachers put significantly less emphasis than American, Australian, and New Zealand on rewards, establishment of rules by pupils, and agreement between teachers and children on rules. The espousal of these values suggests that a teacher cares about the happiness of pupils.

In comparing hostility in drawings of the present five groups with the hostility shown in the world-wide collection of samples, these English-speaking boys rank low and close to one another. As predicted, the American boys rank higher than New Zealanders, but other predictions were not borne out. Since the greatest difference in hostility appeared between the American and Canadian samples, contrasts between the conditions of these two groups of children should be sought in an effort to locate sources of hostility. These Canadian children enjoy a high standard of living in regard to food, space, and advanced social legislation that favors families. A comparison between the American and Canadian schools might yield some explanation of the difference, since the examiners' impressions were that the Canadian buildings and equipment were vastly superior to the American schools in which the investigation took place.

The Australian children ranked first in humor, the Canadians last. The United States was the only country in which girls drew more funny pictures than boys. The overall sex difference was definitely in favor of boys. Sutton-Smith (9) has found that children ask riddles frequently in countries where high authority rests in adults and where ridicule is used. Evidence from Adams (1) shows that in teachers' reports as to having rules about pupil behavior, Australians ranked significantly higher than Americans, English, and New Zealanders. The American group was significantly lower than the other three. (Canadians were not included in Adam's study). It seems possible, then, that the use of humor in drawings serves a purpose similar to the function of riddles in a situation where adults exercise strong authority over children.

2. DRAWING OF A DYAD   Whereas the drawing of a man indicates personality values or abstractions representing a typical or perhaps ideal man in a particular culture, the dyad shows interaction between the self and others. We do not know whether the dyad represents values and ideals for social relationships, or typical social behavior, or both.

United States groups occupied either highest or lowest ranks on all but one of the categories. Lowest in competition, cooperation, work, games and sports, the American children drew the largest number of smiling faces. What *did* the American children show themselves and their friends doing? Very often they were "just standing." If high frequency of smiling drawings indicates a high evaluation of happiness, as we believe Dennis has shown, then it seems as though the American boys and girls show a pervasive desire to be happy. At the same time, they showed relatively little action and involvement with the pursuits that might yield satisfaction. Possibly the passivity suggested is related to heavy use of television by American children. Since preschool children average over 50 hours a week viewing (6), the development of initiative and action patterns may have been stunted from an early age. However,

Canadians have had access to television for many years, and it seems unlikely that their high involvement with games and sports would not have also suffered, were television the main depressant. The only category in which American boys and girls differed greatly in rankings was in showing family members. Girls ranked highest among girls' groups and boys lowest among boys'. The boys from the five countries were almost equal in the percent that showed hostility.

New Zealand children ranked highest in number of adults depicted, and scenes of work. They were very close to the top in showing cooperation; only Canadian girls exceed the New Zealand girls, while New Zealand boys showed the most cooperation in their dyad-drawings. These results are in the hypothesized direction. They occupied middle ranks for competition, smiling, hostility, games and sports, and were second in depicting family members.

Canadian scores were more like the New Zealand pattern than any other. In the smiling category, Canadian children were between American and New Zealand, confirming the high frequency of smiling that Canadians produced in the man. Canadian drawings emphasized cooperation, sports and games, work, and family, suggesting the involvement in action and interaction seen in the New Zealand drawings. Perhaps Canadian children, with an esteem for happiness that almost matches American children's, are more actively engaged in pursuits that might yield satisfaction.

Australian drawings resembled Canadian and New Zealand more than they resembled English or American. Australian boys scored fairly high in competition, and, along with girls, moderate in cooperation and smiling. Australians were in the low ranks for work and family themes, and lowest for drawing adults. In games and sports, Australian boys scored almost the same as English, Canadian and New Zealand boys, all of whom were much higher than American. Australian girls were lower in sports and games than the other British groups, but still higher than American. On the basis of the finding that Australian drawings of the man scored high in humor and zero in fantasy, a tentative generalization is that the pictures suggest self-contained individuals who interact moderately, with preference for peers.

English drawings were lowest in smiling and highest in competition. The profile of English scores was more similar to the Australian than to any other. English scores were moderate to low for cooperation, work, adults, and family.

Since the number of cross-national differences was greater for boys than for girls, one might explain this overall sex difference in terms of the test being more compatible with male modes of expression. However, almost all mental and physical measurements show greater variation in boys than in girls. It therefore seems reasonable that cross-national differences should be greater for males than for females. Girls around the world are thus more alike than are boys. The overall sex differences are interesting in regard to competition and cooperation. While boys indicated much more competition, they showed about the same frequency of cooperation as girls. This result suggests that being competitive does not preclude being cooperative. (Indeed, we have evidence from a study in preparation, on the New Zealand sample used in the present study, that some of the boys switched easily between cooperative and competitive strategies in a game.)

E. CONCLUSIONS

While reliability is a difficult problem in this type of study, we are reassured by the fact that the data on smiling are so consistent with the findings of Dennis and others. Likewise, rankings of hostility data in Gardiner's world-wide samples are indications that our procedures matched those of Dennis and Gardiner and that certain attitudes and beliefs are being consistently tapped.

The results confirm our primary hypothesis, that cooperation would be expressed more frequently in drawings from New Zealand, where the quality of life is high in physical and psychological terms, than in the United States and England, where ecological problems are more severe and the psychological environment less hospitable to children and families. Consistent with this finding and with our predictions are the ranking of Canadian and Australian boys' cooperation scores between those of American and New Zealand boys. Although girls' rankings were slightly different, the results on cooperation are what we expected to find in a healthy environment that supports child growth and family living. As expected from observations and our own research, New Zealand children ranked high in drawing adults and family members. We were mistaken, however, in expecting United States children to rank low in these categories.

Predictions concerning hostility were weakly supported by the man drawing, in which American boys ranked high and Canadians low, but New Zealanders did not differ significantly from others. As expected, English children scored higher in competition, and lower in cooperation than New Zealanders, whose living conditions are most favorable, and whose teachers believe most strongly in cooperative establishment of rules, low punishment, and high rewards. Fulfilling our anticipations, United States children showed very few scenes of sports and games. The other four national groups showed many sports and games, with virtually no differences between them.

We correctly predicted that the first country to split off from the mother country would differentiate more in terms of results in children's drawings. The American scores differ more from the English than do Canadian, Australian, or New Zealand. In fact, the profiles of the three daughter countries, as shown in scores for drawings, are very similar. In general, the striking difference between American drawings and all others is in amount of content indicating action and involvement with other people.

References

1. ADAMS, R. Visiting Scholar Lecture, University of Rhode Island, Kingston, May 2, 1973.
2. BRONFENBRENNER, U. Two Worlds of Childhood. New York: Russell Sage Foundation, 1970.
3. DENNIS, W. Group Values Through Children's Drawings. New York: Wiley, 1966.
4. DENNIS, W., & URAS, A. The religious content of human figure drawings made by nuns. *J. of Psychol.*, 1965, **61**, 263–266.
5. GARDINER, H. W. A cross-cultural comparison of hostility in children's drawings. *J. Soc. Psychol.*, 1969, **79**, 261–263.
6. MORRISETT, L. N. The changing culture of childhood. Paper presented at meetings of the American Psychological Association, Montreal, August, 29, 1973.

7. SMART, M. S., GORDON, A., & SMART, R. C. Values reflected in children's drawings. *New Zealand Psychologist*, 1972, **1**, 4–12.
8. SMART, R. C., & SMART, M. S. New Zealand preadolescents' parent-peer orientation and parent perceptions compared with English and American. *J. Mar. & Fam.*, 1973, **35**, 142–148.
9. SUTTON-SMITH, B. A developmental structural account of riddles. Paper presented at meetings of the Society for Research in Child Development, Philadelphia, March 31, 1973.

The Relationship Between Moral Judgment, Egocentrism, and Altruistic Behavior *

Kenneth H. Rubin and Frank W. Schneider
UNIVERSITY OF WATERLOO

Fifty-five 7-year-old children were administered cognitive measures of communicative egocentrism and moral judgment and were provided with 2 opportunities to display altruistic behavior—(*a*) to donate candy to poor children and (*b*) to help a younger child complete a task. Success on the 2 cognitive measures was positively correlated with the incidence of altruistic behavior in both altruism conditions. With mental age partialled out the correlations between the cognitive measures and donating candy were significantly lower than the correlation between the cognitive measures and helping. The difference between the correlations was accounted for by the fact that only in the candy donation were there cues that helped the subject attend to the possibility of emitting an altruistic act. Finally, the communicative and moral judgment measures were significantly correlated.

A number of studies of altruism in children have indicated that the incidence of helping and sharing behavior increases with age, at least until 10 years of age (e.g., Handlon & Gross, 1959; Midlarsky & Bryan, 1967; Ugurel-Semin, 1952). However, little attention has been directed toward understanding why younger children are, in fact, less altruistic than older children. One explanation may be suggested by Piaget's notions concerning egocentrism (Piaget, 1926) and moral judgments (Piaget, 1932).

According to Piaget (1950), the young child is unable to decenter, that is, to shift his attention from one aspect of an object or situation to another. This inability appears to underlie the preoperational child's egocentric thought and immature moral judgment. For example, during communicative activity, the egocentric child fails to take his auditor's point of view into account. He centers

From *Child Development*, 1973, **44**, 661–665. Copyright © 1973 by The Society for Research in Child Development, Inc. Reprinted by permission.

* The authors express their appreciation to the Windsor School Board for its cooperation during the execution of the study, to Patricia H. Haggith, and Mary C. Tierney who served as the experimenters, and to Dr. Akira Kobasigawa for his helpful suggestions during the preparation of this article.

only on his own viewpoint (e.g., Rubin, 1973). Moreover, when attempting to resolve moral-conflict stories, the child who cannot decenter fails to consider the reciprocal interpersonal aspects of the moral situations (e.g., Lee, 1971). The idea that decentration underlies both moral development and sociocentric thought has received empirical support from studies in which spatial (Lee, 1971; Stuart, 1967) and role-taking (Selman, 1971) skills have been found to be significantly related to moral development. Piaget believes that it is not until later childhood, 7–12 years of age, that the child is able to consider reciprocal relations and the viewpoints of others. In support of Piaget, research has indicated that with increasing age children become less egocentric (Flavell, 1968) and increasingly able to make mature moral judgments (Lee, 1971).

It seems logical to assume that there is a direct link between a child's capacity to decenter and the amount of altruistic behavior he displays. The increase in the child's ability to (a) recognize that another person is in need of help (i.e., to take the other person's point of view) and (b) to understand reciprocal relations should be accompanied by an increase in the likelihood that the child will help others. The fact that the increase in altruism with age is paralleled by a decline in egocentrism and the development of higher-level moral judgments is consistent with this interpretation. Moreover, inasmuch as altruistic behavior is moral behavior, it would seem likely that moral judgment and conduct are highly related. Thus, the present study was undertaken to test the hypothesis that among 7-year-olds, there is a positive relationship between their scores on measures of communicative skill (lack of egocentrism) and moral judgment and the incidence of their altruistic behavior. Two measures of altruism were selected, (a) generosity and (b) helping behavior. The latter measure was included since almost all studies of altruistic behavior in children have been restricted to measures of generosity (Bryan & London, 1970).

METHOD

Subjects   Fifty-five 7-year-olds (28 girls and 27 boys) were drawn from two lower-middle-class public schools in Windsor, Ontario. The mean age of the sample was 89.7 months. Peabody Picture Vocabulary Test (PPVT) I.Qs ranged from 78 to 127 with a mean of 100.89 and a standard deviation of 18.70.

Procedure   The study was conducted in two sessions. During the first session each *S* was individually administered the PPVT by *E* 1, a female graduate assistant. After completion of the PPVT, a communicative egocentrism task was administered in a manner similar to the procedure followed by Glucksberg and Krauss (1967). The task required that two persons communicate with one another about novel, low-encodable, graphic designs. The *E* 1 and the *S* had identical sets of 10 nonsense figures (Glucksberg & Krauss, 1967) drawn on 5 × 7-inch cards. A screen placed in the center of a table prevented *E* 1 and the *S* from seeing each other's cards. The *S*'s cards were turned face down in a single pile in front of him. The cards of *E* 1 were spread randomly before him. The *E* 1 instructed the *S* as follows: "The idea of this game is for us to match as many of our cards together as possible. However, since you cannot see my cards and I cannot see yours, the only way we can match them is if you tell me all you possibly can about each of your cards."

The S proceeded by describing one card at a time. All conversation was tape recorded and transcribed such that the mean number of distinctive features per item could be computed from the S's description. An example of a distinctive feature was, "The top part [of the figure] is shaped like a lemon." A low distinctive feature score indicated a high degree of egocentricity.

Upon completion of the communicative tasks, E 1 led the S behind a partition in the experimental room. On a table were eight nickel boxes of Smarties (Canadian equivalent of M&M's) and a colored box with a small slit in the top. The E 1 informed the S that "you can keep all of these boxes of candy for helping me today. Or, if you want, you can give some of the candy to a group of poor children from Windsor." The E 1 then showed the S four pictures of poor children. Following this, E 1 explained that she would go to the other side of the partition so that she could not see what the S chose to do. The E 1 stated: "If you want to give some of your candy to the poor children, put them in the box. Put all the candy that you want to keep for yourself in this bag on which I've written your name. No one will find out what you did because I will seal the bag for you when you bring it to me. Then in about a week I will give the bag back to you."

The E 1 then left and waited for the S to come back with his bag of candies. The number of boxes donated to poor children served as the first measure of altruism.

During the second experimental session, S and a 6-year-old child of the same sex were brought into another experimental room by E 2, a second female graduate assistant. The children were introduced to each other with reference to their names and ages. Thus S was informed that the second child was younger than he. The E 2 showed the children a number of new toys in the experimental room. The children were told that they would be allowed to play with the toys upon completion of a simple task. The S and the younger child were subsequently seated at opposite sides of a small table on which two stacks of tickets and a shallow box rested. Then E 2 stated: "Do you see these tickets? We are going to sell them to people for a show we are putting on. We must put the tickets into small piles of five tickets each [E 2 demonstrates]. Now this is your pile [to S], and this is your pile [to younger child]. Before you play with the toys, take your tickets and put them into piles of five. Then put a rubber band around them and place them in this small box. When you are finished with your tickets you may play with the toys."

The number of tickets in S's pile ($N = 25$) was exactly one-half the number of those in the younger child's pile ($N = 50$). Interestingly, none of the children remarked about the discrepancy. Then E 2 retired to an observation room where she watched the children's behavior through a one-way mirror. Because S had been given fewer tickets, he finished his task before the younger child. Thus, he could choose between helping the younger child and playing with the toys. While in the observation room, E 2 counted the piles of tickets that S completed for the younger child. The number of ticket piles that S completed for the younger child served as the second measure of altruism.

After 10 minutes, E 2 returned to the experimental room. The younger child was instructed to return to his classroom, after which E 2 administered a measure of moral judgment to each S. Lee's (1971) adaptation of Kohlberg's

(1964) moral-judgment stories and levels was used. The choice of Lee's measures rather than Kohlberg's stemmed from the fact that the moral-conflict stories developed by the latter were considered too complex for the 7-year-old children in this study. Thus, Lee's (1971) three "authority vs. altruism" situations and three "peer vs. altruism" situations were read to each S. All six stories present a conflict between two legitimate alternatives. At the end of each story, S was asked what the main character in the story should do to resolve the conflict and why. The reason given for the solution of each conflict was assigned a score ranging from 1 to 5. These values correspond to Lee's five levels of moral judgment. Briefly, these levels are (1) authority orientation, (2) authority bound but emergence of reciprocity awareness, (3) reciprocity, (4) rules are for societal order, and (5) ideological, based upon principles rather than rules. The sum of the scores attained by S on the six stories served as the measure of moral judgment. Thus, the possible range of moral-judgment scores was from 6 to 30.

RESULTS   A series of t tests revealed that there were no significant sex differences on the measures of egocentrism, moral judgment, altruism, and mental age. Therefore, the male and female data were grouped together. The results were analyzed by means of Pearson product-moment correlations. A correlational matrix for all the variables of interest is presented in Table 1.

The results support the hypothesis that positive relationships exist between children's scores on measures of egocentrism and moral judgment and the incidence of their altruistic behavior. The number of candy boxes donated to poor children was significantly related to both communicative egocentrism, $r = .31$, and to moral judgment, $r = .31$. The number of ticket piles completed for the younger child was also significantly related to egocentrism, $t = .44$, and moral judgment, $r = .40$. Further support for these findings stems from the fact that (a) when the effects of mental age were partialled out the amount of candy donated remained significantly related to egocentrism, $r = .29$, and to moral judgment, $r = .29$; and (b) the number of ticket piles completed remained significantly related to egocentrism, $r = .64$, and to moral judgment,

TABLE 1

Intercorrelations between Measures of Moral Judgment, Egocentrism, Altruism, and Mental Age
(N = 55)

MEASURE	1	2	3	4	5
1. Moral judgment	—	.59†	.31**	.40†	.42†
2. Egocentrism* –	—	—	.31**	.44†	.43†
3. Candy donated	—	—	—	.40†	.18
4. Ticket piles completed	—	—	—	—	−.14
5. Mental age	—	—	—	—	—

* A high score signifies a low degree of egocentrism.
** $p < .05$.
† $p < .01$.

$r = .57$. Moreover, with mental age partialled out, the correlation coefficients between egocentrism and the two measures of altruism were significantly different from each other, $t = 3.08$, $p < .01$. A similar result was found for the relationships between moral judgment and the two altruism conditions, $t = 2.29$, $p < .05$.

In addition, 21 out of the 29 S's scoring at or below the median distinctive features score (median = 1.10) failed to give any help to the younger child on the ticket task; on the other hand, among the 26 S's who scored above the median, all but nine helped, $\chi^2(1) = 6.44$, $p < .02$. Likewise, 22 out of the 30 S's scoring at or below the median moral-judgment score (median = 12) failed to give any help to the younger child on the ticket task. Among the 25 S's who scored above the median, all but eight helped, $\chi^2(1) = 7.80$, $p < .01$. Only five of 55 S's failed to donate any candy to the poor children. Finally, a significant positive relationship was found between egocentrism and moral judgment, $r = .59$.

DISCUSSION

The results of this study provide clear support for the hypothesis that among 7-year-olds there is a positive relationship between decentration skills, as indicated by scores on measures of communicative egocentrism, and moral judgment and the incidence of altruism. It is important to note that when mental age was partialled out the correlations between the two measures of decentration and the measure of helping behavior were significantly greater than the correlation between the decentration measures and the measure of generosity. This may be accounted for by the fact that the generosity measure involved the presentation of a "decentration" cue to the children. The experimenter focused the subject's attention on two alternatives, (a) keeping all candies for himself and (b) giving some of the candy to poor children. Perhaps this cue helped some of the children, who otherwise would have simply centered upon themselves, to simultaneously center both on themselves and on the poor children. If this was so, then the cue may have contributed to the lower correlation coefficient in the generosity condition than in the helping condition where no such cues were given. It is also possible that the instructions in the generosity condition may have served to lower the decentration-generosity correlation coefficients in another way. By providing the child with cues suggesting the possibility of emitting a generous act, the instructions may have reminded the child that, in the past, he had been reinforced for displaying such behaviors. Thus, children who had experienced reinforcement for sharing with others may have donated candy because of the possible reinforcement consequences to themselves.

Apparently, only the classical Hartshorne and May (1930) study has related moral cognition and altruistic behavior. However, the correlations between their eight subscales of "moral knowledge" and "helpful behavior" (Hartshorne & May, 1930, p. 203) were generally lower than those found in the present investigation. We believe that our higher correlations were, in part, a function of differences in the measures used to define moral judgment. In the present study, only Lee's (1971) three "authority vs. altruism" and her three "peer vs. altruism" situations were read to the children. Thus the measure of moral judgment was specific to altruism. However, Hartshorne and May's moral knowledge measures were general, tapping many aspects of moral cognition (e.g., honesty, good manners, bravery, and prejudice). The present results are consistent with more recent research which indicates a positive relationship between levels of moral judgment and other moral behaviors, for example, resistance to temptation (Krebs, 1967) and children's adherence to rules in the absence of authority (Kohlberg, 1964).

Finally, the belief that the ability to decenter is the underlying factor common to measures of egocentrism and moral judgment is supported by the significant relationship between these two measures. This finding supports previous research (Lee, 1971; Selman, 1971; Stuart, 1967). In conclusion, the results of the present study suggest that the increase in altruism with age is, in part, the result of the child's increasing capacity to decenter.

References

BRYAN, J. H., & LONDON, P. Altruistic behavior by children. *Psychological Bulletin*, 1970, **73**, 200–211.

FLAVELL, J. H. *The development of role-taking and communication skills in children*. New York: Wiley, 1968.

GLUCKSBERG, S., & KRAUSS, R. M. What do people say after they have learned how to talk? Studies of the development of referential communication. *Merrill-Palmer Quarterly*, 1967, **13**, 309–316.

HANDLON, B. J., & GROSS, P. The development of sharing behavior. *Journal of Abnormal and Social Psychology*, 1959, **59**, 425–428.

HARTSHORNE, H., & MAY, M. A. *Studies in the nature of character*. Vol. 3. New York: Macmillan, 1930.

KOHLBERG, L. Development of moral character and moral ideology. In M. L. Hoffman & L. N. Hoffman (Eds.), *Review of child development research*, Vol. 1. New York: Russell Sage Foundation, 1964.

KREBS, R. L. Some relationships between moral judgment, attention, and resistance to temptation. Unpublished doctoral dissertation, University of Chicago, 1967.

LEE, L. C. The concomitant development of cognitive and moral modes of thought: a test of selected deductions from Piaget's theory. *Genetic Psychology Monographs*, 1971, **83**, 93–146.

MIDLARSKY, E., & BRYAN, J. H. Training charity in children. *Journal of Personality and Social Psychology*, 1967, **5**, 408–415.

PIAGET, J. *The language and thought of the child*. London: Routledge & Kegan Paul, 1926.

PIAGET, J. *The moral judgment of the child*. London: Kegan Paul, 1932.

PIAGET, J. *The psychology of intelligence*. New York: Harcourt, Brace, 1950.

RUBIN, K. Egocentrism in childhood: a unitary construct? *Child Development*, 1973, **44**, 102–110.

SELMAN, R. L. The relation of role taking to the development of moral judgment in children. *Child Development*, 1971, **32**, 79–91.

STUART, R. B. Decentration in the development of children's concepts of moral and causal judgment. *Journal of Genetic Psychology*, 1967, **111**, 59–68.

UGUREL-SEMIN, R. Moral behavior and moral judgment of children. *Journal of Abnormal and Social Psychology*, 1952, **47**, 463–474.

The Ubiquity of Big Brother*

*Langdon E. Longstreth, Gayle V. Longstreth,
Christopher Ramirez, and Gloria Fernandez*
UNIVERSITY OF SOUTHERN CALIFORNIA

Teachers from grades K through 6 nominated the most physically active and most physically passive students from each sex. Half the schools were attended mainly by low-SES Mexican-American students and half upper-middle-SES Caucasian students. The main finding was that physically active students were more likely to have an older brother than were physically passive students. This effect was independent of sex, grade level, race, SES, and other-sibling combinations. A second study confirmed this relationship when college students rated themselves on the same active-passive dimension.

Among the clearest of the "other-sibling" effects is what we call the "older-brother" effect: characteristics that can be traced to the presence of an older brother. Sutton-Smith and Rosenberg (1970) conclude, for males, that "this male presents us with one of the most consistent pictures of development" (p. 143), and, for females, that "this is a surprisingly unmitigated record of the older male sibling's influence on the younger girl" (p. 151).

The influence is similar in both cases. It seems to center around masculinity, nonconformity, aggressiveness, and physicalness. However, in reviewing these studies, it became apparent to us that the clarity and generality of the effect, although perhaps, considerable in relation to other-sibling effects, leave something to be desired from a broader viewpoint. For example, some of the studies rely on psychometric evidence rather than on behavioral evidence (e.g., Sampson & Hancock, 1967), some confound other-sibling patterns with that of the older brother (e.g., Wohlford, Santrock, Berger, & Liberman, 1971), some sample only a limited age range, and, finally, some do not give the effect, particularly with psychometric measurements (e.g., Sampson & Hancock, 1967). In the present study, the older-brother effect is measured behaviorally as well as psychometrically, a broad age range is sampled as well as race, socioeconomic status, and both sexes, and the possible effects of other confounded sibling patterns are examined.

STUDY 1: EFFECTS OF AGE, SEX, RACE, SES, AND PATTERN

Method   Teachers at four elementary schools in Los Angeles, California, were asked to nominate two children of each sex at each extreme of the following scale: *physically inactive*: physically very conservative, avoids dangerous activi-

From *Child Development*, 1975, **46**, 769–772. Copyright © 1975 by The Society for Research in Child Development, Inc. Reprinted by permission.

* We are indebted to the principals and teachers at the following schools whose fine cooperation made studies 1 and 2 possible: Cowan Avenue School (Mr. Taylor, principal), Kentwood Avenue School (Mr. Avak, principal), Euclid Avenue School (Mr. Ugliano, principal), and Hammel Street School (Mr. Arriola, principal).

ties and rough games, and prefers sedate activities; *physically active*: physically very daring, never turns down a physical challenge, and has plenty of cuts and bruises to show for it.

After the papers were collected, school records were used to obtain sibling and SES data. At the time of the nominations, teachers had not been informed of the purpose of the study but simply that the investigators were interested in children who were at the extremes of the scale.

Two schools were predominantly white in student racial composition and two were predominantly Mexican-American (M-A). All grades, K through 6, were sampled. A total of 48 teachers responded, yielding 192 possible pairs of names. Due to omissions and other causes, however, 170 pairs provided complete information and constituted the sample.[1]

Results   Table 1 shows that the hypothesis is strongly supported for the sample as a whole: children with an older brother were more likely to be nominated for the active end of the scale than other children. The table also shows that SES was fairly constant in all cells of the table (rated on an eight-point scale according to Hollingshead [1956]) but that total number of siblings varied somewhat. Number of siblings was held constant by considering only nominees with one sibling who either was or was not an older brother. Of 48 active nominees with one sibling, 19 had an older brother, as compared with five of 48 inactive nominees. The resulting χ^2 of 9.4, $p < .001$, indicates that the relationship is not dependent on other sibling patterns.

A more complete analysis of sibling pattern is provided in Table 2. Consider older brothers (OB) first. The top part of the table shows that, regardless of the presence of other siblings in addition to an older brother, the result is the same: nomination to the active extreme is more likely than nomination to the inactive extreme. The lower part of the table presents nine non-older-brother combinations, one of which should be ignored because of the small N (YB + OS + YS). Of the remaining eight combinations, six are in the expected direction. In the other two cases (OS's only and single child), the distributions

TABLE 1
*Active-Passive Distribution as a Function of
Older Brother or No Older Brother*

	ACTIVE	PASSIVE
Older brother	91	47
	Sibs = 2.9	Sibs = 3.1
	SES = 3.8	SES = 4.3
No older brother	79	123
	Sibs = .9	Sibs = 1.5
	SES = 3.7	SES = 3.6

NOTE.—$\chi^2_c (1) = 22.6$, $p < .001$.

[1] Interrater reliability was determined in a separate study in which an observer spent 24 hours in each of four classrooms. Percentage agreement with teachers in nominations to the two ends of the scale was 22/24, yielding a point biserial correlation coefficient of .72.

TABLE 2
*Older-Brother and No-Older-Brother Categories
Partitioned into Smaller Groups*

	ACTIVE (SIBS)	PASSIVE (SIBS)
OBs only	21 (1.2)	7 (1.3)
OBs + YBs	12 (2.3)	5 (2.8)
OBs + OSs	32 (3.2)	21 (2.9)
OBs + YSs	8 (2.8)	3 (2.7)
OBs + other	18 (4.7)	11 (5.1)
Total OB	91 (2.9)	47 (3.1)
YBs only	12 (1.2)	23 (1.2)
OSs only	12 (1.3)	10 (1.8)
YSs only	10 (.9)	22 (1.2)
YBs + OSs	4 (4.0)	11 (2.9)
YBs + YSs	3 (2.0)	17 (2.5)
OSs + YSs	2 (3.5)	7 (2.7)
YBs + OSs + YSs	1 (4.0)	1 (4.0)
Twins	1 (1.0)	5 (2.4)
Single child	33	27
Total − OB	78 (.9)	123 (1.5)

NOTE. OB = older brother; −OB = no older brother; YB = younger brother; OS = older sister; YS = younger sister.

are about evenly divided between actives and inactives. In no case is a distribution in the opposite direction found. Thus, it may be said of the table as a whole that a sibling combination of an older brother plus anything else is more likely to be associated with an active nomination than a combination of no older brother plus anything else. The older-brother effect is robust indeed with respect to other-sibling combinations.

SES, Race, Sex, and Age   As implied in Table 1, SES was not a factor in the older-brother effect. The effect also held up independent of race, being significant for both whites and Mexican-Americans. It was also independent of sex, being significant for both boys and girls. Finally, the effect appeared at every grade level, K through 6, and age did not interact with race or sex.

STUDY 2: SELF-RATINGS IN COLLEGE STUDENTS

In this study, a new method was employed at an older age level. Students in a developmental psychology class each obtained self-ratings from 10 college students, using exactly the same scale as employed in study 1. They were asked to rate themselves as they were at age 12 in order to alleviate any anxiety that might have resulted from rating present behavior in an imagined socially deviant direction; it was possible to admit past deviancy while maintaining present normality. Neither students nor subjects were aware of the hypothesis at the time of data collection; students were led to believe that the study was about "only children."

The results showed the same older-brother effect as in study 1, $p < .001$, but only if the older brother was not more than 3 years older; with a greater age spread the effect disappeared completely. The entire study was subsequently replicated on a sample of Belgian students. Again, the effect appeared only with a spacing of 3 years or less. The data of study 1 were then reanalyzed for a possible spacing effect, but unfortunately only one school provided the necessary data (e.g., actual age of siblings instead of simply "older than" or "younger than"). In that school, however, the spacing effect again appeared: a spacing of 4 years or more resulted in a complete disappearance of the older-brother effect. It would appear, then, that age spacing is critical.

DISCUSSION

The major purpose of the present study was to verify the older-brother effect and to test its generality independent of other conditions in which it is usually embedded. It is revealed by ratings of current behavior as well as by retrospective self-reports. It is not restricted to a small age range, sex, race, a certain segment of SES, or other-sibling patterns. It is dependent, however, on the relative age of the older brother. Sutton-Smith and Rosenberg (1970) argue, in fact, that the maximum effect seems to occur at a spacing of 2–4 years, with weaker effects at both shorter and longer intervals. Such a curvilinear relationship was not found in the present data: older-brother spacing was examined at intervals of 0–2, 2–4, and 4 + years as well as at 0–3 and 3 + years. The older-brother effect was equally strong at 0–2 and 2–4 years but entirely nonexistent at more than 4 years. Sutton-Smith and Rosenberg's conjecture, however, was based mainly on intellectual and dependency effects, not simply older-brother activity-inactivity effects, so that the present data do not contradict a limited version of their summary statement.

A fundamental question is the extent to which physical activity as measured in the present study is the main personality trait affected by an older brother, as opposed to being, possibly, a peripheral effect accounted for by the effects on some other, more basic trait. Fortunately, there is some agreement about the personality domain of children as measured by teacher ratings (Becker & Krug, 1964; Cattell & Coan, 1957, 1958; Digman, 1963; Walker, 1967). Physical activity and temerity emerge rather consistently in these studies as a basic personality trait. Becker and Krug, for example, identified five clusters of personality items. One of them is labeled "submissive-dominant," and the "dominant" end is defined by the following eight items: active, tough, adventurous, dominant, extroverted, independent, strong-willed, and individualistic. Digman surveyed a number of factor-analytic studies and concluded that, under one title or another, "energy" consistently appeared as one of six frequently replicated personality traits in children. Measuring all six, Walker (1967) called it "energetic" and defined it as follows: "These children are always active, seem to have great stores of energy. They would rather run than walk." Although the temerity component is not explicitly included here, "fearfulness" was another one of the six traits measured by Walker. It correlated negatively with the energetic scale, $-.35$ for boys, $-.46$ for girls, indicating that "energetic" children also tend to be relatively fearless.

Physical activity-temerity thus appears to be a rather broad trait in its own right rather than a component or derivative of some other, more fundamental trait. Nevertheless, it is meaningful to inquire about its relationship to other components of the personality domain in children, since current models have used oblique factor solutions or have formed clusters of items that can be arranged to form a "circumplex" of interrelated parts. The strongest relationship appears to be with "sociability," defined in terms of "sociable," "interesting," "colorful" (Becker & Krug, 1964) or "friendly," "gregarious," "outgoing" (Walker, 1967), etc., with $r = .50–.60$. Weaker relationships are found with hostility and aggressiveness, $r = .20–.30$, and paradoxically, "happiness" (surgency), $r = .20–.30$. The physically active and daring child thus tends to be seen as a sociable and happy child as well and occasionally as an overbearing, aggressive child, too. Just where the presence of an older brother exerts its maximum effect in this man-made structure remains unanswered.

Just how the effect is produced is equally debatable. Whether it is the shaping and modeling effects of the older brother himself, or differential reactions of the parents, or both, is an unsettled question. On the one hand, there is experimental evidence demonstrating the shaping and modeling influences of one peer on another (Sutton-Smith & Rosenberg, 1970). On the other hand, there is evidence that male infants are more irritable and that they demand, and receive, more care (Moss, 1967), which produces hostility in the mother (Schaefer & Bayley, 1963) that may generalize to second borns (Sears, Maccoby, & Levin, 1957) and produce physical aggressiveness (see Longstreth, [1974] for a review of these studies). But aggressiveness is not the same as the older-brother effect. Furthermore, this explanation would not easily account for its effect on females, since there is evidence that maternal hostility generalizes only to second-born sons and not to second-born daughters (Sears et al., 1957). Finally, direct effects of the older brother are suggested by the tendency for girls but not boys to show self-esteem problems. This sex-related effect is not unexpected from a direct-effects point of view: an activating stabilizing effect on the younger brother but an activating, conflict-inducing effect on the younger sister (Sutton-Smith & Rosenberg, 1970).

References

BECKER, W. C., & KRUG, R. S. A circumplex model for social behavior in children. *Child Development*, 1964, **35**, 371–396.

CATTELL, R. B., & COAN, R. W. Child personality structure as revealed by teachers' behavior ratings. *Journal of Clinical Psychology*, 1957, **13**, 315–327.

CATTELL, R. B., & COAN, R. W. Personality dimensions in the questionnaire responses of six- and seven-year-olds. *British Journal of Educational Psychology*, 1958, **28**, 232–242.

DIGMAN, J. Principal dimensions of child personality as inferred from teachers' judgments. *Child Development*, 1963, **34**, 43–60.

HOLLINGSHEAD, A. B. *Two factor index of social position.* New Haven, Conn.: privately printed, 1956.

LONGSTRETH, L. E. *Psychological development of the child* (2d ed.) New York: Ronald, 1974.

Moss, H. A. Sex, age, and state as determinants of mother-infant interaction. *Merrill-Palmer Quarterly*, 1967, **13**, 19–36.

Sampson, E. E., & Hancock, F. T. An examination of the relationship between ordinal position, personality, and conformity. *Journal of Personality and Social Psychology*, 1967, **5**, 398–407.

Schaefer, E. S., & Bayley, N. Maternal behavior, child behavior, and their intercorrelations from infancy through adolescence. *Monographs of the Society for Research in Child Development*, 1963, **28**(3, Serial No. 87).

Sears, R. R.; Maccoby, E.; & Levin, H. *Patterns of child rearing*. Evanston, Ill.: Row, Peterson, 1957.

Sutton-Smith, B., & Rosenberg, B. G. *The sibling*. New York: Holt, Rinehart & Winston, 1970.

Walker, R. N. Some temperament traits in children as viewed by their peers, their teachers, and themselves. *Monographs of the Society for Research in Child Development*, 1967, **32** (6, Serial No. 114).

Wohlford, P.; Santrock, J. W.; Berger, S. E.; & Liberman, D. Older brother's influence on sex-typed, aggressive, and dependent behavior in father-absent children. *Developmental Psychology*, 1971, **4**, 124–134.

Part Four

THE ADOLESCENT

13

Physical Growth, Health, and Coordination

The puberal growth spurt brings bodily changes that require new physical and psychological responses. New motor coordinations are both possible and necessary. Food intake has to adjust to growth demands. A fast developing body calls for frequent changes in body image, as well as continual re-evaluation of one's own body and self in relation to others'. Newly acquired sexual powers have to be understood and integrated into living. In reworking and elaborating his sense of identity, the young person has to deal with all these aspects of his bodily development.

Because fast growth involves postural changes, the subject of posture is discussed here. David Sinclair traces postural changes with growth, basing it on a description of mechanics in the human body. Postural deformities and the drawbacks of erect posture are discussed.

Physical educators know how to conduct endurance training programs that increase children's physical fitness. The research reported here by Robert W. McGowan, Boyd O. Jarman, and Darhl M. Pedersen demonstrates positive psychological effects of improvement in fitness and endurance. The effects were in self-concept, not in peer attitudes.

The timing of puberty determines the age when the child grows fast and when secondary sex characteristics are established. If the timing is fast or slow, the individual is out of phase with his age mates. Problems faced by children with early and late puberty and incongruous puberal development are discussed by John Money and Richard R. Clopper, Jr. The problems, both social and personal, can be minimized by appropriate education and sometimes helped by endocrine treatment.

One of the most unfortunate teenage physical problems is pregnancy. Teenage pregnancy is not only a physical problem but a psychological and social one as well. Not only does pregnancy affect the body of the girl who has not completed her own growth but it handicaps the baby she bears. Treatments for teenage pregnancy, both preventive and ameliorative, involve social and cultural factors, as well as physical factors. Cynthia P. Green and Susan J. Lowe discussed this topic.

Changes in Posture with Growth; Drawbacks of the Erect Posture

David Sinclair

PERTH MEDICAL CENTRE

CHANGES IN POSTURE WITH GROWTH

The vertebral column of the new-born infant has two primary curvatures which depend largely on the shape of the component bones [Figure 1]. Both are concave forwards, one being in the thoracic region, and the other being formed by the curve of the sacrum, which at this stage consists of separate sacral vertebrae. Later on the sacral curvature becomes permanently fixed by the fusing together of its vertebral components; the thoracic curve allows a certain limited amount of movement, but the intervertebral discs in this region are thin, and this restricts the scope of movement of one vertebra on another; movement is also limited by the oblique set of the spines of the vertebrae and the fact that their laminae overlap each other.

At about 3 months of age the baby begins to hold its head up, and in association with this a secondary curvature appears in the cervical region of the column. This curvature, unlike the two primary ones, is convex forwards, and remains mobile, for its radius depends on the tension of the muscles which stretch across its concavity. The mobility of the cervical curvature is largely due to the thick intervertebral discs, which allow a considerable "play" between one vertebra and its neighbours.

On top of this secondary curvature the skull has to be held balanced. At birth the position on the skull of the facets which articulate with the atlas vertebra is similar in all anthropoids. In apes the portion of the base of the skull in front of the joint grows more than the portion behind, so that the joint shifts backwards and the centre of gravity of the skull and brain falls well forward.

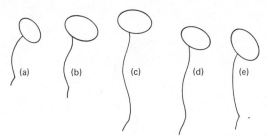

FIGURE 1. *Changes in the spinal curvatures with growth.* (a) Infant. Two primary curvatures. (b) Six months. The secondary cervical curvature has appeared. (c) Adult. Two primary and two secondary curvatures. (d) Old age. The two secondary curvatures, dependent on the discs and the postural muscles, are becoming obliterated. (e) Final stage, corresponding to condition in infant.

From *Human Growth After Birth.* 2nd ed. London: Oxford University Press, 1973. Pp. 113–121. Reprinted by permission.

In man there is much less discrepancy between the growth of the skull in front of the joint and behind it. The result is that the joint comes to lie relatively much further forwards than in the apes, although the centre of gravity of the head is still in front of it. The skull therefore balances reasonably well on top of the vertebral column, but it still requires some muscular effort to keep the gaze horizontal.

When the baby begins to sit up, the lumbar curvature appears. This secondary curvature, like the cervical one, is mobile, depends largely on the discs rather than on the shape of the bones, is controlled by the great postural muscles of the vertebral column, and is convex forwards [Figure 1]. Both the secondary curvatures may fail to develop at the expected time should there be any delay in the development of the postures of sitting and holding the head up.

At the creeping stage the baby is essentially a four-footed animal, albeit with exceptionally mobile forelimbs, and his centre of gravity is supported in a very stable manner by his quadrupedal posture. When this quadruped rears himself up on end in his first efforts to walk, he has an awkward and unstable stance. Since his centre of gravity is high, he must stand with his legs widely apart in order to balance himself securely, and since it lies well forward, partly because of the large liver, there is a compensatory exaggeration of the lumbar curvature in order to bring the upper part of the body into the vertical position; this usually ceases to be necessary about the age of 4 years. In the early stages of walking the baby is often bow-legged [Figure 2]; this corrects itself gradually, and may even be followed by a knock-kneed period. As the baby stands up, so the weight of the body pressing down on the lumbosacral joint forces the upper part of the sacrum forwards and downwards; the posterior part of the sacrum and the coccyx are restrained by the sacrotuberous and sacrospinous ligaments from rotating upwards in consequence of this, with the result that the sacrum sinks more deeply in between the two innominate bones. As the legs straighten and the weight is transmitted through the pelvis to the heads of the

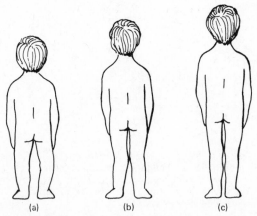

(a)   (b)   (c)

FIGURE 2.   *Development of stance.* (a) *18 months old: bow legs.* (b) *3 years old: knock knees.* (c) *6 years old: legs straight.*

femora, the pelvis becomes steadily remodelled; the force applied to the sacrum tends to lever outwards the lower part of the pelvis, thus broadening the region of the symphysis and increasing the subpubic angle. The acetabula become deeper and the hip joints more stable as the child becomes more active in his newly acquired two-legged freedom.

In the new-born the legs are flexed and the feet inverted; as walking begins the lower limbs straighten out and the feet evert, and at the same time the angle made by the neck of the femur with the shaft decreases gradually from about 160 degrees to the adult value of about 125 degrees.

In the adult the center of gravity is approximately 55 per cent of the total height from the floor, being higher in men than in women. The line of gravity naturally alters constantly according to posture. When standing at rest it falls through the external auditory meatus, behind the hip, in front of the ankle, and half-way between the heel and the balls of the toes [Figure 3]. It passes through the dens of the axis vertebra, the front of the body of the second thoracic vertebra, and the back of the body of the twelfth thoracic vertebra, and the back of the body of the fifth lumbar vertebra [Figure 4]. If the centre of gravity is

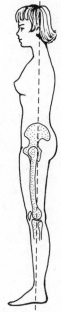

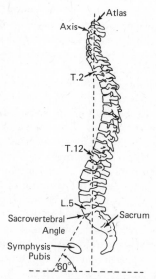

FIGURE 3.   *Position of line of gravity in erect posture. The line passes through the external auditory meatus, the tip of the acromion process of the scapula, and the mid-point between the heel and the balls of the toes. It falls behind the hip joint, through the middle of the knee joint, and in front of the ankle joint.*

FIGURE 4.   *The line of gravity. The line passes through the dens of the axis vertebra, the front of the body of the second thoracic vertebra, the middle of the body of the twelfth thoracic vertebra, and the back of the body of the fifth lumbar vertebra. The angle made with the horizontal by a line passing through the sacral promontory and the upper border of the symphysis pubis is known as the pelvic tilt, and is usually about 60°.*

allowed to fall too far backwards or forwards, muscular effort is needed to prevent falling.

The most important single factor in faulty posture is the tilt of the pelvis in relation to the horizontal. This is defined as the angle with the horizontal made by a line through the sacral promontory and the upper border of the symphysis pubis [Figure 4], which is normally about 60 degrees. The pelvic tilt is determined by the postural pull of the muscles of the back, abdomen, and thighs, and these pulls are in turn influenced by the way the individual habitually stands. A "tense" habit of standing increases the tilt, so that the pelvis rotates forwards on the thighs, carrying the lumbar spine forwards, and with it the centre of gravity. In compensation, the upper part of the body is thrust backwards, so increasing the lumbar curvature. The neck is held stiffly, with the chin tucked in, in order to maintain the horizontal gaze of the eyes. If this posture is held as a routine, the muscles which have pulled the pelvis out of position may shorten and their opponents lengthen, so that after a time the individual is unable to stand in any other way.

The converse of the "tense" posture is the "slack" posture. The pelvic tilt decreases, the center of gravity passes backwards, and the head and thorax are thrust forwards to compensate. There is thus a mild increase in the thoracic curvature, and the neck is extended, the chin being poked forwards. The joints of the lower limb tend to flex, and become mechanically unstable.

Poor posture results from many causes, which are not always as easy to determine as might be thought. The damage may originate in any part of the body, for posture is an integral whole, and anything that tends to upset one part of the mechanism will throw the rest of it out of gear. A good example is the very common defect known as "round shoulders." By this is meant a failure of the muscles of the shoulder girdle to hold the scapulae back towards the spine, so that the whole shoulder girdle drifts round the side of the chest towards the front of the body. This in turn upsets the gravitational equilibrium of the upper part of the body, for arm weight in front of the gravity line must be compensated for by alterations in the curvatures of the spine, and this in turn causes a movement of the pelvis which has repercussions on the posture of the joints of the lower limb and on the distribution of weight in the foot.

Conversely, the wearing of high-heeled shoes, which tip the body weight forwards, can lead to disturbances of the posture of the whole body working upwards through the pelvis to the spine; a complaint of aching pain in the neck can sometimes be cured by wearing a lower heel.

Postural deformities can obviously be caused by injury or disease, but there is also a hereditary factor, and mental attitudes are also of importance in determining how the child "holds himself." Deformities commonly develop in adolescence, when the weight increase at the time of the adolescent spurt may not be accompanied for some time by a corresponding increase in the strength of the postural muscles, especially in girls. Those people who have six lumbar vertebrae instead of five have a greater part of their spinal column unprotected by the leverage of the rib cage, and tend to have trouble in this region. One of the most difficult conditions to explain is scoliosis, which is a twisting deformity affecting the whole column. It is often attributed to faulty working postures in poorly designed school seats and desks, but there are certainly other factors concerned.

DRAWBACKS OF THE ERECT POSTURE

The erect posture brings with it certain advantages. The hands are freed, allowing manipulation of objects and co-ordination between the hands and brain. This in turn is responsible for an increase in the size of the brain, and thus for our capacity to make and use tools. A second advantage is that the eyes are brought further from the ground and made more mobile, since the skull can now be poised more freely on the top of the vertebral column.

But the erect posture also brings with it many disabilities, some of which are apparent quite early in life, while others tend to appear later, when the pull of gravity and the effects of tissue degeneration have been operating for a long time.

In the first place, it is a precarious equilibrium, and consequently a great part of the large central nervous system has to be devoted to maintaining this equilibrium by a complex system of reflexes and controls. These are easily lost as a result of illness, or in old age. Secondly, there is an increased strain on the bones and joints of the lower limb, particularly on the foot, and this is shown by the incidence of flat feet, sprained ankles, etc. These are much in evidence following the adolescent spurt, when violent exercise may throw an intolerable strain on the ankle region, and when periods of prolonged standing at work may place too much gravitational load on the arches of the feet.

There is also a considerable strain on the cantilever structure of the vertebral column, which is not yet fully adapted by evolution to being tipped up on end [Figure 5]. Aches and pains, degenerating joints, and damage to intervertebral discs are all common in the lower part of the column.

The pelvis is also not yet properly adapted, and remains essentially the pelvis of a four-footed animal. Nevertheless, it has to continue to allow the passage of the fetal skull, which in the course of evolution has grown bigger, while at the same time coping with a very large gravitational strain. This mechanical problem is aggravated by the postural burden which a heavy pregnant uterus lying in front of the line of gravity imposes on the vertebral column, and women who have borne several children may have troublesome pain in the lower part of the back resulting from the stress laid upon their lumbosacral and sacro-iliac joints.

In the upright position the forelimbs hang down at the side of the trunk, at right angles to their former "neutral" position. The resulting extensive anatomical alterations in the shoulder region have made some of the nerves and vessels entering the limb liable to compression and injury.

Breathing is hampered, since the whole weight of the chest wall must be raised against the pull of gravity instead of swinging at right angles to it as in the four-footed animal. The rib cage therefore tends to fall in old age, when the muscles are no longer equal to the heavy task of raising it in inspiration; this is responsible for respiratory difficulties due to deficient ventilation. At the same time the thoracic and abdominal viscera descend, and the anterior abdominal wall becomes weakened because of increased pressure on the lower portion of it; this in turn is a factor in the frequency of hernia. Similarly, there is an increased gravitational load on the pelvic floor, and this shows itself in the frequency of the condition of prolapse, in which the uterus and bladder descend through a pelvic diaphragm, weakened or damaged by childbirth.

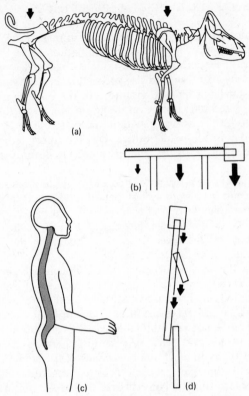

FIGURE 5.   *Stresses in the vertebral column. (a) Skeleton of a pig: the arrows indicate the points at which weight is transferred to the limbs. (b) Compare with the plan of a two-armed cantilever. The solid line indicates compression forces taken by the bones, the dotted line indicates tension forces. The spines of the vertebrae in (a) are long and powerful in order to afford attachment to muscles and ligaments resisting tension forces. (c) and (d) When this structure is stood on end, the stresses which it has to withstand are quite different.*

Finally, the elevation of the brain above the heart means that gravity interferes with its blood supply. The return of blood to the heart from the lower limbs is also impeded by the long vertical haul against gravity. For this reason the autonomic nervous system has had to develop a complicated system of vasomotor controls, and these are not always adequate to the occasion, as is seen in the condition of postural fainting, in which the blood supply to the brain is interrupted when the patient suddenly stands up. The common condition of varicose veins also testifies to the incomplete adaptation of the vascular system.

The erect posture is therefore not an unmixed blessing, and the gradual achievement of it during the first part of childhood carries with it liabilities as well as advantages. In old age many of these liabilities come home to roost, and posture undergoes regressive changes.

Effects of a Competitive Endurance Training Program on Self-Concept and Peer Approval *

Robert W. McGowan, Boyd O. Jarman, and Darhl M. Pedersen

BRIGHAM YOUNG UNIVERSITY

Summary

The purpose of this study was to investigate the effects of a cardiovascular fitness program on the self-concept and peer approval of seventh grade boys. Thirty-seven low self-esteem Ss were randomly divided into a control group (participated in no formal physical education activity) and an experimental group (participated in a special running training program).

At the end of an 18 week training program the two groups were significantly different in cardiovascular endurance, indicating the efficacy of the experimental treatment. There was an increase in self-concept from pretest to posttest for the experimental group only. Neither group had a significant change in peer approval.

A. INTRODUCTION

Physical educators tend to promote physical education on the premise that physical fitness leads to the development of the whole person. It is believed that physical conditioning enhances a number of personal variables including the self-concept and the ability to relate to others. Empirical studies have substantiated these beliefs in part. Tillman (7) found that personality changes occurred for males in a training program if they achieved a high degree of physical fitness. In a similar study Reed (5) showed that winning in competitive activities produced a significantly improved self-concept. Stein (6) and Jones (4) both found positive relationships between physical strength and peer approval. Stronger Ss were rated higher in prowess and social popularity, whereas weaker Ss were less popular, experienced feelings of inferiority, and reported difficulty in social relations.

These studies suggest that by significantly increasing physical fitness through a program of contrived and actual success a person's self-concept and peer relationships should be significantly improved. The purpose of this study was to examine the effects of a success-oriented endurance training program on self-concept and peer approval of seventh grade boys.

B. METHOD

1. SUBJECTS Ss were male seventh grade students enrolled at Farrer Junior High School in Provo, Utah.

2. MEASURING INSTRUMENTS   *a. Tennessee Self Concept Scale*   The Tennessee Self Concept Scale was developed by Fitts (2) and has a reliability

Reprinted from *The Journal of Psychology*, 1974, **86**, 57–60. By permission.

* This experiment was supported in part by a Faculty Research Fellowship granted to Boyd O. Jarman and Darhl M. Pedersen by Brigham Young University.

345

of .92. Ss rated items describing relationships to peers, family, and self as to how descriptive they were of themselves on a five-point scale from strongly agree to strongly disagree.

b. *Cooper's Twelve Minute Run*   This is a measure of cardiovascular fitness which was developed by Cooper (1). The task requires Ss to cover the maximum distance they can by running and walking during a 12 minute time limit. The score is the distance traveled. This score is highly correlated (.90) with the physiological measure of oxygen uptake (VO_2). It is easy to administer and has a high test-retest reliability (.91).

c. *Sociogram*   The Sociogram consisted of a list of all seventh grade males. The Ss indicated their five best friends and circled their own name. It was scored by obtaining the frequency with which each S was selected as a best friend. This was the measure of peer approval utilized in the study.

3. PROCEDURE   During registration in September, 1972, all seventh grade males were given the Tennessee Self Concept Test and the Sociogram in that order. Those who scored 47 or below on the Positive Total Score (a general indicator of self-image) of the Tennessee Self Concept Scale and were chosen by three or fewer peers as "best friend" were retained as subjects. During the first two weeks of school all Ss completed Cooper's Twelve Minute Run.

The students who were selected to participate in the experiment were randomly assigned to one of two groups—an experimental group and a control group. The experimental group was an endurance training group. They followed a training schedule similar to a running training program outlined by Gardner and Purdy (3). However, their program was adapted to a three or four day per week program instead of a seven day per week program. On nonrunning days Ss participated in various competitive activities: viz., floor hockey, basketball, football, and volleyball. Every three to four weeks the experimental group competed against the regular physical education class in a variety of activities including Cooper's Twelve Minute Run.

The endurance training group was positively reinforced for each activity. They were told that they won on each occasion. Sometimes the win was actual and sometimes it was contrived. For the team sports, players were assigned by the experimenter to the teams in such a way as to assure victory for the experimental group. For Cooper's task, average distances were reported to the Ss in favor of the experimental group whether or not they actually had a better mean distance. They also ran mile and two mile races with experimental and physical education groups mixed. Again the mean time for the experimental group was always reported as superior.

The endurance group was divided into three teams. Average times for the one mile, two miles, one-half mile runs were recorded every third week for each team, as well as for each individual. They ran one mile the first week, two miles the second week, and one-half mile the third week. The winning team was rewarded with sweat suits, golf caps, instructor's praise, and free time during the week. The same rewards were given for outstanding individual efforts. It was arranged so that each team won an equal number of times; i.e., success was administered with a variable ratio of 1/3.

The control group attended regular classes with no participation in physical education classes.

At the end of the 18 week semester the experimental group and the control group were retested on the Sociogram and the Tennessee Self Concept Scale.

4. ANALYSIS   The experimental and control groups were compared on each of the three measures by means of a t test to insure equality between the groups on the pretest. A t test for paired data was used to determine whether or not there were significant within-group differences from pretest to posttest over each measure.

C. RESULTS AND DISCUSSION

The t test between groups for the three measures given in the pretest revealed no significant differences, substantiating the randomness of the assignment of Ss to groups. Following the 18 week program the experimental group experienced a positive within-group change in cardiovascular fitness ($t = 8.71$, $p < .005$), indicating the efficacy of the experimental treatment. There was also a significant increase in self-concept ($t = 1.79$, $p < .05$); however, there was no significant difference in peer approval. No significant difference from the pre- to posttesting was found for the control group. This last finding indicates that the scores of the control group Ss on the posttest measures were unaffected by any intervening experiences or by the fact that they had previously taken the measures during the pretest. Thus, it may be concluded that the competitive endurance training program increased self-concept.

References

1. COOPER, K. H. The New Aerobics. New York: Bantam Books, 1972.
2. FITTS, W. H. Tennessee Self Concept Scale. Nashville, Tenn.: Counsel. Recordings & Tests, 1965.
3. GARDNER, J. B., & PURDY, J. G. Computerized Running Training Programs. Los Altos, Calif.: Tafnews Press, 1970.
4. JONES, H. E. Motor Performance and Growth, Berkeley: Univ. California Press, 1949.
5. REED, D. A. The influence of competitive and non-competitive programs of physical education on body image and self-concept. Diss. Abst. Internat., 1969, 19, 4312–4313.
6. STEIN, J. U. Physical fitness in relation to IQ, social distance, and physique of intermediate school mentally retarded boys. Diss. Abst. Internat., 1966, 27, 1253.
7. TILLMAN, K. Relationship between physical fitness and selected personality traits. Res. Quart., 1965, 36, 485–489.

Psychosocial and Psychosexual Aspects of Errors of Pubertal Onset and Development *

John Money and Richard R. Clopper, Jr.
THE JOHNS HOPKINS UNIVERSITY SCHOOL OF MEDICINE

Abstract

Pubertal anomalies fall into two major groups: errors of timing (delayed puberty and precocious puberty) and errors of congruence (for example, adolescent gynecomastia in boys, and hirsutism in girls). In cases of timing errors, the disparity between physique age and chronologic age creates a problem in social age which cannot correspond precisely with either. Social age includes academic age, recreational age, and pyschosexual age. Physique age dictates, in an almost automatic fashion, the expectancies of other people, who, therefore, overestimate the social age in precocious puberty, and underestimate it in delayed puberty. In consequence, the patient receives negative reinforcement when behaving concordantly with chronologic age.

The patient with precocious puberty, for example, is expected by others to behave in a more adult manner than his chronologic age permits. From the patient's point of view, it is a challenge to close the gap between social age and physique age, without the benefit of the usual period in which to learn more mature behavior. When I.Q. and school performance permit, school acceleration has been successfully used to foster precocious social maturation. This, in turn, assists to ameliorate the feeling of being a misfit. Psychosexual maturation is concordant with social age rather than physique age, for the most part. Masturbation may or may not be increased in frequency, relative to chronologic age. Masturbation imagery is dependent upon erotic knowledge. Dating and romance follow the usual chronologic age patterns and do not parallel the precocious maturation of physique. Early and straightforward sex education is imperative and successful in guiding sexual behavior. To date, treatment with antagonistic hormone therapy has been unsuccessful. Consequently, psychologic help is primary to the successful management of cases of precocious puberty.

For the teenager with delayed puberty, the discrepancy between physique age and chronological age induces others to infantilize or juvenilize the delayed boy or girl. In consequence, the patient may react accordingly. Also he may become a social isolate or loner. Psychosexual maturation is typically delayed and may be associated with long-term sexual inertia. Amelioration of problems of age-physique discrepancy in delayed puberty usually requires psychologic counseling and appropriate exogenous sex hormone therapy.

The major problem for people with incongruous pubertal development is to reconcile the self-concept of body image with actual physique. Typically their major concern is the matching of physique and gender identity, by means of appropriate hormonal and/or surgical therapy. Teenagers with incongruous pubertal development tend to withdraw from social relationships—particularly those that may risk their revealing their medical problem to others. Dating and romantic relationships may be disrupted. While psychologic counseling is often helpful it is not always readily available.

From *Human Biology*, 1974, 46, No. 1, 173–181. Copyright © 1974 by Wayne State University Press. Reprinted by permission.

* This research was supported by Grant HD-00325 (USPHS) and by the Erickson Educational Foundation.

Statistically, pubertal development begins around age 11 in girls and age 13 in boys (Marshall and Tanner, 1969, 1970). Normally, this physical development is congruent with the child's gender identity, which differentiates much earlier in life (Money and Ehrhardt, 1972). When puberty occurs on schedule and is congruous with gender identity, psychosocial and psychosexual development proceed with minimal difficulty. However, when pubertal onset occurs too early or too late, or, when pubertal development is unexpectedly incongruous with respect to gender identity, normal psychosocial and psychosexual development become more difficult.

The purpose of this paper is to present the psychologic problems associated with anomalies of pubertal timing and incongruous pubertal development. Most of the information reported below was gathered in the Psychohormonal Research Unit at the Johns Hopkins Hospital and has been summarized recently in Money and Ehrhardt (1972). It is our intention to outline the nature of these adjustment problems, and the therapeutic methods that these researchers have found successful in the amelioration of these problems.

AGE DISPARITY IN INCORRECT PUBERTAL TIMING

The paradigm for understanding the psychologic problems posed by errors of pubertal timing is based on the concepts of chronologic age, psychosocial age, and physique age. The term chronologic age is self-defining while physique age and psychosocial age are not. Physique age refers to the stage of development in physique normally associated with a particular chronologic age. Psychosocial age refers to the stage of development in social behavior normally associated with a particular chronologic age. Psychosocial age includes academic, recreational, and psychosexual age.

In normal individuals chronologic age, physique age, and psychosocial age coincide. For example, a boy 13 years of age looks and behaves like a 13 year old. His physical maturation and psychosocial behavior are appropriate for his chronologic age.

Owing to the usual correspondence between these three ages, the behavioral expectations for conventionally appropriate and inappropriate behavior can readily be made with reasonable accuracy. The most available age, from the point of view of an observer's first impression, is physique age, conveyed through the visual sense. Normally, physique supplies all the information required for an accurate estimate of chronologic age. Thus one's almost automatic response is to expect a person to behave consistently with the chronologic age impression inferred from the physique age. Rewards and punishments for age-appropriate and age-inappropriate behavior can then be administered accordingly.

When physical maturation is grossly disparate from chronologic age, as is the case in atypical pubertal timing, it is virtually certain that all newcomers, meeting the patient for the first time, will erroneously estimate the patient's chronologic age. When the observer's error is not corrected by behavioral feedback appropriate to either the physique age or chronologic age his error is further compounded: his reactions and expectancies are based on either an underestimation or overestimation of chronologic age and also of the reservoir of experience that age normally implies. Herein lies the psychologic problem central to errors of pubertal timing.

ERRORS OF PUBERTAL TIMING

Errors of timing in pubertal physical development are classified as either precocious or delayed. Both occur in males and females. In precocious puberty, the abnormally early onset of pubertal development can appear as early as birth, but more typically occurs around the ages of 4 to 6 years. It is marked by the early onset of the secondary sexual signs of maturation and of the adolescent growth spurt and epiphysial closure. It is related directly to early pituitary stimulation and the release of gonadal sex hormones into the blood stream. Adult height in affected individuals is often around 5 feet, owing to premature epiphysial closure. Reproductive fertility is established as much as six to ten years before the usual age.

Delayed puberty is, with respect to timing, the converse of precocious puberty in that sexual maturation is delayed beyond the normal age of pubertal onset. Delayed pubertal onset is more common in males than females. In females, the more common problem is delay of onset of menstruation rather than delay of onset of pubertal physique. Delayed puberty is related directly to a lack of sex hormones in the blood stream and may be either temporary or chronic in duration. Hormonal lack may itself be secondary to gonadal failure or to hypothalamo-pituitary failure; the latter may be idiopathic or consequent upon a brain lesion. Dependent on diagnosis, the problems of delayed puberty may be transient or chronic. Only the chronic form is referred to in this paper.

PRECOCIOUS PUBERTY

In cases of precocious puberty, physique age rapidly accelerates beyond chronologic age. Social age remains somewhere in between. As a consequence of physique and chronologic age disparity, precocious children automatically and routinely are expected by others, parents and other adults included, to behave in a more adult manner than their chronologic age permits (Money and Alexander, 1969).

The same age discrepancy that creates problems in adult behavioral expectancies also may present problems for the precocious child, himself or herself, in forming friendship and play relationships. Though precocious children prefer to play and make friends with children who resemble them in size and strength, they have difficulty being accepted by older and bigger children (Money and Alexander, 1969). They lack the social expertise, if not the greater physical maturation, of older children. At the same time, however, age mates may have difficulty accepting the precocious child, because of his or her larger physique and greater strength and energy. As a result, precocious children tend to view themselves as freaks or misfits, rather than feeling superior because of their size. They need to close the gap between social age and physical age. School acceleration is one way of helping to close this gap.

Psychosexual development need be no more difficult for precocious children than for pubertally normal children. In boys who are physically precocious (Money and Alexander, 1969), the capacity for erection, ejaculation, and erotic fantasy are precocious in their appearance. The content of erotic fantasy, however, seems to be contingent upon the boy's knowledge of sex and, developmentally, to closely parallel the imagery reported by normal boys. In girls who are physically precocious, Money and Walker (1971) reported that no persistent progression of erotic fantasies was found, and no evidence, including observed or reported masturbation, indicated an early interest in genitopelvic sexual behavior. Romantic and sexual involvements typically did not occur until middle teenage, or later, in precocious boys and girls, and were sometimes complicated by feelings of inferiority and being undesirably different. Precocious sexual development did not lead automatically to sexual promiscuity. Paraphilias were conspicuous by their absence in both males and females.

The successful management of sexually precocious children is, to date, primarily psychologic in nature, since antagonistic sex hormone therapy has not proved entirely successful. School acceleration by 1 to 2 years has been shown to be helpful in fostering an acceleration of social age, but is dependent on I.Q. and prior school achievement (Money and Neill, 1967). Fortunately, I.Q. frequently allows school acceleration (Money and Lewis, 1966; Money and Meredith, 1967; Money and Walker, 1971). Complete and accurate sex education, close to the time of pubertal onset, has proved valuable in guiding sexual behavior. Such education should include the physiology of sex and reproduction, including intercourse, and the social facts of sex such as privacy (Money, 1968), and love education, graded according to social age.

DELAYED PUBERTY

The age discrepancy in cases of delayed puberty is one in which physique age lags behind chronological age, with social age somewhere in between. The psychologic difficulty facing teenagers with delayed puberty is the problem of keeping the social age congruent with chronological age. The almost automatic reaction of both peers and adults is to treat a pubertally delayed teenager according to his physique age rather than his chronologic age. This infantilization makes it easy for the individual to be delayed in social development, since he is too often rewarded for behaving younger than his age, and held back from behaving in a manner appropriate for his age. The tendency toward marking time socially is seen most frequently as a preference for playing with chronologically younger children. Another reaction to disparity between physique and chronologic age may be that of being a loner—often as a consequence of peer rejection. Owing to delayed physical maturation, delayed teenagers often have difficulty competing successfully with their age mates, especially in sports (Money and Alexander, 1967).

Psychosexual development is typically delayed until the time of physical pubertal onset. Sexual inertia, after the induction of puberty with appropriate sex hormone therapy is common, though dependent on the diagnosis and etiology (Bobrow, Lewis, and Money, 1972; Ehrhardt, Greenberg, and Money, 1970; Money and Alexander, 1967; Money and Mittenthal, 1970). Masturbation, which is less frequent in females than in males, is variable in frequency prior to sex hormone treatment and generally increases following such therapy. Its post-treatment frequency, however, is usually lower than for normal individuals.

The frequency of erection and ejaculation is increased by the institution of appropriate sex hormone therapy, and may or may not reach normal levels. Libido or interest in sex is usually low even after exogenous sex hormone treatment. Erotic fantasies are infrequent prior to hormone therapy but they tend to increase following the induction of puberty. Dating and romantic involvements, as well as sexual experience including intercourse, are, with very few exceptions, delayed chronologically until after the onset of puberty. Marriage frequency varies according to the diagnosis. Paraphilias, that is sexual behavior disorders associated with an unusual object stimulus as in fetishism, are rare or nonoccurrent. So also is homosexuality.

The endocrine treatment for delayed puberty depends on the diagnosis and, specifically, on whether the delay is temporary or chronic. Exogenous sex hormone therapy to induce and/or maintain pubertal development must be timed individually, since the administration of sex hormone is accompanied by epiphysial closure and the cessation of linear growth. In cases of statural dwarfism with pubertal delay, the timing of treatment is particularly important because ultimate height is typically of prime concern to the patient.

The psychologic aspects of case management in late puberty include counselling to aid in the maintenance of a social age congruent with chronological age, as well as complete and factual sex education.

BODY IMAGE AND GENDER IDENTITY IN INCONGRUOUS PUBERTAL DEVELOPMENT

The psychologic problems associated with incongruous pubertal development primarily involve the reconciliation of gender identity with a sexually incongruous body image. Usually, gender identity is differentiated as male or female by puberty, though it may be ambivalent. It is not determined exclusively by chromosomal sex, prenatal hormonal sex, or pubertal hormonal sex, but is heavily dependent on postnatal socialization (Money and Ehrhardt, 1972). The male faced with a feminizing puberty, or the female faced with a masculinizing puberty, usually experiences fears of further incongruous development and its unknown consequences. Usually gender identity *per se* is not affected, except in unusual cases in which the pubertal child's gender identity is ambiguous, or when incongruous development is so precocious in its onset as to interfere with gender identity differentiation.

Persistent adolescent gynecomastia or breast growth in the male, may be idiopathic or associated with another endocrinologic and/or cytogenic anomaly. The degree of breast development varies. A mild degree of gynecomastia, in the sense that there is some non-fatty, glandular, or ductal tissue palpable, has been estimated to occur transiently in as many as 70% of pubertal boys (Gallagher, 1968). Because it is self-regressing and creates no visible problem, this minimal degree of gynecomastia needs to be distinguished from the more persistent degree in which the proliferation of breast tissue can approximate the amount normally found in an adolescent girl. The size and persistence of gynecomastia is related directly to the magnitude of the psychologic problem that ensues.

In girls, incongruous pubertal development usually takes the form of abnormal body hair growth (hirsutism), which may be associated with menstrual irregularity or failure. In some untreated syndromes, for example, the adrenogenital syndrome, the development of a masculine skeletal and muscular physique occurs also. Like gynecomastia in males, the origins of hirsutism are only partially understood, but are related to an elevated level of androgen.

PERSISTENT ADOLESCENT GYNECOMASTIA IN THE MALE

Upon reaching puberty and being confronted with the development of breasts in contradiction to gender identity, a boy may fear continued incongruous anatomical development and sex change. Since gender identity disturbances are seldom involved, the primary concern of such a boy is to have his breasts surgically removed. Hormones that feminize the chest do not feminize the mind. The sense of shame experienced by a boy with breasts may lead to self-sabotaging modesty. Such modesty can even delay his seeking medical help. The boy may tend toward social isolation and reclusiveness, to avoid ridicule and teasing from age mates.

Psychosexually, there is no correlation between incongruous pubertal development and either bisexuality or homosexuality. Erotic behavior follows gender identity differentiation. Dating and romantic involvements, however, may be delayed until medical treatment restores an appropriate body appearance.

When breast enlargement does not regress, surgical treatment of adolescent gynecomastia is indicated. Parallel psychologic counseling is desirable also. In rare cases, sex appropriate hormone therapy may be prescribed in addition.

HIRSUTISM IN THE FEMALE

The psychologic problems for a girl with hirsutism closely parallel those of a boy with gynecomastia. Since gender identity is already well differentiated, in the majority of cases, the primary concern of such a girl is the restoration of a female appearance. Hirsutism may breed a sense of shame or freakishness, social reclusiveness, and fear of exposure. Dating and romantic interests are frequently disrupted, though bisexuality and lesbianism are not in general a problem, since sexual behavior and gender identity are typically consistent with sex of assignment and rearing.

The management of these cases usually includes appropriate sex hormone therapy and psychologic counseling.

PROBLEMS OF SECURING PROFESSIONAL GUIDANCE

One difficulty, not yet mentioned, for patients with pubertal anomalies, is the problem of securing adequate professional help. Professional counseling is required when problems reach severe psychologic proportions. Often physicians are hard pressed for time to provide the psychologic help required, even if adequately trained to do so. Psychologists and psychiatrists seldom have an adequate endocrine backgound on which to base their counseling. Ideally, both the psychologic and medical services should be coordinated. This ideal requires the development of new programs in medical psychology for medical students and graduate students.

References

BOBROW, N. A., J. MONEY AND V. G. LEWIS, 1971. Delayed puberty, eroticism, and sense of smell: A psychological study of hypogonadotropinism, osmatic and anosmatic (Kallmann's syndrome). Archs. Sexual Behavior 1: 329–344.

EHRHARDT, A. A., N. GREENBERG AND J. MONEY, 1970. Female gender identity and absence of fetal hormones: Turner's syndrome. Johns Hopkins Med. J. 126: 237–248.

GALLAGHER, J. R., 1968. Adolescents and their disorders. In The Biologic Basis of Pediatric Practice, Edited by R. E. Cooke, McGraw-Hill, New York.

MARSHALL, W. A. AND J. M. TANNER, 1969. Variations in pattern of pubertal changes in girls. Archs. Dis. Childh. 44: 291–303.

———— 1970. Variations in the pattern of pubertal changes in boys. Archs. Dis. Childh. 45: 13–23.

MONEY, J., 1968. Sex errors of the body. Johns Hopkins Press, Baltimore.

MONEY, J. AND D. ALEXANDER, 1967. Eroticism and sexual function in developmental anorchia and hyporchia with pubertal failure. J. Sex Res. 3: 31–47.

———— 1969. Psychosexual development and absence of homosexuality in males with precocious puberty: Review of 18 cases. J. Nerv. Ment. Dis. 148: 111–123.

MONEY, J. AND A. A. EHRHARDT, 1972. Man & woman, boy & girl: Differentiation and dimorphism of gender identity from conception to maturity. Johns Hopkins Press, Baltimore.

MONEY, J. AND V. LEWIS, 1966. I.Q., genetics and accelerated growth: Adrenogenital syndrome. Bull. Johns Hopkins Hosp. 118: 365–373.

MONEY, J. AND T. MEREDITH, 1967. Elevated verbal I.Q. and idiopathic precocious sexual maturation. Ped. Res. 1: 59–65.

MONEY, J. AND S. MITTENTHAL, 1970. Lack of personality pathology in Turner's syndrome: Relation to cytogenetics, hormones, and physique. Behav. Genet. 1: 43–56.

MONEY, J. AND J. NEILL, 1967. Precocious puberty, I.Q., and school acceleration. Clin. Ped. 6: 277–280.

MONEY, J. AND P. A. WALKER, 1971. Psychosexual development, maternalism, non-promiscuity, and body image in 15 females with precocious puberty. Archs. Sexual Behavior 1: 45–60.

Teenage Pregnancy : A Major Problem for Minors

Cynthia P. Green and Susan J. Lowe

Teenagers account for one out of every five births in the U.S., nearly 617,000 births in 1973. A large proportion of these births (70–85%) are unplanned. One in ten teenagers has a child in her teen years. About four in ten teenage mothers are married; three in ten are unmarried, and three in ten marry before giving birth or soon after. In addition, one out of every three abortions is performed on a teenager; teenagers had an estimated 275,000 abortions in 1974.

Teenage pregnancy is a long-standing social problem which has only recently received public attention. Contrary to popular belief, the incidence of teenage

From *Zero Population Growth National Reporter*, 1975, 7:6, 4–5. Reprinted by permission of Zero Population Growth.

pregnancy is not increasing, except for women under the age of 15. From 1972–1973 the birth rate for women under 15 increased eight percent. While women aged 15–19 experienced a four percent decline in fertility during the same period, this was the lowest decline for all age groups from 15–49.

Increased public concern over teenage pregnancy may be attributed to the increasing proportion of teenage births in relation to total births and to the rising proportion of out-of-wedlock births among teenagers.

In the past, pregnant teenagers were pressured to get married or have their babies secretly and put them up for adoption. Previously, pregnant teenagers were routinely expelled from school; today teen mothers are asserting their right to an education, and special classes and programs have been started in many communities. There is growing recognition that social sanctions to punish the teenager neither prevent pregnancy nor solve the problems teen mothers encounter.

In addition to facing higher health risks both for themselves and their children, teenage mothers are often forced to leave school and to forego job training and other opportunities for economic advancement. Unmarried mothers face social disapproval, financial hardship, and difficulty in finding work and child care facilities. If they marry, teenage mothers are more likely to have unstable marriages and financial problems than others of the same age and socioeconomic status. Women who have their first child in their teen years tend to have more children in quicker succession than their peers.

Planned Parenthood officials predict an epidemic of teenage pregnancies due to increased sexual activity, non-use or ineffective use of contraceptives, and lack of contraceptive information and services for teenagers. Nearly three in ten teenage women are sexually experienced; only one in five of those who are sexually experienced consistently uses contraceptives. Moreover, only one-fifth to one-third of the teenagers in need of family planning are being served in organized programs.

DEMOGRAPHIC PROFILE

The Census Bureau estimates that in mid-1974, there were approximately 10.3 million females aged 15–19 and 10.2 million females aged 10–14. With about one million fewer women aged 20–24, the emergence of this large group of young people into their childbearing years will have major significance for future population trends.

The 1970 Census found that school enrollment dropped off rapidly after the age of 16, with 86% of 17-year-old females and 61% of 18-year-old females in school. In the 16–17-year-old age category, 37% of the females were employed full or part-time, as were 56% of those aged 18–19. Over one-quarter (28%) of those 19-year-old females surveyed were married, compared with 12% of the males. Half of all married teenage women had had at least one child at the time of the 1970 Census. Six out of ten females aged 14–19 had an annual income of less than $1,000.

TEEN SEXUAL ACTIVITY RISING

Surveys confirm that a large number of teenage females are sexually active, and there are signs that the age of initiation is decreasing. A 1971 study

TABLE 1
Out-of-Wedlock Births

	NUMBER		PERCENT OF LIVE BIRTHS WHICH ARE OUT-OF-WEDLOCK	
YEAR	Under 15	15–19	Under 15	15–19
1973	10,900	204,900	85	34
1971	9,500	194,100	82	31
1968	approx. 168,600		81	27

AGE-SPECIFIC FERTILITY RATES (number of births per 1,000 women in each age group)

	1973	1970	1960
Under 15	1.3	1.2	.8
Ages 15–19	59.7	68.3	89.1

SOURCE: U.S. Dept. of Health, Education, and Welfare, National Center for Health Statistics, *Monthly Vital Statistics Report Final Natality Statistics, 1968, 1971, and 1974*, Vol. 23, No. 3, 11, June 7, 1974 and Jan. 30, 1975.

of women aged 15–19 found that 28% had some coital experience, and the experience increased with age. The researchers estimated that about three percent of those aged 19 in 1971 had had sexual intercourse by age 15, compared with nine percent of those aged 15 in 1971. The number of unmarried black females aged 15–19 who had had intercourse was twice that of whites— 54% compared with 23%.[1]

More than two million unmarried women age 15–19 are sexually active and at risk of unintended pregnancy.[2]

TEEN CONTRACEPTIVE USE IRREGULAR

Teenage pregnancy is largely the result of non-use or sporadic use of contraception. A 1971 nationwide study found that 53% of the sexually active 15–19-year-olds failed to use any kind of contraception the last time they had intercourse. Teenagers tend to believe that they cannot become pregnant easily. Of those who did not use contraception at last intercourse, 56% stated that they were too young to get pregnant, that they had sex too infrequently to get pregnant, or that they had intercourse at the wrong time of the month.[3]

A recent study of contraception and pregnancy among American teenage women showed that 71% of sexually active teenagers do not use contraception because of ignorance of pregnancy risk and 31% because of inaccessibility of contraceptive services. Eight out of ten (84%) of the non-users of contraceptives did not wish to become pregnant; seven percent of the teenagers wanted to have a baby, and nine percent said that they didn't mind if they became pregnant.

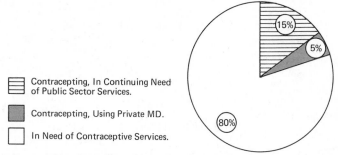

FIGURE 1.   *Percent distribution of currently sexually active never-married women aged 15–19 not desiring pregnancy, by contraceptive use status, United States, 1973 (minimum estimate).*

The study found that teenagers from poor families, those with limited educational backgrounds, and those with low educational aspirations were less likely to use contraceptives. Fewer black teenagers than whites used contraceptives, though this difference in largely related to their poverty status. Catholics reported higher levels of contraceptive use than either Protestants or those with no religious affiliation.[4]

Researchers found no evidence that the availability of abortion would weaken the motivation to use contraception. When asked what they thought a young unmarried girl should do if she finds herself pregnant by a boy she does not love, only one-fifth of the sexually experienced teenagers chose the option of ending the pregnancy.[5]

According to a 1971 study, the condom, withdrawal, and the Pill account for almost three-quarters of all contraceptive use among teenagers. The condom was named the "most recently used" method by 27% of the sexually experienced teenagers, while 24% used withdrawal, 21% used the Pill, six percent used foam, cream, diaphragm, or rhythm, five percent used a douche, and one percent had an IUD. As age increases, non-use of contraception decreases, use of withdrawal decreases, and use of the Pill increases.[6]

PREGNANCY AMONG TEENAGERS

Nearly three in ten teenage women who have premarital intercourse become pregnant, according to a 1971 study. Of these, 35% marry before the outcome of the pregnancy (birth or abortion) and an additional 10% marry after the outcome of the pregnancy. Of the 55% who do not marry, 60% have live births, 19% obtain abortions, and eight percent miscarry.

The study found that whites were more likely to marry as a result of pregnancy; 51% of the whites and nine percent of the blacks married before the outcome of the pregnancy. White teenagers are also more likely to opt for abortion, with 36% of the whites and five percent of the blacks choosing abortion in the 1971 survey.[7]

TEENS HAVE ONE-THIRD OF U.S. ABORTIONS

Single teenagers accounted for at least one-quarter of the abortions performed in the U.S., according to Planned Parenthood Federation of

America. In 1974, some 275,000 abortions were performed on unmarried women under the age of 20.[8]

H. E. W.'s Center for Disease Control found that in 1973 one-third of the legal abortions reported by states were to women under the age of 20. Data from 23 states showed that women under 15 had 1.2 abortions for every live birth, while women aged 15–19 had about two live births for every abortion.[9]

There is evidence that the legalization of abortion has influenced the nationwide decline in out-of-wedlock teenage births between 1970–1971, though it has not substantially reduced out-of-wedlock births. States with liberal abortion laws in 1970–1971 experienced declines in out-of-wedlock births of 14% for white teenagers and eight percent for non-whites. In states prohibiting abortion, out-of-wedlock births declined six percent for white teenagers and rose three percent for non-whites.[10]

Teenagers appear to have somewhat more conservative attitudes toward abortion than adults. In a national survey, a majority supported a woman's right to have an abortion in cases of danger to the woman's health, rape, and possible deformity. Although more than two in five teenagers believed that abortion should be available to a very young unmarried woman, a majority did not believe that this was a strong enough reason for abortion.[11]

CHILDBEARING AMONG TEENAGERS

In 1973, nearly one out of five (19%) of all live births in the U.S. were to teenagers—13,000 to women under 15 and 604,000 to women aged 15–19. Between 1972 and 1973, the number of births to women under 15 increased by six percent, and the birth rate for this group increased by eight percent. In the same period, births to women 15–19 decreased by two percent and the birth rate by four percent.[12]

The proportion of births rises rapidly with age. The National Center for Health Statistics calculated that in 1968, one percent of the 15-year-old females gave birth, three percent of the 16-year-olds, six percent of the 17-year-olds, ten percent of the 18-year-olds, and 13% of the 19-year-olds. Teenagers tend to have their children in quick succession. In 1968, one-quarter of all teenage mothers had more than one child before the age of 20, and 23% of the births to teenagers were second or higher order.[13]

Three out of ten teenage births are out-of-wedlock, and the proportion of births to unmarried teenagers compared with married teens is increasing. With the decline in marital fertility there has been a shift to child bearing outside of marriage for both black and white teenagers. It is estimated that in 1973, more than one-fourth of the babies born to white teenagers and almost three-fourths of the babies born to black teenagers were out-of-wedlock. Increased availability of abortion has slowed the rise in out-of-wedlock births which occurred in the late 1960's, but it has not reversed the trend.

Over half (53%) of the out-of-wedlock births in 1973 were to teenagers—10,900 to women under 15 and 204,000 to women 15–19. Between 1972 and 1973, there was a 19% increase in out-of-wedlock births to white women under 15.

PREGNANCY-RELATED MARRIAGES LIKELY TO FAIL

Early marriage as a result of a premarital pregnancy is fairly common. The National Center for Health Statistics estimates that six out of ten infants born to teenage mothers in 1968 were conceived out-of-wedlock. Studies show that nearly half of all teenage marriages break up within five years and that teenage marriages resulting from pregnancy are three times more likely to dissolve.[14]

Teenage marriages which involve a pregnancy are economically disadvantaged in terms of occupation, income, and assets when compared with couples of similar socio-economic status.[15] Many pregnant teenagers drop out of school, which contributes not only to social and economic difficulties but also leads to repeat pregnancies and larger than average families.[16]

TEEN MOTHERS RUN HEALTH RISK

With improved medical techniques, deaths related to childbearing have been dramatically reduced in the past two decades. Mortality risk for teenagers has declined considerably, although teenagers are more likely to have complications related to pregnancy. For whites, the risk of mortality associated with pregnancy is higher for teenagers than for women aged 20–29, but lower than the rate for women 30 and over. The maternal mortality rate for nonwhites is four times that of whites and increases gradually until the age of 30 when it rises sharply.[17] The most common complications of teenage pregnancy are toxemia, prolonged labor, and iron-deficiency anemia. Poor nutrition, inadequate prenatal care, and physical immaturity contribute to the risk of complications.

Children born to teenage mothers face substantial health risks. Infant mortality for both white and nonwhite mothers under 15 is more than twice as high as for mothers in their early 20's. Children born to both white and nonwhite women aged 19 or younger have higher mortality rates than for mothers in their 20's and 30's.[18] The incidence of prematurity and low birth weight is higher among teenage pregnancies, increasing the risk of such conditions as epilepsy, cerebral palsy, and mental retardation.

CLINIC SERVICES FOR TEEENS INADEQUATE

Until recent years, teenagers had difficulty obtaining contraceptive services unless they had married or produced an out-of-wedlock child. Today, unmarried teenagers are legally entitled to contraceptive services on their own consent in 22 states (47 states for women 18 and over). Despite the more liberal laws, unmarried teenagers in many communities still have trouble locating contraceptive services.

National studies indicate that some two million unmarried women aged 15–19 are in need of contraceptive services and that only one-fifth to one-third of them are being served by organized family planning programs.[19] In 1973, nearly three in ten (28%) of the 3.2 million patients seen in organized family planning programs were teenagers; a large proportion of these 896,000 teenage patients may have been married.[20] Planned Parenthood clinics have seen an eightfold increase in the number of new teenage patients in the past six years (828% between 1968 and 1973).[21]

Studies show that most teenagers seek contraceptive services after they have become sexually active; many of them come to clinics initially for pregnancy tests. Traditional sanctions against premarital sex have not kept teenagers celibate but rather appear to have contributed to the non-use and sporadic use of contraceptives as well as the tendency to select unreliable contraceptive methods. Ironically, moral codes intended to prevent out-of-wedlock pregnancy appear to have had the opposite effect.

LAWS REGARDING MINORS

The last five years have seen expanded rights for teenagers as most states lowered the age of majority to eighteen. At present, an unmarried 18-year-old woman can legally consent to all aspects of medical care including contraception in 47 states and the District of Columbia. In all states but Nebraska and Wyoming she can obtain most pregnancy-related services, abortion, and treatment for venereal disease on her own consent.

Although it is still difficult for young people under age 18 to obtain contraceptive services, 22 states and the District of Columbia now allow minors contraceptive care on their own consent; 17 states and the District of Columbia permit persons under 18 to consent to abortion. The doctrine of the "mature" or "emancipated" minor is gaining acceptance. It holds that a minor intelligent enough to understand the nature and consequences of a particular medical treatment may consent to it. Five states (Ark., Id., Miss., Mont., N.H.) have "mature minor" statutes, and several other states have recognized the doctrine through court decisions.

Although 18-year-old women may obtain abortions on their own initiative in all states except Nebraska and Wyoming, minors face complicated obstacles in obtaining abortions without parental consent. Many states have laws specifically requiring parental consent, and other states which permit contraceptive services to minors on their own consent specifically exclude abortion. A minor's right to privacy has been recognized in court decisions in Colorado, Florida, Kentucky, Massachusetts, Utah, and Washington, where parental consent requirements for abortion were declared unconstitutional.[22]

Much more work needs to be done to educate teenagers and their parents on the problems related to teenage pregnancy and the availability of contraceptive information, counseling, and services. In addition, school authorities, social workers, and health personnel, especially physicians, must be made aware of the special needs of teenagers.

Teenage pregnancy is a complicated problem which will be with us for some time to come. Failing to act today only compounds the high human, social, and economic costs to be borne by teenage mothers, their children, and society in general.

Reference Notes

1. John F. Kantner and Melvin Zelnik, "Sexual Experience of Young Unmarried Women in the United States," *Family Planning Perspectives,* IV:4 — (Oct. 1972), p. 10.

2. JOY G. DRYFOOS, "A Formula for the 1970's Estimating Need for Subsidized Family Planning Services in the U.S.", *Family Planning Perspectives*, V:3 (Summer 1973), p. 145–172.

3. JOHN F. KANTNER and MELVIN ZELNIK, "Contraception and Pregnancy: Experience of Young Unmarried Women in the United States," *Perspectives*, V:1 (Winter 1973), p. 22.

4. KANTNER and ZELNIK (1973), *Ibid*, p. 26.

5. KANTNER and ZELNIK (1973), *Ibid*, p. 26.

6. KANTNER and ZELNIK (1973), *Ibid*, p. 26.

7. MELVIN ZELNIK and JOHN F. KANTNER, "The Resolution of Teenage First Pregnancies," *Perspectives*, VI:2, (Spring 1974), p. 74–80.

8. GENE VADIES and RICHARD POMEROY, "Pregnancy Among Single American Teenagers," unpublished paper delivered at meeting of the Association of Planned Parenthood Physicians, Los Angeles, 1975.

9. U.S. Dept. of Health, Education, and Welfare, Center for Disease Control, *Abortion Surveillance: Annual Summary 1973* (May 1975), p. 1, 16.

10. JUNE SKLAR and BETH BERKOV, "Teenage Family Formation in Postwar America." *Perspectives* VI:2 (Spring 1974), p. 85–86.

11. MELVIN ZELNIK and JOHN F. KANTNER, "Attitudes of American Teenagers Toward Abortion," *Perspectives* VII:2 (Mar./Apr. 1975), p. 89.

12. U.S. Dept. of Health, Education, and Welfare, National Center for Health Statistics, Monthly Vital Statistics Report: *Summary Report, Final Natality Statistics, 1973*, Vol. 23, No. 11, Jan. 30, 1975.

13. U.S. Dept. of Health, Education, and Welfare, National Center for Health Statistics, *Vital Statistics of the U.S.*, Natality, Vol. 1.

14. LOLAGENE C. COOMBS et al., "Premarital Pregnancy and Status before and after Marriage," *American Journal of Sociology*, 75:5 (March 1970), p. 800–820.
   JOHN G. CLAUDY and JAMES M. RICHARDS, Jr. "Psychological and Social Factors in Fertility in the Early Years of Marriage: An Exploratory Study," paper presented at the annual convention of the American Psychological Association, Washington, D.C., Sept. 3–7, 1971.

15. LOLAGENE C. COOMBS et al. *Ibid*.

16. LINDA AMBROSE, "Discrimination Persists Against Pregnant Students Remaining in School," *Perspectives*, IV:1 (Feb. 1975).
   ELIZABETH WHELAN and GEORGE HIGGINS, *Teenage Childbearing: Extent and Consequences* (Washington, D.C.: Child Welfare League of America Inc./Consortium on Early Childbearing and Childrearing, 1973).

17. JANE MENKEN, "The Health and Social Consequences of Teenage Childbearing," *Family Planning Perspectives*, IV:3 (July 1972), p. 49.

18. MENKEN, *Ibid*, p. 47–48.

19. LEO MORRIS, "Estimating the Need for Family Planning Services Among Unwed Teenagers," *Perspectives*, VI:2 (Spring 1972); F. S. JAFFE et al., "Who Needs Organized Family Planning Services?: A Preliminary Projection, 1971–75," *Perspectives*, III:3 (1971).

20. FARIDA SHAH, MELVIN ZELNIK and JOHN F. KANTNER, "Unprotected Intercourse Among Unwed Teenagers," *Prespectives*, VII:1 (Jan./Feb. 1975), p. 39–43.

21. VADIES and POMEROY (1975), *Ibid*.

22. EVE W. PAUL, HARRIET F. PILPEL and NANCY F. WECHSLER, "Pregnancy, Teenagers and the Law, 1974," *Perspectives*, VI:3 (Summer 1974).

23. Commission on Population Growth and the American Future, *Population and the American Future* (Washington, D.C.: U.S. Government Printing Office, 1972), p. 42.

14

Intellectual Development

The following articles contribute to understanding the nature of intelligence and intellectual development in adolescence. They also give information about the processes of intellectual behavior.

Certain families produce children of higher intelligence than do other families. Families provide both heredity and environment for children. Of what does a family's influence on intelligence consist? Some differences in intellectual behavior appear to be hereditary, especially those that seem to be sex-linked. What, if any, environmental factors influence the expression of hereditary control?

Many researchers have been curious about the relationship between birth order and family size to children's cognitive functioning. Hunter M. Breland's study is an effort to provide answers to some of these questions. He obtained a very large number of subjects, nearly 800,000 high school juniors, who took tests for the National Merit Scholarships. Therefore, it was possible to control for socioeconomic variables and for mother's age. Breland's findings were similar to other studies in showing the favorable effects of small family size and wide spacing of children on verbal achievement. Several hypotheses are considered for explaining the results. This article has implications not only for children's verbal learning but also for family planning.

The way in which a child sees herself is the product of her cognitive structure. Contrasts between self-perceptions of children and adolescents are also contrasts between cognition on the level of concrete operations and cognition in formal operations. The paper by Raymond Montemayor and Marvin Eisen compares categories of self-description and gives examples in the subjects' own words, making it easy to get a feeling for the essence of each level of thought. One especially interesting part of the article is a discussion and illustration of the changeover from childhood to adolescence in the mode of self-perception.

Subjects of two cognitive levels are again compared in a cognitive performance, by Lauren J. Harris, Charles Hanley, and Catherine T. Best. The task here is to show understanding of the principle of horizontality by predicting where the water level will be when a bottle is tilted. As well as the expected age-level difference, Harris and his associates found a significant sex difference. Through a series of ingenious tests, developed from cues given by subjects in each previous test, reasons for success and failure were analyzed. The authors concluded that success requires visuo-spatial abilities primarily, rather than logical reasoning. A sex difference in visuo-spatial abilities has already been established by other investigators.

Birth Order, Family Configuration, and Verbal Achievement

Hunter M. Breland

EDUCATIONAL TESTING SERVICE

Two samples of National Merit Scholarship participants tested in 1962 and the entire population of almost 800,000 participants tested in 1965 were examined. Consistent effects in all 3 groups were observed with respect to both birth order and family size (firstborn and those of smaller families scored higher). Control of both socioeconomic variables and mother's age, by analysis of variance as well as by analysis of covariance, failed to alter the relationships. Step-down analyses suggested that the effects were due to a verbal component and that no differences were attributable to nonverbal factors. Mean test scores were computed for detailed sibship configurations based on birth order, family size, sibling spacing, and sibling sex.

The long history of research on relationships between birth position and achievement variables is well documented by numerous reviews (e.g., Altus, 1966; Bayer & Folger, 1967; Bradley, 1968; Hsiao, 1931; Jones, 1933, pp. 204–241, 1954, pp. 667–668; Murphy, Murphy, & Newcomb, 1937, pp. 349–363; Sampson, 1965, pp. 175–222; Schachter, 1963; Schooler, 1972; Sutton-Smith & Rosenberg, 1970). Only those reviews by Altus and by Schachter argued strongly for the existence of a relationship (that early-born, and especially firstborn, have higher achievement). Altus (1965) suggested that the observed relationship was due to a verbal factor. Most of the other reviewers indicate that little evidence exists for a relationship between birth order and intelligence or other achievement indicators.

Recent studies of large samples, however, clearly suggest that highly significant and consistent relationships do exist. Belmont and Marolla (1973), Eysenck and Cookson (1969), and Record, McKeown, and Edwards (1969) all obtained similar patterns of results (firstborn and early-born tended to score higher on various achievement and intelligence measures). The causes of those observed differences have been debated extensively (e.g., Breland, 1973; Schooler, 1973).

The analyses of the present study represented an attempt at verification of such birth-order effects, but with suspected confounding factors controlled. A second objective was to explore the possibility that any observed relationship is due to a verbal factor, as Altus had indicated. Finally, the question of the effects of specific family configurations formed by sibling spacing and sex differences was investigated. It was hypothesized that closely spaced siblings experience sociological influences similar to those of twins.

METHOD

Samples　Two samples of National Merit Scholarship participants tested in 1962 and almost the entire population of participants tested in 1965 were

From *Child Development*, 1974, **45**, 1011–1019. Copyright © 1974 by The Society for Research in Child Development, Inc. Reprinted by permission.

examined. The first sample of 670 subjects consisted of a random selection of the 1962 participants and was termed the "normative sample," The second sample of 1,147 subjects consisted of a random selection of high-scoring 1962 participants; this sample was called the "commended group." The third sample, essentially all participants tested in 1965, was termed the "1965 sample." In the spring of 1965, the National Merit Scholarship Qualification Test (NMSQT) was administered to 794,589 eleventh-grade students from a total of 17,608 different high schools.

Further details of these samples are given in Breland (1972a, 1972b).

Data   All subjects involved were administered the National Merit Scholarship Qualification Test (NMSQT) in the spring of their junior year of high school. In addition, selected subjects tested in 1962 were requested to complete a student questionnaire. Questionnaires were also requested from parents and teachers of these selected participants. From the questionnaire information, a very large number of variables were available for examination. In the present study, particular attention was directed to mother's education, father's education, family income, and mother's age. The second major source of information involved in the present study consisted of NMSQT scores for 1965 participants. For the 1965 administration, all subjects were requested to complete an information grid immediately prior to taking the test. This information grid included an item concerning the position of the subject in his family, whether he or she was a twin, and the sexes and spacing of siblings. Using the ordinal position data collected from this grid, it was possible to categorize subjects into 82 different sibling configurations.

Instruments   The NMSQT consists of five tests: English usage, Mathematics Usage, Social Studies Reading, Natural Science Reading, and Word Usage. The unweighted sum of the five tests, known as the Selection Score, has both Kuder-Richardson 20 and odd-even reliabilities of .97. For the 1962 participants (normative sample and commended group), four additional measures of father's education, mother's education, family income, and mother's age at birth were used. The three socioeconomic variables were obtained from questionnaire items. For the 1965 sample, information on socioeconomic status and mother's age was not available. On the other hand, very detailed information was available concerning the subjects' family structures.

Analyses   The data for the two 1962 samples were analyzed by means of an exact least-squares multivariate analysis of variance and covariance as described by Bock (1963). Computations were performed using the multivariance program of Finn (1972). The design involved two factors, family size and birth order—each having five levels of observation—and four covariates—mother's education, father's education, family income, and mother's age. For the very large 1965 sample, practicalities of data reduction dictated a different approach. No analyses of variance or covariance were performed; however, mean scores were computed for each of the 82 sibship configurations, and these were then combined to test birth-order effects, spacing effects, and sibling-sex effects by means of t tests.

RESULTS

In all three samples, the relationships obtained between birth order and NMSQT Selection Score were similar. Firstborns from small families had the highest scores, and lastborns from large families the lowest. The analyses of variance and covariance of the two 1962 samples showed the effects were statistically significant and that these effects were not appreciably influenced by the covariates. Step-down analyses of the birth-order effects in the 1962 samples suggested that they were verbal in nature, since the more verbal of the NMSQT subtests (such as Word Usage) showed highly significant birth-order differences regardless of step-down orderings, and the least verbal subtests (Math Usage) showed no significant differences for any step-down ordering of subtest scores.

The nature of the relationships among the variables of birth order, family size, and NMSQT Selection Score is most vividly described by the plot of Figure 1, based on the large 1965 sample. Almost all the mean differences represented in Figure 1 are significant beyond the .01 level. But what is perhaps of more interest is the close consistency between the male and female subsamples. Although males score slightly higher overall than females, the pattern of relationships is the same. The plots of Figure 1 are remarkably similar to the one presented in Belmont and Marolla (1973), a study of 400,000 19-year-old men in the Netherlands.

Sibling spacing effects are indicated in Figures 2 and 3 for two-child and three-child families, respectively (larger families were not analyzed with respect to spacing because of the large number of categories involved). Again, the patterns of spacing effects are consistent for both males and females. Combinations of sibling configurations were examined so as to compare categories having different numbers of siblings of a given sex. None of these differences was statistically significant (despite the large number of cases), and no consistent patterns were noted.

Some intriguing results were obtained when each of the 82 sibship configurations were rank ordered by NMSQT Selection Score separately for males and females. The rank-order correlations between sexes, as indicated, is .96. The sibling configurations occupying ranks 1, 6, 10, 14, 20, 62, and 68 are identical for both males and females. Twins occupy rank 72 for males and rank 70 for females, indicating agreement with most twin research (that twins average low on achievement tests, especially tests having large verbal components). That the high correlation of ranks for males and females is not merely an artifact of increasing family size was demonstrated by a similar rank-order correlation within the 36 configurations of three-child families. For this subset of configurations, a rank-order correlation between males and females of .95 was obtained.

DISCUSSION

The analyses of variance and covariance for the 1962 samples confirm the relationship between birth order and achievement often noted in the literature. These analyses suggested also that the observed relationship was not attributable to family differences in father's education, mother's education, and family

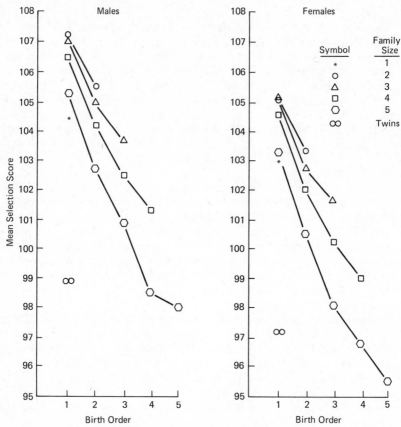

FIGURE 1.   *Mean NMSQT Selection Scores, 1965 sample. Symbols for family size:*
∗ = 1, ○ = 2, △ = 3, □ = 4, ○ = 5, ∞ = *twins.*

income; to family differences in mother's age; or to combinations of these factors. Moreover, the relationship between family size and achievement appeared to be related to some characteristic of family size itself rather than to socioeconomic-status factors associated with family size. Such a result is in close agreement with results obtained and arguments advanced by Nisbet (1953).

That the primary source of the score differences is verbal in nature was indicated by the step-down analyses on the individual NMSQT tests. After all other sources of variation were removed, the birth-order differences for the most purely verbal of the NMSQT tests (Word Usage) remained. Furthermore, when Word Usage was ordered first, all other differences became insignificant.

The detailed classification of family configurations available for the 1965 sample was useful for substantiating the results of the two smaller 1962 samples as well as for investigation of more subtle effects of sibling spacing and sexes. Although several studies have reported significant differences in birth-order

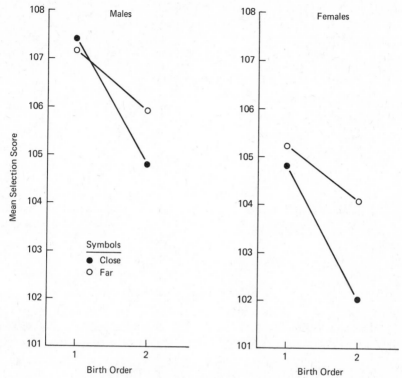

FIGURE 2.   *Spacing effects in two-child families, 1965 sample.* ● = *close*, ○ = *far*.

effects where the number of like-sexed siblings was varied, the present study indicated no consistent differences at all that were related to sibling sexes. Conversely, the analyses of the 1965 sample data suggested some striking effects associated with sibling spacing. Where a sibling followed closely in age (2 years or less), the scores were depressed. But where the age spacing interval was far (3 years or more), the same score depression did not occur.

Because the birth-order effects on NMSQT scores appear to be attributable to a specific ability of a verbal nature, and because of the apparent importance of spacing effects, one is led to believe that these differences are due to environmental causes. Neither physiological theories nor economic theories would explain differences in verbal achievement but not in nonverbal achievement. And although closeness of siblings might be related to socioeconomic status (poor parents have closer children), the fact that scores are depressed primarily for closely following siblings tends to preclude such a possibility.

Therefore, of the three traditional explanations for birth-order effects (physiological, economic, and social-psychological), the last would seem to offer the most promise—but this is not an expectancy theory. A common denominator tying together low achievement for twins, those of larger families,

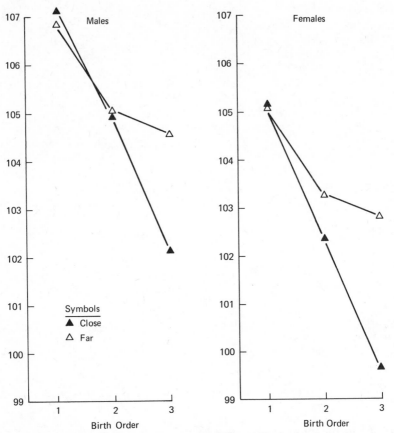

FIGURE 3. *Spacing effects in three-child families, 1965 sample. ▲ = close, △ = far. Spacing for second born refers only to preceding sibling.*

later birth orders, and closely following siblings is what has been called an "isolation hypothesis" (Faris, 1940). That is, children isolated from other children during early developmental stages may have an advantage as far as achievement is concerned. The twin study of Record et al. (1970) serves as an excellent demonstration of the effect of isolation from other siblings. In this study, even though normal twins who grew up to the time of testing (age 11) together had decidedly depressed verbal reasoning scores, surviving twins whose co-twin died at or near birth had scores about the same as nontwins. What is not explained by the isolation hypothesis is the case of the only child. As in the present investigation, Belmont and Marolla (1973) observed that only children do not appear to fit the same pattern as the other sibship configurations. Mean scores for only children tend to fall below those of most other firstborns (see Figure 1). One possible explanation for this anomaly is contained in Kammeyer's (1967) review of birth-order research. According to Kammeyer, some research indicates that the firstborn plays a parent-surrogate role relative to later-born siblings—a role that also may be thought of as a kind of "foreman" role. As long as there are other siblings, therefore, the firstborn serves as interlocutor between parents and later-born. Such a role would appear to be an excellent one for the development of verbal skills.

If one combines the isolation hypothesis with an interlocutor hypothesis, the higher verbal abilities of firstborn in relation to only children would be explained. That is, isolation from other siblings provides for close relationships with parents at their higher verbal level and avoids close relationships with siblings at a low verbal level. But an initial isolation, followed by an interlocutor role, offers the possibility of a further verbal enrichment. What is suggested, then, is a need for a mathematical modeling of these various potential sources of development. It is only with such models that the complex of interacting factors is likely to be understood.

References

ALTUS, W. D. Birth order and scholastic aptitude. *Journal of Consulting Psychology*, 1965, 29, 202–205.

ALTUS, W. D. Birth order and its sequelae. *Science*, 1966, 151, 44–49.

BAYER, A. E., & FOLGER, J. K. The current state of birth-order research. *International Journal of Psychiatry*, 1967, 3, 37–39.

BELMONT, L., & MAROLLA, F. A. Birth order, family size, and intelligence. *Science*, 1973, 182, 1096–1101.

BOCK, R. D. Programming univariate and multivariate analysis of variance. *Technometrics*, 1963, 5, 95–116.

BRADLEY, R. W. Birth order and school-related behavior. *Psychological Bulletin*, 1968, 70, 45–51.

BRELAND, H. M. Birth order and intelligence. (Doctoral dissertation, State University of New York at Buffalo.) Ann Arbor, Mich.: University Microfilms, 1972. No. 72–27. (a)

BRELAND, H. M. Birth order, family configuration, and verbal achievement. *Research Bulletin 72–47*. Princeton, N.J.: Educational Testing Service, 1972. (b)

BRELAND, H. M. Birth order effects: a reply to Schooler. *Psychological Bulletin*, 1973, 80, 210–212.

EYSENCK, H. J., & COOKSON, D. Personality in primary school children: 3-family background. *British Journal of Educational Psychology*, 1969, 40, 117–131.

FARIS, R. E. L. Sociological causes of genius. *American Sociological Review*, 1940, 5, 689–699.

FINN, J. D. Multivariance: univariate and multivariate analysis of variance, covariance, and regression. Ann Arbor, Mich.: National Educational Resources, Inc., 1972.

HSIAO, H. H. The status of the firstborn with special reference to intelligence. *Genetic Psychology Monographs*, 1931, 9, 1–118.

JONES, H. E. Order of birth. In C. Murchison (Ed.), *A handbook of child psychology*. Worcester, Mass.: Clark University Press, 1933.

JONES, H. E. The environment and mental development. In L. Carmichael (Ed.), *Manual of child psychology*. New York: Wiley, 1954.

KAMMEYER, K. Birth order as a research variable. *Social Forces*, 1967, 46, 71–80.

MURPHY, G.; MURPHY, L. G.; & NEWCOMB, T. *Experimental social psychology*. New York: Harper, 1937.

NISBET, J. Family environment and intelligence. *Eugenics Review*, 1953, 45, 31–42.

RECORD, R. G.; McKEOWN, T.; & EDWARDS, J. H. The relation of measured intelligence to birth order and maternal age. *Annals of Human Genetics*, 1969, 33, 61–69.

RECORD, R. G.; McKEOWN, T.; & EDWARDS, J. H. An investigation of the difference in measured intelligence between twins and single births. *Annals of Human Genetics,* 1970, **84,** 11–20.

SAMPSON, E. E. Study of ordinal position. In B. A. Maher (Ed.), *Progress in experimental personality research.* Vol. 2. New York: Academic Press, 1965.

SCHACHTER, S. Birth order, eminence, and higher education. *American Sociological Review,* 1963, **28,** 757–767.

SCHOOLER, C. Birth-order effects: not here, not now! *Psychological Bulletin,* 1972, **78,** 161–175.

SCHOOLER, C. Birth-order effects: a reply to Breland. *Psychological Bulletin,* 1973, **80,** 213–214.

SUTTON-SMITH, B., & ROSENBERG, B. G. *The sibling.* New York: Holt, Rinehart and Winston, 1970.

The Development of Self-Perceptions in Children and Adolescents*

Raymond Montemayor and Marvin Eisen
BROOKLYN COLLEGE AND CALIFORNIA STATE UNIVERSITY AT SAN DIEGO

A small body of research exists in the area of self-concept development. Investigators have concerned themselves with age changes in such things as self-esteem, body image, and the disparity between perceived self and idealized self. However, in few of these studies is self-concept development conceived of as at least partly an outcome of changes in cognitive processes. Yet, developmental changes in self-perceptions and attitudes, and the organization of those perceptions and attitudes may reflect underlying cognitive changes.

The purpose of the present investigation is to explore one implication of such a conception. Specifically, it is hypothesized that with increasing age, self-perceptions, or more accurately self-descriptions, become less concrete and more abstract. It is suggested that young children primarily describe and define themselves in terms of concrete characteristics such as appearance, likes and dislikes, and possessions, while adolescents conceive of themselves more abstractly and describe themselves in psychological and interpersonal terms. This formulation is in agreement with Werner's notion that development leads to increased integration as reflected in the use of abstract constructs.

Few studies in the area of self-concept development bear on this question. However, investigations of the development of impression formation or person perception have consistently found that, with increasing age, other people

Presented at meetings of The Society for Research in Child Development, Denver, 1975. Printed by permission.

* Parts of this research were supported by a grant to the first author from the Faculty Research Award Program of the City University of New York, No. 10702, and by a grant to the second author from the NIH Biomedical Sciences Support Program to Michigan State University.

are viewed in a way that is increasingly more interpersonal, complex, and abstract. To the extent that developmental changes in self-perceptions are similar to changes in person perceptions, one would expect a similar result, i.e., an increasing use of psychological and abstract terms to describe the self.

One hundred and thirty-six males and 126 females served as subjects in this study. The subjects were drawn from five grades—4, 6, 8, 10 and 12—and the average age for the students within each grade was 10, 12, 14, 16, and 18 years, respectively. The subjects were white, middle-class, average and above in intelligence and were from a suburban, academic, midwestern community. Subjects were administered the Twenty Statements Test in class groups. The Twenty Statements Test simply asks the respondent to give 20 answers to the question, "Who am I?" The test takes approximately 15 minutes to complete. A 30-category scoring system, devised by Gordon (1968) was used to classify each answer. Table 1 shows the scoring system and gives a few illustrative examples for each category. For example, category 10, Social Status, was

T A B L E 1
Who Am I Scoring Categories with Typical Examples

1. *Sex*: a boy, a sister, a guy.
2. *Age*: 9½, a teenager, a senior.
3. *Name*: Susan, Bobby.
4. *Racial* or *National Heritage*: White, a Negro, Italian.
5. *Religious Categorization*: a Catholic, Jewish, Methodist.
6. *Kinship Role*: a son, a sister, engaged.
7. *Occupational Role*: hoping to become a doctor, paper-boy.
8. *Student Role*: a student, getting bad grades, a "B" student.
9. *Political Affiliation*: a Democrat, an Independent.
10. *Social Status*: middle-class, from a rich family.
11. *Territoriality, Citizenship*: an American, living on Oak Street.
12. *Membership in Interacting Group*: on the football team, in the science club.
13. *Existential, Individuating*: Me, myself, nothing, I.
14. *Membership in an Abstract Category*: a person, a human, a speck in the universe.
15. *Ideological and Belief References*: a liberal, a pacifist.
16. *Judgments, Tastes, Likes*: hate school, like sports.

17. *Intellectual Concerns*: a thinker, likes to read.
18. *Artistic Activities*: a dancer, singer, poet.
19. *Other Activities*: a hiker, a stamp collector, a swimmer.
20. *Possessions, Resources*: have a bike, own a dog.
21. *Physical Self, Body Image*: 5′ 10″, 125 lbs., fat.
22. *Sense of Moral Worth*: bad, good, honest, a liar.
23. *Sense of Self-Determination*: ambitious, a hardworker.
24. *Sense of Unity*: mixed up, a whole person, in harmony.
25. *Sense of Competence*: good at many things, creative.
26. *Interpersonal Style (how I typically act)*: friendly, fair, shy, cool, nice.
27. *Psychic Style, Personality (how I typically think and feel)*: happy, sad, in love, calm.
28. *Judgments Imputed to Others*: popular, well-liked, loved.
29. *Situational References*: going on a date tonight, bored with this.
30. *Uncodable Responses*: the sea, a flower, dead.

(Adapted from Gordon, 1968).

defined as any reference to the individual's or family's socioeconomic situation, such as middle-class or from a rich family. Category 22, Sense of Moral Worth, was any reference to a moral evaluation of the self. The categories are reasonably exhaustive and rarely was an answer classified as uncodable.

Two undergraduates were trained in the use of the system. Interjudge agreement was tested by having both coders score a sample of 20 tests drawn from the experimental population. Interjudge agreement was 85% (average agreement per test, 17/20 responses). Responses were then summarized for each age group by sex in terms of the number of subjects who answered each category at least once. Age changes for each sex were then determined by chi-square tests performed on each category. Since there were 60 separate chi-square tests performed, the possibility that a test would be significant by chance was high. Therefore, only p values less than .001 were considered significant. Table 2 shows the per cent of subjects at each age using a category at least once.

The results indicated that there were no developmental pattern differences for males and females, i.e., if the use of a category tended to increase or decrease, it tended to increase or decrease for both males and females. However, changes in the use of some categories were significant for only one sex. Females showed a decrease between childhood and adolescence in the use of the categories Name and Territory; while males showed a decrease in the use of the categories Tastes and Likes, and Possessions. Both sexes were more likely to use physical descriptions in childhood than in adolescence.

In addition, for both males and females, there was a significant increase between childhood and adolescence in the use of the following categories: Existential, e.g., I, myself; Abstract Category, a person, a human; Self-Determination, ambitious, a hardworker; Interpersonal Style, friendly, nice; and finally Psychic Style, happy, calm.

The pattern of the data indicates that there is very often more of a change in self-descriptions between ages 10 and 12 than at any other time. Thus, 12-year-olds are to some extent more like 18-year-olds than 10-year-olds. Perhaps reading a few of the protocols will illustrate this finding and will give a better idea of what children at different ages say about themselves. (Original spellings and emphasis have been retained).

These first responses are from a boy, age 9, in the 4th grade. Notice the concrete flavor of his self-descriptions; the almost exclusive use of the categories Sex, Age, Name, Territory, Likes, and Physical Self.

> My name is Bruce C. I have brown eyes. I have brown hair. I have brown eyebrows. I'am nine years old. I *love*! Sports. I have seven people in my family. I have great! eye site. I have lots! of friends. I live on 1923 P. Dr. I'am going on 10 in September. I'am a boy. I have a uncle that is almost 7 feet tall. My school is P. My teacher is Mrs. V. I play Hockey! I'am almost the smartest boy in the class. I *love*! food. I love fresh air. I *love* School.

Next is a girl, age 11½, in the 6th grade. Note that although she uses the category Tastes and Likes quite frequently, there is a heavy emphasis on interpersonal and personality characteristics.

> My name is A. I'm a human being. I'm a girl. I'm a truthful person. I'm not pretty. I do so-so in my studies. I'm a very good cellist. I'm a very good pianist.

TABLE 2

Percent of Subjects at Each Age Using Category at Least Once

	FEMALES					MALES				
AGE	10	12	14	16	18	10	12	14	16	18
Category										
Sex	43	83	46	47	70*	47	63	30	48	74*
Age	33	26	29	21	45	3	44	30	29	37
Name	62	4	4	6	30†	38	15	11	16	32*
Race	0	4	0	12	25**	9	4	4	13	5
Religion	10	0	4	3	15	3	0	4	6	5
Kinship	43	40	25	21	50	31	15	11	29	63**
Occupation	5	9	21	29	50**	3	15	37	26	37**
Student	71	74	29	50	70**	63	44	44	58	74
Politics	0	0	7	6	5	0	0	0	0	5
Social Status	5	0	0	3	5	3	0	0	0	0
Territory	52	17	11	12	5†	44	15	30	13	16*
Inter. Grp.	57	52	46	53	60	56	26	22	23	53**
Existential	0	52	18	26	55†	0	15	19	26	53†
Abstract Category	0	78	39	44	45†	3	81	22	45	59†
Ideological	5	13	32	21	40*	3	15	15	26	37*
Tastes, Likes	71	70	79	50	35*	66	59	81	39	26†
Intellectual	43	26	36	21	20	28	30	44	26	26
Artistic	24	35	29	30	25	22	37	30	26	10
Other Acts.	57	65	75	65	45	69	59	89	84	74
Possessions	52	22	18	18	10*	53	22	30	10	5†
Physical Self	90	65	39	59	15†	84	48	52	39	16†
Moral Worth	5	30	11	21	20	3	15	22	35	32*
Self-Determination	0	4	29	47	45†	9	11	22	42	53†
Unity	0	0	18	18	20	0	0	11	16	21*
Competence	33	26	29	41	40	38	48	59	55	32
Interpersonal	33	96	96	82	90†	50	56	85	90	95†
Psychic Style	29	65	89	74	80†	25	19	41	87	63†
Judgments	24	26	25	21	60*	22	19	22	35	53
Situation	5	9	21	26	10	13	4	19	13	11
Uncodable	10	0	0	6	0	28	30	19	6	16
N	21	23	28	34	20	32	27	27	31	19

* Chi-square significant at .05 level.
** Chi-square significant at .01 level.
† Chi-square significant at .001 level.

I'm a little bit tall for my age. I like several boys. I like several girls. I'm old-fashioned. I play tennis. I am a *very* good swimmer. I try to be helpful. I'm always ready to be friends with anybody. Mostly I'm good, but I lose my temper. I'm not well-liked by some girls and boys. I love sports and music. I don't know if I'm liked by boys or not.

Finally, are the responses from a girl, age 17 who is in the 12th grade. Here, note the strong emphasis on interpersonal descriptions, characteristic mood states, and the large number of ideological and belief references, the beginnings of the establishment of a world view.

> I am a human being. I am a girl. I am an individual. I don't know who I am. I am a Pisces. I am a moody person. I am an indecisive person. I am an ambitious person. I am a very curious person. I am a confused person. I am not an individual. I am a loner. I am an American (God help me). I am a Democrat. I am a liberal person. I am a radical. I am a conservative. I am a pseudo-liberal. I am an atheist. I am not a classifiable person (i.e.—I don't want to be).

Contrast the responses of the previous 11-year-old with both the 9- and 17-year-old and I think you can see that the 11-year-old sounds more like the 17- than the 9-year-old. There may be a transitional period between the ages of 10 and 12 in the area of self-descriptions that corresponds to the transitional period from concrete to formal cognitive operations. To the extent that the 12-year-olds in this sample have begun to acquire the formal operational skills of hypothetical-deductive thinking and propositional logic, their thinking may more closely resemble those older adolescents who are in a similar stage rather than the younger children in a previous stage. Similarily, conceptualizations of the self by the 12-year-old boy may also be more like the older group than the younger group.

As Inhelder and Piaget have pointed out, adolescent thinking is a "second order system" in the sense that the adolescent does not solve problems in terms of concrete givens, but uses those concrete facts to form hypotheses about an underlying reality. Young children seem to characterize themselves in terms of descriptions of their behaviors. One might almost think of them as naïve behaviorists. Adolescents, however, seem to infer from their behavior the existence of an underlying personality trait. For example, it is not uncommon for young children to say that they like to play baseball, football, hockey, soccer, and so on. An adolescent, however will rarely present a list of behaviors such as that. Much more common would be to say: "I am an athlete," or "I like athletics." Thus, there is an integration of behaviors which leads the adolescent to infer a superordinate category.

It might be useful to think of the relationship between increasing cognitive abilities and self-descriptions as an attempt to more accurately and uniquely characterize the essence of the self. One notes an increasing use of descriptions which result in a sharper and more focused picture of the self, and which lead to a clearer differentiation of the self from others. For example, to describe oneself as a boy, 9-years-old, with brown hair and good eyesight is not to say much that will allow for a specific and unique characterization of the self. But, to describe the self as moody, indecisive, confused and a loner results in a picture of this adolescent that is reasonably specific and differentiated from others.

In conclusion, one might say that what appears to be the self for the child is only a set of elements from which the adolescent infers a constellation of philosophical and psychological categories that uniquely characterize himself.

Reference

GORDON, C. Self-conceptions: Configurations of content. In C. Gordon and K. Gergen (Eds.) *The self in social interaction.* Vol. I. New York: Wiley, 1968.

Conservation of Horizontality : Sex Differences in Sixth-Graders and College Students

Lauren J. Harris, Charles Hanley, and Catherine T. Best
MICHIGAN STATE UNIVERSITY

In the classical demonstration of the test for representation of horizontality (Piaget and Inhelder, 1956), the child is shown a bottle half-filled with water, asked to notice the position of the water in the bottle, and then to predict where the water level will be when the bottle is tipped. According to Piaget and Inhelder (1956), the principle that the water level will remain horizontal is mastered by about 12 years of age, the start of the so-called formal operational stage.

Recent studies have shown, however, that many 12-year-olds and even young adults do *not* know the principle (e.g., Liben, 1973; Morris, 1971; Rebelsky, 1964; Thomas et al., 1973), the majority of whom are females—in the case of college-age women, an estimated 50 per cent (Thomas et al., 1973).

This sort of failing of what seems to be a basic principle about nature has sparked much interest generally because it is puzzling in itself, for some psychologists because of its apparent violation of Piagetian theory, and finally because of the sex difference. Why *do* females lag behind? It occurred to us that in all earlier investigations known to us, the subject had to draw or otherwise construct the predicted waterline. With notions about "perception-performance lag" partly in the back of our minds, we wondered what would have happened had the subjects—especially college-age—simply been required to recognize the waterline expected. To find out, we designed a test that required the subject merely to pick that one of several drawings of tilted containers that correctly represented the water level of a standard container shown in upright orientation. We showed a variety of containers, shown in Figure 1—open containers, bottles, and pouring pitchers—one flat-bottomed, one round-bottomed of each type—in questions like those illustrated in Figure

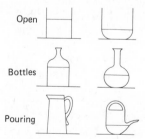

FIGURE 1.   *Container types.*

Presented at meetings of The Society for Research in Child Development, Denver, 1975. Printed by permission.

If the bowl holding the water, marked X at the left, is tipped, which numbered bowl shows where the waterline will be?

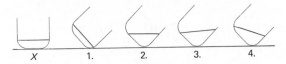

If the sprinkling can holding the water, marked X at the left, is tilted, which numbered can shows how the water will look?

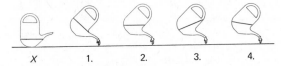

If the can holding water, marked X at the left, is tilted, which numbered can shows how the water will look?

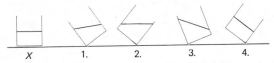

FIGURE 2.   *Types of questions.*

2. For each question, there was one standard in upright orientation with the water horizontal, and four foils showing various degrees and directions of tilt. One foil showed the liquid level at the true horizontal. The other three showed, in various combinations, the water level tilted 10, 20, or 30 degrees, in relation to the true horizontal, or parallel to the base of the container.

Sixteen such questions were printed in booklets. The instructions, appearing above each question read, "If the [container name] holding the water, marked X at the left, is tipped, which numbered [container name] shows how the waterline will look?" [Note: for half the questions, counterbalanced for choice, the instructions ended," . . . how the waterline will be?"] Rebelsky (1964) writes of her college-age subjects who had failed to conserve on a standard drawing task: "Even with a glass of water before them, some *S*s saw the water level was not as they had drawn it, but felt the water level did not look horizontal. A few tried to verify this by looking through the glass at a horizontal plane. *S*s noted that the water was "really" horizontal but reported it "looked" tilted" (pp. 373–374).

We therefore supposed that the wording "which . . . container shows how the waterline will look?" might encourage "phenomenalistic" answers or judgments, even in individuals who knew the principle of invariance, while the wording ". . . how the waterline will be?" would encourage "realistic" answers even for subjects who, like Rebelsky's, might feel that the water level did not actually *look* horizontal. The subject merely had to pick that one of the four foils in which the water level matched the level shown in the standard. It seemed ridiculously simple—to us who had made up the test!—and at least for the adults, we expected practically everybody to pick up the correct foil.

EXPERIMENT 1

Subjects The subjects in Experiment 1 were 158 undergraduates (48 men and 110 women) and 61 sixth-grade children (33 boys and 28 girls). Both groups were tested in their classrooms.

Results Contrary to our expectation, many of the university students did not conserve, most of them women. The results are displayed as histograms in Figure 3, which shows the percentages of males and females scoring from 0 to 16 correct for the 16 questions. The adults' scores are on the left. The men averaged 13.4 correct of 16 questions, or 84%; the women, 9.4 correct, or 59%. The difference was significant ($t = 5.16$, $df = 156$, $p < .01$)

The children's scores appear on the right. They did much worse, but once again males were ahead, boys averaging 9.3 correct, or 58%, as well as the university women had done; the girls, 5.9, or 37% ($t = 5.16$, $df = 59$, $p < .01$). Twenty-seven per cent of the boys got from 14–16 correct (15% with perfect scores) compared to only 4% of the girls (all with scores of 14). So a fair number of persons—children and adults alike—did *not* make the horizontal judgment even when they merely had to pick the one horizontal line out of the four foils— and females failed in this respect more than males.

As for the two different wordings of the instructions, item analyses failed to disclose any difference between them. It may be that the subjects simply failed to read them as significantly different instructions (i.e., took them as non-meaningful variants of each other), or that the different wordings were not sufficiently emphasized.

EXPERIMENT 2

One of the men in Experiment 1 who had made predominantly horizontal choices afterwards remarked that he had felt constrained to choose a *non-*

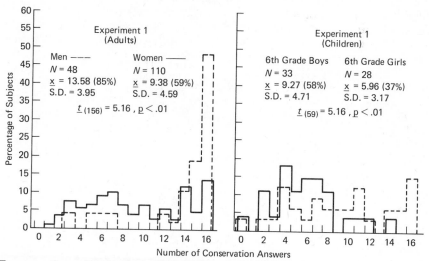

FIGURE 3. *Percentage of subjects* (*men, women, boys, girls*) *giving specified numbers of conservation answers.* (*Experiment 1.*)

horizontal foil in some cases because the correct foil—the foil showing the water level to be horizontal—did not show the same *volume* of water as the standard. He therefore was unsure whether the test was about water level or water volume. To our chagrin, we discovered that he was right: in making the drawings, we indeed had failed several times to conserve the volume of water in the tilted containers—how fragile are these principles even in the sophisticated!

We doubted that this failing in the test was related to the sex differences found, for if it were, it would mean that females, more than males, had answered on the basis of water volume rather than level—which seemed unlikely. But to be sure, we corrected the mistakes and repeated the test with a new group of undergraduates, 53 men and 105 women. The results were unchanged: the men averaged 13.77 correct (86%), the women 10.3 (64%) ($t = 5.08$, $df = 156$, $p < .01$). As the histograms show, in Figure 4, the distributions of scores were very similar to those for the university sample in Experiment 1.

The question may be raised whether persons with very low or middle scores were simply guessing. Item analyses showed that they were not: errors were *not* distributed haphazardly across the various choices; instead, foils showing the 10 degree tilt—the smallest degree included—were chosen far more often than the others. And the foil showing the water level parallel to the base of the tilted figure was chosen less than 5% of the times it appeared, though more often by females. So the subjects— males and females alike—were making their incorrect choices systematically, usually picking the smallest degree of tilt as though they expected that the water level would be close to but not at the horizontal.

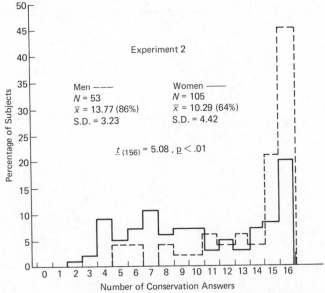

FIGURE 4.   *Percentage of men and women giving specified numbers of conservation answers.* (*Experiment 2.*)

It is tempting to suppose that the subject's errors were "perceptual"—that they were mistaking the 10 degree tilt for the true horizontal. But the 10 degree tilt was appreciable (adults, men and women alike, have no trouble picking out the foil showing a horizontal line when they are expressly asked to do so, or setting a line at the true horizontal, as other investigators have found; Thomas and Jamison, 1975; Willemsen and Reynolds, 1973), and, besides, the foil showing the true horizontal was always available for choice.

So far, then, we merely had satisfied ourselves that the nonconserver's difficulty in previous studies did not stem from the requirement that the predicted waterline be drawn or otherwise constructed, and that females were more affected in this regard than males. Some subjects themselves gave us a clue as to what the real problem might be. These were university students who had failed to conserve and who argued that the instructions ("If the container holding the water . . . is tipped . . .") implied that the water was in motion at that very moment and therefore tilted. As one subject put it, as the container was being tipped, the water would roll to one side. The subject was correct provided the container was tipped quickly and abruptly. But if tipped more smoothly and slowly the water would remain level. Though our instructions did not mention the speed with which the container is tipped, the possibility nevertheless arose that the subjects who failed to conserve horizontality had interpreted the instructions as meaning that the container at that moment was being tipped (quickly and abruptly), and that, for some reason, proportionately more female than males had made this inference. We studied this possibility in a further experiment.

EXPERIMENT 3

Procedure   In Experiment 3, two kinds of instructions were used, in a between-subjects design, with the 16 drawings used in the previous studies. One instruction (Figure 5—top) was designed to imply that the container was still in motion and read, "The pictures . . . show containers of water while they are being tilted. Which picture shows how the waterline will look?" The other instruction (Figure 5—bottom) was designed to imply that the container was still, and read, "The pictures . . . show . . . containers of water, which, several minutes before were tilted at various angles. Which picture shows how the waterline will look?"

Note that we have eliminated the upright standard in this experiment, and that the instructions now imply that the four foils show four *different* containers. With a standard present, as in Experiments 1 and 2, and with instructions saying that all the foils are variants of the standard, it was understandable that at least one subject had been encouraged to compare the foils against the standard in the basis of volume. Even though we were careful, in Experiment 2, to conserve volume in the foils, we worried nonetheless that some subjects would continue to make their judgments in terms of volume in addition to, or instead of, orientation of the waterline. These individuals therefore might make an incorrect choice of orientation because the volumes, in fact equal, nonetheless might appear unequal. This problem is eliminated by eliminating the standard.

"... While Being Tilted"

The pictures below show containers of water while they are being tilted at various angles. Which picture shows how the waterline would look?

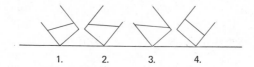

1.   2.   3.   4.

"... Several Minutes Before"

The pictures below show containers of water which, several minutes before, were tilted at various angles. Which picture shows how the waterline would look?

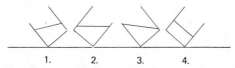

1.   2.   3.   4.

F IGURE 5.   *Examples of questions asked in Experiment 3.*

Subjects   The subjects were a new group of 221 college undergraduates; 45 men and 65 women had test booklets with the "several minutes before" instructions, and 48 men and 63 women had the "while being tilted" instructions.

Results   The results (Figure 6) seemed to have had no effects. In the "while being tilted" and "several minutes before" condition, the men's average scores were 14.1 correct (88%) and 13.4 (84%), respectively, not significantly different from each other or from the combined average for the adult men of Experiments 1 and 2 (all t's < 1.0). The women's average scores were 11.03 correct (69%) and 11.95 (75%), also not significantly different from each other (t < 1.0), though slightly better than the combined average of women in Experiments 1 and 2. And in both conditions, the women's scores were behind the men's—by a significant margin in the "while being tilted" condition (t = 3.88, df = 109, p < .01), and marginally so in the "several minutes before" condition (t = 1.73, df = 108; .05 < p < .10, two-tailed). We nevertheless were reluctant to give up on the idea that inferred motion was an underlying factor in the performance of the nonconservers. Perhaps the instructions should have been more explicit. We decided to try again.

EXPERIMENT 4

Procedure   This time we determined to leave no room for doubt as to whether the water was or was not in motion at the moment the subject is asked to represent its level in the container. In one condition, illustrated at the top of Figure 7, the instructions read, "The pictures ... show containers of water being tilted at various angles. Imagine that this is being done right now, and

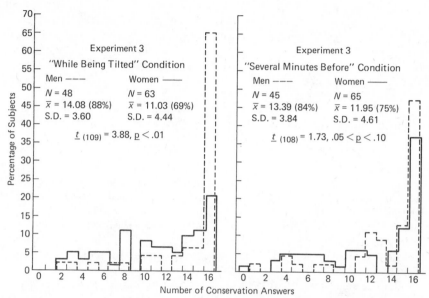

FIGURE 6. *Percentage of men and women giving specified numbers of conservation answers.*
(*Experiment 3.*)

"Water in Motion"

The pictures below show bottles of water being tilted at various angles. Imagine that this is being done right now, and that the water is still in motion. Which picture shows how the waterline will look?

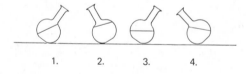

1.   2.   3.   4.

"Water at Rest"

The pictures below show bottles of water which have been tilted at various angles. Imagine that this was done several minutes ago, and that the water has come to rest. Which picture shows how the waterline will look?

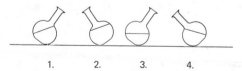

1.   2.   3.   4.

FIGURE 7. *Examples of questions asked in Experiment 4.*

that the water *is still in motion*. Which picture shows how the waterline will look?" The other instructions (bottom of Figure 7) read, "The pictures ... show containers of water which have been tilted at various angles. Imagine that this was done several minutes ago, and that the water *has come to rest*." Once again, we eliminated the standard, and this time also shortened the test from 16 to 12 questions.

Subjects   The subjects were a new group of 135 undergraduates. Fourteen men and 55 women had the test booklet with the "water at rest" instructions, and 16 men and 50 women had the "water in motion" instructions.

Results   The results are shown in Figure 8. In the "water in motion" condition—shown at the left—both the men's and women's scores were low, the men averaging 7.37 correct out of 12 (61%), the women, 5.37 (45%). The difference between them was not significant ($t = 1.76$, $df = 64$, $.05 < p < .10$). The subjects given the "water at rest" instructions—shown at the right—did better, the men averaging 9.7 correct out of 12 (81%), the women, 9.58 (80%). For the first time the women's score was clearly equal to the men's (t [difference in men's and women's scores] < 1.0).

This seemed neat: if we assume that the instructions we used in Experiments 1 and 2 ("If the container ... is tipped ...") are ambiguous as to the motion of the water, then we now see that where the water is *explicitly* stated to be in motion, men do poorly (about as poorly as women do ordinarily—in

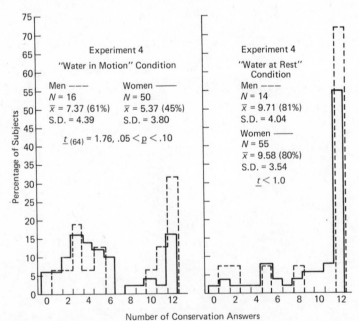

F I G U R E 8.   *Percentage of men and women giving specified numbers of conservation answers.*
(*Experiment 4.*)

Experiments 1 and 2—with "ambiguous" instructions; and women do poorly too, but no *worse* than they do with ambiguous instructions. And in the "water at rest" condition, men do well, but no better than they do with ambiguous instructions; and women do *better* than they do with ambiguous instructions.

These results suggest a possibly important role for inferred motion on the horizontality task and suggest that the usual male lead stems from men's normally interpreting the task as though the water were still; while women are more likely to think of the water as moving. Unfortunately, it proved to be not quite so neat as this. Again it was a remark by one of the subjects that cued us. This woman was puzzled: "I understand why," she said, "when the water is at rest, it will be level with the tabletop. But as long as the water is in motion, it would have to be tilted." The experimenter allowed how this could be true only if the container was tilted abruptly and quickly, but would stay level if the glass was tilted more slowly and smoothly. In that case, the subject declared, the water would remain level only because the water was *not* in motion.

In fact, of course, she was wrong. When a container of water is tilted, the water moves relative to the container, and the container moves relative to the water, and this is true however quickly or slowly the container is tilted, and however little or much the water "sloshes" around inside. But the subject's error is understandable. It is the container that is actively tilted by some*one*, and so from the subject's point of view—or at least from *some* subjects' point of view—it is the container, and not the water in it, that moves. The psychologically more appropriate way to put the question therefore would have been to emphasize the motion or lack of motion of the *container* rather than the water inside. We therefore did a fifth experiment incorporating this change in instructions.

EXPERIMENT 5

Procedure   In one condition—top of Figure 9—the instructions read, "The pictures . . . show containers of water being tilted at various angles. Imagine that this is being done right now, and that the containers *are still in motion* . . . ." The other instructions—bottom of Figure 9—read, "The pictures . . . show containers of water which have been tilted at various angles. Imagine that this was done several minutes ago, and that the containers are *no longer in motion*. Which picture shows how the water in the container will look?"

Subjects   The subjects were a new group of 220 undergraduates, with 58 men and 52 women assigned to each instruction condition.

Results   The results are shown in Figure 10. The "container in motion" instructions—shown at the left—had nearly the same effect as the "water in motion" instructions in Experiment 4. Both the men's and women's scores again were low, the men averaging only 7.29 correct (61%), again as low as *women* usually do; the women, 6.85 (57%), as poorly as they usually do. Once again men's and women's scores were not different from each other ($t = 1.33$, $df = 101$, $p < .05$).

So for both men and women, and to nearly equal degrees, saying that the *container* is in motion works *against* horizontality conservation. This finding

"Container in Motion"

The pictures below show sprinkling cans of water being tilted
at various angles. Imagine that this is being done right now,
and that the sprinkling cans <u>are still in motion.</u> Which picture
shows how the water in the sprinkling can will look?

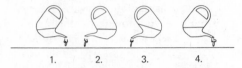

1.   2.   3.   4.

"Container at Rest" (No Longer in Motion)

The pictures below show sprinkling cans of water which have
been tilted at various angles. Imagine that this was done
several minutes ago, and that the sprinkling cans are
<u>no longer in motion.</u> Which picture shows how the water in
the sprinkling can will look?

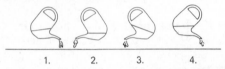

1.   2.   3.   4.

FIGURE 9.   *Examples of questions asked in Experiment 5.*

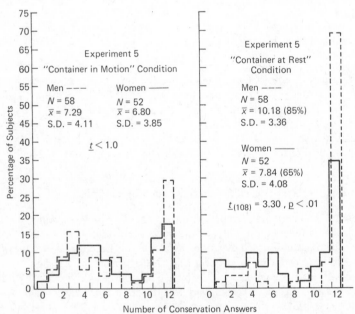

FIGURE 10.   *Percentage of men and women giving specified numbers of conservation answers.*
(*Experiment 5.*)

bolsters our surmise in Experiment 4 that inferred motion is important, and that men typically excel because they conceptualize the water as still, while women see it as moving. Why men and women should be so differently inclined —if indeed they are—we do not know.

This conclusion, however reasonable it may seem, is thrown into doubt when we consider the effects of the "container at rest" instructions—shown at the right. In the "*water at rest*" condition in Experiment 4, both the men and women had done well, the men averaging 81% correct, the women, 80% correct. In the "container at rest" condition in Experiment 5, the men, as expected, again did well, averaging 10.18 correct (85%), with 76% of the subjects getting at least 11 of 12 correct, and only 9% getting as few as 0–3 correct. But the women, as a group, did not do so well. Only 45% got 11 or 12 correct, and 21% got as few as 0–3 correct. As a group, the women averaged only 7.84 (65%), significantly less than the men ($t = 3.30$, $df = 108$, $p < .01$), and also significantly less than the 9.58 (80%) score by the women in the "water at rest" condition of Experiment 4 ($t = 2.35$, $df = 105$, $p < .01$).

Apparently, the "container at rest" instructions are functionally equivalent to the "water at rest" instructions for men but not for women. Describing the *container* requires the subject to *infer* something about the appearance of the water *inside* the container. And women, it seems, are less able, or less likely, than men to make the correct inference. Thus if it is the case that women and girls, more than men and boys, tend to interpret the situation as dynamic—as involving motion—this cannot wholly explain their poorer performance.

Nor can a tendency to infer motion explain certain exceptions to the general findings: combining the "in motion" conditions of Experiments 4 and 5, 29% of the women and 45% of the men gave 10–12 conservation answers. And combining the two "at rest" conditions, 14% of the women and 10% of the men gave as few as 0–3 conservation answers. That is, more than a quarter of the women and nearly half the men *conserved* horizontality even with instructions designed, for the large part successfully, to discourage it; while a small proportion of men and women alike failed in the task even with instructions designed, again for the large part successfully, to make the correct answer obvious.

Perhaps we are thinking about the horizontality task in quite the wrong way. What really seems to puzzle many cognitive developmental psychologists about it is that they conceive of the principle that water seeks its own level, that horizontality is invariant, as strictly a milestone in *logical*, *analytical* thinking like the principles assessed in tests of abstract reasoning. On these other tasks, adults, for the most part, perform at their expected level of competence, and women are just as good as men, and sometimes better.

But note how Piaget and Inhelder (1956) themselves speak of the water level test, in discussing children's performance:

> Now although it is doubtful whether failure to predict horizontality at this age is by itself proof of inability to conceive of a coordinate system—since it could be due to lack of interest, inattention, and so on—the repeated difficulty in appreciating the material facts themselves carries an entirely different implication. It undoubtedly indicates an inability to evaluate the perceptual data in terms of the orientation of lines and planes, and thereby suggests a failure on the part of

coordination as such. What indeed is a system of coordinates but a series of comparisons between objects in different positions and orientations (p. 390)?

This description sounds not so much like a description of a task involving *logical* principles but of visuo-spatial skills—e.g., perceiving and comparing spatial patterns; turning or rotating an object in 3-space and recognizing a new appearance or position after the prescribed manipulation. In high school seniors, just a bit younger than the college undergraduates we tested, performance on a test of horizontality is correlated significantly with performance on standard tests of spatial visualization (Spatial Subtest or Differential Aptitude Test; Liben, unpublished report), and it is well-established that in this *very particular* skill, males do better than females. The horizontality test, therefore, may well be *primarily* a test of visuo-spatial ability. Like any spatial test, it can be made harder, so that more people fail, or simpler, so that more people do well, though females, on average, still find it more difficult than males do.

The difficulty that many adults and older children have on this task, in particular the greater difficulty experienced by females, therefore might better be examined within the context of current theories about visuo-spatial ability, among them the view that the male's visuo-spatial superiority reflects greater right-hemisphere specialization for visuo-spatial processing (e.g., Knox and Kimura, 1970; McGlone and Kertesz, 1973), and the hypothesis, supported in several studies (e.g., Bock, 1973; Bock and Kolakowski, 1973; Corah, 1965; Hartlage, 1970; Stafford, 1961) that visuo-spatial ability is a sex-linked recessive-gene characteristic (see Harris, 1975, for review).

References

BOCK, R. D. Word and image: sources of the verbal and spatial factors in mental test scores. *Psychometrika*, 1973, 38, 437–457.

BOCK, R. D. and KOLAKOWSKI, D. Further evidence of sex-linked major-gene influence on human spatial visualizing ability. *American Journal of Human Genetics*, 1973, 25, 1–14.

CORAH, N. L. Differentiation in children and their parents. *Journal of Personality*, 1965, 33, 300–308.

HARRIS, L. J. Sex differences in spatial ability: possible environmental, genetic, and neurological factors. To appear in M. Kinsbourne, Ed., *Hemispheric asymmetries of function*. Cambridge: Cambridge University Press (expected publication, 1975).

HARTLAGE, L. C. Sex-linked inheritance of spatial ability. *Perceptual and Motor Skills*, 1970, 31, 610.

KNOX, C. and KIMURA, D. Cerebral processing of non-verbal sounds in boys and girls. *Neuropsychologia*, 1970, 8, 227–238.

LIBEN, L. S. Operative understanding of horizontality and its relation to long-term memory. Paper presented at *Biennial Meetings of the Society for Research in Child Development*. Philadelphia, Pa., 1973.

LIBEN, L. S. Individual differences and performance on Piagetian spatial tasks. Unpublished report (mimeo., 28 pages, undated).

McGLONE, J. and KERTESZ, A. Sex differences in cerebral processing of visuo-spatial tasks. *Cortex*, 1973, 9, 313–320.

MORRIS, B. B. Effects of angle, sex, and cue on adults' perception of the horizontal. *Perceptual and Motor Skills*, 1971, 32, 827–830.

PIAGET, J. and INHELDER, B. *The child's conception of space*. New York: Humanities Press, 1956 (paperback edition: New York: W. W. Norton & Company, Inc., 1967).

REBELSKY, F. Adults' perception of the horizontal. *Perceptual and Motor Skills*, 1964, **19**, 371–374.

STAFFORD, R. E. Sex differences in spatial visualization as evidence of sex-linked inheritance. *Perceptual and Motor Skills*, 1961, **13**, 428.

THOMAS, H. and JAMISON, W. On the acquisition of understanding that still water is horizontal. *Merrill-Palmer Quarterly of Behavior and Development*, 1975, **21**, 31–44.

THOMAS, H., JAMISON, W., and HUMMEL, D. D. Observation is insufficient for discovering that the surface of still water is invariantly horizontal. *Science*, 1973, **181**, 173–174.

WILLEMSEN, E. and REYNOLDS, B. Sex differences in adults' judgments of the horizontal. *Developmental Psychology*, 1973, **8**, 309.

15

Parents, Peers, and the Quest for Identity

The sense of identity is an integrating concept in the study of adolescent personality development. Identity is approached from many different perspectives. Physiological development produces changes that a person must integrate into the self-concept. Cognitive transformations equip the individual to think in more complex ways about the self and its relation to the world, the past, present, and future. Emotional experiences add another dimension. Two of the articles in this chapter place the adolescent in a broad context. The third deals with limited aspects of teenage and parent behavior.

The excerpt from Erik H. Erikson's book is very concentrated in meaning, although short in length, summarizing his ideas on the development of the sense of identity in adolescence. We hope that this small piece from Erikson will stimulate students to read his books. Erikson is a model for human developmentalists in relating the individual to his bodily and intellectual growth, to his personal history, and to his society and its place in history.

In analyzing support systems, or where adolescent boys go for help, Benjamin H. Gottlieb also gives much information about the social structure of a high school. He describes variety and meaning in peer relationships, illustrating them vividly with direct quotations. Gottlieb, like Erikson, takes a broad viewpoint of the ways in which adolescents interact with many different representatives of the social environment.

Jack O. Balswick and Clitos Macrides consider adolescent rebellion, as interpreted by adolescents themselves, in relation to the parents' marriage and disciplinary practices with children. Erikson's article offers a framework in which to view the relevance of both rebellion and parental behavior to the whole of the development of adolescent personality. Balswick and Macrides focus on a small area of the whole scene, as must be done in order to understand these particular relationships. However, the reader should not exaggerate the importance of what parents do, even though it is shown to relate to one aspect of adolescent behavior.

Excerpt from "'Identity Crisis' in Autobiographic Perspective"

Erik H. Erikson

To say, then, that the identity crisis is psycho *and* social means that:

1. It is a subjective sense as well as an observable quality of personal sameness and continuity, paired with some belief in the sameness and continuity of some shared world image. As a quality of unself-conscious living, this can be gloriously obvious in a young person who has found himself as he has found his communality. In him, we see emerge a unique unification of what is irreversibly given—that is, body type and temperament, giftedness and vulnerability, infantile models and acquired ideals—with the open choices provided in available roles, occupational possibilities, values offered, mentors met, friendships made, and first sexual encounters.

2. It is a state of being and becoming that can have a highly conscious (and indeed, self-conscious) quality and yet remain, in its motivational aspects, quite unconscious and beset with the dynamics of conflict. This, in turn, can lead to contradictory mental states, such as a sense of aggravated vulnerability and yet also an expectation of grand individual promise.

3. It is characteristic of a *developmental period*, before which it cannot come to a head, because the somatic, cognitive, and social preconditions are only then given; and beyond which it must not be unduly delayed, because the next and all future developments depend on it. This stage of life is, of course, *adolescence and youth.* The advent and solution of the identity crisis thus partially depends on *psychological* factors, which secure the somatic basis for a coherent sense of vital selfhood. On the other hand, *psychosocial* factors can prolong the crisis (painfully, but not necessarily unduly) where a person's idiosyncratic gifts demand a prolonged search for a corresponding ideological and occupational setting, or where historical change forces a postponement of adult commitment.

4. It is dependent on the *past* for the resource of strong identifications made in childhood, while it relies on new models encountered in youth, and depends for its conclusion on workable roles offered in young adulthood. In fact, each subsequent stage of adulthood must contribute to its preservation and renewal.

The "socio" part of identity, then, must be accounted for in that communality within which an individual finds himself. No ego is an island to itself. Throughout life the establishment and maintenance of that strength which can reconcile discontinuities and ambiguities depends on the support of parental as well as communal models. For youth depends on the ideological coherence of the world it is meant to take over, and therefore is sensitively aware of whether the system is strong enough in its traditional form to "confirm" and to be confirmed by the identity process, or so rigid or brittle as to suggest renovation,

From *Life History and the Historical Moment,* Copyright © 1975 by Rikan Enterprises Ltd. Pp. 18–22. Reprinted by permission.

reformation, or revolution. Psychosocial identity, then, also has a *psycho-historical* side, and suggests the study of how life histories are inextricably interwoven with history. The study of psychosocial identity, therefore, depends on three complementarities—or are they three aspects of one complementarity? —namely, the personal coherence of the individual and role integration in his group; his guiding images and the ideologies of his time; his life history—and the historical moment.

All this sounds probable enough and, especially when shorn of its unconscious dimension, appears to be widely, and sometimes faddishly, acceptable in our day. The unconscious complexities often ignored can be grouped thus:

1. Identity formation normatively has its dark and negative side, which throughout life can remain an unruly part of the total identity. Every person and every group harbors a *negative identity* as the sum of all those identifications and identity fragments which the individual had to submerge in himself as undesirable or irreconcilable or which his group has taught him to perceive as the mark of fatal "difference" in sex role or race, in class or religion. In the event of aggravated crises, an individual (or, indeed, a group) may despair of the ability to contain these negative elements in a positive identity. A specific rage can be aroused wherever identity development thus loses the promise of an assured wholeness: an as yet uncommitted delinquent, if denied any chance of communal integration, may become a "confirmed" criminal. In periods of collective crisis, such potential rage is shared by many and is easily exploited by psychopathic leaders, who become the models of a sudden surrender to total doctrines and dogmas in which the negative identity appears to be the desirable and the dominant one: thus the Nazis fanatically cultivated what the victorious West as well as the more refined Germans had come to decry as "typically German." The rage aroused by threatened identity loss can explode in the arbitrary violence of mobs, or it can—less consciously— serve the efficient destructiveness of the machinery of oppression and war.

2. In some young people, in some classes, at some periods in history, the personal identity crisis will be noiseless and contained within the rituals of passage marking a second birth; while in other people, classes, and periods, the crisis will be clearly marked off as a critical period intensified by collective strife or epidemic tension. Thus, the nature of the identity conflict often depends on the latent panic or, indeed, the intrinsic promise pervading a historical period. Some periods in history become identity vacua caused by the three basic forms of human apprehension: *fears* aroused by new facts, such as discoveries and inventions (including weapons), which radically expand and change the whole world image; *anxieties* aroused by symbolic dangers vaguely perceived as a consequence of the decay of existing ideologies; and, in the wake of disintegrating faith, the *dread* of an existential abyss devoid of spiritual meaning. But then, again, a historical period may (as, for example, the American Revolution did) present a singular chance for a collective renewal which opens up unlimited identities for those who, by a combination of unruliness, giftedness, and competence, represent a new leadership, a new elite, and new types rising to dominance in a new people.

If there *is* something to all this, why would insights concerning such universal matters first come from psychoanalysis, a clinical science? The fact is that in all periods of history, mental disturbances of epidemiological significance or special fascination highlight a specific aspect of man's nature in conflict with "the times" and are met with by innovative insights: as happened to hysteria in Freud's early days. In our time, a state of *identity confusion*, not abnormal in itself, often seems to be accompanied by all the neurotic or near psychotic symptoms to which a young person is prone on the basis of constitution, early fate, and malignant circumstance. In fact, young individuals are subject to a more malignant disturbance than might have manifested itself during other stages of life, precisely because the adolescent process can induce the individual semi-deliberately to give in to some of his most regressed or repressed tendencies in order, as it were, to test rock bottom and to recover some of his as yet undeveloped childhood strengths. This, however, is safe only where a relatively stable society provides collective experiences of a ceremonial character, or where revolutionary leaders (such as Luther) provide new identity guidelines which permit the adolescent individual to take chances with himself. Historical crises, in turn, aggravate personal crises; and, indeed, many young people have in the recent past been judged to suffer from a chronic malignant disturbance, where we now know that an aggravated developmental crisis was dominant. This, then, is the clinical anchorage for the conception of an identity crisis.

The Contribution of Natural Support Systems to Primary Prevention Among Four Social Subgroups of Adolescent Males

Benjamin H. Gottlieb
UNIVERSITY OF GUELPH

In a recent chapter of the *Annual Review of Psychology*, "Social and Community Interventions," Cowen (1) presents an overview of the fields of community mental health and community psychology. While acknowledging that this title is "little more than a polymorphous, perverse locus designator," he nevertheless identifies a preventive orientation in mental health programming as its critical hallmark, based on his readings of the theoretical underpinnings of these community approaches. Following his review of specific avenues toward implementing a preventive model, however, he voices two strong reservations about the field: a lack of programming efforts in *primary* prevention and a deficit of empirical research.

This paper describes one pathway toward establishing an empirical research base in primary prevention with a population of adolescents. It centers upon an examination of natural support systems in the community which aid

From *Adolescence*, 1975, **10**, 207–220. Reprinted by permission of Libra Publishers, Inc.

the coping efforts of adolescents. The natural support system is composed of two categories of informal helping agents: community gatekeepers or caretakers such as family physicians, employers, clergymen, teachers, counselors and school administrators. These persons' normal work roles in the community bring them into contact with large segments of the population and they are therefore in strategic frontline positions to aid the coping efforts of people who are experiencing problems in living. The second category of informal helpers are primary group members including kin and kith. Research on the contribution of natural support systems to primary prevention integrate three theoretical propositions underlying the community mental health movement: an orientation toward practice which aims to promote health, not to remediate illness; a programmatic orientation toward serving the needs of groups or populations-at-risk, not individuals and a commitment to utilizing all the mental health resources within any locality, not only the professional clinical services. Interlacing these propositions, this study assesses how the coping efforts of a population of adolescents are strengthened by the helping relationships they form with a range of informal community resources.

Two considerations prompted the specific choice of high school seniors as a critical population for the study of informal helping relationships. First, a number of important decisions and problems are compacted within the last year of high school and are fequently accompanied by emotional and role strains within the family and peer group contexts. This period of heightened stress thus offers an excellent opportunity for documenting the helping transactions which occur. Second, the use of adolescent subjects presents an opportunity to determine whether contrasting social subgroups within a given population prefer and value different qualities in the helping agents whom they engage for the management of problems.

Elsewhere (4), the author has presented a detailed account of the procedure used to reliably identify peer social subgroups within the Senior class of high school adolescents. Essentially, this procedure called for 20 peer raters who independently classified a random half of their classmates into social subgroups, and provided descriptions of the bases of their classification. That report also presented an analysis of the quantitative data gathered about the major current concerns of each of the four identified social subgroups and their contrasting preferences for informal help sources.[1] This paper begins with a summary of these latter findings and sketches a profile of the social characteristics of each subgroup of youth. The major focus of this paper, however, is on qualitative data which illuminates the bases of group preferences for different informal help sources. Specifically, the qualitative data are the recurrent themes expressed by the members of each social subculture in describing the qualities of helping relationships which they prize most highly. These emergent themes provide a sensitive record, from the adolescents' interior perspectives, of the helping experiences which have an impact on their lives.

PROFILES OF THE FOUR SUBGROUPS

The first three group sketches below are derived from the common perceptions of the fourteen reliable peer raters. These were the raters who inde-

[1] Copies of this report, including analysis details of the procedure used to identify social subgroups and their members, are available on request from the author, Dr. Gottlieb.

pendently generated these group classifications and were in agreement about their memberships. The membership of the fourth group was also generated by the peer rating procedure, but since this group's classification rested on its members' anonymity to the raters, the group's descriptive profile is based solely on self-report data drawn from its members' family background and social activities questionnaires. Thus the final sample of 20 adolescents interviewed in this study was composed of the five youths in each subgroup who received the highest interrater agreement scores. No single label can faithfully describe each group. For ease of reference, however, assignments have been made on the basis of the raters' consensus about the outstanding typing characteristic of the group as a whole.

Elites   Members of this group are highly visible, competitive, and successful in both academic and extra-curricular school programs, especially in varsity athletics, the major prerequisite for entry into this high status social subgroup. Raters perceived the group as cliquish, populated by talented, but conceited individuals. In the words of one rater: "They stick together; they've got their own clique; in the hall you know them right away; the in-crowd. They're all very good at something. Everybody knows it; they know it too." Members of this group are described as moderate users of both alcohol and marijuana.

Isolates   Members of this social subgroup are involved exclusively in the school's academic program. Raters describe members as lacking self-confidence and as deficient in those social skills demanded by extra-curricular group participation. The major typing characteristic of the group is its members' isolation from the overall peer social structure of the class. A typical rater comment was: "They have no true friends; they keep to themselves; they just don't know how to relate." Isolates are "straights" who abstain both from drug and liquor use.

Deviants   These youths are involved neither in the academic nor in the extra-curricular programs of the high school. The hallmark of the group is its members' tendencies to engage in certain excesses of behavior which are perceived as inappropriate within the school setting and directly linked to members' high use of soft drugs. This low status social subgroup included only a small number of students who neither constitute a cohesive group nor maintain ties to the overall peer social structure. One rater noted: "They have their own group, but it's not that big; they don't have too much to do with other people; they tend to go to more extremes than others; they come to school high."

Outsiders   A more limited sketch of the anonymous social subgroup is drawn from members' self-reports of family background, involvement in social and extra-school activities and future plans following high school. First, three of the five group members do not participate in any school or community-based social clubs or teams. In comparison to the three other social subgroups, the group contains the largest number of youths who plan to work full time during the coming year while they attend the local junior college. Four of the five group members are employed and have been working 35-hour weeks for the past ten months. Two of the members have already left home and the majority report that their best friends are located at their places of employment. Taken together, these findings help to account for the apparent anonymity of these youths within the high school and the complementary salience of extra school settings in their lives. The commonalities between this group and the others include similar middle class status on socio-economic indicators (Father's and Mother's Educations, Father's Occupation), similar family sizes and similar lengths of school and community tenure.

MAJOR PROBLEMS AND PREFERRED HELP SOURCES

Intensive private interviews were conducted with the 20 youths, five from each of the four social subgroups. Each youth was requested to review a list of twelve everyday problems, whose relevance to the youths' lives was suggested by pretest interviews with adolescent informants and underscored by the litera-ture on the tasks of adolescent development including the instrumental (goal achievement), expressive (relationship), and integrative (values and identity) domains. After reviewing the list, the youth was asked to rate his relative current concern about each problem. The interview then focused on the three problems rated of greatest relative concern, inquiring in particular about the help sources the youth had involved in his attempts to cope with these problems. A summary follows of the differences among the major life concerns of the four subgroups and their contrasting preferences for informal helping agents.

Elites   Three problems are of greater concern to Elites than to any other group: their current school performance, their plans following graduation and their fears about disappointing their parents. The first concern is congruent with raters' characterizations of group members as high achievement competitors, and the second complements the self-reported intentions of four of the five group members to attend college outside the local area on a full-time basis. Clearly, the two concerns mesh since Senior grades have an important bearing on college admission. Members' third major concern about disappointing parents is also tied to the former concerns since these youths' parents are highly invested in their son's successes. These parents not only passively com-municate their high expectations, but represent the single most active helping agents engaged by Elites.

School-based adult personnel rank second, and account for 37% of all mentions of help sources used by the Elites for current problems. This figure is twice as large as any other group's percentage use of school-based sources and is inflated by the Elite's access to and engagement of a team coach who appears to serve in an exclusive and comprehensive helping role to members. Teachers and counselors are also engaged by members, but represent second and third preference, respectively, as helping agents in the school. These findings appear consistent with raters' description of Elites as highly visible and successful in the athletic and academic programs of the high school.

The third outstanding finding is that peers account for only 7% of all mentions of help sources used by Elites, while peers represent at least 30% of the mentions for each of the other subgroups in the study. This is particularly striking in view of members' reputed participation in a cohesive peer group and their shared team memberships. This finding is best accounted for in the following section which reveals that peers do not possess qualities which Elites value in a helping relationship.

Isolates   Problems within the expressive task domain are of great concern to Isolates and reflect members' social isolation. Specifically, they are more worried than are members of other groups about their relations with peers, family members and girls, and deviate most sharply from other group scores in their high concern about "What classmates think of me." A single problem in the instrumental task domain is of greatest concern of all, however: "Managing my time better." In members' detailed accounts of this problem, they express an inability to initiate or complete daily responsibilities, such as school assignments, finding employment and submitting applications to college. For instance, one youth summarized his feelings about the problems of tasks left undone:

> I should be getting out but I don't have the drive. Not motivated I guess. I want to move too, you know. It kinda motivates me a little bit to see them [peers] going . . . I want to go too. It might motivate me for a while. I do care but I just haven't got on it.

These examples, combined with our knowledge of members' social isolation, yield a group portrait of unmotivated, passive individuals.

Isolates' passivity, however, does not extend to their help seeking behavior. Theirs is the most inclusive pattern of choices, revealing an almost even distribution of relationships with all helping agents, including parents, kin, peers, counselors, teachers, employers, and clergymen. Only peers are favored slightly more than others. Thus Isolates' passivity is complemented by a coping style which communicates their dependency on any other persons in the natural environment who can either stimulate them to action or simply provide interpersonal contact and feedback. One of the Isolates' remarks about his inability to complete school assignments illustrates this point:

> Every time I've tried, I get going good for a couple of weeks and then, Bang!, I'm right back where I started from. It goes on and off. When somebody like you talks to me . . . a counselor, my parents or somebody . . . then it sort of motivates me.

It is likely that this bond of passivity and dependence contributes to their peers' rejection of them, and so perpetuates members' social isolation.

Deviants   The portrait composed from the raters' comments about the Deviant subgroup highlighted members' reputed heavy drug use and their tendency to engage in unconventional, even bizarre behavior in school. Within the group, these perceptions are mirrored in two integrative problems which members experience most intensely, relative to the other groups: they feel a need to achieve a greater measure of understanding of themselves and their "hang-ups," and they express concern about their drug involvements. The two problems are interdependent since members feel that their use of drugs may be retarding or compromising their own personal development. One youth expressed this relationship as follows:

> The main reason I started drugs was because at the time, people were telling me that drugs create peace, love, harmony and great insight. You can find your problems. Well, it took me a long time to find out that it wasn't, so I'm just starting back where I was.

Their desire to gain a deeper insight into themselves is, in part, an expression of their felt need to alter those aspects of their behavior which feed peers' stereotype of them as "dopers."

Primary group members, including parents, siblings, and peers, constitute 70% of the mentions of helping sources engaged by Deviants for their problems. No single other category is prominent among the remaining help sources mentioned. In the category of school-based personnel, a single work-study program teacher is mentioned three times and is described by members as unconventional because he reaches out to help both within and outside school.

Outsiders   Relative to the other groups, Outsiders express greatest concern about two problems which reflect their marginal status in their families and their preoccupation with problems of economic self-maintenance in the community: "Getting a job to have enough money" and "Worry about family members." Since two of the members have already left home, one is paying rent at home and all are more highly employed than members of the other groups, decreased contact with home naturally prompts a greater concern about family welfare. Their intense involvement with matters which pertain to supporting themselves in the community also helps to explain their relative anonymity to peers at school and their low relative concern about school performance.

Of all groups, the Outsiders reveal the strongest preference for peer helping sources, who account for 57% of all mentions. The peers who are cited, however, are encountered outside the school setting. The unique relational qualities which characterize these helping transactions are discussed in the following section. Parents rank second in preference as helping resources, receiving 30% of all mentions. Mere contact with parents constitutes help since it reassures members of family well-being.

VALUED QUALITIES OF THE HELPING RELATIONSHIPS

Follow-up interviews were conducted with two members of each of the social subgroups for the purpose of gaining greater insight into the qualities differentiating more from less preferred helping agents. The two youths were selected on the basis of the fit between the pattern of preferences for helping agents which they reported in the first interview and the pattern of preferences which emerged for their group as a whole. It was felt that individuals who approximated their group preference pattern most closely would be in the best position to serve as spokesmen in communicating the bases of these preferences. Thus, each youth was given a "feedback card," which displayed, in categories of high, moderate, and low, the total subgroups' profile of preferences for helping agents. Only those themes appearing in both youths' descriptions of the valued qualities of the most preferred helping agents are presented below.

Elites Elites prefer helping relationships with expert sources of help who recognize and reinforce their high social status. Particularly, they value helpers whose past experience can be drawn upon in those areas of instrumental tasks which are of greatest concern: their current school performance and future career plans. They do not mention process variables in their accounts— the opportunity to share their feelings and reflect upon their own psychological selves—but instead stress the importance of outcome decisions and problem resolutions which expert sources of advice can provide. Members also prefer helping agents who acknowledge, or even call attention to their "significant" status in the school, which separates them from the mass of students. The coach is one prototype of the ideal help source. He combines authoritative advice in specific task areas with the exclusivity of attention the Elites desire. In the words of one youth:

> My coach has done everything for me—got a job for me, given me advice during football and stuff like that; helped me extra. You can always count on him to give you some pretty good advice. He'll give you both sides but he'll tell you what he thinks is best for you. He knows me, too. I mean that's a different thing. He's seen me in action, I guess.

Parents as help sources, however, are most highly valued and most frequently engaged since they combine expert knowledge with the greatest investment of all persons in their sons' special academic and athletic status.

Teachers and counselors, sources of help potentially available to all students, do not meet members' needs for special attention which reinforces their status. One youth dismissed teachers and counselors because ". . . they've got too many kids to worry about, and the don't really get to know me."

Peer sources of help are strongly rejected, since contemporaries experience precisely the same problems, can therefore not impart expertise and perhaps could harm the youth by offering misleading advice. One youth summed up his opinion of friends as helpers:

> Sometimes they let other things influence them, stuff like that. I'd just rather go to somebody who knows a little bit more about the situation . . . gone through that time and can look back and give you the best advice.

And, according to the second youth:

> Maybe I don't trust them as much. I don't know if I'd want to listen to them as much. Someone your own age—they're not experienced as much.

The matter of trust among peers is especially salient for the Elites since a facade of "machismo" may be required among athletes, inhibiting the disclosure of personal emotional problems which both signify weakness and endanger in-group status.

Isolates The Isolates do not identify any specific valued qualities among the helpers they prefer, nor do they engage others for outcomes. What they deem most important in a helping relationship are feelings of ease in the partner's company and a sense of security that the partner values their company. Those rare social transactions which contain an element of mutuality are highly prized since Isolates do not participate in cooperative group activities at school. The theme of reciprocity is expressed in one youth's account of an important helping relationship with a peer: "Frank and I exchange ideas and feelings about a lot of problems. I feel more at ease with him than I do with my parents."

Isolates welcome occasions to convene with a peer: such meetings offer a pleasurable break from isolation, as well as an opportunity for realistic social comparison. Peers provide more solid feedback about how members are perceived, while members themselves compare their feelings and responses to events with those of their peers. In the words of one Isolate:

> Mostly from talking to them [peers] I get to understand my problems. Sometimes I don't exactly understand what's going on and by talking to my friends I sort of like analyze myself. It's kinda a funny way of doing it, but it works a lot.

Isolates report that interpersonal problems with girls and parents—problems which members rate of high concern—are the main subjects of these dyadic exchanges.

A second theme drawn from the Isolates' reports of helping relationships is that of "appropriateness." They firmly believe that the problem should be suited to the helper's formal role specialization. Thus, all community-based and school-based adult gatekeepers are deemed inappropriate for addressing personal emotional problems, although they are used for their specialized functions. For example, in reference to his employer, one youth remarked:

> I would be inclined to take some problems to him, but not all. I think that I would trust him to some extent—it would be more like the Principal—I would tend to take more of a work problem to him instead of a personal problem.

In response to a question about approaching counselors and teachers for help with personal problems, the second youth interviewed responded:

> With them it goes back to what I said about the boss and family doctor. They're for school-related problems only. It's their role, and I think that's their place.

Deviants   The Deviants value helping relationships which permit the expression of mutual authenticity. Regardless of the helper's formal role, members engage for help persons who allow the stereotype of the "Doper" to recede, and who take a genuine interest in and appreciate the member's personal identity. The following remarks of one member not only reveal the link between his drug use and his desire to renegotiate his public and private identity, but also suggest that only intimates, not "people in general," are acceptable helping agents:

> I have a hard time being myself around *people in general*, 'cause like, I play a part, and as time progresses, you get tired of the part you're playing, and you try to change, and people act as if they expect you to be your old self . . . the drug-crazed hippy, which I played pretty good.

Congruent with their high concern about obtaining a deeper understanding of themselves is the fact that Deviants prize helping relationships with persons who accept their expression of more idiosyncratic and private feelings. Primary group helpers—close peers and parents—are thus the preferred helping sources. As one youth explained:

> Well, the people who know me really well are really close . . . the others are people you try to put up a front for . . . like a teacher . . . to get a better grade; your kin . . . to make your parents look good; your family doctor . . . just be healthy; a boss . . . you're always kind, precise, and polite around him. These people make me be more an outgoing person, like friendly. But it's kinda like a front.

Neither requirements of helper's formal expertise, experience, status or age are prerequisite to the helping relationships preferred by Deviants. Nor do the formal roles of school- and community-based adult gatekeepers prevent their engagement as personal helpers if they are open and sincere. As an example, one member described the qualities which he feels make the school biology teacher an approachable helping resource:

> I think that I would probably talk to him about anything, [even though] everybody thinks that he's a nut. He's an honest guy . . . he's open about stuff . . . if he feels one way or the other about things he just tells you—he doesn't try to hide anything or put on a show or cover up about anything.

Outsiders   The following description of several friends in the community captures the qualities which the Outsiders value most highly in their preference for helping relationships with peers:

> When I'm around them, I don't feel apprehensive, just relaxed. They make me feel comfortable. We're pretty good friends and none of us would want to do anything to hurt the other person. We've all had hassles with our parents and stuff like that—some a little worse than others.

Outsider's preference for helpers who share their life style and values is partially based upon the fear that others, both peers and adults, who live more conventional lives will use the helping relationship as an opportunity to make negative judgments or to prescribe solutions to problems which demand that Outsiders conform to age-graded norms. Thus, in supplying reasons why teachers and counselors were least preferred sources of help, one Outsider maintained:

> Oh, it just doesn't seem that there would be that much they could do for me . . . the most they could do is tell you to cut it out and that kind of stuff. So, if that's what they're going to say, why bother?

Peers who are on their own and working in the community, however, hold values which are generated from life experiences compatible with members', and are therefore naturally most relevant as helpers. One member described the basis of his willingness to confide in his roommate as follows:

> He's lived and had everything that you shouldn't have had . . . you know, and he's come out of it pretty decent. Any time we want to share a problem I feel open towards him . . . more open than towards other people.

Far from attaching any stigma to the Outsider, friends who have prematurely opted out of traditional home life also provide a substitute for family support and personal warmth. Nevertheless, Outsiders remain ambivalent about preserving their emotional ties to parents since, on the one hand, they express the highest relative concern of all groups about family welfare, yet on the other hand, they must safeguard their own independence from the family.

DISCUSSION

Before offering any firm recommendations for future program design in primary prevention with adolescents, this study or a variant should be replicated on a larger scale and with a strictly representative population of adolescents. Similarly, a group-based case study such as this cannot yield conclusive statements regarding the theoretical properties of informal support systems engaged by adolescents. The purpose of this study has been to generate, not test, hypotheses.

One outstanding pattern in the results which begs for future probing is the fit of each social subgroup's major life problems and preferred qualities of help sources with the group's observed social characteristics. Each group occupies a unique ecological niche within the overall peer social structure of the class. Members' original assignment to these niches and their subsequent tenure is, in part, a function of the labelling process — practiced by school-based peers and adults. Certain values, attitudes, needs, and pressures are unique to each group niche and members experience common emotional and interpersonal stresses. Similarly, each group expresses distinctive preferences for resources in the environment. Some categories of persons are less attractive as helpers because of their cultural distance from members and the accompanying censure they reflect, while others are attractive because of the coincidence of values and the esteem and cultural acceptance they offer. Thus, the cultural environment of each social subgroup mediates both the particular stresses which members experience and their access to and preferences for different helping agents. This hypothesis appears to support the social ecology model of research and theory which examines the reciprocal and dynamic interplay of person and setting variables on the behaviors of persons occupying a given ecological niche. Thus, this hypothesis represents a specific example of the general proposition which asserts the importance of the ecological niche in the organization of behavior:

> . . . the understanding of behavior requires systematic study of the characteristics of the environmental pattern defining the ecologic niche of each species and the adaptations required by that environment as well as of response processes (5, p. 48).

Several issues arise in considering the implications of this study for programmatic efforts in primary prevention. First, the study reveals the existence of a natural support system which aids the coping efforts of adolescents in the community. To the degree that these informal helpers are available during the early stages of problem recognition and crystallization, and are accepted as naturally relevant during the problem-solving process, they function as a first line of defense against potential loss of social and emotional equilibrium. As such, their early intervention makes a contribution toward secondary prevention. More important for primary prevention, however, is the fact that repeated occasions of collaborative management of stress generate independent problem-solving skills and the social competence necessary for successful coping with future developmental and situational stressors. There is no implication here that the individual will become autonomous, functioning apart from his personal support community. Rather, we suggest with Erikson (2, 3) that the successful resolution of developmental crises throughout life instills enhanced ego functioning and increased openness to alternative sources of support available in the environment.

Practically, the findings of this study suggest that mental health professionals must re-examine their assumption that community gatekeepers are in need of further education through consultation in mental health helping skills. In fact, helping professionals may risk injury to the process of natural support by replacing intuition and compassion with technique and objectivity. Instead, this study suggests that a close collaboration between professional and lay helper is desirable on account of the benefits which the professional would receive. These benefits would accrue both from more extensive diagnostic consultation with laymen who have been involved in the early pre-referral stages of problem-solving with adolescents, and from directly involving the subculturally appropriate informal helpers in the process of strengthening a fragile or incomplete support system in the adolescent's natural environment.

References

1. COWEN, E. "Social and Community Interventions," *Annual Review of Psychology*, 1973, 24, 423–472.
2. ERIKSON, E. H. *Childhood and Society*. New York: Norton, 1950.
3. ERIKSON, E. H. "Identity and the Life Cycle," *Psychol Issues*, 1959, 1, No. 1.
4. GOTTLIEB, B. H. "Natural Support Systems: An Analysis of Preferred Helping Relationships Among Four Social Subgroups of Adolescent Males," Unpublished Manuscript, 1974.
5. SELLS, S. B. "Ecology and the Science of Psychology," in R. H. Moos and P. M. Insel (Eds.), *Issues in Social Ecology*. Palo Alto, California: National Press Books, 1974, pp. 45–64.

Parental Stimulus for Adolescent Rebellion *

Jack O. Balswick and Clitos Macrides
UNIVERSITY OF GEORGIA AND LANITION GYMNASIUM (CYPRUS)

Abstract
Utilizing the responses of 417 college students to questionnaires, self-defined adolescent rebellion is correlated with perceived parental marital happiness, restrictive-permissiveness of child rearing practices, and division of authority.

From *Adolescence*, 1975, **10**, 253–266. Reprinted by permission of Libra Publishers, Inc.

* We wish to acknowledge our thankfulness to Daniel Hobbs for his most helpful critical reading of the paper.

Adolescent rebellion is found to be the product of a home thought to be patriarchal and unhappy, patriarchal and very restrictive, and patriarchal and very permissive. Whether parents are restrictive or permissive is not as important as the extent of their restrictiveness or permissiveness. A very restrictive home leads to frustration and then to aggression, while a very permissive home leads to frustration, in not knowing what the parental expectations are, which then leads to aggression, in search of norms. Frustration-aggression theory is used to explain how parental stimulus can produce frustration in an adolescent child which can result in the child's aggression.

INTRODUCTION

Research on adolescent rebellion has focused attention on cultural conditions at large. Most of the literature has followed the trend initiated by such pioneer social scientists as Margaret Mead and, later, Kingsley Davis. Mead (1928) was perhaps the first to demonstrate that adolescence *per se* is not necessarily a time of stress and strain, but cultural conditions may make it so. Davis (1940) identified certain "universals" in the parent-child relation (e.g., the age differential between parents and child) which tended to produce conflict. He suggested that cultural variables (e.g., the rate of social change) will determine whether or not the universals produce conflict.

The present paper deviates from the above explanations and suggests that certain structural components *from within* the family may be contributing factors to adolescent rebellion. Although youth in American society may be exposed to the cultural variables discussed above, the nature of the actual parent-child relationship may vary greatly, producing little or no conflict or rebellion.

Although this is an exploratory study, and it is designed more as an attempt toward hypothesis-forming than hypothesis-testing, it is motivated by research which has been conducted within the frustration-aggression hypothesis. A recent summary of the research conducted on the frustration-aggression hypothesis can be seen in Zigler and Child's chapter on "Socialization" in *The Handbook of Social Psychology* (1969). Radke (1946), based on a number of early studies, concluded that parental behavior is a key variable in explaining frustration of the child which results in aggression. Sears (1953) found that frustration itself depends upon such factors as the child's perception of other's behavior, and Berkowitz (1964, 1965) found that the type of frustration-produced-aggression that will occur depends to a large extent upon the kind of stimuli present. Using these studies as a starting point, the parents (or the child's perception of parental behavior) become the stimuli in producing his frustration-aggression level. One of the dynamics of family interaction especially present when the child is a teenager, is parentally induced frustration which leads to the adolescent's aggression. The possibility of heightened frustration-aggression interaction during the parental-adolescent period suggests the fruitfulness of examining the relationship between adolescent rebellion and certain perceived parental conditions. The specific questions with which this study was concerned included the correlation between the extent of a youth self-defined rebellion and 1) perceived parental marital happiness; 2) the restrictiveness or permissiveness of perceived child rearing practices; and 3) perceived division of authority between parents. Another concern was with the possible inter-relationship between each of these variables and the differences which may exist between males and females in regard to each of the above.

METHODOLOGY

This study is based upon the responses to mailed questionnaires of an entire student body of 720 undergraduate students attending a small mid-western liberal arts college. The actual data are drawn from the 417 (59%) returned questionnaires. The characteristics of the sample include an average age of 20 years, 43% male, 57% female, and 95% white and 5% black. The liberal arts college is a church related school which might be considered theo-logically conservative although not predominantly fundamentalistic.

Four scales, consisting of forced category responses to four questions, were used to measure the four major variables. Adolescent rebellion was measured by the following scale: Some teenagers seem to go through a period of stress and strain or rebellion toward parents and other authorities. During this period would you say that you were: Extremely rebellious; Very rebellious; Slightly rebellious; Not rebellious at all. Perceived parental marital happiness was measured by the following scale: Taking all things together; how would you describe your parent's marriage? Very unhappy; Not too happy; Just about average; A little happier than average; Extremely happy.

Perceived parental restrictive/permissive child rearing practice was meas-ured by the following scale: In regard to bringing you up, would you de-scribe your parents' child rearing as: Very restrictive; Slightly restrictive; Just about average; Slightly permissive; Very permissive. Perceived division of authority between parents was measured by the following scale: Taking all things together, how would you describe the division of authority between your mother and your father: Would you say your: Mother had much more authority than your father; Mother had slightly more authority than your father; Mother and father had equal authority; Father had slightly more authority than your mother; Father had much more authority than your mother.

In the initial analysis of the data all of the separate categories within each variable were maintained in cross-tabulating the variables. In collapsing the categories care was taken not to obscure any nonlinear relationships. In con-sidering the relationship between each of the three independent variables and rebellion, the remaining two variables were held constant.

FINDINGS

In the sample as a whole, 14% of the males and 21% of the females replied that they did not go through a period of rebellion, 65% of the males and 56% of the females replied that they had experienced slight rebellion and 21% of the males and 23% of the females replied that they were very rebellious or extremely rebellious.

PARENTAL HAPPINESS AND REBELLION   Table 1 shows that youths who see their parents' marriage as unhappy rather than happy, are more likely to rebel. This relationship holds when sex, rearing practices, and parental

TABLE 1

*Parental Happiness and Rebellion**

PARENTAL HAPPINESS**	TOTAL SAMPLE		SEX				REARING PRACTICES						AUTHORITY†			
			Male		Female		Very Restrictive or Very Permissive		Slightly Restrictive or Slightly Permissive		Average		Non-Patriarchal		Patriarchal	
	%	N	%	N	%	N	%	N	%	N	%	N	%	N	%	N
Unhappy	29	(137)	29	(55)	30	(81)	49	(33)	23	(69)	22	(35)	27	(70)	31	(67)
Happy	19	(280)	18	(125)	19	(155)	23	(47)	21	(155)	10	(78)	22	(93)	17	(187)
	$\chi^2 = 6.06$		G = .32		G = .27		G = .51		G = .05		G = .44		G = .15		G = .38	
	P < .01															

* In this and all following tables, the number in each cell represents the percentages who are rebellious and the number in parenthesis represents the N upon which the percentage is based. "Rebellious" includes the categories "extremely rebellious" and "very rebellious" of the Rebellion Scale. χ^2 is the symbol for Chi Square and G is the symbol for Gamma. As a rule of thumb, two Gammas which differ by at least .20 will be discussed as significantly different. For a discussion of the use of Gamma as the choice for a measurement of Association see Costner (1965).

** In this and all following tables "Happy" includes the categories "a little happier than average," and "extremely happy," while "unhappy" includes "just about average," "not too happy," and "very unhappy."

† In this and all following table, Non-Patriarchal includes the categories "mother much more than father" and "mother slightly more than father" and "mother and father had equal authority," while Patriarchal includes "father much more than mother," and "father slightly more than mother."

authority are held constant. However, there is the tendency for rebellion to be associated with the combined conditions of unhappy parental marriage and very restrictive or very permissive rearing practices, and for low rebellion to be associated with the combined conditions of a happy marriage and average restrictive/permissiveness in rearing practices. There is also the tendency for parental happiness and rebellion to be more strongly related where the home is patriarchal.

PARENTAL CHILD REARING PRACTICES AND REBELLION   The child rearing scale measures child rearing on a continuum from very restrictive to very permissive. Table 2 shows that when the five points on this continuum are related to rebellion, the resulting relationship is bimodal rather than linear. Although rebellion is higher where parents are perceived as being very permissive or slightly permissive rather than very restrictive or slightly resrictive, rebellion is higher the more the child rearing practice is in either the permissive or restrictive direction. The data were reorganized into a new ordinal scheme with the three categories of very permissive or restrictive, slightly permissive or restrictive, and about average in restrictive/permissiveness. The logic behind and justification for using the data in this way will be elaborated on in the discussion section.

Table 3 shows that there is a positive relationship between the extremes in child rearing practices and rebellion. Thirty-four percent of those who defined their parents' child rearing as very restrictive or permissive are rebellious, 22% of those who define their parents as slightly restrictive or permissive are rebellious, while only 14% of those who define their parent child rearing as average are rebellious. The relationship continues to hold when sex, parental happiness and parental authority are used as control variables. Females (42%) are more likely to rebel under very restrictive or permissive child rearing practices than are males (23%). Parental authority seems to have a specifying effect upon the positive relationship between extremes in child rearing practices and rebellion; the relationship declines among those who perceive their home as non-patriarchal and is intensified among those who perceive their home as patriarchal.

PARENTAL AUTHORITY AND REBELLION   The relationship between parental authority and rebellion is not linear (See Figure 1). The highest

TABLE 2
Parental Child Rearing Practices for All Five Child Rearing Categories

	PERCENTAGE REBELLION IN TOTAL SAMPLE	
	%	N
Very Restrictive	29	(60)
Slightly Restrictive	19	(142)
About Average	14	(113)
Slightly Permissive	24	(82)
Very Permissive	45	(20)

TABLE 3

Parental Child Rearing Practices and Rebellion

	Total Sample %	N	Sex Male %	N	Female %	N	Parental Happiness Unhappy %	N	Happy %	N	Parental Authority Non-Patriarchal %	N	Patriarchal %	N
Very Restrictive or Permissive	34	(80)	23	(31)	42	(48)	49	(33)	23	(47)	30	(30)	36	(50)
Slightly Restrictive or Permissive	22	(224)	24	(103)	20	(121)	23	(69)	21	(155)	25	(88)	20	(136)
Average	14	(113)	13	(46)	15	(67)	22	(35)	10	(78)	18	(45)	12	(68)
	$\chi^2 = 10.47$ $P < .005$		$G = .20$		$G = .40$		$G = .35$		$G = .29$		$G = .20$		$G = .40$	

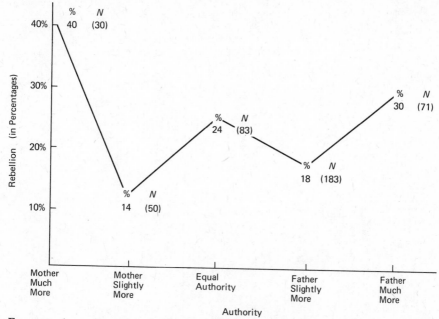

F I G U R E 1.   *Parental authority and rebellion: All five authority categories. (This table is presented in graph form so as to illustrate the tri-modal curve in this relationship.)*

amount of rebellion occurs in homes where either the mother or the father is perceived as having much more authority than the other, with a considerably higher percentage where it is the mother who has greater authority. The lowest amount of rebellion occurs in homes where either the mother or the father is seen as having only slightly more authority than the other. An equalitarian marriage relationship tends to be related to a moderate amount of rebellion.

The lack of linear relationship between parental authority and rebellion makes it almost impossible to collapse the authority categories in further analyzing the relationship. Therefore, a choice was made to collapse the categories into traditional patterns of parental authority (patriarchal) and non-traditional patterns (non-patriarchal).

Table 4 demonstrates that parental authority, based upon the patriarchal-non-patriarchal distinction, is not related to rebellion. However, an examination of how the control variables affect this relationship is of interest. In regard to child rearing practices, the relationship between parental authority and rebellion is highest among those who see their parents as moderate in rearing practices, declines among those with slightly restrictive or permissive parents, and becomes a negative relationship among those who feel they have very restrictive or permissive parents. Parental happiness has a similar effect upon the relationship between parental authority and rebellion: Among unhappy parents it is a negative relationship and among happy parents it is a positive relationship. The greatest amount of youth rebellion occurs where the marriage

TABLE 4
Parental Authority and Rebellion: Non-Patriarchal/Patriarchal

| | Total Sample | | Sex | | | Rearing Practices | | | | | | Parental Happiness | | | |
| | | | Males | | Females | | Very Restrictive or Permissive | | Slightly Restrictive or Permissive | | Average | | Unhappy | | Happy | |
	%	N	%	N	%	N	%	N	%	N	%	N	%	N	%	N
Non-Patriarchal	24	(163)	25	(59)	23	(103)	30	(30)	25	(88)	18	(45)	27	(70)	22	(93)
Patriarchal	21	(254)	19	(121)	23	(133)	36	(50)	20	(136)	12	(68)	31	(67)	17	(187)
	χ^2 = .53 NS		G = .19		G = .02		G = −.14		G = .15		G = .24		G = −.10		G = .14	

relationship is patriarchal and unhappy, while the least amount of rebellion occurs where the marriage relationship is patriarchal and happy.

DISCUSSION

PARENTAL HAPPINESS The evidence presented in this paper suggests that parental variables may help to explain youth rebellion. The finding that rebellion is higher in unhappy homes than in happy homes is not surprising, as unhappy homes have been found to be related to juvenile delinquency (Glueck and Glueck, 1950; Monahan, 1957) and mental illness (Nye, 1957). Parental unhappiness may produce frustrations in the youth, resulting in aggression expressed in the form of rebelling. Where parents are perceived as being unhappy in their marital relationship the child is likely to discount them as a desirable source of authority and may even see this as an opportunity to "conquer the divided." A child may find it much easier to justify a defiant attitude toward parents who have not shown themselves to be models of contentment, than he would if his parents were getting along well. Unhappiness undoubtedly involves a certain amount of verbal and/or physical aggression on the part of the parents, thus providing aggression models to the child who comes to be aggressive also. Applicable here would be Bandura and Walters' (1963) modeling theory of aggression, where aggressiveness on the part of the child is seen as an imitation of the aggressiveness on the part of his parents. In the unhappy home the child may find aggression models in the parents and come to aggress also if he observes parental aggression. Also, children of unhappy parents may participate in strong rebellion as a way of expressing their distinctiveness from their unhappy parents.

CHILD REARING PRACTICES The traditional argument between the restrictive and the permissive school of child rearing may be an over-simplified one. The question is not whether parents are restrictive or permissive, but rather concerns the extent of their restrictiveness or permissiveness. Extremes in either of the two directions tend to be associated with high rebellion. The dynamics of the parent-child relationship can be described as the process of the child moving through time from a state of rather complete dependence upon his parents, to a state of relative independence from his parents. The change from a dependent to an independent relationship may be smoother when parents are moderate in their disciplinary practices. The overly restrictive parent holds the reins too tight upon his children, and does not allow for a gradual development of independence. This tight hold on children creates a situation where independence can come about only by the child initiating a drastic break with his parents. High parental restrictiveness leads to frustration in the child. The frustrated child then becomes aggressive toward his parents and sometimes toward society in general; this aggressiveness is then interpreted as rebellion.

The extremely permissive home may produce a state of confusion for the child, within which the parents are so permissive that the child does not perceive any clearly defined rules for behavior. The extremely permissive parent not only allows the child to make his own decisions, but he may also fail to set the limits for the child's behavior. Dr. Spock has emphasized that he had been greatly misinterpreted by modern parents. Whereas he has argued for greater permissiveness in the sense that a child should be free to begin making his own decisions, he feels that he has been falsely interpreted as proposing that parents not set any limits upon their children. When parents don't clearly state what the rules and limits are, the child has only the option to behave in increasingly extreme ways in an attempt to discover the parental limitations. The brand of permissiveness which may be exemplified by permissive American parents may include a great deal of ambiguity about just how the child is expected to behave. This ambiguity produces behavior which is defined as rebellion, but which in fact may be considered behavior in search of norms.

An alternative interpretation of the relationship between high permissiveness and high rebellion may be that the child of permissive parents interprets this permissiveness as a lack of interest in him. Parents are seen as permissive because they just don't care what the child does. Having reached such a conclusion, the child then rebels as a way of receiving attention from his neglecting parents.

PARENTAL AUTHORITY   The relationship between the division of parental authority and adolescent rebellion is both interesting and confusing. A trimodal relationship develops where rebellion is high at the extremes (where either the father or mother has much authority), low where either parent has moderate authority, and high in an equalitarian home (See Figure 1). Tentatively, it may be suggested that extreme inequality in parental authority may result in a state of confusion for the child as to the nature of the disciplinarian role of the subordinate parent. When authority is perceived as being primarily in the hands of one parent, the child may have problems interacting with both parents as authority figures. Rebellion may then be the best solution to this confused situation. Much authority on the part of one parent may also mean much domination over the child. Such domination, regardless of the tyrant, is still frustrating to the child and may result in aggressiveness. Thus the frustration-aggression hypothesis may also be applied here. A different type of confusion may be experienced in the equalitarian home, where the problem for the child is one of not being able to identify with whom the ultimate authority resides. The situation where least rebellion will occur will then be in the home where one of the parents clearly has a little more authority over the other, but the authority is not so complete as to usurp the authoritative role of the other or to put the other down. Parental authority may be best where one of the parents has enough more authority than the other as to be a "tie breaker" in the decision making process, but who can break the tie in a non-authoritarian way.

Both the extreme highs and extreme lows in adolescent rebellion seem to be produced in a patriarchal home. The two combinations of a patriarchal and unhappy home and patriarchal and very restrictive or permissive home both produce a high rate of rebellion. The lowest amount of rebellion is produced when the home is patriarchal and happy and patriarchal and average in permissiveness. When the home is matriarchal and very restrictive or permissive, rebellion is less than it is when it is patriarchal. When a child aggresses toward his father, it may be tolerated, but when he aggresses toward his mother it will not be tolerated. Children are taught not to aggress toward females in general, and especially not toward *mother* in particular. The child may be in a bind when his mother is in control of the home, for although she may act very restrictively or permissively and thus produce frustration in the child, the child must be gentle toward her.

CONCLUSION

The frustration-aggression hypothesis may be relevant in both very restrictive and very permissive situations. A very restrictive home leads to frustration and then to aggression and to further frustration, etc. A very permissive home leads to frustration, in not knowing what the parental expectations are, which then leads to aggression—in search of norms. But where there are no checks on the aggression, there is then an increased amount of aggression expressed.

This study has been concerned with perceived parental conditions which may contribute to adolescent rebellion. Further research is needed which is based upon more exacting measurements of the major variables. With this suggestion it may be helpful to offer the following tentative hypotheses in conclusion:

1. The lower the parental marital happiness, the greater will be the adolescent rebellion.

2. The greater the parental restrictiveness or permissiveness, the greater will be the adolescent rebellion.

3. The less the parental marital happiness and the greater the father's authority, the greater will be the adolescent rebellion.

4. The greater the parental restrictiveness or permissiveness and the greater the father's authority, the greater will be the adolescent rebellion.

5. The greater the parental marital happiness and the greater the father's authority, the less will be the adolescent rebellion.

6. The less the parental restrictiveness or permissiveness and the greater the father's authority, the less will be the adolescent rebellion.

It could be argued that the hypotheses do not have a clear cut theoretical tie to the frustration-aggression hypothesis. Some researchers may, in fact, wish to use the above hypotheses as part of an alternative theoretical framework in explaining adolescent rebellion. It is hoped that this paper will serve as a challenge to researchers to further explore the possible effects of familial variables upon the phenomena of adolescent rebellion.

References

BANDURA, A. and R. H. WALTERS. *Social Learning and Personality Development*. New York: Holt, Rinehart, and Winston, 1963.

BERKOWITZ, L. "Aggressive Cures in Aggressive Behavior and Hostility Catharsis," *Psychological Review*, 71, 104–122, 1964.

"The Concept of Aggressive Drive: Some Additional Considerations," *Advances in Experimental Social Psychology*, edited by L. Berkowitz. Vol. 2. New York: Academic Press, 301–329, 1965.

COSTNER, H. L. "Criteria for Measures of Association," *American Sociological Review*, 30, 341–353, 1965.

DAVIS, K. "The Sociology of Parent-Youth Conflict," *American Sociological Review*, 2, 523–535, 1940.

GLUECK, S. and E. GLUECK. *Unraveling Juvenile Delinquency*. Cambridge, Mass.: Harvard University Press, 1950.

MEAD, M. *Coming of Age in Samoa*. New York: William Morrow and Co., 1928.

MONAHAN, T. "The Trend in Broken Homes Among Delinquent Children," *Marriage and Family Living*, 362–365, 1957.

NYE, F. I. "Child Adjustment in Broken and in Unhappy Homes," *Marriage and Family Living*, 356–361, 1957.

RADKE, M. "Relation of Parental Authority to Children's Behavior and Attitudes," *University of Minnesota Institute of Child Welfare Monograph*, No. 22, 1946.

SEARS, R. and J. WHITING, V. NOWLIS, and P. SEARS. "Some Childrearing Antecedents of Aggression and Dependency in Young Children," *Genetic Psychology Monograph*, 47, 135–236, 1953.

ZIGLER, E. and I. CHILD. "Socialization," *The Handbook of Social Psychology*, Vol. 3. 450–589, 1969.

16

Growth in Self-Direction

This chapter is concerned with the adolescent's control of his own life. Significant topics include moral thought and behavior, beliefs about source of power and influence, planning, and the ability to influence society as well as oneself.

Recent literature on moral development abounds in cognitive interpretations, or how and what children think about moral questions. Another line of inquiry yields information on altruistic behavior, the motivations behind this behavior, and the circumstances under which children share or help. In his article, "Legal Socialization," Robert Hogan pulls together many different threads of thought. He provides an account of moral development that integrates cognitive and motivational sources of morality, and acknowledges the historical sources of his ideas. Furthermore, Hogan draws upon the new ethological views of human beings as having inherited potential for cooperative social behavior that has survival value for the group.

Following a comprehensive study on United States high school students, Amos Handel investigated the relationships of certain attitudes, beliefs, and aspirations to cognitive functioning in Israeli students. Locus of control, self-concept, and educational aspiration were found to be more predictive of achievement and intelligence than were socioeconomic, home, and parental education measures. This study and the United States studies suggest that the particular salience of each measure may vary with the ethnic or socioeconomic group studied.

Legal Socialization

Robert Hogan

THE JOHNS HOPKINS UNIVERSITY

By human goodness is meant not fineness of physique, but a right condition of the psyche. That being so, it is evident that the statesman ought to have some inkling of psychology.

Aristotle, *The Nichomachean Ethics*

Reprinted by permission of the publisher, from *Psychology and the Law* by Battelle Memorial Institute (Lexington, Mass.: Lexington Books, D.C. Heath and Company, 1976).

I. AN OVERVIEW OF LEGAL SOCIALIZATION

As the foregoing quotation suggests, Aristotle thought there was a natural relationship between law and psychology. The two disciplines are most clearly joined in what psychologists call the socialization process. The *Oxford English Dictionary* defines the verb "to socialize" as "to render social, to make fit for living in society." As used by social psychologists, socialization refers to those events that cause people to develop their particular (and usually favorable) orientations to the rules, values, and customs of their society. Legal socialization, then, is concerned with the development of people's attitudes and behaviors with regard to a particular set of social rules, the manifest law.

Since the mid-1950's social psychologists have become increasingly interested in legal socialization. Their writing on this topic can be divided into two broad classes depending on whether it is concerned with content or process. The content literature describes children's attitudes toward the law at various age levels. Adelson, Green, and O'Neil (1969), Gallatin and Adelson (1971), Hess and Torney (1968), and Tapp and Kohlberg (1971) have made important contributions to this topic. It is a rather extensive literature, difficult to summarize briefly, but Adelson et al.'s findings convey the flavor, i.e., over time children are increasingly able to think in terms of legal principles, to see law in a relativistic, pragmatic, utilitarian way as an instrument for achieving social ends.

There are two principle process theories of legal socialization. The first, outlined by Hess and Torney originally in the context of political socialization, assumes four different processes underlying the manner in which children orient themselves to the legal system:

(a) The Accumulation model describes legal socialization as a process wherein children steadily acquire over time units of knowledge about the law; the Accumulation model explains the contribution of the school system to legal socialization.

(b) The Interpersonal Transfer model holds that a child transfers to authority figures (policemen, judges, etc.) attitudes and behavior developed *vis à vis* its parents; this model is used to explain the emotional loading of a child's relationship to authority.

(c) The Identification model describes legal socialization in terms of a child directly imitating adult attitudes toward some aspect of the law rather than transferring their attitudes from an earlier object; this model would explain such phenomena as a child's attitude toward capital punishment.

(d) The Cognitive-Developmental model maintains that a child's conception of the law is modified by its stage of intellectual development; this model is primarily useful for explaining how a child develops complex and abstract legal ideas such as distributive justice and natural rights.

The second process theory of legal socialization, described in detail by Tapp and Levine (1974) and Tapp and Kohlberg (1971), is probably the best known view of this subject. Here legal socialization is equated with the development of legal reasoning (defined in terms of how laws are justified); this reasoning is seen as evolving through three levels. At the preconventional level, legal reasoning is grounded in physical fear of authority and deference to power. At the second or law maintenance level, laws are justified in terms of their ability to regulate society. Level three is called post-conventional; it is a "law-creating, legislative perspective" wherein laws are justified in terms of certain abstract and personally defined conceptions of justice. This second process theory is primarily concerned with the development of conscious, publicly stated attitudes toward the law; as such it is a very "rational" model: ". . . the ultimate appeal of a cognitive-developmental explanation of legal thought is its emphasis on rationality and its refusal to accept the preeminence of irrationality" (Tapp & Levine, 1974, p. 11).

These two process theories of legal socialization were imported from other (related) fields—Hess and Torney are students of political socialization, the Tapp and Kohlberg model comes from moral development—and this is no accident. Only content studies of legal socialization contain subject matter specific to the field. Process theories necessarily belong to the study of socialization broadly defined, and they take *legal* socialization as a special case.

The process models discussed above are important contributions to the study of legal socialization and they have stimulated some very useful research. At the same time, however, they tend to foster a serious misconception—i.e., that a child's consciousness of rules is important in itself, that its actual behavior with regard to these rules is irrelevant or at least not very important. Process research consists almost exclusively of inquiring about children's conscious attitudes toward the law, or of asking them to comment on hypothetical legal dilemmas and situations. But this resarch repeatedly demonstrates that even fairly young children distinguish between what they think they should do or say in a situation, and what they actually would do or say (cf. Zellman and Sears, 1971, p. 119). That children can do this points up the importance of Ichheiser's (1970) distinction between "views in principle" and "views in fact." As Ichheiser notes, views in principle are those we have about social and legal issues in general, and they have no serious implications for our actions; they reveal only how we think we would or should act in certain hypothetical situations. In contrast with our views in principle, our views in fact actually determine our actions. The problem is that most people don't know what their views in fact actually are, and when asked, they typically state their views in principle. The point is that to the degree that legal socialization research studies only children's theoretical legal judgments, it is sampling their views in principle and is studying the social psychological equivalent of phlogiston.

There is a second misconception fostered by this research. The rationalist view that motivates it—the view that people's conscious opinions and judgments are the cause (or at least a major determinant) of their actions —represents what Freud, Jung, and William James called the intellectualist fallacy (cf. McDougall, 1908; p. 323; Rawls, 1971, p. 470). The problem is that once we know a person can state a rule or legal principle, why should we assume that person will follow it? Similarly, this rationalism accounts for the fact that these models contain no reference to the moral passions, no mention of guilt, remorse, and painful moral introspection, no description of man's irrational sense of honor; they seem unconcerned with the kinds of conflicts between private belief and respect for public authority that can cause one to resign from high public office, or push one to the edge of madness and despair. We have instead tepid accounts of how children's theoretical legal attitudes change over time.

II. AN ALTERNATIVE MODEL OF LEGAL SOCIALIZATION

In a very influential analysis, Kelman (1961) identified three sets of reasons for following a socially defined rule, three types if you will of legal socialization. The first set of reasons, labeled *compliance*, results in relatively superficial rule observance. Compliance occurs when one follows a rule with the hope of gaining a favorable reaction from certain others. Here rule observance is a function of the degree to which one is observed by the relevant others. In the second case, which Kelman calls *identification*, one follows a rule in order to preserve a social relationship that is personally rewarding, a relationship that enhances one's feelings of self-esteem. If a person finds a particular relationship satisfying he will tend to act in accordance with the expectations of the others with whom he is involved, and these expectations coincidentally will reflect the norms and rules of the group. Identification is similar to compliance in that the rules aren't seen as intrinsically worthwhile; it differs from compliance in that the person actually believes in the norms and rules that he adopts. Moreover, the person will follow these rules in private as long as the role relationship remains satisfying.

Kelman's third type of rule compliance is called *internalization*. It occurs when a law is seen as congruent with a person's own value system. In such cases the law is assimilated effortlessly to a person's character structure and it is thereafter followed and defended in an unambivalent, almost unconscious manner. Kelman emphasizes that internalization is not necessarily or even primarily a rational process. Laws are internalized essentially without regard for their logical consistency with one's existing values, and they are subsequently observed whether or not one is being watched and regardless of the wishes of one's friends and associates.

Only when laws have been internalized in Kelman's sense can legal socialization be considered complete. The next question is, What social experiences and development processes produce an internalized orientation to the law?

In the remainder of this paper I will describe a model of legal socialization that focuses on the processes underlying internalization of the law. Like the Tapp and Kohlberg theory described earlier, this model was initially derived from the study of moral development. Before moving into the details of the model itself, I should describe the assumptions on which it is based—the model assumes that beyond his survival requirements man needs social interaction, predictability and order, and that his cultural and legal systems reflect these needs.

Three separate lines of research support these assumptions. For example, recent work in anthropology suggests that for the major portion of his time on earth man lived in small hunting groups and seemed largely concerned with killing game and members of competing groups as efficiently as possible. Individual survival depended on the quality of the group rather than the talent of particular members; efficient social organization (defined in terms of laws, language, leadership structure, etc.) rather than brain size promoted man's survival and ultimately his evolutionary success. This line of reasoning suggests, then, that man has a deep organic need for his culture, and that legal systems are not arbitrary accretions of history continually threatened with obsolescence. Rather, part of what it means to be human is to have a system of law.

A second line of research, ably summarized by Bowlby (1969), suggests that children (and people in general) require social interaction with preferred others on a predictable basis. Conversely, they fear unpredictability and isolation. (In man's evolutionary past he was most vulnerable when alone and in a strange environment.) People seem happiest in the company of familiar companions in a predictable environment; infants in particular become severely disturbed—in some cases even die—when these requirements aren't met.

A third line of research, conducted by my colleagues at Johns Hopkins, points to the conclusion that children need social interaction (probably from birth), and they rapidly develop (i.e., by age $3\frac{1}{2}$) a considerable range of conventional, rule-governed means for carrying out this interaction. Moreover, the rules that structure their interaction often become so important that many small children stop playing rather than allow the rules to be broken—e.g., when playing with girls many little boys will quit rather than be "Mommy."

Restating the main point, three lines of research suggest that man needs social interaction on a predictable and orderly basis, and that his cultural and legal systems reflect these needs. In brief, we have the image of man as a rule-formulating and rule-following animal, and these rule-oriented tendencies reflect human biology and promote human survival. With this image in mind we can now turn to a discussion of how internalized attitudes toward the law develop.

Starting from an initial unsocialized state, internalized compliance with legal and social rules seems to pass through three forms or levels; the attainment of each level is precipitated by changes in a child's life circumstances. The first is characterized by *attunement to rules*; the second is marked by *sensitivity to social expectations and concern for the well-being of others*; the third is defined by *ideological maturity*. As a graduate student I came to these three levels from a consideration of what counts as an adequate explanation of social conduct. I have subsequently discovered that at least three distinguished writers have proposed the same stages, although arriving at them from very different perspectives. Emile Durkheim (1961) described a person's integration into his social groups as passing through three stages. The first is defined by a sense of loyalty and duty to the rules of the group; the second is achieved by adopting impersonal, group-defined goals for one's actions; the third is reached by a conscious and rational understanding of the group's purposes. William McDougall (1908) described moral development in terms of three stages. In the first, one's conduct is regulated by fear of punishment; in the second, conduct is governed by social praise and blame; and in the third, one's conduct and sense of self-worth depend on the maintenance of certain abstract moral principles.

Rawls (1971) elaborates his discussion of a theory of justice by describing moral development in terms of three stages that he calls the ethics of authority, the ethics of association, and the ethics of principle. The parallels between Rawls' views and those presented below are obvious and extensive.

A. ATTUNEMENT TO RULES

Among the many problems confronting a very young child, two stand out—procuring care and attention from adult caretakers, and making sense out of the social world that surrounds it. For the social scientist a key problem is to explain why the initially amoral infant would allow itself to be guided by adult rules. This is a puzzle because, as Rawls (1971) notes, "The child's having a morality of authority [being attuned to rules] consists in his being disposed without the prospect of reward and punishment to follow certain precepts that not only may appear to him largely arbitrary but which in no way appeal to his original inclinations" (p. 466). This distinguishing feature of the first level of internalization has nothing to do with the rules *per se*, i.e., the child doesn't internalize a set of rules much as it would eat a box of cookies. Rather, the critical transformation concerns the accommodation that a child makes to adult authority. If a child sees its parents as benevolent and trustworthy sources of support and guidance, it will be disposed to accept their rules and commands regardless of their content. If the parents are not so viewed, a child will tend to regard authority with suspicion and even resentment—it will be resistant to rules regardless of their content.

The specific chemistry of the parent–child interaction that engenders attunement to rules is not well understood. Nonetheless, two points about this early transformation are apparent. First, Waddington (1967) points out that the survival of culture necessarily requires the role of authority accepter; children would be unable to learn language (or the safe foods to eat, or danger signs) unless they were willing to accept the arbitrary pairing of certain random sounds with various meanings. And there is in principle no difference between language learning and the acquisition of any other rule system or aspect of culture. Second, there is evidence to suggest that within the first twelve months of life, maternal warmth and sensitivity to an infant's needs are sufficient to produce compliance to maternal commands; given the "proper" parent–child atmosphere, infants seem innately disposed toward compliance (cf. Stayton, Hogan & Ainsworth, 1971). As an infant begins to creep around, however, its caretakers must increasingly restrict its behavior. Generally speaking, a child will be most attuned to rules if it is treated in a warm but restrictive fashion, if it receives love and nurturance combined with prompt and consistent disapproval for disobedience. Warm but permissive parents, on the other hand, produce self-confident children who are not attuned to rules. Cold restrictive parents tend to have children who are hostile toward authority but who publicly conform to rules. Cold permissive parents tend to produce delinquent children.

To restate the point, the first level of legal socialization (in developing internalized compliance with the law) involves attunement to rules; this entails recognizing that social situations are governed by rules, learning what they are, and adjusting to them in an effortless, unambivalent way. Moreover, by adopting parental rules (e.g., language, etc.), a child is able simultaneously to secure parental care and to begin making sense of its environment. As Rawls (1971) notes, a child will become attuned to the rules under the following conditions: "First, the parents must love the child and be worthy objects of his admiration. In this way they arouse in him a sense of his own value and the desire to become the sort of person that they are. Secondly, they must enunciate clear and intelligible (and of course justifiable) rules adapted to the child's level of comprehension. In addition they should set out the reasons for these injunctions in so far as these can be understood, and they must also follow these precepts insofar as they apply to them as well. The parents should exemplify the morality which they enjoin, and make explicit its underlying principles as time goes on (pp. 465–466)." The point, however, is that a child doesn't internalize rules *per se*, rather it becomes attuned to the existence and operation of rules so that when it enters any given situation it expects rules to apply; its job is to determine what they are.

Understanding this permits us to make sense of some otherwise rather curious findings in the legal socialization literature. For example, Torney (1971) notes that relative to lower-class and to upper-middle-class children, lower-middle class children have favorable attitudes toward the police. She explains these findings in terms of different social-class-related experiences with policemen. Her explanation requires that lower-middle-class children have generally positive experiences with the police while the experiences of lower-class and upper-middle-class children must be generally negative. But how many normal seven-year-olds have had significant contact with the police? A more parsimonious answer is that social class differences in child rearing lead to differences in attunement to rules and orientation to adult authority generally.

Finally, I might note that if a child is attuned to rules, if it loves and trusts its parents, it will tend to feel guilty when it breaks these rules. The guilt associated with this stage is a composite of fear of parental punishment and fear of parental rejection—rejection in particular is a blow to a child's self-esteem and symbolizes parental abandonment. Rawls (1971) disagrees; he observes that ". . . love and trust will give rise to feelings of guilt once the parental injunctions are disobeyed. Admittedly in the case of the child it is sometimes difficult to distinguish feelings of guilt from the fear of punishment, and especially from the dread of the loss of parental love and affection . . . I have supposed, however, that even in the child's case we can separate (authority) guilt feelings from fear and anxiety" (p. 465).

B. SENSITIVITY TO SOCIAL EXPECTATIONS

The second level of legal socialization entails developing internalized compliance with the norms, values, and principles of one's society. How does this come about? Throughout the history of mankind very young children have been faced with the problem of making an accommodation to adult authority. Typically, however, by the time a child is five it has been replaced at the center of family attention by a younger sibling. Changes within the family in conjunction with a child's naturally expanding sociability cause it to spend increasing time away from its parents, usually with its peers. Making one's way in the peer group is a major problem at this point in life, and to the degree that a child remains scrupulously loyal to parental rules and adult authority, its way will be hindered. At this point, a child must accommodate itself to a greatly altered (i.e., more general and abstract) set of rules or risk becoming a social isolate. To the degree that the children of a culture are sensibly supervised, the norms of the peer group will approximate the norms of adult society.

As Mead (1934) and Piaget (1964) pointed out so well, the major vehicle for the socialization of children at this age is games and the experience of cooperation. Through games children are exposed to a range of adult values, including most importantly the norms of reciprocity and the concept of fairness. In the first period of legal socialization children become attuned to *rules*. In the second period, however, they develop internalized compliance with adult *norms* and *values*—through peer group experience. And, as Rawls (1971) points out, the notions of reciprocity and fairness in childhood turn into the concept of justice in adulthood.

Although the preadolescent child is able to articulate many adult values and principles (cf. Adelson et al., 1969), the question remains as to how they become internalized. In very general terms, this is a function of the development of empathy (Hogan, 1973), which can be broken down into two psychological processes. The first is sensitivity to social expectations. I remember a boy in my seventh grade class who was vastly unpopular; he routinely alienated his classmates and was sublimely indifferent to their attempts to socialize him. He was one of the most obtuse and insensitive people I have ever met—and remained so into adulthood. I watched him one day in the company of his parents at a supermarket. The parents obviously worshipped the ground the boy walked on; apparently their solicitude and unqualified affection made it unnecessary for him to develop the introspection and attentiveness to social cues that leads to sensitivity to social expectations. This sensitivity in turn provide cues for regulating one's behavior.

The second process that seems to engender internalized compliance with norms and values is concern for the welfare of those people with whom one interacts—in a child's case, the extended family and the peer group. How do people come to care about the welfare of their social groups? Freud (1960) suggested that when people work together toward a common goal, ties of affection "naturally" spring up. Rawls (1971) is more specific. Sensitivity to social expectations develops as children experience reciprocity in the family, school, neighborhood, and peer group. "Thus if those engaged in a system of social cooperation regularly act with evident intention to uphold its just (or fair) rules, bonds of friendship and mutual trust tend to develop among them, thereby holding them even more securely to the scheme" (Rawls, 1971, p. 470). Thus, ". . . the evident intention to honor one's obligations and duties is seen as a form of good will, and this recognition arouses feelings of friendship and trust in return" (p. 471). These bonds of friendship and trust lead to a concern for the welfare of others and to an internalized orientation to the norms and values appropriate to this second level of legal socialization.

Once a set of norms and values has been internalized, a person will tend to feel guilty if it is violated. These feelings of guilt are perhaps rooted in fear of social disapproval; they are manifested in a willingness to make reparations, to admit blame, and to be less indignant when others violate the same norms. If this capacity for guilt is missing, then there are no genuine ties of friendship and mutual trust among the members of the group, and one's compliance with these norms and values is not internalized.

To summarize this discussion, the second level of legal socialization consists in developing an internalized orientation to the norms, values, and principles implicit in the laws of one's society. This process starts when a child leaves the exclusive care of its parents and begins to accommodate itself to the demands of its peer group, neighborhood, and school. Being required to cooperate with others, experiencing reciprocity in peer play, perceiving that certain ideals are upheld by attractive members of the group, all these factors sensitize a child to social expectations and engender a concern for the welfare of the group. This leads to what Rawls (1971) calls the ethics of association; here the ideals and norms of one's social group are seen as one's own, and one feels guilty when these norms are violated.

C. IDEOLOGICAL MATURITY

According to Jung (1934) the critical problem facing an adolescent is choosing a mate and a career. According to Erikson (1950), however, neither choice is possible unless a person has a sense of personal identity, some knowledge of who he is and what he stands for. Another way of putting this, it seems to me, is to say that a major problem for an adolescent is to make sense of the competing and often contradictory lessons learned in the family, neighborhood, and peer group. From the viewpoint of legal socialization, the problem is to explain a person's internalized compliance with the rules and principles of law when such compliance runs counter to the wishes and expectations of his parents and peer group. From the viewpoint of social theorists the problem is that a person who is attuned to rules, sensitive to social expectations, and concerned about the welfare of his social groups will be necessarily committed to the status quo. Consequently, a proper model of legal socialization must make provisions for constructive nonconformity, for prosocial deviation from established patterns of conduct.

At the first level of legal socialization one must learn to live with authority; at the second level, one must learn to live with other people; but at the third level, one must learn to live with oneself. Rawls (1971) calls this final level of internalized compliance with the law the ethics of principle. As he remarks, although a person at the second level ". . . understands the principles of justice, his motive for complying with them . . . springs largely from his ties of friendship and fellow feeling for others, and his concern for the approbation of wider society . . .. Once a morality of principle is accepted, however, moral attitudes are no longer connected solely with the well-being and approval of particular individuals and groups, but are shaped by a conception of right chosen irrespective of these contingencies" (p. 475).

We are concerned here with what in another context I called autonomy or autonomous observance of legal and social rules. The problem of autonomy has vexed social psychology for years. Part of the difficulty is methodological—e.g., it is hard to distinguish autonomous behavior from simple, immature anti-conformity (cf. Hollander and Willis, 1967). Perhaps the biggest problem, however, is conceptual and definitional. The tradition of ethical individualism exemplified by Friedrich Nietzsche, for example, defines autonomous moral behavior as conformity to internal rather than external laws; truly moral (and autonomous) conduct is guided by one's personally derived standards of right and wrong. Although this individualistic view is widely popular (e.g., Kohlberg, 1963), it is untenable for practical and psychological reasons. On the one hand, society would be impossible if citizens refused to comply with any laws but their own. On the other hand, the unpredictable and anomic society that would follow from the Nietzschean ethic violates man's need for a predictable and orderly social environment. Nietzschean autonomy, like the existentialist's notion of authentic existence, presupposes a stable social order; if everyone adopted Kohlberg's stage six post-conventional morality, there would soon be no society in terms of which they could be post-conventional.

It seems to me then that autonomous conduct has to be defined not with regard to the rules, values, and principles of a society, but with regard to other people—peers and authority. The autonomous or principled person upholds the moral and legal ideals of his society without regard for their contemporary popularity.

How does autonomous or principled rule compliance come about? The best empirical work on the subject has been conducted by Baumrind (1971). She has identified a set of child-rearing practices that characterize "authoritative" parents. Such parents provide clear guidelines for their children's behavior, explain their rules, allow for rational discussion of specific prescriptions, but adhere to the principle that there will be some rules in any event. Perhaps the truly critical feature of such parents is that they are themselves autonomous—they provide models of autonomous adult behavior, and this may be more important than any discrete pattern of child-rearing practices.

William James and William McDougall proposed definitions of autonomy similar to that presented above; i.e., that one is autonomous with regard to other people rather than social rules and principles. They explained the development of autonomous rule observance in terms of what is today known as reference group theory. That is, over time some people come to be concerned about the approval and censure of a group of judges more distinguished or elevated than their own family and friends. These judges may be historical personages, even in the case of Socrates, for example, semi-fictional characters. They no longer have a temporal existence and they embody the best traditions of one's culture or society. By being concerned with their approval rather than that of one's peers, one achieves a measure of autonomy while remaining generally in tune with the rules and precepts of one's society. McDougall was particularly clear about this; as he remarked: "The man who stands up against the prevailing public opinion . . . has found some higher court of appeal, the verdict of which he esteems more highly . . . and whose approval he desires more strongly, than that of the mass of mankind . . . . In short, he has learned to judge his conduct as it would appear to a purely ideal spectator . . . . In this way . . . a man may become, as it is said, a 'law unto himself'" (1923, pp 441–442).

There is an alternative view, however, that emphasizes the role of ideology in promoting autonomous rule compliance. As mentioned above, one of the major problems facing an adolescent is to integrate the conflicting requirements of parents, peers, school, and neighborhood. This integration is made possible through ideological maturity. Ideological maturity is a function of having organized one's experiences and aspirations in terms of a coherent philosophy, political perspective, religion, or set of family ideals. To achieve ideological maturity the adolescent needs two supporting features in the environment—adult models of autonomy, and a history, a tradition, a political philosophy, or a culturally based ideology on which he can draw. Problems will develop, of course, when the relevant adult models and cultural traditions are absent.

Erikson (1950) also emphasizes the role of ideology in adolescent identity formation, and Gallatin and Adelson (1971) provide evidence that 18 year olds are in fact inclined to formulate ideologies. As they remark: "To lend coherence to his anticipated adult life, some order to his decisions, the adolescent needs to develop what Erikson (1959) has loosely termed an 'ideology of religion' or what Inhelder and Piaget (1958) call 'a feeling for ideals'" (p. 105).

In addition to providing a structure for organizing his life, an ideology also gives an adolescent a sacred rationalization for the rules adopted from his parents, and the norms and principles learned in the peer group. The sacred or numinous quality of ideologies in part accounts for the extraordinary tenacity and independence of the views of persons at this level of legal socialization. When the rules and principles of one's culture have been organized under an ideology, they become a part of one's identity, and their violation produces the most profound psychological distress.

III. CONCLUSION

The complete argument can now be stated very quickly. For the rules, values, and principles of one's society to be fully internalized in Kelman's (1961) sense, legal socialization must pass through three levels. In the first, one internalizes *rules* by accommodating oneself to loving but controlling parents. At the second level, one internalizes *principles* by accommodating oneself to a peer community in which certain standards (e.g., fairness, cooperation) are maintained by virtue of judicious adult supervision. At the third level, one organizes these rules and principles under an ideology usually by accommodating oneself to one's cultural and ethnic history; this gives the rules and principles acquired earlier a sacred quality that makes their violation almost unimaginable.

References

ADELSON, J., GREEN, B., & O'NEIL, R. Growth of the idea of law in adolescence. *Developmental Psychology*, 1969, **4**, 327–332.

BAUMRIND, D. Current patterns of parental authority. *Developmental Psychology Monograph*, Part 2, January, 1971, pp. 1–103.

BOWLBY, J. *Attachment and loss* (Vol. I): *Attachment*. New York: Basic Books, 1969.

DURKHEIM, E. *Moral education*. New York: Free Press, 1961.

ERIKSON, E. *Childhood and society*. New York: Norton, 1950.

ERIKSON, E. Identity and the life cycle. *Psychological Issues*, 1959, **1**(1, Whole Monograph 1).

FREUD, S. *Group psychology and the analysis of the ego*. New York: Bantam, 1960.

GALLATIN, J., & ADELSON, J. Legal guarantees of individual freedom: A cross-national study of the development of political thought. *Journal of Social Issues*, 1971, **27**, 93–108.

HESS, R. D., & TORNEY, J. V. *The development of political attitudes in children*. New York: Anchor Books, 1968.

HOGAN, R. Moral conduct and moral character. *Psychological Bulletin*, 1973, **79**, 217–232.

HOLLANDER, E. P., & WILLIS, R. H. Some current issues in the psychology of conformity and nonconformity. *Psychological Bulletin*, 1967, **68**, 62–76.

ICHHEISER, G. *Appearances and reality*. San Francisco: Jossey-Bass, 1970.

INHELDER, B., & PIAGET, J. *The growth of logical thinking from childhood to adolescence*. New York: Basic Books, 1958.

JUNG, C. G. *Modern man in search of a soul*. New York: Harcourt Brace, 1934.

KELMAN, H. C. Processes of opinion change. *Public Opinion Quarterly*, 1961, **25**, 57–78.

KOHLBERG, L. The development of children's orientation towards a moral order. *Vita Humana*, 1963, **6**, 11–33.

McDOUGALL, W. *Social psychology*. London: Methuen, 1908.

McDOUGALL, W. *Outline of psychology*. New York: Scribners, 1923.

MEAD, G. H. *Mind, self, and society*. Chicago: University of Chicago Press, 1934.

PIAGET, J. *The moral judgment of the child*. New York: Free Press, 1964.

RAWLS, J. *A theory of justice*. Cambridge, Mass.: Harvard University Press, 1971.

STAYTON, D., HOGAN, R., & AINSWORTH, M. D. S. Infant obedience and maternal behavior: The origins of socialization reconsidered. *Child Development*, 1971, **32**, 1057–1069.

TAPP, J. L., & KOHLBERG, L. Developing senses of law and legal justice. *Journal of Social Issues*, 1971, **27**, 65–92.

TAPP, J. L., & LEVINE, F. J. Legal socialization: Strategies for an ethical legality. *Stanford Law Review*, 1974, **27**, 1–72.

TORNEY, J. V. Socialization of attitudes toward the legal system. *Journal of Social Issues*, 1971, **27**, 137–154.

WADDINGTON, C. H. *The ethical animal*. Chicago: University of Chicago Press, 1967.

ZELLMAN, G. L., & SEARS, D. O. Childhood origins of tolerance for dissent. *Journal of Social Issues*, 1971, **27**, 109–136.

Attitudinal Orientations and Cognitive Functioning Among Adolescents [*]

Amos Handel

UNIVERSITY OF HAIFA

The purpose of this study was to examine the pattern of relations of attitudinal orientations to cognitive functioning in a sample of Israeli seventh-grade students ($N = 950$). Following Coleman et al.'s 1966 study, attitudinal orienta-

From *Developmental Psychology*, 1975, **11**, 667–675. Copyright © 1975 by The American Psychological Association. Reprinted by permission.

[*] This research was supported by a grant from the University Research Council, University of Haifa. The author is indebted to D. Yagil, S. Shur, T. Spanglet, and S. Bar for their assistance in various phases of the investigation and to M. Lakin for his most helpful and constructive criticism of the manuscript.

tions were represented by measures of locus of control, self-concept, and educational aspirations. Multiple regression analyses showed that 18.1% to 31.6% of the total variance in four measures of cognitive functioning was associated with attitudinal orientations, while only 10.6% to 18.9% of the total variance in these measures was associated with socioeconomic background variables. In the economically least advantaged group, locus of control was the most potent attitude variable; in the complementary two groups of higher socioeconomic status, more of the variance in cognitive functioning was associated with self-concept and aspirations than with locus of control.

In their survey of equality of educational opportunity, Coleman and his co-workers (Coleman, Hobson, McPartland, Mood, Weinfeld, & York, 1966) included brief measures of three attitudinal orientations: (a) academic self-concept, (b) interest in school and educational aspirations, and (c) sense of control of the environment. These student orientations, along with sets of measures of family background and of characteristics of their schools, were examined in relation to the dependent variable of verbal achievement. One of the striking findings in the Coleman report is the indication that of all independent variables measured in the survey, attitudinal orientations showed a strong relation to verbal achievement and contributed more of its variance than did a set of eight family background and socioeconomic variables.

While Coleman et al. (1966) based this conclusion on attitudes expressed by the students themselves, other investigators arrived at similar conclusions based on measures of parents' achievement-related attitudes and of their stimulation of the child. Such measures, obtained through extensive home interviews, contributed more to variance in cognitive performance of the child than did various indices of the socioeconomic status of the family (Marjoribanks, 1972a, 1972b; Plowden, 1967; Werner, 1969; Wolf, 1966).

The growing interest in various expressions of attitudinal orientations seems to reflect a recent trend in studies of the determinants of cognitive development. This trend focuses on process variables, that is, the actual experiences of children which contribute to their cognitive growth, rather than on status variables (social class, race), which are presumed to represent only surface characteristics of the environment (Wolf, 1964, 1966). This trend has been stimulated by the anticipation that investigation of attitudinal orientations and process variables could have one of the following advantages: (a) increase the predictability of cognitive functioning above the level of predictions afforded by standard indices of socioeconomic status (SES); (b) elucidate the factors underlying the observed correlations between SES and the level of cognitive functioning (Deutsch & Katz, 1968; Jensen, 1968); or (c) indicate a class of variables that would be amenable to intervention and manipulation (Wolf, 1966; Whiteman & Deutsch, 1968). However, in spite of the consistency of social class differences in cognitive functioning across various countries (Thorndike, 1962), no attempt has yet been made to examine the cross-cultural consistency of Coleman et al.'s (1966) frequently cited finding about the prepotency of students' attitudinal orientations in relation to achievement.

Coleman et al. (1966) also found substantial differences in the relative amount of variance associated with the three attitudinal orientations within the racial and ethnic groups included in his survey. Thus, for blacks, sense of control of environment was clearly the most important attitude, associated with from two to several times as much of the variance as either of the other two attitudinal orientations. For whites (and native-born Orientals), the order of importance was different: Self-concept was more highly related to the level of verbal ability than was sense of control of environment.

The implications of these findings for the education of disadvantaged children have been widely discussed (Coleman et al., 1966; Hess, 1970; Katz, 1967, 1969; Pettigrew, 1968; Tulkin, 1972). Notwithstanding this extensive discussion, no attempt has ever been made to determine whether these findings are unique to the social structure of the United States or would be duplicated in other sociocultural settings.

The purpose of the present study was to examine the pattern of relations of attitudinal orientations to cognitive functioning in a sample of adolescents in Israel. There were two specific goals for this study: (a) to determine whether the class of attitudinal orientations is associated with more of the variance in various measures of cognitive functioning than is the class of socioeconomic background variables, as indicated by Coleman et al. (1966); and (b) to determine whether the particular patterns of relations of attitudinal orientations reported by Coleman et al. (1966) for whites and blacks obtain among the more and less advantaged students in Israel.

METHOD

Most of the measures used by Coleman et al. (1966) were adopted with only slight modifications, In addition, the following modifications were made in the design of the present study in order to extend the scope of its relevance and increase its potential significance:

1. The criterion of cognitive functioning was extended to include measures of scholastic achievement and measures of nonverbal intelligence in addition to verbal ability, which was the primary criterion of achievement in the analyses presented by Coleman et al. (1966). The choice of both verbal and nonverbal criterion measures was made in view of differences found in the degree of relation of verbal and nonverbal abilities with socioeconomic status (Cropley, 1964; Karp, Silberman, & Winters, 1969; MacArthur & Elley, 1963; Marjoribanks, 1972a, 1972b) and with parents' achievement-related attitudes (Marjoribanks, 1972a, 1972b).

2. A second questionnaire, in addition to that used by Coleman et al. (1966), was used to measure control of environment in view of the importance accorded to this orientation in their report.

3. Socioeconomic background variables were restricted to measures of "objective" background conditions (crowdedness of home, items in the home which indicate its economic standing) and did not include such "subjective" factors as parental educational aspirations for the child.[1] This differs from the Coleman et al. (1966) study in which these subjective factors were contained within the class of socioeconomic background variables.

[1] This more limited definition of the home background seemed to be called for in order to contrast the relative contributions of socioeconomic background and of attitudinal orientations to the variance in cognitive functioning. Moreover, the broad definition originally used by Coleman et al. (1966) appears to have eventually obscured differences in the relationships of objective and subjective background variables to achievement (Smith, 1972).

4. The differentiation between more and less advantaged students was based on a measure of socioeconomic background (crowdedness ratio of the home) rather than on a criterion of ethnicity[2] as in the Coleman et al. (1966) study. This was done on the assumption that the use of a direct measure of socioeconomic background is preferable to the use of ethnic classifications, which generally represent a confounded index of socioeconomic background (Edwards, 1974; Hess, 1970).

5. The degree of association of attitudinal orientations with the variance in cognitive measures was determined with socioeconomic background variables held constant. Likewise, attitudinal orientations were partialed out in estimating the degree of association of socioeconomic background variables with the variance in cognitive measures. Unlike this symmetric approach to the two classes of independent variables, Coleman et al. (1966) only controlled for family background variables and did not assess their degree of association with attitudes partialed out.

MEASURES OF COGNITIVE FUNCTIONING   Four tests were used to assess the relevant areas of cognitive functioning: a comprehensive test of scholastic achievement, a verbal intelligence test, and two nonverbal intelligence tests. These tests were (a) Achievement Test A, covering the areas of arithmetic, Hebrew language, and social studies; this multiple-choice test was prepared by the Ministry of Education in Israel (Ortar, 1967) and was originally used in 1958 for selection and guidance of graduates of all elementary schools throughout the country; (b) Otis, a modified Hebrew version (Handel, 1973a) of the Otis Beta Quick-Scoring Mental Ability Test; (c) Standard Progressive Matrices, Raven's (1960) nonverbal intelligence test; (d) The D48 Test (Centre de Psychologie Appliquée, 1959), a nonverbal analogies test that shares about 45% of its variance with Progressive Matrices among adolescents (Handel, 1973a).

The information about socioeconomic background and attitudinal orientations was gathered by a student questionnaire. Most of its items were adopted, with slight modifications, from the 6th- and 9th-grade questionnaire used in the survey of Coleman et al. (1966).

MEASURES OF SOCIOECONOMIC BACKGROUND   The assessment of socioeconomic background was based on information provided by the student about items in his home, crowdedness conditions in his home, and education of his parents.

All six "items in home" listed in Coleman et al.'s (1966) questionnaire were included and coded 1 and 2 for presence or absence, respectively, of each in the home (TV, telephone, record player, refrigerator, automobile, vacuum cleaner).

Crowdedness ratio of the home (number of persons divided by number of rooms) provided another index of economic level, as used in studies of SES

[2] Ethnicity in the Jewish population in Israel is defined by the country of origin of the parents. Two major groups are distinguished: (a) the Oriental Jews whose origin is Asia (usually, the Arab countries of the Middle East) and North Africa; (b) the Western group whose origin is Europe and North and South America. Oriental Jews are predominant in the Israeli lower class; the Western group is usually of a higher socioeconomic status.

effects in the United States (Bloom, Whiteman, & Deutsch, 1965; Deutsch, 1967; Tulkin, 1968; Tulkin & Newbrough, 1968), in Canada (Marjoribanks, 1972a), in England (Swift, 1967), and in Israel (Handel, 1973c; Yaffe & Smilansky, 1958).

The information obtained about education of parents was eventually discarded because 25% of the students responded "don't know" with respect to father's education and 32% with respect to mother's education. These two items received similarly high rates of "don't know" responses (36% and 31%) among sixth-graders in the Coleman et al. (1966) survey (Jencks, 1972).

MEASURES OF ATTITUDINAL ORIENTATIONS   Self-reports of students provided measures of self-concept, educational aspirations, and locus of control (control of environment).

Self-Concept   Academic self-concept was assessed by three items from the Coleman et al. (1966) questionnaire: (a) How good a student are you? (3-point scale, from 1 = low self-esteem to 3 = high self-esteem); (b) I sometimes feel I just can't learn (1 = agree—low self-concept, 2 = disagree—high self-concept); (c) I would do better in school if teachers didn't go so fast (1 = agree—low self-concept, 2 = disagree—high self-concept).

Educational Aspirations   Included were two items from the Coleman et al. (1966) questionnaire, both scored on a 5-point scale: (a) Mark the highest grade you want to finish in school (from 1 = low aspirations—finishing elementary school to 5 = high aspirations—finishing college); (b) how good a student do you want to be in school? (from 1 = high aspirations to 5 = low aspirations).

Locus of Control   This orientation (subsequently referred to as "control") was assessed by three items adopted from the Coleman et al. (1966) questionnaire: (a) People like me don't have much of a chance to be successful in life. (b) Every time I try to go ahead, something or somebody stops me. (c) Good luck is more important than hard work for success. Each of the three items was dichotomously scored (1 = agree—external control, 2 = disagree—internal control). In addition, a specifically constructed scale of internal control was used. This scale was developed from a pool of items selected from the Intellectual Responsibility Questionnaire (Crandall, Katkowsky, & Crandall, 1965) and from the Internal–External Control Scale (Rotter, 1966). Experimental versions of this scale were applied to different groups of adolescents in Israel. The final version of the scale (Handel, 1973b) was composed of 20 forced-choice items. Each item of this scale referred to a positive achievement experience in the student's daily life or to various success and failure experiences of people in general. Each item was followed by two alternatives representing an internal and external control interpretation of these events. The score was the total number of internal choices endorsed by the student. The Kuder–Richardson (KR 20) estimate of internal consistency of this scale in a sample of 161 seventh-grade pupils yielded a value of .63, which is comparable to estimates of internal consistency reported by Rotter (1966) for his original scale.

The tests and questionnaires were administered to groups of 12–15 students at a time during a 2-month period at the beginning of the autumn term in 1969. The testing was conducted by two male and two female graduate students.

SUBJECTS   The sample, which intended to draw from all socioeconomic groups, consisted of seventh-grade students in four newly established junior high schools in Haifa. It included all seventh-grade students enrolled in these schools in 1969, with $N = 950$, 440 boys and 510 girls. The range of ages was from 11 years 9 months to 13 years 3 months, with about the same mean for the boys (12 years 4 months) and the girls (12 years 3 months) and a standard deviation of 5 months for both groups.

The socioeconomic composition of this sample corresponded closely with the 1969 census data for the total Jewish population in Israel (Central Bureau of Statistics, 1970, Table F/16, p. 181). This comparison was based on the crowdedness index as a gross and comprehensive indicator of socioeconomic status. The medians of this index in our sample and in the census data were 1.58 and 1.60, respectively. The percentage of those living in relatively crowded conditions (dwellings with a crowdedness ratio of 2.0 or more) were also highly similar: 25.7% in our sample and 27.7% in the total Jewish population.

The ethnic composition of this sample also corresponded closely with the 1969/1970 census data for the junior high schools in Israel (Central Bureau of Statistics, 1972), with the following proportions of students of a distinctly Oriental origin: 15.2% in our sample and 13.2% in the total population of students in junior high schools. The corresponding complement (84.8% and 86.8%) comprised children of a distinctly Western origin and second-generation Israeli children of either Western or Oriental origin.

ANALYSES OF DATA   The relations of individual background and attitude variables with each measure of cognitive functioning were analyzed by means of zero-order correlations between these variables. These data provided a base line from which to view the results of multiple regression analyses inasmuch as the latter procedure was the primary method used to analyze the pattern of relations obtained in the total sample and in its subgroups.

Multiple regression analyses were used to assess the degree to which the two major classes of independent variables—attitudinal orientations (nine variables) and socioeconomic background variables (seven variables)—were associated with each dependent (cognitive) measure. It was recognized that significant relations between the class of attitudinal orientations and cognitive measures might be spurious due to the common variance shared by both of these with the background variables. Therefore, the degree of association of attitude variables with the dependent measures was determined both before and after partialing out of background variables. Similarly, the degree of association of background variables with the dependent measures was computed with and without partialing out of attitude variables.

Multiple regression analyses were also applied to three sets of variables within the class of attitudinal orientations: measures of aspirations (two variables), self-concept (three variables), and control (four variables).

TABLE 1

Zero-Order Correlations Between Independent Variables and Cognitive Measures

INDEPENDENT VARIABLE	ACHIEVE-MENT TEST A	OTIS	PRO-GRESSIVE MATRICES	THE D48 TEST
Items in home				
TV	− 03	− 02	− 05	− 03
Telephone	− 27†	− 32†	− 24†	− 26†
Record player	− 15†	− 16†	− 10**	− 09**
Refrigerator	− 07*	− 11†	− 09**	− 07*
Automobile	− 21†	− 26†	− 20†	− 22†
Vacuum cleaner	− 18†	20†	− 16†	− 20†
Crowdedness ratio	− 32†	− 36†	− 27†	− 28†
Aspirations				
Highest grade	37†	36†	28†	31†
Achievements	− 24†	− 25†	− 17†	− 15†
Self-concept				
Achievements	35†	27†	17†	18†
Can't learn	20†	19†	18†	15†
Teachers' pace too fast	31†	37†	31†	27†
Control				
Don't have chance	27†	29†	25†	22†
Don't go ahead	19†	19†	21†	17†
Luck more important	27†	30†	21†	21†
Internal control	32†	31†	24†	21†

Note. Direction of scores is as follows: for items in home, crowdedness ratio, and the second item (achievements) of aspirations, a high score = absence of item in home, high crowdedness, and low aspirations; for the first item (highest grade) of aspirations and for variables of self-concept and control, a high score = high aspirations, high self-concept, and internal control. All decimal points have been omitted.
* $p < .05$.
** $p < .01$.
† $p < .001$.

The relation of each of the three sets of attitude variables with measures of cognitive functioning was further examined in three distinct SES groups. For this purpose, the distribution of scores of the crowdedness ratio was divided at two points that roughly coincided with the values of Q_1 and Q_3 in the distribution of these scores for the total Jewish population in Israel (Central Bureau of Statistics, 1970). The resultant three subgroups were as follows:

low crowdedness: ratio of 1.1 and below, $N = 224$
average crowdedness: ratio of 1.2 to 2.2, $N = 583$
high crowdedness: ratio of 2.3 and above, $N = 143$.

Separate regression analyses were also performed to identify possible differences in the pattern of relationship in each sex group.

RESULTS

ATTITUDINAL ORIENTATIONS AND SOCIOECONOMIC BACKGROUND VARIABLES   All attitude measures and background variables, with the exception of one (possession of TV), are significantly related to each of the four measures of cognitive functioning (Table 1).

The multiple regression analyses computed for successive sets of the independent background and attitude variables (Table 2) clearly indicate that attitudinal orientations as a group (Set J) are associated with more of the variance than is the class of socioeconomic background variables (Set C). This major finding applies to each of the four measures of cognitive functioning. Furthermore, predictions from even two attitudinal orientations (Sets G, H, I) are superior to predictions based on the total class of socioeconomic background variables.

The data in Table 3 further demonstrate the relatively strong relation between the dependent cognitive variables and the class of attitudinal orientations. With the total class of background variables partialed out, attitudinal

TABLE 2
Multiple Regression Analyses (R^2) of Cognitive Measures by Sets of Independent Variables

INDEPENDENT VARIABLE	TOTAL NO. OF MEASURES IN EACH SET	OTIS	ACHIEVEMENT TEST A	PROGRESSIVE MATRICES	THE D48 TEST
A = crowdedness*	1	.13	.10	.07	.08
B = items in home	6	.15	.10	.08	.10
C = A + B = background	7	.19	.14	.11	.12
D = aspirations	2	.16	.16	.09	.10
E = self-concept	3	.18	.19	.12	.10
F = control	4	.18	.16	.10	.12
G = D + E	5	.25	.26	.16	.15
H = E + F	7	.26	.26	.17	.14
I = D + F	6	.27	.26	.17	.16
J = D + E + F = attitudes	9	.32	.31	.20	.16
K = C + J	16	.40	.36	.24	.23

Note. All R^2 values are significant ($p < .001$).
* For crowdedness ratio, R^2 values are based on zero-order correlations.

TABLE 3

Proportions of Variance of Cognitive Measures Accounted for by
Classes of Independent Variables

	% Variance (R^2) Accounted for		
Independent Variable*	Total Sample	Boys ($n = 440$)	Girls ($n = 510$)
Otis			
K	39.5	37.2	42.6
J	31.6	29.3	34.5
C	18.9	17.3	20.7
L	7.9	7.9	8.1
M	20.6	19.9	21.9
Achievement Test A			
K	36.5	34.5	39.2
J	31.3	29.5	33.7
C	14.2	17.3	15.8
L	5.2	5.0	5.5
M	22.3	17.2	23.4
Progressive Matrices			
K	23.7	20.1	27.3
J	19.8	15.9	23.8
C	10.6	9.6	11.5
L	3.9	4.2	3.5
M	13.1	10.5	15.8
The D48 Test			
K	23.5	22.3	26.0
J	18.1	16.6	20.8
C	12.2	11.4	13.4
L	5.4	5.7	5.2
M	11.3	10.9	12.6

Note. The total numbers of measures included in each class of independent variables are: 16 in K, 9 in J, and 7 in C.
* K = background + attitudes; J = attitudes; C = background; L = K − J = background, attitudes partialed out; M = K − C = attitudes, background partialed out.

orientations are associated with from two to four times as much of the variance in cognitive measures as is the class of background variables with attitudes partialed out. This is true for the total sample as well as for both sex groups.

ATTITUDINAL ORIENTATIONS WITH MORE AND LESS ADVANTAGED SUBGROUPS The estimates of variance associated with the three sets of attitudinal orientations are much the same both in the total sample (Table 2, Sets D, E, and F) and in the two sex groups. Further comparisons of these estimates within the subgroups of low, average, and high crowdedness, however, indicate highly consistent differences[3] between the proportions of variance associated within each subgroup (Table 4).

For the high-crowdedness group, control seems to be the most important attitude and shows the strongest relation to performance on different measures of cognitive functioning. In this group, the variable of control is associated with considerably more of the variance than are either of the other two attitude variables, and the association of measures of control (Set O) is even larger than the association of the combined set of variables of self-concept and aspirations (Set N).

In the average- and low-crowdedness group, the variables of self-concept and aspirations are of more importance, and their joint association with the variance in cognitive measures is about two to four times as large as the association of the measures of control.

The apparent similarity of the pattern of relations between attitude and cognitive measures in the two groups of higher socioeconomic status was further examined by a cross-validation analysis. For this purpose, regression weights from the low-crowdedness subgroup were applied to scores of students in the average-crowdedness subgroup, and vice versa. The resultant R^2 values[4] are very similar in magnitude to the original R^2 values in both subgroups, especially for Otis and Achievement Test A, thus indicating the comparability of the pattern of relations between attitude and cognitive measures in the two subgroups of higher socioeconomic status.

DISCUSSION

The results of this study suggest that attitudinal orientations represent meaningful constructs and potent correlates of the cognitive functioning of adolescents in Israel. Specifically, our data support the consistency of two major findings of Coleman et al. (1966): (a) Attitudinal orientations are more highly associated with the variation in cognitive functioning than are socioeconomic background variables. (b) For the disadvantaged group, locus of control shows the strongest relation to cognitive functioning, while for the more advantaged subjects, self-concept and educational aspirations seem to be of more importance.

The specific estimates of variance associated with attitudinal orientations and socioeconomic background variables also show close agreement with estimates reported in the United States (Coleman et al., 1966; Kohn & Rosman,

[3] These differences are not attributable to differences in the sizes of variances of these measures, since these variances do not differ widely (see Footnote 4).
[4] The table containing the results of this cross-validation analysis (Table A) and the table of the means and variances of all measures in the total sample and in the three subgroups of crowdedness conditions (Table B) may be obtained from the author, Dr. Handel.

TABLE 4

Proportions of Variance in Cognitive Measures Accounted for by Sets of Attitude Variables in Subgroups of High, Average, and Low Crowdedness

INDEPENDENT VARIABLE	CROWDEDNESS SUBGROUP*	% VARIANCE (R^2) ACCOUNTED FOR			
		Otis	Achievement Test A	Progressive Matrices	Test D48
J = aspirations + self-concept + control	High	35.0	31.9	22.3	15.8
	Average	29.1	30.2	18.0	16.7
	Low	25.7	20.7	13.7	14.2
D = aspirations	High	8.5	9.8	2.8	5.3
	Average	16.9	17.6	10.2	10.9
	Low	11.9	8.6	4.0	4.9
E = self-concept	High	14.9	14.0	12.2	4.6
	Average	14.8	17.4	9.4	8.3
	Low	15.4	15.3	9.5	8.2
F = control	High	28.6	23.6	16.5	12.5
	Average	13.6	12.4	8.9	7.0
	Low	11.6	8.4	5.9	6.8
G = D + E = aspirations + self-concept	High	22.6	22.5	14.1	9.2
	Average	23.9	26.0	15.2	15.0
	Low	19.4	17.5	10.6	10.0
N = J – F = aspirations + self-concept: control partialed out	High	6.4	8.3	5.8	3.3
	Average	15.5	17.8	9.1	9.7
	Low	14.1	12.3	7.8	7.4
O = J – G = control; aspirations + self-concept partialed out	High	12.4	9.4	8.2	6.6
	Average	5.2	4.2	2.8	1.7
	Low	6.3	3.2	3.1	4.2

* ns for high-, average-, and low-crowdedness subgroups are 143, 583, and 224, respectively.

1973) and in Canada (Marjoribanks, 1972a). Thus, the estimates of total variance for the criterion of verbal ability (Otis) in this study, and the corresponding estimates in the study of Coleman et al. (1966) for ninth-grade[5] whites, are as follows: 39.5% and 38.8% for the attitude and socioeconomic variables, 31.8% and 31.1% for the attitude measures, and 18.9% and 23.3% for the socioeconomic variables, respectively. Comparable estimates of variance associated with multiple indices of socioeconomic background were found by Kohn and Rosman (1973) for the Stanford Binet (19.1%) and for the Caldwell Preschool Inventory (22.0%), and by Marjoribanks (1972a) for the verbal subtests of SRA Primary Mental Abilities (28.1%).

Furthermore, the fact that Otis and Achievement Test A seem to be more predictable than the nonverbal tests of Progressive Matrices and D48 by both attitude and socioeconomic measures further replicates the findings from multiple regression analyses of Marjoribanks (1972a) for the SRA Primary Mental Abilities.

In contrast to the consistencies and similarities in the findings discussed so far, two findings deviate from this general trend. These findings pertain to further characteristics of the economically disadvantaged group in our sample (high-crowdedness group) and to the characteristics of the complementary two groups of higher socioeconomic status.

First, the disadvantaged group scored one standard deviation or less below the mean of the most advantaged group on the measures of cognitive functioning and about one half of a standard deviation below its mean on various measures of attitudinal orientations (see Footnote 4). In contrast, Coleman et al. (1966) found that southern blacks scored about one standard deviation or more below the mean of northern whites on different measures of cognitive functioning, and fell even farther behind in their level of internal control, while their academic self-concept and educational aspirations were as high as those of the northern whites.

Unlike the low-achieving black student who showed lack of realism in his educational aspirations (Coleman et al., 1966) and may have used expressions of high ambition and interest in education as a verbal substitute for behaviors he is unable to enact (Katz, 1968), the typical low-achieving student from the economically disadvantaged group in our sample seemed to be more diffident in the expressions of his academic self-concept and educational aspirations. Furthermore, his feelings about low control of the environment were consonant with the level of his other attitudinal orientations, unlike the discrepancy found between the level of focus of control and that of the other two attitudinal orientations among southern blacks (Coleman et al., 1966).

Second, the data of the present study indicate the similarity of the two groups of average and high socioeconomic status. This is suggested by the fact that students living in homes of average and low crowdedness differ only slightly in their scores on the dependent cognitive measures, while they score about the same on the independent attitude measures and produce highly

---

[5] For this comparison, the ninth-grade data were selected from the Coleman et al. (1966) survey, since Grade 9 was the lowest grade at which students were tested by uncurtailed scales of attitude measures in this survey.

similar patterns of relations between the two classes of variables (see Footnote 4).

Thus, the division of SES between average- and high-crowdedness conditions yields two relatively homogeneous groups. This might reflect a particular characteristic of the measure chosen to represent the continuum of SES in the present study, or a particular feature of the social structure of the Jewish population in Israel, or both.[6]

Alternatively, the division in terms of crowdedness might be viewed in the context of other observations which suggest that social class variation does not represent a psychologically equidistant continuum (Kohn, 1963; Lorion, 1973; Pavenstedt, 1965). Specifically, dichotomization at a point near the lower end of the continuum of social class variation is especially relevant to the psychological functioning of individuals from low-SES groups. Such individuals may lack sufficient resources and relevant experiences to develop a favorable view of self in school-related activities and of the environment. Consequently, they have feelings of inadequate control of the environment, low self-esteem, and depressed aspirations in contrast to the more favorable outlook of individuals located anywhere above the critical point of social class variation.

Further exploration of the determinants of attitudinal orientations at different ages, under different cultural conditions, may indicate the generality of this interpretation and further contribute to the clarification of some critical questions in the research on disadvantaged groups: (a) the extent to which the characteristic patterns of attitudinal orientations of children from poverty groups are directly influenced by various objective "realities of life" and the extent to which the impact of these "reality" factors is mediated by parental styles and socialization practices (Allen, 1970; Gurin & Gurin, 1970; Hess, 1970; Tulkin, 1972); (b) the extent to which the attitudinal orientations of disadvantaged groups are amenable to educational intervention and modifiable in a time perspective of years or decades (cf. Rappaport, 1974; Sarason, 1973); and (c) the extent to which changes in the attitudinal orientations of these groups will be reflected in corresponding changes in the level of their cognitive performance (cf. Hunt & Hardt, 1969).

Reference Note

1. OKADA, T., COHEN, W. M., & MAYSKE, G. W. *Growth in achievement for different racial, regional, and socioeconomic groupings of students.* Washington, D.C.: U.S. Office of Education mimeograph, May 16, 1969.

[6] Such a particularistic interpretation may be at least partially defended in view of the specific form of the regressions of the various cognitive measures on the crowdedness ratio in the total sample. While no significant deviations from linearity were found for these regressions, the increments in the level of cognitive performance at the lower end of the SES continuum (between high and average crowdedness) consistently exceeded the increments at the upper end (between average and low crowdedness) for the various criteria of cognitive functioning (see Footnote 4). This is at variance with the findings of monotonicity in the relationships between cognitive performance and indicators of SES in the original data of the Coleman et al. (1966) survey (Okada, Cohen, & Mayeske. Note 1), as well as with other findings that suggest either monotonicity (Curry, 1962; Deutsch & Brown, 1964) or infrequent departures from this type of relationship (Kohn & Rosman, 1973).

References

ALLEN, V. E. Theoretical issues in poverty research. *Journal of Social Issues*, 1970, **26**, 149–167.

BLOOM, R., WHITEMAN, M., & DEUTSCH, M. Race and social class as separate factors related to social environment. *American Journal of Sociology*, 1965, **70**, 471–476.

Central Bureau of Statistics. *Statistical Abstract of Israel*, 1970, **21**.

Central Bureau of Statistics. *Demographic characteristics of pupils in kindergartens and schools 1963/4–1969/70*. Jerusalem, Israel: Author, 1972.

Centre de Psychologie Appliquée. *Manuel: Test D48*. Paris: Editions du Centre de Psychologie Appliquée, 1959.

COLEMAN, J. S., HOBSON, C. J., McPARTLAND, JR., MOOD, A. M., WEINFELD, F. D., & YORK, R. L. *Equality of educational opportunity*. Washington, D.C.: U.S. Government Printing Office, 1966.

CRANDALL, V. C., KATKOWSKY, W., & CRANDALL, V. J. Children's beliefs in their own control of reinforcement in intellectual-academic achievement situations. *Child Development*, 1965, **36**, 91–109.

CROPLEY, A. J. Differentiation of abilities, socioeconomic status, and the WISC. *Journal of Consulting Psychology*, 1964, **28**, 512–517.

CURRY, R. L. The effect of socio-economic status on the scholastic achievement of sixth-grade children. *British Journal of Educational Psychology*, 1962, **32**, 46–49.

DEUTSCH, M. Minority groups and class status as related to social and personality factors in scholastic achievement. In M. Deutsch et al. (Eds.), *The disadvantaged child*. New York: Basic Books, 1967.

DEUTSCH, M., & BROWN, B. Social influences in Negro–white intelligence differences. *Journal of Social Issues*, 1964, **20**, 24–35.

DEUTSCH, M., & KATZ, I. Introduction. In M. Deutsch, I. Katz, & A. R. Jensen (Eds.), *Social class, race, and psychological development*. New York: Holt, 1968.

EDWARDS, D. W. Blacks versus whites: When is race a relevant variable? *Journal of Personality and Social Psychology*, 1974, **29**, 39–49.

GURIN, G., & GURIN, P. Expectancy theory in the study of poverty. *Journal of Social Issues*, 1970, **26**, 83–104.

HANDEL, A. The applicability of the WISC for pre-school children. *Megamot*, 1973, **19**, 255–267. (a)

HANDEL, A. Cognitive styles among adolescents in Israel. *International Journal of Psychology*, 1973, **8**, 255–267. (b)

HANDEL, A. The D48 as a measure of general ability among adolescents in Israel. *Journal of Cross-Cultural Psychology*, 1973, **4**, 302–213. (c)

HESS, R. D. Social class and ethnic influences upon socialization. In P. H. Mussen (Ed.), *Carmichael's manual of child psychology* (3rd ed.). New York: Wiley, 1970.

HUNT, D. E., & HARDT, R. H. The effect of upward bound programs on the attitudes, motivation and academic achievement of Negro students. *Journal of Social Issues*, 1969, **25**, 177–229.

JENCKS, C. S. The quality of data collected by the equality of educational opportunity survey. In F. Mosteller & D. P. Moynihan (Eds.), *On equality of educational opportunity*. New York: Random House, 1972.

JENSEN, A. R. Basic processes in intellectual development: Introduction. In M. Deutsch, I. Katz, & A. R. Jensen (Eds.), *Social class, race, and psychological development*. New York: Holt, 1968.

KARP, S. A., SILBERMAN, L., & WINTERS, S. Psychological differentiation and socioeconomic status. *Perceptual and Motor Skills*, 1969, **28**, 55–60.

KATZ, I. Some motivational determinants of racial differences in intellectual achievement. *International Journal of Psychology*, 1967, **2**, 1–12.

KATZ, I. Academic motivation and equal educational opportunity. *Harvard Educational Review*, 1968, **38**, 57–64.

KATZ, I. A critique of personality approaches to Negro performance, with research suggestions. *Journal of Social Issues*, 1969, **25**, 13–27.

KOHN, L. M. Social class and parent–child relationships: An interpretation. *American Journal of Sociology*, 1963, **68**, 471–480.

KOHN, M., & ROSMAN, B. L. Cognitive functioning in five-year-old boys as related to social-emotional and background-demographic variables. *Developmental Psychology*, 1973, **8**, 277–294.

LORION, R. P. Socioeconomic status and traditional treatment approaches reconsidered. *Psychological Bulletin*, 1973, **79**, 263–270.

MACARTHUR, R. J., & ELLEY, W. B. The reduction of socioeconomic bias in intelligence testing. *British Journal of Educational Psychology*, 1963, **33**, 107–119.

MARJORIBANKS, K. E. Environment, social class, and mental abilities. *Journal of Educational Psychology*, 1972, **63**, 103–109. (a)

MARJORIBANKS, K. E. Ethnicity and learning patterns: A replication and explanation. *Sociology*, 1972, **6**, 417–431. (b).

ORTAR, G. Educational achievements of primary school graduates in Israel as related to their socio-cultural background. *Comparative Education*, 1967, **4**, 23–34.

PAVENSTEDT, E. A. A comparison of the child rearing environment of upper-lower and very low lower-class families, *American Journal of Orthopsychiatry*, 1965, **35**, 89–98.

PETTIGREW, T. F. Race and equal educational opportunity. *Harvard Educational Review*, 1968, **38**, 66–76.

PLOWDEN, B. *Children and their primary schools* (Report to the Central Advisory Council for Education, England). London: Her Majesty's Stationery Office, 1967.

RAPPAPORT, H. Jewishness, blackishness, and the impending retreat of psychology. *American Psychologist*, 1974, **29**, 570–571.

RAVEN, J. C. *Guide to the Standard Progressive Matrices: Sets A, B, C, D, and F*. London: Lewis, 1960.

ROTTER, J. C. Generalized expectancies for internal versus external control of reinforcement. *Psychological Monographs*, 1966, **80** (1, Whole No. 609).

SARASON, S. B. Jewishness, blackishness, and the nature–nurture controversy. *American Psychologist*, 1973, **28**, 962–971.

SMITH, M. S. Equality of educational opportunity: The basic findings reconsidered. In F. Mosteller & D. P. Moynihan (Eds.), *On equality of educational opportunity*. New York: Random House, 1972.

SWIFT, D. F. Family environment and 11+ success: Some basic predictors. *British Journal of Educational Psychology*, 1967, **37**, 10–21.

THORNDIKE, R. L. International comparison in the achievement of 13-year-olds. In, *Educational achievements of thirteen-year-olds in twelve countries*. Hamburg: UNESCO Institute for Education, 1962.

TULKIN, S. R. Race, class, family, and school achievement. *Journal of Personality and Social Psychology*, 1968, **9**, 31–37.

TULKIN, S. R. An analysis of the concept of cultural deprivation. *Developmental Psychology*, 1972, **6**, 326–339.

TULKIN, S. R., & NEWBROUGH, J. R. Social class, race, and sex differences on the Raven (1956) Standard Progressive Matrices. *Journal of Consulting and Clinical Psychology*, 1968, **32**, 400–406.

WERNER, E. E. Sex differences in correlations between children's IQs and measures of parental ability, and environmental ratings. *Developmental Psychology*, 1969, **1**, 280–285.

WHITEMAN, M., & DEUTSCH, M. Social disadvantage as related to intellective and language development. In M. Deutsch, I. Katz, & A. R. Jensen (Eds.), *Social class, race, and psychological development*. New York: Holt, 1968.

WOLF, R. *The identification and measurement of environmental process variables related to intelligence*. Unpublished doctoral dissertation, University of Chicago, 1964.

WOLF, R. The measurement of environment. In A. Anastasi (Ed.), *Testing problems in perspective*. Washington, D.C.: American Council on Education, 1966.

YAFFE, E., & SMILANSKY, M. The extent and causes of early school leaving. *Megamot*, 1958, **9**, 275–285.

Part Five

SUMMARY

17

An Overview of Human Life and Growth

In an earlier, and possibly in some ways happier, time, man was considered the final and triumphant item of creation, the master and user of other living things. Even the early evolutionary biologists considered that man stood at the apex of evolution; they did not seem aware of the possibility that the process of evolution might continue, resulting in the appearance of new species. They seemed even less aware of the possibility that the evolutionary process of man resulted in a creature who had within him the seeds of his own destruction, like the sabre-toothed tiger, whose overdeveloped canine teeth prevented him from ingesting his prey.

Ecology is the branch of biology that studies the relationship of living things to their environment, including other living things. Recently ecologists have included man as the subject of their study. In general, the results of their investigations have been frightening. Especially in North America man is seen as a fouler of his environment—air, water, and soil—to such an extent that ecologists say that if present trends go unchecked, man may make his continued existence impossible.

In the first article in this chapter, William W. Ballard, a biologist, describes some of the facts about man's evolutionary development and speculates about the future. He makes the important distinction between man as a species and men as individuals who together make up the species. Each individual has characteristics of the species that have arisen during the course of evolution, but each individual has his own personal history, during which he has learned some ways of behaving that may be, in the long run, maladaptive for the species. Ballard's article has been very useful to us in teaching child development courses. We found ourselves referring frequently to his notion of the two computers when we discussed opposing processes or ideas in all sorts of contexts.

Lawrence K. Frank, the author of the second article, gave form, direction, and impetus to the field of child development. Frank's genius provided a flow of ideas for research, education, and theory. He was responsible for establishing child development centers, the parent education movement, and interdisciplinary research. In the article presented here, Frank demonstrates his characteristic warmth and wonder while analyzing the growth processes at work in infants. He describes how the child elaborates his individuality through interaction. In the terms used by Ballard in the first article, Frank shows how the "second computer" begins, based on the beginnings of the "first computer."

Erikson and Piaget, the authors of the third and fourth selections, are also primarily concerned with the development of the "second computer." But both are explicit in their statement that their theories are based on biology. Although both are dealing with psychological material, they start from biological characteristics of man.

The epigenetic theory of Erik H. Erikson is represented by the next essay, taken from his book Identity, Youth and Crisis. An artist, teacher, and philosopher thoroughly trained in Freudian psychoanalysis, Erikson has made enormous contributions to the field of child development. His theory is built upon Freudian theory, which he extends and develops into a way of understanding and describing the healthy personality throughout life. Erikson describes stages of personality growth, showing for each one a relation of personality to bodily development and to interaction with the culture. Each stage is derived from and built upon the one preceding it. The organization of this book is shaped by Erikson's stages in childhood and adolescence. The content is influenced by his thinking.

Jean Piaget, the world-famous Swiss psychologist, is the author of the fourth piece in this section. Piaget is primarily a genetic epistemologist, a scientist-philosopher who investigates the production of knowledge. He has developed a comprehensive theory of the mental structures through which human beings build their concept of reality and deal with it. Piaget has stimulated psychological research all over the world. Americans have produced hundreds of studies in response to his theories and findings. Like Erikson's theory of personality development, Piaget's account of the growth of intelligence is epigenetic and interactional. Piaget's theory is very compatible with a child development point of view, because the child's mind is seen as resulting from biologically given beginnings actively engaged with the environment.

The Rise and Fall of Humanity

William W. Ballard

The reading that follows is the last part of a lecture titled " The Rise and Fall of Humanity." In the first part Ballard summarizes the development of living things during the course of four billion years of earth history, the accelerating growth of knowledge in the last few thousand years, and the serious threats to man's continued existence that have stemmed from this knowledge. Basically, Ballard says, the present crisis has arisen because there are too many people on the earth and they are demanding more than the earth can provide. These events have occurred because man as a species of animal is composed of men and women as individuals.

To maximize the amount of life that can be supported in a given ecosystem, a large number of species of plants, animals, and decomposers are brought into balance, each occupying its own niche and following its own instructions to make the best of the things available to it while contributing to the flow of energy and the recycling of materials. If one species in the ecosystem gets out of balance the whole community develops an instability that may either result in an irreversible change in its character, or in the control or rejection of the destabilizing element.

From *Dartmouth Alumni Magazine*, 1970, **62** (6), 60–64. Reprinted by permission of the author, the Dartmouth Alumni College, and the *Dartmouth Alumni Magazine*.

The human species has been manipulating its environment since the invention of agriculture, favoring the plants and animals that serve it for food, repressing or even exterminating others. Where this was overdone—e.g., Mesopotamia, the Near East, Yucatan—ghost cities and records of dead cultures remain to show how powerfully nature can strike back. Quite recently we have begun to use the treasure trove of fossil fuels to grow the food to satisfy the multiplying demands of our own population, and we congratulate ourselves on having temporarily freed ourselves from the normal restrictions of the natural world. It is a dangerous game we are playing.

No good asking why the human *species* takes these risks. A species is an invention of the mind, a generalization. Only human *individuals* actually walk and breathe and make decisions and it is the collection of individuals who have been doing what I say the species has been doing. What went wrong with human individuals, that they have gotten their species and their environment into such a mess? The other face of this question is, what is an indvidual supposed to be doing, and within what limits is he supposed to be held?

THE PRIMARY COMPUTER   To simplify, I shall restrict the latter question to animals rather than plants or decomposers. I shall pick animals that are not on a rampage, animals that have (so far as we can tell) no conscious reasoning ability, no thoughts, loyalties, hopes, or faiths. Some kind of earthworm or some frog will do. I assume that whatever one of these animals does, any choice that it makes, is determined by its inherited computer system. It receives from its ancestors a scanning mechanism which reports what all the circumstances around and inside it are at the moment. This information is checked against an inherited memory encoded in its central nervous system. The computer then not only orders up the strategy and tactics that had met that sort of situation successfully before, but directs what every cell, what every organ, what the whole earthworm or frog must be doing to contribute to that response. (Directions for unsuccessful responses are not encoded in this primary computer, because they simply are not inherited.)

To see what this genetic computer requires the individual worm or frog to do, let us follow his life history, watching him obey and reconstructing from what he does the nature of the commands.

1. As a member of a bisexual species he (or she) starts as a fertilized egg, a single diploid individual with unique heterozygous genic individuality. First, *he develops*. Since the fertilized egg is insulated to a degree from the outside world, his computer works at first mostly on internal information. It refers to the inherited memory in the chromosomes and brings out instructions of various intricate sorts to the ultrastructures of the cell, programmed so that the cell divides into two, then four, then eight cells . . . until the word gets back to the multiplied computers in the multiplied cells that it is time to activate their inherited instructions for differentiation. Tissues and organs are formed, in such sorts and such patterns as have enabled the species to survive so far. The new individual acquires the sensory and neural apparatus for bringing in more and more information from the outside, and this is referred to the more and more specialized computer developing out of the inherited instructions, in a central nervous system (in the case of a frog, a brain and spinal cord). He begins

to move about, respire, feed, excrete, defend himself, in directions and at rates calculated to be appropriate to the sensed state of affairs from moment to moment. This is quite a trick for a self-built computer to bring off, and as an embryologist I wish I understood more of how it is done.

2. The young earthworm or pollywog, having broken loose from its protective envelopes and used up its dowry of yolk, is next under orders to *reach adulthood*. He recognizes dangers and opportunities by continually referring the information flowing in from his sensory apparatus to his inherited memory. He certainly has not learned his behavioral responses from his parents, never having met them. It is the inherited computer which tells him what to do from one millisecond to the next. He survives or not, partly by luck but also partly according to whether his own inherited variant of the species-specific computer will deliver the right answers to the problems of his own day and place. (The *species* survives by offering up enough varieties so that some individuals will have what the new situations demand, the wastage of the other individuals being a necessary part of the cost. No other way has yet been discovered for meeting the demands of an unpredictable future, i.e. winning a game the rules for which have not yet been written.)

3. Our earthworm or frog, if lucky, finds himself a sexually mature individual, with his instructions to reproduce now turned on. These instructions, activated by seasonal or other environmental signals, operate upon particular genes, particular cells, particular organs, and particular behavioral mechanisms set off through the nervous system. Without knowing it, much less knowing why, the animals seeks out a mate, copulates, and shares in the production of fertilized eggs that bring us again to phase 1 of the cycle.

4. Having blindly and without thought followed his instructions to (1) develop, (2) make do, survive, gain strength, and (3) reproduce, our earthworm or frog subsequently (4) *dies*. It is the ancient law. So far as the interests of the individual are concerned, it is absurd.

But now how about man? How unique is he? Does he not learn by experience and education, manage his own life, consciously determine what jobs he shall tackle, what ends he shall serve? My argument that he too is run by an inherited computer program rests partly on the observed fact that (1) he develops, (2) he makes every effort to reach maturity, (3) if lucky enough he sets the cycle going again, and (4) he dies. There is nothing unique about that. Experience, learning, individual preferences serve only for minor embellishments.

I select one case to illustrate that an animal's program is mostly inherited. Four to six weeks after fertilization (depending on temperature) a salamander embryo will have used up its yolk and must by then have acquired an elaborate repertoire of locomotor, hunting-sensory, food-grabbing, and swallowing behavior to keep itself fed and growing. Does the individual learn this behavior by trial and error? No. Starting a day before any of his muscles were mature enough to contract, you can rear him in a dilute anesthetic solution until he has reached the feeding stage. Put him back into pond water, and in twenty minutes the anesthetic will have worn off and he is swimming, hunting, grabbing, and swallowing like a normal tadpole. One is seeing here the computer-controlled maturation of a computer-controlled behavior. No practice, no learning.

The individual within which this remarkable apparatus matures is an expendable pawn, and the apparatus is not for his enjoyment of life, it is to keep the species going.

THE SECONDARY COMPUTER   There is such an inherited program in the human individual, but there is much more. The baby does not so much learn to walk as to develop the inherited capacity to walk; but then he can learn a dance that no man has ever danced before, he can paint a picture with a brush clasped between his toes. During late fetal life and his first six or eight years he gradually matures a second computer system superimposed on, controlling and almost completely masking the ancient frog-type computer. The evolutionary history of this new device is traceable back to, and in some respects beyond, the time of origin of the modern mammals 70 million or more years ago. It has progressed farthest in particular mammalian orders—the carnivores, hoofed animals, bats, whales and primates, and least in the egg-laying mammals and marsupials.

The new trend has worked certain real advantages, and has been kept under reasonable control, in the higher mammals, but it is my strong suspicion that its over-development in man is the root of our trouble. Like the dinosaurs, we contain in our own structure the reason why we will have to go. Robinson Jeffers[1] said it: "We have minds like the fangs of those forgotten tigers, hypertropied and terrible."

Up to a point, the development of brain and spinal cord follows the same course in frog and man. Sense organs, cranial and spinal nerves, principal subdivisions of the brain, basic fiber tract systems, all form in strictly comparable fashion in both. But the adult human brain is a far different thing from the adult frog brain. It continues the multiplication and interconnection of neurons during a far longer growth period, and adds to the elementary or frog-type apparatus two principal complicating tissues that far overshadow the earlier developments. One is often called reticular substance, the other is the cerebral cortex.

The reticular substance is so called because it is an interweaving of small centers of gray substance with short bundles and interspersed mats of axons (the white substance), quite different from the simple contrast between gray and white substance seen in primitive animals and in early embryos. The frog brain is not without this sort of tissue, but in the brains of advanced vertebrates like the teleost fishes, the reptiles, and the birds, it becomes indescribably complex. The modern mammals push this development to still higher orders of magnitude.

Although neurological science is not yet ready with answers to most specific questions about what happens where in the central nervous system, the new techniques of exploration within the brain suggest that in and through the reticular substance the connections for integrating sensory information with the devices for evaluation and for making decisions and coordinated responses are multiplied exponentially.

Thus, an electrode planted within a single neuron in the reticular substance of the hindbrain can give startling evidence that this one cell is receiving and

[1] R. Jeffers, "Passenger Pigeons," in *The Beginning and the End.*

reacting to sensations reported from widely scattered parts of the body, and sending out coded pulses as a calculated response. Your own brain contains hundreds of millions, probably billions of such cells, every one individually a computer.

The neurologists can now stimulate chosen localized areas through implanted electrodes, either hooked up to wires dangling from the cage ceiling or activated through miniaturized transmitters healed in under the scalp and controlled by radio transmission. In such experiments, stimuli delivered to many parts of the reticular substance cause the animal to react as though he were flooded with agreeable sensation. If the cat or rat or monkey learns how to deliver the stimulus to himself by pressing a pedal, he will do so repeatedly and rapidly, until he falls asleep exhausted. As soon as he wakes up, he goes to pounding the pedal again.

There are other reticular areas which have the reverse effect. If the stimulus comes at rhythmical intervals and the animal discovers that he can forestall it by pressing the pedal, he quickly learns to regulate his life so as to be there and step on it just in time. What kind of sensation such a stimulus produces in him can only be guessed by the experimenter. One might suppose that these areas of reticular substance which have such opposite effects are there to add into the computer's analysis of the situation at the moment a go signal or a stop signal for particular alternative choices, or a sense of goodness or badness, satisfaction or distress, urgency or caution, danger or relaxation. A value judgment, in other words.

It is not difficult to see the survival value of such a device. No doubt the basic mechanism exists in the brains of fishes and frogs, though I am not aware that experiments have been done to locate it. In the reticular substance of mammals, however, we see it hugely developed. The result of overdoing this might produce an awareness of the good and bad features of so very many facets of a situation as to delay and perplex the individual in calculating his single coordinated response.

Mammals are also conspicuously good at remembering experiences from their own lives as individuals, and these memories are loaded with value judgments. There is still no clear answer as to where or in what coded form these new personal memories are stored. But an animal with all this added to the ancestral memory, enhanced with perhaps casually acquired and unwisely generalized connotations of goodness and badness, might predictably be endowed with excessive individuality, prone to unnecessarily variable behavior, chosen more often for self-satisfaction than in the interest of species survival.

The other evolutionary development, the formation of the cerebral cortex, is almost unknown in vertebrates other than mammals, and is feeble in some of these. Cerebral cortex is a tissue of awesome complexity, and our techniques for analyzing what happens in it are still highly inadequate. Stimulation of willing human subjects, in chosen spots exposed surgically, or radio stimulation of these areas through permanently installed electrodes operated by healed-in transistor devices, evoke feelings referred to a particular part of the body, or cause normal-appearing localized movements, e.g. the flexion of an arm or a finger, time and again, upon repetition of the signal. Other areas produce more generalized sensory or motor or emotional or physiologic effects. The patient, his brain exposed under local anesthesia, does not know when the stimulus is applied. When the electrode touches a particular spot of his cortex he may report that he is suddenly remembering a scene identifiable as to time and place, but the memory blacks out when the current is cut off. Stimulation of other areas may elicit emotions of sexual attraction or anxiety or rage graded according to the intensity of the signal.

More wide-ranging experiments with cats, monkeys, or barnyard stock, singly or in groups, free to move in large caged areas, show the possibility of turning on and off a great range of complex emotions, behavior, and even personality traits, by local stimulation.[2] The effect produced through a permanently planted electrode is area specific. Though not predictable before the first stimulus is given, the response is repeated with each stimulus, many times a day or over periods of months or years.

In subjective comparison of mammals with greater or less personal individuality one gets the impression that the degrees of freedom of choice, of imaginative recognition of possible ways to react to situations, of storage capacity and retentiveness of memory, and the richness of association, are correlated with the intricacy and amount of the cerebral cortex and reticular substance. Animals highest on both scales include porpoises, elephants, cats and dogs, apes, and people.

One cannot underestimate the effects on the human species of other evolutionary trends that came to a climax in us, for instance the development of upright posture that frees the hands, the reshaping of the fingers for grasping and manipulating, the perfection of binocular vision that can bring into focus either the hands or the far distance at will. Far more significant than these was the development of speech, made possible by and controlled in a particular small area of the new cerebral cortex. This expanded the powers of the human secondary computer by orders of magnitude, even in comparison with that of close relatives like apes.

We no longer communicate with each other by baring teeth, raising hackles and flaunting rumps, but in symbolic language. We can make abstractions and generalizations, and artificial associations. Through speech we can feed into the recording apparatus of each others' secondary computers not only the vast and rather accidental store of individually acquired and long-lasting memories of our own experience, but also the loads of approval or disapproval which we deliberately or unwittingly put upon them. We increasingly remove ourselves into created worlds of our own, calculating our choices by reference to a memory bank of second-hand ghosts of other people's experiences and feelings, prettied up or uglified with value judgments picked up who knows where, by whom, for what reason.

Language gave a fourth dimension to the powers of the secondary computer, and writing a fifth dimension. We can now convince each other that things are good or bad, acceptable or intolerable, merely by agreeing with each other, or by reciting catechisms. With writing we can color the judgments of people unborn, just as our judgments are tailored to the whim of influential teachers in the past.

[2] J. M. R. Delgado, 1969, *Physical Control of the Mind.*

Symbols have given us the means to attach a value judgment to some abstract noun, some shibboleth, and transfer this by association to any person or situation at will. We invent, we practice, we delight in tricks for saying things indirectly by poetry and figures of speech, that might sound false or trite or slanderous or nonsensical if we said them directly. A more normally constructed animal, a porpoise or an elephant, mercifully spared such subtleties, might well look at human beings and see that each one of us has become to some degree insane, out of touch with the actual world, pursuing a mad course of options in the imagined interest of self rather than of species.

The primary computer is still there, programmed in the interest of species survival. With his new powers, man should do better than any other animal at understanding the present crisis and generating an appropriate strategy and tactics. Instead, the effort is drowned out in the noise, the flicker-bicker, the chattering flood of directives from the personalized secondary computer. In pursuit of his own comfort and his own pleasure, man wars against his fellows and against the good earth.

The frame of each person is like a racing shell with two oarsmen in it, back to back, rowing in opposite directions. The one represents the ancient computer system, comparing the personal situation of the moment with an inherited value system and driving the person to perform in such a way that the species will survive, irrespective of how absurd his own expendable life may be. The other represents the secondary computer system, probably located in reticular substance and cerebral cortex, surveying chiefly the memories of childhood and adult life, and deciding how to act according to the value-loaded store of personal experience.

It is this runaway evolutionary development of our superimposed second computer that has produced our inventors, our artists, our saints and heroes, our poets, our thinkers. Our love and hate, ecstasy and despair. The infinite variety of human personalities. It has also atomized the species into a cloud of ungovernable individuals. We split our elections 48 to 52, make laws to break them, and either ignore community priorities or establish them by political blind-man's-buff in frivolous disregard of real emergencies. Six experts will come violently to six different decisions on how to meet a crisis because their personal histories lead them to weigh the same data differently. Each of us can see bad logic and conflicts of interest affecting the judgment of most of our associates; it is more difficult to detect them in ourselves. Our individually acquired prejudices have been built into our secondary computers.

Yet it is a glorious thing to feel the uniqueness, the power of decision, the freedom of being human. Who would prefer to be even so wonderful a creature as a dog, an elephant, a horse, a porpoise? I believe nevertheless that just this ungovernable power of the human individual, the essence of our humanity, is the root of the trouble.

The California biologist Garrett Hardin, in a famous essay called "The Tragedy of the Commons," showed that this accounts for practically all the facets of our apocalyptic crisis, from the population explosion to runaway technology.[3] He is referring to the community pasture where anyone may feed

[3] G. Hardin, 1968, *Science* **162**: 1243. "The Tragedy of the Commons."

his animals. Overgrazing will bring erosion and irreversible deterioration in it. Each herdsman, calculating the advantage and disadvantage to himself of putting out one more animal to graze, balancing his small share of the possible damage against his sole ownership of the extra income, adds another animal in his own interest, and another, and another. All do, and all lose together. The tragedy is the inescapable disaster when each herdsman pursues his own advantage without limit, in a limited commons. This is the tragedy that leaves us with too many human mouths to feed, soil impoverished and washed or blown away, forests skinned off, lakes ruined, plastic bottles and aluminium cans scattered over the countryside, rivers clogged with dead fish, bilge oil spreading on public waters, streets and highways made obscene with advertisements. It is what gives us choking smog, the stink and corruption below paper mills and slaughter houses, the draining of one well by another in a falling water table, the sneaking of radioactive wastes into the air and the oceans.

All these, Hardin makes clear, are problems with *no technological solution.* To be sure, the technology stands ready, but the trouble starts with some individual, you, me, whose response to a situation is to give highest priority to his personal chance of profit, or his family's, or his country's. He has a vivid sense of the value to himself of his own freedom, but the total effects of all such freedoms on the species and on the natural world which supports it is invisible or far out of focus. The technology might just as well not exist.

Some of these problems that will not be solved by technology alone can indeed be brought under control by compacts, treaties, and other agreements between willing groups, or by laws imposed by the majority upon a minority in the common interest. Hardin, however, puts the finger on the population problem as the worst example of the worst class of problems, in which all of us must restrict the freedom of all of us, when none of us want to. He is properly skeptical of conscience or altruism as forces for uniting the community when nearly all of us are still daring to gamble on the continued capacity of the commons to withstand collapse. What is needed, he says, is a fundamental extension of morality.

My way of agreeing with him is to say that human nature is our chief enemy because the species-preserving function of our primary computer has not yet been built into the secondary computer which generates our human nature. It is by now clear that our nature as individuals is not so much inherited as learned by babies as they grow into people, in and from their individual, accidental, and culture-bound experiences. We need to incorporate into the decision-making apparatus that will really control them a new survival morality, a system of values the principal axiom of which is that anything which threatens the welfare of the species is bad, anything that serves to bring the species into harmony with its environment is good. We must, each of us, because of this inner drive, regulate our numbers and our selfish wants as rigorously as the forces of natural selection would have done had we not learned how to set them aside.

Do we know how to create a human nature that can keep the species going without undue sacrifice of the privilege and joy of being human? How much freedom must we give up? Do we want to? Is there time?

Basic Processes in Organisms

Lawrence K. Frank

If we are to understand the infant as a persistent, but ever changing, organism, we need to think in terms that are dynamic, which calls for a recognition of the ongoing processes by which the infant grows, develops, matures, and ages while continually functioning and behaving. As a young mammalian organism, the human infant lives by much the same basic physiological processes as other mammals.

The recognition of process has come with the acceptance of such recently formulated conceptions as that of self-organization, self-stabilization, self-repair, and self-direction which are characteristic not only of organisms but of various man-made machines such as computers and systems designed to operate a planned sequence of activities with the use of positive and negative feedbacks (Wiener 1961; Von Foerster and Zopf 1962). The organism may be said to be "programmed" by its heredity but capable of flexible functioning through the life cycle.

Moreover, it must be re-emphasized that each infant differs to a greater or lesser extent from all other infants, exhibiting not only individual variation but also displaying a considerable range of intra-individual variability, or continually changing functioning and physiological states, especially during the early months of life when the infant is not yet fully organized or capable of adequate self-stabilization.

Since most of our knowledge of infancy and childhood is derived from observations and measurements of selected variables, responses to stimuli, at a given time or a succession of times, we do not gain an adequate conception of the continuous, dynamic processes of living organisms, especially since we tend to focus upon the outcomes, without recognizing the processes which produce them. Accordingly, some account of these basic processes and how they operate may provide a conceptual model for understanding the multidimensional development of infants during the first year of life. Whatever is done to and for the infant, what privations, frustrations and deprivations he may suffer, what demands and coercions he must accept, what spontaneous activity and learning he displays, may be viewed as expressions of his basic functioning processes.

Every experience in the life of an infant evokes some alteration in these organic processes whereby he manages not only to survive but to grow and develop, to learn while carrying on his incessant intercourse with the surrounding world. Thus, by focusing on the organic processes we may discover what is taking place when we speak of adjustment, learning, adaptation, and the transitions encountered at critical stages in his development.

The concept of mechanism indicates or implies a deterministic relationship between antecedent and consequent, usually as a *linear* relationship in which the consequent is proportional to the antecedent. The concept of *process* involves a dynamic, *non-linear* operation, whereby the same process, depending upon where, what, how, and in what quantities or intensities it operates, may produce different products which may be all out of proportion to that which initiates or touches off the process. For example the process of fertilization and gestation operates in all mammals to produce the immense variety of mammalian young. But different processes may produce similar or equivalent products, an operation which has been called "equifinality" by Bertalanffy (1950).

A brief discussion of the six basic processes operating in organisms will indicate how the infant organism is able to persist and survive by continually changing and is thereby able to cope with the particular version of infant care and rearing to which he is subjected.

These six processes are: The Growth Process, The Organizing Process, The Communicating Process, The Stabilizing Process, The Directive or Purposive Process, and The Creative Process. (Frank, 1963).

THE GROWTH PROCESS   The infant who has been growing since conception continues, with a brief interruption and often some loss of weight, to grow incrementally, adding gradually to his size and weight. His growth may be slowed down by inadequate or inappropriate feeding, by some difficulties in digesting and assimilating whatever foodstuff he be given, or by a variety of disturbances and dysfunctions. A continuing upward trend in weight is expected as an expression of normal development, although recent cautions have been expressed on the undesirability of too rapid increase in weight and the vulnerability of a fat, waterlogged infant.

This incremental growth in size and weight indicates that the infant is maintaining an excess of growth over the daily losses through elimination of urine and feces, through skin and lungs, and also in the replacement of many cells that are discarded. Thus, millions of blood corpuscles are destroyed and replaced each day, the iron of those destroyed being salvaged and reused. Likewise, cells of the skin and lining of the gastrointestinal tract, of the lungs, kidneys, liver, indeed of almost all organ systems, except the central nervous system and brain, are continually being replaced at different rates.

Probably more vitally significant but less clearly recognized is the continual replacement of the chemical constituents of cells, tissues, and bony structures, like the skeleton and the teeth in which different chemicals are discarded and new materials are selected out of the blood stream to replace them. Here we see a dramatic illustration of the statement that an organism is a configuration which must continually change in order to survive, a conception which is wholly congruous with the recently formulated assumption of the world as an aggregate of highly organized complexes of energy transformations.

Growth, incremental and replacement, is a major functioning process, gradually producing an enlarging infant as the growing cells differentiate, specialize and organize to give rise to the varied tissues and organ systems in the developing embryo and fetus. In this prenatal development the creative process is also operating to produce the unique, unduplicated human infant along with the operation of the organizing process.

THE ORGANIZING PROCESS   Only recently has the process of self-organization been recognized in scientific thinking as basic to all organisms which start with some kind of genetic inheritance and undergo multiplication and duplication of cells with differentation and specialization of components that become organized into a living organism. (Von Foerster and Zopf, 1962). Thus the initial development of an infant takes place through the operation of the growth and the organizing processes which continue to operate throughout its life, maintaining the organism as it undergoes various transitions and transformations and copes with the many discontinuities encountered in its life cycle.

Since the normal infant arrives fully equipped with all the essential bodily components and organ systems, the growth process and the organizing process operate to incorporate the intakes of food, water, and air into its ever changing structure-functioning. Most of the highly organized foodstuffs, proteins, fats, and carbohydrates, are progressively broken down, disorganized, and randomized, and the products of these digestive operations are then circulated through the blood stream from which the constituent cells, tissues, and fluids select out what they need for metabolism and organize these into their specialized structure-functioning components. The recent dramatic findings in molecular biology show how this organizing process operates within the cell as the DNA (the carrier of the genetic information) of the genes directs the production of the various proteins and the utilization of the minerals and vitamins for the growth and multiplication of cells and the maintenance of their functioning.

Also of large significance for the understanding of organic processes are the sequential steps in the utilization of food stuffs for metabolism involving many steps and numerous specialized enzymes and catalysts. Unfortunately some infants suffer from so-called metabolic errors when one or more of these steps in the metabolic sequence is missing or inadequate and therefore his growth and development and healthy functioning are jeopardized.

In the self-organizing organism we encounter circular and reciprocal operations in which every component of the organism by its specialized functioning, gives rise to, and maintains, the total organism of which it is a participant; concurrently, the total organism reciprocally governs when, what, and how each of these components must function and operate to maintain the organized whole. This capacity for self-organizing arises from the autonomy of each component of an organism which over millions of years of evolution has developed its own highly individualized and specialized functioning within the total organic complex but functions according to the requirements of the organism in which it operates.

COMMUNICATION PROCESS   Obviously, these autonomous components which give rise to growth and organization must continually communicate, internally and with the external "surround." The infant has an inherited communication network in his nervous system, his circulatory system, and his lymphatic system. Through these several channels every constituent of an organism continually communicates with all others, directly or indirectly, and with different degrees of speed in communication. Each component continually sends and receives messages whereby its functioning operations are regulated, synchronized, articulated, and related to all others, with greater or less immediacy. The infant is born with most of these internal communications already functioning, having been in operation for varying periods of its prenatal development but with the central nervous system still immature. The infant also has the sensory apparatus for various inputs, of light, of sound, touch, taste and smell, also for pain, heat and cold, and for gravity and for atmospheric pressure changes. But the infant is also initially prepared for dealing with the varying intensities and durations of these intakes and impacts, gradually increasing his capacity for filtering, buffering, mingling, and transducing these inputs whereby he may monitor these sensory communications according to his ever changing internal, physiological states and the kinesthetic and proprioceptive messages by which he continually orients himself and gradually achieves an equilibrium in space.

The infant must carry on this incessant intercourse with the world more or less protected by adults from too severe or hazardous impacts and provided with the food and care required by his helpless dependency. But the infant often must try to defend himself from what his caretakers try to impose on him or compel him to accept, as in feeding, toilet training, etc. Under this treatment much of the infant's energies may be expended in these efforts to maintain his stability and integrity against unwelcomed and uncongenial treatment which may interfere with his normal functioning and compromise his growth and development and learning as a unique organism. Thus we may say that the growth and organizing processes contribute to and are dependent upon the communication process, which operates through the inherited receptors of the infant which may become progressively altered, refined, and increasingly sensitized through learning. Quite early the infant may become receptive to nonverbal communications such as tones of voice, smiling, tactile comforting, or painful treatment.

STABILIZING PROCESS   Since the world presents so many different and continually varying messages and impacts, organisms must be able to cope with the ever changing flux of experience and maintain their integrity and functional capacities by monitoring all their organic functions. While all other organisms have evolved with their species-specific range of sensory awareness and capacity for perception and for living in their ancestral life zones, the human infant, and a few other mammals are able to live in a wide variety of climates and habitations and maintain their internal world within fairly close limitations upon intraorganic variability. This becomes possible through the operation of the stabilizing process.

The stabilizing process operates through a network of physiological feedbacks, both negative and positive, to maintain a dynamic equilibrium and is not limited to the concept of homeostasis which Cannon used to describe the maintenance of the fluid internal environment. The stabilizing process maintains continually changing physiological states. At birth it is not fully developed or operationally effective and hence the infant needs continual care, protection, and appropriate nutrition. But as he grows and develops he increasingly regulates his internal functioning by responding appropriately to the various inputs and outputs, intakes, and outlets. Obviously an infant who must grow, both incrementally and by replacement, cannot tolerate too stable an internal environment which might prevent or limit such growth and adaptive functioning. With his increasing exposure to the world the infant learns to calibrate all his sensory inputs and increasingly to "equalize his thresholds," as Kurt Goldstein (1939) has pointed out.

Not the least significant and often stressful experience under which an infant must maintain his internal stability are the varying practices of child care and feeding, the efforts of parents to regularize his functioning and compel him to conform to whatever regimen of living they wish to establish. Clearly the stabilizing process is essential to the infant's survival and to his continuing growth and development and the variety of learning which he must master. Happily, most infants achieve a progressive enlargement of their capacity for living and for self-regulation and self-stabilization to assume an autonomy expressing their integrity in the face of often uncongenial treatment and surroundings.

THE DIRECTIVE OR PURPOSIVE PROCESS   With the achievement of motor coordination and locomotion, by creeping and crawling, and then assuming an erect posture and learning to walk, the infant enlarges the purposive or goal seeking process which involves continual scanning, probing, and exploring the world and developing his selective awareness and patterned perception, and especially the ability to ignore or to reject what may interfere or distract him in his endeavour to attain remote or deferred goals. Obviously, the purposive process cannot operate effectively until the infant has achieved a considerable degree of internal stabilization and of neuro-muscular coordination, and the ability to cope with a three dimensional, spatial world.

Since the child initially is attracted or impelled by whatever he may become aware of or has an impulse to seek, to handle, to put into his mouth, or otherwise to manipulate, the purposive process is frequently blocked and the child may be severely punished in his attempts to develop his autonomous mastery of his small world. Thus the purposive process operates differentially in each infant who is likely to be attracted by and responsive to different dimensions of his environment at different times; these early explorations provide an endless sequence of learning experiences which involve, not only the actual world of nature, but the wide range of artifacts and of highly individuated personalities with whom he is in contact. With language the infant learns to deal with people and verbal symbols of language for goal seeking.

THE CREATIVE PROCESS   As noted earlier, the creative process begins to operate early in gestation to produce a unique infant as a human organism with the same basic organic functions and similar or equivalent components which, however, are different in each infant. From birth on, therefore, each infant is engaged in creating a highly selective environment or a "life space" that is as congenial and appropriate for his individualized organism, with its peculiar needs and capacities, as is possible under the constraints and coercions imposed by others upon his growth, development, functioning, and learning. In infancy and childhood the individual is more creative than in any other period in his life cycle, but this creativity may be either ignored or discouraged by those who are intent upon making the child conform as nearly as possible to their image or ideal of attainment.

Within recent years the purposive and creative processes have become major foci in the studies of early child growth, development, and education, but it must be remembered that the purposive and creative processes cannot operate independently because they are inextricably related to and dependent upon the other four basic processes which reciprocally contribute to the operation of these two processes.

Most of the training and education of the infant and young child involves curbing, regulating, focusing, and patterning, and also evoking the communicating and stabilizing and directive processes which are more amenable to intervention and control by others. Through supervision and regulation of these processes the child is largely molded, patterned, and oriented into the kind of organism-personality favored by his parents and appropriately prepared for living in his cultural and social order. As he grows older the infant is expected to learn the required conduct for group living and to master the various symbol systems by which he can relate cognitively to the world and negotiate with other people. It appears that learning as an expression of the purposive and the creative processes may be compromised and sometimes severely distorted or blocked when the child is expected or compelled to alter the organizing, communicating, and stabilizing processes, as required by his parents and other more experienced persons.

In the discussion of humanization we will see how the young mammalian organism is transformed into a personality for living in a symbolic cultural world and for participating in a social order, through the various practices of infant care and rearing that are focused upon, and directly intervene in, the operation of these six basic organic processes. But each infant is a highly individualized organism who develops his own idiosyncratic personality through the development and utilization of his basic organic processes.

References

BERTALANFFY, L. VON, "Theory of Open Systems in Physics and Biology," *Science*, CXI, 1950, pp. 27–29. See also Yearbooks of Society for General Systems Research.

FRANK, L. K., "Human Development—An Emerging Discipline," in *Modern Perspectives in Child Development*, In honor of Milton J. E. Senn, Eds. Albert J. Solnit and Sally Provence, New York: International Universities Press, 1963.

——. "Potentiality: Its Definition and Development," in *Insights and the Curriculum*, Yearbook, Association for Supervision and Curriculum Development, Washington, D.C.: National Education Association, 1963.

GOLDSTEIN, KURT, *The Organism*, New York: American Book Company, 1939.

VON FOERSTER, HEINZ, and ZOPF, JR., GEORGE W., Eds., *Principles of Self Organizing Systems*, London: Pergamon Press, 1962.

WIENER, NORBERT, *Cybernetics*, Cambridge and New York: M.I.T. Press and John Wiley and Sons, Inc., 1961.

The Life Cycle : Epigenesis of Identity

Erik H. Erikson
HARVARD UNIVERSITY

Whenever we try to understand growth, it is well to remember the *epigenetic principle* which is derived from the growth of organisms *in utero*. Somewhat generalized, this principle states that anything that grows has a ground plan, and that out of this ground plan, the parts arise, each part having its time of special ascendancy, until all parts have arisen to form a functioning whole. This, obviously, is true for fetal development where each part of the organism has its critical time of ascendance or danger of defect. At birth the baby leaves the chemical exchange of the womb for the social exchange system of his society, where his gradually increasing capacities meet the opportunities and limitations of his culture. How the maturing organism continues to unfold, not by developing new organs but by means of a prescribed sequence of locomotor, sensory, and social capacities, is described in the child-development literature. As pointed out, psychoanalysis has given us an understanding of the more idiosyncratic experiences, and especially the inner conflicts, which constitute the manner in which an individual becomes a distinct personality. But here, too, it is important to realize that in the sequence of his most personal experiences the healthy child, given a reasonable amount of proper guidance, can be trusted to obey inner laws of development, laws which create a succession of potentialities for significant interaction with those persons who tend and respond to him and those institutions which are ready for him. While such interaction varies from culture to culture, it must remain within " the proper rate and the proper sequence" which governs all epigenesis. Personality, therefore, can be said to develop according to steps predetermined in the human organism's readiness to be driven toward, to be aware of, and to interact with a widening radius of significant individuals and institutions.

It is for this reason that, in the presentation of stages in the development of the personality, we employ an epigenetic diagram analogous to the one employed in *Childhood and Society* for an analysis of Freud's psychosexual stages.[1] It is, in fact, an implicit purpose of this presentation to bridge the theory of infantile sexuality (without repeating it here in detail) and our knowledge of the child's physical and social growth.

In Diagram 1 the double-lined squares signify both a sequence of stages and a gradual development of component parts. In other words, the diagram formalizes a progression through time of a differentiation of parts. This indicates (1) that each item of the vital personality to be discussed is systematically related to all others, and that they all depend on the proper development in

[1] See Erik H. Erikson, *Childhood and Society*, 2nd ed., New York: W. W. Norton & Company, Inc., 1963, Part I.

DIAGRAM 1

	1	2	3	4	5	6	7	8
VIII								INTEGRITY vs. DESPAIR
VII							GENERATIVITY vs. STAGNATION	
VI						INTIMACY vs. ISOLATION		
V	Temporal Perspective vs. Time Confusion	Self-Certainty vs. Self-Consciousness	Role Experimentation vs. Role Fixation	Apprenticeship vs. Work Paralysis	IDENTITY vs. IDENTITY CONFUSION	Sexual Polarization vs. Bisexual Confusion	Leader- and Followership vs. Authority Confusion	Ideological Commitment vs. Confusion of Values
IV				INDUSTRY vs. INFERIORITY	Task Identification vs. Sense of Futility			
III			INITIATIVE vs. GUILT		Anticipation of Roles vs. Role Inhibition			
II		AUTONOMY vs. SHAME, DOUBT			Will to Be Oneself vs. Self-Doubt			
I	TRUST vs. MISTRUST				Mutual Recognition vs. Autistic Isolation			

the proper sequence of each item; and (2) that each item exists in some form before "its" decisive and critical time normally arrives.

If I say, for example, that a sense of basic trust is the first component of mental vitality to develop in life, a sense of autonomous will the second, and a sense of initiative the third, the diagram expresses a number of fundamental relations that exist among the three components, as well as a few fundamental facts for each.

Each comes to ascendance, meets its crisis, and finds its lasting solution in ways to be described here, toward the end of the stages mentioned. All of them exist in the beginning in some form, although we do not make a point of this fact, and we shall not confuse things by calling these components different names at earlier or later stages. A baby may show something like "autonomy" from the beginning, for example, in the particular way in which he angrily tries to wriggle his hand free when tightly held. However, under normal conditions, it is not until the second year that he begins to experience the whole critical alternative between being an autonomous creature and being a dependent one, and it is not until then that he is ready for a specifically new encounter with his environment. The environment, in turn, now feels called upon to convey to him its particular ideas and concepts of autonomy in ways decisively contributing to his personal character, his relative efficiency, and the strength of his vitality.

It is this encounter, together with the resulting crisis, which is to be described for each stage. Each stage becomes a crisis because incipient growth and awareness in a new part function go together with a shift in instinctual energy and yet also cause a specific vulnerability in that part. One of the most difficult questions to decide, therefore, is whether or not a child at a given stage is weak or strong. Perhaps it would be best to say that he is always vulnerable in some respects and completely oblivious and insensitive in others, but that at the same time he is unbelievably persistent in the same respects in which he is vulnerable. It must be added that the baby's weakness gives him power; out of his very dependence and weakness he makes signs to which his environment, if it is guided well by a responsiveness combining "instinctive" and traditional patterns, is peculiarly sensitive. A baby's presence exerts a consistent and persistent domination over the outer and inner lives of every member of a household. Because these members must reorient themselves to accommodate his presence, they must also grow as individuals and as a group. It is as true to say that babies control and bring up their families as it is to say the converse. A family can bring up a baby only by being brought up by him. His growth consists of a series of challenges to them to serve his newly developing potentialities for social interaction.

Each successive step, then, is a potential crisis because of a radical change in perspective. Crisis is used here in a developmental sense to connote not a threat of catastrophe, but a turning point, a crucial period of increased vulnerability and heightened potential, and therefore, the ontogenetic source of generational strength and maladjustment. The most radical change of all, from intrauterine to extrauterine life, comes at the very beginning of life. But in postnatal existence, too, such radical adjustments of perspective as lying relaxed, sitting firmly, and running fast must all be accomplished in their own good time.

With them, the interpersonal perspective also changes rapidly and often radically, as is testified by the proximity in time of such opposites as "not letting mother out of sight" and "wanting to be independent." Thus, different capacities use different opportunities to become full-grown components of the ever-new configuration that is the growing personality.

Equilibrium

Jean Piaget
UNIVERSITY OF GENEVA

The psychological development that starts at birth and terminates in adulthood is comparable to organic growth. Like the latter, it consists essentially of activity directed toward equilibrium. Just as the body evolves toward a relatively stable level characterized by the completion of the growth process and by organ maturity, so mental life can be conceived as evolving toward a final form of equilibrium represented by the adult mind. In a sense, development is a progressive equilibration from a lesser to a higher state of equilibrium. From the point of view of intelligence, it is easy to contrast the relative instability and incoherence of childhood ideas with the systematization of adult reason. With respect to the affective life, it has frequently been noted how extensively emotional equilibrium increases with age. Social relations also obey the same law of gradual stabilization.

An essential difference between the life of the body and that of the mind must nonetheless be stressed if the dynamism inherent in the reality of the mind is to be respected. The final form of equilibrium reached through organic growth is more static and, above all, more unstable than the equilibrium toward which mental development strives, so that no sooner has ascending evolution terminated than a regressive evolution automatically starts, leading to old age. Certain psychological functions that depend closely on the physical condition of the body follow an analogous curve. Visual acuity, for example, is at a maximum toward the end of childhood, only to diminish subsequently; and many other perceptual processes are regulated by the same law. By contrast, the higher functions of intelligence and affectivity tend toward a "mobile equilibrium." The more mobile it is, the more stable it is, so that the termination of growth, in healthy minds, by no means marks the beginning of decline but rather permits progress that in no sense contradicts inner equilibrium.

It is thus in terms of equilibrium that we shall try to describe the evolution of the child and the adolescent. From this point of view, mental development is

From *Six Psychological Studies*, by Jean Piaget, translated by Anita Tenzer, edited by David Elkind. Copyright © 1967 by Random House, Inc. Reprinted by permission of Random House, Inc. and Hodder & Stoughton Educational.

a continuous construction comparable to the erection of a vast building that becomes more solid with each addition. Alternatively, and perhaps more appropriately, it may be likened to the assembly of a subtle mechanism that goes through gradual phases of adjustment in which the individual pieces become more supple and mobile as the equilibrium of the mechanism as a whole becomes more stable. We must, however, introduce an important distinction between two complementary aspects of the process of equilibration. This is the distinction between the variable structures that define the successive states of equilibrium and a certain constant functioning that assures the transition from any one state to the following one.

There is sometimes a striking similarity between the reactions of the child and the adult, as, for example, when the child is sure of what he wants and acts as adults do with respect to their own special interests. At other times there is a world of difference—in games, for example, or in the manner of reasoning. From a functional point of view, i.e., if we take into consideration the general motives of behavior and thought, there are constant functions common to all ages. At all levels of development, action presupposes a precipitating factor: a physiological, affective, or intellectual need. (In the latter case, the need appears in the guise of a question or a problem.) At all levels, intelligence seeks to understand or explain, etc. However, while the functions of interest, explanation, etc., are common to all developmental stages, that is to say, are "invariable" as far as the functions themselves are concerned, it is nonetheless true that "interests" (as opposed to "interest") vary considerably from one mental level to another, and that the particular explanations (as opposed to the function of explaining) are of a very different nature, depending on the degree of intellectual development. In addition to the constant functions, there are the variable structures. An analysis of these progressive forms of successive equilibrium highlights the differences from one behavioral level to another, all the way from the elementary behavior of the neonate through adolescence.

The variable structures—motor or intellectual on the one hand and affective on the other—are the organizational forms of mental activity. They are organized along two dimensions—intrapersonal and social (interpersonal). For greater clarity we shall distinguish six stages or periods of development which mark the appearance of these successively constructed structures:

1. The reflex or hereditary stage, at which the first instinctual nutritional drives and the first emotions appear.
2. The stage of the first motor habits and of the first organized percepts, as well as of the first differentiated emotions.
3. The stage of sensorimotor or practical intelligence (prior to language), of elementary affective organization, and of the first external affective fixations. These first three stages constitute the infancy period—from birth till the age of one and a half to two years—i.e., the period prior to the development of language and thought as such.
4. The stage of intuitive intelligence, of spontaneous interpersonal feelings, and of social relationships in which the child is subordinate to the adult (ages two to seven years, or "early childhood").

5. The stage of concrete intellectual operations (the beginning of logic) and of moral and social feelings of cooperation (ages seven to eleven or twelve, or "middle childhood").
6. The stage of abstract intellectual operations, of the formation of the personality, and of affective and intellectual entry into the society of adults (adolescence).

Each of these stages is characterized by the appearance of original structures whose construction distinguishes it from previous stages. The essentials of these successive constructions exist at subsequent stages in the form of substructures onto which new characteristics have been built. It follows that in the adult each stage through which he has passed corresponds to a given level in the total hierarchy of behavior. But at each stage there are also temporary and secondary characteristics that are modified by subsequent development as a function of the need for better organization. Each stage thus constitutes a particular form of equilibrium as a function of its characteristic structures, and mental evolution is effectuated in the direction of an ever-increasing equilibrium.

We know which functional mechanisms are common to all stages. In an absolutely general way (not only in comparing one stage with the following but also in comparing each item of behavior that is part of that stage with ensuing behavior), one can say that all action—that is to say, all movement, all thought, or all emotion—responds to a need. Neither the child nor the adult executes any external or even entirely internal act unless impelled by a motive; this motive can always be translated into a need (an elementary need, an interest, a question, etc.).

As Claparède (1951) has shown, a need is always a manifestation of disequilibrium: there is need when something either outside ourselves or within us (physically or mentally) is changed and behavior has to be adjusted as a function of this change. For example, hunger or fatigue will provoke a search for nourishment or rest; encountering an external object will lead to a need to play, which in turn has practical ends, or it leads to a question or a theoretical problem. A casual word will excite the need to imitate, to sympathize, or will engender reserve or opposition if it conflicts with some interest of our own. Conversely, action terminates when a need is satisfied, that is to say, when equilibrium is re-established between the new factor that has provoked the need and the mental organization that existed prior to the introduction of this factor. Eating or sleeping, playing or reaching a goal, replying to a question or resolving a problem, imitating successfully, establishing an affective tie, or maintaining one's point of view are all satisfactions that, in the preceding examples, will put an end to the particular behavior aroused by the need. At any given moment, one can thus say, action is disequilibrated by the transformations that arise in the external or internal world, and each new behavior consists not only in re-establishing equilibrium but also in moving toward a more stable equilibrium than that which preceded the disturbance.

Human action consists of a continuous and perpetual mechanism of re-adjustment or equilibration. For this reason, in these initial phases of construction, the successive mental structures that engender development can be considered as so many progressive forms of equilibrium, each of which is an advance upon its predecessor. It must be understood, however, that this functional mechanism, general though it may be, does not explain the content or the structure of the various needs, since each of them is related to the organization of the particular stage that is being considered. For example, the sight of the same object will occasion very different questions in the small child who is still incapable of classification from those of the older child whose ideas are more extensive and systematic. The interests of a child at any given moment depend on the system of ideas he has acquired plus his affective inclinations, and he tends to fulfill his interests in the direction of greater equilibrium.

Before examining the details of development we must try to find that which is common to the needs and interests present at all ages. One can say, in regard to this, that all needs tend first of all to incorporate things and people into the subject's own activity, i.e., to "assimilate" the external world into the structures that have already been constructed, and secondly to readjust these structures as a function of subtle transformations, i.e., to "accommodate" them to external objects. From this point of view, all mental life, as indeed all organic life, tends progressively to assimilate the surrounding environment. This incorporation is effected thanks to the structures of psychic organs whose scope of action becomes more and more extended. Initially, perception and elementary movement (prehension, etc.) are concerned with objects that are close and viewed statically; then later, memory and practical intelligence permit the representation of earlier states of the object as well as the anticipation of their future states resulting from as yet unrealized transformations. Still later intuitive thought reinforces these two abilities. Logical intelligence in the guise of concrete operations and ultimately of abstract deduction terminates this evolution by making the subject master of events that are far distant in space and time. At each of these levels the mind fulfills the same function, which is to incorporate the universe to itself, but the nature of assimilation varies, i.e., the successive modes of incorporation evolve from those of perception and movement to those of the higher mental operations.

In assimilating objects, action and thought must accommodate to these objects; they must adjust to external variation. The balancing of the processes of assimilation and accommodation may be called "adaptation." Such is the general form of psychological equilibrium, and the progressive organization of mental development appears to be simply an ever more precise adaptation to reality.

Reference

CLAPARÈDE, E. *Le développement mental*. Neuchâtel: Delachaux et Niestlé, 1951.

Author Index

Italic numbers indicate that the author is mentioned in the *References* section that follows the reading. **Boldface** numbers indicate that the author is the author of a reading.

Abrahams, R. D., *222*
Adams, D., 20, *28*
Adams, R., 314, *323*
Adelson, J., 414, 420, *423, 424*
Ainsworth, M. D. S., 90, *92, 418, 424*
Alexander, D., 20, *28,* 350, 351, *354*
Allen, S., 300, 301, *302*
Allen, V. E., 436, *437*
Almy, M., *206–209*
Altus, W. D., 363, *369*
Amatruda, C. S., 121, *131,* 174, *176*
Ambrose, L., 359, *361*
Ambuel, J., 20, *27*
Ames, L. B., 174, *176*
Andersson, T., 210–212, 218, *222*
Annett, M., 140, *148*
Arciniega, T. A., 212, *222, 223*
Aristotle, *413*
Astrand, P. O., 253, 255, *261*

Bailey, D. A., **251–262**
Baldwin, C. P., 157, 163, *164*
Ballard, W. W., **443–450**
Balswick, J. O., **401–412**
Balzer, R. H., **293–297**
Bandura, A., 409, *411*
Bannister, R., 254, *261*
Barnes, R. H., 132, *137*
Barnett, C. R., 20, 26, *27, 28*
Bartlett, F. C., 130, *131*
Bates, E. B., 216, *222*
Baumrind, D., 422, 423

Bayer, A. E., 363, *369*
Bayley, N., 68, 69, *74,* 334, *335*
Beach, F. A., 109, *111*
Becker, W. C., 333, *334*
Bell, R. D., 255, *261*
Bell, R. Q., 99, *111,* 112, 113, *120*
Belmont, L., 363, 365, 368, *369*
Bender, E., 167, *176*
Benitez, M., 210, *222*
Benton, A. L., 121, 130, *131*
Berger, S. E., 330, *335*
Berkov, B., 358, *361*
Berkowitz, L., 402, *411*
Berlyne, D. E., 293, 294, 296, *297*
Berman, S., 284, *291*
Bernstein, A. C., *263–283*
Bertalanffy, L. von, 452, *456*
Best, C. T., **375–387**
Birch, H., 191, 192, *194*
Birch, H. G., **121–132,** 132, 136, *137*
Bloom, B. S., 67, *74*
Bloom, L., 157, *164*
Bloom, R., 428, *437*
Blurton-Jones, N., 173, *175,* 192, *194*
Blurton-Jones, N. G., 109, *111*
Board of Regents of New York Department of Education, 211, *222*
Bobrow, N. A., 351, *354*
Bock, R. D., 364, *369, 386*
Borke, H., 176, 171, *181,* **182–191**
Borth, A. M., **303–311**
Bortner, M., 130, *131*
Botkin, P. T., 176, *181,* 182, *190*

465